Charles H. Spurgeon

Ichthus Publications · Apollo, Pennsylvania

Published over a four-year period between 1877 and 1881 in London by Passmore & Alabaster, Charles Spurgeon's "The Shilling Series" was originally a collection of seven books that each sold for the same price—a shilling. The text for this reprint comes from the original editions. Spelling, language, grammar, and punctuation have been gently updated.

Our goal is to provide high-quality, thought-provoking books that foster encouragement and spiritual growth. For more information regarding bulk purchases, other IP books, or our publishing services, visit us online or write to support@ichthuspublications.com.

Printed in the United States of America.

Copyright © 2021 Ichthus Publications
ISBN: 978-1946971715

www.ichthuspublications.com

Contents

BOOK ONE: Christ's Glorious Achievements

Preface | 9
1 Christ the End of the Law | 11
2 Christ the Conqueror of Satan | 25
3 Christ the Overcomer of the World | 41
4 Christ the Maker of All Things New | 56
5 Christ the Spoiler of Principalities and Powers | 72
6 Christ the Destroyer of Death | 86
7 Christ the Seeker and Savior of the Lost | 102

BOOK TWO: Seven Wonders of Grace

Preface | 119
1 Manasseh; or, the Outrageous Rebel | 121
2 The Woman that was a Sinner; or, the Loving Penitent | 138
3 The Dying Thief; or, the Lone Witness | 155
4 Saul of Tarsus; or, the Pattern Convert | 167
5 The Philippian Jailor; or, the Good Officer Improved | 182
6 Onesimus; or, the Runaway Servant | 196
7 The Greatest Wonder of All | 211

BOOK THREE: The Spare Half-Hour

Preface | 225
1 Honeywood Park; or, a Tale of My Grandfather | 227
2 Two Episodes in My Life | 231
3 Ten Thousand Skulls | 239
4 The Dropping Well of Knaresborough | 245
5 Voices from Pompeii | 253

6 Ghost Stories for Christmas | 259
7 The Great Pot and the Twenty Loaves | 269
8 The Saint of the Smithy | 281
9 In a Fog | 291
10 A Visit to Christ's Hospital | 298
11 St. Brelade's Bay | 311
12 Sundew, a Strange Plant | 318
13 Two Sights which I Shall Never Forget | 323
14 "Oh, You Wretch!" | 328

BOOK FOUR: The Mourner's Comforter

Preface | 337
1 The Anointed Messenger and his Work | 339
2 The Proclamation of Acceptance and Vengeance | 354
3 Gracious Appointments for Zion's Mourners | 371
4 Beauty for Ashes | 386
5 The Oil of Joy for Mourning | 402
6 The Garment of Praise | 415
7 Trees of Righteousness | 431

BOOK FIVE: The Bible and the Newspaper

Preface | 445
1 A Voice from the Sea | 447
2 Calling Out the Reserves | 452
3 Ladies' Dress | 457
4 The Deceiver and the Victim | 460
5 Floods in the Streets | 462
6 The Race and its Spectators | 467
7 Double-Minded | 470
8 A Fox in the Pulpit | 472
9 The Evil wrought by One Man | 474
10 Sympathy Created by Kindred Experience | 476
11 The Morning Drummer and the Preacher | 479
12 Have to Have More | 481
13 Conscientious Separation | 484
14 On Exposing Others to Peril | 487
15 Want of Light | 490

16 Tale-Bearing | 492
17 Tempting Temptation | 494
18 Review at Aldershot | 496
19 *"Quis Separabit?"* | 498
20 Life Versus Machinery | 501
21 Homesickness | 505
22 Religious Sluggards | 510
23 The Withering of Unbelief | 512
24 Sympathy | 514
25 Benefit of Trial | 516
26 Watching | 518
27 Moore's Remonstrance | 521
28 H. C. Wants Money | 523
29 Sinking of the Ironclad | 526
30 Tests for Diamonds | 529
31 A Path Strewn with Blessings | 533
32 The Fickleness of Mankind | 536
33 Pearls | 539
34 Safe—Not Saved | 543
35 Diplomacy and Duplicity | 545
36 Labor in Vain | 548
37 Chaotic Theology | 550
38 Want of Stamina | 552
39 Blasting Prohibited | 555
40 Deserters | 558
41 Blame the Scale-Maker | 562
42 Spurious Imitations | 564
43 The Watch Tower | 568
44 Battered Scripture | 571
45 The True Wrestler | 573
46 The Best Preparation for the Second Advent | 575

BOOK SIX: Eccentric Preachers

Preface | 581
1 What Is Eccentricity? | 583
2 Who Have Been Called Eccentric? | 598
3 Causes of Eccentricity | 613
4 Hugh Latimer (1480–1555) | 630

5 Hugh Peters (1599–1660) | 633
6 Daniel Burgess (1645–1713) | 636
7 John Berridge (1716–1793) | 639
8 Rowland Hill (1744–1833) | 643
9 Matthew Wilks (1746–1829) | 647
10 William Dawson (1773–1841) | 651
11 Jacob Gruber (1778–1850) | 656
12 Edward Taylor (1793–1871) | 669
13 Edward Brooke (1779–1871) | 675
14 Billy Bray: The Uneducated Soul-Winner | 683
Conclusion | 691

BOOK SEVEN: Be of Good Cheer

Preface | 695
1 Good Cheer from Christ's Call and from Himself | 697
2 Good Cheer from Forgiven Sin | 710
3 Good Cheer from Grace Received | 722
4 Good Cheer from Christ's Real Presence | 736
5 Good Cheer from Christ's Victory over the World | 745
6 Good Cheer from Past and Future Service | 758
7 Good Cheer from Faith in the Divine Truthfulness | 764

Book One

Christ's Glorious Achievements

Set Forth in Seven Sermons

Preface

This little volume consists of seven discourses in honor of our Lord Jesus. Upon no theme is the true minister so much at home, and yet no subject more completely surpasses his ability. We love the subject, though we are lost in it. It is possible to describe all other things more or less accurately; but words are not capable of setting forth the redeeming grace and dying love of Jesus; yet we would fain be confined to this one topic for life, and be set free to speak of nothing else but our Beloved. As the harp of Anacreon refused all other themes and would resound "love alone," so would we gladly become forever silent save only upon the famous deeds and adorable person of our Lord. "Arms and the Man" we sing, but ah how feebly! Certainly we can never speak well enough of him whose name is Wonderful, for his work is honorable and glorious and his righteousness endureth forever. We cannot content ourselves with anything which we can write concerning him, for, as the pen glides along, the heart glows yet more and more.

> My Christ he is the Lord of lords,
>   He is the King of kings
> He is the Sun of righteousness
>   With healing in his wings.
>
> My Christ, he is the heaven of heaven
>   My Christ what shall I call?
> My Christ is first, my Christ is last,
>   My Christ is All in All.

May the readers of these sermons be enabled by the Spirit of God in some degree to make increase in their knowledge of Christ. He alone is worth knowing; all other wisdom will fade away. Right well we know that none can reveal

Christ to the heart but the Holy Ghost, and therefore with prayer for his divine enlightening we commit these pages to his condescending care, asking that they may prove to be good for edification.

May the Lord Jesus be glorified by this little work.

Thus humbly prays,

C. H. Spurgeon

1

Christ the End of the Law

"For Christ is the end of the law for righteousness to every one that believeth" (Rom. 10:4).

To be the end of the law is one of the most glorious achievements of our Lord, and it will be a great blessing to us all to know him in that character.

The reason why many do not come to Christ is not because they are not earnest, after a fashion, and thoughtful and desirous to be saved, but because they cannot brook God's way of salvation. "They have a zeal for God, but not according to knowledge," We do get them by our exhortation so far on the way that they become desirous to obtain eternal life, but "they have not submitted themselves to the righteousness of God." Mark, "submitted themselves," for it needs submission. Proud man wants to save himself, he believes he can do it, and he will not give over the task till he finds out his own helplessness by unhappy failures. Salvation by grace, to be sued for *in forma pauperis*, to be asked for as an undeserved boon from free, unmerited grace, this it is which the carnal mind will not come to as long as it can help it: I beseech the Lord so to work that some of you may not be able to help it. And oh, I have been praying that, while this morning I am trying to set forth Christ as the end of the law, God may bless it to some hearts, that they may see what Christ did, and may perceive it to be a great deal better than anything they can do; may see what Christ finished, and may become weary of what they themselves have labored at so long, and have not even well commenced at this day. Perhaps it may please the Lord to enchant them with the perfection of the salvation that is in Christ Jesus. As Bunyan would say, "It may, perhaps, set their mouths a watering after it," and when a sacred appetite begins it will not be long before the feast is enjoyed. It may be that when they see the raiment of wrought gold, which Jesus so freely bestows on naked souls, they will throw away their own filthy rags which now they hug so closely.

I am going to speak about two things, this morning, as the Spirit of God shall help me: and the first is, *Christ in connection with the law*—he is "the end of the law for righteousness"; and secondly, *ourselves in connection with Christ*—"to everyone that believeth Christ is the end of the law for righteousness."

I. First, then, CHRIST IN CONNECTION WITH THE LAW. The law is that which, as sinners, we have above all things cause to dread; for the sting of death is sin, and the strength of sin is the law. Towards us the law darts forth devouring flames, for it condemns us, and in solemn terms appoints us a place among the accursed, as it is written, "Cursed is every one that continueth not in all things that are written in the book of the law to do them." Yet, strange infatuation! Like the fascination which attracts the gnat to the candle which burns its wings, men by nature fly to the law for salvation, and cannot be driven from it. The law can do nothing else but reveal sin and pronounce condemnation upon the sinner, and yet we cannot get men away from it, even though we show them how sweetly Jesus stands between them and it. They are so enamored of legal hope that they cling to it when there is nothing to cling to; they prefer Sinai to Calvary, though Sinai has nothing for them but thunders and trumpet warnings of coming judgment. O that for awhile you would listen anxiously while I set forth Jesus my Lord, that you may see the law in him.

Now, what has our Lord to do with the law? He has everything to do with it, for he is its end for the noblest object, namely, for righteousness. He is the "end of the law." What does this mean? I think it signifies three things: first, that Christ is *the purpose and object* of the law; secondly, that he is *the fulfillment* of it; and thirdly, that he is *the termination* of it.

First, then, *our Lord Jesus Christ is the purpose and object of the law.* It was given to lead us to him. The law is our schoolmaster to bring us to Christ, or rather our attendant to conduct us to the school of Jesus. The law is the great net in which the fish are enclosed that they may be drawn out of the element of sin. The law is the stormy wind which drives souls into the harbor or refuge.

The law is the sheriff's officer to shut men up in prison for their sin, concluding them all under condemnation in order that they may look to the free grace of God alone for deliverance. This is the object of the law: it empties that grace may fill, and wounds that mercy may heal. It has never been God's intention towards us, as fallen men, that the law should be regarded as a way to salvation to us, for a way of salvation it can never be. Had man never fallen, had his nature remained as God made it, the law would have been most helpful to him to show him the way in which he should walk: and by keeping it he would have lived, for "he that doeth these things shall live in them." But ever since man has fallen the Lord has not proposed to him a way of salvation by works, for he knows it to be impossible to a sinful creature. The law is already broken; and whatever man can do he cannot repair the damage he has already done: therefore he is out of court as to the hope of merit. The law demands perfection, but man has already fallen short of it; and therefore let him do his best. He cannot accomplish what is absolutely essential. The law is meant to lead the sinner to faith in Christ, by showing the impossibility of any other way. It is the black dog to fetch the sheep to the shepherd, the burning heat which drives the traveler to the shadow of the great rock in a weary land.

Look how the law is adapted to this; for, first of all, *it shows man his sin*. Read the Ten Commandments and tremble as you read them. Who can lay his own character down side by side with the two tablets of divine precept without at once being convinced that he has fallen far short of the standard? When the law comes home to the soul it is like light in a dark room revealing the dust and the dirt which else had been unperceived. It is the test which detects the presence of the poison of sin in the soul. "I was alive without the law once," said the apostle, "but when the commandment came sin revived and I died." Our comeliness utterly fades away when the law blows upon it.

Look at the commandments, I say, and remember how sweeping they are, how spiritual, how far-reaching. They do not merely touch the outward act, but dive into the inner motive and deal with the heart, the mind, the soul. There is a deeper meaning in the commands than appears upon their surface. Gaze into their depths and see how terrible the holiness which they require is. As you understand what the law demands you will perceive how far you are from fulfilling it, and how sin abounds where you thought there was little or none of it. You thought yourself rich and increased in goods and in no need of anything, but when the broken law visits you, your spiritual bankruptcy and utter penury stare you in the face. A true balance discovers short weight, and such is the first effect of the law upon the conscience of man.

The law also shows *the result and mischief of sin*. Look at the types of the old Mosaic dispensation, and see how they were intended to lead men to Christ by making them see their unclean condition and their need of such cleansing as only he can give. Every type pointed to our Lord Jesus Christ. If men were put apart because of disease or uncleanness, they were made to see how sin separated them from God and from his people; and when they were brought back and purified with mystic rites in which were scarlet wool and hyssop and the like, they were made to see how they can only be restored by Jesus Christ, the great High Priest. When the bird was killed that the leper might be clean, the need of purification by the sacrifice of a life was set forth. Every morning and evening a lamb died to tell of daily need of pardon, if God is to dwell with us.

We sometimes have fault found with us for speaking too much about *blood*; yet under the Old Testament the blood seemed to be everything, and was not only spoken of but actually presented to the eye. What does the apostle tell us in the Hebrews?

> Whereupon neither the first testament was dedicated without blood. For when Moses had spoken every precept to all the people according to the law, he took the blood of calves and of goats, with water, and scarlet wool, and hyssop, and sprinkled both the book, and all the people saying, this is the blood of the testament which God hath enjoined unto you. Moreover he sprinkled with blood both the tabernacle, and all the vessels of the ministry. And almost all things are by the law purged with blood; and without shedding of blood is not remission.

The blood was on the veil, and on the altar, on the hangings, and on the floor of the tabernacle: no one could avoid seeing it. I resolve to make my ministry of the same character, and more and more sprinkle it with the blood of atonement. Now that abundance of the blood of old was meant to show clearly that sin has so polluted us that without an atonement God is not to be approached: we must come by the way of sacrifice or not at all. We are so unacceptable in ourselves that unless the Lord sees us with the blood of Jesus upon us he must away with us. The old law, with its emblems and figures, set forth many truths as to men's selves and the coming Savior, intending by every one of them to preach Christ. If any stopped short of him, they missed the intent and design of the law. Moses leads up to Joshua, and the law ends at Jesus.

Turning our thoughts back again to the moral rather than the ceremonial law, it was intended to teach men *their utter helplessness.* It shows them how short they fall of what they ought to be, and it also shows them, when they look at it carefully, how utterly impossible it is for them to come up to the standard. Such holiness as the law demands no man can reach of himself. "Thy commandment is exceeding broad." If a man says that he can keep the law, it is because he does not know what the law is. If he fancies that he can ever climb to heaven up the quivering sides of Sinai, surely he can never have seen that burning mount at all. Keep the law! Ah, my brethren, while we are yet talking about it we are breaking it; while we are pretending that we can fulfil its letter, we are violating its spirit, for pride as much breaks the law as lust or murder. "Who can bring a clean thing out of an unclean? Not one." "How can he be clean that is born of a woman?" No, soul, thou canst not help thyself in this thing, for since only by perfection thou canst live by the law, and since that perfection is impossible, thou canst not find help in the covenant of works. In grace there is hope, but as a matter of debt there is none, for we do not merit anything but wrath. The law tells us this, and the sooner we know it to be so the better, for the sooner we shall fly to Christ.

The law also shows us *our great need*—our need of cleansing, cleansing with the water and with the blood. It discovers to us our filthiness, and this naturally leads us to feel that we must be washed from it if we are ever to draw near to God. So the law drives us to accept of Christ as the one only person who can cleanse us, and make us fit to stand within the veil in the presence of the Most High. The law is the surgeon's knife which cuts out the proud flesh that the wound may heal. The law by itself only sweeps and raises the dust, but the gospel sprinkles clean water upon the dust, and all is well in the chamber of the soul. The law kills, the gospel makes alive; the law strips, and then Jesus Christ comes in and robes the soul in beauty and glory. All the commandments, and all the types direct us to Christ, if we will but heed their evident intent. They wean us from self, they put us off from the false basis of self-righteousness, and bring us to know that only in Christ can our help be found. So, first of all, Christ is the end of the law, in that he is its great purpose.

And now, secondly, he is *the law's fulfillment*. It is impossible for any of us to be saved without righteousness. The God of heaven and earth by immutable necessity demands righteousness of all his creatures. Now, Christ has come to give to us the righteousness which the law demands, but which it never bestows. In the chapter before us we read of "the righteousness which is of faith," which is also called "God's righteousness"; and we read of those who "shall not be ashamed" because they are righteous by believing unto righteousness." What the law could not do Jesus has done. He provides the righteousness which the law asks for but cannot produce. What an amazing righteousness it must be which is as broad and deep and long and high as the law itself. The commandment is exceeding broad, but the righteousness of Christ is as broad as the commandment, and goes to the end of it. Christ did not come to make the law milder, or to render it possible for our cracked and battered obedience to be accepted as a sort of compromise. The law is not compelled to lower its terms, as though it had originally asked too much; it is holy and just and good, and ought not to be altered in one jot or tittle, nor can it be.

Our Lord gives the law all it requires, not a part, for that would be an admission that it might justly have been content with less at first. The law claims complete obedience without one spot or speck, failure, or flaw, and Christ has brought in such a righteousness as that, and gives it to his people. The law demands that the righteousness should be without omission of duty and without commission of sin, and the righteousness which Christ has brought is just such an one that for its sake the great God accepts his people and counts them to be without spot or wrinkle or any such thing. The law will not be content without spiritual obedience, mere outward compliances will not satisfy. But our Lord's obedience was as deep as it was broad, for his zeal to do the will of him that sent him consumed him. He says himself, "I delight to do thy will, O my God, yea thy law is within my heart." Such righteousness he puts upon all believers. "By the obedience of one shall many be made righteous"; righteous to the full, perfect in Christ.

We rejoice to wear the costly robe of fair white linen which Jesus has prepared, and we feel that we may stand arrayed in it before the majesty of heaven without a trembling thought. This is something to dwell upon, dear friends. Only as righteous ones can we be saved, but Jesus Christ makes us righteous, and therefore we are saved. He is righteous who believeth on him, even as Abraham believed God and it was counted unto him for righteousness. "There is therefore, now no condemnation to them that are in Christ Jesus," because they are made righteous in Christ. Yea, the Holy Spirit by the mouth of Paul challengeth all men, angels, and devils, to lay anything to the charge of God's elect, since Christ hath died. O law, when thou demandest of me a perfect righteousness, I, being a believer, present it to thee; for through Christ Jesus faith is accounted unto me for righteousness. The righteousness of Christ is mine, for I am one with him by faith, and this is the name wherewith he shall be called—"The Lord our righteousness."

Jesus has thus fulfilled the original demands of the law, but you know, brethren, that since we have broken the law there are other demands. For the remission of past sins something more is asked now than present and future obedience. Upon us, on account of our sins, the curse has been pronounced, and a penalty has been incurred. It is written that he "will by no means clear the guilty," but every transgression and iniquity shall have its just punishment and reward. Here, then, let us admire that the Lord Jesus Christ is the end of the law as to penalty. That curse and penalty are awful things to think upon, but Christ has ended all their evil, and thus discharged us from all the consequences of sin. As far as every believer is concerned the law demands no penalty and utters no curse. The believer can point to the Great Surety on the tree of Calvary, and say, "See there, oh law, there is the vindication of divine justice which I offer to thee. Jesus pouring out his heart's blood from his wounds and dying on my behalf is my answer to thy claims, and I know that I shall be delivered from wrath through him." The claims of the law both as broken and unbroken Christ has met: both the positive and the penal demands are satisfied in him. This was a labor worthy of a God, and lo, the incarnate God has achieved it. He has finished the transgression, made an end of sins, made reconciliation for iniquity, and brought in everlasting righteousness. All glory be to his name.

Moreover, not only has the penalty been paid, but Christ has put great and special honor upon the law in so doing. I venture to say that if the whole human race had kept the law of God and not one of them had violated it, the law would not stand in so splendid a position of honor as it does today when the man Christ Jesus, who is also the Son of God, has paid obeisance to it. God himself, incarnate, has in his life, and yet more in his death, revealed the supremacy of law; he has shown that not even love nor sovereignty can set aside justice. Who shall say a word against the law to which the Lawgiver himself submits? Who shall now say that it is too severe when he who made it submits himself to its penalties? Because he was found in fashion as a man, and was our representative, the Lord demanded from his own Son perfect obedience to the law, and the Son voluntarily bowed himself to it without a single word, taking no exception to his task. "Yea, thy law is my delight," saith he, and he proved it to be so by paying homage to it even to the full. Oh wondrous law under which even Emmanuel serves! Oh matchless law whose yoke even the Son of God does not disdain to bear, but being resolved to save his chosen was made under the law, lived under it and died under it, "obedient to death, even the death of the cross."

The law's stability also has been secured by Christ. That alone can remain which is proved to be just, and Jesus has proved the law to be so, magnifying it and making it honorable. He says, "Think not that I am come to destroy the law, or the prophets: I am not come to destroy, but to fulfill. For verily I say unto you, till heaven and earth pass, one jot or one tittle shall in no wise pass from the law, till all be fulfilled." I shall have to show you how he has made an end of the law in another sense, but as to the settlement of the eternal principles of right and wrong, Christ's life and death have achieved this forever.

"Yea, we established the law." said Paul, "we do not make void the law through faith." The law is proved to be holy and just by the very gospel of faith, for the gospel which faith believes in does not alter or lower the law, but teaches us how it was to the uttermost fulfilled. Now shall the law stand fast forever and ever, since even to save elect man God will not alter it. He had a people, chosen, beloved, and ordained to life, yet he would not save them at the expense of one principle of right. They were sinful, and how could they be justified unless the law was suspended or changed? Was, then, the law changed? It seemed as if it must be so, if man was to be saved, but Jesus Christ came and showed us how the law could stand firm as a rock, and yet the redeemed could be justly saved by infinite mercy. In Christ we see both mercy and justice shining full orbed, and yet neither of them in any degree eclipsing the other. The law has all it ever asked, as it ought to have, and yet the Father of all mercies sees all his chosen saved as he determined they should be through the death of his Son. Thus I have tried to show you how Christ is the fulfillment of the law to its utmost end. May the Holy Ghost bless the teaching.

And now, thirdly, he is the end of the law in the sense that he is *the termination of it*. He has terminated it in two senses. First of all, his people are not under it as a covenant of life. "We are not under the law, but under grace." The old covenant as it stood with father Adam was "do this and thou shalt live": its command he did not keep, and consequently he did not live, nor do we live in him, since in Adam all died. The old covenant was broken, and we became condemned thereby, but now, having suffered death in Christ, we are no more under it, but are dead to it. Brethren, at this present moment, although we rejoice to do good works, we are not seeking life through them, we are not hoping to obtain divine favor by our own goodness, nor even to keep ourselves in the love of God by any merit of our own.

Chosen, not for our works, but according to the eternal will and good pleasure of God; called, not of works, but by the Spirit of God, we desire to continue in this grace and return no more to the bondage of the old covenant. Since we have put our trust in an atonement provided and applied by grace through Christ Jesus, we are no longer slaves but children, not working to be saved, but saved already, and working because we are saved. Neither that which we do, nor even that which the Spirit of God worketh in us is to us the ground and basis of the love of God toward us, since he loved us from the first, because he would love us, unworthy though we were; and he loves us still in Christ, and looks upon us not as we are in ourselves, but as we are in him; washed in his blood and covered in his righteousness. Ye are not under the law, Christ has taken you from the servile bondage of a condemning covenant and made you to receive the adoption of children, so that now ye cry, Abba, Father.

Again, Christ is the terminator of the law, for we are no longer under its curse. The law cannot curse a believer, it does not know how to do it; it blesses him, yea, and he shall be blessed; for as the law demands righteousness and looks at the believer in Christ, and sees that Jesus has given him all the righteousness it demands, the law is bound to pronounce him blessed. "Blessed is he whose transgression is forgiven, whose sin is covered. Blessed is the man unto whom the Lord imputeth not iniquity, and in whose spirit there is no guile."

Oh, the joy of being redeemed from the curse of the law by Christ, who was "made a curse for us," as it is written, "Cursed is every one that hangeth on a tree." Do ye, my brethren, understand the sweet mystery of salvation? Have you ever seen Jesus standing in your place that you may stand in his place? Christ accused and Christ condemned, and Christ led out to die, and Christ smitten of the Father, even to the death, and then you cleared, justified, delivered from the curse, because the curse has spent itself on your Redeemer. You are admitted to enjoy the blessing because the righteousness which was his is now transferred to you that you may be blessed of the Lord world without end. Do let us triumph and rejoice in this evermore. Why should we not? And yet some of God's people get under the law as to their feelings, and begin to fear that because they are conscious of sin they are not saved, whereas it is written, "he justifieth the ungodly."

For myself, I love to live near a sinner's Savior. If my standing before the Lord depended upon what I am in myself and what good works and righteousness I could bring, surely I should have to condemn myself a thousand times a day. But to get away from that and to say, "I have believed in Jesus Christ and therefore righteousness is mine," this is peace, rest, joy, and the beginning of heaven! When one attains to this experience, his love to Jesus Christ begins to flame up, and he feels that if the Redeemer has delivered him from the curse of the law he will not continue in sin, but he will endeavor to live in newness of life. We are not our own, we are bought with a price, and we would therefore glorify God in our bodies and in our spirits, which are the Lord's. Thus much upon Christ in connection with the law.

II. Now, secondly, OURSELVES IN CONNECTION WITH CHRIST—for "Christ is the end of the law *to everyone that believeth.*" Now see the point "to everyone that believeth," there the stress lies. Come, man, woman, dost thou believe? No weightier question can be asked under heaven. "Dost thou believe on the Son of God?" And what is it to believe? It is not merely to accept a set of doctrines and to say that such and such a creed is yours, and there and then to put it on the shelf and forget it. To believe is to trust, to confide, to depend upon, to rely upon, to rest in. Dost thou believe that Jesus Christ rose from the dead? Dost thou believe that he stood in the sinner's stead and suffered the just for the unjust? Dost thou believe that he is able to save to the uttermost them that come unto God by him? And dost thou therefore lay the whole weight and stress of thy soul's salvation upon him, yea, upon him alone? Ah then, Christ is the end of the law for righteousness to thee, and thou art righteous. In the righteousness of God thou art clothed if thou believest. It is of no use to bring forward anything else if you are not believing, for nothing will avail. If faith be absent the essential thing is wanting: sacraments, prayers, Bible reading, hearings of the gospel; you may heap them together, high as the stars, into a mountain, huge as high Olympus, but they are all mere chaff if faith be not there. It is thy believing or not believing which must settle the matter. Dost thou look away from thyself to Jesus for righteousness? If thou dost he is the end of the law to thee.

Now observe that there is no question raised about the previous character, for it is written, "Christ is the end of the law for righteousness to *every one that believeth.*" But, Lord, this man before he believed was a persecutor and injurious, he raged and raved against the saints and haled them to prison and sought their blood. Yes, beloved friend, and that is the very man who wrote these words by the Holy Ghost, "Christ is the end of the law for righteousness to every one that believeth." So if I address one here this morning whose life has been defiled with every sin, and stained with every transgression we can conceive of, yet I say unto such, remember "all manner of sin and of blasphemy shall be forgiven unto men."

If thou believest in the Lord Jesus Christ thine iniquities are blotted out, for the blood of Jesus Christ, God's dear Son, cleanseth us from all sin. This is the glory of the gospel that it is a sinner's gospel; good news of blessing not for those without sin, but for those who confess and forsake it. Jesus came into the world, not to reward the sinless, but to seek and to save that which was lost; and he, being lost and being far from God, who cometh nigh to God by Christ, and believeth in him, will find that he is able to bestow righteousness upon the guilty. He is the end of the law for righteousness to everyone that believeth, and therefore to the poor harlot that believeth, to the drunkard of many years standing that believeth, to the thief, the liar, and the scoffer who believeth, to those who have aforetime rioted in sin, but now turn from it to trust in him. But I do not know that I need mention such cases as these; to me the most wonderful fact is that Christ is the end of the law for righteousness *to me*, for I believe in him. I know whom I have believed, and I am persuaded that he is able to keep that which I have committed to him until that day.

Another thought arises from the text, and that is, that there is nothing said by way of qualification as to the strength of the faith. He is the end of the law for righteousness to everyone that believeth, whether he is Little-faith or Great-heart. Jesus protects the rear rank as well as the vanguard. There is no difference between one believer and another as to justification. So long as there is a connection between you and Christ the righteousness of God is yours. The link may be very like a film, a spider's line of trembling faith, but, if it runs all the way from the heart to Christ, divine grace can and will flow along the most slender thread. It is marvelous how fine the wire may be that will carry the electric flash. We may want a cable to carry a message across the sea, but that is for the protection of the wire, the wire which actually carries the message is a slender thing. If thy faith be of the mustard-seed kind, if it be only such as tremblingly touches the Savior's garment's hem, if thou canst only say "Lord, I believe, help thou mine unbelief," if it be but the faith of sinking Peter, or weeping Mary, yet if it be faith in Christ, he will be the end of the law for righteousness to thee as well as to the chief of the apostles.

If this be so then, beloved friends, all of us who believe are righteous. Believing in the Lord Jesus Christ we have obtained the righteousness which those who follow the works of the law know nothing of. We are not completely sanctified, would God we were; we are not quit of sin in our members, though we hate it; but still for all that, in the sight of God, we are truly righteous and being qualified by faith we have peace with God. Come, look up, ye believers that are burdened with a sense of sin. While you chasten yourselves and mourn your sin, do not doubt your Savior, nor question his righteousness. You are black, but do not stop there, go on to say as the spouse did, "I am black, *but comely.*"

> Though in ourselves deform'd we are,
>   And black as Kedar's tents appear,

> Yet, when we put Thy beauties on,
> Fair as the courts of Solomon.

Now, mark that the connection of our text assures us that being righteous we are saved; for what does it say here, "If thou shalt confess with thy mouth the Lord Jesus, and shalt believe in thine heart that God hath raised him from the dead, thou shalt be *saved*." He who is justified is saved, or what were the benefit of justification? Over thee, O believer, God hath pronounced the verdict "*saved*," and none shall reverse it. You are saved from sin and death and hell; you are saved even now, with a present salvation; "He hath saved us and called us with a holy calling." Feel the transports of it at this hour. "Beloved, now are we the sons of God."

And now I have done when I have said just this. If anyone here thinks he can save himself, and that his own righteousness will suffice before God, I would affectionately beg him not to insult his Savior. If your righteousness sufficeth, why did Christ come here to work one out? Will you for a moment compare your righteousness with the righteousness of Jesus Christ? What likeness is there between you and him? As much as between an ant and an archangel. Nay, not so much as that: as much as between night and day, hell and heaven. Oh, if I had a righteousness of my own that no one could find fault with, I would voluntarily fling it away to have the righteousness of Christ, but as I have none of my own I do rejoice the more to have my Lord's.

When Mr. Whitefield first preached at Kingswood, near Bristol, to the colliers, he could see when their hearts began to be touched by the gutters of white made by the tears as they ran down their black cheeks. He saw they were receiving the gospel, and he writes in his diary "as these poor colliers had no righteousness of their own they therefore gloried in Him who came to save publicans and sinners." Well, Mr. Whitefield, that is true of the colliers, but it is equally true of many of us here, who may not have had black faces, but we had black hearts. We can truly say that we also rejoice to cast away our own righteousness and count it dross and dung that we may win Christ, and be found in him. In him is our sole hope and only trust.

Last of all, for any of you to reject the righteousness of Christ must be to perish everlastingly, because it cannot be that God will accept you or your pretended righteousness when you have refused the real and divine righteousness which he sets before you in his Son. If you could go up to the gates of heaven, and the angel were to say to you, "What title have you to entrance here?" and you were to reply, "I have a righteousness of my own," then for you to be admitted would be to decide that your righteousness was on a par with that of Immanuel himself. Can that ever be? Do you think that God will ever allow such a lie to be sanctioned? Will he let a poor wretched sinner's counterfeit righteousness pass current side by side with the fine gold of Christ's perfection? Why was the fountain filled with blood if you need no washing? Is Christ a superfluity? Oh, it cannot be. You must have Christ's righteousness or be unrighteous, and being unrighteous you will be unsaved, and being unsaved you must remain lost forever and ever.

Has it all come to this, then, that I am to believe in the Lord Jesus Christ for righteousness, and to be made just through faith? Yes, that is it: that is the whole of it. Trust Christ alone and then live as I like! You cannot live in sin after you have trusted Jesus, for the act of faith brings with it a change of nature and a renewal of your soul. The Spirit of God who leads you to believe will also change your heart. You spoke of "living as you like," you will like to live very differently from what you do now. The things you loved before your conversion you will hate when you believe, and the things you hated you will love.

Now, you are trying to be good, and you make great failures, because your heart is alienated from God; but when once you have received salvation through the blood of Christ, your heart will love God, and then you will keep his commandments, and they will be no longer grievous to you. A change of heart is what you want, and you will never get it except through the covenant of grace. There is not a word about conversion in the old covenant, we must look to the new covenant for that, and here it is—"A new heart also I will give you, and a new spirit will I put within you: and I will take away the stony heart out of your flesh, and I will give you an heart of flesh." This is one of the greatest covenant promises, and the Holy Ghost performs it in the chosen. Oh that the Lord would sweetly persuade you to believe in the Lord Jesus Christ, and that covenant promise shall be fulfilled to you. O Holy Spirit of God, send thy blessing on these poor words, for Jesus' sake.

2

Christ the Conqueror of Satan

"And I will put enmity between thee and the woman, and between thy seed and her seed; it shall bruise thy head, and thou shalt bruise his heel" (Gen. 3:15).

This is the first gospel sermon that was ever delivered upon the surface of this earth. It was memorable discourse indeed, with Jehovah himself for the preacher, and the whole human race and the prince of darkness for the audience. It must be worthy of our heartiest attention.

Is it not remarkable that this great gospel promise should have been delivered so soon after the transgression? As yet no sentence had been pronounced upon either of the two human offenders, but the promise was given under the form of a sentence pronounced upon the serpent Not yet had the woman been condemned to painful travail, or the man to exhausting labor, or even the soil to the curse of thorn and thistle. Truly "mercy rejoiceth against judgment." Before the Lord had said "dust thou art and unto dust thou shalt return," he was pleased to say that the seed of the woman should bruise the serpent's head. Let us rejoice, then, in the swift mercy of God, which in the early watches of the night of sin came with comfortable words unto us.

These words were not directly spoken to Adam and Eve, but they were directed distinctly to the serpent himself, and that by way of punishment to him for what he had done. It was a day of cruel triumph to him such joy as his dark mind is capable of had filled him, for had he indulged his malice, and gratified his spite. He had in the worst sense destroyed a part of God's works, he had introduce sin into the new world, he had stamped the human race with his own image, and gained new forces to promote rebellion and to multiply transgression, and therefore he felt that sort of gladness which a fiend can know who bears a hell within him. But now God comes in, takes up the quarrel personally, and causes him to be disgraced on the very battle-field upon which he had gained a temporary success. He tells the dragon that he will undertake to deal with him; this quarrel shall not be between the serpent and man, but between God and the serpent. God saith, in solemn words, "I will put enmity between thee and the woman, between thy seed and her seed," and he promised that there shall rise in fullness of time a champion, who, though he suffer, shall smite in a vital part the power of evil, and bruise the serpent's head.

This was the more, it seems to me, a comfortable message of mercy to Adam and Eve, because they would feel sure that the tempter would be punished, and as that punishment would involve blessing for them, the vengeance due to the serpent would be the guarantee of mercy to themselves. Perhaps, however, by thus obliquely giving the promise, the Lord meant to say, "Not for your sakes do I this, O fallen man and woman, nor for the sake of your descendants; but for my own name and honor's sake, that it be not profaned and blasphemed amongst the fallen spirits. I undertake to repair the mischief which has been caused by the tempter, that my name and my glory may not be diminished among the immortal spirits who look down upon the scene." All this would be very humbling but yet consolatory to our parents if they thought of it, seeing that mercy given for God's sake is always to our troubled apprehension surer than any favor which could be promised to us for our own sake. The divine sovereignty and glory afford us a stronger foundation of hope than merit, even if merit can be supposed to exist.

Now we must note concerning this first gospel sermon that on it the earliest believers stayed themselves. This was all that Adam had by way of revelation, and all that Abel had received. This one lone star shone in Abel's sky; he looked up to it and he believed. By its light he spelt out "sacrifice," and therefore he brought of the firstlings of his flock and laid them on the altar, and proved in his own person how the seed of the serpent hated the seed of the woman, for his brother slew him for his testimony. Although Enoch the seventh from Adam prophesied concerning the Second Advent, yet he does not appear to have uttered anything new concerning the first coming, so that still this one promise remained as man's sole word of hope. The torch which flamed within the gates of Eden just before man was driven forth lit up the world to all believers until the Lord was pleased to give more light, and to renew and enlarge the revelation of his covenant, when he spoke to his servant Noah. Those ancient fathers who lived before the flood rejoiced in the mysterious language of our text, and resting on it, they died in faith. Nor, brethren, must you think it a slender revelation, for, if you attentively consider, it is wonderfully full of meaning. If it had been on my heart to handle it doctrinally this morning, I think I could have shown you that it contains all the gospel. There lie within it, as an oak lies within an acorn, all the great truths which make up the gospel of Christ.

Observe that here is the grand mystery of incarnation. Christ is that seed of the woman who is here spoken of; and there is a hint not darkly given as to how that Incarnation would be effected. Jesus was not shadowed of the Holy Ghost, and "the holy thing" which was born of her was as to his humanity the seed of the woman only; as it is written, "Behold a virgin shall conceive and bear a son, and they shall call his name Immanuel." The promise plainly teaches that the deliverer would be born of a woman, and carefully viewed, it also foreshadows the divine method of the Redeemer's conception and birth. So also is the doctrine of the two seeds plainly taught here—"I will put enmity between thee and the woman, between thy seed and her seed." There was evidently to be in the world a seed of the woman on God's side against the serpent, and a seed of the serpent that should always be upon the evil side even as it is unto this day. The church of God and the synagogue of Satan both exist. We see an Abel and a Cain, an Isaac and an Ishmael, a Jacob and an Esau; those that are born after the flesh, being the children of their father the devil, for his works they do, but those that are born again—being born after the Spirit, after the power of the life of Christ, are thus in Christ Jesus the seed of the woman, and contend earnestly against the dragon and his seed. Here, too, the great fact of the sufferings of Christ is clearly foretold—"Thou shalt bruise his heel." Within the compass of those words we find the whole story of our Lord's sorrows from Bethlehem to Calvary. "It shall bruise thy head": there is the breaking of Satan's regal power, there is the clearing away of sin, there is the destruction of death by resurrection, there is the leading of captivity captive in the ascension, there is the victory of truth in the world through the descent of the Spirit, and there is the latter-day glory in which Satan shall be bound, and there is, lastly, the casting of the evil one and all his followers into the lake of fire.

The conflict and the conquest are both in the compass of these few fruitful words. They may not have been fully understood by those who first heard them, but to us they are now full of light. The text at first looks like a flint, hard and cold; but sparks fly from it plentifully, for hidden fires of infinite love and grace lie concealed within. Over this promise of a gracious God we ought to rejoice exceedingly.

We do not know what our first parents understood by it, but we may be certain that they gathered a great amount of comfort from it. They must have understood that they were not then and there to be destroyed, because the Lord had spoken of a "seed." They would argue that it must be needful that Eve should live if there should be a seed from her. They understood, too, that if that seed was to overcome the serpent and bruise his head, it must auger good to themselves: they could not fail to see that there was some great, some mysterious benefit to be conferred upon them by the victory which their seed would achieve over the instigator of their ruin. They went on in faith upon this, and were comforted in travail and in toil, and I doubt not both Adam and his wife in the faith thereof entered into everlasting rest.

This morning I intend to handle this text in three ways. First, we shall notice *its facts*; secondly, we shall consider *the experience within the heart of each believer which tallies to those facts*; and then, thirdly, *the encouragement* which the text and its connection as a whole afford to us.

I. *THE FACTS*. The facts are four, and I call your earnest attention to them. The first is *enmity was excited*. The text begins, "I will put enmity between thee and the woman." They had been very friendly; the woman and the serpent had conversed together. She thought at the time that the serpent was her friend; and she was so much his friend that she took his advice in the teeth of God's precept, and was willing to believe bad things of the great Creator, because this wicked, crafty serpent insinuated the same. Now, at the moment when God spoke, that friendship between the woman and the serpent had already in a measure come to an end, for she had accused the serpent to God, and said, "The serpent beguiled me, and I did eat." So far, so good. The friendship of sinners does not last long; they have already begun to quarrel, and now the Lord comes in and graciously takes advantage of the quarrel which had commenced, and says, "I will carry this disagreement a great deal further, I will put enmity between thee and the woman." Satan counted on man's descendants being his confederates, but God would break up this covenant with hell, and raise up a seed which should war against the Satanic power.

This we have here God's first declaration that he will set up a rival kingdom to oppose the tyranny of sin and Satan, that he will create in the hearts of a chosen seed an enmity against evil, so that they shall fight against it, and with many a struggle and pain shall overcome the prince of darkness. The divine Spirit has abundantly achieved this plan and purpose of the Lord, combating the fallen angel by a glorious man: making man to be Satan's foe and conqueror. Henceforth the woman was to hate the evil one, and I do not doubt that she did so. She had abundant cause for so doing, and as often as she thought of him it would be with infinite regret that she could have listened to his malicious and deceitful talk. The woman's seed has also evermore had enmity against the evil one. I mean not the carnal seed, for Paul tells us, "They which are the children of the flesh, these are not the children of God: but the children of the promise are counted for the seed." The carnal seed of the man and the woman are not meant, but the spiritual seed, even Christ Jesus and those who are in him.

Wherever you meet these, they hate the serpent with a perfect hatred. We would if we could destroy from our souls every work of Satan, and out of this poor afflicted world of ours we would root up every evil which he has planted. That seed of the woman, that glorious *One*—for he speaks not of seeds as of many but of seed that is one—you know how he abhorred the devil and all his devices. There was enmity between Christ and Satan, for he came to destroy the works of the devil and to deliver those who are under bondage to him. For that purpose was he born; for that purpose did he live; for that purpose did he die; for that purpose he has gone into the glory, and for that purpose he will come again, that everywhere he may find out his adversary and utterly destroy him and his works form amongst the sons of men. This putting of the enmity between the two seeds was the commencement of the plan of mercy, the first act in the program of grace. Of the woman's seed it was henceforth said, "Thou lovest righteousness, and hatest wickedness: therefore God, thy God, hath anointed thee with the oil of gladness above thy fellows."

Then comes the second prophecy, which has also turned into a fact, namely *the coming of the champion*. The seed of the woman by promise is to champion the cause, and oppose the dragon. That seed is the Lord Jesus

Christ. The prophet Micah saith, "But thou, Bethlehem Ephratah; though thou be little among the thousands of Judah, yet out of thee shall he come forth unto me that is to be ruler in Israel; whose goings forth have been from of old, from everlasting. Therefore will he give them up, until the time that she which travaileth hath brought forth." To none other than the babe which was born in Bethlehem of the blessed Virgin can the words of the prophecy refer. She it was who did conceive and bear a son, and it is concerning her son that we sing, "Unto us a child is born, unto us a son is given: and his name shall be called Wonderful, Counsellor, the Mighty God, the Everlasting Father, the Prince of Peace." On the memorable night at Bethlehem, when angels sang in heaven, the seed of the woman appeared, and as soon as ever he saw the light the old serpent, the devil, entered into the heart of Herod if possible to slay him, but the Father preserved him, and suffered none to lay hands on him.

As soon as he publicly came forward upon the stage of action, thirty years after, Satan met him foot to foot. You know the story of the temptation in the wilderness, and how there the woman's seed fought with him who was a liar from the beginning. The devil assailed him thrice with all the artillery of flattery, malice, craft and falsehood, but the peerless champion stood unwounded, and chased his foeman from the field. Then our Lord set up his kingdom, and called one and another unto him, and carried the war into the enemy's country. In divers places he cast out devils. He spoke to the wicked and unclean spirit and said, "I charge thee come out of him," and the demon was expelled. Legions of devils flew before him: they sought to hide themselves in swine to escape from the terror of his presence. "Art thou come to torment us before our time?" was their cry when the wonder-working Christ dislodged them from the bodies which they tormented.

Yea, and he made his own disciples mighty against the evil one, for in his name they cast out devils, till Jesus said, "I beheld Satan as lightning fall from heaven." Then there came a second personal conflict, for I take it that Gethsemane's sorrows were to a great degree caused by a personal assault of Satan, for our Master said, "This is your hour, and the power of darkness." He said also, "The Prince of this world cometh." What a struggle it was. Though Satan had nothing in Christ, yet did he seek if possible to lead him away from completing his great sacrifice, and there did our Master sweat as it were great drops of blood, falling to the ground, in the agony which it cost him to contend with the fiend. Then it was that our Champion began the last fight of all and won it to the bruising of the serpent's head. Nor did he end till he had spoiled principalities and powers and made a show of them openly.

> Now is the hour of darkness past,
>   Christ has assumed his reigning power;
> Behold the great accuser cast
>   Down from his seat to reign no more.

The conflict our glorious Lord continues in his seed. We preach Christ crucified, and every sermon shakes the gates of hell. We bring sinners to Jesus by the Spirit's power, and every convert is a stone torn down from the wall of Satan's mighty castle. Yea, and the day shall come when everywhere the evil one shall be overcome, and the words of John in the Revelation shall be fulfilled. "And the great dragon was cast out, that old serpent, called the Devil, and Satan, which deceiveth the whole world: he was cast out into the earth, and his angels were cast out with him. And I heard a loud voice saying in heaven, Now is come salvation, and strength, and the kingdom of our God, and the power of his Christ: for the accuser of our brethren is cast down, which accused them before our God day and night." Thus did the Lord God in the words of our text promise a champion who should be the seed of the woman, between whom and Satan there should be war for ever and ever: that champion has come, the man-child has been born, and thought the dragon is wroth with the woman, and made war with the remnant of her seed which keep the testimony of Jesus Christ, yet the battle is the Lord's, and the victory falleth unto him whose name is Faithful and True, who in righteousness doth judge and make war.

The third fact which comes out in the text, though not quite in that order, is that *our Champion's heel should be bruised*. Do you need that I explain this? You know how all his life long his heel, that is, his lower part, his human nature, was perpetually being made to suffer. He carried our sicknesses and sorrows. But the bruising came mainly when both in body and in mind his whole human nature was made to agonize; when his soul was exceeding sorrowful even unto death, and his enemies pierced his hands and his feet, and he endured the shame and pain of death by crucifixion. Look at your Master and your King upon the cross, all disdained with blood and dust! There was his heel most cruelly bruised. When they take down that precious body and wrap it in fair white linen and in spices, and lay it in Joseph's tomb, they weep as they handle the casket in which the Deity had dwelt, for there again Satan had bruised his heel. It was not merely that God had bruised him, "though it pleased the Father to bruise him," but the devil had let loose Herod, and Pilate, and Caiaphas, and the Jews, and the Romans, all of them his tools, upon him whom he knew to be the Christ, so that he was bruised of the old serpent.

That is all, however! It is only his heel, not his head, which is bruised! For lo, the Champion rises again; the bruise was not mortal nor continual. Though he dies, yet still so brief is the interval in which he slumbers in the tomb that his holy body hath not seen corruption, and he comes forth perfect and lovely in his manhood, rising from his grave as from a refreshing sleep after so long a day of unresting toil! Oh the triumph of that hour! As Jacob only halted on his thigh when he overcame the angel, so did Jesus only retain a scar in his heel, and that he bears to the skies as his glory and beauty. Before the throne he looks like a lamb that has been slain, but in the power of an endless life he liveth unto God.

Then comes the fourth fact, namely, that while his heel was being bruised, *he was to bruise the serpent's head*. The figure represents the dragon as inflicting an injury upon the champion's heel, but at the same moment the champion himself with that heel crushes in the head of the serpent with fatal effect. By his sufferings Christ has overthrown Satan, by the heel that was bruised he has trodden upon the head which devised the bruising.

> Lo, by the sons of hell he dies;
>   But as he hangs 'twixt earth and skies,
> He gives their prince a fatal blow,
>   And triumphs o'er the powers below.

Though Satan is not dead, my brethren, I was about to say, would God he were, and though he is not converted, and never will be, nor will the malice of his heart ever be driven from him, yet Christ has so far broken his head that he has missed his mark altogether. He intended to make the human race the captives of his power, but they are redeemed from his iron yoke. God has delivered many of them, and the day shall come when he will cleanse the whole earth from the serpent's slimy trail, so that the entire world shall be full of the praises of God. He thought that this world would be the arena of his victory over God and good, instead of which it is already the grandest theatre of divine wisdom, love, grace, and power.

Even heaven itself is not so resplendent with mercy as the earth is, for here it is the Savior poured out his blood, which cannot be said even of the courts of paradise above. Moreover he thought, no doubt, that when he had led our race astray and brought death upon them, he had effectually marred the Lord's work. He rejoiced that they would all pass under the cold seal of death, and that their bodies would rot in the sepulcher. Had he not spoiled the handiwork of his great Lord? God may make man as a curious creature with intertwisted veins and blood and nerves, and sinews and muscles, and he may put into his nostrils the breath of life; but, "Ah," saith Satan, "I have infused a poison into him which will make him return to the dust from which he was taken." but now, behold, our Champion whose heel was bruised has risen from the dead, and given us a pledge that all his followers shall rise form the dead also. Thus is Satan foiled, for death shall not retain a bone, nor a piece of a bone, of one of those who belonged to the woman's seed. At the trump of the archangel from the earth and from the sea they shall arise, and this shall be their shout, "O death, where is thy sting? O grave, where is thy victory?" Satan, knowing this, feels already that by the resurrection his head is broken. Glory be to the Christ of God for this!

In multitudes of other ways the devil has been vanquished by our Lord Jesus, and so shall he ever be till he shall be cast into the lake of fire.

II. Let us now view *OUR EXPERIENCE AS IT TALLIES WITH THESE FACTS*. Now, brothers and sisters, we were by nature, as many of us as have been saved, the heirs of wrath even as others. It does not matter how godly our parents were, the first birth brought us no spiritual life, for the promise is not to them which are born of blood, or of the will of the flesh, or of the will of man, but only to those who are born of God, "That which is born of the flesh is flesh"; you cannot make anything else and there it abides, and the flesh, or carnal mind, abideth in death; "it is not reconciled to God, neither indeed can be." He who is born into this world but once, and knows nothing of the new birth, must place himself among the seed of the serpent, for only by regeneration can we know ourselves to be the true seed. How does God deal with us who are his called and chosen ones? He means to save us, and how does he work to that end?

The first thing he does is, he comes to us in mercy, and *puts enmity between us and the serpent*. That is the very first work of grace. There was peace between us and Satan once; when he tempted we yielded; whatever he taught us we believed; we were his willing slaves. But perhaps you, my brethren, can recollect when first of all you began to feel uneasy and dissatisfied; the world's pleasures no longer pleased you; all the juice seemed to have been taken out of the apple, and you had nothing at all. Then you suddenly perceived that you were living in sin, and you were miserable about it, and though you could not get rid of sin yet you hated it, and sighed over it, and cried, and groaned. In your heart of hearts you remained no longer on the side of evil, for you began to cry, "O wretched man that I am, who shall deliver me from the body of this death?" You were already from of old in the covenant of grace ordained to be the woman's seed, and now the decree began to discover itself in life bestowed upon you and working in you. The Lord in infinite mercy dropped the divine life into your soul. You did not know it, but there it was, a spark of the celestial fire, the living and incorruptible seed which abideth forever. You began to hate sin, and you groaned under it as under a galling yoke; more and more it burdened you, you could not bear it. So it was with you: is it so now? Is there still enmity between you and the serpent? Indeed you are more and more the sworn enemies of evil, and you willingly acknowledge it.

Then came the Champion: that is to say, "Christ was formed in you the hope of glory." You heard of him and you understood the truth about him, and it seemed a wonderful thing that he should be your substitute and stand in your room and place and stead, and bear your sin and all its curse and punishment, and that he should give his righteousness, yea, and his very self, to you that you might be saved. Ah, then you saw how sin could be overthrown, did you not? As soon as your heart understood Christ then you saw that what the law could not do, in that it was weak through the flesh, Christ was able to accomplish, and that the power of sin and Satan under which you had been in bondage, and which you now loathed, could and would be broken and destroyed because Christ had come into the world to overcome it.

Next, do you recollect how you were led to see *the bruising of Christ's heel* and to stand in wonder and observe what the enmity of the serpent had wrought in him? Did you no begin to feel the bruised heel yourself? Did not sin torment you? Did not the very thought of it vex you? Did not your own heart become a plague to you? Did not Satan begin to tempt you? Did he not inject blasphemous thoughts, and urge you on to desperate measures; did he not teach you to doubt the existence of God, and the mercy of God, and the possibility of your salvation, and so on? This was his nibbling at your heel. He is at his old tricks still. He worries whom he can't devour with a malicious joy. Did not your worldly friends begin to annoy you? Did they not give you the cold shoulder because they saw something about you so strange and foreign to their tastes? Did they not impute your conduct to fanaticism, pride, obstinacy, bigotry, and the like?

Ah, this persecution is the serpent's seed beginning to discover the woman's seed, and to carry on the old war. What does Paul say? "But as then he that was born after the flesh persecuted him that was born after the Spirit, even so it is now." True godliness is an unnatural and strange thing to them, and they cannot away with it Though there are no stakes in Smithfield, nor racks in the Tower, yet the enmity of the human heart towards Christ and his seed is just the same, and very often shows itself in "trials of cruel mockings" which to the tender hearts are very hard to bear. Well, this is your heel being bruised in sympathy with the bruising of the heel of the glorious seed of the woman.

But, brethren, do you know something of the other fact, namely, that *we conquer, for the serpent's head is broken in us?* How say you? Is not the power and dominion of sin broken in you? Do you not feel that you cannot sin because you are born of God? Some sins which were masters of you once, do not trouble you now. I have known a man guilty of profane swearing, and from the moment of his conversion he has never had any difficulty in the matter. We have known a man snatched from drunkenness, and the cure by divine grace has been very wonderful and complete. We have known persons delivered from unclean living, and they have at once become chaste and pure, because Christ has smitten the old dragon such blows that he could not have power over them in that respect. The chosen seed sin and mourn it, but they are not slaves to sin; their heart goeth not after it they have to say sometimes "the thing I do," but they are wretched when it is so. They consent with their heart to the law of God that it is good, and they sigh and cry that they may be helped to obey it, for they are no longer under the slavery of sin; the serpent's reigning power and dominion is broken in them.

It is broken next in this way: that the guilt of sin is gone. The great power of the serpent lies in unpardoned sin. He cries "I have make you guilty: I brought you under the curse." 'No,' say we, "we are delivered from the curse and are now blessed, for it is written, 'Blessed is the man whose transgression is forgiven, whose sin is covered.' We are no longer guilty, for who shall lay anything to the charge of God's elect? Since Christ hath justified, who is he that condemneth? Here is a swinging blow for the old dragon's head, such as he never will recover.

Oftentimes the Lord also grants us to know what it is to overcome temptation, and so to break the dead of the fiend, Satan allures us with many baits; he has studied our points well he knows the weakness of the flesh: but many and many a time blessed be God, we have foiled him completely to his eternal shame! The devil must have felt himself mean that day when he tried to overthrow Job, dragged him down to a dunghill, robbed him of everything, covered him with sores, and yet could not make him yield. Job conquered when he cried, "Though he slay me yet will I trust in him." A feeble man had vanquished a devil who could raise the wind and blow down a house, and destroy the family who were feasting in it. Devil as he is, and crowned prince of the power of the air, yet the poor bereaved patriarch sitting on the dunghill covered with sores, being one of the woman's seed, through the strength of the inner life won the victory over him.

> Ye sons of God oppose his rage.
>   Resist, and he'll be gone:
> Thus did our dearest Lord engage
>   And vanquish him alone.

Moreover, dear brethren, we have this hope that the very being of sin in us will be destroyed. The day will come when we shall be without spot or wrinkle or any such thing; and we shall stand before the throne of God, having suffered no injury whatever from the fall and from all the machinations of Satan, for are "they are without fault before the throne of God." What triumph that will be! "The Lord will tread Satan under your feet shortly." When he has made you perfect and free from all sin, as he will do, you will have bruised the serpent's head indeed.

And your resurrection, too, when Satan shall see you come up from the grave like one that has been perfumed in a bath of spices, when he shall see you arise in the image of Christ, with the same body which was sown in corruption and weakness raised in incorruption and power, then will he feel an infinite chagrin, and know that his head is bruised by the woman's seed.

I ought to add that every time any one of us is made useful in saving souls we do as it were repeat the bruising of the serpent's head. When you go, dear sister, among those poor children, and pick them up from the gutters, where they are Satan's prey, where he finds the raw material for thieves and criminals, and when through your means, by the grace of God, the little wonderers become children of the living God, then you in your measure bruise the old serpent's head, I pray you do not spare him. When we by preaching the gospel turn sinners from the error of their ways, so that they escape from the power of darkness, again we bruise the serpent's head. Whenever in any shape of way you are blessed to the aiding of the cause of truth and righteousness in the world, you, too, who were once beneath his power, and even now have sometimes to suffer from his nibbling at your heel, you tread upon his head. In all deliverances and victories you overcome, and prove the promise true,—"Thou shalt tread upon the lion and adder; the young lion and the dragon shalt thou trample under feet. Because he hath set his love upon me, therefore will I deliver him I will set him on high, because he hath known my name."

III. Let us speak awhile upon THE ENCOURAGEMENT which our text and the context yields to us; for it seems to me to abound.

I want you, brethren, to exercise faith in the promise and be comforted. The text evidently encouraged Adam very much. I do not think we have attached enough importance to the conduct of Adam after the Lord had spoken to him. Notice the simple but conclusive proof which he gave of his faith. Sometimes an action may be very small and unimportant, and yet, as a straw shows which way the wind blows, it may display at once, if it be thought over, the whole state of the man's mind. Adam acted in faith upon what God had said, for we read, "And Adam called his wife's name Eve (or Life); because she was the mother of all living" (v. 20). She was not a mother at all, but as the life was to come through her by virtue of the promised seed, Adam marks his full conviction of the truth of the promise though at the time the woman had borne no children. There stood Adam, fresh from the awful presence of God, what more could he say? He might have said with the Prophet, "My flesh trembleth fro the fear of thee," but even then he turns round to his fellow-culprit as she stands there trembling too, and he calls her Eve, mother of the life that is yet to be.

It was grandly spoken by Father Adam: it makes him rise in our esteem. Had he been left to himself he would have murmured or at least despaired, but no, his faith in the new promise gave him hope. He uttered no word of repining against the condemnation to till with toil the unthankful ground, nor on Eve's part was there a word of repining over the appointed sorrows of motherhood; they each accept the well-deserved sentence with the silence which denotes the perfection of their resignation; their only word is full of simple faith. There was no child on whom to set their hopes, nor would the true seed be born for an age, still Eve is to be the mother of all the living, and he calls her so.

Exercise like faith, my brother, on the far wider revelation which God has given to you, and always extract the utmost comfort from it. Make a point, whenever you receive a promise from God, to get all you can out of it if you carry out that rule, it is wonderful what comfort you will gain. Some go on the principle of getting as little as possible out of God's word. I believe that such a plan is the proper way with a man's word; always understand it at the minimum, because that is what he means; but God's word is to be understood at the maximum, for he will do exceeding abundantly above what you ask or even think.

Notice by way of further encouragement that we may regard our reception of Christ's righteousness as an installment of the final overthrow of the devil. The twenty-first verse says, "Unto Adam also and to his wife did the Lord God made coats of skins, and clothed them." A very condescending, thoughtful, and instructive deed of divine love! God heard what Adam said to his wife, and saw that he was a believer, and so he comes and gives him the type of the perfect righteousness, which is the believer's portion—he covered him with lasting raiment. No more fig leaves, which were a mere mockery, but a close fitting garment which had been procured through the death of a victim; the

Lord brings that and puts it on him, and Adam could no more say, "I am naked." How could he, for God had clothed him. Now, beloved, let us take out of the promise that is given us concerning our Lord's conquest over the devil this one item and rejoice in it, for Christ has delivered us from the power of the serpent who opened our eyes and told us we were naked, by covering us from head to foot with a righteousness which adorns and protects us, so that we are comfortable in heart, and beautiful in the sight of God, and are no more ashamed.

Next, by way of encouragement in pursuing the Christian life, I would say to young people, expect to be assailed. If you have fallen into trouble through being a Christian, be encouraged by it; do not at all regret of fear it, but rejoice ye in that day, and leap for joy, for this is the constant token of the covenant. There is enmity between the seed of the woman and the seed of the serpent still, and if you did not experience any of it you might begin to fear that you were on the wrong side. Now that you smart under the sneer of sarcasm and oppression rejoice and triumph, for now are ye partakers with the glorious seed of the woman in the bruising of his heel.

Still further encouragement comes from this. Your suffering as a Christian is not brought upon you for your own sake; ye are partners with the great seed of the woman, ye are confederates with Christ. You must not think the devil cares much about you: the battle is against Christ in you. When, if you were not in Christ, the devil would never trouble you. When you were without Christ in the world you might have sinned as you like, your relatives and workmates would not have been at all grieved with you, they would rather have joined you in it; but now the serpent's seed hates Christ in you. This exalts the sufferings of persecution to a position far above all common afflictions. I have heard of a woman who was condemned to death in the Marian days, and before her time came to be burned a child was born to her, and she cried out in her sorrow. A wicked adversary, who stood by said, "how will you bear to die for your religion if you make such ado?" "Ah," she said, "Now I suffer in my own person as a woman, but then I shall not suffer, but Christ in me." Nor were these idle words, for she bore her martyrdom with exemplary patience, and rose in her chariot of fire in holy triumph to heaven. If Christ be in you, nothing will dismay you, but you will overcome the world, the flesh, and the devil by faith.

Last of all, let us resist the devil always with this belief that he has received a broken head. I am inclined to think that Luther's way of laughing at the devil was a very good one, for he is worthy of shame and everlasting contempt. Luther once threw and inkstand at his head when he was tempting him very sorely, and though the act itself appears absurd enough, yet it was a true type of what that greater reformer was all his life long, for the books he wrote were truly a flinging of the inkstand at the head of the fiend. That is what we have to do: we are to resist him by all means. Let us do this bravely, and tell him to his teeth that we are not afraid of him. Tell him to recollect his bruised head, which he tries to cover with a crown of pride, or with a popish cowl, or with an infidel doctor's hood. We know him, and see the deadly wound he bears. His power is gone; he is fighting a lost battle; he is contending against omnipotence. He has set himself against the oath of the Father; against the blood of the incarnate Son; against the eternal power and Godhead of the blessed Spirit, all of which are engaged in the defense of the seed of the woman in the day of battle. Therefore, brethren, be ye steadfast in resisting the evil one being strong in faith, giving glory to God.

> Tis by thy blood, immortal Lamb,
>   Thine armies tread the tempter down;
> 'tis by thy word and powerful name
>   They gain the battle and renown.
>
> Rejoice ye heavens; let every star
>   Shine with new glories round the sky;
> Saints, while ye sing the heavenly war,
>   Raise your Deliverer's name on high.

3

Christ the Overcomer of the World

"Be of good cheer; I have overcome the world" (John 16:33).

When these words were spoken our Savior was about to leave his disciples to go to his death for their sakes. His great anxiety was that they might not be too much cast down by the trials which would come upon them. He desired to prepare their minds for the heavy sorrows which awaited them, while the powers of darkness and the men of the world accomplished their will upon him.

Now observe, beloved, that our Lord Jesus, in whom dwells infinite wisdom, knew all the secret springs of comfort, and all the hallowed sources of consolation in heaven and under heaven, and yet in order to console his disciples he spoke, not of heavenly mysteries nor of secrets hidden in the heart of God, but he spoke concerning himself. Does he not herein teach us that there is no balm for the heart like himself, no consolation of Israel comparable to his person and his work? If even such a divine Barnabas, such a firstborn son of consolation as the Lord himself must point to what he himself has done, for only by this can he make his followers to be of good cheer, then how wise it must be in ministers to preach much about Jesus by way of encouragement for the Lord's afflicted, and how prudent it is for mourners to look to him for the comfort they need. "Be of good cheer," he says, "*I*" — something about himself — "*I have* overcome the world." So then, beloved, in all times of depression of spirit hurry away to the Lord Jesus Christ; whenever the cares of this life burden you, and your way seems hard for your weary feet, flee to your Lord. There may be, and there are, other sources of consolation, but they will not at all times serve your purpose; but in him there dwells such a fulness of comfort, that whether it is in summer or in winter the streams of comfort are always flowing. In your high estate or in your low estate, and from whatever quarter your trouble may arise, you can resort at once to him and you shall find that he strengthens the hands that hang down and confirms the feeble knees.

A further remark suggests itself that the Lord Jesus must be more than man from the tone which he assumed. There are certain people who deny the Godhead of our Lord and yet think well of Jesus as a man; indeed, they have uttered many highly complementary things with regard to his character: but I wonder that it should not strike them that there is a great deal of assumption, presumption, pride, egotism, and all that form of folly in this man if he is nothing more than a man. For what good man whom you would wish to imitate would say to others "Be of good cheer: I have overcome the world." This is altogether too much for a mere man to say.

The Lord Jesus Christ frequently spoke about himself and about what he has done, and commended himself to his disciples as one who was only a man and of a lowly mind could never have done. The Lord was certainly meek and lowly in heart, but no man of that character would have told others so. There is an inconsistency here which no one can account for except those who believe him to be the Son of God. Understand him to be divine, put him in his true position as speaking down from the excellency of his deity to his disciples, and then you can comprehend his speaking like that, yes, it becomes infinitely seemly and beautiful. Deny his Godhead, and I for one am quite unable to understand how the words before us, and others like them, could ever have fallen from his lips, for no one will dare to say that he was boastful. Blessed are you, oh Son of man, you are also Son of God, and therefore you not only speak to us with the sympathizing tenderness of a brother man, but also with the majestic authority of the Only Begotten of the Father. Divinely condescending are your words, "I have overcome the world."

If you look at this claim of Jesus without the eye of faith, does it not wear an extraordinary appearance? How could the betrayed man of Nazareth say, "I have overcome the world?" We can imagine Napoleon speaking like this when he had crushed the nations beneath his feet, and reshaped the map of Europe to his will. We can imagine Alexander speaking like this when he had rifled the palaces of Persia and led her ancient monarchs captive. But who is this who speaks like this? It is a Galilean, who wears a peasant's garment, and consorts with the poor and the fallen! He has neither wealth nor worldly rank nor honor among men, and yet speaks of having overcome the world. He is about to be betrayed by his own base follower into the hands of his enemies, and then he will be led out to judgment and to death, and yet he says, "I have overcome the world."

He is casting an eye towards his cross with all its shame, and to the death which ensued from it, and yet he says, "I have overcome the world." He did not have anywhere to lay his head, he never had a disciple who would stand up for him, for he had just said, "You shall be scattered, every man to his own, and shall leave me alone"; he was to be charged with blasphemy and sedition, and brought before the judge, and find no man to declare his generation; he was to be given up to brutal soldiers to be mocked and despitefully used and spat upon; his hands and feet were to be nailed to a cross, so that he might die a felon's death, and yet he says, "I have overcome the world."

How marvelous, and yet how true! He did not speak after the manner of the flesh nor after the sight of the eye. We must use eyes of faith here and look within the veil, and then we shall see not only the despised bodily person of the Son of man, but also the indwelling, noble, all-conquering soul which transformed shame into honor, and death into glory. May God the Holy Spirit enable us to look through the external to the internal, and see how marvelously the ignominious death was the rough garment which concealed the matchless victory from the blind eyes of carnal man.

During the last two Sunday mornings I have spoken of our Lord Jesus Christ: first, as the end of the law; and secondly, as the conqueror over the old serpent; now we come to speak of him as *the overcomer of the world*, addressing his disciples he said, "Be of good cheer; I have overcome the world."

Now, *what is this world that he speaks about?* And, *how has he overcome it?* Also, *what good cheer is there in the fact for us?*

I. *WHAT IS THIS WORLD WHICH HE IS REFERRING TO?*

I scarcely know a word which is used with so many senses as this word "world." If you will turn to your Bibles you will find the word "world" used in widely varying meanings, for there is a world which Christ made, "He was in the world and the world was made by him"—that is, the physical world. There is a world which God so loved that he gave his only-begotten Son that whoever believes in him might not perish. There are several forms of this favorable meaning. Then there is a world, the world meant here, which "lies in the wicked one," a world which does not know Christ, but which is always opposed to him: a world for which he says that he does not pray, and a world which he would not have us love—"Do not love the world, neither the things which are in the world." Without going into these various meanings, and shades of meaning, which are very abundant, let us just say that we scarcely know how to define what is meant here in so many words, though we know well enough what is meant. Scripture does not give us definitions, but uses language in a popular manner, since it speaks to common people. "The world" is very much the equivalent of the "seed of the serpent," of which we spoke last Sunday. The world here means the visible embodiment of that spirit of evil which was in the serpent, and which now works in the children of disobedience; it is the human form of the same evil force with which our Lord contended when he overcame the devil; it means the power of evil in the unregenerate mass of mankind, the energy and power of sin as it dwells in that portion of the world which remains in death and lies in the wicked one. The devil is the god of this world, and the prince of this world, and therefore he who is the friend of this world is the enemy of God. The world is the opposite of the church. There is a church which Christ has redeemed and chosen out of the world and separated to himself, from among men, and of these as renewed by the power of divine grace, he says, "You are not of the world, even as I am not of the world"; and again, "Because you are not of the world, but I have chosen you out of the world, therefore the world hates you."

Now, the rest of mankind not included among the chosen, the redeemed, the called, the saved, are called the world. Of these our Lord said, "Oh, righteous Father, the world has not known you"; and John said, "The world does not know you because it did not know him." This is the power which displays a deadly enmity against Christ and against his chosen; hence it is called "this present evil world," while the kingdom of grace is spoken of as "the world to come." This is the world of which it is said, "He who is born by God overcomes the world."

You will see that "the world" includes the ungodly themselves, as well as the force of evil in them, but it singles them out, not as creatures nor even as men who have sinned, but as unregenerate, carnal and rebellious, and therefore as the living embodiments of an evil power which works against God; and so we read of "the world of the ungodly."

Perhaps I ought to add that there has grown up out of the existence of unconverted men and the prevalence of sin in them certain customs, fashions, maxims, rules, modes, manners, and forces, all of which go to make up what is called "the world," and there are also certain principles, desires, lusts, governments and powers which also make up a part of the evil thing called "the world." Jesus says "My kingdom is not of this world." James speaks of keeping ourselves "unspotted from the world." John says, "the world passes away and its lust"; and Paul says, "do not be conformed to this world, but be transformed."

Moreover, I may say that the present constitution and arrangement of all things in this fallen state may be summed up in the term "world," for everything has come under vanity by reason of sin, and things are not today according to the original plan of the Most High, as designed for man in his innocence. Behold there are trials and troubles springing out of our very existence in this life of which it is said, "in the world you shall have tribulation." To many a child of God there have befallen hunger and disease and suffering, and unkindness, and various forms of evil which do not belong to the world to come, nor to the kingdom which Christ has set up, but which come to them because they are in this present evil world, which has become like this because the race of men have fallen under the curse and consequence of sin.

Now the world is all these matters put together, this great conglomeration of mischief among men, this evil which dwells here and there and everywhere wherever men are scattered—this is the thing which we call the world. Every one of us knows better what it is than we can tell to anyone else, and perhaps while I am explaining I am rather confounding than expounding. You know just what the world is to some of you—it is not more than your own little family, with respect to outward form, but much more with respect to influence. Your actual world may be confined to your own house, but the same principles enter into the domestic circle which pervade kingdoms and states. To others the world takes a wide sweep as they necessarily meet ungodly men in business, and this we must do unless we are to go altogether out of the world, which is not part of our Lord's plan, for he says, "I do not pray that you should take them out of the world."

To some who look at the whole mass of mankind, and are called thoughtfully to consider them all because they have to be God's messengers to them, the tendencies and outgoings of the human mind towards what is evil, and the spirit of men's actions as done against God in all nations and ages—all these go to make up for them "the world." But whatever it is, it is a thing out of which tribulation will be sure to come to us, Christ tells us so. It may come in the form of temporal trial of some form or other; it may come in the form of temptation which will alight upon us from our fellow men, it may come in the form of persecution to a greater or lesser extent according to our position: but it will come. "In the world you shall have tribulation." We are sojourners in an enemy's country, and the people of the land where we tarry are not our friends, and will not help us on our pilgrimage to heaven. All spiritual men in the world are our friends, but then, like ourselves, they are in the world but they are not of it. From the kingdom of this world of which Satan is lord we must expect fierce opposition against which we must contend even to victory if we are to enter into everlasting rest.

II. Now this brings me to the more interesting topic in the second point of HOW HAS CHRIST OVERCOME THE WORLD? And we answer, first he did so *in his life:* then *in his death:* and then *in his rising and his reigning.*

First, Christ *overcame the world in his life.* This is a wonderful study, the overcoming of the world in the life of Christ. I imagine that those first thirty years of which we know so little were a wonderful preparation for his conflict with the world, and that though only in the carpenter's shop, and obscure, and unknown to the great outside world, yet in fact he was not merely preparing for the battle, but he was then beginning to overcome it. In the patience which made him bide his time we see the dawn of the victory. When we are intent upon doing good, and we see mischief and sin triumphant everywhere, we are eager to begin: but suppose it were not the great Father's will that we should be immediately engaged in the fray, how strongly would the world then tempt us to go forward before our time. A transgression of discipline may be caused by too much zeal, and this as much breaks through the law of obedience as dullness or sloth would do. The Roman soldier was judged guilty who, when the army was left with the orders that no man should strike a blow in the leader's absence, nevertheless stepped forward and killed a Gaul; the act was one of valor, but it was contrary to military discipline, and might have had most baleful results, and so it was condemned. So it is sometimes with us, before we are ready, before we have received our commission, we are in a hurry to step forward and strike the foe. That temptation must have come to Christ from the world: many a time as he heard of what was going on in the reign of error and hypocrisy his benevolent impulses might have suggested to him to be up and doing, had it not been that he was incapable of wrong desires. Doubtless he was willing to be healing the sick. Was not the land full of sufferers? He would gladly be saving souls—were they not going down to the pit by thousands? He would gladly have confuted error, for falsehood was doing deadly work, but his hour was not yet come. Yet our Lord and Master had nothing to say until his Father told him to speak. We know he was strongly under an impulse to be at work, for when he went up to the temple he said, "Did you not know that I must be about my Father's business?" That utterance revealed the fire that burned within his soul, and yet he was not preaching nor healing, nor disputing, but still remained in obscurity all those thirty years, because God would have it so. When the Lord would have us quiet we are doing his will best by being quiet, but yet to be still and calm for so long a time was a wonderful example of how all his surroundings could not master him not even when they seemed to work with his philanthropy; he still remained obedient to God, and thus proved himself the overcomer of the world.

When he appears upon the scene of public action you know how he overcomes the world in many ways. First, *by remaining always faithful to his testimony*. He never modified it, not even by so much as a solitary word to please the sons of men. From the first day in which he began to preach even to the closing sentence which he uttered it was all truth and nothing but truth, truth uncolored by prevailing sentiment, untainted by popular error. He did not, after the manner of the Jesuit, disguise his doctrine by so framing it so that men would hardly know that it was the very error in which they had been brought up, but he came out with plain-speaking, and set himself in opposition to all the powers which ruled the thought and creed of the age. He was no guarder of truth. He allowed truth to fight her own battles in her own way, and you know how she bares her breast to her antagonist's arrows, and finds in her own immutable, immortal, and invulnerable life her shield and her spear. His speech was confident, for he knew that truth would conquer in the long run, and therefore he proclaimed his doctrine without respect to the age or its prejudices. I do not think that you can say that about anyone else's ministry, not even of the best and bravest of his servants.

We can see, in looking at Luther, great and glorious Luther, how Romanism tinged all that he did more or less; and the darkness of the age cast some gloom even over the serene and steadfast soul of Calvin; of each one of the reformers we must say the same: bright stars as all of these were, yet they did not keep themselves untarnished by the sphere in which they shone. Every man is more or less affected by his age, and we are obliged, as we read history, to make continual allowances, for we all admit that it would not be fair to judge the men of former times by the standard of this century. But, sirs, you may test Christ Jesus if you will by this century's light, if it is light; you may judge him by any century, indeed, you may try him by the bright light of the throne of God: his teaching is pure truth without any adulteration, it will stand the test of time and of eternity. His teaching was not affected by the fact of his being born a Jew, nor by the prevalence of the Rabbinical traditions, nor by the growth of the Greek philosophy, nor by any other of the particular influences which were then abroad. His teaching was in the world, but it was not of it, nor tinged by it. It was the truth as he had received it from the Father, and the world could not make him add to it, or take from it, or change it in the least degree, and therefore in this respect he overcame the world.

Observe him next in *the deep calm which pervaded his spirit at times when he received the approbation of men*. Our Lord was popular to a very high degree at certain times. How the people thronged around him as his benevolent hands scattered healing on all sides. How they approved of him when he fed them; but how clearly he saw through that selfish approbation, and said, "You seek me because of the loaves and fishes." He never lost his self-possession: you never find him elated by the multitudes following him. There is not an expression that he ever used which even contains a suspicion of self-glorification. Amid their hosannas his mind is quietly reposing in God. He leaves their acclamations and applause to refresh himself by prayer upon the cold mountains, in the midnight air. He communed with God, and so lived above the praises of men. He walked among them, holy, harmless, undefiled and separate from sinners, even when they would have taken him by force and made him a king. Once he rides in triumph, as he might often have done if he had pleased, but then it was in such a humble style that his pomp was far other than that of kings, a manifestation of lowliness rather than a display of majesty. Amid the willing hosannas of little children, and of those whom he had blessed, he rides along, but you can see that he indulges none of the thoughts of a worldly conqueror, none of the proud ideas of the warrior who returns from the battle stained with blood. No, he is still as meek and as gentle and as kindly as he ever was, and his triumph has not a grain of self-exaltation in it. He had overcome the world. What could the world give him, brethren? An imperial nature like his, in which the manhood held such close communion with Deity as is not readily to be imagined, what was there here below to cause pride in him? If the trumpet of fame had sounded out its loudest note, what could it have been compared with the songs of cherubim and seraphim to which his ear had been accustomed throughout all ages? No, allied with his deity, his manhood was superior to all the arts of flattery, and to all the honors which mankind could offer him. He overcame the world.

He was the same when the world tried the other plan upon him. *It frowned at him, but he was still calm.* He had scarcely begun to preach before they would have cast him headlong from the brow of the hill. Do you not expect, as they are hurrying him to the precipice, to see him turn around upon them and denounce them at least with burning words, such as Elijah used? But no, he does not speak an angry word; he passes away and is gone out of their midst. In the synagogue they often gnashed their teeth upon him in their malice, but if ever he was moved to indignation it was not because of anything directed against himself; he always bore it all, and scarcely ever spoke a word by way of reply to merely personal attacks.

If calumnies were heaped upon him he went on as calmly as if they had not abused him, nor desired to kill him. When he is brought before his judges what a difference there is between the Master and his servant Paul. He is struck, but he does not say like Paul, "God shall strike you, you whited wall"; no, but like a lamb before her shearers he is dumb and does not open his mouth. If they could have made him angry they would have overcome him; but he was still loving; he was gentle, quiet, patient, however much they provoked him. Point me to an impatient word—there is not even a tradition of an angry look that he gave on account of any offence rendered to himself.

They could not drive him from his purposes of love, nor could they make him say anything or do anything that was contrary to perfect love. He calls down no fire from heaven: no she-bears come out of the woods to devour those who have mocked him. No, he can say, "I have overcome the world," for whether it smiles or whether it frowns, in the perfect peace and quiet of his spirit, in the delightful calm of communion with God, the Man of Sorrows holds on his conquering way.

His victory will be seen in another form. He overcame the world concerning *the unselfishness of his aims*. When men find themselves in a world like this they generally say, "What is our market? What can we make out of it?" This is how they are trained from childhood. "Boy, you have to fight your own way, be careful to look to your own interests and rise in the world." The book which is commended to the young man shows him how to make the best use of all things for himself, he must take care of "number one," and look out for the best opportunities. The boy is told by his wise instructors "You must look after yourself or no one else will look after you: and whatever you may do for others, be doubly sure to guard your own interests." That is the world's prudence, the essence of all her politics, the basis of her political economy—every man, and every nation must take care of themselves: if you wish for any other politics or economics you will be considered to be foolish theorists and probably a little touched in the head. Self is the man, the world's law of self-preservation is the sovereign rule, and nothing can go on properly if you interfere with the gospel of selfishness so the commercial and political Solomons assure us.

Now, look at the Lord Jesus Christ when he was in the world and you will learn nothing about such principles, except their condemnation: the world could not overcome him by leading him into a selfish mode of action. Did it ever enter into his soul, even for a moment, what he could do for himself? There were riches, but he had nowhere to lay his head. The little money he had he committed to the trust of Judas, and as long as there were any poor in the land they were sure to share in what was in the bag. He set so little value on estate, and stock, and funds that no mention is made of such things by any of his four biographers. He had wholly and altogether risen above the world in that respect; for with whatever evil the most spiteful infidels have ever charged our Lord they have never, to my knowledge, accused him of avarice, greed, or selfishness in any form. He had overcome the world.

Then again the Master overcame the world in that *he did not stoop to use its power*. He did not use that form of power which belongs to the world even for unselfish purposes. I can conceive a man even apart from the Spirit of God rising superior to riches, and desiring only the promotion of some great principle which has possessed his heart; but you will usually notice that when men have done so, they have been ready to promote good by evil, or at least they have judged that great principles might be pushed on by force of arms, or bribes, or policy. Mohammed had grasped a grand truth when he said, "There is no God but God." The unity of the Godhead is a truth of the utmost value; but then here comes the means to be used for the propagation of this grand truth—the scimitar. "Off with the infidels' heads! If they have false gods, or will not acknowledge the unity of the Godhead, they are not fit to live."

Can you imagine our Lord Jesus Christ doing this? Why then the world would have conquered him. But he conquered the world in that he would not employ in the slightest degree this form of power. He might have gathered a troop around him, and his heroic example, together with his miraculous power, must soon have swept away the Roman empire, and converted the Jew; and then across Europe and Asia and Africa his victorious legions might have gone trampling down all manner of evil, and with the cross for his banner and the sword for his weapon, the idols would have fallen, and the whole world must have been made to bow at his feet. But no, when Peter takes out the sword, he says, "Put up your sword into its sheath, those who take the sword shall perish with the sword." Well did he say, "My kingdom is not of this world, otherwise my servants would fight."

And he might if he had pleased have allied his church with the state, as his mistaken friends have done in these degenerate times, and then there might have been penal laws against those who dared to dissent, and there might have been forced contributions for the support of his church and such like things. You have read, I dare say, of such things being done, but not in the Gospels, nor in the Acts of the Apostles. These things are done by those who forget the Christ of God, for he uses no instrument but love, no sword but the truth, no power but the Eternal Spirit, and, in the very fact that he put all the worldly forces aside, he overcame the world.

So, brethren, he overcame the world by *his fearlessness of the world's elite*, for many a man who has braved the frowns of the multitude cannot bear the criticism of the few who think they have monopolized all wisdom. But Christ meets the Pharisee, and pays no honor to his phylactery; he confronts the Sadducee and does not yield to his cold philosophy, neither does he conceal the difficulties of the faith to escape his sneer; and he braves also the Herodian, who is the worldly politician, and he gives him an unanswerable reply. He is the same before them all, master in all positions, overcoming the world's wisdom and supposed intelligence by his own simple testimony to the truth.

And he overcame the world in his life best of all *by the constancy of his love*. He loved the most unlovely men, he loved those who hated him, he loved those who despised him. You and I are readily turned aside from loving when we receive ungrateful treatment, and thus we are conquered by the world, but he kept to his great object—"he saved others, but he could not save himself"; and he died with this prayer on his lips, "Father, forgive them, for they do not know what they are doing."

Not soured in the least, oh blessed Savior, you are at the last just as tender as at the first. We have seen fine spirits, full of generosity, who have had to deal with a crooked and perverse generation, until they have at last grown hard and cold. Nero, who weeps when he signs the first death-warrant of a criminal, at last comes to gloat in the blood of his subjects. Thus do sweet flowers wither into noxious corruption. As for you, oh precious Savior, you are always fragrant with love. No spot comes upon your lovely character, though you traverse a miry road. You are as kind towards men at your departure as you were at your coming, for you have overcome the world.

I can only say on the next point that *Christ by his death overcame the world* because, by a wondrous act of self-sacrifice, the Son of God struck to the heart the principle of selfishness, which is the very soul and life-blood of the world. There, too, by redeeming fallen man he lifted man up from the power which the world exercises over him, for he taught men that they are redeemed, that they are no longer their own but bought with a price, and thus redemption became the note of liberty from the bondage of self-love, and the hammer which breaks the fetters of the world and its lusts.

By reconciling men to God through his great atonement, he has also removed them from the despair which otherwise had kept them down in sin, and made them the willing slaves of the world. Now they are pardoned, and, being justified, they are made to be the friends of God, and being the friends of God they become enemies to God's enemies, and are separated from the world, and so the world by Christ's death is overcome.

But chiefly he has overcome *by his rising and his reigning,* for when he rose he bruised the serpent's head, and that serpent is the prince of this world, and has dominion over it. Christ has conquered the world's prince and led him in chains, and now Christ has assumed the sovereignty over all things here below. God has put all things under his feet. The keys of providence are at his belt; he rules among the multitude and in the council chambers of kings. Just as Joseph governed Egypt for the good of Israel, so Jehovah Jesus governs all things for the good of his people. Now the world can go no further in persecuting his people than he permits. Not a martyr can burn, nor a confessor be imprisoned without the permission of Jesus Christ who is the Lord of all; for the government is upon his shoulders and his kingdom rules over all. Brethren, this is a great joy for us to think of the reigning power of Christ as having overcome the world.

There is this other thought that he has overcome the world *by the gift of the Holy Spirit.* That gift was practically the world's conquest. Jesus has set up a rival kingdom now: a kingdom of love and righteousness; already the world feels its power by the Spirit. I do not believe that there is a dark place in the center of Africa which is not to some extent improved by the influence of Christianity; even the wilderness rejoices and is glad for him. No barbarous power dares to do what it once did, or if it does there is such a clamor raised against its cruelty that very soon it has to say *peccavi* ("I have sinned") and confess its faults. This moment the stone cut out of the mountain without hands has begun to strike old Dagon, it is breaking his head and breaking his hands and the very stump of him shall be dashed in pieces yet. There is no power in this world so vital, so potent as the power of Christ at this day. I say nothing just now of heavenly or spiritual things; but I speak only of temporal and moral influences—even in these the cross is at the forefront. He of whom Voltaire said that he lived in the twilight of his day, is going from strength to strength. It was true it was the twilight, but it was the twilight of the morning and the full noon is coming. Every year the name of Jesus brings more light to this poor world; every year hastens on the time when the cross which is the Pharos of humanity, the world's lighthouse amid the storm, shall shine out more and more brightly over the troubled waters until the great calm shall come. The word shall become more and more universally true, "I, if I am lifted up, will draw all men to me." Thus he has overcome the world.

III. Now, lastly, WHAT CHEER IS THERE HERE FOR US?

Why, this first, that if the man Christ Jesus has overcome the world at its worst, we who are in him shall overcome the world too through the same power which dwelt in him. He has put his life into his people, he has given his Spirit to dwell in them, and they shall be more than conquerors. He overcame the world when it attacked him in the worst possible form, for he was poorer than any of you, he was more sick and sad than any of you, he was more despised and persecuted than any of you, and he was deprived of certain divine consolations which God has promised never to take away from his saints, and yet with all possible disadvantages Christ overcame the world: therefore be assured we shall conquer also by his strength.

Besides, he overcame the world when no one else had overcome it. It was as it were a young lion which had never been defeated in a fight: it roared upon him out of the thicket and leaped upon him in the fullness of its strength. Now if our greater Samson tore this young lion as though it were a kid and flung it down as a vanquished thing, you may depend upon it that now it is an old lion, and grey and covered with the wounds which he gave it of old, we, having the Lord's life and power in us, will overcome it too. Blessed be his name! What good cheer there is in his victory. He as good as says to us, "I have overcome the world, and you in whom I dwell, who are clothed with my Spirit, must overcome it too."

But then, next, remember he overcame the world as our Head and representative, and it may truly be said that if the members do not overcome, then the head has not perfectly gained the victory. If it were possible for the members to be defeated, why then, the head itself could not claim a complete victory, since it is one with the members. So Jesus Christ, our Covenant-Head and representative, in whose loins lay all the spiritual seed, conquered the world for us and we conquered the world in him. He is our Adam, and what was done by him was actually done for us and virtually done by us. Have courage then, for you must conquer; it must happen to you as it happened to your head: where the head is the members shall be, and just as the head is so must the members be: therefore be assured of the palm branch and the crown.

And now, brethren, I ask you whether you have not found it so? Is it not true at this moment that the world is overcome in you? Does *self* govern you? Are you working to acquire wealth for your own aggrandizement? Are you living to win honor and fame among men? Are you afraid of men's frowns? Are you the slave of popular opinion? Do you do things because it is the custom to do them? Are you the slaves of fashion? If you are, you know nothing about this victory. But if you are true Christians I know what you can say: "Lord, I am your servant, you have released my bonds; henceforth the world has no dominion over me; and though it tempts me, and frightens me, and flatters me, yet still I rise superior to it by the power of your Spirit, for the love of Christ constrains me, and I do not live for myself and for things that are seen, but for Christ and for things that are not visible." If it is so, who has done this for you? Who except Christ the Overcomer, who is formed in you the hope of glory: therefore be of good cheer, for you have overcome the world by virtue of his dwelling in you.

So, brethren, let us go back to the world and its tribulations without fear. Its trials cannot harm us. In the process we shall get good, just as the wheat does from the threshing. Let us go out to combat the world, for it cannot overcome us. There was never a man yet with the life of God in his soul whom the whole world could subdue; no, all the world and hell together cannot conquer the weakest babe in the family of the Lord Jesus Christ. Lo, you are harnessed with salvation, you are panoplied with omnipotence, your heads are covered with the aegis of the atonement, and Christ himself, the Son of God, is your captain. Take up your battle-cry with courage, and do not fear, for more is he who is for you than all those who are against you. It is said of the glorified saints, "They overcame through the blood of the Lamb"; "and this is the victory which overcomes the world, even our faith," therefore be steadfast, even to the end, for you shall be more than conquerors through him who has loved you. Amen.

4

Christ the Maker of All Things New

"Therefore if any man is in Christ, he is a new creature: old things are passed away; behold, all things are become new" (2 Cor. 5:17).

We shall try to preach this morning of Christ as the Author of the new creation, and may we be enabled by the Holy Spirit to speak to his glory. To create all things new is one of his most famous achievements; may we not only gaze upon it but be partakers in it.

What does Solomon say in the book of Ecclesiastes? Does he not tell us there that "the thing that has been shall be, and what is done is what shall be done, and there is no new thing under the sun?" No doubt Solomon was correct in this declaration, but he wrote about this world and not about the world to come of which we speak; for behold, in the world to come, that is to say, in the kingdom of our Lord Jesus Christ, all things are new. To the wisest mind, if unrenewed, there is nothing new, but to the most humble of the regenerated ones all things have become new.

The word "new" seems to harmonize sweetly with the name and work of our Lord Jesus, inasmuch as he comes in after the old system had failed, and begins anew with us as the father and head of a chosen race. He is the Mediator of the new covenant, and has come to place us in a new relationship with God. As the second Adam he has delivered us from the old broken covenant of works where we lay under the curse, and he has placed us under the new infallible covenant of grace where we are established by his merit. The blood of Jesus Christ is said to be "the blood of the new covenant"; there is thus a connection with newness even in the most vital point of our dear Redeemer's person. The blood is even to him its life, and apart from that blood he can bestow no remission of sin; thus there is a newness about that essential life flood, for when he gives us to drink of his cup of remembrance he says "This is my blood of the *new* testament, which is shed for many for the remission of sins." "Now he has obtained a more excellent ministry, by how much also he is the Mediator of a better covenant, which was established upon better promises." The old covenant, the old ceremonial law, the old spirit of bondage, and all of the old leaven Jesus has purged out of the house, and he has ushered in a new age in which grace reigns through righteousness to eternal life.

When our Lord Jesus came into the world his birth of a virgin by the power of the Holy Spirit was a new thing, for thus the prophet Jeremiah had said of old in the name of the Lord, "How long will you go around, oh you backsliding daughter? for the Lord has created a new thing in the earth, a woman shall encompass a man." To us a child is born who is the virgin's son, in whom we rejoice because he comes into the world without taint of original sin, after a new fashion, as never a man was born before. Coming thus into the old world, he proclaims new doctrine, for his doctrine is called gospel, or good news. It is the freshest news that an anxious heart can hear; it is the most novel music by which a troubled heart can be soothed. Jesus Christ's teaching is still the best news of these days, as it was centuries ago. Though the world has had nearly two millennia of the glad tidings, the gospel has the dew of its youth upon it, and when men hear it they still ask, as the Greeks did of old, "What new doctrine is this?"

Our Lord Jesus has come to set up, by the preaching and teaching of the gospel, a new kingdom, a kingdom having new laws, new customs, a new charter, and new riches, a kingdom which is not of this world, a kingdom founded upon better principles and bringing infinitely better results to its subjects than any other dominion that has ever been. Into that kingdom he introduces only new men, who are made new creatures in Christ Jesus, who therefore love his new commandment and serve him in newness of spirit and not in the oldness of the letter. Moreover, Christ has opened for us an entrance into the kingdom of heaven above, for now we come to God "by a new and living way, which he has consecrated for us through the veil, that is to say, his flesh." When in days to come we shall meet him again there will still be novelty, for he has said, "I will not drink henceforth of the fruit of the vine until that day when I drink it new with you in my Father's kingdom."

Indeed, concerning our Lord and Master everything is new, and was it not so prophesied? For did not Isaiah say in the forty-third chapter, eighteenth verse, "Do not remember the former things, neither consider the things of old. Behold, I will do a new thing; now it shall spring forth; shall you not know it?" And to the same effect his prophecy in the sixty-fifth chapter, seventeenth verse: "For, behold, I create new heavens and a new earth: and the former shall not be remembered, nor come into mind. But be glad and rejoice for ever in what I create: for, behold, I create Jerusalem as a rejoicing, and her people a joy." This newness of everything was to be a leading feature in Messiah's reign, and it has already been so; but this shall be seen far more in the latter days. Does not John say in Rev. 21:5, "He who sat upon the throne said, 'Behold, I make all things new.'" Foretold in former ages as the Creator of the new heavens and a new earth, our Lord shall at last, in the summing up, be plainly seen to be the Maker of all things new. Do you wonder, beloved, that if a man is in Christ he is a new creature? If everything that Christ touches is made new, if he refreshes and revives, if he reestablishes and re-edifies, and creates anew wherever he goes, are you at all astonished that those who live nearest to his heart, indeed, are in vital union with his blessed person, should also be made new? It would be very astonishing if it were not so.

Let us direct our attention then to the teaching of the text, "If any man is in Christ he is a new creature."

I. We shall first consider with brevity THE BASIS OF THE NOVELTY which is here spoken of.

It is, "If any man is *in Christ*, he is a new creature," not otherwise. No man comes to be a new creature by any process apart from Christ. "If any man is in Christ, he is a new creature," but if any man is not in Christ he is not a new creature, nor can he become so except by connection with him of whom it is written that he is "the beginning of the creation of God." As in the old creation "without him was not anything made that was made," so it is in the new. He makes all things new, but the things that are apart from him have become old and are ready to perish, neither can they renew their youth. As well might the face of the earth hope to be renewed with spring apart from the sun, as for a soul to hope for spiritual renewal apart from Jesus. The wonderful newness produced by regeneration and new creation is the work of the Holy Spirit and his operations are all in union with the Lord Jesus and aimed at his glory. "He who believes on the Son has everlasting life: and he who does not believe the Son shall not see life, but the wrath of God rests on him."

But how come a man is indeed a new creature if he is in Christ? I answer, first, it comes necessarily from *the representative character of Christ* towards those who are in him. If you wanted a man to be made a new creature, and were omnipotent, what process would suggest itself to you? I think a double one. To make an old creature into a new creature there must first be the stroke which ends him, and then the touch which begins him anew: to put it more plainly, there must be death and then life. Now, has that taken place upon those who are in Christ? Of course it has, if it has taken place upon Christ himself, because he is the Head, and represents the members. Just as Adam acted for the seed in him, so Christ has acted for the seed in him. See, then, beloved, Christ has died; he came before the judgment seat with our sins upon him, the representative of those of whom he is the head; and in him death, which was the penalty of sin, was fulfilled to the letter, its bitterest dregs being drunk up. Jesus died. We are certain that he died, for the executioners did not break his legs because they saw that he was dead already, but one of the soldiers with a spear pierced his side, and immediately blood and water flowed out from there. We know that he died, for the jealous eyes of his enemies would not have permitted him to have been taken down from the cross unless the life had assuredly departed. He was laid in the grave, assuredly dead, under the dominion of death for the time being; and you and I who are in him, at that time died in him. "If one died for all then all died." Such is the proper translation of that passage. We died, for he died in our name. Our sin, was punished in him by the death which he endured.

See, then, brethren, we are dead, dead by virtue of our federal union with Jesus Christ. I do not mean all of you, unless you are all in Christ Jesus. Judge whether it is so with you or not. But I mean as many as the Father gave to Christ, as many as Christ in his intention specifically redeemed by becoming their substitute: these were in him, and in him they died, being crucified with him. In him also all his people rose again when he rose. On the third day he burst the bonds of death and left the grave on our behalf. See how the Holy Spirit, by his servant Paul, identifies us with all this. "Now if we are dead with

Christ, we believe that we shall also live with him: knowing that Christ being raised from the dead dies no more; death has no more dominion over him. For in that he died, he died to sin once: but in that he lives, he lives to God. Likewise consider also yourselves to be dead indeed to sin, but alive to God through Jesus Christ our Lord."

As far as he was our representative he was a new man when he rose. The law had no claims upon him: he had been dead, and so had passed out of its jurisdiction. The law never had any claim upon the risen Christ: it had a claim upon him when he came under the law, but when he had satisfied it to the last jot and tittle, by death, he was completely clear. Has the law of our country any claim upon a man after he is dead? If a dead man can be raised again all his past offences are done away with, he begins a new life, and is not under the old law. And so with Christ and so with us, for here is the point of union, we are risen with him by faith in the resurrection of Christ. We have been dead and buried, and now we are risen, and thus this, which is the very best and surest process for making a person a new creature has been undergone by all God's elect, by reason of the representative and sacrificial death of Jesus Christ and his glorious representative resurrection on their behalf.

But, beloved, there is another meaning. *We are made new creatures by an actual process* as well as by the legal process which I have described, and here also the same thing is done. We are made vitally one with Jesus Christ when we believe in him, and then we spiritually die and are made to live again. Our faith comprehends the dying of Christ, and we feel at the same time the sentence of death in ourselves. We see how we deserve to die for sin, and we accept the sentence, confessing our guiltiness before the Most High, and there is proclaimed throughout the powers and passions of the soul a decree from God that the flesh shall die, with all its lusts. We consider sin as henceforth dead to us, and ourselves as dead to it. We labor to mortify all our evil desires and the lusts of the flesh, and all that comes from the flesh. When we believe in Jesus a sword goes through the very loins of sin, and the arrows of the Lord stick firm in the hearts of the King's enemies that lurk within our spirit. There also comes a new life into us as we behold Jesus risen from the dead. When we believe in Jesus we receive from God a new vital principle, of superior and heavenly character, akin to Deity: there drops into our soul a sacred seed from the hand of the eternal Spirit, living and incorruptible, which remains forever, and forever produces fruit after its kind. As we believe in Christ living we live in Christ and live according to the way of Christ, and the Spirit of him who raised up Christ from the dead dwells in our mortal bodies, making us to live in newness of life.

Now, beloved, do you know anything about this? Have you been made new creatures by death and resurrection? If you have been baptized you have professed that it has been so with you. "Do you not know, that so many of us as were baptized into Jesus Christ were baptized into his death? Therefore we are buried with him by baptism into death: that just as Christ was raised up from the dead by the glory of the Father, even so we also should walk in newness of life. For if we have been planted together in the likeness of his death, we shall also be in the likeness of his resurrection."

In the ordinance of baptism, by burial in the water, and rising up from it, there is an exemplifying as in a type and figure of our Lord's burial and resurrection, and at the same time it is an emblem of the process by which we become new creatures in him. But is it *really* so in your souls? Are you now henceforth dead to the world, and dead to sin, and quickened into the life of Christ? If you are so, then the text will bear to you a third and practical meaning, for it will not merely be true that your old man is condemned to die and a new nature is bestowed, but *in your common actions you will try to show this by newness of actual conduct.* Evils which tempted you at one time will be unable to beguile you now because you are dead to them: the charms of the painted face of the world will no longer attract your attention, for your eyes are blind to such deceitful beauties. You have obtained a new life which can only be satisfied by new delights, which can only be motivated by new purposes and constrained by new principles suitable to its own nature. This you will continually show. The life of God within you will make your actions instinct with holiness, and its end shall be everlasting life. Your faith in Christ clearly evinces you to be a new creature, for it kills your old confidences and makes you build upon a new foundation: your love for Christ also shows your newness, for it has killed your old desires, and captured your heart only for Jesus: and your hope, which is also a gift from the blessed Spirit, is set upon new things altogether, while your old hopes are things of which you are now ashamed.

Thus it is that first by the headship of Christ you are legally dead and alive again; next by your vital union with Christ you are dead and alive again as a matter of experience, and now it is practically proven in your life from day to day that you are dead and your life is hidden with Christ in God: in all these three ways you are new creatures by the double process of dying and quickening. You are under a new Adam, and so start life afresh as new creatures; you are under a new covenant, and begin to act under different principles, and so are new creatures: you are quickened by a new Spirit, and so in thought and word and deed are seen to be new creatures. But all this is *in Christ*, and if you are not in Christ you are still in the old world which must shortly be destroyed.

As "by the Word of God the heavens were made, and all the host of them by the breath of his mouth," so you have been created by Jesus, the Eternal Word, and quickened by his Spirit, or else you still remain in death. If your faith has never laid her hand upon Christ's sacrifice for sin then your soul has never felt the regenerating influence of the Holy Spirit, and all the baptismal regeneration and everything else of human invention that may now comfort you is only a vain deceit. You must be born again, but it can only be in Christ Jesus, for to "as many as received him, he gave to them power to become the sons of God, even to those who believe on his name." "He who has the Son has life; and he who does not have the Son of God does not have life." Oh, that we may all believe in him, and enter into the new life.

> Author of the new creation,
>   Come with all thy Spirit's power;
> Make our hearts thy habitation,
>   On our souls thy graces shower.

II. I shall in the second place lead you to consider the *essence of this novelty*. "If any man is in Christ, he is *a new creature*."

Read, and the reading will be accurate, "He is a new creation." This is a very sweeping statement. A man in Christ is not the old man purified, nor the old man improved, nor the old man in a better humor, nor the old man with additions and subtractions, nor the old man dressed in gorgeous robes. No, he is a new creature altogether. As for the old man, what is to be done with him? Can he not be sobered, reformed, and made to do us useful service? No, he is crucified with Christ, and bound to die by a lingering but certain death. The capital sentence is passed upon him, for he cannot be mended and therefore must be ended. "The carnal mind is enmity against God: for it is not subject to the law of God, neither indeed can be." You cannot change the old nature, it is immutably bad, and the sooner it is put away as a filthy and unclean thing the better for us.

The believer, as far as he is in Christ, is a new creation: not the old stuff put into a new shape, and the old material worked up into an improved form, but absolutely a new creation. To create is to make out of nothing, and that is precisely how the new-born life came into us; it is not a development, or an outgrowth, but a creation, a heavenly something called into being by a power from above. The new man in us is made out of nothing that was in us before, for nature does not assist grace but is opposed to it. Christ has not found light stored away in our darkness, nor life amid the corruption of our spiritual death. The new birth is from above, and the life produced by it is a new creation, and not the goodness of nature educated until it becomes grace. They are conjuring up a notion in certain quarters that the children of pious parents, if not of all mankind, are the children of God by their first birth, and only need certain training and influences to be brought to bear upon them and then they will develop into Christians as they grow up into manhood and womanhood.

One divine says that our children ought not to need conversion. This theory is false throughout, for the best of children are by nature heirs of wrath even as others. The grace of God in the soul is a new creation, and not the natural development of a pious education and training working upon the innate goodness of men: indeed there is no such goodness there at all; it is a dream altogether. The new man in Christ is not the old creature washed and sent out to school, and elevated by "modern thought and culture." No, the Ethiopian cannot change his skin, nor the leopard his spots; do what you wish with him he will still be an Ethiopian and a leopard; but the new man in Christ is another creature altogether.

Notice that it is not said that the man has something new about him, but he, himself, is new. It is not merely that in a spiritual sense he has new eyes, new hands, and new feet, but he, he, he, he, himself, is a new creation. Notice that. Do you not see then that salvation is the work of God? You cannot create yourself, and you cannot create anything at all. Try and create a flea first, and then you may dream of being able to create a new heart and a right spirit in another person, but even then it would be quite another matter to create yourself anew. Is not the very idea an absurdity? Shall nothing create something?

Shall darkness create light? Shall sin create holiness? Shall death create life? Shall the devil create God? None of these questions are more absurd than the idea of the sinner's being able to create himself anew.

No, beloved, regeneration is an extraordinary work, demanding omnipotence to accomplish it; it is, in fact, a divine work, for it is the supreme prerogative of God to create.

> Know that the Lord is God alone,
> He can create, and he destroy.

If any man is in Christ it is not only said that he is a creation, but a *new* creation, and the word here translated "new," as has been well observed, does not mean *recent*, but something altogether different from what previously existed. A book may be new, and yet it may be only a fresh copy of some old work; but that is not the case in this example. The creature is not a new specimen of the same kind as the old, but another and different creation. We might almost read the text as if it said, "If any man is in Christ he is a fresh creation, a new kind of creature altogether." The new creation differs essentially from the old, although the first is an instructive emblem of the second. The first creation was the work of physical power, the second a work of spiritual power: the first created for the most part materialism in its various forms, but the new creation deals with spiritual things, and reveals the most sublime attributes of the divine character. God in nature is glorious, but in grace he is all glorious. The second is a creation nearer to the heart of God than the first creation was; for when he made the world he simply said it was good, but when he makes the new creation, it is written, "He shall rest in his love; he shall rejoice over you with singing." So gladdening to his heart is the sight of the new creature which his grace has made, that he sings a joyful hymn.

Furthermore, we must notice that if any man is in Christ he is a new creature, and the creation of him bears some resemblance to the creation of the world. I have at other times gone through that wonderful first chapter of the book of Genesis, which is a Bible in miniature, and I have shown you how it illustrates the spiritual creation. Behold by nature we lie like chaos: a mass of disorder, confusion, and darkness. As in the old creation so in the new, the Spirit of God broods over us and moves upon the face of all things. Then the word of the Lord comes and says within us, as previously in chaos and old night, "Let there be light," and there is light. After light there comes a division of the light from the darkness, and we learn to call them by their names. The light is "day" and the darkness is "night."

So to us there is a knowing and a naming of things, and a discerning of differences in matters which before we confounded when we thought darkness was light. After a while there comes out in us the lower forms of spiritual life. As in the earth there came grasses and herbs, so in us there come desire, hope, and sorrow for sin. Eventually there appeared on the globe fowl and fish, and beasts, and living things, and life beyond all count. So also in the new creation, from having life we go on to have it more abundantly. God by degrees created all his works, until at last he had finished all the host of them, and even so he works on until he completes in us the new creation and looks upon us with rejoicing. Then he brings to us a day of rest, blessing us and causing us to enter into his rest because of his finished work. We could draw a very beautiful parallel if we had time, but you can think it out for yourselves.

Now, notice very carefully that if *any man* is in Christ he is a new creature, and this certifies that a new creation has taken place upon every man who is in Christ, whether by nature he was a Jew or Gentile, a moralist or a rake, a philosopher or a fool. When a man is converted and brought to Christ he has invariably become a new creature. If he has believed in Jesus only three minutes yet he is a new creature; and if he has known the Lord seventy years he can be no more. A new creation is a new creature, and in this matter there is no difference between the babe in grace and the father in Israel.

Just as this creation is common to all the saints, so it is *immediate and present*. "If any man is in Christ he *is* a new creature": it is not spoken of as something that is to happen to him in the last article of death, when some seem to hope that many wonderful changes will be accomplished in them; but he who is in Christ is a new creature *now*. "Neither circumcision nor uncircumcision avails anything, but a new creature": and that new creature is now possessed, and I may add consciously possessed too: for albeit that there may arise occasional doubts upon this question, yet in a man's innermost self he finds a reason to know that there has passed upon him a marvelous change which only God himself could have accomplished.

This change is *universal in the man*; the new man is not full-grown in every part, nor in fact in any part, and yet in all the portions of his regenerated nature he is a new creature. I mean this, if any man is in Christ it is not his mental *eye* that is a new creation merely, but he himself is a new creation. He has a new heart according to the promise, "I will also give you a new heart, and I will put a new spirit within you." He has new ears, hearing what he refused to hear before; he has a new tongue, and can pray with it as he never prayed before; he has new feet, and these delight to run in the ways of God's commandments. I refer of course only to his inner man, that is altogether new, and not any one part of it only. If a man is merely enlightened in understanding, what is that? It is good, but it is not salvation; a new brain is not all that is needed to make a new man. A new man is spiritually created anew from head to foot. Although only a babe in grace, and not fully developed in any one part, yet he is new, "created in Christ Jesus to good works which God has before ordained that we should walk in them."

Thus I have tried to show you the essence of the novelty.

III. Let us next consider THE EXTENT OF THE NOVELTY. "If any man is in Christ he is a new creature; *old things are passed away, behold all things have become new.*"

It seems then that not only is the man a new creature, but he has entered into a new creation; he has opened his eyes in a new world. Imagine Adam falling asleep at the gates of Paradise just under the cherubim's flaming sword, with the thorns and thistles springing up before him, and the serpent's trail behind him: and then further picture him lying there in a deep sleep until the Lord touches him, makes him open his eyes, and causes him to find himself in a better paradise than the one he had lost. It was not so in reality, but can you imagine such a thing? If so, it may serve as a symbol of what the Lord has done for us. We are made new, and find ourselves in a new world.

What about *the old things*? The text says they have passed away, and the Greek word gives the idea of their having passed away spontaneously. I cannot compare it to anything that I know of better than the snow which melts in the sun. You wake up one morning, and all the trees are festooned with snowy wreaths, while down below upon the ground the snow lies in a white sheet over everything. Lo, the sun has risen, its beams shed a congenial warmth; and in a few hours where is the snow? It has passed away. If you had hired a thousand carts and horses and machines to sweep it away it could not have been more effectively removed. It has passed away. That is what the Lord does in the new creation: his love shines on the soul, his grace renews us, and the old things pass away as a matter of course. Where are your old views about which you used to be so positive? Where are those old opinions for which you could freely have knocked a man down? Where are those old sneers against God's people? Where are those old pleasures which you took so much delight in? Where are those old engrossing pursuits? Had you a hard tug to get away from these bonds? Where are those old joys, those old hopes, those old trusts, those old confidences? Was it difficult to shake these off? Ah, no! Under the power of the Holy Spirit they have passed away. You hardly know how it is, but they have gone, and gone completely. As a dream when one awakens you have despised their image, and your heart knows them no more. It is marvelous in this new creation how the Lord makes confusion and old night to vanish. You may call for them and say, "Chaos, where are you?" and no answer comes back, for old things are passed away. Our Lord Jesus Christ causes all this. Where his blessed face beams with grace and truth, as the sun with warmth and light, he dissolves the bands of sin's long frost, and brings on the spring of grace with newness of buds and flowers.

But when you remove the old what is to take its place? Do you not observe that *new things have come*, "Behold all things are become new." Now the man has new views, new notions, new ambitions, new convictions, new desires, new hopes, new dreads, new aims, new principles, and new affections: he is led by a new spirit and follows a new course of life; everything in fact about him is as if he had come fresh from the hand of God. Even as with the cleansed leper, his flesh came again to him as the flesh of a little child, and he was clean, so it is with the heart renewed by grace.

Beloved, it is delightful to read in the book of Revelation and anticipate the things which are to be hereafter. How full that book is of novelties which illustrate our subject, for there you read of a *new name* which the Lord bestows upon those who overcome. Perhaps some of you used to be actually known by some nickname or vulgar epithet while you lived in the world and were a lover of it. Now in all probability you are called by quite a different name among your Christian friends. Saul the persecutor is called Paul when he becomes an apostle. Moreover, there is a new name which the mouth of the Lord shall name, which no man knows except he who receives it. You have been named with the name of the Father, and of the Son, and of the Holy Spirit, and you wear henceforth that name by which the whole family in heaven and earth is named. Grace also has taught you a *new song*, "He has put a new song into my mouth and established my goings." You are rehearsing the music of that glorious band of whom it is written, "They sang a new song, saying, 'You are worthy to take the book and to open its seals.'" Now you are a citizen of a *new city*, the new Jerusalem which comes down out of heaven from God, which shall be established among the sons of men, in the last days as the world's metropolis, concerning which they shall say, "The temple of God is with men and he dwells among them."

Beloved, each one of you has now become part of *one new man*. Do you know what I mean by that? There were once the Jews and the Gentiles, but now, Paul says, Christ "has broken down the middle wall of partition; for to make in himself from two one new man, so making peace." The mystical body of Christ is the one new man, and we are members of that body. Henceforth we have communion with all saints, and to us "there is neither Greek nor Jew, bound nor free, but Christ is all, and in all." Even now we have begun to live in a new heaven and walk upon a new earth, and we are anticipating the time when literally on this very earth where we have struggled there shall be set up a new condition of things, for the first heaven and the first earth shall have passed away and there shall be no more sea. Those blue heavens shall be rolled up like a scroll, and the elements shall melt with fervent heat; nevertheless, we, according to his promise, look for new heavens and a new earth, to which in expectation we are always drawing near, and pressing forward with inward yearning, for already in Christ Jesus we are a part of that new creation which is more fully to be revealed.

IV. Fourthly let us consider THE RESULT OF THIS NOVELTY. "If any man is in Christ, he is a new creature."

Well, the result of this novelty is, first, that the man is already a great wonder to himself. You know the Pythagorean doctrine of the transmigration of souls, the soul passing first into one body and then into another, and so existing under different conditions. We do not believe that fiction for a moment, but if it had been true, the memories of such souls must have been stored with varied information, surpassingly strange to hear. Ours is another transformation, it is death and resurrection: the old passing away and the new being created: but how remarkable are the experiences of the men who have been so transformed! Here is a man who is a new creature, and he has a very distinct memory of the time when he was something far other than what he now is. What a change he has undergone!

Suppose a swine could suddenly be turned into a man and yet remember what it did when it was one of the herd; what an experience it would have to tell! If you could take a hog from the trough and turn it into an emperor, that would not be half so great a change as is accomplished when an unregenerated sinner becomes a saint; but I warrant you the emperor would not find much cause for glorifying in his former swinish state; he would be silent and ashamed when others mentioned it. If he alluded to that state it would always be with the blushes of humiliation and the tears of gratitude. If anyone began to talk about it, and he knew that there might be others around him who might be helped by hearing what the Lord had done, he would begin to tell in a gentle, modest way how the Lord transformed him from a swine into a monarch, but he would never, never boast: how could he? In such a case the poor swine would have no responsibility, and could not be blamed for wallowing in the mire, but this cannot be said of us; for when we acted as swine we knew better, and sinned wilfully. Still, what a change it is! How I wonder about myself! How I marvel about the goodness of my God! How I adore that sacred power which has made me the child of two births, the subject of two creations: he first made me in the fashion of a man, and then made me in the image of the man Christ Jesus. I was first born to die, and then born to live eternally. Let us bless God and be full of lowly wonder this morning.

The next result of this new creation is, however, that the man does not feel at home in this present evil world, for this is the old creation, and the new man, the twice-born man, feels as if he were out of his element and not in a congenial country. He resides in a body which is nothing better than a frail, uncomfortable, easily removed tent, in which he groans, earnestly desiring to enter his own house at home, the house not made with hands, eternal in the heavens. Wherever he goes things seem out of order with the rule which is set up in his soul. He does not love the world, neither the things in the world; the world's glories do not charm him, and its treasures do not enchant him. Earth's music grates upon his refined ear, which is tuned to heavenly harmony; its dainties do not delight the taste, which has learned to enjoy the bread of heaven. The new creatures pine to be in the new creation. And beloved, while we are pining we are preparing: the Spirit of God is working us into this very same thing, and filling us with groans and pangs of strong desire, which indicate that we are becoming more and more fit to be partakers with the saints in light, who see the face of the Beloved without a veil, and drink in ever new delights.

Notice once more, while the new creature is thus watching and waiting for the new creation he is meanwhile extending an influence more or less unconscious over the old world in which he dwells. Just as our Lord has gone to heaven to prepare a place for us, so we, his people, are staying here to prepare a place for him. We are winning men from the world to Christ, we are raising the tone of morals, we are spreading light and truth on all sides by the power of the Spirit, and so we are helping to make the world more ready to receive the great King. We are seeking out his jewels, we are bringing his rebellious subjects to his feet. The life that is in us seems out of place in this mortal frame, for the body is dead because of sin, and therefore we groan, being burdened. As for the world itself, it is not our rest, for it is polluted. It seems a dreadful thing for the living Spirit to be dwelling in this graveyard of a world, but there is a necessity for us to be here.

We are linked with a creation made subject to vanity, because it was thus subjected, not willingly, but by reason of him who has subjected the same in hope that the creation itself also "shall be delivered from the bondage of corruption into the glorious liberty of the children of God." We are here as links between the spiritual and the material, and we are working out divine purposes for the fuller display of the divine glory. Therefore comfort each other with these words, and as new creatures in Jesus Christ look for the new heavens and the new earth, and for the coming of your Lord and Savior. Do you not know that when he shall appear then you shall also appear with him in glory? Let us even now bow before him and greet him with the language of our hymn.

> To thee the world its treasure brings;
>   To thee its mighty bow;
> To thee the church exulting springs;
>   Her Sovereign, Savior Thou!

Beneath thy touch, beneath thy smile,
   New heavens and earth appear;
No sin their beauty to defile,
   Nor dim them with a tear.

5

Christ the Spoiler of Principalities and Powers

"And having spoiled principalities and powers, he made a shew of them openly, triumphing over them in it" (Col. 2:15).

To the eye of reason the cross is the center of sorrow and the lowest depth of shame. Jesus dies a malefactor's death. He hangs upon the gibbet of a felon and pours out his blood upon the common mount of doom with thieves for his companions. In the midst of mockery, and jest, and scorn, and ribaldry, and blasphemy, he gives up the ghost. Earth rejects him and lifts him from her surface, and heaven affords him no light, but darkens the mid-day sun in the hour of his extremity. Deeper in woe the Savior dived, imagination cannot descend. A blacker calumny than was cast on him satanic malice could not invent. He hid not his face from shame and spitting; and what shame and spitting it was! To the world the cross must ever be the emblem of shame: to the Jew a stumbling-block, and to the Greek foolishness. How different however is the view which presents itself to the eye of faith.

Faith knows no shame in the cross, except the shame of those who nailed the Savior there; it sees no ground for scorn, but it hurls indignant scorn at sin, the enemy which pierced the Lord. Faith sees woe, indeed, but from this woe it marks a fount of mercy springing. It is true it mourns a dying Savior, but it beholds him bringing life and immortality to light at the very moment when his soul was eclipsed in the shadow of death. Faith regards the cross, not as the emblem of shame, but as the token of glory. The sons of Belial lay the cross in the dust, but the Christian makes a constellation of it, and sees it glittering in the seventh heaven. Man spits upon it, but believers, having angels for their

BOOK ONE: *Christ's Glorious Achievements*

companions, bow down and worship him whoever liveth though once he was crucified. My brethren, our text presents us with a portion of the view which faith is certain to discover when its eyes are anointed with the eye-salve of the Spirit. It tells us that the cross was Jesus Christ's field of triumph. There he fought, and there he conquered, too. As a victor on the cross he divided the spoil. Nay, more than this; in our text the cross is spoken of as being Christ's triumphal chariot in which he rode when he led captivity captive, and received gifts for men. Calvin thus admirably expounds the last sentence of our text:

> The expression in the Greek allows, it is true, of our reading—*in himself*; the connection of the passage, however, requires that we read it otherwise; for what would be meagre as applied to Christ, suits admirably well as applied to the cross. For as he had previously compared the cross to a signal trophy or show of triumph, in which Christ led about his enemies, so he now also compares it to a triumphal car in which he showed himself in great magnificence. For there is no tribunal so magnificent, no throne so stately, no show of triumph so distinguished, no chariot so elevated, as is the gibbet on which Christ has subdued death and the devil, the prince of death; nay, more, has utterly trodden them under his feet.

I shall this morning, by God's help, address you upon the two portions of the text. First, I shall endeavor to describe *Christ as spoiling his enemies on the cross*; and having done that I shall lead your imagination and your faith further on to see *the Savior in triumphal procession upon his cross,* leading his enemies captive, and making a show of them openly before the eyes of the astonished universe.

I. First, our faith is invited this morning to behold CHRIST MAKING A SPOIL OF PRINCIPALITIES AND POWERS. Satan, leagued with sin and death, had made this world the home of woe. The Prince of the power of the air, fell usurper, not content with his dominions in hell, must need invade this fair earth. He found our first parents in the midst of Eden; he tempted them to forego their allegiance to the King of heaven; and they became at once his bondslaves—bondslaves forever, if the Lord of heaven had not interposed to ransom them The voice of mercy was heard while the fetters were being riveted upon their feet, crying, "Ye shall yet be free!" In the fullness of time there shall come one who shall bruise the serpent's head, and shall deliver his prisoners from the house of their bondage. Long did the promise tarry. The earth groaned and travailed in its bondage. Man was Satan's slave, and heavy were the clanking chains which were upon his soul.

At last, in the fullness of time, the Deliverer came forth, born of a woman. This infant conqueror was but a span long. He lay in the manger—*he* who was one day to bind the old dragon and cast him into the bottomless pit, and set a seal upon him. When the old serpent knew that his enemy was born, he conspired to put him to death; he leagued with Herod to seek the young child that he might destroy him. But the providence of God preserved the future conqueror; he went down into Egypt, and there was he hidden for a little season. Anon, when he had come to fullness of years, he made his public advent, and began to preach liberty to the captives, and the opening of the prison to them that were bound. Then Satan again shot forth his arrows, and sought to end the existence of the woman's seed. Once the Jews took up stones to stone him; nor did they fail to repeat the attempt. They sought to cast him down from the brow of a hill headlong. By all manner of devices they labored to take away his life, but his hour was not yet. Dangers might surround him, but he was invulnerable till the time was come. At last the tremendous day arrived. Foot to foot the conqueror must fight with the dread tyrant. A voice was heard in heaven, "This is your hour, and the power of darkness." And Christ himself exclaimed, "Now is the crisis of this world; now must the prince of darkness be cast out."

From the table of communion the Redeemer arose at midnight, and marched forth to the battle. How dreadful was the contest! In the very first onset the mighty conqueror seemed himself to be vanquished. Beaten to the earth at the first assault, he fell upon his knees and cried, "My Father, if it be possible let this cup pass from me." Revived in strength, made strong by heaven, he no longer quailed, and from this hour never did he utter a word which looked like renouncing the fight. From the terrible skirmish all red with bloody sweat, he dashed into the thick of the battle. The kiss of Judas was, as it were, the first sounding of the trumpet; Pilate's bar was the glittering of the spear; the cruel lash was the crossing of the swords. But the cross was the center of the battle; there, on the top of Calvary, must the dread fight of eternity be fought. Now must the Son of God arise, and gird his sword upon his thigh.

Dread defeat or glorious conquest awaits the Champion of the church. Which shall it be? We hold our breath with anxious suspense while the storm is raging. I hear the trumpet sound. The howlings and yells of hell rise in awful clamor. The pit is emptying out its legions. Terrible as lions, hungry as wolves, and black as night, the demons rush on in myriads. Satan's reserve forces, those who had long been kept against this day of terrible battle, are roaring from their dens. See how countless their armies, and how fierce their countenances. Brandishing his sword the arch fiend leads the van, bidding his followers fight neither with small nor great, save only with the King of Israel. Terrible are the leaders of the battle. Sin is there, and all its innumerable offspring, spitting forth the venom of asps, and infixing their poison-fangs in the Savior's flesh. Death is there upon his pale horse, and his cruel dart rends its way through the body of Jesus even to his inmost heart. He is "exceeding sorrowful, even unto death."

Hell comes, with all its coals of juniper and fiery darts. But chief and head amongst them is Satan; remembering well the ancient day Christ hurled him from the battlements of heaven, he rushes with all his malice yelling to the attack. The darts shot into the air are so thick that they blind the sun. Darkness covers the battlefield, and like that of Egypt it was a darkness which might be felt. Long does the battle seem to waver, for there is but one against many. One man—nay, tell it, lest any should misunderstand me, one *God* stands in battle array against ten thousands of principalities and powers. On, on they come, and he receives them all. Silently at first he permits their ranks to break upon him, too terribly enduring hardness to spare a thought for shouting. But at last the battle-cry is heard. He who is fighting for his people begins to shout, but it is a shout which makes the church tremble.

He cries, "I thirst." The battle is so hot upon him, and the dust so thick that he is choked with thirst. He cries, "I thirst." Surely, now, he is about to be defeated? Wait awhile; see ye yon heaps; all these have fallen beneath his arm, as for the rest fear not the issue. The enemy is but rushing to his own destruction. In vain his fury and his rage, for see the last rank is charging, the battle of ages is almost over. At last the darkness is dispersed. Hark how the conqueror cries, "It is finished." And where now are his enemies? They are all dead. There lies the king of terrors, pierced through with one of his own darts! There lies Satan with his head all bleeding, broken! Yonder crawls the broken-backed serpent, writhing in ghastly misery! As for sin, it is cut in pieces, and scattered to the winds of heaven! "It is finished," cries the conqueror, as he came with dyed garments from Bozrah, "I have trodden the wine-press alone, I have trampled them in my fury, and their blood is sprinkled on my garments."

And now he proceeds to *divide the spoil*.

We pause here to remark that when the spoil is divided it is a sure token that the battle is completely won. The enemy will never suffer the spoil to be divided among the conquerors as long as he has any strength remaining. We may gather from our text of a surety, that Jesus Christ has totally routed, thoroughly defeated once for all, and put to retreat all his enemies, or else he would not have divided the spoil.

And now, what means this expression of Christ dividing the spoil? I take it that it means, first of all, that *he disarmed all his enemies*. Satan came against Christ; he had in his hand a sharp sword called the Law, dipped in the poison of sin, so that every wound which the law inflicted was deadly. Christ dashed this sword out of Satan's hand, and there stood the prince of darkness disarmed. His helmet was cleft in twain, and his head was crushed with a rod of iron. Death rose against Christ. The Savior snatched his quiver from him, cut them in two, gave Death back the feather end, but kept the poisoned barbs from him, that he might never destroy the ransomed. Sin came against Christ; but sin was utterly cut in pieces. It had been Satan's armor bearer, but its shield was cast away, and it lay dead upon the plain.

Is it not a noble picture to behold all the enemies of Christ—nay, my brethren, all your enemies, and mine—totally disarmed? Satan has nothing left him now wherewith he may attack us. He may attempt to injure us, but wound us he never can, for his sword and spear are utterly taken away. In the old battles, especially among the Romans, after the enemy had been overcome, it was the custom to take away all their weapons and ammunition; afterwards they were stripped of their armor and their garments, their hands were tied behind their backs, and they were made to pass under the yoke. Now, even so hath Christ done with sin, death, and hell: he hath taken away their armor, spoiled them of all their weapons, and made them all to pass under the yoke; so that now they are our slaves, and we in Christ are conquerors of them who were mightier than we.

I take it this is the first meaning of dividing the spoil—total disarming of the adversary.

In the next place, when the victors divide the spoil they carry away not only the weapons but all the treasures which belong to their enemies. They dismantle their fortresses, and rifle all their stores, so that in future they may not be able to renew the attack. Christ has done the like with all his enemies. Old Satan had taken away from us all our possessions. Paradise, Satan had added to his territories. All the joy, and happiness, and peace of man, Satan had taken—not that he could enjoy them himself, but that he delighted to thrust us down into poverty and damnation. Now, all our lost inheritances Christ hath gotten back to us. Paradise is ours, more than all the joy and happiness that Adam had, Christ hath brought back to us.

O robber of our race, how art thou spoiled and carried away captive! Didst thou despoil Adam of his riches? The second Adam hath rent them from thee! How is the hammer of the whole earth cut asunder and broken, and the waster is become desolate. Now shall the needy be remembered, and again shall the meek inherit the earth. "Then is the prey of a great spoil divided, the lame take the prey."

Moreover, when victors divide the spoil, it is usual to take away all the ornaments from the enemy, the crowns and the jewels. Christ on the cross did the like with Satan. Satan had a crown on his head, a haughty diadem of triumph. "I fought the first Adam," he said; "I overcame him, and here's my glittering diadem." Christ snatched it from his brow in the hour when he bruised the serpent's head. And now Satan cannot boast of a single victory, he is thoroughly defeated. In the first skirmish he vanquished manhood, but in the second battle manhood vanquished him. The crown is taken from Satan. He is no longer the prince of God's people. His reigning power is gone. He may tempt, but he cannot compel; he may threaten, but he cannot subdue; for the crown is taken from his head, and the mighty are brought low. O sing unto the Lord a new song, all ye his people, make a joyful noise unto him with psalms, all ye his redeemed; for he hath broken in sunder the gates of brass, and cut the bars of iron, he hath broken the bow and cut the spear in sunder, he hath burned the chariots in the fire, he hath dashed in pieces our enemies, and divided the spoil with the strong.

And now, what says this to us? Simply this. If Christ on the cross hath spoiled Satan, let us not be afraid to encounter this great enemy of our souls. My brethren, in all things we must be made like unto Christ. We must bear our cross, and on that cross we must fight as he did with sin, and death and hell. Let us not fear. The result of the battle is certain, for as the Lord our Savior hath overcome once even so shall we most surely conquer in him. Be none of you afraid with sudden fear when the evil one cometh upon you. If he accuse you, reply to him in these words: "Who shall lay anything to the charge of God's elect?" If he condemn you, laugh him to scorn, crying, "Who is he that condemneth? It is Christ that died, yea rather hath risen again." If he threaten to divide you from Christ's love, encounter him with confidence: "I am persuaded that neither things present nor things to come, nor height nor depth, nor any other creature shall be able to separate us from the love of God which is in Christ Jesus your Lord." If he let loose your sins upon you dash the hell-dogs aside with this: "If any man sin, we have an advocate with the Father, Jesus Christ the righteous." If death should threaten you, shout in his very face: "O grave where is thy sting" O death, where is thy victory?"

Hold up the cross before you. Let that be your shield and buckler and rest assured that as your master not only routed the foe but afterwards took the spoil, it shall be even so with you. Your battles with Satan shall turn to your advantage. You shall become all the richer for your antagonists. The more numerous they shall be, the greater shall be your share of the spoil. Your tribulation shall work patience, and your patience experience, and your experience hope—a hope that maketh not ashamed. Through this much tribulation shall you inherit the kingdom, and by the very attacks of Satan shall you be helped the better to enjoy the rest which remaineth to the people of God. Put yourselves in array against sin and Satan. All ye that bend the bow shoot at them, spare no arrows, for your enemies are rebels against God.

Go up against them, put your feet upon their necks, fear not, neither be dismayed, for the battle is the Lord's and he will deliver them into your hands. Be ye very courageous, remembering that you have to fight with a stingless dragon. He may hiss, but his teeth are broken and his poison fang extracted. You have to battle with an enemy already scarred by your Master's weapons. You have to fight with a naked enemy. Every blow you give him tells upon him, for he has nothing left to protect him. Christ hath stripped him naked, and divided his armor, and left him defenseless before his people. Be not afraid. The lion may howl, but rend you in pieces he never can. The enemy may rush in upon you with hideous noise and terrible alarms, but there is no real cause for fear. Stand fast in the Lord. Ye war against a king who hath lost his crown; ye fight against an enemy whose cheek-bones have been smitten, and the joints of whose loins have been loosed. Rejoice, rejoice ye in the day of battle, for it is for you but the beginning of an eternity of triumph.

I have thus endeavored to dwell upon the first part of the text, Christ on the cross divided the spoil and he would have us do the same.

II. The second part of our text refers not only to the dividing of the spoil, but to THE TRIUMPH. When a Roman general had performed great feats in a foreign country, his highest reward was that the senate should decree him a triumph. Of course there was a division of spoil made on the battlefield, and each soldier, and each captain, took his share; but every man looked rapturously to the day when they should enjoy the public triumph. On a certain set day the gates of Rome were thrown open; all the houses were decorated with ornaments; the people climbed to the tops of the houses, or stood in great crowds along the streets. The gates were opened, and by-and-bye the first legion began to stream in with its banners flying and its trumpets sounding. The people saw the stern warriors as they marched along the street returning from their blood-red fields of battle. After one half of the army had thus defiled, your eye would rest upon one who was the center of all attraction: riding in a noble chariot drawn by milk-white horses, there came the conqueror himself, crowned with the laurel crown and standing erect. Chained to his chariot were the kings and mighty men of the regions which he had conquered. Immediately behind them came part of the booty. There were carried the ivory and the ebony, and the beasts of the different countries which he had subdued.

After these came the rest of the soldiery, a long, long stream of valiant men, all of them sharing the triumphs of their captain. Behind them came banners, the old flags that had floated aloft in the battle, the standards which had been taken from the enemy. And after these, large painted emblems of the great victories of the warrior. Upon one there would be a huge map depicting the rivers which he had crossed, or the seas through which his navy had found its way. Everything was represented in a picture, and the populace gave a fresh shout as they saw the memorial of each triumph. And then, behind, together with the trophies, would come the prisoners of lesser rank. Then the rear would be closed with sound of trumpet, adding to the acclamation of the throng. It was a noble day for old Rome. Children would never forget these triumphs; they would estimate their years from the time of one triumph to another. High holiday was kept. Women cast down flowers before the conqueror, and he was the true monarch of the day.

Now, our apostle had evidently seen such a triumph, or read of it, and he takes this as a representation of what Christ did on the cross. He says, "Jesus made a show of them openly, triumphing over them in it." Have you ever thought that the cross could be the scene of a triumph? Most of the old commentators can scarcely conceive of it as true. They say, "This must certainly refer to Christ's resurrection and ascension." But, nevertheless, so saith the Scripture, even on the cross Christ enjoyed a triumph. Yes! While those hands were bleeding, the acclamations of angels were being poured on his head. Yes, while those feet were being rent with the nails, the noblest spirits in the world were crowding round him in admiration. And when upon that blood-stained cross he died in agonies unutterable, there was heard a shout such as never was heard before for the ransomed in heaven, and all the angels of God with loudest harmony chanted his praise. There was sung, in fullest chorus, the song of Moses, the servant of God and of the Lamb, for he had indeed cut Rahab and sorely wounded the dragon. Sing unto the Lord, for he hath triumphed gloriously. The Lord shall reign for ever and ever, King of kings and Lord of lords.

I do not feel able, however, this morning, to work out a scene so grand, and yet so contrary to everything that flesh could guess as a picture of Christ actually triumphing on the cross—in the midst of his bleeding, his wounds, and his pains, actually being a triumphant victor, and admired of all. I choose, rather, to take my text thus: the cross is the ground of Christ's ultimate triumph. He may be said to have really triumphed there, because it was by that one act of his, that one offering of himself, that he completely vanquished all his foes, and for ever sat down at the right hand of the Majesty in the heavens. In the cross, to the spiritual eye, every victory of Christ is contained. It may not be there in fact, but it is there virtually; the germ of his glories may be discovered by the eye of faith in the agonies of the cross.

Bear with me while I humbly attempt to depict the triumph which now results from the cross.

Christ has forever overcome all his foes, and divided the spoil upon the battle field, and now, even at this day is he enjoying the well-earned reward and triumph of his fearful struggle. Lift up your eyes to the battlements of heaven, the great metropolis of God. The pearly gates are wide open, and the city shines with her bejeweled walls like a bride prepared for her husband. Do you see the angels crowding to the battlements? Do you observe them on every mansion of the celestial city, eagerly desiring and looking for something which has not yet arrived? At last, there is heard the sound of a trumpet, and the angels hurry to the gates—the vanguard of the redeemed is approaching the city. Abel comes in alone, clothed in a crimson garb, the herald of a glorious army of martyrs. Hark to the shout of acclamation! This is the first of Christ's warriors, at once a soldier and a trophy that has been delivered.

Close at his heels there follow others, who in those early times had learned of the coming Savior's fame. Behind them a mighty host may be discovered of patriarchal veterans, who have witnessed to the coming of the Lord in a wanton age. See Enoch still walking with his God, and singing sweetly—"Behold the Lord cometh with ten thousand of his saints." There too is Noah, who had sailed in the ark with the Lord as his pilot. Then follow Abraham, Isaac, and Jacob, Moses and Joshua, and Samuel, and David, all mighty men of valor.

Hearken to them as they enter! Every one of them waving his helmet in the air, cries, "Unto him who loved us, and washed us from our sins in his blood, unto him be honor, and glory, and dominion, and power, for ever and ever!" Look, my brethren, with admiration upon this noble army! Mark the heroes as they march along the golden streets, everywhere meeting with an enthusiastic welcome from the angels who have kept their first estate. On, on they pour, those countless legions—was there ever such a spectacle? It is not the pageant of a day, but the "show" of all time.

For four thousand years, on streams the army of Christ's redeemed. Sometimes there is a short rank, for the people have often been diminished and brought low; but, anon, a crowd succeeds them, and on, on, still on they come, all shouting, all praising him who loved them and gave himself for them. But, see, *he* comes! I see his immediate herald, clad in a garment of camel's hair, and a leathern girdle about his loins. The Prince of the house of David is not far behind. Let every eye be open.

Now, mark, how not only the angels, but the redeemed crowd the windows of heaven! He comes! He comes! It is Christ himself! Lash the snow-white coursers up the everlasting hills; "Life up you heads, O ye gates, and be ye lifted up, ye everlasting doors, that the King of glory may come in." See, he enters in the midst of acclamations. It is he! but he is not crowned with thorns. It is he! but though his hands wear the scar, they are stained with blood no longer. His eyes are as a flame of fire, and on his head are many crowns, and he hath on his vesture and on his thigh written, KING OF KINGS AND LORD OF LORDS. He stands aloft in that chariot which is "paved with love for the daughters of Jerusalem." Clothed in a vesture dipped in blood, he stands confessed the emperor of heaven and earth. On, on he rides, and louder than the noise of many waters and like great thunders are the acclamations which surround him!

See how John's vision is become a reality, for now we can see for ourselves and hear with our ears the new song, whereof he writes,

> They sung a new song, saying, thou art worthy to take the book, and to open the seals thereof: for thou was slain, and hast redeemed us to God by thy blood out of every kindred, and tongue, and people, and nation; and has made us unto our God kings and priests: and we shall reign on the earth. And I beheld, and I heard the voice of many angels round about the throne and the beasts and the elders: and the number of them was ten thousand times ten thousand, and thousands of thousands; saying with a loud voice, worthy is the Lamb that was slain to receive power, and riches, and wisdom, and strength, and honour, and glory, and blessing. And every creature which is in heaven, and on the earth, and under the earth, and such as are in the sea, and all that are in them, heard I saying, blessing, and honour, and glory, and power, be unto him that sitteth upon the throne, and unto the Lamb for ever and ever. And the four beasts said, amen. And the four and twenty elders fell down and worshipped him that liveth for ever and ever.

But who are these at his chariot wheels? Who are these grim monsters that come howling in the rear? I know them. First of all there is the arch enemy. Look at the old serpent, bound and fettered, how he writhes his ragged length along; his azure hues all tarnished with trailing in the dust, his scales despoiled of their once-vaunted brightness.

Now is captivity led captive, and death and hell shall be cast into the lake of fire. With what derision is the chief of rebels regarded. How is he become the object of everlasting contempt. He that sitteth in the heavens doth laugh, and the Lord doth have him in derision. Behold now how the serpent's head is broken, and the dragon is trampled underfoot. And now regard attentively yon hideous monster—*sin*—chained hand in hand with his satanic sire. See how he rolls his fiery eye-balls, mark how he twists and writhes in agonies. Mark how he glares upon the holy city, but is unable to spit his venom there, for he is chained and gagged, and dragged along an unwilling captive at the wheels of the victor. And there, too, is old Death, with his darts all broken and his hands behind him—the grim king of terrors, he too is a captive. Hark to the songs of the redeemed, of those who have entered in Paradise, as they see these mighty prisoners dragged along! "Worthy is he," they shout, "to live and reign at his Almighty Father's side, for he hath ascended up on high, he hath led captivity captive, and received gifts for men."

And now behind him I see the great mass of his people streaming in. The apostles are the first to arrive in one goodly fellowship hymning their Lord; and then their immediate successors; and then a long array of those who through cruel mockings and blood, through flame and sword, have followed their Master. These are those of whom the world was not worthy, brightest among the stars of heaven. Regard also the mighty preachers and confessors of the faith, Chrysostom, Athanasius, Augustine, and the like. Witness their holy unanimity in praising their Lord. Then let your eye run along the glittering ranks till you come to the days of Reformation. I see in the midst of the squadron, Luther, Calvin, and Zwingli—three holy brothers. I see just before them Wycliffe, and Huss, and Jerome of Prague—all marching together. And then I see a number that no man can number, converted to God through these mighty reformers, who now follow in the rear of the King of kings and Lord of lords. And looking down to our own time I see the stream broader and wider.

For many are the soldiers who have in these last times entered into their Master's triumph. We may mourn their absence from *us,* but we must rejoice in their presence with the Lord. But what is the unanimous shout, what is the one song that still rolls from the first rank to the last? It is this: "Unto him that loved us, washed us from our sins in his own blood, to him be glory and dominion for ever and ever!" Have they changed the tune? Have they supplanted his name by another? Have they put the crown upon another head, or elevated another hero into the chariot? Ah, no: they are content still to let the triumphant procession stream along its glorious length; still to rejoice as they behold fresh trophies of his love, for every soldier is a trophy, every warrior in Christ's army is another proof of his power to save, and his victory over death and hell.

I have not the time to enlarge further, or else I might describe the mighty pictures at the end of the procession; for in the old Roman triumphs, the deeds of the conqueror were all depicted in paintings. The towns he had taken, the rivers he had passed, the provinces he had subdued, the battles he had fought, were represented in pictures and exposed to the view of the people, who with great festivity and rejoicing, accompanied him in throngs, or beheld him from the windows of their houses, and filled the air with their acclamations and applauses. I might present to you first of all the picture of hell's dungeons blown to atoms. Satan had prepared deep in the depth of darkness a prison-house for God's elect; but Christ has not left one stone upon another.

On the picture I see the chains broken in pieces, the prison doors burnt with fire, and all the depths of the vast deep shaken to their foundations. On another picture I see heaven open to all believers; I see the gates that were fast shut heaved open by the golden lever of Christ's atonement. I see one, another picture, the grave despoiled; I behold Jesus in it, slumbering for a while, and then rolling away the stone and rising to immortality and glory. But we cannot stay to describe these mighty pictures of the victories of his love. We know that the time shall come when the triumphant procession shall cease, when the last of his redeemed shall have entered into the city of happiness and joy, and when with the shout of a trumpet heard for the last time, he shall ascend into heaven, and take his people up to reign with God, even our Father, even for ever and ever, world without end.

Our only question, and with that we conclude, is, have we a good hope through grace that we shall march in that tremendous procession? Shall we pass under view in that day of pomp and glory? Say, my soul, shalt thou have a humble part in that glorious pageant? Wilt thou follow at his chariot wheels? Wilt thou join in the thundering hosannas? Shall thy voice help to swell the everlasting chorus? Sometimes, I fear it shall not. There are times when the awful question comes—what if my name should be left out when he should read the muster roll? Brethren, does not that thought trouble you? Can you answer it? Will you be there—shall you see this pomp? Will you behold him triumph over sin, death and hell at last? Canst thou answer this question? There is another, but the answer will serve for both—dost thou believe on the Lord Jesus Christ? Is he thy confidence and thy trust? Hast thou committed thy soul to his keeping? Reposing on his might canst thou say for thine immortal spirit—

> Other refuge have I none,
>> Hangs my helpless soul on thee?

If thou canst say that, thine eyes shall see him in the day of his glory; nay, thou shalt share his glory, and sit with him upon his throne, even as he has overcome and sits down with his Father upon his throne. I blush to preach as I have done this morning on a theme far beyond my power; yet I could not leave it unsung, but, as best I might, sing it. May God enlarge your faith, and strengthen your hope, and inflame your love, and make you ready to be made partakers of the inheritance of the saints in light, that when he shall come with flying clouds on wings of wind, ye may be ready to meet him, and may with him ascend to gaze forever on the vision of his glory.

May God grant this blessing, for Christ's sake. Amen.

6

Christ the Destroyer of Death

"The last enemy that shall be destroyed is death" (1 Cor. 15:26).

In the five previous discourses we have been following our Lord and Master through his great achievements: we have seen him as the end of the law, as the conqueror of Satan, as the overcomer of the world, as the creator of all things new, and now we behold him as the destroyer of death. In this and in all his other glorious deeds let us worship him with all our hearts.

May the Spirit of God lead us into the full meaning of this, which is one of the Redeemer's grandest achievements.

How wonderfully is our Lord Jesus *one with man!* For when the Psalmist David had considered "the heavens the work of God's fingers," he said, "Lord, what is man that you are mindful of him, or the son of man that you visit him?" He was speaking of Christ. You would have thought he was thinking of man in his humblest estate, and that he was wondering that God should be pleased to honor so frail a being as the poor fallen son of Adam. You would never have dreamed that the glorious gospel lay hidden within those words of grateful adoration. Yet in the course of that meditation David went on to say, "You made him to have dominion over all the works of your hands, you have put all things under his feet."

Now, had it not been for the interpretation of the Holy Spirit, we should still have considered that he was speaking of men in general, and of man's natural dominion over the brute creation, but behold while that is true, there is another and a far more important truth concealed within it, for David, as a prophet, was all the while chiefly speaking of the man of men, the model man, the second Adam, the head of the new race of men. It was of Jesus, the Son of man, as honored by the Father, that the psalmist sang, "He has put all things under his feet." Was it not strange that when he spoke of man he must of necessity speak also of our Lord? And yet, when we consider the thing, it is only natural and according to truth, and only remarkable for us because in our minds we too often consider Jesus and man as far removed, and too little regard him as truly one with man.

Now, see how the apostle infers from the psalm the necessity of the resurrection, for if all things must be put under the feet of the man Christ Jesus, then every form of evil must be conquered by him, and death among the rest. "He must reign until he has put all enemies under his feet." It must be so, and therefore death itself must ultimately be overcome. So from that simple sentence in the psalm, which we should have read far otherwise without the light of the Holy Spirit, the apostle deduces the doctrine of the resurrection. The Holy Spirit taught his servant Paul how by a subtle chemistry he could distil from simple words a precious fragrant essence, which the common reader never suspected to be there.

Texts have their secret drawers, their box within a box, their hidden souls which lie asleep until he who placed them on their secret couches awakens them so that they may speak to the hearts of his chosen. Could you ever have guessed resurrection from the eighth Psalm? No, nor could you have believed, had it not been told to you, that there is fire in the flint, oil in the rock, and bread in the earth we tread upon. Man's books have usually far less in them than we expect, but the book of the Lord is full of surprises, it is a mass of light, a mountain of priceless revelations. We little know what still lies hidden within the Scriptures. We know the form of sound words as the Lord has taught it to us, and by it we will abide, but there are inner storehouses into which we have not peered; chambers of revelation lit up with bright lamps, perhaps too bright for our eyes at this present time.

If Paul, when the Spirit of God rested upon him, could see so much in the songs of David, the day may come when we also shall see even more in the epistles of Paul, and wonder about ourselves that we did not understand better the things which the Holy Spirit has so freely spoken to us by the apostle. May we at this time be enabled to look deep and far, and behold the sublime glories of our risen Lord.

To the text itself then: (1) death is an enemy; (2) death is an enemy to be destroyed; and, (3) death is an enemy to be destroyed last: "the last enemy that shall be destroyed is death."

I. *Death is an enemy.*

It was so born, even as Haman the Agagite was the enemy of Israel by his descent. Death is the child of our direst foe, for "sin when it is finished results in death." "Sin entered into the world and death by sin." Now, what is distinctly the fruit of transgression cannot be other than an enemy of man. Death was introduced into the world on that gloomy day which saw our fall, and he who had its power is our arch-enemy and betrayer, the devil: from both of which facts we must regard it as the obvious enemy of man. Death is an alien in this world, it did not enter into the original design of the unfallen creation, but its intrusion mars and spoils it all. It is no part of the Great Shepherd's flock, but it is a wolf which comes to kill and to destroy.

Geology tells us that there was death among the various forms of life from the first ages of the globe's history, even when as yet the world was not outfitted for the dwelling of man. This I can believe and still regard death as the result of sin. If it can be proved that there is such an organic unity between man and the lower animals that they would not have died if Adam had not sinned, then I see in those deaths before Adam the antecedent consequences of a sin which was then uncommitted.

If by the merits of Jesus there was salvation before he had offered his atoning sacrifice then I do not find it hard to conceive that the foreseen demerits of sin may have cast the shadow of death over the long ages which came before man's transgression. Of that we know little, nor is it important that we should, but it is certain that as far as this present creation is concerned death is not God's invited guest, but an intruder whose presence mars the feast. Man in his folly welcomed Satan and sin when they forced their way into the high festival of Paradise, but he never welcomed death: even his blind eyes could see in that skeleton form a cruel foe. As the lion to the herds of the plain, as the scythe to the sowers of the field, as the wind to the sere leaves of the forest, such is death to the sons of men. They fear it by an inward instinct because their conscience tells them that it is the child of their sin.

Death is well called an enemy for *it does an enemy's work* towards us. For what purpose does an enemy come except to root up, and to pull down, and to destroy? Death tears in pieces that beautiful handiwork of God, the fabric of the human body, so marvelously formed by the fingers of divine skill. Casting this rich embroidery into the grave among the armies of the worm, to its fierce soldier's death divides "to everyone colorful embroidered garments, highly embroidered garments"; and they ruthlessly rend in pieces the spoil. This building of our manhood is a house fair to look upon, but death the destroyer darkens its windows, shakes its pillars, closes its doors and causes the sound of the grinding to cease. Then the daughters of music are brought low, and the strong men bow themselves. This Vandal spares no work of life, however full of wisdom, or beauty, for it releases the silver cord and breaks the golden bowl. Lo, at the fountain the costly pitcher is utterly broken, and at the cistern the well-formed wheel is dashed to pieces. Death is a fierce invader of the realms of life, and where it comes it fells every good tree, plugs all wells of water, and mars every good piece of land with stones. Look at a man when death has accomplished his will upon him, what a ruin he is! How his beauty is turned to ashes and his good appearance to corruption. Surely an enemy has done this.

Look, my brethren, at the course of death throughout all ages and in all lands. What field is there without its grave? What city without its cemetery? Where can we go to find no sepulchers? Just as the sandy shore is covered with the upcastings of the worm, so are you, oh earth, covered with those grass covered mounds beneath which sleep the departed generations of men. And you, oh sea, even you, are not without your dead! As if the earth were all too full of corpses and they jostled each other in their crowded sepulchers, even into your caverns, oh mighty main, the bodies of the dead are cast. Your waves must become defiled with the carcasses of men, and on your floor must lie the bones of the slain! Our enemy, death, has marched as it were with sword and fire ravaging the human race. Neither Goth, nor Hun, nor Tartar could have slain so universally all who breathed, for death has allowed no one to escape. Everywhere it has withered household joys and created sorrow and sighing; in all lands where the sun is seen it has blinded men's eyes with weeping. The tear of the bereaved, the wail of the widow, and the moan of the orphan—these have been death's war music, and he has found a song of victory in it.

The greatest conquerors have only been death's slaughtermen, journeymen butchers working in his butcher shop. War is nothing better than death holding carnival, and devouring his prey a little more quickly than is his common custom.

Death has done the work of an enemy towards those of us who have as yet escaped his arrows. Those who have recently stood around a newly made grave and buried half their hearts can tell you what an enemy death is. It takes the friend from our side, and the child from our bosom, neither does it care for our crying. He has fallen who was the pillar of the household; she has been snatched away who was the brightness of the hearth. The little one is torn out of his mother's bosom though his loss almost breaks her heartstrings; and the blooming youth is taken from his father's side though the parent's fondest hopes are crushed by it.

Death has no pity for the young and no mercy for the old; he pays no regard to the good or to the beautiful; his scythe cuts down sweet flowers and noxious weeds with equal ease. He comes into our garden, tramples down our lilies and scatters our roses on the ground; yes, and even the most modest flowers planted in the corner, and hiding their beauty beneath the leaves so that they may blush unseen, death discovers even these, and cares nothing for their fragrance, but withers them with his burning breath. He is your enemy indeed, you fatherless child, left for the pitiless storm of a cruel world to beat upon, with no one to shelter you. He is your enemy, oh widow, for the light of your life is gone, and the desire of your eyes has been removed with a stroke. He is your enemy, husband, for your house is desolate and your little children cry for their mother of whom death has robbed you.

He is the enemy of us all, for what head of a family among us has not had to say to him, "You have bereaved me again and again!" Death is especially an enemy to the living when he invades God's house and causes the prophet and the priest to be numbered with the dead. The church mourns when her most useful ministers are struck down, when the watchful eye is closed in darkness, and the instructive tongue is mute. Yet how often does death war against us like this! The earnest, the active, the indefatigable are taken away. Those mightiest in prayer, those most affectionate in heart, those most exemplary in life, those are cut down in the midst of their labors, leaving behind them a church which needs them more than tongue can tell. If the Lord only threatens to permit death to seize a beloved pastor, the souls of his people are full of grief, and they view death as their worst foe, while they plead with the Lord and entreat him to let their minister live.

Even *those who die* may well consider death to be their enemy: I mean not now that they have risen to their seats, and, as disembodied spirits, behold the King in his beauty, but previously while death was approaching them. He seemed to their trembling flesh to be a foe, for it is not in nature, except in moments of extreme pain or aberration of mind, or of excessive expectation of glory, for us to be in love with death. It was wise of our Creator to constitute us so that the soul loves the body and the body loves the soul, and they desire to dwell together as long as they may, otherwise there would have been no care for self-preservation, and suicide would have destroyed the race.

> For who would bear the whips and scorns of time,
>   The oppressor's wrong, the proud men's contumely,
> When he himself might his quietus make
>   With a bare bodkin?

It is a first law of our nature that skin for skin, yes, all that a man has he will give for his life, and thus we are nerved to struggle for existence, and to avoid what would destroy us. This useful instinct renders death an enemy, but it also aids in keeping us from that crime of all crimes the most sure of damnation if a man commits it wilfully and in his sound mind; I mean the crime of self-murder.

When death comes even to the good man he comes as an enemy, for he is attended by such terrible heralds and grim outriders as do greatly scare us.

> Fever with brow of fire;
>   Consumption wan; palsy, half-warmed with life,
> And half a clay-cold lump; joint-torturing gout,
>   And ever-gnawing rheum; convulsion wild;
> Swol'n dropsy; panting asthma; apoplex
>   Full gorged.

None of these add to the prospect of death a bit of beauty. He comes with pains and griefs; he comes with sighs and tears. Clouds and darkness are all around him, an atmosphere laden with dust oppresses those whom he approaches, and a cold wind chills them even to the marrow. He rides on the pale horse, and where his steed sets its foot the land becomes a desert. By the footfall of that terrible steed the worm is awakened to gnaw the slain. When we forget other grand truths and only remember these dreadful things, death is the king of terrors for us. Hearts are sickened and courage is lost, because of him.

But, indeed, he is an enemy, for what does he come to do to our body? I know he does what ultimately leads to its betterment, but still it is what in itself, and for the present, is not joyous, but grievous. He comes to take the light from the eyes, the hearing from the ears, the speech from the tongue, the activity from the hand, and the thought from the brain. He comes to transform a living man into a mass of putrefaction, to degrade the beloved form of brother and friend to such a condition of corruption that affection itself cries out, "Bury my dead out of my sight." Death, you child of sin, Christ has transformed you marvelously, but in yourself you are an enemy before whom flesh and blood tremble, for they know that you are the murderer of all those born of woman, whose thirst for human prey the blood of nations cannot slake.

If you think for a few moments about this enemy, you will observe some of his points of character. He is the *common* foe of all God's people, and the enemy of all men: for however some have been persuaded that they should not die, yet there is no discharge in this war; and if in this conscription a man escapes the draft many and many a year until his greybeard seems to defy the winter's hardest frost, yet the man of iron must yield at last. It is appointed to all men once to die. The strongest man has no elixir of eternal life to renew his youth amid the decays of age: nor has the wealthiest prince a price by which to bribe destruction. To the grave must you descend, oh crowned monarch, for scepters and shovels go together. You must go down to the sepulcher, oh mighty man of valor, for sword and spade are made of the same metal. The prince is brother to the worm, and must dwell in the same house. Of our whole race it is true, "Dust you are, and to dust you shall return."

Death is also a *subtle* foe, lurking everywhere, even in the most harmless things. Who can tell where death has not prepared his ambushes? He meets us both at home and abroad; at the table he assails men in their food, and at the fountain he poisons their drink. He waylays us in the streets, and he seizes us in our beds; he rides on the storm at sea, and he walks with us when we are on our way upon the solid land. Where can we flee to escape from you, oh death, for from the summit of the Alps men have fallen to their graves, and in the deep places of the earth where the miner goes down to find the precious ore, there you have sacrificed many thousands of precious lives. Death is a subtle foe, and with noiseless footfalls follows close at our heels when we least think of him.

He is an enemy whom *none of us will be able to avoid*, take what bypaths we may, nor can we escape from him when our hour is come. Into this fowler's nets, like the birds, we shall all fly; in his great *seine* must all the fishes of the great sea of life be taken when their day is come. As surely as the sun sets or as the midnight stars at length descend beneath the horizon, or as the waves sink back into the sea, or as the bubble bursts, so must we all early or late come to our end, and disappear from earth to be known no more among the living.

Sudden, too, very often, are the assaults of this enemy.

> Leaves have their time to fall,
>   And flowers to wither at the north wind's breath,
> And stars to set—but all,
>   Thou hast all seasons for thine own, oh Death!

Such things have happened as for men to die without a moment's notice; with a psalm upon their lips they have passed away; or engaged in the daily business they have been summoned to turn in their account. We have heard of one who, when the morning paper brought him news that a friend in business had died, was drawing on his boots to go to his accounting house, and observed with a laugh that as far as he was concerned, he was so busy he had no time to die. Yet, before the words were finished, he fell forward and was a corpse. Sudden deaths are not so uncommon as to be marvels if we dwell in the centre of a large circle of mankind. Therefore death is a foe not to be despised or trifled with. Let us remember all his characteristics, and we shall not be inclined to think lightly of the grim enemy whom our glorious Redeemer has destroyed.

II. Secondly, let us remember that death is AN ENEMY TO BE DESTROYED. Remember that our Lord Jesus Christ has already accomplished a great victory upon death so that he has delivered us from lifelong bondage through its fear. He has not yet *destroyed death*, but he has come very close to it, for we are told that he has "abolished death and has brought life and immortality to light through the gospel." This surely must come very near to having destroyed death altogether.

In the first place, our Lord has subdued death in the very worst sense by having delivered his people from spiritual death. "And he has quickened you who were dead in trespasses and sins." Once you had no divine life whatever, but the death of original depravity remained upon you, and so you were dead to all divine and spiritual things; but now, beloved, the Spirit of God, even he who raised up Jesus Christ from the dead, has raised you up into newness of life, and you have become new creatures in Christ Jesus. In this sense death has been subdued.

Our Lord in his lifetime also conquered death by restoring certain individuals to life. There were three memorable cases in which at his bidding the last enemy resigned his prey. Our Lord went into the ruler's house, and saw the little girl who had recently fallen asleep in death, around whom they wept and lamented: he heard their scornful laughter, when he said, "She is not dead but sleeps," and he put them all out and said to her, "Maid, arise!" Then the spoiler was spoiled, and the dungeon door was flung open. He stopped the funeral procession at the gates of Nain, from where they were carrying out a young man, "the only son of his mother, and she was a widow," and he said, "Young man, I say to you arise." When that young man sat up and our Lord delivered him to his mother, then again the prey was taken from the mighty. Chief of all when Lazarus had laid in the grave so long that his sister said, "Lord, by this time he stinks," when, in obedience to the word, "Lazarus come out!" out came the raised one with his grave-clothes still around him, but yet really quickened, then death was seen to be subservient to the Son of man. "Loose him and let him go," said the conquering Christ, and death's bonds were removed, for the lawful captive was delivered. When at the Redeemer's resurrection many of the saints arose and came out of their graves into the holy city then the crucified Lord was proclaimed to be victorious over death and the grave.

Still, brethren, these were only preliminary skirmishes and mere foreshadowings of the grand victory by which death was overthrown. The real triumph was achieved upon the cross—

> He hell in hell laid low;
>   Made sin, he sin o'erthrew:
> Bow'd to the grave, destroy'd it so,
>   And death, by dying, slew.

When Christ died he suffered the penalty of death on the behalf of all his people, and therefore no believer now dies by way of punishment for sin, since we cannot dream that a righteous God would exact the penalty for one offense twice. Death since Jesus died is not a penal infliction upon the children of God: as such he has abolished it, and it can never be enforced. Why then do the saints die? Why, because their bodies must be changed before they can enter heaven. "Flesh and blood" as they are "cannot inherit the kingdom of God."

A divine change must take place upon the body before it will be fit for incorruption and glory; and death and the grave are, as it were, the refining pot and the furnace by means of which the body is made ready for its future bliss. Death, it is true you are not yet destroyed, but our living Redeemer has so changed you that you are no longer death, but something other than your name! Saints do not die now, but they are dissolved and depart.

Death is the releasing of the cable so that the bark may freely sail to the Fair Havens. Death is the fiery chariot in which we ascend to God: it is the gentle voice of the Great King, who comes into his banqueting hall, and says "Friend, come up higher." Behold, on eagle's wings we mount, we fly, far from this land of mist and cloud, into the eternal serenity and brilliance of God's own house above. Yes, our Lord has abolished death. The sting of death is sin, and our great Substitute has taken that sting away by his great sacrifice. Stingless, death remains among the people of God, but it so little harms them that to them "it is not death to die."

Further, Christ vanquished death and thoroughly overcame him when he rose. What a temptation one has to paint a picture of the resurrection, but I will not be led aside to attempt more than a few touches. When our great Champion awoke from his brief sleep of death and found himself in the drawing-room of the grave, he quietly proceeded to take off the garments of the tomb. How leisurely he proceeded! He folded up the napkin and placed it by itself, so that those who lose their friends might wipe their eyes with it; and then he took off the winding sheet and laid the grave-clothes by themselves so that they might be there when his saints come there, so that the room might be well furnished, and the bed ready sheeted and prepared for their rest. The sepulcher is no longer an empty vault, a dreary tomb, but a room of rest, a dormitory furnished and prepared, hung with the rich tapestry which Christ himself has bequeathed. It is now no more a damp, dark, dreary prison: Jesus has changed all that.

> 'Tis now a cell where angels use
> To come and go with heavenly news.

The angel from heaven rolled away the stone from our Lord's sepulcher and let in the fresh air and light again upon our Lord, and he stepped out more than a conqueror. Death had fled. The grave had capitulated.

> Lives again our glorious King!
> "Where, oh death, is now thy sting?"
> Once he died our souls to save;
> "Where's thy victory, boasting grave?"

Well, brethren, as surely as Christ rose so he guaranteed as an absolute certainty the resurrection of all his saints into a glorious life for their bodies, the life of their souls never having paused even for a moment. In this he conquered death; and since that memorable victory, every day Christ is overcoming death, for he gives his Spirit to his saints, and having that Spirit within them they meet the last enemy without alarm: often they confront him with songs, perhaps more frequently they face him with calm countenance, and fall asleep with peace. I will not fear you, death, why should I? You look like a dragon, but your sting is gone. Your teeth are broken, oh old lion, why should I fear you? I know you are no more able to destroy me, but you are sent as a messenger to conduct me to the golden gate where I shall enter and see my Savior's unveiled face forever. Expiring saints have often said that their last beds have been the best they have ever slept upon. Many of them have enquired,

> Tell me, my soul, can this be death?

To die has been so different a thing from what they expected it to be, so cheerful, and so joyous; they have been so unloaded of all care, have felt so relieved instead of burdened, that they have wondered whether this could be the monster they had been so afraid of all their days. They find it a pin's prick, whereas they feared it would prove to be a sword thrust: it is the shutting of the eye on earth and the opening of it in heaven, whereas they thought it would have been a stretching upon the rack, or a dreary passage through a dismal region of gloom and dread. Beloved, our exalted Lord has overcome death in all these ways.

But now, observe, that this is not the text: the text speaks of something yet to be done. The last enemy that *shall be* destroyed is death, so that death in the sense meant by the text is not destroyed yet. He is to be destroyed, and how will that be?

Well, I take it death will be destroyed in the sense that first, at the coming of Christ, *those who are alive and remain shall not see death*. They shall be changed; there must be a change even to the living before they can inherit eternal life, but they shall not actually die. Do not envy them, for they will have no preference beyond those who sleep; rather I think theirs to be the inferior lot of the two in some respects. But they will not know death: the multitude of the Lord's own who will be alive at his coming will pass into glory without needing to die. So death, as far as they are concerned, will be destroyed.

But the sleeping ones, the myriads who have left their flesh and bones to molder back to earth, death shall be destroyed even for them, for when the trumpet sounds they shall rise from the tomb. *The resurrection is like destruction of death.* We never taught, nor believed, nor thought that every particle of everybody that was put into the grave would come back to its companion, and that the absolutely identical material would rise; but we do say that the identical body will be raised, and that as surely as there comes out of the ground the seed that was put into it, though in a very different form, for it does not come out as a seed but as a flower, so surely shall the same body rise again. The same material is not necessary, but there shall come out of the grave, indeed, come out of the earth, if it never saw a grave, or come out of the sea if devoured by monsters, that very same body for true identity which was inhabited by the soul while here below. Was it not so with our Lord? Then so it shall be with his own people, and then the saying that is written shall be brought to pass, "Death is swallowed up in victory. Oh death, where is your sting! Oh grave where is your victory!"

There will be this feature in our Lord's victory, that death will be fully destroyed because *those who rise will not be one whit the worse for having died.* I believe concerning those new bodies that there will be no trace upon them of the feebleness of old age, none of the signs of long and wearying sickness, none of the scars of martyrdom. Death shall not have left his mark upon them at all, except it is some glory mark which shall be to their honor, like the scars in the flesh of the Well-Beloved, which are his chief beauty even now in the eyes of those for whom his hands and feet were pierced. In this sense death shall be destroyed because he shall have done no damage to the saints at all, the very trace of decay shall have been swept away from the redeemed.

And then, finally, there shall, after this trumpet of the Lord, be *no more death*, neither sorrow, nor crying, for the former things have passed away. "Christ being raised from the dead dies no more, death has no more dominion over him"; and so also the quickened ones, his own redeemed, they too shall die no more. Oh dreadful, dreadful supposition, that they should ever have to undergo temptation or pain, or death a second time. It cannot be. "Because I live," says Christ, "they shall live also." Yet the doctrine of the natural immortality of the soul having been given up by some, certain of them have felt obliged to give up with the eternity of future punishment the eternity of future bliss, and assuredly as far as some great proof texts are concerned, they stand or fall together. "These shall go away into everlasting punishment, and the righteous into life eternal"; if the one state is short so must the other be: whatever the adjective means in the one case it means in the other. To us the word means endless duration in both cases, and we look forward to a bliss which shall never know end or duration. Then in the tearless, sorrowless, graveless country death shall be utterly destroyed.

III. And now last of all, and the word "last" sounds fitly in this case, DEATH IS TO BE DESTROYED LAST.

Because he came in last he must go out last. Death was not the first of our foes: first came the devil, then sin, then death. Death is not the worst of enemies; death is an enemy, but he is much to be preferred to our other adversaries. It would be better to die a thousand times than to sin. To be tested by death is nothing compared with being tempted by the devil. The mere physical pains connected with dissolution are comparative trifles compared with the hideous grief which is caused by sin and the burden which a sense of guilt causes to the soul. No, death is only a secondary mischief compared with the defilement of sin. Let the great enemies go down first; strike the shepherd and the sheep will be scattered; let sin, and Satan, the lord of all these evils, be struck first, and death may well be left to the last.

Notice, that death is the last enemy for each individual Christian and the last to be destroyed. Well now, if the word of God says it is the last I want to remind you of a little piece of practical wisdom—leave him to be the last. Brother, do not dispute the appointed order, but let the last be last. I have known a brother wanting to vanquish death long before he died. But, brother, you do not need dying grace until dying moments. What would be the good of dying grace while you are yet alive? A boat will only be necessary when you reach a river. Ask for living grace, and glorify Christ by it, and then you shall have dying grace when dying time comes. Your enemy is going to be destroyed, but not today.

There is a great host of enemies to be fought today, and you may be content to leave this one alone for a while. This enemy will be destroyed, but concerning the times and the seasons we are in ignorance; our wisdom is to be good soldiers of Jesus Christ as the duty of every day requires. Take your trials as they come, brother! As the enemies march up kill them, rank upon rank, but if you fail in the name of God to strike the front ranks, and say, "No, I am only afraid of the rear rank," then you are playing the fool. Leave the final shock of arms until the last adversary advances, and meanwhile hold your place in the conflict. God will in due time help you to overcome your last enemy, but meanwhile see to it that you overcome the world, the flesh, and the devil. If you live well you will die well. That same covenant in which the Lord Jesus gave you life contains also the grant of death, for "All things are yours, whether things present or things to come, or life or death, all are yours, and you are Christ's, and Christ is God's."

Why is death left to the last? Well, I think it is because Christ can make much use of him. The last enemy that shall be destroyed is death, because death is of great service before he is destroyed. Oh, what lessons some of us have learned from death! "Our dying friends come over us like a cloud to damp our brainless ardors," to make us feel that these poor fleeting toys are not worth living for; that just as others pass away so must we also be gone, and so they help to make us hold this world loosely, and urge us to take wing and mount towards the world to come. There are, perhaps, no sermons like the deaths which have happened in our households; the departure of our beloved friends have been to us solemn discourses of divine wisdom, which our heart could not help hearing. So Christ has spared death to make him a preacher to his saints.

And you know, brethren, that if there had been no death the saints of God would not have had the opportunity to exhibit the highest ardor of their love. Where has love for Christ triumphed most? Why, in the death of the martyrs at the stake and on the rack. Oh Christ, you never had such garlands woven for you by human hands as they have brought you who have come up to heaven from the forests of persecution, having waded through streams of blood. By death for Christ the saints have glorified him most.

So it is in their measure with saints who die from ordinary deaths; they would have had no such test for faith and work for patience as they now have if there had been no death. Part of the reason for the continuance of this world is that the Christ of God may be glorified, but if believers never died, the supreme consummation of faith's victory must have been unknown. Brethren, if I may die as I have seen some of our church members die, I court the grand occasion. I would not wish to escape death by some back road if I may sing as they sang. If I may have such hosannas and hallelujahs beaming in my very eyes as I have seen as well as heard from them, it would be a blessed thing to die. Yes, as a supreme test of love and faith, death is well respited awhile to let the saints glorify their Master.

Besides, brethren, without death we should not be so conformed to Christ as we shall be if we fall asleep in him. If there could be any jealousies in heaven among the saints, I think that any saint who does not die, but is changed when Christ comes, could almost meet you and me, who probably will die, and say, "My brother, there is one thing I have missed, I never lay in the grave, I never had the chilly hand of death laid on me, and so in that I was not conformed to my Lord. But *you* know what it is to have fellowship with him, even in his death." Did I not well say that those who were alive and remain should have no preference over those who are asleep? I think the preference if anything shall belong to us who sleep in Jesus, and wake up in his likeness.

Death, beloved, is not yet destroyed, because he brings the saints home. He only comes to them and whispers his message, and in a moment they are supremely blessed,

> Have done with sin and care and woe,
>   And with the Savior rest.

And so death is not destroyed yet, for he serves useful purposes.

But, beloved, he is going to be destroyed. He is the last enemy of the church collectively. The church as a body has had a number of foes to contend with, but after the resurrection we shall say, "This is the last enemy. No other foe is left." Eternity shall roll on in ceaseless bliss. There may be changes, bringing new delights; perhaps in the eternity to come there may be eras and ages of even more amazing bliss, and still more superlative ecstasy; but there shall be,

> No rude alarm of raging foes,
>   No cares to break the last repose.

The last enemy that shall be destroyed is death, and if the last is slain there can be no future foe. The battle is fought and the victory is won forever. And who has won it? Who except the Lamb who sits on the throne, to whom let us all ascribe honor, and glory, and majesty, and power, and dominion, and might, for ever and ever. May the Lord help us in our solemn adoration. Amen.

7

Christ the Seeker and Savior of the Lost

"For the Son of Man has come to seek and to save that which was lost" (Luke 19:10).

We have now considered six of the glorious achievements of our Divine Lord and Savior, and it is time to conclude the series. How shall we crown the edifice? The best wine should be kept for the last, but where shall we find it? The choice is wide, but amid so many wonders, which shall we select? What shall be the seventh great work concerning which we shall extol Him? Many marvels suggested themselves to me and each one was, assuredly, worthy to occupy the place, but as I could not take all, I resolved to close with one of the simplest and most practical. His saving sinners seemed to me to be practically the chief of all His works, for it was for this purpose that the rest of His achievements were attempted and performed. Had it not been for the salvation of men, I know not that we had ever known our Lord as the Destroyer of Death or the Overcomer of Satan and, certainty, if He had not saved the lost, I am unable to perceive what Glory there would have been in the overcoming of the world, or in the creation of all things new.

The salvation of men was the prize of His life's race—for this He girded up His loins and distanced every adversary! The salvation of the lost was "the joy which was set before Him," for the sake of which He "endured the Cross, despising the shame." Although it seems, at first sight, that in selecting our present topic we have descended from the transcendent glories of our Champion to more common things, it is, indeed, *not* so. The victories of our Lord which are written in the Book of the wars of the Lord, when He led captivity captive and robbed death of his sting, may strike us as more astounding, but yet in very truth this is the summing-up of His great works—this is the issue, the flower, and crown of all! "The Son of Man is come to seek and to save that which was lost," is a sentence as majestic as Prophet ever penned when in fullest Inspiration he extolled the Prince of Peace!

I. Notice, first, OUR LORD'S GRACIOUS MISSION—"*The Son of Man is come.*" When He was here among men, He could use the present tense and say, "*is come.*" That was an improvement upon what Prophets had to say, for they only spoke of Him as The Coming One—as One who, in the fullness of time, would be manifested. The promise was amazing, but what shall I say of the actual performance when the Word made flesh could say, "The Son of Man *is* come"? To us, today, the coming of Christ to seek and to save the lost is an accomplished fact, a matter of history, most sure and certain. And what a fact it is!

You have often thought of it, but have you ever worked your mind into the very heart of it—that God has actually visited this world in human form—that He before whom angels bow has actually been here, in fashion like ourselves, feeding the hungry crowds of Palestine, healing their sick and raising their dead? I know not what may be the peculiar boast of other planets, but this poor star cannot be excelled, for on this world the Creator has stood! This earth has been trodden by the feet of God and yet it was not crushed beneath the mighty burden because He designed to link His Deity with our humanity! The Incarnation is a wonder of wonders, but it does not belong to the realm of imagination or even of expectation, for it has actually been beheld by mortal eyes!

We claim your faith for a fact which has really taken place. If we asked you by faith to expect a marvel yet to come, we trust the Spirit of God would enable you to do so, that, like Abraham, you might foresee the blessing and be glad. But the miracle of miracles has been worked! The Son of the Highest *has been here*. From Bethlehem to Calvary, He has traversed life's pilgrimage. Thirty years or more yonder canopy of sky hung above the head of Deity in human form. O wondrous joy! Say rather, O matchless hive of perfect sweets, for a thousand joys lie close compacted in the word, "Immanuel," God With Us!

> Welcome to our wondering sigh.
> Eternity within a span!

> Summer in winter! Day in night!
> Heaven in earth! And God in man!
> > Great Little One, whose glorious birth
> Lifts the earth to Heaven, stoops Heaven to earth.

Our Lord had come upon His sacred mission as soon as He was really the Son of Man, for before He was known only as the Son of God. Others had borne the name of "son of man," but none deserved it so well as He. Ezekiel, for reasons which we need not now stay to consider, is called, "son of man," a very large number of times. Perhaps, like John in Christ's own day, Ezekiel had much of the spirit and character which were manifest in our Lord—and so the name was the more suitable to him. Certainly he had Christ's eagle eyes, Christ's spiritual Nature and was filled with light and knowledge—and so, as if to remind him that he who is like his Lord in excellence must also have fellowship with Him in lowliness, he is again and again reminded that he is still "the son of man."

When our Lord came into this world, He seemed to select that title of "Son of Man" for Himself and make it His own special name—and worthily so, for other men are the sons of this man or that, but His is no restricted humanity—it is manhood of the universal type. Jesus is not born into the race of the Jews so much as into the human family. He is not to be claimed for any age, place, or nationality—He is "the Son of Man"—and this, I say, is how He comes to man. So that as long as Christ is the Son of Man, we may still say of Him that He comes to seek and to save the lost! I know that, in Person, He has gone back to Heaven. I know that the cloud has received Him out of our sight. But the very taking upon Himself of our humanity was a coming down to seek and save the lost—and as He has not laid that Humanity aside, He is still with men, continuing to seek and to save even to this day! "He is able to save them to the uttermost that come unto God by Him, seeing He ever lives to make intercession for them."

So that, if I treat the text as if Jesus were still among us, I would not err, for He is here in the sense of seeking the same end, though it is by His Spirit and by His servants rather than by His own bodily Presence! He has said, "Lo, I am with you always, even unto the end of the world," and that saying is found in connection with the agency which He has established for seeking and saving lost men, by making men disciples and teaching them the way of life! As long as this dispensation lasts, it will still be true that the great Savior and Friend of man has come among us and is seeking and saving the lost!

II. Now, secondly, let us see HIS MAIN INTENT IN COMING HERE BELOW—"The Son of Man is come *to seek and to save that which was lost*." The intent breaks itself up into two points: *the persons*—the lost, and *the purpose*—the seeking and the saving of them.

Christ's main intent in coming here bore upon *the lost*. Proud men do not like us to preach this Truth of God. It was but yesterday that I saw it alleged against Christianity that it discourages virtue and patronizes the guilty. They say that we ministers lift the sinful into the most prominent place and give them the preference above the moral and excellent in our preaching. This is a soft impeachment to which, in a better sense than is intended by those who bring it, we are glad to plead guilty!

We may well be excused if our preaching seeks the lost, for these are the persons whom our Lord has come to seek and to save. The main stress and intent of the Incarnation of God in the Person of Christ lies with the guilty, the fallen, the unworthy, the lost; His errand of mercy has nothing to do with those who are good and righteous in themselves, if such there is, but it has to do with sinners—real sinners, guilty not of nominal but of actual sins—and who have gone so far therein as to be lost! Why do you quibble at this? Why should He come to seek and to save that which is not lost? Should the Shepherd seek the sheep which has not gone astray? Answer me. Why should He come to be the Physician of those who are not lost? Should He light a candle and sweep the house to look for pieces of silver which are not lost, but lie bright and untarnished in His hand? To what purpose would this be? Would you have Him paint the lily and gild it with refined gold? Would you make Him a mere busybody offering superfluous aid? With those who think themselves pure, what has the cleaning blood of Jesus to do? Is the Savior a needless Person and was His work a needless business? It must be so if it is intended for those who do not need it!

Who wants a Savior most? Answer this. Should not mercy exercise itself where there is most need for it? This world is like a battlefield over which the fierce hurricanes of conflict have swept and the surgeons have come to deal with those who lie upon its plains. To whom shall they go first? Shall they not turn first to those who are most terribly wounded and who are bleeding almost to the death? Will you quarrel with us if we declare that the first to be taken to the hospital should be those who are in direst need? Will you be angry if we say that the liniment is for the wounded, that the bandages are for the broken limbs and that the medicine is for the sick? A strange quarrel this would be! If ever it should begin, a fool must begin it, for no wise man would ever raise the question! Blessed Christ of God, we will not quibble because You also come in Your mercy to those who need You most, even to the lost!

And who, think you, will love Him best and so reward Him best if He comes to them? The proud Pharisee in his perfection of imaginary holiness—will he value the Christ who tells him that He comes to wash away his sin? He turns upon his heels with scorn! What sin has *he* to wash away? The self-satisfied moralist who dares to say, "All these commands I have kept from my youth up: what lack I yet?"—is he likely to become a disciple of the Great Teacher whose first lessons are, "Yet must be born again," and, "Except you are converted and become as little children you shall not enter into the Kingdom of Heaven"? The fact is that Jesus has no form nor comeliness to those who have a beauty of their own!

Christ gets most love where He pardons most sin. And the sweetest obedience to His command is rendered by those who once were most disobedient, but who are gently led beneath His sway by the force of grateful love. Yon sterile hills of fancied holiness yield Him no harvest and, therefore, He leaves them to their own boastfulness. But meanwhile, He scatters plenteous grain among the lowlands where the ground is broken and lies ready for the seed. He preaches pardon to those who know that they have sinned and confess the same—but those who have no sin, have no Savior.

But after all, dear friends, if Jesus did not direct His mission of salvation to the lost, to whom else could He have come? For truth to say, there are none but the lost on the face of this whole earth! The proudest Pharisee is but a sinner and all the more a sinner for his pride. And the moralist who thinks himself so clean is filthy in the sight of God! Though he labors to conceal the spots, the self-righteous man is a leper and will forever remain so unless Jesus cleanses Him. It is a thrice-blessed fact that Christ came to save the lost, for such are we all—and had He not made lost ones the object of His searching and saving, there would have been no hope for us!

What is meant by "*the lost*"? Well, "lost" is a dreadful word. I would need much time to explain it, but if the Spirit of God, like a flash of light, shall enter into your heart and show you what you are by nature, you will accept that word, "lost," as descriptive of your condition and understand it better than a thousand words of mine could enable you to do! Lost by the Fall! Lost by inheriting a depraved nature! Lost by your own acts and deeds! Lost by a thousand omissions of duty and lost by countless deeds of overt transgressions! Lost by habits of sin! Lost by tendencies and inclinations which have gathered strength and dragged you downward into deeper and yet deeper darkness and iniquity! Lost by inclinations which never turn of themselves to that which is right, but which resolutely refuse Divine Mercy and Infinite Love! We are lost willfully and willingly—lost perversely and utterly! But still lost of our own accord which is the worst kind of being lost that can possibly be! We are lost to God, who has lost our heart's love, lost our confidence, and lost our obedience! We are lost to the Church, which we cannot serve; lost to the Truth of God which we will not see; lost to right, whose cause we do not uphold; lost to Heaven, into whose sacred precincts we can never come! Lost—so lost that unless Almighty Mercy shall intervene, we shall be cast into the Pit that is bottomless to sink forever! "LOST! LOST! LOST!"

The very word seems to me to be the knell of an impenitent soul. "*Lost! Lost! Lost!*" I hear the dismal tolling! A soul's funeral is being celebrated! Endless death has befallen an immortal being! It comes up as a dreadful wail from far beyond the boundaries of life and hope, forth from those dreary regions of death and darkness where spirits dwell who would not have Christ to reign over them. "*Lost! Lost! Lost!*" Ah me, that ever these ears should hear that doleful sound! Better a whole world on fire than a lost soul! Better every star quenched and yon skies a wreck than a single soul to be lost!

Now, it is for souls that soon will be in that worst of all conditions and are already preparing for it, that Jesus came here seeking and saving. What joy is this! In proportion as the grief was heavy, the joy is great. If souls can be delivered from going down into such a state, it is a feat worthy of God, Himself. Glory be to His holy name!

Now note the purpose—He "came *to seek and to save* that which was lost." Ah, this is a Truth of God worth preaching—this Doctrine that Jesus Christ came to seek and to save sinners. Some people tell me that He comes "to make men salvable"—to put all men into such a condition that it is possible that they may be saved. I believe that men *may* be saved, but I see no very great wonder in the fact. It does not stir my blood, or incite me to dance for joy. I do not know that it makes even the slightest impression upon me! I can go to sleep and I am sure I shall not wake up in the night and long to get up at once to preach such poor news as that Jesus came to make men salvable! I would not have become a minister to preach so meager a Gospel! But that our Lord came to *save* men—that is substantial and satisfying news, far exceeding the other! To make men salvable is a skeleton, bones and skin—but to save them is a living blessing! To make men salvable is a farthing blessing, but to save them is untold wealth!

They say also that Jesus came into the world to let men be saved if they will. I am glad of that. It is true and good. I believe that every truly willing soul may be saved, yes, such a one is, in a measure, saved already! If there is a sincere will towards salvation—understand, towards *true salvation*—that very will indicates that a great change has commenced within the man and I rejoice that it is written, "Whoever will, let him take the water of life freely." But now just read our text as if it ran thus—"The Son of Man is come that whoever wills to be saved may be saved." The sense is good, but very feeble! How the wine is mixed with water!

But, oh, what flavor, what essence, what marrow, what fatness there is in this, "The Son of Man is come *to seek and to save that which was lost!*" This is the Gospel! And the other is but a part of the Good News. Again, read the text another way, "The Son of Man is come to help men to save themselves." This will not do at all. It is something like helping men to march who have no legs, or helping blind men to judge colors, or helping dead men to make themselves alive. Help to those who can do nothing at all is a miserable mockery. No, we cannot have our Bibles altered that way! We will let the text stand as it is—in all its fullness of Divine Grace!

Nor is it even possible for us to cut down our text to this, "The Son of Man is come to save those who seek Him." If it ran so, I would bless God forever for it, for it would be a glorious Gospel text even then. There are Scriptures which teach that Doctrine and it is a blessed Truth for which to be supremely grateful. But my text goes very much further, for it says, "The Son of Man has come to seek and to save that which was lost." I met with a question and answer the other day, "Where did the Samaritan woman find the Savior? She found Him at the well." I do not quibble at that mode of expression, but mark you, that is not how I would ask the question! I should rather enquire, "Where did the Savior find the woman?" For, surely, she was not seeking Him—I see no indication that she had any such idea in her mind! She was looking after water from the well—and if she had found that—she would have gone home satisfied.

No, those are the finders, surely, who are the seekers! And so it must be that Christ found the woman, for He was looking after her. While I bless my Lord that He will save you if you seek Him, I am still more thankful that there are men and women whom He will seek as well as save! No, that there never was a soul saved yet but Christ sought it first! He is the Author as well as the Finisher of faith. He is the Alpha and the Omega, the Beginning and the Ending of the work of Grace! Let His name be praised for it! The text must stand as it is and we will adore the length and breadth, the height and depth of the love which has made it true! Successful seeking and complete saving belong to the Son of Man—some of us have experienced both. Oh, that all of us might yet do so!

III. Now we pass on, thirdly, to notice A DOUBLE DIFFICULTY.

We see Christ's errand and we at once perceive that He has come to deal with people who are lost in two senses and in each sense a miracle of Grace is needed for their deliverance. They are so lost that they need *saving*, but they are also so lost that they need *seeking*. Persons may be so lost on land or on sea as to need saving and not seeking—but we were spiritually lost so as to need both saving and seeking too.

I heard, a little while ago, of a party of Friends who went to the lakes of Cumberland and endeavored to climb the Langdale Pikes. One of the many found the labor of the ascent too wearisome and so resolved that he would go back to the little inn from which they started. Being a wiser man than some, in his own esteem, he did not take the winding path by which they had ascended. He thought he would go straight down, for he could see the house just below, and fancied he should pitch upon it all of a sudden and show the mountaineers that a straight line is the nearest road! Well, after descending and descending, leaping many a rugged place, he found himself, at last, on a ledge from which he could go neither up nor down. After many vain attempts, he saw that he was a prisoner. In a state of wild terror, he took off his garments and tore them into shreds to make a line and, tying the pieces together, he let them down, but he found that they reached nowhere at all in the great and apparently unfathomable abyss which yawned below him. So he began to call aloud, but no answer came from the surrounding hills except the echo of his own voice! He shouted by the half-hour together, but there was no answer, neither was there anyone within sight. His horror nearly drove him out of his wits. At last, to his intense joy, he saw a figure move in the plain below and he began to shout again. Happily it was a woman, who, hearing his voice, stopped. And as he called again, she came nearer and called out, "Stay where you are. Do not stir an inch. Stay where you are!" He was lost, but he no longer needed seeking, for some friendly shepherds soon saw where he was. All he needed was saving—and so the mountaineers descended with a rope, as they were known to do when rescuing lost sheep—and soon brought him out of danger. He was lost, but he did not need seeking—they could see where he was.

A month or two ago, you must have noticed in the papers a notice about a gentleman who had left Wastwater some days before to go over the hills, and had not been heard of since. His friends had to *seek* him so that, if still alive, he might be saved. And there were those who traversed hill and moor to find him, but they were unable to save him because they could not find him. If they could have found out where he was, I do not doubt that had he been in the most imminent peril, the bold hill-men would have risked their lives to rescue him. But, alas, he was never found or saved—his lifeless corpse was the only discovery which was ultimately made. This last is the true image of our deplorable condition—we are by nature, lost—so that nothing but seeking and saving together will be of a service to us.

Let us see how our Lord accomplished *the saving*. That has been done, completely done. My dear Friends, you and I were lost in the sense of having broken the Law of God and having incurred His anger. But Jesus came and took the sin of men upon Himself and, as their Surety and their Substitute, He bore the wrath of God so that God can henceforth be just and yet the Justifier of him that believes in Jesus. I would like to die talking of this blessed Doctrine of Substitution and I intend, by Divine Grace, to live proclaiming it, for it is the keystone of the Gospel! Jesus Christ did literally take upon Himself the transgression and iniquity of His people and was made a curse for them, seeing that they had fallen under the wrath of God! And now every soul that believes in Jesus is saved because Jesus has taken away the penalty and the curse due to sin. In this let us rejoice! Christ has also saved us from the power of Satan. The Seed of the woman has bruised the serpent's head so that Satan's power is broken. Jesus has, by His Almighty Power, set us free from Hell's horrible yoke by vanquishing the Prince of Darkness and has, moreover, saved us from the power of death, so that to Believers it shall not be death to die! Christ has saved us from sin and all its consequence by His most precious death and Resurrection—

> See God descending in the Human frame,
>   The Offended suffering in the offender's name!
> All your deeds to Him imputed see,
>   And all His Righteousness devolved on thee.

Our Lord's saving work is, in this sense, finished, but there is always going on in the world His *seeking* work—and I want you to think of it.

He can save us, blessed be His name! He has nothing more to do in order to save any soul that trusts Him. But we have wandered very far away, and are hidden in the wilds of the far country. We are very hungry and though there is bread enough and to spare, what is the use of it while we are lost to the home in which it is so freely distributed? We are very ragged—there is the best robe and it is ready to be put on us—but what is the good of it while we are so far away? There are the music and the dancing to make us glad and to cheer us, but what is the use of them while we still tarry among the swine? Here, then, is the great difficulty. Our Lord must find us, follow our wanderings and, treating us like lost sheep, He must bear us back upon His shoulders rejoicing!

Many need seeking because they are lost in bad company. Evil companions gather around men and keep them away from hearing the Gospel by which men are saved. There is no place to be lost in like a great city. When a man wants to escape the police, he does not run to a little village—he hides away in a thickly populated town. So this London has many hiding places where sinners get out of the Gospel's way! They lose themselves in the great crowd and are held captives by the slavish customs of the evil society into which they are absorbed. If they do but relent for a moment, some worldling plucks them by the sleeve and says, "Let us be merry while we may! Why are you so melancholy?" Satan carefully sets a watch upon his younger servants to prevent their escaping from his hands. These pickets labor earnestly to prevent the man from hearing the good news of salvation lest he should be converted. Sinners therefore need seeking out from among the society in which they are imbedded—they need as much seeking after as the pearls of the Arabian Gulf!

The Lord Jesus Christ, in seeking men, has to deal with deep-seated prejudices. Many refuse to hear the Gospel—they would travel many miles to escape its warning message! Some are too wise, or too rich to have the Gospel preached to them. Pity the poor rich! The poor man has many missionaries and evangelists seeking him out, but who goes after the great ones? Some come from the East to worship, but who comes from the West? Many more will find their way to Heaven out of the back slums than ever will come out of the great mansions and palaces! Jesus must seek His elect among the rich under great disadvantages, but blessed be His name, He does seek them!

See how vices and depraved habits hold the mass of the poor classes! What a seeking out is needed among working men, for many of them are besotted with drunkenness! Look at the large part of London on the Lord's Day—what have the working population been doing? They have been reading the Sunday newspaper and loafing about the house in their shirtsleeves and waiting at the posts of the doors—not of wisdom, but of the drink shop! These have been thirsting, but not after righteousness. Baachus still remains the god of this city and multitudes are lost among the beer barrels and the spirit casks! In such pursuits men waste the blessed Sabbath hours. How shall they be sought out? The Lord Jesus is doing it by His Holy Spirit!

Alas, through their ill ways, men's ears are stopped, their eyes are blinded and their hearts hardened so that the messengers of mercy have need of great patience! It would be easy work to save men if they could but be made willing to receive the Gospel, but they will not even *hear* it. When you do get them for a Sabbath-Day beneath the sound of a faithful ministry, how they struggle against it! They need seeking out 50 times over! You bring them right up to the Light of God and flash it upon their eyes, but they willfully and deliberately close their eyelids to it! You set before them life and death, and plead with them even unto tears that they would lay hold on eternal life—but they choose their own delusions. So long and so patiently must they be sought that this seeking work as much reveals the gracious heart of Jesus as did the saving work which He fulfilled upon the bloody tree!

Notice how He is daily accomplishing His search of love. Every day, Beloved, Jesus Christ is seeking men's *ears*. Would you believe it? He has to go about with wondrous wisdom even to get a hearing. They do not want to know the love message of their God. "God so loved the world"—they know all about that and do not want to hear any more. There is an Infinite Sacrifice for sin— they turn on their heels at such stale news. They would rather read an article in an infidel Review or a paragraph in the *Police News*. They want to know no more of spiritual matters! The Lord Jesus, in order to get at their ears, cries aloud by many earnest voices. Thank God He has ministers yet alive who mean to be heard and will not be put off with denials! Even the din of this noisy world cannot drown their testimony. Cry aloud, my Brother! Cry aloud and spare not, for cry as you may, you will not cry too loudly, for man will not hear if he can help it. Our Lord, to win men's ears, must use a variety of voices—musical or rough—as His wisdom judges best. Sometimes He gains an audience by an odd voice whose quaintness wins attention—He will reach men when He means to save them! That was an odd voice—surely the oddest I ever heard of—which came a little time ago in an Italian town to one of God's elect ones there. He was so depraved that he actually fell to worshipping the devil rather than God!

It chanced, one day that a rumor went through the city that a Protestant was coming there to preach. The priest, alarmed for his religion, told the people from the altar that Protestants worshipped the devil and he charged them not to go near the meeting room. The news, as you may judge, excited no horror in the devil-worshipper's mind. "Yes," he thought, "then I shall meet with brethren!" And so he went to hear our beloved missionary who is now laboring in Rome. Nothing else would have drawn the poor wretch to hear the Good Word—but this lie of the priest's was overruled to that end! He went and heard, not of the devil, but of the devil's Conqueror—and before long was found at Jesus' feet—a sinner saved!

I have known my Lord, when His ministers have failed, take out an arrow from His quiver and fix upon it a message, put it to His bow and shoot it right into a man's bosom till it wounded him. And as it wounded him and he lay moaning upon his bed, the message has been and accepted. I mean, that many a man in sickness has been brought to hear the message of salvation. Often, losses and crosses have brought men to Jesus' feet. Jesus seeks them so. When Absalom could not get an interview with Joab, he said, "Go and set his barley field on fire." Then Joab came down to Absalom and said, "Why have your servants set my field on fire?" The Lord sometimes sends losses of property to men who will not otherwise hear Him—and at last their ears are gained! Whom He seeks, He in due time finds!

Well, after my Lord has sought men's ears, He next seeks their *desires*. He will have them long for a Savior—and this is not an easy thing to accomplish! But He has a way of showing men their sins—and then they wish for mercy. He shows them at other times the great joy of the Christian life—and then they wish to enter into the same delight. I pray that at this hour He may lead some of you to consider the danger you are in while you are yet unconverted, that so you may begin to desire Christ and in this way may be sought and found by Him!

Then He seeks their *faith*. He seeks that they may come and trust Him—and He has ways of bringing them to this, for He shows them the suitability of His salvation and the fullness and the freeness of it! And when He has exhibited Himself as the sinners' Savior, and such a Savior as they need, then do they come and put their trust in Him. Then has He found them and saved them!

He seeks their *hearts*, for it is their hearts that He has lost. And oh, how sweetly does Christ, by the Holy Spirit, win men's affection and hold them fast! I shall never forget how He won mine—how first He gained my ear and then my desires, so that I wished to have Him for my Lord! And then He taught me to trust Him. And when I had trusted Him and found that I was saved, then I loved Him and I love Him still! So, dear Hearer, if Jesus Christ finds you, you will become His loving follower forever! I have been praying that He would bring this message under the notice of those whom He means to bless. I have asked Him to let me sow in good soil. I hope that among those who read these pages, there will be many whom the Lord Jesus has specially redeemed with His most precious blood—and I trust that He will appear at once to them and say to each one of them, "I have loved you with an everlasting love: therefore with loving kindness have I drawn you." May the eternal Spirit open your ears to hear the still small voice of love! By grace omnipotent may you be made to yield to the Lord with the cheerful consent of your conquered will and accept that glorious Grace which will bring you to praise the seeking and saving Savior in Heaven!

Book Two

Seven Wonders of Grace

Preface

He who never wonders has no mind. "The wise man only wonders once in his life, and that is always." This is especially true of the kingdom of grace, where everything is marvelous. When the great God comes to deal with offending men in the way of mercy the mere idea of such grace is wonderful, but when he for the sake of sinners gives his Son to die it is a world of wonders in one.

A dogmatic writer has said that "all wonder is but the effect of novelty upon ignorance," but assuredly it is not so when the work of redemption is the theme; here the more we know the more we wonder, and years of familiar acquaintance and growing understanding do but increase our astonishment. The name whereby our ever-blessed Lord is called is "Wonderful," and well does he deserve the title, for his person, his birth, his life, his death, his teachings, and his actions are all wonderful. Out of the proclamation of the amazing story of the love of Jesus other wonders grow, for signs and wonders are the witnesses of the gospel's power. Newborn souls are "set for wonders in Israel"; and those who delight to search out the glorious works of the Lord are filled with holy admiration and astonishment as they see the heart and hand of the Lord revealed in each individual.

To set forth some of the "wonders of grace" this little book was prepared. Come, reader, and see the various characters upon which grace operates, and it may be, if you are unsaved, you will find here a something to arouse or to encourage you. May the Holy Spirit bless these our utterances to the souls of many, and lead them to the wonder-working Lord who of his own free grace forgives sin, renews the heart, and preserves the spirit.

We have said in our heart,

> Surely I will remember thy wonders of old (Ps. 77:11),

and here is the result of our musings.

Reader, if thou be a regenerated man or woman, pray for thy servant in Christ,

C. H. Spurgeon

1

Manasseh;

or

The Outrageous Rebel

"And when he was in affliction, he besought the Lord his God, and humbled himself greatly before the God of his fathers, and prayed unto him: and he was intreated of him, and heard his supplication, and brought him again to Jerusalem into his kingdom. Then Manasseh knew that the Lord he was God" (2 Chron. 33:12, 13).

When we wish to recommend a physician to a friend who is very ill we are in the habit of mentioning certain cures which he has wrought; and when we can produce several astonishing instances we feel that we are going the right way to work to convince the judgment of our friend and to win his confidence in the doctor. Now, it is our impression that very many are anxious to be saved by the grace of God who, nevertheless, have not dared to trust the great Healer of souls: they know that they are in great danger, but they are reluctant to go to "the beloved physician." They are grievously afraid because of the greatness of their sins, and they are filled with doubt and unbelief as to the possibility of their salvation on account of their singular sinfulness. Therefore it struck me that if I could set before them a number of scriptural instances of wonderful conversions it might tend to encourage hope in Christ in their hearts, and, under the blessing of the Holy Spirit, it might be the means of leading them to trust and try our Lord Jesus, out of whose very garment virtue flows.

Perhaps, dear friends, as you shall see how the Lord, the Healer, has looked on one and another, and restored them from the horrible disease of sin, you, too, who feel yourselves far gone, may pluck up courage and say, "If he healed others, why should he not also heal me? I too will touch his garment's hem and see if he will not make me perfectly whole." How I wish that poor souls knew how ready my Lord Jesus is to save them: they would not keep back if they knew how eager he is to have mercy on the guilty. I pine within my soul to lead you to Jesus that you may be blest. That is the desire of my heart in introducing to you the case of Manasseh, whom I select from the Old Testament as a very prominent instance of glaring sin and of amazing grace.

We do not find many of what we can accurately call conversions in the Old Testament. It is a record of a dim dispensation in which we rather see the types of things than the things themselves; but I should suppose that the priests, if they had been inspired to write what they often heard, would have been able to tell of many instances of deep conviction which would be made known in connection with the sin offerings and the trespass offerings, and they probably saw many instances of persons who henceforth led a new life and ceased from the sin which they had confessed over the victim's head. Of conviction, confession, and conversion they must have seen a great deal, but records we have none. On this account the story of the madly wicked king who was led to humble himself greatly before God is all the more valuable, and it is matter for thankfulness that it is so remarkable. Every item of it reflects glory upon the amazing grace of God, and, indeed, compels us to exclaim, "Who is a God like unto thee, passing by transgression, iniquity, and sin?"

We will waste no time on a preface, but come at once to the life-story of Manasseh, and look, first, at *his circumstances*; then consider him as *a great sinner*; and afterwards, with greater comfort, view him as *a remarkable convert*.

I. First, let us notice HIS CIRCUMSTANCES; because a man's sin may be heightened by his position, or on the other hand, the condition in which he is placed may suggest some alleviating considerations which, in all fairness, should be remembered. Now, with regard to Manasseh, we find that *he was the child of an eminently godly father:* the son of a king who, with all his mistakes, was sound in heart towards God. Hezekiah "wrought that which was good, and right, and truth before the Lord his God." He was a man mighty in prayer, and found deliverance thereby in the hour of great peril through the invasion of Sennacherib, a man whose life was so precious in the sight of the Lord that, in answer to his cries, he gave him a new lease of life, and spared him yet another fifteen years.

It is a great thing for a youth to have a godly father to train his tender mind; and, even though such a parent should be early taken away, yet the privilege is an eminent one. As for Manasseh's mother, we cannot say with certainty that she was a godly woman, but let us hope that as her name was Hephzibah—"My delight is in her"—she, too, was delightful for grace and piety. Isaiah seems to have taken her name and to have applied it to the church: "thou shalt be called Hephzibah, for the Lord delighteth in thee," and we may suppose that he would hardly have done so unless there had been some sweet associations therewith. Let us trust that Queen Hephzibah was indeed God's delight; and, if so, Manasseh had the special favor of having two parents who would train him up in the way he should go. Such a happy start in life renders his after sin the more heinous.

But, in all truthfulness, we have to mention next that *he was a child born to his father in his later years*, after his life had been lengthened by special license from above. He was the child of his parent's desire, an heir born after the father had expected to die childless, and therefore, it is not at all unlikely that he was a spoiled child. It is very possible that being highly prized he was also greatly indulged, and if so he was in special danger. Those children who are doted upon by their parents are greatly to be pitied, for they are apt to be allowed to have their own way, and a youth's own way is sure to be a wrong one.

Fathers, in such cases, are apt to play the part of Eli, of whom we read that his sons made themselves vile, and he restrained them not. It was no wonder that Adonijah disturbed the dying moments of David when we read that "his father had not displeased him at any time in saying, Why hast thou done so?" Nor need we marvel that Absalom almost broke his father's heart, if this was the manner of his bringing up. Even though at twelve years of age Manasseh could not have fully developed his character, yet it may have been warped by those early days of admiration and indulgence.

Parents, take note of this, and you petted children do the same. Recollect that *Manasseh lost his father at twelve years of age*. I do not know a greater trial for a family than for the head of the house to be taken away while the children are young. Just when the guiding, encouraging, and restraining power of the father is wanted it is mournful to see it removed. How mysterious it seems to us when a large family loses the wise guide of the household at the very time when his influence is most needed by the growing up of boys and girls. Too often in such a case the young people have broken away from all restraint, and the loss of their father has been the loss of everything. Manasseh, the prince who seemed born under such favorable circumstances for the production of a gracious character, was much to be pitied when the good king his father was called away, and his tender son was left alone amid flatterers and idolaters.

Remember, too, that *Manasseh was placed in a giddy position as a child*, for he mounted the throne at twelve years of age. A child upon a throne is a child out of its natural place. Such high and hard places are not for boys. Now and then such a child turns out to be a Josiah, the very delight of mankind; but the probabilities are very much against its being so. "Woe unto thee, O land, when thy king is a child," It is ill for a child to sway a scepter, but "it is good for a man that he bear the yoke in his youth."

A fierce fire of temptation blazes around a youthful throne. Sycophants and flatterers are sure to surround a boy prince, pandering to his worst desires, and arousing that part of his nature which most needs to be repressed. No doubt there were good people whom Hezekiah had gathered in his courts, but then they could not flatter so well as the evil party which had been repressed for a while but still remained strong in the land. Though Hezekiah had set up the worship of God everywhere, and had done his best to root out idolatry, yet the idolatrous party was far from being extinct, and the common people were sadly careless and irreligious.

Isaiah in his opening chapter describes the condition of the land by saying, "Israel doth not know, my people doth not consider." "Except the Lord of hosts had left unto us a very small remnant, we should have been as Sodom, and we should have been like unto Gomorrah." The nation was not steadfast like King Hezekiah: it worshipped Jehovah when compelled by royal authority, but it was ready enough to turn aside to its idols. The idolatrous party—which I might liken to the papists; and the people who worshipped on the high places—who were the ritualistic party of the day; came around the young king, fawning, flattering, and cajoling. By pleasing the taste of the boy-king, and indulging his vices, they undermined in his esteem the orthodox worshippers of God, whom I may call the evangelical school. He yielded himself up readily to their influence, and when he was old enough became the head of the idolatrous party, throwing his whole soul into it, and, with all the might of his nature, and the force of his authority laboring to stamp out the pure worship of the most high God, and to set up those debasing idolatries which his father Hezekiah had be much abhorred.

Look at him, then, as a mere child placed in a condition of great danger, led astray at first, and afterwards becoming a ringleader in iniquity. If I should address any young person who finds himself, too early for his good, set free from the restraint of parents and placed in a position of considerable power and influence over others, I pray him to flee to the Lord for help, or his ruin will be certain. The Lord can teach the young men wisdom, the babes knowledge and discretion. Look to your Bible, the mercy-seat, and your God, or you will make shipwreck of the life which God has entrusted to you. There are responsibilities upon you too heavy for you to carry alone: because your burdens are heavier seek for yourself more power from on high: because your restraints are fewer put yourself under the restraints of divine love. The youth who is so much trusted by providence as to be left alone without a guardian, and to have power confided to him which usually needs the wisdom of age, ought to be the more careful and the more guarded, and cry the more earnestly to God that he may have grace given to him, lest of him it should be said, as it was said of Manasseh, he "did evil in the sight of the Lord."

These are some of the circumstances of Manasseh's life.

II. Now I have a heavy task, and one which saddens me, though it is concerning one who lived so many hundreds of years ago: I have mournfully to describe Manasseh as *A GREAT SINNER*. If you will turn to the second of Chronicles, chapter 33 and will follow the verses, you will get a view of this atrocious offender. In the second verse we read, "He did that which was evil in the sight of the Lord." That is a description of his life as a whole. Take his fifty-five years' reign in the bulk, notwithstanding the repentance of his later years, it is a true estimate of it all to say that "he did evil in the sight of the Lord." He was a son of David, but he was the very reverse of that king, who was always faithful in his loyalty to the one only God of Israel. David's blood was in his veins, but

David's ways were not in his heart. He was a wild, degenerate shoots of a noble vine.

Nay, the description of his life is more intensely black than the summary might suggest, for it is said that "he did evil in the sight of the Lord, like unto the abominations of the heathen, whom the Lord had cast out before the children of Israel." He seemed to have taken for his models the men whom God condemned to die for capital offences against his law. How deplorable that one who was cradled in piety must, notwithstanding, not be satisfied until the very scum of society, which God had skimmed off as from the pot and thrown away with detestation, should be his models and his tutors. Yet we have known young men to be doubly perverse, possessed as it were by the devil, if not by seven devils at once.

We are all depraved, but in some that depravity manifests itself in an extraordinary love of low, coarse society, and of everything that is irreligious and unlovely. I have in my mind's eye now—and it makes my heart melt as I remember it—sons of men with whom I have been glad to associate, and who were always happy to aid me in the Lord's work, but now their sons find their most congenial company amongst the drunken and profane, the gamblers and debauchees; and if perchance they see their father's friend they look aside or slink away, anxious to be unobserved by him, scarcely brooking to have it known that they know the man. This is the unhappiest thing that can occur to us parents. You who have buried your little children, you who have wept so bitterly when your dear babes were snatched from your bosoms, may far prefer that sorrow to having your sons and your daughters live to dishonor your name by plunging into glaring sin. Manasseh was a son of this character, and could his father have foreseen what he would live to do he would have preferred death rather than have lived to be the sire of such a monster of iniquity.

It is noted concerning him, in the next place, that *he undid what his father had done*. In the third verse we read, "He built again the high places which Hezekiah, his father, had broken down." I have known many a man who has had no respect for God who, nevertheless, has had such a regard for his father's memory that he would not scoff at things which his father held sacred. But this man had cast off all filial reverence. He cared not what his godly parent might have thought, he gloried in building up what his father had thrown down, and throwing down what his father had built up.

This is a great evil; for a man in order to be guilty of it has to do violence to some of the strongest and best instincts of his nature. Is that your case, my friend? Are you doing exactly that which you know would have broken your father's heart? Is your conduct such that your mother would have been brought to her grave by it had she been here? Are you fighting against the Lord God of your father? May the Lord in mercy stay your guilty hand lest the curse of Absalom come upon you. Turn not aside from your father's God, follow in the godly footsteps of your mother, and set not yourself to act contemptuously against that which was your parents' reverence.

Manasseh next sinned in a great variety of ways, for, according to the third verse, he seemed eager to be meddling with all forms of idolatry. He was not satisfied with one false god, or one set of idolatrous rites, but he reared up altars for Baalim and made groves, and worshipped the host of heaven; nor yet content with all this he adored Moloch, and passed his children through the fire in the valley of the son of Hinnom. He heaped up vile idolatries, not only sending far and wide to find out what were the gods of the different nations, but reviving the old cast-off gods of the Canaanites, whom God had destroyed for their crimes. One form of insult to the living God was not enough for him, he heaped together his rebellions. There are men to whom to sin with one hand is not sufficient: they must transgress with greediness. One vice does not content them, they cannot be satisfied to go to hell except with four steeds to their chariot, and these they drive like Jehu the furious. They never seem content except with all their might they are fighting against the Lord, and pulling down his wrath upon their heads.

These sins of Manasseh were not merely various, but *some of them were peculiarly foul*. The worship of Baalim and Ashtaroth was associated with such abominations that one is sorry even to have known of them, and especially the *ashera*, or symbols, wrongly translated "groves," were so lascivious that I shall not so much as hint at what they were. Such worship must have unutterably defiled the mind of the worshipper, and rendered him fit for vice of the most degrading kind. Think of obscenity made into a religion: vice an ingredient of adoration.

O God, that every man should have come down to this! Worse still that a king of Judah and a son of Hezekiah should patronize and ordain orgies which polluted the mind beyond conception. It sufficed not that he adored the sun when it shined, and kissed his hand to the moon walking in her brightness; the sin of star worship was not enough, but he must needs set up graven images and worship the idols of the Philistines, of Egypt, Assyria, and Tyre. The calves of Bethel did not sufficiently provoke the Lord, but the idols of Baal and the lewdness of Ashtaroth must defile the whole land from end to end. Instead of the holy worship of Jehovah the worship of devils was ordained by the king's authority, and Judah's land became a den of abominations.

But Manasseh went to the utmost in evil, and *added gross impudence and insult to his crimes*, so as to defy the Lord to his face, for "he built altars in the house of the Lord, whereof the Lord had said, In Jerusalem shall my name be for ever. And he built altars for all the host of heaven in the two courts of the house of the Lord." Oh, the infinite patience of the Most High, that he bore with such a daring insult as this! There were all the hills of Judah and the valleys thereof. Were they not enough for Manasseh's idols and their altars? Must the hill of Zion also be profaned? Was there no spot but that which the Lord had set apart for himself, and of which it had been said, "The Lord is there"? Must Jehovah's own courts be desecrated with the image of jealousy? Must the altars to the hosts of heaven be set up where only the Lord of hosts should have been adored! Yet Manasseh dared to do this, carrying rebellion against the Lord to its utmost extent.

Another proof of his inveterate sinfulness is found *in his treatment of his children:* he was not satisfied with sinning in his own person, his offspring must be handed over to the evil one. "He caused his children to pass through the fire in the valley of the son of Hinnom." Moloch is said to have been represented by a great hollow image made of brass, which was heated red hot and filled with fire till the flames came pouring forth from its mouth. Into the red-hot arms of this image some parents placed their babes, so that they were consumed alive; but others, like Manasseh, passed their children between these burning arms, so that they received "a baptism of fire." It was a cruel consecration of the poor helpless infants to the monstrous demon Moloch, whose altar stood conspicuous in the valley of Hinnom, outside the walls of Jerusalem. It was an atrocious crime that children, and children of the seed of Abraham, who were under covenant with God according to the flesh, should be thus profanely made to share in abominable rites. Yet nothing would content this man but that his own children should be the sworn adversaries of God, and from their birth be scorched in unhallowed flames.

Alas, Manasseh is not alone, for many fathers and mothers seem bent upon ruining their children's souls. What shall I say of the man who teaches his boy to drink, who instructs him in vice by his example, and compels him to learn profanity from his father's lips? Can anything be worse? How much better is the woman who consecrates her daughter to fashion, and all its follies, and teaches her worldliness, love of finery, gaiety, and vain company? Do not many train their boys to avarice and their girls to be lovers of pleasure? I might say even worse, but surely the passing of children through the fire to Bacchus, to Mammon, to Venus, to the very devil himself, is common enough still, and who shall estimate the enormity of the crime?

Nor is this all. *Manasseh went to extremes in personal, deliberate sin*, for it is said of him that for himself, and on his own account, he "observed times"—that is "lucky" and "unlucky" days, and he "used enchantments"—those different devices by which men think they can produce certain events or foretell them. "And he used witchcraft, and dealt with a familiar spirit, and with wizards." It matters nothing whether these things were deceits by which he was duped, or were real dealings with demons—the sin is the same, because in the man's intent forbidden intercourse was carried on, such intercourse as is abominable in the sight of the Most High, and to be abhorred by every believer. Whether true or pretended, attempts at necromancy, and witchcraft, and communion with spirits mark a mind far gone astray from God. Remember that such persons cannot enter heaven, for "without are dogs and sorcerers," and they are placed with whoremongers and liars, who are declared to be shut out of the holy city.

Manasseh was eager and greedy in these detestable pursuits, he could never have enough of them. Witches, wizards, familiar spirits, and enchantments—all sorts of cheats he trusted in: he who would not believe in God could freely yield his faith to lying wonders. How sad to see a mind capable of thought and reason bowed down at the feet of witches and mutterers of spells! How horrible to see a man making a league with death and a covenant with hell! Still, if a man should have gone this length he may yet be recovered out of the snare of the devil by almighty grace. Friend, if you have even wandered into this infamous wickedness you need not despair, for Jesus lives to save the vilest of the vile.

The picture is awful enough already, surely, say you. Ay, but we have other strokes to add, for Manasseh *repeated these sins and exaggerated them each time.* After one forbidden idol had been enshrined he set up another yet more foul, and after building altars in the courts of the temple he ventured further, and "set a carved image, the idol which he had made, in the house of God, of which God had said to David and to Solomon his son, In this house, and in Jerusalem, which I have chosen before all the tribes of Israel, will I put my name for ever." Thus he piled up his transgressions and multiplied his provocations.

All this while *he was leading thousands with him in his desperate course:* both by his influence and authority he was compelling the nation to blaspheme. The whole land followed its king, save only a remnant according to the election of grace, and these bore all the fury of his wrath. The nation was prone to fall into idolatry, and willingly went with the court; when the king bade them worship Baalim, they joyfully replied "so would we have it;" and even when the most polluted emblems were set up for worship, the mass of the people greedily went after the abominations. A few wept and sighed in secret, and spoke often one to another, but they had no power to alter the sad state of things, for the king was too strong for them.

How sad to see a royal personage become a ringleader of iniquity! For princely example is infectious and its power for evil is boundless. Do I speak to one whose life leads others astray? Are you a man of mark? Are you placed in a position of influence? Are you a parent with children about you who will inevitably copy you? Are you the foreman in the workshop, or the head of a club, so that what you say and do becomes law to feebler minds than your own? Ah, you have the power to sin a hundred times at once, for you make others commit the sin in which you indulge. Your sin brings forth many at a birth, and as by means of mirrors the image of an object can be multiplied, so is your sin reflected in scores of others. The voice of your evil life is repeated by a thousand echoes. Think of this and beware. Why should you destroy others as well as yourself? Do not be guilty of the blood of your neighbors. Do not murder your own children's souls. Consent not to be a jackal for the lion of the pit, or a net in the devil's hand, for if you are such your sin is infinite.

Nor was this all, for though it is not recorded in the Chronicles, yet you will find in the second book of Kings, at the 21st chapter, that *he persecuted the people of God very furiously.* "Moreover, Manasseh shed innocent blood very much, till he had filled Jerusalem from one end of it to another." He was so zealous in carrying out his idolatries that he could not endure the sight of a man who would not bow before his images. He hated those ancient Nonconformists, those Protestants, those separatists, those Puritans, and he made laws to put them down, so that the worshippers of Jehovah were "stoned and were sawn asunder, they wandered about in sheep skins and goat skins, destitute, afflicted, tormented."

We cannot vouch for the tradition that the prophet Isaiah was put to death by him by being sawn in sunder, but terrible as is the legend it is not at all improbable. Manasseh had his Bartholomew Massacre and his unholy Inquisition. He was a bloody persecutor during much of his long life, and left marks of his reign of terror all over the land. Persecution is one of the most heinous of sins, and greatly provokes the Most High, for the Lord has said concerning his people," He that toucheth you toucheth the apple of my eye." Manasseh did, as it were, thrust his finger into the eye of God. This was a heaven-provoking crime! In these days the law does not allow the shedding of innocent blood, but there are people in the world who go as far as they can in persecution. There are modes of torture which can be used against a believing wife, such as will hardly be imagined. Children can be provoked and grievously afflicted by unchristian parents. "Trials of cruel Blockings," are mentioned by the apostle, and they are very cruel and trying too. We have known persons use towards brothers and sisters, and even towards children, such threats and modes of abuse, and such taunts and jeers, that they have made their lives bitter as with heavy bondage. This is against God a very high offense. You cannot anger a man more than by ill-using his little ones. Touch his children and you bring the color into his face directly, and the man's temper is up; and he who insults, and mocks, and grieves God's children will one day find that the Lord will avenge his own elect though he bear long with them.

Only one more touch to finish this dark picture—was there ever a blacker?—and it is this which is contained in the tenth verse: "And the Lord spake to Manasseh, and to his people, but they would not hearken." *Manasseh refused warning.* He did not sin without being rebuked. God did try the bit and bridle upon him, but they were of no use, for this wild horse took the bit between his teeth and dashed on in utter madness. He could not, he would not, bow before the loving admonition of the Most High. This makes sin to be exceedingly sinful, for, "He, that being often reproved hardeneth his neck, shall suddenly be destroyed, and that without remedy." Without rebuke a man's sin may be far less than it must be after the rejection of admonitions from the mouth of God. To stifle conscience, and refuse loving warning is to incur fearful guilt.

Such was this Manasseh—the very chief of sinners. I feel certain that among those whom I address there is not a grosser sinner than he was, and I might almost say there never lived a worse; he has an evil eminence among the lovers of iniquity, *and yet he was saved by divine grace!* O you who hear these words or read them never dare to doubt the possibility of your being forgiven. If such a wretch as Manasseh was brought to repentance, surely no one need despair.

III. Now listen to what almighty grace, nevertheless, did for Manasseh, whom we will now think of as A REMARKABLE CONVERT. His conversion began, or *was wrought at its commencement, instrumentality, by his afflictions.* The king of Assyria came against him, and he was unable to resist his assault. Sennacherib, a former king of Assyria, had invaded the land in the days of Hezekiah, and the Lord had delivered his people, but there was no God to deliver Manasseh, and so the armies of Assyria overran the land, and the royal idolater found his idols fail him. For fear of being captured in Jerusalem he fled and concealed himself in a thorn brake, but was soon captured or "taken among the thorns," and led in chains to Babylon. He seems to have been very severely handled by the king, who was, probably, Esarhaddon, king of united Assyria and Babylon, for he is spoken of as taken with hooks, such as large fish are taken with, or held by a ring such as is often passed through the noses of wild beasts.

If this be only a figure, it represents Manasseh as regarded by the Assyrian king as an unmanageable beast to be subdued by rigor even as a bull is managed by a ring in his nose. We are also told that he was loaded with double fetters of brass, and was taken down to Babylon, to be kept in a close dungeon. The Assyrians were notoriously a fierce people, and Manasseh having provoked them, felt all the degradation, scorn, and cruelty which anger could invent. He who had trusted idols was made a slave to an idolatrous people; he who had shed blood very much was now in daily jeopardy of the shedding of his own; he who had insulted the Lord must now be continually insulted himself.

That which he had meted out was measured into his own bosom. He was the prodigal in actual life, in a far country where he fain would have filled his belly with the husks that the swine did eat, and no man gave unto him. While fast chained in prison, the iron entered into his soul, and his thoughts troubled him. How vain now to cry to Baal or Ashtaroth. The stars that peered through the grated bars of his dungeon upbraided him for his foolish worship, and the sun and moon took up the tale of rebuke. Familiar spirits were familiar no longer, and magic with its lying wonders could not release him; no, nor the witches and wizards with their enchantments. There he lies, and fears that there he will lie and rot; but in his extremity infinite mercy visits him, and *his soul finds vent for its misery in prayer.* "He besought the Lord God of his fathers."

I admire the historian's words. He had dishonored his father as well as his God, but now he bethinks him of his godly ancestors and their holy faith. Surely his desire to return to his father's faith bore some likeness to that more spiritual resolve of the prodigal, "I will arise and go unto my father." It has often happened that men have been by grace the more readily led to God because he was their father's or their mother's God; human lore is thus dissolved in the nobler passion. Manasseh thinks, meditates, considers, reviews his life, and loathes himself; he remembers how his father prospered by Jehovah's aid, and perhaps also recollects the marvelous story of how Jehovah heard his father's prayer when he was near to die, and raised him to life again. At any rate, in the dungeon he imitated his father, turned his face to the wall and wept sore and prayed. "If," said he, "God saved my father's life, peradventure he may forgive my sin and bring me out of this horrible captivity." Thus hopefully he cried unto the Lord. O friend, will not you also cry unto the God whom you have offended? Will not you say, "God be merciful to me a sinner?" Try, I beseech thee, the power of prayer.

But notice what went with his prayer; for, O sinner, if thou wouldst have mercy of God it must go with thine: "he humbled himself greatly." Ah, he had been a great man before: he was high and mighty Manasseh who would have his own way and dared defy the Lord to his face; but now he sings another song, he lies low as a penitent and begs as a sinner. How would he now use the language of his forefather David—"Have mercy upon me, O God, and blot out my transgressions." There is in the Apocrypha a book entitled "The Prayer of Manasseh," which was probably composed to gratify the curiosity which would like to know how so great a transgressor prayed.

Of course it is spurious, but it contains some good and humble language almost meet for the lips of so great a penitent, though far more coherent and oratorical than his words are likely to have been. What a broken prayer Manasseh's must have been, and what groans and sobs and sighs were heard and seen by the great Father of spirits, as his erring child sought his face in the gloomy cells of Babylon! Let such be your frame of mind, O sinner. Be ashamed at your sin and folly. Confess it with mourning, and abhor yourself on account of it. May the Holy Spirit bring you to this mind.

Brethren, *the Lord heard Manasseh!* Glory be to infinite grace, the Lord heard him. Bloodstained hands were lifted to heaven, and yet the Lord accepted the prayer. A heart that had been the palace of Satan, a heart which had conceived mischief and brought forth cruelty, a proud rebellious heart humbled itself before God, and the Lord pardoned and smiled upon the penitent, and, as a testimony of his infinite mercy, he moved the king of Assyria to take Manasseh out of prison and restore him to his throne. The Lord doeth great marvels, and showeth great mercy unto the very chief of sinners. O that this might persuade some to test and try this gracious God. Manasseh had not such a clear revelation as you have; you have heard of God in Christ Jesus reconciling the world unto himself, not imputing their trespasses unto them. Let the wounds of Jesus encourage you, let his intercession for sinners cheer you. God is ready to pardon, and his bowels yearn towards you. Come even now and seek his face, ye vilest among men.

Now, can you picture Manasseh going back from Babylon attended by a cohort of Assyrian soldiery? The poor believers in Jerusalem have had a little respite while he has been in durance. Perhaps they even ventured to the temple, and restored the worship of Jehovah; at any rate, they crept out of the holes and corners in which they had laid hid, and breathed more freely. But now it is rumored that the persecuting king is coming back—that the hunter of the souls of men is again abroad. What dread seized the minds of the timid among the godly, and how earnestly the brave-spirited steeled their hearts for the conflict. More stonings, more sawings assunder! Can it be that these horrors are to be renewed? The righteous meet and sorrowfully plead with God that he would not permit the light to be quite quenched, nor give over his people like sheep to the slaughter. What a day of foreboding it must have been when the king came through the city gates. But, perhaps, some of them watched him, and when he passed by a shrine of Baal, they noticed that he did not bow.

The image of Ashtaroth stood in the high place, but they observed that he turned away his head as though he would not look in that direction; and what was their joy when they afterwards read his proclamation, that, from henceforth, Judah should worship Jehovah alone. What hanging down of the heads for the ritualistic, idolatrous party, and what joy among the evangelicals that the king himself had come over to their side—for now the truth and the true-hearted would have the upper hand. What triumph was felt by the saints, when the king sent the cleansers to the temple to pull down the carved image—the blessed virgin, which stood in its own niche, and to take down altar and reredos and rood and relic, which denied the house of the Lord. Loud was the psalm of delight when they saw the king standing to offer peace offerings and thank-offerings to Jehovah, and knew that henceforth there was to be no Baal worship, no Ashtaroth worship, no more of the obscene symbols; for all these things were swept away. Then went up their hymns, and they blessed the Lord with all their hearts, singing, "In Judah is God known: his name is great in Israel. There brake he the arrows of the bow, the shield, and the sword, and the battle." O that such songs might be sung in the church of Christ because of some of you.

Manasseh also *did his best to undo what he had done,* and to restore what he had damaged; for those who are really converted show it practically. Restitution must be made for wrong done, or repentance is a sham. All the evil we have done we must labor to remedy, or our penitence is only skin deep. That conversion which does not convert or turn the life is no conversion at all; Manasseh's life ran in a course directly opposite to its former direction, for the Lord had turned him and he was turned indeed. Glory be to God for his mighty work in this royal sinner's case, honor and praise be unto the love eternal, the grace unbounded, the power omnipotent, which changed such a wretch, so that the fierce destroyer became a defender of the faith and a reformer in the house of the Lord. Can he not do the like with you? Can he not cause you also to be turned from the power of Satan unto God?

One or two things remain to be said by way of practical address. First, dear friend, *adore divine grace*. Never limit its power, but believe it able to convert the most abandoned; believe that it can save you. Since our Lord Jesus ever liveth to intercede for those who come unto God by him, he is able also to save them unto the uttermost. You cannot have too large ideas of divine grace, for where sin abounded grace does much more abound.

But, secondly, *never turn it into an excuse for continuing in sin*, for this case of Manasseh, with all its mercy, is still a sad one. Though we have seen how grace gave it a good ending, yet, take it for all in all, it is a sad case, and as a life Manasseh's was wasted, misspent, and full of wretchedness. Although he sought to mend matters, he could not fully undo what he had done. The people were nothing like as eager to follow the right as they were the wrong; and after many years of royal patronage of idolatry it was not easy for the masses to turn round on a sudden, and so the people sacrificed on their high places, though only to Jehovah, and their hearts went after their idols still. The polluting idolatries had degraded the people; licentiousness had taken possession of them, and from this evil there was no drawing them back.

Indeed, their sin was so great that God resolved that the sin of Judah under Manasseh should never be forgiven, and it never was. A respite was given, for Josiah reigned a little time, but it was God's mind and purpose that the sin should never be put away. If you read in the twenty-third chapter of the Second Book of Kings, and the twenty-sixth verse, you will see that though Manasseh himself was saved as a penitent yet the transgression of Judah in having followed him in all that sin still remained. "Notwithstanding, the Lord turned not from the fierceness of his great wrath, wherewith his anger was kindled against Judah, because of all the provocations that Manasseh had provoked him withal." And so in the twenty fourth, at the third verse, "Surely, at the commandment of the Lord came this upon Judah, to remove them out of his sight, for the sins of Manasseh, according to all that he shed (for he filled Jerusalem with innocent blood), which the Lord would not pardon." So, though a man may be pardoned, yet he may have been the occasion of sin in others, which never will be blotted out. How strange is this! A man may lead others into such evil that in it they will abide and perish, although through mighty grace he may himself be forgiven. Will any of you venture upon such a hazardous business? Even if you knew that your own house would be saved, would you burn other men's houses? Would you wish to be the cause of other men's ruin even if you were sure that in the end you would repent? No, be not so base. Lay hold on Jesus and eternal life even now, that you may not have a misspent life to mourn over.

Note well that Manasseh after death had no honor. It does not say of him as of Hezekiah, that they buried him in the sepulchers of the kings, but they buried him in the palace garden. As Matthew Henry very well says, "A pardoned sinner may get back his comfort, but he can never get back his credit." It is hard to live an ill life for years, and yet die in honorable repute, because of late repentance. Even if grace comes in to make the conclusion of your career to be bright with salvation, it is an awful thing to have led a life which, taken as a whole, is rather a curse to mankind than a blessing. So when I tell you what divine grace can do, do not continue in sin to try that grace. You have sinned enough already. Do pray God to do more for you than for Manasseh—namely, save you from Manasseh's sins, and make you to lead a life which from this moment to its end shall glow with the grace of God. How much better to live like Josiah than like Manasseh! Who would not infinitely prefer to lead the life of Moses, perpetually serving God, than that of a hoary sinner who is saved at the last "so as by fire."

The last word is, *seek for mercy, all of you:* do not neglect it because of its greatness, but the rather hasten to receive it. Since we all need more mercy than we imagine, let us cry for it at once in hearty earnest. Let us come to the fountain which is opened for the house of David and for the inhabitants of Jerusalem, and wash therein. Let us, by faith in Jesus' blood, wash and be clean. The Lord make us to do so, for Jesus' sake, Amen.

2

The Woman That Was A Sinner;
or
The Loving Penitent

"And, behold, a woman in the city, which was a sinner, when she knew that Jesus sat at meat in the Pharisee's house, brought an alabaster box of ointment, and stood at his feet behind him weeping, and began to wash his feet with tears, and did wipe them with the hairs of her head, and kissed his feet, and anointed them with the ointment" (Luke 7:37, 38).

Manasseh's case gave us an opportunity of dwelling upon the dark side of conversion: we saw in him the darkness from which a man needs to be turned, and how grace is able to turn him. The Scripture has presented his lost estate with remarkable fullness, and therefore we have dwelt upon it at considerable length, our hope being that some far-gone rebel would take encouragement from it to seek the Lord, If any man tested the longsuffering of God to the utmost degree it was surely Manasseh, yet that longsuffering held out and worked his salvation. May some of the chief of sinners see in this the needlessness and folly of despair, and take heart of hope that the Lord will pardon them also.

In the case of "the woman that was a sinner," details of her sin are very scanty, as is natural in a book so delicate and tender as the New Testament; but we have quite a narrative of her penitence and its fruits, and in these she shines resplendently as a wonder of grace. We have seen enough of the disease in Manasseh, let us see the cure in this loving woman. The wayward king shows us the stone in the rough, in the woman we shall see it polished after the similitude of a palace. Manasseh reveals the lion in the unrenewed nature, and the woman shows us the lion tamed into a lamb. Our last subject taught us to lament the depravity engendered by the fall, our present will lead us to rejoice in the restoration wrought by redemption.

We will consider the life of this famous penitent under three heads, and notice, first, *her former character;* then, *her deed of love which showed her new character;* and, thirdly, *our Lord's treatment of her.*

I. Let us very briefly look at THE WOMAN'S CHARACTER, to begin with, in order that we may see the horrible pit out of which she was taken.

We do not know much about her. Roman Catholic expositors generally insist upon it that she was Mary Magdalene, but this appears to other writers to have been quite impossible. Certainly it does not seem probable that a woman possessed with seven devils should follow the trade of "a sinner." Demoniacal possession was akin to madness, and it was frequently accompanied by epilepsy, and one would think that Magdalene was more fit to be a patient at an infirmary than an inmate of a reformatory. Some have even been so mistaken as to suppose this woman to have been Mary of Bethany, but this will never do. One cannot associate with the lovely household of Martha and Mary the horrible course of pollution implied in the vice which earned for this woman the special name of "a sinner." Besides, although both women anointed our Lord, yet the place, the time, the manner were all different. I need not stay to show you the difference, for that is not the point in hand.

This woman was distinguished by the title of "a sinner," and her touch was regarded by Simon the Pharisee as defiling. We are all sinners, but she was a sinner by profession, sin was her occupation, and probably her livelihood. The name in her case had an emphatic sense which involved shame and dishonor of the worst kind. The city streets wherein she dwelt could have told you how well she deserved her name. Poor fallen daughter of Eve, she had forsaken the guide of her youth, and forgotten the covenant of her God. She was one of those against whom Solomon warns young men, saying, "Her house inclineth unto death, and her paths unto the dead." Yet as Rahab was saved by faith, even so was she, for grace covereth even a harlot's sins.

She was *a well-known sinner:* ill fame had branded her, so that Simon the Pharisee recognized her as one of the town's unhallowed sisterhood. Her way of life was common town talk; persons of decent character would not associate with her, she was cut off from respectable society, and, like a leper, put outside the camp of social life. She was a sinner, marked and labelled: there was no mistaking her, infamy had set its seal upon her.

She was one who had evidently *gone a great way in sin*, because our Savior, who was far from being prejudiced against her, as Simon was, and never uttered a word that would exaggerate the evil in any one, yet spoke of "her sins, which are many." She loved much, for much had been forgiven; she was the five hundred pence debtor as compared with Simon, who owed but fifty. It is not difficult to imagine her unhappy story, because that story is so commonly repeated around us. We know not how she was at first led into evil ways. Perhaps her trustful heart was deceived by flattering words and promises; perhaps the treachery of one too dearly loved led her into sin, and afterwards deserted her to loneliness and shame. Perhaps her mother's heart was broken, and her father's head was bowed down with sorrow; but she became bold enough to pursue the sin into which she had at first been betrayed, and became the decoyer of others.

That long hair of hers, I fear, is rightly called by Bishop Hall "the net which she was wont to spread to catch her amorous companions." She was a sinner of the city in which she dwelt, and though her name is not mentioned, it was far too well known in her own day. She had lived an evil life we know not how long, but, certainly, she had greatly sinned, for her own flowing tears as well as the Savior's estimate of her life prove that she had been no ordinary offender. Let equal sinners be encouraged to go to Jesus as she did.

But *all her sin was known to Jesus*. I mention this, not at all as a fact you do not know, but as one which any trembling sinner may do well to remember. If you have fallen into the same vice in a greater or less degree, whether others know it or not, Jesus knows all about it. Our Lord allowed her to wash his feet with her tears, but he knew well what those eyes had looked upon. When he allowed those lips to kiss his feet, he knew right well what language those lips had used in years gone by; and when he suffered her to show her love to him he knew how foul her heart had aforetime been with every unhallowed desire. Her lustful imaginations and unchaste desires, her wanton words and shameless acts were all before the Savior's mind far more vividly than they were before her own, for she had forgotten much; but he knew all. With all her tender sense of sin, she herself did not apprehend all the heinousness of her guilt as the perfect mind of Jesus did: and yet though she was a sinner, a well-known sinner, and known best of all to the Savior to be such, yet, glory be to divine grace, she was not cast out when she came to Jesus, but she obtained mercy, and is now shining in heaven as a bright and special star to the glory of the love of Christ.

When this woman stood in the house of Simon she was *a believing sinner.* We do not know how she became a convert, but according to the harmony of the gospels this particular incident fits in just after Matthew 11; that is to say, if Luke has written his story with the intent of chronological correctness—and if the harmonies are right, this passage comes in after the following blessed word, "Come unto me all ye that labour and are heavy laden, and I will give you rest: take my yoke upon you and learn of me, for I am meek and lowly of heart, and ye shall find rest unto your souls, for my yoke is easy and my burden is light." Did this woman hear this gracious invitation? Did she feel that she was laboring and heavy laden? Did she look into the face of the great Teacher and feel that he spoke the truth, and did she come to him and find rest? Doubtless her faith came by hearing: did she hear in some crowd in the street the sweet wooing voice of the Sinner's Friend? Was this the means of making "the woman that was a sinner" into the woman that anointed Jesus' feet?

We are not informed as to the particular means, nor is it of any consequence. She was converted, and that is enough; how it came about is a small matter. Perhaps even she herself could not have told us the precise words which impressed her mind, for many are most assuredly brought to Jesus, but the work has been so gentle, gradual, and gracious that they feel themselves renewed; but hardly know how it came about. On the other hand, from the marked change in her character it is highly probable that she did know the day and the hour and the precise means: and if so, dear were the words which called her from the ways of folly, sin, and shame, I do not suppose that our Savior had, at that time, delivered the memorable parable of the prodigal son, but it may have been some similar discourse which won her attention, when she made one of a crowd of publicans and sinners who drew near to hear the Lord Jesus. Pressing forward among the men to catch those silver tones, so full of music, she wondered at the man whose face was so strangely beautiful, and yet so marvelously sad, whose eyes were so bright with tears, and whose face so beamed with love and earnestness. The very look of that mirror of love may have affected her, a glance at that holy countenance may have awed her, and his tones of deep pity and tender warning—all these held her fast, and drew her to abhor her sin and accept the joyful message which the great Teacher had come to proclaim. She believed in Jesus, she was saved, and therefore she loved her Savior. When she came to the Pharisee's house she was *a forgiven sinner*. She carried an alabaster box in her hand with which to anoint him, because she felt that he had been a priest to her, and had cleansed her. She brought her choicest treasure to give to him because he had bestowed on her the choicest of all gifts, namely, the forgiveness of sin. She washed his feet because he had washed her soul, she wept because she believed, and loved because she trusted. She was, when she entered the room, in a condition of rest as to her forgiveness, for men are seldom deeply grateful for mercies which they are not sure of having obtained. Though after that deed she rose a step higher, and became fully assured of her acceptance, even at her first coming she was conscious of forgiven sin, and for that reason she paid her vows unto the forgiving Lord, whom her soul loved.

Our text begins with a "behold"; and it may well be so, for a forgiven sinner is a wonder to heaven, and earth, and hell. A forgiven sinner! Though God has made this round world exceeding fair, yet no work of creation reflects so much of his highest glory as the manifestation of his grace in a pardoned sinner. If you range all the stars around, and if it be so that every star is filled with a race of intelligent beings, yet, methinks, among unfallen existences there can be no such marvel as a forgiven sinner. At any rate he is a wonder to himself, and he will never cease admiring the grace which pardoned and accepted him. What a miracle to herself must this woman have been. For a case like hers she had seen no precedent, and this must have made it the more surprising to her: when your case also appears to stand out by itself alone as a towering peak of grace, refrain not from wondering and causing others to wonder, "All glory to God," may some say, "I whose name could not be mentioned without making the cheek of modesty to crimson, I am washed in the blood of the Lamb! I who was a blasphemer, who sat on the drunkard's bench, who gloried in being an infidel, and denied the Godhead of Christ, I, even I, am saved from wrath through him. I who played a dis, honest part, who respected not the laws of man any more than those of God, I who went to an excess of riot, even I am made whiter than snow through faith in Christ Jesus.

> Tell it unto sinners, tell,
> I am, I am saved from hell.

Let all know it upon earth, and let heaven know it, and let the loud harps ring in yon celestial halls, because of matchless grace.

Behold, then, this woman's character; and, remember, however fallen you may have been, the grace of God can yet save you.

II. Now, secondly, let us consider, at some length, THE DEED OF LOVE WHICH INDICATED HER CONVERSION. Her conduct as a convert was wide as the poles asunder from that of her unregenerate state: she became as evidently a penitent as she had been a sinner. One of the expositors upon this passage says that he cannot so much expound it as weep over it; and I think every Christian must feel very much in that humor. O that our eyes were as ready with tears of repentance as hers were! O that our hearts were as full of love as hers, and our hands as ready to serve the forgiving Lord. If she has exceeded some of us in the publicity of her sin, yet has she not exceeded all of us in the fervency of her affection?

Let us notice what she did, and the first of twelve matters to which I shall call your attention is *the earnest interest which she took in the Lord Jesus.* "Behold, a woman in the city, which was a sinner, when she knew that Jesus sat at meat." She had a quick ear for anything about Jesus. When she heard the news it did not pass in at one ear and out at the other, but she was interested in the information, and straightway went to the Pharisee's house to find him. There were hundreds in that city who did not care a farthing where Jesus was. If they heard the general gossip about him it did not concern them in the least, he was nothing to them; but when *she* knew it, she was in motion at once to come even to his feet. Jesus never again will be an object of indifference to a forgiven sinner. If the Lord has pardoned you, you will henceforth feel the deepest interest in your Savior, and in all things which concern his kingdom and work among men.

Now, if you have to remove to any place you will want to know first— "Where can I hear the gospel? Are there any lovers of Jesus there?" If you are informed about a town or country, the information will not be complete till you have enquired, "How is the cause of God prospering there?" As you look upon your fellow men the thought will strike you, "How do they stand towards Christ?" When yon attend a place of worship it will not matter much to you whether the edifice is architecturally beautiful, or the preacher a learned man, and a great orator, you want to know whether you can hear of Jesus in that place, and be likely to meet with him in that assembly. Your cry will be, "Tell me, O thou whom my soul loveth, where thou feedest?" If you perceive a sweet savor of Christ in the place, you feel that you have had a good Sabbath-day; but if Jesus Christ be wanting, you consider everything to be wanting, and you groan over a lost Sabbath. A soul that has tasted Christ's love cannot be put off with anything short of him, it hungers and thirsts after him, and any good word about him is sweet unto the taste. Is it so with you?

Notice, next, *the readiness of her mind to think of something to be done for Jesus.* "When she knew that Jesus sat at meat in the Pharisee's house she brought an alabaster box of ointment"—she was quick and ready in her thoughts of service. She would not appear before the Lord empty, but the resolve to bring an offering, and the selection of that offering, were quickly made. She would get that alabaster box of aromatic balsam, the daintiest and costliest perfume that she had, and she would anoint his feet to do him honor. Many minds are inventive for the things of the world, but they seem to have no quickness of thought in reference to the service of Christ: they proceed with dull routine, but never flash out with spontaneous deeds of love. This woman showed an original genius in her love, she was no copier of a former example, her plan of service had the dew of freshness upon it.

Mary of Bethany did something like it, but that was afterwards: this was the woman's own original idea. Her thoughtful soul struck out this new path for itself. It is a great thing for Christian people to carry on works commenced by others, for what should we do if the established agencies of the church should come to a standstill? But it is pleasant to see quick wits and thoughtful faculties exercising themselves for Jesus and devising means to serve him. It is well, for instance, when a beloved sister is so fired with the love of Jesus that she feels—"I am somewhat different from other women, both in character and past experience, and I have peculiarities of gifts and disposition, therefore I will let my soul follow the bent of her gracious inclination, and I will give myself to work which is unusual in the church, but which will be specially suitable for me."

Oh, for more of that voluntary service which, so far from requiring to be urged, does not even need to be instructed, but shows a sacred suggestiveness and affection which supplies the place of teaching and example. We need more contriving, inventing, and planning for Christ. See how we act towards those we love: we consider what will please them, and plot and plan some pleasant surprise for them. We put our heads together and ask—"What shall it be? Let us think of something new and off the common." That thoughtfulness is half the beauty of the act. I wish that loving believers would lay their heads together and say, "What shall be done unto him whom the Lord delighteth to honor? What shall we do for Jesus our Redeemer? What could we do best, and what is most needed to be done just now?" For, you see, this woman did the most fitting thing that could be done. Simon had not washed his feet, it was most proper that *she* should wash them: Simon had not kissed him, but somebody should do so, for he deserved every honor, and therefore she did it. Simon had not poured oil upon his head, or shown him any token of respect; but her warm heart, by the Holy Spirit, who is the creator and fosterer of all love, devised and carried out the right thing at the right time, as earnest believers always do when they are willing to give full liberty to the warm dictates of their loving hearts. Note that.

Notice, thirdly, *her promptness of action*. She did not merely think that she had an alabaster box to give, but she took it at once, and hastened to pour out its contents. Dear friend, you have been saved by grace, and you have an alabaster box upstairs which you have long meant to bring down, but it is there still. Half-a-dozen times or more, when you have had your heart warmed by the love of Christ, you have felt that now was the time to bring out the box, but it remains sealed up still. You were so pleased with yourself for having such earnest feelings and generous resolutions that you stopped to admire yourself, and forgot to carry out your resolutions. You have done nothing, though you have intended a great deal. Do you not sometimes feel as self-contented as if you had done something wonderful when, after all, you have only mapped out what you think you may possibly do at some future time? Indeed, it is a mighty easy thing to make yourself believe that you have really done what you have only dreamed about. This is wretched child's play, and the woman before us would have none of it. She saw the occasion and she seized it. Jesus might not be in her city again, and she might not be able to find him for many a day. The thought struck her, and she struck the thought while yet the iron was hot, and she fashioned it into a fact. It is usually true that second thoughts are best, but it is not so in the service of our Lord. The first suggestions of love, like the first beams of the morning, are not to be excelled for beauty and freshness. Good things had better be done at once, without a second thought. "I consulted not with flesh and blood," said the apostle. Is it a right thing? Is it for Jesus? Why, then, do it. Get it done first, and even then do not think of it, but go on to something yet beyond. In this sacred work "he gives twice who gives quickly." Promptness of action is the bloom upon the fruit which delay would brush off. What grace had the Lord given to this poor fallen woman! She shames the best of us.

Observe, in the fourth place, *her courage*. She knew that Jesus was at meat in the Pharisee's house, and she soon found him reclining, in the oriental fashion, with his feet near the door, for Simon was so uncivil that he was sure to give him a poor place at the table. Seeing the Lord, she ventured in. It needed no small bravery for her to enter the house of a Pharisee, who above all things dreaded to be touched by such a character. In her bad times she had seen the holy man gather up his garments, and leave her a broad space on the streets for fear that she should pollute his sacred person. She must have felt, as all penitent sinners do, an inward shrinking from the cold, hard, self-righteous professor of purity. She would have gone anywhere in that city rather than into Simon's house. It must have cost her a great struggle to face his frowns and severe remarks.

Perhaps, however, I am wrong; indeed, I think I am, for she was so full of the desire to show her love and to honor the Lord Jesus that she forgot the Pharisee. Ay, and if the devil had been there instead of Simon, she would have dared him in his den to reach her Lord. Still there was much courage needed for one so lowly in her penitence to be able to bear the cold contemptuous look of the master of the house. Conscious that she had been a castaway from society, yet she courageously fulfilled her mission, fearless of cruel remarks and taunting charges. O poor timid seeking soul, the Lord can give to thee also the courage of a lion in his cause, though now thou art timid as a hare.

When, then, the penitent had reached the Master's feet, note well how one grace balanced another, and observe *her humility* tempering her courage. Her boldness was not forwardness nor indelicate impertinence; no, she was as bashful as she was brave. She did not advance to our Lord's head, or thrust herself where he would readily see her, much less did she presume to address him, but she stood at his feet behind him, weeping. She was probably but a little way in the room, she courted no observation; she was near Jesus, but it was near his feet, and weeping there. To weep at his feet was honor high enough for her; she sought no uppermost seat at the banquet. Ah, dear friends, it is a blessed thing to see young converts bold, but it is equally delightful to see them humble, and they are none the worse for being very retiring if they have been great sinners.

I have been very sorry when I have seen a lack of modesty where it ought to have super-abounded. There is more grace in a blush than in a brazen forehead, far more propriety in holy shamefacedness than in pious impudence. Good Bishop Hall says, "How well is the case altered! She had wont to look boldly in the face of her lovers, and now she dares not behold the awful countenance of her Savior. She had been accustomed to send alluring beams forth into the eyes of her paramours, but now she casts dejected eyes to the earth, and dares not so much as-raise them up to see those eyes, from which she desired commiseration." Lowliness goes well with penitence. One would not wish humility to be corrupted into cowardice, nor courage to be poisoned into pride. This repenting sinner had both excellences in proper proportion, and the two together put her exactly in the place where a woman that was a sinner ought to be when saved by grace.

We see before us our reclaimed sister looking down upon the Lord's blessed feet, and as we mark her flowing tears we pause to speak of *her contrition*. She gazed upon our Lord's feet, and I wonder whether that sight suggested to her how her feet had wandered and how travel worn had become the feet of the Lord, who had sought and found her.

> She knew not of the bitter way
>   Those sacred feet had yet to tread,
> Nor how the nails would pierce one day
>   Where now her costly balms were shed.

But she saw those feet to be all unwashed, for Jesus had been neglected where he ought to have been honored; and she saw therein the memory of her own neglects of him who had so freely loved her soul. She wept at the memory of her sins, but she wept over *his* feet; she grieved most because she had grieved him. She wept because she had sinned so much, and then wept because he had forgiven her so freely. Love and grief in equal measures made tip those precious tears. The divine Spirit was at work within her dissolving her very soul, even as it is written, "He causeth his wind to blow, and the waters flow"; and again, "He smote the rock, and the waters gushed out." Do you marvel that she stood and wept? Thinking of herself, and then thinking of him, the two thoughts together were far too much for her, and what could she do but both relieve her heart and express it in a shower of tears? Wherever there is a real forgiveness of sin there will be real sorrow on account of it. He who knows that his sin is pardoned is the man who most acceptably exercises repentance. Our hymn puts it on the right footing when it points, not to the horrors of hell, but to the griefs of Immanuel, by which our pardon is certified to us as the deep source of sorrow for sin.

> My sins, my sins, my Savior,
>   How sad on thee they fall!
> Seen through thy gentle patience
>   I tenfold feel them all.
>
> I know they are forgiven,
>   But all their pain to me
> Is all the grief and anguish
>   They laid, my Lord, on thee.

After admiring this woman's contrition, notice *her love*. The Holy Spirit took delight in adorning her with all the graces, and she came behind in nothing, but she excelled in love. Our Lord Jesus Christ when he translated her act of anointing his feet, expressed it in the one word "love": he said, "she loved much." I cannot speak much with you concerning love, for it is rather to be felt than to be described. Words have no power to bear the weight of meaning which lies in love to Christ. O how she loved! Her eyes, her hair, her tears, herself, she counted all as nothing for his dear sake: words failed her as they fail us, and therefore she betook herself to deeds in order to let her heart have vent. Alabaster box and ointment were all too little for him, the essence of her heart was distilled to bathe his feet, and the glory of her head was unbound to furnish him with a towel. He was her Lord, her all in all: if she could have laid kingdoms at his feet she would have rejoiced to do so; as it was, she did her best, and he accepted it.

This love of hers led her to *personal service.* Her hand was the servant of her heart, and did its part in the expression of her affection. She did not send the alabaster box to Jesus by her sister, or ask a disciple to pass it to him, but she performed the anointing with her own hand, the washing with her own tears, and the wiping with her own hair. Love cannot be put off with proxy service; she seeks no substitute, but offers her own person. I grant, dear brothers and sisters, that we can serve the Lord a great deal by helping others to serve him, and it is right and proper to help those who are able to labor better and more widely than we can; but still it is not meet that we should rest content with that, we ought to be ambitious to render tribute to our Lord with our own hands.

We cannot deny ourselves the pleasure of doing some little thing for our well-beloved Lord. Suppose this loving woman had had a sister who loved the Master even as she did, and suppose like a loving sister she had said to her, "I fear it will be too heavy a task for you to face cold-hearted Simon, I will take the box and anoint our blessed Lord, and tell him that I did it for you, and so he shall know your love." Do you think she would have consented to the proposal? Ah, no, it would not have answered the purpose at all. Love refuses sponsors. She must anoint those blessed feet *herself.*

Now, dear friends, you who hope that you have been forgiven, are you doing anything for Jesus? Are you in your own person serving him? If not, let me tell you, you are missing one of the greatest delights that your souls can ever know, and, at the same time, you are omitting one of the chief fruits of the Spirit. "Simon, son of Jonas, lovest thou me?" is the question, and if you wish to answer it with proof positive, then go and with your own and feed the Savior's sheep. Surely you cannot love him as you should unless each day has its deed of love, its sacrifice of gratitude.

Observe, next, that *her service was rendered to the Lord himself.* Read the passage and place an emphasis upon the words which refer to the Lord: "She stood at *his* feet, behind *him*, weeping, and began to wash *his* feet, and did wipe *them* with the hairs of her head, and kissed *his* feet, and anointed *them* with the ointment." It was not for Peter and James and John that she acted as servitor. I have no doubt she would have done anything for any of his disciples, but at this time her thoughts were with her Lord, and all her desire was to honor *him*. It is a delightful thing for Christian people to lay themselves out distinctly for the Lord Jesus. There should be more ministering unto him, more definite aiming at his glory. To give money to the poor is good, but sometimes it is better to spend it upon Jesus more distinctly, even though some Judas or other should complain of waste.

> Love is the true economist,
>   She breaks the box and gives her all;
> Yet not one precious drop is miss'd,
>   Since on *his* head and feet they fall.

One is glad to serve the church; who would not wait upon the bride for the bridegroom's sake? One is glad to go into the streets and lanes of the city to gather in poor sinners, but our main motive is to honor the Savior. See, then, how she who was once a harlot has become a zealous lover of the Lord, and is ready to wash her Lord's feet, or perform any service which may be permitted her, if so be she may work a good work upon him.

Further, remark, that what she did she did very *earnestly*. She washed his feet, but it was with tears; she wiped them, but it was with those luxurious tresses which were all unbound and disheveled, that she might make a towel of them for his blessed feet. She kissed his feet, and she did it again and again, for she did not cease to kiss his feet, or if she made a moment's pause, it was only that she might pour on more of the balsam. She was altogether taken up with her Lord and his work; her entire nature concurred in what she did, and aroused itself to do it well. True love is intense: its coals burn with vehement heat; it makes all things around it living. Dead services cannot be endured by living hearts. I know some people, I hope they are Christian people, but they belong to the coldblooded animals, you never perceive the smallest warmth in them; they are patent refrigerators, walking masses of ice. If you shake hands with them, you think you have got a dead fish in your hand, there is nothing hearty and warm about them. If such people speak about Jesus Christ, it is in the coolest possible terms. If they preach, their sermons are best appreciated on a hot summer's day, when you need something cool and airy: but the man who feels he has been forgiven much, and owes much to the Savior, throws his whole heart into what he has to say for him. Give me a woman that is full of love to Jesus, and you shall see how she will labor in the Redeemer's service.

I have heard of a preacher who was so intensely earnest that, when one complained of his sermon being short, an old farmer replied, "Short, yes, but look at the weight of it. Every word he spoke weighed half-a-hundred weight." I like a preacher of that kind who is so full of love that every word is a power. Everything we do for Jesus should be done intensely, earnestly, vehemently. To keep back part of the price from him would be shameful, to be neither cold nor hot would be fatal, to be consumed with zeal for him is no more than his due. To do no more than you feel obliged to do, and that in about as slovenly a style as you well can—this is a poor, dead way of living, unworthy of a soul redeemed of blood. He who loves much cannot endure a sleepy religion: he devotes himself to the Lord Jesus with all his heart.

Furthermore, notice the woman's *absorption in her work*. There she stood anointing his feet with ointment and kissing them again and again. Simon shook his head, but what of that? He frowned and cast black looks at her, but she ceased not to wash his feet with her tears. She was too much occupied with her Lord to care for scowling Pharisees. Whether any one observed her or not, or whether observers approved or censured, was a very small matter to her, she went quietly on, accomplishing the suggestion of her loving heart.

And what she did was so *real*, so *practical*, so *free* from the mere froth of profession and pretense. She never *said* a word: and why not? Because it was all act and all heart with her. Words! Some abound in them, but what wretched things words are wherewith to express a heart. As in a glass darkly can we see the reflection of a soul's love in its most passionate utterances. Actions are far more loud-voiced and have a sweeter tone than words. This woman had done with speech, for the time being, at any rate, and tears and disheveled hair, and poured-out balsam must speak for her. She was too much in earnest to call anyone's attention to what she was doing, or to care for anyone's opinion, much less to court commendation, or to answer the ugly looks of the proud professor who scorned her. This thorough oblivion of all except her Lord constituted in a measure the charm of her deed of love; it was whole-hearted and entire loyalty which her homage revealed.

Now, dearly beloved in the Lord Jesus Christ, I do pray that you and I, as pardoned sinners, may be so taken up with the service of our Lord Jesus Christ that it may not matter to us who smiles or who frowns; and may we never take the trouble to defend ourselves if people find fault, or even wish for anybody to commend us, but be so taken up with *him* and the work he has given us to do, and with the love we feel to *him*, that we know nothing else. If all others run away from the work, if all discourage us, or if they all praise us, may we take but small notice of them, but keep steadily to our loving service of Jesus. If grace enables us to do this it will be greatly magnified.

See, dear friends, what grace made of "the woman that was a sinner." Perhaps you thought her worse than yourselves in her carnal estate, what think you when you see her as a penitent? What think ye of yourselves if you stand side by side with her? Do you not blush for very shame, and ask for forgiveness of your Lord for the slenderness of your affection?

III. Lastly, let us see THE SAVIOR'S BEHAVIOR TO HER. What did he do? First, *he silently accepted her service*. He did not move his feet away, did not rebuke her, or bid her be gone. He knew that reflections were being cast upon his character by his allowing her to touch him, yet he did not forbid her, but, on the contrary, continued quietly enjoying the feast of repentance, gratitude, and love, which she spread for him. He was refreshed by seeing such grace in one who aforetime had been so far from God. The perfumed balsam was not so grateful to his feet as her love was to his soul, for Jesus delights in love, especially in penitent love. Her tears did not fall in vain, they refreshed the heart of Jesus, who delights in the tears of repentance. The applause of a nation would not have solaced him one half so much as this woman's pure, grateful, contrite, humble love. His silence gave consent, yea, even approbation, and she was happy enough to be allowed to indulge herself in expressions of adoring affection.

Then the Lord went a little farther. He turned round and *looked at her*, and said to Simon, "Seest thou this woman?" That glance of his must have encouraged her, and made her heart dance for joy. As soon as ever that eye of his lighted on her she could see that all was right; she knew that, whoever frowned, there were no frowns on that brow, and she was filled with supreme content.

Next, *the Lord spoke, and defended her triumphantly*, and praised her for her deed: yes, and he went beyond that, and *personally spoke to her*, and said, "Thy sins be forgiven thee," setting a seal to the pardon which she had received, and making her assurance doubly sure. This was a joy worth worlds.

> Oh might I hear thy heavenly tongue
>   But whisper, "Thou art mine";
> That heavenly word should raise my song
>   To notes almost divine.

She had a choice blessing in hearing from his own lips that her faith was firmly based, and that she was indeed forgiven. Then she received a direction from him as to what to do—"Go in peace." A forgiven sinner is anxious to know what he may do to please his Lord, "Show me what thou wouldst have me to do," was Paul's prayer. So our Lord Jesus seemed to say, "Beloved, do not stop here battling with these Pharisees. Do not tarry in this crowd of cavilers. Go home in perfect peace; and as you have made home unhappy by your sin, make it holy by your example." That is just, I think, what the Lord Jesus would have me say to my dear friends who have followed me in this discourse. You see what grace can do, go home and let your family see it.

If any of you are conscious of great sin, and have received great forgiveness, and therefore wish to show your love to Jesus, do what is on your heart, but at the same time remember that he would have you go in peace. Let a holy calm abide in your breasts. Do not enter into the vain janglings and endless controversies of the hour. Do not worry yourself with the battles of the newspapers and magazines that are everlastingly worrying poor souls with modern notions. Go in peace. You know what you do know; keep to that. You know your sin, and you know Christ your Savior; keep to him, and live for him, Go home into the family circle, and do there everything you can to make home happy, and to bring your brothers and sisters to Christ, and to encourage your father and mother, if they have not yet found the Savior.

Home is especially a woman's sphere. There she reigns as a queen: let her reign well. Around the hearth and at the table, in the sweets of domestic relationships and quiet friendships, a woman will do more for the glory of the Lord

Jesus Christ than by getting up to preach. In the cases of men also, many who long to flash in public had better by far shine at home. Go home in peace, and by a happy, holy life, show to others what saints God can make out of sinners. You have seen what sin and the devil can do to degrade, go and prove what grace and the Holy Spirit can do to elevate, and may many, cheered by your example, come and trust your Lord.

3

The Dying Thief;
or,
The Lone Witness

"And one of the malefactors which were hanged railed on him, saying, If thou be Christ, save thyself and us. But the other answering rebuked him, saying, Dost not thou fear God, seeing thou art in the same condemnation. And we indeed justly; for we receive the due reward of our deeds: but this man hath done nothing amiss. And he said unto Jesus, Lord, remember me when thou comest into thy kingdom. And Jesus said unto him, Verily I say unto thee, To-day shalt thou be with me in Paradise" (Luke 23:39–43).

The dying thief was certainly a very great wonder of grace. He has generally been looked upon from one point of view only, as a sinner called at the eleventh hour, and therefore an instance of special mercy because he was so near to die. Enough has been made of that circumstance by others: to my mind it is by no means the most important point in the narrative. Had the thief been predestined to come down from the cross and live for half a century longer his conversion would have been neither more nor less than it was. The work of grace which enabled him to die in peace would, if it had been the Lord's will, have enabled him to live in holiness. We may well admire divine grace when it so speedily makes a man fit for the bliss of heaven, but it is equally to be adored when it makes him ready for the battle of earth. To bear a saved sinner away from all further conflict is great grace; but the power and love of God are, if anything, even more conspicuous when like a sheep surrounded by wolves, or a spark in the midst of the sea, a believer is enabled to live on in the teeth of an ungodly world and maintain his integrity to the end.

Dear friend, whether you die as soon as you are born again, or remain on earth for many years, is comparatively a small matter, and will not materially alter your indebtedness to divine grace. In the one case the great Husbandman will show how he can bring his flowers speedily to perfection; and in the other he will prove now he can preserve them in blooming beauty despite the frosts and snows of earth's cruel winter: in either case your experience will reveal the same love and power.

There are other things, it seems to me, to be seen in the conversion of the thief besides the one single matter of his being brought to know the Lord when near to death's door.

Observe the singular fact that our Lord Jesus Christ should die in the company of two malefactors. It was probably planned in order to bring him shame, and it was regarded by those who cried, "Crucify him! Crucify him!" as an additional ignominy. Their malice decreed that he should die *as* a criminal, and *with* criminals, and in the center, between two, to show that they thought him the worst of the three; but God in his own way baffled the malice of the foe, and turned it to the triumph and glory of his dear Son; for, had there been no dying thief hanging at his side, then one of the most illustrious trophies of his love would not have been gained, and we should not have been able to sing to his praise—

> The dying thief rejoiced to see
>   That fountain in his day;
> And there have I, though vile as he,
>   Washed all my sins away!

His enemies gave our Lord Jesus an opportunity for still continuing the seeking as well as the saving of the lost. They found him an occasion for manifesting his conquering grace when they supposed they were heaping scorn upon him. How truly did the prophet in the psalm say—"He that sitteth in the heavens shall laugh, the Lord shall have them in derision"; for that which was meant to increase his misery revealed his majesty. Moreover, though it was intended to add an ingredient of bitterness to his cup, I do not doubt that it supplied him with a draught of comfort. Nothing could so well have cheered the heart of Jesus, and taken his mind for just an instant off from his own bitter pangs, as having an object of pity before him upon whom he could pour his mercy. The thief's confession of faith and expiring prayer must have been music to his Savior's ear, the only music which could in any degree delight him amid his terrible agonies. To hear and to answer the prayer, "Lord, remember me when thou comest into thy kingdom," afforded our Lord a precious solace. An angel strengthened him in the garden, but here it was a man, nailed up at his side, who ministered consolation by the indirect but very effective method of seeking help at his hands.

Furthermore, the long continued testimony and witness for Christ among men was at that time exceedingly feeble and ready to expire, and the thief's confession maintained it. The apostles—where were they? They had fled. Those disciples who ventured near enough to see the Lord scarcely remained within speaking distance. They were poor confessors of Christ, scarcely worthy of the name. Was the chain of testimony to be broken? Would none declare his sovereign power? No, the Lord will never let that testimony cease, and lo I he raises up a witness where least you would expect it—on the gibbet. One just ready to die bears witness to the Redeemer's innocence and to his assured coming to a kingdom. As many of the boldest testimonies to Christ have come from the stake, so here was one that came from the gibbet, and gained for the witness the honor of being the last testifier to Christ before he died.

Let us always expect, then, dear friends, that God will overrule the machinations of the foes of Christ so as to get honor from them. At all times of the world's history, when things appear to have gone to pieces, and Satan seems to rule the hour, do not let us despair, but be quite sure that, somehow or other, light will come out of darkness, and good out of evil.

We will now come close up to the dying thief, and look, first, at *his faith*; secondly, at *his confession of faith*; thirdly, at *his prayer of faith*; and fourthly, at *the answer to his faith*.

I. First, then, may the Holy Ghost help us concerning this dying malefactor, to consider HIS FAITH.

It was of the operation of the Spirit of God, and there was *nothing in his previous character to lead up to it*. How came that thief to be a believer in Jesus? You who carefully read the gospels will have noticed that Matthew says, "the thieves also, which were crucified with him, cast the same in his teeth" (27:44). Mark also says, "They that were crucified with him reviled him"

(Mark 15:32). These two evangelists plainly speak of both thieves as reviling our Lord. How are we to understand this? Would it be right to say that those two writers speak in broad terms of the thieves as a class, because one of them so acted, just as we in common conversation speak of a company of persons doing so and so, when in fact the whole matter was the deed of one man of the party? Was it a loose way of speaking? I think not: I do not like the look of suppositions of error in the inspired volume. Would it not be more reverent to the word of God to believe that the thieves did both revile Jesus? May it not be true that, at the first, they both joined in saying, "If thou be the Christ save thyself and us," but that afterwards one, by a miracle of sovereign grace, was led to a change of mind, and became a believer? Or would this third theory meet the case, that at the first the thief who afterwards became a penitent, having no thought upon the matter, by his silence gave consent to his fellow's reviling so as fairly to come under the charge of being an accomplice therein: but when it gradually dawned upon his mind that he was under error as to this Jesus of Nazareth, it pleased God in infinite mercy to change his mind, so that he became a confessor of the truth, though he had at first silently assented to the blasphemy of his companion? It would be idle to dogmatize, but we will gather this lesson from it—that faith may enter the mind, notwithstanding the sinful state in which the man is found. Grace can transform a reviling thief into a penitent believer.

Neither do we know the outward means which led to this man's conversion. We can only suppose that he was affected by seeing the Lord's patient demeanor, or, perhaps, by hearing that prayer," Father, forgive them, for they know not what they do." Surely there was enough in the sight of the crucified Lord with the blessing of God's Spirit to turn a heart of stone into flesh. Possibly the inscription over the head of our Lord may have helped him—"Jesus of Nazareth, the King of the Jews." Being a Jew, he knew something of the Scriptures, and putting all the facts together, may he not have seen in the prophecies a light which gathered around the head of the sufferer, and revealed him as the true Messiah? Possibly the malefactor remembered Isaiah's words, "He is despised and rejected of men; a man of sorrows, and acquainted with grief: and we hid as it were our faces from him; he was despised, and we esteemed him not." Or perhaps the saying of David, in the twenty-second Psalm, rushed upon his memory, "They pierced my hands and my feet." Other texts which he had learned in his youth at his mother's knee may have come before his mind, and putting all these together, he may have argued, "It may be. Perhaps it is. It is. It must be. I am sure it is. It is the Messiah, led as a lamb to the slaughter." All this is but our supposition, and it leads me to remark that there is much faith in this world which cometh, "not with observation," but is wrought in men by unknown instrumentalities, and so long as it really exists it matters very little how it entered the heart, for in every case it is the work of the Holy Ghost. The history of faith is of small importance compared with the quality of faith.

We do not know the origin of this man's faith, but we do know that *it was amazing faith under the circumstances*. I very gravely question whether there was ever greater faith in this world than the faith of this thief; for he, beyond all others, realized the painful and shameful death of the Lord Jesus, and yet believed. We hear of our Lord's dying upon the cross, but we do not realize the circumstances; and, indeed, even if we were to think upon that death very long and intently, we shall never realize the shame and weakness and misery which surrounded our Lord as that dying thief did, for he himself was suffering the pangs of crucifixion at the Savior's side, and therefore to him it was no fiction, but a vivid reality. Before him was the Christ in all his nakedness and ignominy surrounded by the mocking multitude, and dying in pain and weakness, and yet he believed him to be Lord and King. What think you, dear people? Some of you say you find it hard to believe in Jesus, though you know that he is exalted in the highest heavens; but had you seen him on the cross, had you seen his marred countenance and emaciated body, could you then have believed on him, and said, "Lord, remember me when thou comest into thy kingdom"? Yes, you could have done so if the Spirit of God had created faith in you like to that of the thief; but it would have been faith of the first order, a jewel of priceless value. As I said before, so say I again, the vivid sympathy of the thief with the shame and suffering of the Lord rendered his faith remarkable in the highest degree.

This man's faith, moreover, was singularly clear and decided. He rolled his whole salvation upon the Lord Jesus and said, "Lord, remember me when thou comest into thy kingdom." He did not offer a single plea fetched from his doings, his present feelings, or his sufferings; but he cast himself upon the generous heart of Christ, "Thou hast a kingdom: thou are coming to it. Lord, remember me when thou comest into it." That was all. I wish that some who have been professors for years had as clear a faith as the thief; but they are too often confused between law and gospel, works and grace, while this poor felon trusted in nothing but the Savior and his mercy. Blessed be God for clear faith. I do rejoice to see it in such a case as this, so suddenly wrought and yet so perfect—so outspoken, so intelligent, so thoroughly restful.

That word "restful" reminds me of a lovely characteristic of his faith, namely, *its deep peace-giving power*. There is a world of rest in Jesus, in the thief's prayer, "Lord, remember me when thou comest into thy kingdom." A thought from Christ is all he wanted, and after the Lord said, "Today shalt thou be with me in paradise," we never read that the petitioner said another word. I did think that perhaps he would have said, "Blessed be the name of the Lord for that sweet assurance. Now I can die in peace;" but his gratitude was too deep for words, and his peace so perfect that calm silence seemed most in harmony with it. Silence is the thaw of the soul, though it be the frost of the mouth; and when the soul flows most freely it feels the inadequacy of the narrow channel of the lips for its great waterfloods. "Come, then, expressive silence, muse his praise." He asked no alleviation of pain, but in perfect satisfaction died as calmly as saints do in their beds.

This is the kind of faith which we must all have if we would be saved. Whether we know how we come by it or not, it must be a faith which rolls itself upon Christ and a faith which consequently brings peace to the soul. Do you possess such faith, dear friend? If you do not, remember that you may die on a sudden, and then into Paradise you will never enter. Look well to this, and believe in the Lord Jesus at once.

II. Secondly, we are going to look at this man's CONFESSION OF FAITH. He had faith, and he confessed it. He could neither be baptized nor sit at the communion table, nor unite with the church below; he could not do any of those things which are most right and proper on the part of other Christians, but he did the best he could under the circumstances to confess his Lord.

He confessed Christ, first of all, almost of necessity, because *a holy indignation made him speak out*. He listened for a while to his brother thief, but while he was musing, the fire burned, then spoke he with his tongue, for he could no longer bear to hear the innocent sufferer reviled. He said, "Dost not thou fear God, seeing thou art in the same condemnation? And we indeed justly; for we receive the due reward of our deeds: but this man hath done nothing amiss." Did this poor thief speak out so bravely, and can some of you silent Christians go up and down the streets, and hear men curse and blaspheme the name of Christ, and not feel stirred in spirit to defend his cause? While men are so loud in their revilings can you be quiet? The stones you tread on may well cry out against you. If all were Christians, and the world teemed with Jesus' praise, we might, perhaps, afford to be silent; but, amidst abounding superstition and loud-mouthed infidelity, we are bound to show our colors, and avow ourselves on Christ's side. We doubt not that the penitent thief would have owned his Lord apart from the railing of his comrade; but, as it happened, that reviling was the provoking cause. Does no such cause arouse *you*? Can you play the coward at such a time as this?

Observe next, that *he made a confession to an unsympathetic ear*. The other thief does not seem to have made any kind of reply to him, but it is feared that he died in sullen unbelief. The believing thief made his confession where he could not expect to gain approbation, yet he made it none the less clearly. How is it that some dear friends who love the Lord have never confessed their faith, even to their Christian brethren? You know how glad we should be to hear of what the Lord has done for you, but yet we have not heard it. There is a mother who would be so happy if she did but know that her boy was saved, or that her girl was converted, and you have refused her that joy by your silence. This poor thief spoke for Jesus to one who did not enter into his religions experience, and you have not even told yours to those who would have communed with you and rewarded you with comfort and instruction. I cannot understand cowardly lovers of Christ. How you manage to smother your love so long I cannot tell. Love is usually like a cough, which speaks for itself, or a candle which must be seen, or a sweet perfume which is its own revealer: how it is that you have been able to conceal the day which has dawned in your hearts? What can be your motive for coming to Jesus by night only? I cannot understand your riddle, and I hope you will explain it away. Do confess Jesus if you love him, for he bids you do it, and says, "He that confesseth me before men, him will I confess before my Father which is in heaven."

Observe well that this poor thief's confession of faith *was attended with a confession of sin*. Though he was dying a most horrible death by crucifixion, yet he confessed that he was suffering justly. "We indeed justly." He made his confession not only to God but to men, justifying the law of his country under which he was then suffering. True faith confesses Christ, and, at the same time, confesses its sin. There must be repentance of sin and acknowledgment of it before God if faith is to give proof of its truth. A faith that never had a tear in its eye, or a blush on its cheek, is not the faith of God's elect. He who never felt the burden of sin, never felt the sweetness of being delivered from it. This poor thief is as clear in the avowal of his own guilt as in his witness to the Redeemer's innocence. Reader, could we say the same of you?

The thief's confession of faith *was exceedingly honoring to the Lord Jesus Christ*. He confessed that Jesus of Nazareth had done nothing amiss, when the crowd around the cross were condemning him with speech and gesture. He honored Christ by calling him Lord while others mocked him; by believing in his kingdom while he was dying on across, and by entreating him to remember him though he was in the agonies of death. Do you say that this was not much? Well, I will make bold to ask many a professor whether he could honestly say that throughout the whole of his life he has done as much to honor Christ as this poor thief did in those few minutes. Some of you certainly have not, for you have never confessed him at all; and others have confessed him in such a formal manner that there was nothing in it.

Oh, there have been times when, had you played the man, and said right straight out, in the midst of a ribald crew, "I do believe in him whom you scoff, and I know the sweetness of that dear name, which you trample under foot," you might have been the means of saving many souls; but you were silent, and whispered to yourself that prudence was the better part of valor, and so you allowed the honor of your Master to be trailed in the mire. Oh, had you, my sister, taken your stand in the family—had you said, "You may do what you will, but as for me, I will serve the Lord"—you might have honored God far more than you have done; for I fear you have been living in a halting, hesitating style, giving way to a great deal which you knew was wrong, not bearing your protest, not rebuking your brother in his iniquity, but studying your own peace and comfort instead of seeking the Redeemer's glory. We have heard people talk about this dying thief as if he never did anything for his Master; but let me ask the Christian church if it has not members in its midst—gray-haired members, too, who have never, through fifty years of profession, borne one such bravely honest and explicit testimony for Christ as this man did while he was agonizing on the cross. Remember, the man's hands and feet were tortured, and he himself was suffering from that natural fever which attends upon crucifixion; his spirit must have melted within him with his dying griefs, and yet he was as bold in rebuke, as composed in prayer, and as calm in spirit as if he was suffering nothing, and thus he reflected much glory upon his Lord.

One other point about this man's confession is worthy of notice, namely, that *he was evidently anxious to change the mind of his companion*. He rebuked him, and he reasoned with him. Dear friends, I must again put a personal question. Are there not many professing Christians who have never manifested a tithe as much anxiety for the souls of others as this thief felt? You have been a church member ten years, but did you ever say as much to your brother as this dying thief said to the one who was hanging near him? Well, you have meant to do so. Yes, but did you ever do it? You reply that you have been very glad to join others in a meeting. I know that too, and so far, so good; but did you ever personally say as much to another as this dying man did to his old companion? I fear that some of you cannot say so. I, for my part, bless and magnify the grace of God which gave this man one of the sweet fruits of the Spirit, namely, holy charity towards the soul of another, so soon after he himself had come to believe in Jesus. May we all of us have it yet more and more!

III. So much for the confession of his faith: now a little, in the third place, about HIS PRAYER or faith, "Lord, remember me when thou comest into thy kingdom."

He addressed the dying Savior as divine. Wonderful faith this, to call him Lord who was "a worm and no man," and was hanging there upon the cross to die. What shall we say of those who, now that he is exalted in the highest heavens, yet refuse to own his deity? This man had a clearer knowledge of Christ than they have. The Lord take the scales from their eyes, and make them to pray to Jesus as divine.

He prayed to him also as having a kingdom. That needed faith, did it not? He saw a dying man in the hands of his foes nailed to a cross, and yet he believed that he would come into a kingdom. He knew that Jesus would die before long, the marks of the death-agony were upon him, and yet he believed that he would come to a kingdom. O glorious faith! Dear friend, dost thou believe in Christ's kingdom? Dost thou believe that he reigns in heaven, and that he will come a second time to rule over all the earth? Dost thou believe in Christ as King of kings and Lord of lords? Then pray to him as such, "Lord, remember me when thou comest into thy kingdom." May God give you the faith which set this thief praying in so excellent a fashion.

Observe that *his prayer was for a spiritual blessing only*. The other thief said, "Save thyself and us": he meant, "Save us from this cross. Deliver us from the death which now threatens us." He sought temporal benefits, but this man asked only to be remembered by Christ in his kingdom. Do your prayers ran that way, dear friends? Then I bless the Lord that he has taught you to seek eternal rather than temporal blessings. If a sick man cares more for pardon than for health it is a good sign. Soul mercies will be prized above all others where faith is in active exercise.

Observe how humbly he prays. He did not ask for a place at Christ's right hand; he did not, in fact, ask the Lord to do anything for him, but only to "remember" him. Yet that "remember" is a great word, and he meant much by it. "Do give a thought to thy poor companion who now confesses his faith in thee. Do in thy glory dart one recollection of thy love upon poor me, and think on me for good." It was a very humble prayer, and all the sweeter for its lowliness. It showed his great faith in Jesus, for he believed that even to be remembered by him would be enough. "Give me but the crumbs that fall from thy table, and they shall suffice me: but a thought, Lord Jesus, but one thought from thy loving mind, and that shall satisfy my soul."

Did not his prayer drip with faith as a honeycomb with honey? It seems to me as if laid soaking in his faith till it was saturated through and through with it, for *he prays so powerfully*, albeit so humbly. Consider what his character had been, and yet he says "Lord, remember *me* when thou comest into thy kingdom." Note well that it is a thief—an outcast, a criminal on the gallows-tree who thus prays. He is an outcast by his country's laws, and yet he turns to the King of heaven and asks to be remembered. Bad as he is he believes that the Lord Jesus will have mercy upon him. Oh, brave faith!

We see how strong that faith was, because he had no invitation so to pray. I do not know that he had ever heard Christ preach. No apostle had said to him, "Come to Christ, and you will find mercy," and yet he came to Jesus. Here comes an uninvited guest in the sweet bravery of holy confidence in Christ's majestic love; he comes boldly and pleads, "Lord, remember me." It was strong faith which thus pleaded. Remember, too, that he was upon the verge of death. He knew that he could not live very long, and probably expected the Roman bone-breaker to give him very soon the final blow; but in the very hour and article of death he cried, "Lord, remember me," with the strong confidence of a mighty faith. Glory be to God who wrought such a faith in such a man as this.

IV. We have done when we have mentioned, in the fourth place, THE ANSWER TO HIS FAITH.

We will only say that *his faith brought him to paradise*. We had a paradise once, and the first Adam lost it. Paradise has been regained by the second Adam, and he has prepared for believers an Eden above fairer than that first garden of delights below. Faith led the dying thief *to be with Christ* in paradise, which was best of all. "Today shalt thou be *with me* in paradise." Whatever the joy of Christ, and the glory of Christ, the thief was there to see it and to share it as soon as Christ himself.

And it brought him paradise *that very day*. Sometimes a crucified man will be two or three days a-dying; Jesus, therefore, assures him that he shall not have long to suffer, and confirms it with a "verily," which was our Lord's strong word of asseveration—"Verily I say unto thee, today shalt thou be with me in paradise." Such a portion will faith win for each of us, not today it may be, but one day. If we believe in Jesus Christ, who died for our sins, we shall be with him in the delights and happiness of the spirit-world, and with him in the paradise of everlasting glory. If we commenced to believe at once, and were to die immediately, we should be with Christ at once, as surely as if we had been converted fifty years ago. You cannot tell how short your life will be, but it is well to be ready. A friend was here last Sabbath-day of whom I heard this morning that he was' ill, and in another hour that he was dead. It was short work; he was smitten down, and gone at once. That may be the lot of any one of you; and if it should be, you will have no cause whatever to fear it if you now like the thief trust yourself wholly in Jesus' hands, crying, "Lord, remember me when thou comest into thy kingdom."

The lesson of our text is not merely that Christ can save in our last extremity, though that is true, but that now at this moment Jesus is able to save us, and that if saved at all, salvation must be an immediate and complete act, so that, come life or come death, we are perfectly saved. It will not take the Lord long to raise the dead—in a moment, in the twinkling of an eye, the dead shall be raised incorruptible; and the Lord takes no time in regenerating a soul. Dead souls live in an instant when the breath of the Spirit quickens them. Faith brings instantaneous pardon. There is no course of probation to go through, there are no attainments to be sought after, and no protracted efforts to be made in order to be saved. Thou art saved if thou believest in Jesus. The finished work of Christ is thine. Thou art God's beloved, accepted, forgiven, adopted child. Saved thou art, and saved thou shalt be for ever and ever if thou believest.

Instantaneous salvation! Immediate salvation! This the Spirit of God gives to those who trust in Jesus. Thou needest not wait till to-morrow's sun has dawned. Talk not of a more convenient season. Sitting where thou art, the almighty grace of God can come upon thee and save thee, and this shall be a sign unto thee that Christ is born in thy heart the hope of glory—when thou believest in him as thy pardon, righteousness, and all in all, thou shalt have peace. If thou dost but trust thyself in Jesus' hands thou art a saved soul, and the angels in heaven are singing high praises to God and the Lamb on thine account. Farewell.

4

Saul of Tarsus;

or,

The Pattern Convert

"Howbeit for this cause I obtained mercy, that in me first Jesus Christ might shew forth all longsuffering, for a pattern to them which should hereafter believe on him to life everlasting" (1 Tim. 1:16).

It is a vulgar error that the conversion of the apostle Paul was an uncommon and exceptional event, and that we cannot expect men to be saved now-a-days after the same fashion. It is said that the incident was an exception to all rules, a wonder altogether by itself. Now, my text is a flat contradiction to that notion, for it assures us that instead of the apostle as a receiver of the longsuffering and mercy of God being at all an exception to the rule, he was a model convert, and is to be regarded as a type and pattern of God's grace in other believers. The apostle's language in the text, "for a pattern," may mean that he was what printers call a 'first proof, an early impression from the engraving, a specimen of those to follow. He was the typical instance of divine longsuffering, the model after which others are fashioned. To use a metaphor from the artists' studio, Paul was the ideal sketch of a convert, an outline of the work of Jesus on mankind, a cartoon of divine longsuffering. Just as artists make sketches in charcoal as the basis of their work, which outlines they paint out as the picture proceeds, so did the Lord in the apostle's case make as it were a cartoon or outline sketch of his usual work of grace. That outline in the case of each future believer he works out with infinite variety of skill, and produces the individual Christian, but the guiding lines are really there. All conversions are in a high degree similar to this pattern conversion. The transformation of persecuting Saul of Tarsus into the apostle Paul is a typical instance of the work of grace in the heart. We will have no other preface, but proceed at once to two or three considerations.

The first is that IN THE CONVERSION OF PAUL THE LORD HAD AN EYE TO OTHERS, AND IN THIS PAUL IS A PATTERN. In every case, the individual is saved not for himself alone, but with a view to the good of others. Those who think the doctrine of election to be harsh should not deny it, for it is scriptural; but they may to their own minds soften some of its hardness by remembering that elect men bear a marked connection with the race. The Jews as an elect people were chosen in order to preserve the oracles of God for all nations and for all times. Men personally elected unto eternal life by divine grace are also elected that they may become chosen vessels to bear the name of Jesus unto others. While our Lord is said to be the Savior specially of them that believe, he is also called the Savior of all men; and while he has a special eye to the good of the one person whom he has chosen, yet through that person he has designs of love to others, perhaps even to thousands yet unborn.

The apostle Paul says, "I obtained mercy, that in me foremost Jesus Christ might shew forth all longsuffering, for a pattern to them which should hereafter believe." Now, I think I see very clearly that *Paul's conversion had an immediate relation to the conversion of many others*. It had a tendency, had it not, to excite an interest in the minds of his brother Pharisees? Men of his class, men of culture, who were equally at home with the Greek philosophers and with the Jewish rabbis, men of influence, men of rank, would be sure to enquire, "What is this new religion which has fascinated Saul of Tarsus? That zealot for Judaism has now become a zealot for Christianity: what can there be in it?" I say that the natural tendency of his conversion was to awaken enquiry and thought, and so to lead others of his rank to become believers. And, my dear friend, if you have been saved, you ought to regard it as a token of God's mercy to your class. If you are a working man, let your salvation be a blessing to the men with whom you labor. If you are a person of rank and station, consider that God intends to bless you to some with whom you are on familiar terms.

If you are young, hope that God will bless the youth around you, and if you have come to older years, hope that your conversion, even at the eleventh hour, may be the means of encouraging other aged pilgrims to seek and find rest unto their souls. The Lord, by calling one out of any society of men, finds for himself a recruiting officer who will enlist his fellows beneath the banner of the cross. May not this fact encourage some seeking soul to hope that the Lord may save him, though he be the only thoughtful person in all his family, and then make him to be the means of salvation to all his kindred.

We notice that *Paul often used the narrative of his conversion as an encouragement to others*. He was not ashamed to tell his own life-story. Eminent soul-winners such as Whitefield and Bunyan frequently pleaded God's mercy to themselves as an argument with their fellowmen. Though great preachers of another school, such as Robert Hall and Chalmers, do not mention themselves at all, and I can admire their abstinence, yet I am persuaded that if some of us were to follow their example we should be throwing away one of the most powerful weapons of our warfare. What can be more affecting, more convincing, more overwhelming than the story of divine grace told by the very man who has experienced it? It is better than a score tales of converted Africans, and infinitely more likely to win men's hearts than the most elaborate essays upon moral excellence.

Again and again Paul gave a long narrative of his conversion, for he felt it to be one of the most telling things that he could relate. Whether he stood before Felix or Agrippa, this was his plea for the gospel. All through his epistles there are continual mentions of the grace of God towards himself, and we may be sure that the apostle did right thus to argue from his own case: it is fair and forcible reasoning and ought by no means to be left unused because of a selfish dread of being called egotistical. God intends that we should use our conversion as an encouragement to others, and say to them, "Come and hear, all ye that fear God, and I will tell you what he has done for my soul." We point to our own forgiveness and say, "Do but trust in the living Redeemer, and you shall find, as we have done, that Jesus blotteth out the transgressions of believers."

Paul's conversion was an encouragement to him all his life long to have hope for others. Have you ever read the first chapter of the Epistle to the Romans?

Well, the man who penned those terrible verses might very naturally have written at the end of them—"Can these monsters be reclaimed? It can be of no avail whatever to preach the gospel to people so sunken in vice." That one chapter gives as daring an outline as delicacy would permit of the nameless, shameful vices into which the heathen world had plunged, and yet, after all, Paul went forth to declare the gospel to that filthy and corrupt generation, believing that God meant to save a people out of it. Surely one element of his hope for humanity must have been found in the fact of his own salvation; he considered himself to be in some respects as bad as the heathen, and in other respects even worse: he calls himself the *foremost* of sinners (that is the word); and he speaks of God having saved him foremost, that in him he might show forth all longsuffering. Paul never doubted the possibility of the conversion of a person however infamous after he had been converted himself. This strengthened him in battling with the fiercest opponents—he who overcame such a wild beast as I was, can also tame others and bring them into willing captivity to his love.

There was yet another relation between Paul's conversion and the salvation of others, and it was this: *It served as an impulse*, driving him forward in his lifework of bringing sinners to Christ. "I obtained mercy," said he, "and that same voice which spoke peace to me said, I have made thee a chosen vessel unto me to bear my name among the Gentiles." And he did bear it, my brethren. Going into regions beyond that, he might not build on another man's foundation, he became a master builder for the Church of God. How indefatigably did he labor! With what vehemence did he pray! With what energy did he preach! Slander and contempt he bore with the utmost patience. Scourging or stoning had no terrors for him. Imprisonment, yea death itself, he defied; nothing could daunt him. Because the Lord had saved him he felt that he must by all means save some. He could not be quiet. Divine love was in him like a fire, and if he had been silent he would before long have had to cry with the prophet of old, "I am weary with restraining." He is the man who said, "Necessity is laid upon me, yea woe is unto me if I preach not the gospel," Paul, the extraordinary sinner, was saved that he might be full of extraordinary zeal and bring multitudes to eternal life. Well could he say,

> The love of Christ doth me constrain

> To seek the wandering souls of men;
> With cries, entreaties, tears to save,
> To snatch them from the fiery wave.
> My life, my blood I here present,
> If for Thy truth they may be spent;
> Fulfill Thy sovereign counsel, Lord!
> Thy will be done, Thy name adored!

Now, I will pause here a minute to put a question. You profess to be converted, my dear friend. What relation has your conversion already had to other people? It ought to have a very apparent one. Has it had such? Mr. Whitefield said that when his heart was renewed his first desire was that his companions with whom he had previously wasted his time might be brought to Christ. It was natural and commendable that he should begin with them. Remember how one of the apostles, when he discovered the Savior, went immediately to tell his brother. It is most fitting that young people should spend their first religious enthusiasm upon their brothers and sisters.

As to converted parents, their first responsibility is in reference to their sons and daughters. Upon each renewed man his natural affinities, or the bonds of friendship, or the looser ties of neighborhood should begin to operate at once, and each one should feel—"No man liveth unto himself." If divine grace has kindled a fire in you it is that your fellow men may burn with the same flame. If the eternal fount has filled you with living water it is that out of the midst of you should flow rivers of living water. You are blessed that you may bless; whom have you blessed yet? Let the question go round. Do not avoid it. This is the best return that you can make to God, that when he saveth you, you should seek to be the instruments in his hands of saving others. What have you done yet? Did you ever speak with the friend who shares your pew? He has been sitting there for a long time, and may perhaps be an unconverted person; have you pointed him to the Lamb of God? Have you ever spoken to your servants about their souls? Have you yet broken the ice sufficiently to speak to your own sister, or your own brother?

Do begin, dear friend. That Christianity which is consistent with selfishness is not consistent with Christ. You do not possess the spirit of Christ if the only thing you seek for is your own salvation; and if any man have not the Spirit of Christ he is none of his.

Are you ashamed of your negligence in the past, then bestir yourself for the future. Vain regrets cannot redeem lost opportunities, but holy resolves may prevent future omissions. Come now, what can you do? What will you do? Take counsel with a grateful heart and be no longer a dumb dog, a fruitless tree, a blot and a blank in the church of God.

You cannot tell what mysterious threads connect you with your fellow men and their destiny. There was a cobbler once, as you know, in Northamptonshire. Who could see any connection between him and the millions of India? But the love of God was in his bosom, and Carey could not rest till at Serampore he had commenced to translate the Word of God and preach to his fellow men. We must not confine our thoughts to the few whom Carey brought to Christ, though to save one soul is worthy of a life of sacrificed but Carey became the forerunner and leader of a missionary band which will never cease to labor till India bows before Immanuel. That man mysteriously drew, is drawing, and will draw India to the Lord Jesus Christ.

Brother, you do not know what your power is. Awake and try it. Did you never read this passage: "Thou hast given him power over all flesh, that he should give eternal life to as many as thou hast given him"? Now, the Lord has given to his Son power over all flesh, and with a part of that power Jesus clothes his servants. Through you he will give eternal life to certain of his chosen; by you and by no other means will they be brought to himself. Look about you, regenerate man. Your life may be made sublime. Rouse yourself! Begin to think of what God may do by you! Calculate the possibilities which lie before you with the eternal God as your helper. Shake yourself from the dust and put on the beautiful garments of disinterested love to others, and it shall yet be seen how grandly gracious God has been to hundreds of men by having converted you.

So far, then, Paul's salvation, because it had so clear a reference to others, was a pattern of all conversions.

II. Now, secondly, PAUL'S FOREMOST POSITION AS A SINNER DID NOT PREVENT HIS BECOMING FOREMOST IN GRACE, AND HEREIN AGAIN HE IS A PATTERN TO US. Foremost in sin, he became also foremost in service. Saul of Tarsus was a *blasphemer*, and he is to be commended because he has not recorded any of those blasphemies. We can never object to converted burglars and chimney-sweepers, of whom we hear so much, telling the story of their conversion; but when they go into dirty details they had better hold their tongues. Paul tells us that he was a blasphemer, but he never repeats one of the blasphemies. We invent enough evil in our own hearts without being told of other men's stale profanities. If, however, any of you are so curious as to want to know what kind of blasphemies Paul could utter, you have only to converse with a converted Jew and he will tell you what horrible words some of his nation will speak against our Lord. I have no doubt that Paul in his evil state thought as wickedly of Christ as he could—considered him to be an impostor, called him so, and added many an opprobrious epithet. He does not say of himself that he was an unbeliever and an objector, but he says that he was a blasphemer, which is a very strong word, but not too strong, for the apostle never went beyond the truth. He was a downright, thorough-going blasphemer, who also caused others to blaspheme. Will these lines meet the eye of a profane person who feels the greatness of his sin? May God grant that he may be encouraged to seek mercy as Saul of Tarsus did, for "all manner of sin and of blasphemy did he forgive unto men."

From blasphemy, which was the sin of the lips, Saul proceeded to *persecution*, which is a sin of the hands. Hating Christ, he hated his people too. He was delighted to give his vote for the death of Stephen, and he took care of the clothes of those who stoned that martyr. He haled men and women to prison, and compelled them to blaspheme. When he had "printed all Judea as closely as he could he obtained letters to go to Damascus, that might do the same in that place. His eye had been compelled to quit Jerusalem and fly to more remote places, but "being exceeding mad against them he persecuted them unto strange cities." He was foremost in blasphemy and persecution. Will a persecutor read or hear these words? If so, may he be led to see that even for him pardon is possible. Jesus who said, "Father, forgive them; for they know not what they do," is still an intercessor for the most violent "of his enemies.

He adds, next, that he was *injurious*, which I think Bengel considers to mean that he was a despiser: that eminent critic says—blasphemy was his sin towards God, persecution was his sin towards the church, and despising was his sin in his own heart. He was injurious—that is, he did all he could to damage the cause of Christ, and he thereby injured himself. He kicked against the pricks and injured his own conscience. He was so determined against Christ that he counted no cost too great by which he might hinder the spread of the faith, and he did hinder it terribly. He was a ringleader in resisting the Spirit of God which was then working with the church of Christ. He was foremost in opposition to the cross of Christ.

Now, notice that he was saved as a pattern, which is to show you that if you also have been foremost in sin you also may obtain mercy as Paul did: and to show you yet again that if you have not been foremost, the grace of God, which is able to save the chief of sinners, can assuredly save those who are of less degree. If the bridge of grace will carry the elephant it will certainly carry the mouse. If the mercy of God could bear with the hugest sinners it can have patience with you. If a gate is wide enough for a giant to pass through, any ordinary sized mortal will find space enough. Despair's head is cut off and stuck on a pole by the salvation of "the chief of sinners." No man can now say that he is too great a sinner to be saved, because the chief of sinners was saved eighteen hundred years ago. If the ringleader, the chief of the gang, has been washed in the precious blood, and is now in heaven, why not I? Why not *you*?

After Paul was saved he became a foremost saint. The Lord did not allot him a second-class place in the church. He had been the leading sinner, but his Lord did not, therefore, say, "I save you, but I shall always remember your wickedness to your disadvantage." Not so: he counted him faithful, putting him into the ministry and into the apostleship, so that he was not a whit behind the very chief of the apostles. Brother, there is no reason why, if you have gone very far in sin, you should not go equally far in usefulness. On the contrary there is a reason why you should do so, for it is a rule of grace that to whom much is forgiven the same loveth much, and much love leads to much service. What man was clearer in his knowledge of doctrine than Paul? What man more earnest in the defense of truth? What man more self-sacrificing? What man more heroic? The name of Paul in the Christian church stands in some respects the very next to the Lord Jesus. Turn to the New Testament and see how large a space is occupied by the Holy Spirit speaking through his servant Paul; and then look over Christendom and see how greatly the man's influence is still felt, and must be felt till his Master shall come.

Oh, great sinner, if thou art even now ready to scoff at Christ, my prayer is that he may strike thee down at this very moment, and turn thee into one of his children, and make thee to be just as ardent for the truth as thou art now earnest against it, as desperately set on good as now thou art on evil. None make such mighty Christians and such fervent preachers as those who are lifted up from the lowest depths of sin and washed and purified through the blood of Jesus Christ. May grace do this with thee, my dear friend, whoever thou mayest be.

Thus we gather from our text that the Lord showed mercy to Paul that in him foremost it might be seen that prominence in sin is no barrier to eminence in grace, but the very reverse.

III. Now I come to where the stress of the text lies. *PAUL'S CASE WAS A PATTERN OF OTHER CONVERSIONS AS AN INSTANCE OF LONGSUFFERING.* "That in me foremost Jesus Christ might show forth all longsuffering for a cartoon or pattern to them which should hereafter believe." Thoughtfully observe the great longsuffering of God to Paul: he says, "He showed forth all longsuffering." Not only all the longsuffering of God that ever was shown to anybody else, but all that could be supposed to exist—*all* longsuffering.

> All thy mercy's height I prove,
>   All its depth is found in me,

as if he had gone to the utmost stretch of his tether in sin, and the Lord also had strained his longsuffering to its utmost.

That longsuffering was seen first in sparing his life when he was rushing headlong in sin, breathing out threatenings, foaming at the mouth with denunciations of the Nazarene and. his people. If the Lord had but lifted his finger Saul would have been crushed like a moth, but almighty wrath forbore, and the rebel lived on. Nor was this all; after all his sin the Lord allowed mercy to be possible to him. He blasphemed, and persecuted at a red-hot rate; and is it not a marvel that the Lord did not say," Now at last you have gone beyond all bearing, and you shall die like Herod, eaten of worms"? It would not have been at all wonderful if God had so sentenced him; but he allowed him to live within the reach of mercy, and, better still, he in due time actually sent the gospel to him, and laid it home to his heart. In the very midst of his rebellion the Lord saved him. He had not prayed to be converted, far from it; no doubt he had that very day along the road to Damascus, profaned the Savior's name, and yet mighty mercy burst in and saved him purely by its own spontaneous native energy. Oh mighty grace, free grace, victorious grace! This was longsuffering indeed!

When divine mercy had called Paul it swept all his sin away, every particle of it, his blood shedding and his blasphemy, all at once, so that never man was more assured of his own perfect cleansing than was the apostle. "There is therefore now," saith he, "no condemnation to them which are in Christ Jesus." "Therefore being justified by faith, we have peace with God." "Who shall lay anything to the charge of God's elect?" You know how clear he was about that; and he spoke out of his own experience. Longsuffering had washed all his sins away. Then that longsuffering reaching from the depths of sin lifted him right up to the apostleship, so that he began to prove God's longsuffering in its heights of favor. What a privilege it must have been to him to be permitted to preach the gospel. I should think sometimes when he was preaching most earnestly he would half stop himself and say, "Paul, is this you?" When he went down to Tarsus especially he must have been surprised at himself and at the mighty mercy of God. He preached the faith which once he had destroyed. He must have said many a time after a sermon when he went home to his bedchamber, "Marvel of marvels! Wonder of wonders that I who once could curse have now been made to preach—that I, who was full of threatening and even breathed out slaughter, should now be so inspired by the Spirit of God that I weep at the very sound of Jesus's name, and count all things but loss for the excellency of the knowledge of Christ Jesus my Lord."

Oh, brothers and sisters, you do not measure longsuffering except you take it in all its length from one end to the other, and see God in mercy, not remembering his servant's sin, but lifting him into eminent service in his church. Now, this was for a pattern, to show you that he will show forth the same longsuffering to those who believe. If you have been a swearer he will cleanse your blackened mouth, and put his praises into it. Have you had a black, cruel heart, full of enmity to Jesus? He will remove it and give you a new heart and a right spirit. Have you dived into all sorts of sins? Are they so shameful that you dare not think of them? Think of the precious blood which removes every stain. Are your sins so many that you could not count them? Do you feel as if you were almost damned already in the very memory of your life? I do not wonder at it, but he is able to save to the uttermost them that come unto God by him.

You have not gone farther than Saul had gone, and therefore all longsuffering can come to you, and there are great possibilities of future holiness and usefulness before you. Even though you may have been a street-walker or a thief, yet if the grace of God cleanses you it can make something wonderful out of you: full many a lustrous jewel of Immanuel's crown has been taken from the dunghill. You are a rough block of stone, but Jesus can fashion and polish you and set you as a pillar in his temple. Brother, do not despair. See what Saul was and what Paul became, and learn what you may be. Though you deserve the depths of hell, yet up to the heights of heaven grape can lift you. Though now you feel as if the fiends of the pit would be fit companions for such a lost spirit as yourself, yet believe in the Lord Jesus and you shall one day walk among the angels as pure and white as they. Paul's experience of longsuffering grace was meant to be a pattern of what God will do for you.

> Scripture says, "Where sin abounded,
>   There did grace much more abound:"
> Thus has Satan been confounded,
>   And his own discomfit found.
>
> Christ has triumph'd!
>   Spread the glorious news around.
> Sin is strong, but grace is stronger;
>   Christ than Satan more supreme;
>
> Yield, oh, yield to sin no longer,
>   Turn to Jesus, yield to Him—
> He has triumph'd!
>   Sinners, henceforth Him esteem.

IV. Again, THE MODE OR PAUL'S CONVERSION WAS ALSO MEANT TO BE A PATTERN, and with this I shall finish. I do not say that we may expect to receive the miraculous revelation which was given to Paul, but yet it is a sketch upon which any conversion can be painted. The filling up is not the same in any two cases, but the outline sketch of Paul's conversion would serve for an outline sketch of the conversion of any one of us. How was that conversion wrought? Well, it is clear that *there was nothing at all in Paul to contribute to his salvation.*

You might have sifted him in a sieve, without finding anything upon which you could rest a hope that he would be converted to the faith of Jesus. His natural bent, his early training, his whole surroundings, and his life's pursuits, all fettered him to Judaism, and made it most unlikely that he would ever become a Christian. The first elder of the church that ever talked to him about divine things could hardly believe in his conversion. "Lord," said he, "I have heard by many of this man, how much evil he hath done to thy saints at Jerusalem." He could hardly think it possible that the ravening wolf should have changed into a lamb. Nothing favorable to faith in Jesus could have been found in Saul; the soil of his heart was very rocky, the ploughshare could not touch it, and the good seed found no foothold. Yet the Lord converted Saul, and he can do the like by other sinners, but it must be a work of pure grace and of divine power, for there is not in any man's fallen nature a holy spot of the size of a pin's point on which grace can light. Transforming grace can find no natural lodgment in our hearts, it must create its own soil; and, blessed be God, it can do it, for with God all things are possible. Nature contributes nothing to grace, and yet grace wins the day. Humbled soul, let this cheer thee. Though there is nothing good in thee, yet grace can work wonders, and save thee by its own might.

Paul's conversion was an instance of divine power, and of that alone, and so is every true conversion. If your conversion is an instance of the preacher's power you need to be converted again; if your salvation is the result of your own power it is a miserable deception, from which may you be delivered. Every man who is saved must be operated upon by the might of God the Holy Spirit: every jot and tittle of true regeneration is the Spirit's work. As for our strength, it wars against salvation rather than for it. Blessed is that promise, "Thy people shall be willing in the day of thy power." Conversion is as much a work of God's omnipotence as the resurrection; and as the dead do not raise themselves, so neither do men convert themselves.

But Saul was changed immediately. His conversion was once done and done at once. There was a little interval before he found peace, but even during those three days he was a changed man, though he was in sadness. He was under the power of Satan at one moment, and in the next he was under the reign of grace. This is also true in every conversion. However gradual the breaking of the day there is a time when the sun is below the horizon and a moment when he is no longer so. You may not know the exact time in which you passed from death to life, but there was such a time, if you are indeed a believer. A man may not know how old he is, but there was a moment in which he was born. In every conversion there is a distinct change from darkness to light, from death to life, just as certainly as there was in Paul's. And what a delightful hope does the rapidity of regeneration present to us! It is by no long and laborious process that we escape from sin. We are not compelled to remain in sin for a single moment. Grace brings instantaneous liberty to those who sit in bondage. He who trusts Jesus is saved on the spot. Why then abide in death? Why not lift up your eyes to immediate life and light? *Paul proved his regeneration by his faith*. He believed unto eternal life. He tells us over and over again in his epistles that he was saved by faith, and not by works.

So is it with every man; if saved at all it is by simply believing in the Lord Jesus. Paul esteemed his own works to be less than nothing, and called them dross and dung, that he might win Christ, and so every converted man renounces his own works that he may be saved by grace alone. Whether he has been moral or immoral, whether he has lived an amiable and excellent life or whether he has raked in the kennels of sin, every regenerate man has one only hope, and that is centered and fixed in Jesus alone. Faith in Jesus Christ is the mark of salvation, even as the heaving of the lungs or the coming of breath from the nostrils is the test of life. Faith is the grace which saves the soul, and its absence is a fatal sign. How does this fact affect you, dear friend? Hast thou faith or no?

Paul was very positively and evidently saved. You did not need to ask the question, Is that man a Christian or not?, for the transformation was most apparent. If Saul of Tarsus had appeared as he used to be, and Paul the apostle could also have come in, and you could have seen the one man as two men, you would have thought them no relation to one another. Paul the apostle would have said that he was dead to Saul of Tarsus, and Saul of Tarsus would have gnashed his teeth at Paul the apostle. The change was evident to all who knew him, whether they sympathize in it or not. They could not mistake the remarkable difference which grace had made, for it was as great as when midnight brightens into noon. So it is when a man is truly saved: there is a change which those around him must perceive.

Do not tell me that you can be a child at home and become a Christian and yet your father and mother will not perceive a difference in you. They will be sure to see it. Would a leopard in a menagerie lose his spots and no one notice it? Would an Ethiopian be turned white and no one hear of it? You, masters and mistresses, will not go in and out amongst your servants and children without their perceiving a change in you if you are born again. At least, dear brother or sister, strive with all your might to let the change be very apparent in your language, in your actions, and in your whole conduct. Let your conversation be such as becometh the gospel of Christ, that men may see that you as well as the apostle are decidedly changed by the renewal of your minds.

May all of us be the subjects of divine grace as Paul was: stopped in our mad career, blinded by the glory of the heavenly light, called by a mysterious voice, conscious of natural blindness, relieved of blinding scales, and made to see Jesus as one all in all. May we prove in our own persons how speedily conviction may melt into conversion, conversion into confession, and confession into consecration.

I have done when I have enquired, How far we are conformed to the pattern which God has set before us? I know we are like Paul as to our sins, for if we have neither blasphemed nor persecuted, yet have we sinned as far as we have had opportunity. We are also conformed to Paul's pattern in the great longsuffering of God which we have experienced, and I am not sure that we cannot carry the parallel farther: we have had much the same revelation that Paul received on the way to Damascus, for we too have learned that Jesus is the Christ. If any of us sin against. Christ it will not be because we do not know him to be the Son of God, for we all believe in his Deity, because our Bibles tell us so. The pattern goes so far: I would that the grace of God would operate upon you, unconverted friend, and complete the picture, by giving you like faith with Paul. Then will you be saved as Paul was. Then also you will love Christ above all things as Paul did, and you will say: "But what things were gain to me, those I counted loss for Christ. Yea doubtless, and I count all things but loss for the excellency of the knowledge of Christ Jesus my Lord." He rested upon what Christ had done in his death and resurrection, and he found pardon and eternal life at once, and became, therefore, a devoted Christian.

What sayest thou, dear friend? Art thou moved to follow Paul's example? Does the Spirit of God prompt thee to trust Paul's Savior, and give up every other ground of trust and rely upon him? Then do so and live. Does there seem to be a hand holding thee back, and dost thou hear an evil whisper saying, "Thou art too great a sinner"? Turn round and bid the fiend depart, for the text gives him the lie. "In me *foremost* hath Jesus Christ showed forth all longsuffering for a pattern to them which should hereafter believe on his name." God has saved Paul. Back, then, O devil! The Lord can save any man, and he can save me. Jesus Christ of Nazareth is mighty to save, and I will rely on him. If any poor heart shall reason thus its logic will be sound and unanswerable. Mercy to one is an argument for mercy to another, for there is no difference, but the same Lord over all is rich unto all that call upon him.

Now I have set the case before you, and I cannot do more; it remains with each individual to accept or refuse. One man can bring a horse to the trough, but a hundred cannot make him drink. There is the gospel; if you want it take it, but if you will not have it then I must discharge my soul by reminding you that even the gentle gospel—the gospel of love and mercy has nothing to say to you but this—"He that believeth not shall be damned." It is not the law which speaks thus sternly, but the gospel. It shakes the dust from off its feet against you if you reject its loving invitations.

If you count yourselves unworthy of infinite mercy, that very forgiveness which you now may have for nothing, will if rejected become the surest evidence of your black-hearted enmity against the Lord.

> How they deserve the deepest hell
>   That slight the joys above;
> What chains of vengeance must they feel
>   Who break the bonds of love.

God grant that you may yield to mighty love, and find peace in Christ Jesus.

5

The Philippian Jailor;
or,
The Good Officer Improved

"Who, having received such a charge, thrust them into the inner prison, and made their feet fast in the stocks. And at midnight Paul and Silas prayed, and sang praises unto God: and the prisoners heard them. And suddenly there was a great earthquake, so that the foundations of the prison were shaken: and immediately all the doors were opened, and every one's bands were loosed. And the keeper of the prison awaking out of his sleep, and seeing the prison doors open, he drew out his sword, and would have killed himself, supposing that the prisoners had been fled. But Paul cried with a loud voice, saying, Do thyself no harm: for we are all here. Then he called for a light, and sprang in, and came trembling, and fell down before Paul and Silas. And brought them out, and said, Sirs, what must I do to be saved! And they said, Believe on the Lord Jesus Christ, and thou shalt be saved, and thy house. And they spake unto him the word of the Lord, and to all that were in his house. And he took them the same hour of the night, and washed their stripes; and was baptized, he and all his, straightway. And when he had brought them into his house, he set meat before them, and rejoiced, believing in God with all his house" (Acts 16:24–34).

The work of God at Philippi went on very quietly and successfully in the hands of Paul and Silas. It was the commencement of the gospel in Europe, and very auspicious were its circumstances. The good work was intimately connected with prayer-meetings, which for this reason should always wear a charm for Europeans. Godly women met together for devotion, Paul spoke to them, and households were converted and baptized. The work went on delightfully, but the devil, as usual, must needs put his foot in. To any who judged according to the sight of the eyes it must have seemed a most unfortunate circumstance that a poor woman having a spirit of divination came in Paul's way. It was a sad ruffling of the gentle stream of prosperity when, on account of his casting the demon out of her, the apostle and his companion were dragged by the mob before the magistrates, shamefully beaten, and thrown into prison.

Now the preacher's mouth would be stopped, so far as the people of Philippi outside the jail gates were concerned. No more of those delightful prayer-meetings and Bible readings, and openings up of the Scriptures. Surely there was cause for the deepest regret. It might have appeared so, but like a great many other incidents connected with Christian work, the matter could not be judged by the outward appearance, for the Lord had a secret and blessed design, which was being answered by the apparent disaster. Servants of Jesus Christ, never be discouraged when you are opposed, but when things run counter to your wishes expect that the Lord has provided some better thing for you. He is driving you away from shallow waters and bringing you into deeper seas, where your nets shall bring you larger draughts. Paul and Silas must go to prison because a chosen person was to be converted in the prison, who could not otherwise be reached.

Nay, it was not one person only who was to be saved, but eternal love had fixed its eye upon a whole house. The members of this elect family could by no other means be brought to Christ but through Paul and Silas being cast into prison; and, therefore, into prison they must go, to do more by night in their bonds than they could have done by day if they had been free, and to bring to Christ some that would be more illustrious trophies of the grace of God than any they could have gathered had they been preaching in the streets of Philippi. God knows where it is best for his servants to be, and how it is best for them to be. If he foresees that they will do more good with their backs scarred than they would have done if they had escaped the flagellation, then their bodies must bear the marks of the Lord Jesus, and they must rejoice to have it so. Brethren, we do not like the sick bed; we would not choose aching limbs, especially those of us who are of an active disposition, and would fain be perpetually telling out the love of Christ; and yet in our temporary imprisonment we have seen the Lord's wisdom, and have had to look back with thankfulness upon it. Oh, children of God, your Father knows best. Leave everything in his hands, and be at peace, for all is well. May the Holy Ghost work quietness of heart in you.

Our subject is the jailor of Philippi: and, first, we shall say a little as to *what kind of man he was before conversion*; secondly, we shall consider *what was the occasion of his conversion*; and then, thirdly, we will notice *what sort of convert he made* when the grace of God brought him to Jesus' feet.

I. First, then, WHAT SORT OF MAN WAS THIS JAILOR? The jailor is a remarkable instance of the power of divine grace, but he ought not to be spoken of as a notably great transgressor, for of this there is no trace whatever. He was, like ourselves, full of sin and iniquity, but we find no record of anything especially bad about him. I see no reason why Mr. Wesley should so severely stigmatize him as he does in his lines:

> What but the power which wakes the dead
>   Could reach a stubborn gaoler's heart,
> In cruelty and rapine bred,
>   Who took the ancient murderer's part?
> Could make a harden'd ruffian feel,
>   And shake him o'er the mouth of hell?

On the contrary, we shall be able to show that the jailor's salvation is an instance of the grace of God saving one of an admirable moral character, one in whom there were most commendable points, a man of such regularity and decision, that he was not so much saved from vice as from self-righteousness. I take it, from the little we know of him, that he was a fine specimen of stern Roman discipline, *a man full of respect for those in authority, and prompt in obedience to orders*. He was a jailor, and he had to act, not on his own responsibility, but on the command of others, and he scrupulously did so. When we read, "having received *such a charge*," we infer that he carefully followed the tenor of his orders, and attentively observed the weight which the magistrates threw into them. He therefore thrust the apostle and his friend into the inner prison and made their feet fast in the stocks. You can see that he was thorough-going in obedience to authority; for afterwards, although he might have liked to retain the apostle and Silas in his house, yet, when the magistrates sent him word, he spoke to his beloved guests as an official was bound to do, waiving, in some respects, the friend, and tersely saying, "The magistrates have sent to let you go; now, therefore depart, and go in peace." It strikes me that he was an old soldier—a legionary who had fought and done rough work in his younger days, and then settled down, appointed on account of his good behavior to the important post of governor of the jail of Philippi. With his family about him, he occupied himself in attending to his duties as a jailor, and carried them out with the strictest regularity. For this he is to be commended; for, it is expected of men that they be found faithful.

I say, then, that I regard him as an instance of a man whose mind was molded according to the Roman type, a person subservient to discipline, and strict in obedience to rule. I grant that there was a little harshness about his fulfilling the orders concerning Paul and Silas, for he seems to have "thrust" them into the dungeon with some violence; but we cannot object to their being placed in the inner prison, or to their feet being made fast in the stocks, because his orders were that he should keep them safely, and he was only doing his best to do so. He was not responsible for the order of the magistrates; and when the prisoners were brought to him fresh from the lictor's rods with a strict charge, what was he to do but to obey it to the letter? He did so, and does not deserve to be called a ruffian for it. His ruling idea was that he was a servant of the government and bound to carry out his instructions, and was he not right? Such men are very needful in government employ, and I cannot tell how public business could be done without them.

Notice that before he went to bed he saw that the prison doors were all fastened, and the lights put out. Even Roman jailors were open to bribes, and though lights had to be extinguished at a certain hour of the night, it was possible to burn your lamp still, if you placed a little oil upon the jailor's palm. But there was no lamp in the jail of Philippi, for when the keeper himself wanted a light he had to call for it. All lamps were out at the proper time, and all chains were on every person; for the narrative says that, by the earthquake, "Every man's bands were loosed," which they could not be if they were already unbound. The inmates were all secured in their cells, and the whole building was in due order. This shows that the keeper of the prison attended to his business thoroughly, nothing turning him aside from the most correct observance of his instructions.

Well, all being shut up, he has gone to bed, and is fast asleep, as he should be, in the middle of the night, so as to be fit for *his morning's work*. But what happens?

> Paul and Silas, in their prison,
> Sang of Christ, the Lord arisen;
> And an earthquake's arm of might
> Broke their dungeon gates at night.

See how every timber in the house quivers, and he awakes out of his sleep. What is his first thought? To my mind it is fine to observe that he has no terror for himself or family, but at once rushes from his room to look to the prison below. Seeing the prison doors open, he was alarmed. He does not seem to have been in any alarm about his wife and his family, though the earthquake must have shaken the rooms in which they were, but his one concern was his prison and its contents. Under the seal and authority of the Roman emperor he was bound to keep the prisoners safely, and when he wakes his first thought concerns his duty. I wish that all Christians were as faithful in their offices as this man! When as yet he was unenlightened, he *was faithful to those who employed him*. It is a grand thing when a man, placed in an office of responsibility, has his work so much upon his mind that if he starts up in the middle of the night and finds the floor under him reeling with an earthquake, the main thing he thinks about is the duty which he has engaged to fulfil. It ought to be so with Christian servants, with Christian trustees, managers, and confidential clerks, and indeed with all Christian men and women placed in offices of trust. Your chief concern should be to be found faithful; it was so with the jailor.

Now notice, as he finds the prison-doors open, this stern Roman *fears that he shall be disgraced*, for he feels sure that the prisoners must have fled. Naturally they would escape when the doors were open, and as he could not confront the charge of unfaithfulness in his office, he drew his sword in haste, and would have killed himself. For this proposed suicide he is to be most severely censured; but still note the stern Brutus-like fidelity of the man. He cannot endure the charge of having allowed his prisoners to escape, but would rather kill himself. Is it not singular that this Philippi was the place where Cassius committed suicide? Where Brutus also slew himself? Here this man would have added another name to those who laid violent hands upon themselves, and all because he feared that he would lose his character. He preferred death to dishonor. All these things show that he was a man sternly upright, and determined to perform his duty. I am always doubly glad when such men are saved, because it does not often happen. Such persons too often wrap themselves up in the sense of having walked uprightly towards their fellow men, and because, after the lapse of many years they stand high in public esteem, and everybody says the country never had better servants, they are apt to forget their Master in heaven, and their obligations to their Lord—apt to have a blind eye towards their own shortcomings, and to be little inclined to sit as little children at the feet of Jesus, unless some wondrous deed of grace is wrought upon them. Hence we admire the grace of God which brought such a man trembling to the apostle's feet.

The jailor was *a person of few words*; he was not a great talker, but a prompt actor. We only know three things that he said. First, he called for a light, and next he cried, "Sirs, what must I do to be saved?" a terse, laconic question, respectful, earnest, to the point, having not a word too much or too little in it. His other speech to Paul was of the same order when he said, "The magistrates have sent to let you go; now, therefore, depart and go in peace." You would not expect a jailor to use very flowery language, he was accustomed to measure his syllables when he spoke to his prisoners, never uttering a word beyond the statute in that case made and provided. Thus he had acquired a hard business-like style of speech. Men of such a type are often cold as so many statues. We find it hard to warm their hearts, and therefore we bless the grace of God, which made this man's heart to burn within him and snapped the bonds of cold routine, so that, after his conversion, he feasted the ministers of Christ and rejoiced with all his house.

It may be well to make one more remark. It is evident that he was *a man of action, of precision and decision*. Once let him know what is to be done, and he does it. He acts as a man under authority having warders under him, he saith to this man, "Go, and he goeth;" and he himself acts mechanically as his superiors command him. He was a man who, I suppose, opened the prison doors always to a minute at the right time in the morning for those who went out to exercise, measured out the meals of the prisoners to the ounce, and shut up the cells and put out the lights exactly at the fixed hour at night. I see it in him.

Precise obedience is his main point. When he was bidden to believe he believed; he was also baptized straightway. What he lacked in speech he made up in deeds. He obeyed the Lord Jesus immediately, there and then.

I love to see a man brought to Christ who has orderliness and decision about him. Some of us are rough beings, needing a deal of combing to bring us into shape; but certain others are shapely after their way from the first, and all that they need is spiritual life. When the divine life comes their habits are in beautiful consistency with the inward law of obedience and holy order. Still, it is not often that persons of this class are saved; for these very orderly people frequently think that they have no sin, and so the warnings addressed to sinners do not come home to them. For instance, a man says, "Never since I took my position as manager of my master's business have I wasted an hour of his time, or a shilling of his substance." This is well, but the devil is ready with the suggestion, "Thou art a good and faithful servant. What need hast thou to humble thyself before Christ, and seek mercy and grace?" It is a most blessed thing when this tendency is overcome. I see the divine splendor of grace as much in the conversion of the faultless moralist as in the repentance of Manasseh, or of that woman which was a sinner, of whom we spoke a little while ago. It is as hard to deliver a man from self-righteousness as from unrighteousness, as difficult to deliver one man from the frostbite of his own orderliness as to save another from the heat of his unbridled passions. Converts like the jailor are very precious, and very sweetly display the love and power of God.

II. Now, secondly, WHAT OCCASIONED THE JAILOR'S CONVERSION? The narrative is short, and we cannot therefore get much out of it. I think, however, that we are warranted in believing that this man had received some measure of instruction before the earnest midnight cry of, "What must I do to be saved?" Perhaps the often repeated testimony of the Pythoness had been reported to him, for it must have been a matter of general notoriety throughout the town of Philippi that this woman, who was supposed to be inspired, had testified that Paul and Silas were "servants of the Most High God." It is also very possible that when he was fitting on the irons to these holy men, and roughly thrusting them into the inner prison, their quiet manner, like sheep at the slaughter, and perhaps their godly words also, may have carried information to his mind. What he saw and heard did not savingly impress him, for he showed the apostles no sort of courtesy, but, as I have already said, was somewhat harsh with them. "He thrust them into the inner prison, and made their feet fast in the stocks:" so that at that time he had no belief in their mission, and but small respect for their character. He felt, it is clear, no compunction, for he went up to his chamber and fell asleep; nothing of any importance was on his mind notwithstanding what the apostles may have said to him. A young divine in a flowery sermon described the jailor as converted through hearing Paul and Silas sing at midnight. A very beautiful picture he made of it, but it had the drawback of being untrue, for the jailor did not hear them sing, "The prisoners heard them," for they were all down in the vaults under the jailor's house; but it is clear that the keeper of the prison did not hear them, for he was asleep until the earthquake startled him.

I have also heard it said that he was converted through fear of death; a most ridiculous remark, for how could he be afraid to die who was going to kill himself? No, he was too brave a man to be moved by terror. He was afraid of nothing but of being suspected of neglect of duty; he was a soldier, without fear and without reproach, dreading dishonor infinitely more than death. He was a stern disciplinarian, and thought little of his own life or the lives of others. He would have ridden in the charge of Balaclava, with all the rest of them, bravely enough—

> His not to reason why;
>   His but to dare and die.

You can see that it was not fear that brought him to the feet of the apostle. I do not doubt that some are brought to Christ by fear of death, but one is a little suspicious of such conversions; for he who is frightened to the Savior by of death may possibly run away from him when he perceives that his fear has no immediate cause.

Others, too, have thought that he was made to tremble because he was afraid of being brought before Caesar for permitting his prisoners to escape. That fear may have hurried him into the desperate intent of suicide, but it was not the cause of his conversion, for all distress upon that point was gone before he cried out, "Sirs, what must I do to be saved?" In fact, he came to Paul and Silas because that- fear had been banished by hearing the calm and brave voice of the apostle as he said, "Do thyself no harm: we are all here." It was not even a fear of censure from the magistrates which compelled him to tremble, for that also had been removed by finding the prisoners still in their cells; and, though the whole of these things together make up the circumstances of his conversion they cannot be put down as the cause of it, since this last especially had ceased to operate upon him when he fell trembling at the apostle's feet.

What was it, then, which led to the jailor's faith and baptism? I answer, partly the miracle that the doors were opened and the prisoners' bonds loosed by an earthquake; and coupled with that the fact that none of them had escaped. What gladness filled his bosom! He would not be arraigned after all for being unfaithful to his trust. How strange that the prisoners were all there. What a conflict was there in his spirit! What anxiety, and what sudden quelling of his alarm! There was no need to commit suicide lest he should be blamed, for there was nothing for which to blame him. What a deliverance for him! An awful power was abroad, and yet it had taken care of him. A mingled feeling of mystery and gladness created astonishment and gratitude in his bosom. He could not make it out, it was so singular: he had been brought to the verge of a precipice, and yet was safe, "Do thyself no harm; we are all here," rang out like music in his ear. He felt a solemn awe of those two prisoners whose voice had reassured him. Their voice had been to him as the very voice of God sounding forth along those corridors out of the innermost cells. Their bold, truthful, confident, calm tones had astonished him. He had seen before something very singular about those two men, but now the very tone in which they conveyed to him the glad intelligence which banished his worst fear filled him with deep reverence towards them: and he feels that no doubt these men are the servants of the Most High God, and therefore he calls for a light, breaks in upon their darkness, and brings them out.

While this was transpiring, he was brought very near to the world to come by the fact of the sword having been so near his breast, by the earthquake that had started all the stones of the dungeon, by the singular power of God miraculously holding every free man as fast as if he had been bound, and by the presence of men whom he perceived to be linked with deity. This nearness to things unseen caused him to look over his past life. He was calm despite the confusion of the night, for he was not a man to be frightened; but conscience, which in him was quick and prompt from the very habit of obedience, reviewed his past life, judged it and condemned it, and he felt that he was a lost man because of his multiplied shortcomings before the living God, whose servants were there present. For this reason he cried out, "Sirs, what must I do to be saved?" It was none other than the blessed and eternal Spirit, unfolding before him his life which he had thought to be so correct, making him to see the evil of it, and striking him down with a sense of guilt and a dread of consequent punishment. So far we trace his convictions to an awakened conscience visited by the Spirit of God.

His full conversion grew out of the further instructions of the apostles. That answer was very like his short question in fullness of meaning: "Believe on the Lord Jesus Christ, and thou shalt be saved, and thy house." This was condensed gospel for him; and then followed a blessed commentary upon it, when the apostle spoke the word of the Lord both to him and to all his house; all this lit up his mind which was already willing to receive the truth, a mind which, from the very habit of obedience, was quick and prompt to accept the sway of the Lord Jesus. He received the word in the love of it most sweetly, God the Holy Spirit blessing it to him while he listened. There was plain teaching, and a simple heart to receive it, and the two together made quick work of it, and made resident that strange midnight which was henceforth in that house regarded as the beginning of days.

Now, dear friend, I want you to thank God for the circumstances which surround any man's conversion, for all things are well ordered. If the Lord has been pleased to call you by his grace, do not begin judging your conversion because the circumstances were not very remarkable, and do not suspect your friend's sincerity because there was no earthquake in connection with his new birth, for the Lord may not be in the earthquake, nor in the wind, nor in the fire, but in that "still small voice" which calls the heart to Jesus. The matter is not how you came to Christ, but are you there? It is not *what* brought you so much as *who* brought you. Did the Spirit of God lead you to repentance, and are you resting at the cross? If so, then, whether, like Lydia, your heart was gently opened, or, like this jailor, you were startled and awakened, and thus made to perceive grand truths to which you had been a stranger before, it does not matter so long as Christ is believed in and your heart yields itself to his blessed sway.

III. Our third point—and may the Spirit of God help us in it—is to notice WHAT SORT OF CONVERT THIS MAN MADE.

First, you are quite sure he made a very *believing* convert. The gospel command came to him—"Believe in the Lord Jesus Christ, and thou shalt be saved, and thy house"; and he did believe, believed firmly, without raising questions or discussions, without delays, or hesitations. How many there are among those whose conversion we seek after, who meet us always with a "but." We put the truth plainly, and they reply, "Yes, but—." Then we go over it again, and put it in another shape, and they still say "but." We tell them that salvation is by believing in Jesus Christ, and they answer "but." This man, however, had no "buts." He was told to believe and he did believe, and who would not who knows how true the gospel is? Who will not believe what is true? Who will not rely upon that which is divinely certified? Why should we reject what thousands have proved to be true by a gladsome experience? Ah, unbelief, what an enemy thou art to multitudes who hear the gospel! But thou wast utterly cast out of the jailor: he heard the command to believe, and, though he had received slender instruction, he nevertheless believed unto eternal life. He was a convert full of faith.

Next, what a *humble* Christian he was. He fell down at the feet of the servants of God, not feeling himself worthy to stand in their presence; and then, though their jailor, he took them up into his house and waited upon them with gladness. The man who is really born again does not demand the best seat in the synagogue, nor disdain to perform the meanest service. It is poor evidence of a renewed heart when a man must always be the fore- horse in the team, or else he will do nothing at all. He who knows the Lord loves to sit at Christ's feet: the lower the place the better for him. He is glad even to wash the saints' feet, yea, he thinks it an honor. If you, Christian people, must dispute about precedence always fight for the lowest place. If you aspire to be last and least you will not have many competitors; there will be no need to demand a poll, for the lowest seat is undisputed. Humility is the way to a peaceful life, and the jailor began to practice it in his behavior to his prisoners, who were *nor* his pastors.

What a *ready* convert he was! In that one midnight he passed through several stages: hearing, believing, baptizing, service, rejoicing and fellowship, and all within an hour. No long waiting for him! I wish more converts were like him. What slow-coaches we have to deal with. You travel by broad-wheeled wagon to heaven, even you who rush along by express train in the world's business. Yes, you must attend to the world, and my Lord and Master may wait your convenience, as Felix put it; but this should not be. As soon as you know what your Lord would have you to do, every moment of unnecessary delay is a sin. The jailor had been prompt in other duties, and he was just as decided with regard to divine things: he was such a convert as we like to have in our churches, to set an example of quick obedience to the Great Captain of our salvation. Soldierly habits sanctified by grace are greatly needed in the church of God; would God we saw more of them.

Then, see, what a *practical* convert he was! "He took them the same hour of the night and washed their stripes, and set meat before them." All that he could do he did at once, and his wife and children were all busy to help him. It is not easy to fit up a feast in the middle of the night, but the good wife did her best; cold meats were brought forth from the stores, and such good cheer as they had was set out, so that the two good men, who, no doubt, needed refreshment, were sufficiently supplied. I think I see that midnight festival even now. How the young children caught up every word which was spoken by the holy men, and how glad they were to see them at their table! They all believed and were all baptized, and therefore they were all eager to do something for the men of God. How pleased they were to fetch the good men up into the best parlor—how eager to put them into the easiest chairs and let them sit in comfort, or recline at their ease. They did not wait till morning, but showed kindness without delay. This is the sort of convert the church needs: one who delights to serve the Lord, and is no sooner converted than he sets to work in his own hearty way. May the Lord send us scores of such conversions!

Friend, have you ever done anything for the Lord or his cause? "No, sir. Nobody has set me anything to do." What, live in these busy times, and want somebody to find you Christian employment! Why, you are not worth setting to work! He who lives in a great city and cannot find something to do for God, had better not get off his knees till he has asked his Lord to have mercy upon his lazy soul. Here are people dying all round us, and being lost forever, through ignorance and drunkenness and sin of every kind, and yet a young man of one-and-twenty stands up and says that he cannot find anything to do! You are idle. You are very idle. Does not Solomon say, "Whatsoever thy hand findeth to do, do it with thy might"? You need not open your eyes to find good work to do, only put out your hand and there it is. For the love of Jesus, begin to serve him as this jailor and his wife and family did.

Notice again that they were very *joyful* converts. He "rejoiced, believing in God with all his house." The apostle was happy that night. His poor back was smarting, but his heart was leaping within him; and Silas too, who had shared the scourging, he also shared the joy. How lovingly the jailor looked upon his two instructors, how tenderly he washed their stripes. As he had thrown them into the inner prison, so he brought them into his own house. What overflowing joy was in his heart! Methinks while he was waiting at the table he would every now and then stop and wonder at what grace had done. Would he not ask the apostle to teach him that psalm which had been sung below stairs? I am sure he would have sung heartily had he known that hymn which you so much delight in, wherein each one declares, "I am so glad that Jesus loves me." Joy ruled at that midnight feast, and well it might, for the prison had become a palace, and the jailor an heir of heaven.

This man was an *influential* convert, for through his conversion, all his house was led to believe; and he was also a *sensible* convert, which is worth notice, for it is not every Christian man that is wise and prudent. Some zealous people are in a hurry to give up their secular callings. Such would say, "I cannot be a jailor any longer. I must give it up." A Roman jailor would have much to do which would grate upon Christian feelings, but there was nothing positively wrong in the office. Somebody must be jailor, and who so fit for the post as a man who knows the Lord and will therefore manifest a gentle, humane spirit? Who so fit to have poor creatures entrusted to him as one who will not swear at them, or treat them roughly, but who will seek their good? Why, methinks, if a man wanted to be a missionary to those who needed him most, he might desire to be a sailor, for he would be sure to get at the very people who most require the gospel. The Philippian convert was in his right place, and instead of saying, "Ah, I must give up my situation, and live with Christian people," he was wise enough to stay at the jail, and abide in his calling. Observe that when the magistrates tell him that Paul is to go he does not violate their order out of zeal for the faith. He had no right to keep Paul as a guest in his house against the magistrates' will, or he would gladly have retained him; but being bound by his office and by the fact that his apartments were part of the jail, when Paul was bidden to go, he said to him, "Now, therefore, go in peace."

The words look somewhat curt, but no doubt he uttered them in such a kind and courteous manner that the apostle quite understood him. Then Paul went down to Lydia's house, and I dare say the jailor came down to see him there; so that if they could not meet at the jail without breach of regulations, they could meet at Lydia's hospitable abode. He was quite right in maintaining the discipline of the jail and his sincere affection for the apostle at the same time.

My own belief is that he and Lydia were ever afterwards two of the kindest friends that the apostle ever had, and were chief among those who contributed of their substance to his necessities. Paul took no money from any but the Philippians. Though other churches offered to contribute, Paul declined; but when the Philippians sent to him once and again, he accepted their gifts as a sacrifice of sweet smell. He said within himself, "All the family send this gift; all Lydia's household and all the jailer's household are believers, so that no member of the family will grudge what is sent to me." One likes to see brought into the Christian church those who will continue in their business and make money for Jesus Christ, and lay themselves out to serve the Lord in a practical fashion. Many a man gets into a pulpit and spoils a congregation who, if he had stuck to his business and made money that he might help the poor or aid the cause of missions or support the church of God, would have been more truly serving the great cause. He was a sensible convert, this jailor, and I rejoice in him.

And now, if I have been addressing anybody not a jailor, but a person in a position of trust, and if you have a feeling that you have done faithfully, I am glad of it, I am not going to dispute your claim to integrity towards man, nor to undervalue honesty and faithfulness; but oh, remember, you need to be saved. Notwithstanding your moral excellence you will be lost unless you believe in the Lord Jesus Christ. Do see to this. May the Holy Spirit lead you at once to accept the gospel of grace, for you need it even as others. May you become a firm believer in Jesus, and may the Church find in you a willing and earnest helper.

6

Onesimus;

or,

The Runaway Servant

"I beseech thee for my son Onesimus, whom I have begotten in my bonds: which in time past was to thee unprofitable, but now profitable to thee and to me: whom I have sent again: thou therefore receive him, that is, mine own bowels: whom I would have retained with me, that in thy stead he might have ministered unto me in the bonds of the gospel: but without thy mind would I do nothing; that thy benefit should not be as it were of necessity, but willingly. For perhaps he therefore departed for a season, that thou shouldest receive him for ever; not now as a servant, but above a servant, a brother beloved, specially to me, but how much more unto thee, both in the flesh and in the Lord?" (Phil. 1:10–16).

Onesimus was a runaway servant in Rome, but he had been converted under Paul's preaching in that great city, and henceforth the apostle regarded him as his own son. I do not know why Onesimus when he reached Rome found his way to Paul. Perhaps he went to him as a great many scapegraces have come to me—because their fathers or relatives knew me; and so, as Onesimus's master had known Paul, the servant applied to his master's friend, perhaps to beg some little help in his extremity. Anyhow, Paul seized the opportunity and preached the gospel to him, and the runaway slave, became a believer in the Lord Jesus Christ. Paul watched him, admired the character of his convert, was glad to be served by him, and became intensely attached to him. When he thought it right that he should return to his master, Philemon, he took a deal of trouble to compose a letter of apology for him, which we now call "the Epistle to Philemon." Paul, as you know, was not accustomed to write letters with his own hand, but dictated to an amanuensis. It is supposed that he had an affection of the eyes, and therefore when he did write he used large capital letters, for he says in one of his shorter epistles, "Ye see how large a letter I have written unto you with my own hand." The letter to Philemon, at least, part of it, was not dictated, but was written by his own hand. See the eighteenth and nineteenth verses—"If he have wronged thee, or oweth thee ought, put that on mine account; I Paul have written it with mine own hand, I will repay it." It is the only note of hand which I recollect in Scripture, but there it is—an IOU for whatever amount Onesimus may have stolen.

Let us cultivate a large-hearted spirit, and sympathize with new converts when we find them in trouble through past wrong-doing. It is not ours to say that it serves them right, but to see how we can extricate them from their difficulties. Let us try and set the fallen ones on their feet again, and give them, as we say," a fair start in the world." If God has forgiven them, surely we may, and if Jesus Christ has received them they cannot be too bad for us to receive. Let us do for them what Jesus would have done had he been here, so shall we truly be the disciples of Jesus.

Thus, I introduce the text, and we notice concerning it, first, that it contains *a singular instance of divine grace*. Secondly, it brings before us *a case of sin overruled*. And, thirdly, it may be regarded as *example of relationship improved by* for now Onesimus, who had been a slave for a season, would abide with Philemon all his lifetime, and be no more a servant but a brother beloved.

I. First, let us look at Onesimus as AN INSTANCE OF DIVINE GRACE.

We see the grace of God in his *election*. He was a slave. In those days slaves were very ignorant, untaught, and degraded. Being barbarously used, they were for the most part themselves sunk in the lowest barbarism, neither did their masters attempt to raise them out of it. It is possible that Philemon's endeavor to do good to Onesimus may have been irksome to the man, and he may therefore have fled from his house. His master's prayers, warnings, and Christian regulations may have been disagreeable to him, and therefore he ran away. He wronged his master, which he could scarcely have done if he had not been treated to some extent as a confidential servant. Possibly the unusual kindness of Philemon, and the trust he reposed in his slave may have been too much for his untrained nature. We know not what he stole, but evidently he had taken something, for the apostle says, "If he hath wronged thee, or oweth thee ought, put that on mine account." He ran away from Colossae, therefore, and, thinking that he would be less likely to be discovered by the ministers of justice, he sought the city of Rome, which was then as large as London now is, and perhaps larger. There in those back slums of the Jews' quarter Onesimus could hide; or he would obtain shelter amongst those gangs of thieves which infested the imperial city. He thought that he would not be known or be heard of any more, and could live the free and easy life of one who has no ties, and no particular calling. Yet, mark you, the Lord looked out of heaven with an eye of love, and set that eye on Onesimus. Oh that he may look on any reckless youth who has left his father's house because he cannot bear the just restraints of the parental rule.

Were there no free men, that God must elect a slave? Were there no faithful servants, that he must choose one who had embezzled his master's money? Were there none of the educated and polite, that he must needs look upon a barbarian? Were there none among the moral and the excellent, that infinite love should fix itself upon this degraded being, who was now mixed up with the very scum of society? And what the scum of society was in old Rome I should not like to think. The upper classes were about as brutalized in their general habits as we can very well conceive; and what the lowest must have been, none of us can tell. Bad as we now are, society is by no means so unutterably vile in its habits as in the days of Nero and Caligula: indeed, men would not tolerate in the most filthy haunts of vice the deeds which were then done openly by all ranks. The world was deeply depraved, and Onesimus was among the worst of the worst; and yet eternal love, which passed by kings and princes, and left Pharisees and Sadducees, philosophers and magi, to stumble in the dark, fixed its eye upon this poor benighted creature that he might be made a vessel unto honor, fit for the Master's use.

This is ever the way of grace, it glories in selecting those whom human partiality would have passed by, that it may abase the pride of man and reveal the sovereignty of God.

"I will have mercy on whom I will have mercy, and I will have compassion on whom I will have compassion," are sentences which roll like thunder alike from the cross of Calvary and from the mount of Sinai. The Lord is a sovereign, and doeth as he pleases. Let us admire that marvelous electing love which selected such a one as Onesimus!

Grace also is to be observed, in the next place, in the *conversion* of this runaway slave.

Look at him! How unlikely he appears to become a convert. He was an Asiatic slave of about the same grade as an ordinary Lascar, or "heathen Chinee." He was, however, worse than the ordinary Lascar, who is certainly free, and probably an honest man, if he is nothing else: this man was a slave and a thief, and was without home or family, for after taking his master's property he had left all the associations of the town in which he had been brought up, and had run away to Rome. He was like a derelict vessel, without owner or helmsman, drifting to sure destruction, with no man to care what became of him. But everlasting love means to convert the man, and converted he shall be. He had probably heard Paul preach at Colossae, but he had not been impressed by the word. At Rome, Paul was not preaching in St. Peter's: it was in no such noble building, but it was probably down there at the back of the Palatine hill, where the Praetorian Guard had their lodgings, and where there was a military prison called the Praetorium. In a bare room in the barrack prison Paul sat with a soldier chained to his hand, preaching to all who were admitted to hear him, and there it was that the grace of God reached the heart of the wild runaway, the embezzler of his master's goods. What a change it made in him immediately! Now you see him repenting of his sin, grieved to think he has wronged a good master, vexed at his own folly, and confounded as he beholds the depravity of his heart as well as the error of his life. He weeps as Paul preaches of judgment to come: the glance of joy is in his eye as he hears of redeeming love: and from that heavy heart a load is taken. New thoughts light up his dark mind; his heart is relieved from despair, his face is changed, and the entire man renewed, for the grace of God has in his case turned the lion to a lamb, the raven to a dove.

Some of us, I have no doubt, are quite as wonderful instances of divine election and effectual calling as Onesimus was. Let us, therefore, record the loving-kindness of the Lord, and let us say to ourselves, "Christ shall have the glory of it. The Lord hath done it; and unto the Lord be honor, world without end."

The grace of God was conspicuous *in the character which it wrought in Onesimus* upon his conversion, for he appears to have been helpful, useful, and profitable. So Paul says. Paul was willing to have had him as an associate, and this is greatly in his favor; it is not every man that is converted that we should altogether choose as a companion. There are odd people to be met with who will go to heaven we have no doubt, for they are pilgrims on the right way, but we have no wish for much of their company on the road. They are cross-grained, crabbed, and cantankerous, with a something about them that one's nature can no more delight in than the palate can take pleasure in nauseous physic. They are a sort of spiritual hedgehogs; they are alive and useful, and no doubt they illustrate the wisdom and patience of God, but they are not good companions: one would not like to carry them in his bosom. But Onesimus was evidently of a kind, tender, loving spirit. Paul called him, "my son Onesimus, whom I have begotten in my bonds," and even says, "Receive him, that is, mine own bowels." He said that he would have retained him that he might have ministered to him in the bonds of the gospel, had he not thought it better to have his master's full consent first. When Paul bade him return, was it not a clear proof of change of heart in Onesimus that he would go back?

Away as he was in Rome he might have passed on from one town to another, have avoided the authorities, and have remained perfectly free; but feeling that he was under obligation to his master—especially since he had injured him—he takes Paul's advice and returns to his old position. He will go back, and take a letter of apology or introduction to his master, for he feels that it is his duty to make reparation for the wrong he has done. A resolve to make restitution of former wrongs is a test of sincerity in people who profess to be converted. If they have taken money or goods wrongfully they ought to repay it; it were well if they returned sevenfold. If we have in any way robbed or wronged another, the first instincts of grace in the heart will suggest compensation in all ways within our power. Do not think it is to be got over by saying, "God has forgiven me, and therefore I may leave it."

No, dear friend; but inasmuch as God has forgiven you, try to undo all the wrong, and prove the sincerity of your repentance by restitution. So Onesimus was content to go back to Philemon, and work out his term of years with him, or do as Philemon wishes, for though he might have preferred to wait upon Paul, his service was due to the man whom he had injured. That showed a gentle, humble, honest, upright spirit; and let Onesimus be commended for it: nay, let the grace of God be extolled for it. Look at the difference between the man who robbed his master and ran away and the new man who came back of his own accord to be profitable to the master he had defrauded.

What wonders the grace of God has done! What wonders the grace of God can do! Many plans are employed in the world for the reformation of the wicked and the reclaiming of the fallen, and to every one of these, as far as they are rightly bottomed, we wish good success; for whatsoever things are lovely, and pure, and of good report, we wish them God speed. But mark this word—the true reforming of the drunkard lies in giving him a new heart: and the real reclaiming of the harlot is to be found in a renewed nature. Let others do what they will, but God forbid that I should glory save in the cross of our Lord Jesus Christ. I see certain of my brethren fiddling away at the branches of the tree of vice with their wooden saws; but, as for the gospel, it lays the axe at the root of every tree in the whole forest of evil, and if it be fairly received into the heart it fells all the upas trees at once, and causes instead of them the fir tree, the pine tree, and the box tree together, to spring up and flourish, to beautify the house of our Master's glory. Let us, since we see what the Spirit of God can do for men, publish abroad the gospel of the grace of God, and extol the Lord with all our might.

II. And now, secondly, we have in our text, and its connection, a very interesting *INSTANCE OF SIN OVERRULED*.

Onesimus had no right to rob his master and run away; but God was pleased to make use of that crime for his conversion. His dishonesty drove him to Rome, and so led him to the spot where Paul was preaching, and thus it brought him to Christ, and to his right mind. Now, when we speak of this, we must be cautious, lest we seem to excuse the guilt which incidentally led up to the great blessing. When Paul says, "Perhaps he departed for a season, that thou shouldest receive him for ever," he does not apologize for the absconding of Onesimus, but he generously suggests a reason for his master's forgiving him the wrong. He does not make it out that Onesimus did right—not for a moment. Sin is sin, and, whatever it may be overruled to do, yet sin is still evil and only evil. The crucifixion of our Savior has brought the greatest conceivable blessings upon mankind, yet none the less it was "with wicked hands" that they took Jesus and crucified him. The selling of Joseph into Egypt was the means in the hand of God of the preservation of Jacob, and his sons, in the time of famine; but his brethren were none the less guilty for having sold him for a slave.

Let it always be remembered that the faultiness or virtue of an act is not contingent upon the result of that act. If, for instance, a man who has been set on a railway to turn the switch forgets to do it, you call it a very great crime if the train comes to mischief and a dozen people are killed. Yes, but the crime is the same if nobody is killed. It is not the result of the carelessness, but the carelessness itself which deserves punishment. If it were the man's duty to turn the switch in such-and-such a way, and his not doing so should even by some strange accident turn to the saving of life, the man would be equally blameworthy. There would be no credit due to him for good results, for if his duty lies in a certain line his fault also lies in a certain line, namely, the neglecting of that duty. So if God overrules sin for good, as he sometimes does, it is none the less sin; only there is so much the more glory to the wonderful wisdom and grace of God who, out of evil, brings forth good. Onesimus is not excused, then, for having embezzled his master's goods, nor for having left him without right; he is still a transgressor, but God's grace is glorified.

Remember, too, that when Onesimus left his master he was performing an action the results of which, in all probability, would have been ruinous to himself. He was living as a trusted dependent beneath the roof of a kind master, who had a church in his house. If I read the epistle rightly, he had a godly mistress and a godly master, and he had an opportunity of learning the gospel continually; but this reckless young blade, very likely, could not bear it, and could have lived more contentedly with a heathen master, who would have beaten him one day and made him drunk another. He threw away the opportunities of salvation, and went to Rome, and he doubtless went into the lowest part of the city, and associated, as I have already told you, with the most depraved company.

Now, had it come to pass that he had joined in the insurrections of the slaves which took place frequently about that time, as he in all probability would have done had not grace prevented, he would have been put to death as others had been. Short shrift was given to rebel slaves in Rome: half suspect a man, and off with his head was the rule towards slaves and vagabonds. Onesimus was just the very man that would have been likely to be hurried to death and to eternal destruction. When a young man suddenly leaves home and goes to London, we know what that means. When his friends do not know where he is, and he does not want them to know, we are aware, within a little, where he is and what he is at. What Onesimus was doing I do not know, but he was certainly doing his best to ruin himself. His course, therefore, is to be judged, as far as he is concerned, by what it was likely to bring him to; and though it did not bring him to ruin, that was no credit to him, but all the honor of his rescue was due to the overruling power of God.

See how God overruled all. Thus had the Lord purposed. Nobody shall be able to touch the heart of Onesimus but Paul. Onesimus is living at Colossae; Paul cannot come there, he is in prison. It is needful, then, that Onesimus should be brought to Paul. Suppose the kindness of Philemon's heart had prompted him to say to Onesimus, "I want you to go to Rome, and find Paul out and hear him." This naughty servant would have said, "I am not going to risk my life to hear a sermon. If I go with a letter I shall deliver it, but I want none of his preaching."

Sometimes, when persons are brought to hear a preacher, with the view of their being converted, if they have any idea that such is the object, it is about the last thing likely to happen, because they resolve to be fire-proof against the gospel, and so the preaching does not come home to them: and it would, probably, have been so with Onesimus. No, no, he was not to be won in that Way, he must be drawn to Rome by some other method. How shall it be done? Well, the devil shall do it, not knowing that he will be losing a willing servant thereby. The devil tempts Onesimus to steal. Onesimus yields to the temptation, and then, fearful of being discovered, he makes tracks for Rome as quickly as he can, and gets down among the back slums, and there he feels what the prodigal felt—a hungry belly, which to many is one of the best preachers in the world: their conscience is reached through their being made to feel the result of their wrong-doing. Being very hungry, not knowing what to do, and no man giving anything to him, he considers whether there is anybody in Rome that would pity him. He does not know a single person in the city, and is likely to starve.

Perhaps one morning a Christian woman was going to hear Paul, and seeing this poor man fainting upon the steps of a temple, she went to him and spoke about his soul, "Soul," said he, "I care nothing about that, but my body would thank you for something to eat. I am starving." She replied, "Come with me, then," and she gave him bread, and as she did so she said, "I do this for Jesus Christ's sake." "Jesus Christ!" he said, "I have heard of him. I used to hear of him over at Colossae." "Whom did you hear speak of him?" the woman would ask. "Why, a short man, with weak eyes, a great preacher, named Paul, who used to come to my master's house." "Why, I am going to hear him preach," the woman would say, "will you go with me?" "Yes, I think I should like to see the man again. He always had a kind word to say to the poor." So he goes in and pushes his way among the soldiers, and Paul's Master incites the apostle to speak the right word. It may have been so, or it may have been the other way—that not knowing anybody else, he remembered that Paul was there a prisoner, and went to the prison to ask his help. He goes down to the Praetorium and finds him there, tells him of his extreme poverty, and Paul reasons with him and so he becomes a Christian. It may have been in either of these ways that the man's heart was won; at any rate, the Lord must have Onesimus in Rome to hear Paul, and the sin of Onesimus, though perfectly voluntary on his part, so that God had no hand in it, was yet overruled by a mysterious providence to bring him where the gospel was blest to his soul.

Now, I want to speak to some of you Christian people about this matter. Have you a son who has left home? Is he a wilful, wayward young man, who has gone away because he could not bear the restraints of a Christian family? It is a sad thing it should be so—a very sad thing, but do not despond, much less despair about him. You do not know where he is, but God does; and you cannot follow him, but the Spirit of God can. He is going a voyage to Shanghai. Ah, there may be a Paul at Shanghai who is to be the means of his salvation, and as that Paul is not in England your son, must go there. Is it to Australia that he is sailing? There may be a word spoken there by the blessing of God to your son, which is the only word that will ever reach him. I cannot speak it, nobody in London can speak it; but a man in the far-off land will be directed to do so; and God, therefore, is letting your boy go away in all his willfulness and folly that he may be brought under the means of grace, which will prove effectual to his salvation. Many a sailor boy has been wild, reckless, Godless, Christless, and at last has got into a foreign hospital.

Ah, if his mother knew that he was down with the yellow fever, how sad her mind would be, for she would conclude that her dear son will die away from home, and that she will not even have the mournful privilege of weeping over his grave. Yet, perhaps, the mother's fears are all groundless, for it is just in that hospital that God means to save her boy. A sailor writes to me somewhat as follows. He says, "My mother asked me to read a chapter of the Bible every day, but I never did. I got into the hospital at Savannah, and, when I lay there, a man near to me was dying; but before he departed he said to me, 'Mate, could you come here? I want to speak to you. I have got something here that is very precious to me. I was a wild fellow, but reading this packet of sermons has brought me to the Savior, and I am dying with a good hope through grace. Now, when I am dead and gone, will you take these sermons and read them, and may God bless them to you. And will you write a letter to the man who preached those sermons, to tell him that through them I have learned to die in peace.'"

It was a packet of my sermons, and God was pleased to make them useful to that young man, so that he became a Christian. I have no doubt whatever that he was sent to the hospital by a gracious providence that there he might receive the books which the Holy Spirit would employ in his regeneration. You do not know, dear mother, you do not know the deep designs of divine grace. The worst thing that can occur to a young man is sometimes the best thing that can happen to him. I have sometimes thought, when I have seen young men of position and wealth taking to racing and all sorts of dissipation, "Well, it is a dreadfully bad thing, but it may by a roundabout process lead to repentance. They will get through their money very quickly, and when they have come down to beggary, they will be like the young gentleman in the parable who returned to his father because he could not live away from him. 'When he had spent all, there arose a mighty famine in that land, and he began to be in want. And he said, "I will arise and go to my father."'" Perhaps the disease which often follows upon vice—perhaps the poverty which comes like an armed man after extravagance and debauch—is but love in another form, sent to compel the sinner to come to himself and consider his ways, and seek the ever-merciful God.

You Christian people often see the little gutter children—the poor little Arabs in the street, and you feel much pity for them, as well you may; but I have often thought that the poverty and hunger of these poor little children has a louder voice to most hearts than their vice and ignorance. God knew that we were not ready and able to hear the cry of the child's soul, and so he added the child's hunger of body to that cry, that it might pierce our hearts. People could live in sin, and be happy after their own poor fashion, if they were well-to-do and rich; and if sin did not make parents poor and wretched, and their children miserable, we should not so clearly see it, and therefore we should not arouse ourselves to grapple with it. It is a benefit in some diseases when the patient can throw the complaint out upon the skin: and oftentimes outward sin and outward misery are a sort of throwing out of the disease of natural depravity, so that the eye of those who know where the healing medicine is to be had is thereby drawn to the mischief, and the soul's secret malady is dealt with.

Onesimus might have stopped at home, and he might never have been a thief, and yet he might have been lost through self-righteousness. But now he has absconded his sin is visible. The scapegrace has displayed the depravity of his heart, and now it is that he comes under Paul's eye and Paul's prayer, and becomes converted. Do not, I pray you, ever despair of man or woman or child because you see their sin upon the surface of their character. On the contrary, say to yourself, "This is placed where I can see it, that I may pray about it. It is made sadly visible to my eye that I may the more earnestly concern myself to bring this poor soul to Jesus Christ, the mighty Savior, who can save the most forlorn sinner." Look at vice with the eye of earnest, active benevolence, and rouse yourselves to conquer it. Our duty is to hope on and to pray on so long as life lingers in the object of our prayer. We cannot tell the designs of God, but we may rest assured that believing prayer cannot fail. Perhaps the boy has been so wayward that his sin may come to a crisis, and a new heart may be given him. Perhaps your daughter's evil has been developed that the Lord may convince her of sin and bring her to the Savior's feet. At any rate, if the case be ever so bad, hope in God and pray on.

III. Once more. Our text may be viewed as AN EXAMPLE OF RELATIONS IMPROVED. "He therefore departed for a season, that thou shouldest receive him for ever; *not now as a servant, but a brother beloved, specially to me, but how much more unto thee?*" We are a long while learning great truths. Perhaps Philemon had not found out that it was wrong for him to hold a slave. Some men who were very good in their time did not know the sin of it. John Newton did not know that he was doing wrong by engaging in the slave trade, and George

Whitefield, when he left slaves, which had been willed to him, to the orphanage of Savannah, did not think for a moment that he was doing anything more than if he had been dealing with horses, or gold and silver. Public sentiment was not enlightened, although the gospel has always struck at the very root of slavery. The essence of gospel precept is that we are to do to others as we would that they should do to us, and nobody would wish to be another man's slave, and therefore he has no right to hold another man in bondage.

Perhaps when Onesimus ran away and came back again, this letter of Paul may have opened Philemon's eyes as to his own position. He may have been an excellent master, and have trusted his servant, and treated him not as a slave, but as a confidential servant; but perhaps he had not regarded him as a brother man; and now Onesimus has come back he will be a better servant, but Philemon will also be a better master, and a slave-holder no longer. He will regard his former servant as a brother in Christ.

Now, this is what the grace of God does when it comes into a family. It does not alter the relations; it does not give the child a right to be pert, and refuse obedience to his parents; it does not give the father a right to lord it over his family without wisdom and love, for it tells him that he is not to provoke his children to anger, lest they be discouraged; it does not give the servant the right to be a master, neither does it take away from the master his position, or allow him to exaggerate his authority, but all round it softens and sweetens. Rowland Hill used to say that he would not give a halfpenny for a man's piety if his dog and his cat were not better off after he was converted. There was much weight in that remark. Everything in the house goes better when grace oils the wheels. The mistress is, perhaps, naturally rather sharp, quick, tart; but her constitution is marvelously sweetened when she receives the grace of God. The servant may be apt to loiter, may be late up of a morning, very slovenly, fond of a gossip at the door; but, if she is truly converted, all that kind of thing comes to an end. She is conscientious, and attends to her duty as she ought. The master, when he is a truly Christian man, has gentleness, suavity, and considerateness about him. The husband is the head of the wife, but when renewed by grace he is a very loving head. The wife also keeps her place, and seeks, by gentleness and wisdom to make the house as happy as she can. I do not believe in your religion, dear friend, if it belongs to the chapel and the prayer meeting, and not to your home. The best religion in the world is that which smiles at the table, works at the sewing machine, and is pleasant in the chimney-corner and amiable in the drawing-room. Give me the religion which blacks boots, and shines them well; cooks the food so that it can be eaten; measures out yards of calico, and does not make them half-an-inch short; sells a hundred yards of an article, and does not label ninety as a hundred, as many tradespeople do.

That is true Christianity which affects the whole of life. If we are truly Christians we shall be changed in our relationships to our fellow men, and hence we shall regard those whom we call our inferiors with quite a different eye. It is wrong in Christian people when they are so sharp upon little faults that they see in servants, especially if they are Christian servants. That is not the way to correct them. Some mistresses see a little something wrong, and they are down upon the poor girls, as if they had been guilty of murder or high treason. If your Master, and mine, were to treat us in that style, I wonder how long we should be found in his service. How quick some are in discharging their maids for small errors. No excuse, no trying her again: she must go, and where she goes is no concern of ours. Is this doing as a Christian should do?

Many a young man has been turned out of a situation for the veriest trifle by a Christian employer, who must have known that he would expose his servant to all sorts of risks; and many a domestic has been sent adrift as if she were a dog, with no sort of thought whether another position could be found, and without anything being done to prevent her going astray. Do let us think of others, especially of those whom Christ loves even as he does us. Philemon might have said, "No, no, I don't take you back, Onesimus, not I. Once bit, twice shy, sir, I never ride a broken-kneed horse. You stole my money; I am not going to have your finger in my till a second time." I have heard that style of talk, have not you? Did you ever *feel* like it yourself? If you have, go home and pray to God to get such a feeling out of you, for it is bad stuff to harbor in your soul. You cannot take such hard selfishness to heaven, and it is a great defilement to you on earth. When the Lord Jesus Christ has forgiven you so freely, are you to take your fellow-servant by the throat and say," Pay me what thou owest?" God forbid that we should continue in such a temper. Be pitiful, easily entreated, ready to forgive. It is a deal better that you should suffer a wrong than do a wrong: much better that you should overlook a fault which you might have noticed, than notice a fault which you ought to have overlooked.

I want to bring forward one more point, and then I have done. If the mysterious providence of God was to be seen in Onesimus getting to Rome, may there not be a providence in your reading this book at this time, or in your being at this hour where you may hear the gospel? People come to the Tabernacle who never meant to come. If anyone had prophesied that they would listen to the gospel they would have poured contempt upon the prophecy, and yet they come. With all manner of twists and turns they have gone about, but they have been landed where the truth is proclaimed. Did you ever miss a train, and so step in to a service to while away the time? Was the sailing of your ship delayed when you little expected it, and so were you able to hear a sermon? I do pray you, then, consider this question with your own heart—"Does not God mean to bless me? Has he not given me an opportunity to yield my heart to Jesus as Onesimus did?"

My dear friend, if thou believest on the Lord Jesus Christ, thou shalt have immediate pardon for all sin, and shalt be saved. The Lord has brought thee in his infinite wisdom where thou canst hear his loving invitation, and I hope that he has also brought thee where thou wilt accept it, and so go thy way altogether changed. Some three years ago I was talking with an aged minister: he began fumbling about in his waistcoat pocket, but he was a long while before he found what he wanted. At last he brought out a letter that was well-nigh worn to pieces, and as he unfolded it, he exclaimed, "God Almighty bless you! God Almighty bless you!" I said, "Friend, what is it?" He said, "I had a son. I thought he would be the stay of my old age, but he disgraced himself, and he went away from me, and I could not tell where he went, only he said he was going to America. He took a ticket to sail for America from the London Docks, but the ship did not sail on the day appointed." This aged minister bade me read the letter, and I read it, and it ran like this: "Father, I am here in America, I have found a situation, and God has prospered me. I write to ask your forgiveness for the thousand wrongs that I have done you, and the grief I have caused you, for, blessed be God, I have found the Savior. I have joined the church of God here, and hope to spend my life in the Redeemer's service. It happened thus: I did not sail for America on the day I expected to start, and having a leisure hour I went down to the Tabernacle to see what it was like, and there God met with me. Mr. Spurgeon said, 'Perhaps there is a runaway son here. The Lord call him by his grace.' And he did call me." "Now," said the old gentleman, as he folded up the letter and put it into his pocket, "that son of mine is dead, and he is in heaven, and I love you, and I shall do so as long as I live, because you were the means of bringing him to Christ." Do I speak to a similar character, or does one of that sort read these pages? The Lord in mercy gives you another opportunity of turning from the error of your ways. I pray you lift your eye at once to heaven, and say, "God be merciful to me a sinner," and he will accept you. Believe in the sinner's Savior and he will be *your* Savior. Then go home to your father and tell him what the grace of God has done for you, and make him wonder at the love which brought you to Christ.

Thus have we brought before you another wonder of grace. Our soul longs, yea, even faints to hear of others in like manner reclaimed. O poor unsaved souls, by the love of Jesus we pray you turn unto him and live. God save you by his Holy Spirit. Amen.

7

The Greatest Wonder of All

"And I was left" (Ezek. 9:8).

Salvation never shines so brightly to any man's eyes as when it comes to himself. Then is grace illustrious indeed when we can see it working with divine power upon ourselves. To our apprehension, our own case is ever the most desperate, and mercy shown to us is the most extraordinary. We see others perish, and wonder that the same doom has not befallen ourselves. The horror of the ruin which we dreaded, and our intense delight at the certainty of safety in Christ unite with our personal sense of unworthiness to make us cry in amazement, "And I was left."

Ezekiel, in vision, saw the slaughtermen smiting right and left at the bidding of divine justice, and as he stood unharmed among the heaps of the slain, he exclaimed with surprise, "I was left." It may be, the day will come when we, too, shall cry with solemn joy, "And I, too, by sovereign grace, am spared while others perish." Special grace will cause us to marvel. Especially will it be so at the last dread day.

Read the story of the gross idolatry of the people of Jerusalem, as recorded in the eighth chapter of Ezekiel's prophecy, and you will not wonder at the judgment with which the Lord at length overthrew the city. Let us set our hearts to consider how the Lord dealt with the guilty people. "Six men came from the way of the higher gate, which lieth toward the north, and every man with a slaughter weapon in his hand." The destruction wrought by these executioners was swift and terrible, and it was typical of other solemn visitations. All through history the observing eye notices lines of justice, red marks upon the page where the Judge of all the earth has at last seen it needful to decree a terrible visitation upon a guilty people. All these past displays of divine vengeance point at a coming judgment even more complete and overwhelming. The past is prophetic of the future. A day is surely coming when the Lord Jesus, who came once to save, will descend a second time to judge. Despised mercy has always been succeeded by deserved wrath, and so must it be in the end of all things. "But who may abide the day of his coming? or who shall stand when he appeareth?" When sinners are smitten, who will be left? He shall lift the balances of justice, and make bare the sword of execution. When his avenging angels shall gather the vintage of the earth, who among us shall exclaim in wondering gratitude, "And I was left"? Such an one will be a wonder of grace indeed; worthy to take rank with those marvels of grace of whom we have spoken in the former discourses of this book. Reader, will- you be an instance of sparing grace, and cry, "And I was left"?

We will use the wonderfully descriptive vision of this chapter that we may with holy fear behold *the character of the doom* from which grace delivers us, and then we will dwell upon the exclamation of our text, "I was left," considering it as the joyful utterance of *the persons who are privileged to escape the destruction.*

By the help of the Holy Spirit, let us first solemnly consider THE TERRIBLE DOOM from which the prophet in vision saw himself preserved, regarding it as a figure of the judgment which is yet to come upon all the world.

Observe, first, that it was *a just* punishment inflicted upon those who had been often warned; a punishment which they wilfully brought upon themselves. God had said that if they set up idols he would destroy them, for he would not endure such an insult to his Godhead. He had often pleaded with them, not with words only, but with severe providences, for their land had been laid desolate, their city had been besieged, and their kings had been carried away captive; but they were bent on backsliding to the worship of their idol gods. Therefore, when the sword of the Lord was drawn from its scabbard, it was no novel punishment, no freak of vengeance, no unexpected execution. So, in the close of life, and at the end of the world, when judgment comes on men, it will be just and according to the solemn warnings of the word of God. When I read the terrible things which are written in God's book in reference to future punishment, especially the awful things which Jesus spoke concerning the place where their worm does not die and their fire is not quenched, I am greatly pressed in spirit. Some there be who sit in judgment upon the great Judge, and condemn the punishment which he inflicts as too severe. As for myself, I cannot measure the power of God's anger; but let it burn as it may, I am sure that it will be just. No needless pang will be inflicted upon a single one of God's creatures: even those who are doomed forever will endure no more than justice absolutely requires, no more than they themselves would admit to be the due reward of their sins, if their consciences would judge aright. Mark you, this is the very hell of hell that men will know that they are justly suffering. To endure a tyrant's wrath would be a small thing compared with suffering what one has brought upon himself by wilful wanton choice of wrong. Sin and suffering are indissolubly bound together in the constitution of nature; it cannot be otherwise, nor ought it to be. It is right that evil should be punished.

Those who were punished in Jerusalem could not turn upon the executioners and say, "We do not deserve this doom!" But every cruel wound of the Chaldean sword and every fierce crash of the Babylonian battle-axe fell on men who in their consciences knew that they were only reaping what they themselves had sown. Brethren, what wonders of grace shall we be if from a judgment which we have so richly deserved we shall be rescued at the last!

Let us notice very carefully that this slaughter was *preceded by a separation* which removed from among the people those who were distinct in character. Before the slaughtermen proceeded to their stern task a man appeared among them clothed in linen with a writer's inkhorn by his side, who marked all those who in their hearts were grieved at the evil done in the city. Until these were marked the destroyers did not commence their work. Whenever the Lord lays bare his arm for war he first gathers his saints into a place of safety. He did not destroy the world by the flood till Noah and his family were safe in the ark. He would not suffer a single fire drop to fall on Sodom till Lot had escaped to Zoar. He carefully preserves his own; nor flood nor flame, nor pestilence, nor famine shall do them ill. We read in the Revelation that the angel said, "Hurt not the earth, neither the sea, nor the trees, till we have sealed the servants of our God in their foreheads." Vengeance must sheathe her sword, till love has housed its darlings. When Christ cometh to destroy the earth, he will first catch away his people. Before the elements shall melt with fervent heat, and the pillars of the universe shall rock and reel beneath the weight of wrathful deity, he will have caught up his elect into the air so that they shall be ever with the Lord. When he cometh he shall divide the nations as a shepherd divideth his sheep from the goats; no sheep of his shall be destroyed: he shall without fail take the tares from among the wheat, but not one single ear of wheat shall be in danger.

Oh that we may be among the selected ones and prove his power to keep us in the day of wrath. May each one of us say amid the wreck of matter and the crash of worlds, "And I was left." Dear friend, are you marked in the forehead, think you? If at this moment my voice were drowned by the trumpet of resurrection, would you be amongst those who awake to safety and glory? Would you be able to say, "The multitude perished around me, but I was left"? It will be so if you hate the sins by which you are surrounded, and if you have received the mark of the blood of Jesus upon your souls; if not, you will not escape, for there is no other door of salvation but his saving name. God grant us grace to belong to that chosen number who wear the covenant seal, the mark of him who counteth up the people.

Next, this judgment was placed *in the Mediator's hands*. I want you to notice this. Observe that, according to the chapter, there was no slaughter done except where the man with the writer's inkhorn led the way. So again we read in the tenth chapter, that "One cherub stretched forth his hand from between the cherubims unto the fire that was between the cherubims, and took thereof and put it into the hands of him that was clothed with linen; who took it, and went out," and cast it over the city. See you this: God's glory of old shone forth between the cherubim, that is to say, over the place of propitiation and atonement, and as long as that glow of light remained no judgment fell on Jerusalem, for God in Christ condemns not. But by-and-by, "The glory of the God of Israel was gone up from the cherub, whereupon he was, to the threshold of the house," and then judgment was near to come. When God no longer deals with men in Christ his wrath burns like fire, and he commissions the ambassador of mercy to be the messenger of wrath. The very man who marked with his pen the saved ones threw burning coals upon the city and led the way for the destruction of the sinful. What does this teach but this—"The Father judgeth no man, but hath committed all judgment unto the Son"? I know of no truth more dreadful to meditate upon. Think of it, ye careless ones: the very

Christ who died on Calvary is he by whom you will be sentenced. God will judge the world by this man Christ Jesus: he it is that will come in the clouds of heaven, and before him shall be gathered all nations; and when those who have despised him shall look upon his face they will be terrified beyond conception. Not the lightnings, not the thunders, not the dreadful sound of the last tremendous trump shall so alarm them as that face of injured love. Then will they cry to the mountains and hills to hide them from the face of him that sitteth upon the throne. Why, it is the face of him that wept for sinners, the face which scoffers stained with bloody drops extracted by the thorny crown, the face of the incarnate God who, in infinite mercy, came to save mankind! But because they have despised him, because they would not be saved, because they preferred their own lusts to infinite love, and would persist in rejecting God's best proof of kindness, therefore will they say, "Hide us from the face," for the sight of that face shall be to them more accusing, and more condemning, than all else besides. How dreadful is this truth! The more you consider it, the more will it fill your soul with terror! Would to God it might drive you to fly to Jesus, for then you will behold him with joy in that day.

This destruction, we are told, *began at the sanctuary*. Suppose the Lord were to visit London in his anger, where would he begin to smite? "Oh," somebody says, "of course the destroying angel would go down to the low music halls and dancing rooms, or he would sweep out the back slums and the drink palaces, the jails and places where women of ill life do congregate." Turn to the Scripture which surrounds our text. The Lord says, "Begin at my sanctuary." Begin at the churches; begin at the chapels; begin at the church members; begin at the ministers; begin at the bishops; begin at those who are teachers of the gospel. Begin at the chief and front of the religious world; begin at the high professors who are looked up to as examples. What does Peter say?" The time is come that judgment must begin at the house of God and if it first begin at us, what shall the end be of them that obey not the gospel of God? And if the righteous scarcely be saved, where shall the ungodly and the sinner appear?"

The first thing the slaughtermen did was to slay the ancient men which were before the temple, even the seventy elders of the people, for they were secret idolaters. You may be sure that the sword which did not spare the chief men and fathers made but short work with the baser sort. Elders of our churches, ministers of Christ, judgment will begin with us; we must not expect to find more lenient treatment than others at the last great assize; nay, rather, if there shall be especially careful testing of sincerity it will be for us who have taken upon ourselves to lead others to the Savior. For this cause let us see well to it that we be not deceived or deceivers, for we shall surely be detected in that day.

To play the hypocrite is to play the fool. Will a man deceive his Maker, or delude the Most High? It cannot be. You church members, all of you, should look well to it, for judgment will begin with you. God's fire is in Zion and his furnace in Jerusalem. In the olden time the people fled to churches and holy places for sanctuary; but how vain will this be when the Lord's avengers shall come forth, since there the havoc will begin! How fiercely shall the sword sweep through the hosts of carnal professors, the men who called themselves servants of God, while they were slaves of the devil; who drank of the cup of the Lord but were drunken with the wine of their own lusts: who could lie and cheat and commit fornication, and yet dared to approach the sacred table of the Lord? What cutting and hewing will there be among the base-born professors of our churches! It were better for such men that they had never been born, or, being born, that their lot had fallen amid heathen ignorance, so that they might have been unable to add sin to sin by lying unto the living God. "Begin at my sanctuary." The word is terrible to all those who have a name to live and are dead. God grant that in such testing times when many fail we may survive every ordeal and through grace exclaim in the end, "And I was left."

After the executioners had begun at the sanctuary it is to be observed that they *did not spare any except those upon whom was the mark*. Old and young, men and women, priests and people, all were slain who had not the sacred sign; and so in the last tremendous day all sinners who have not fled to Christ will perish. Our dear babes that died in infancy we believe to be all washed in the blood of Jesus and all saved; but for the rest of mankind who have lived to years of responsibility there will be only one of two things—they must either be saved because they had faith in Christ, or else the full weight of divine wrath must fall upon them. Either the mark of Christ's pen or of Christ's sword must; be upon every one. There will be no sparing of one man because he was rich, nor of another because he was learned, nor of a third because he was eloquent, nor of a fourth because he was held in high esteem. Those who are mailed with the blood of Christ are safe! Without that mark all are lost! This is the one separating sign—do you wear it? Or will you die in your sins? Low down at once before the feet of Jesus and beseech him to mark you as his own, that so you may be one of those who will joyfully cry, "And I was left."

Now, secondly, I have to call your very particular attention to THE PERSONS WHO ESCAPED, who could each say, "And I was left." We are told that those were marked for mercy who did "sigh and cry for the abominations that were done in the midst thereof." Now we must be very particular about this. It is no word of mine, remember: it is God's word, and therefore I beg you to hear and weigh it for yourselves. We do not read that the devouring sword passed by those quiet people who never did anybody any harm: no mention is made of such an exemption. Neither does the record say that the Lord saved those professors who were judicious, and maintained a fair name and repute until death. No; the only people that were saved were those who were exercised in heart, and that heart-work was of a painful kind: they sighed and cried because of abounding sin. They saw it, protested against it, avoided it, and last of all wept over it continually. Where testimony failed it remained for them to mourn; retiring from public labors they sat them down and sighed their hearts away because of the evils which they could not cure; and when they felt that sighing alone would do no good they took to crying in prayer to God that he would come and put an end to the dreadful ills which brooded over the land.

I would not say a hard thing, but I wonder, if I were able to read the secret lives of professors of religion whether I should find that they all sigh and cry over the sins of others? Are the tenth of them thus engaged? I am afraid that it does not cause some people much anxiety when they see sin rampant around them. They say that they are sorry, but it never frets them much, or causes them as much trouble as would come of a lost sixpence or a cut finger. Did you ever feel as if your heart would break over an ungodly son? I do not believe that you are a Christian man if you have such a son and have not felt an agony on his behalf. Did you ever feel as if you could lay down your life to save that daughter of yours? I cannot believe that you are a Christian woman if you have not sometimes come to that. When you have gone through the street and heard an oath, has not your blood chilled in you? Has not horror taken hold upon you because of the wicked? There cannot be much grace in you if that has not been the case. If you can go up and down in the world fully at ease because you are prospering in business, and things go smoothly with you, if you forget the woe of this city's sin and poverty, and the yet greater woe which cometh upon it, now dwelleth the love of God in you?

The saving mark is only set on those who sigh and cry, and if you are heartless and indifferent there is no such mark on you. "Are we to be always miserable?" asks one. Far from it. There are many other things to make us rejoice, but if the sad state of our fellow men does not cause us to sigh and cry, then we have not the grace of God in us. "Well," says one, "but every man must look to himself." That is the language of Cain—"Am I my brother's keeper?" That kind of talk is in keeping with the spirit of the wicked one and his seed, but the heir of heaven abhors such language. The genuine Christian loves his race, and therefore he longs to see it made holy and happy. He cannot bear to see men sinning, and so dishonoring God and ruining themselves. If we really love the Lord we shall sometimes lie awake at night sighing to think how his name is blasphemed, and how little progress his gospel makes. We shall groan to think that men should despise the glorious God who made them, and who daily loads them with benefits. It sometimes lies upon my heart like a huge mountain which crushes my spirit to think that Jesus should be rejected, and that in this land of Bibles, where Latimer lit a candle which shall never be put out, the old madness is returning, and many are again bowing before the images of jealousy which the priests have set up.

Yes, we have priests among us again. You can see them in their long and ugly garments in every street. And women have begun to confess to them! Shame! Shame! I marvel that the crimson blush does not mantle the cheek of every one who dares to ask or answer the questions appointed for the confessional, and yet the questions are asked, and modesty is outraged, and the multitudes tamely look on. My countrymen are going back to Rome. Their fathers' noble blood was shed for God, and none was left for the veins of their sons. In vain the conflicts of the years gone by! In vain a Cromwell's mighty arm and the purging of the land! In vain the Puritans driven from their pulpits and witnessing in poverty and persecution! England must needs go back again to wear the fetters forged by papal Rome. My God, prevent it! Prevent it if it cost the lives of thousands of us, for we would be glad to die to save our country from so dire a curse. If you never sigh and cry because of the spread of Ritualism, I do not understand you. What stuff are you made of? "Oh, but my business goes on exceedingly well." Yes, and so does mine when souls are saved, but when they are led away into error my business cannot prosper, but I have loss upon loss. I am happy enough when I think Christ's kingdom comes; but nothing beneath the sky can give me solid satisfaction if my Lord's work is at a standstill. I would to God we were all so taken up with the glory of God that the wickedness of mankind would grieve us to the heart.

But it was not their mourning which saved those who escaped—it was the mark which they all received which preserved them from destruction. We must all bear the mark of Jesus Christ. What is that? It is the mark of faith in the atoning blood. That sets apart the chosen of the Lord, and that alone. If you have that mark—and you have it not unless you sigh and cry over the sins of others—then in that last day no sword of justice can come near you. Did you read that word, "But come not nigh any man upon whom is the mark."

Come not even near the marked ones lest they be afraid. The grace-marked man is safe even from the near approach of ill. Christ bled for him, and therefore he cannot, must not, die. Let him alone, ye bearers of the destroying weapons. Just as the angel of death, when he flew through the land of Egypt, was forbidden to touch a house where the blood of the lamb was on the lintel and the two side posts, so is it sure that avenging justice cannot touch the man who is in Christ Jesus. Who is he that condemned since Christ has died? Have you, then, the blood mark? Yes or no. Do not refuse to question yourself upon this point. Do not take it for granted, lest you be deceived. Believe me, your all hangs upon it. If you are not registered by the man clothed in linen you will not be able to say, "And I was left."

This brings me to this last point which I desire to speak of. *What were the prophet's emotions when he said, "And I teas left"?* He saw men falling right and left, and he himself stood like a lone rock amidst a sea of blood; and he cried in wonder, "And I was left."

Let us hear what he further says—"I fell on my face." He lay prostrate with *humility*. Have you a hope that you are saved? Fall on your face, then! See the hell from which you are delivered, and bow before the Lord. Why are you to be saved more than anyone else? Certainly not because of any merit in you. It is due to the sovereign grace of God alone. Fall on your face and own your indebtedness.

> Why was I made to hear thy voice,
> And enter while there's room,
> When thousands make a wretched choice,
> And rather starve than come?

"And I was left."

If a man has been a drunkard, and has at length been led to flee to Christ, when he says, "And I was left," he will feel the hot tears rising to his eyes, for many other drinkers have died in delirium. One who has been a public sinner, when she is saved will not be able to think of it without astonishment. Indeed, each saved man is a marvel to himself. Nobody here wonders more at divine grace in his salvation than I do myself. Why was I chosen, and called, and saved? I cannot make it out, and I never shall; but I will always praise, and bless, and magnify my Lord for casting an eye of love upon me. Will you not do the same, beloved, if you feel that you by grace are left? Will you not fall on your face and bless the mercy which makes you to differ?

What did the prophet do next? Finding that he was left he began to pray for others. "Ah, Lord," said he, "wilt thou destroy all the residue of Israel?" Intercession is an instinct of the renewed heart. When the believer finds that he is safe he must pray for his fellow-men. Though the prophet's prayer was too late, yet, blessed be God, ours will not be. We shall be heard. Pray, then, for perishing men. Ask God, who has spared you, to spare those who are like you. Somebody has said, there will be three great wonders in heaven, first, to see so many there whom we never expected to meet in glory; secondly, to miss so many of whom we felt sure that they must be safe; and thirdly, the greatest wonder of all will be to find ourselves there. I am sure that everyone who has a hope of being in glory feels it to be a marvel; and he resolves, "If I am saved, I will sing the loudest of them all, for I shall owe most to the abounding mercy of God."

Let me ask a few questions, and I have done. The first—and let each man ask it of himself—shall I be left when the ungodly are slain? Answer it now to yourselves. Men, women, children, will you be spared in that last great day? Are you in Christ? Have you a good hope in him? Do not lie unto yourselves. You will be weighed in the balances; will you be found wanting or not?" Shall I be left?" Let that question burn into your souls.

Next, will my relatives be saved? My wife, my husband, my children, my brother, my sister, my father, my mother—will these all be saved? Happy are we who can say, "Yes, we believe they will," as some of us can joyfully hope. But if you have to say, "No, I fear that my boy is unconverted, or that my father is unsaved"; then do not rest till you have wrestled with God for their salvation. Good woman, if you are obliged to say, "I fear my husband is unconverted," join me in prayer. Bow your heads at once and cry unto your God, "Lord, save our children! Lord, save our parents! Lord, save our husbands and wives, our brothers and sisters; and let the whole of our families meet in heaven, unbroken circles, for thy name's sake!"

May God hear that prayer if it has come from the lips of sincerity! I could not endure the thought of missing one of my boys in heaven: I hope I shall see them both there, and therefore I am in deep sympathy with any of you who have not seen your households brought to Christ. Oh for grace to pray earnestly and labor zealously for the salvation of your whole households.

The next earnest enquiry is, if you and your relatives are saved, how about your neighbors, your fellow-workmen, your companions in business? "Oh," say you, "many of them are scoffers. A good many of them are still in the gall of bitterness." A sorrowful fact, but have you spoken to them? It is wonderful what a kind word will do? Have you tried it? Did you ever try to speak to that person who meets you every morning as you go to work? Suppose he should be lost! Oh, it will be a bitter feeling for you to think that he went down to the pit without your making an effort to bring him to God. Do not let it be so. "But we must not be too pushing," says one. I do not know about that. If you saw poor people in a burning house nobody would blame you for being officious if you helped to save them. When a man is sinking in the river, if you jump in and pull him out nobody will say, "You were rude and intrusive, for you were never introduced to him!" This world has been lost, and it must be saved; and we must not mind manners in saving it. We must get a grip of sinking sinners somehow, even if it be by the hair of their heads, ere they sink, for if they sink they are lost forever. They will forgive us very soon for any roughness that we use; but we shall not forgive ourselves if, for want of a little energy, we permit them to die without a knowledge of the truth.

Oh, beloved friends, if you are left while others perish, I beseech you, by the mercies of God, by the bowels of compassion which are in Christ Jesus, by the bleeding wounds of the dying Son of God, do love your fellow men, and sigh and cry about them if you cannot bring them to Christ. If you cannot save them you can weep over them. If you cannot give them a drop of cold water in hell, you can give them your heart's tears while yet they are in this body.

But are you in very deed reconciled to God yourselves? Reader, are you cured of the awful disease of sin? Are you marked with the blood-red sign of trust in the atoning blood? Do you believe in the Lord Jesus Christ? If not, the Lord have mercy upon you! May you have sense enough to have mercy upon yourself. May the Spirit of God instruct you to that end. Amen.

Book Three

The Spare Half-Hour

Preface

The occasional papers, rescued from the pages of our monthly magazine, *The Sword and the Trowel*, are preserved in this form from the oblivion which awaits the bulk of periodical literature. We are in hopes that spare "half-hours" may be profitably spent in reading these brief essays. The book should be allowed to lie about in the parlor, the kitchen, or the waiting-room: it may catch the eye by its title, and interest by its contents. Our life has been mainly spent in *direct* religious teaching, and to that work we would dedicate our main strength; but men need also to hear common, everyday things spoken of in a religious manner, for to some of them this roundabout road is the only way to their hearts. Theology is dull reading to the unconverted; but mixed with a story, or set forth by a witty saying, they will drink in a great amount of religious truth and find no fault. They like their pills gilded, or at least sugar-coated, and if by that means they may be really benefited, who will grudge them the gilt or the sugar?

In these papers the reader will find considerable variety, but not much of finish; and he will not wonder that it is so when he remembers that they were written by a very busy man in the intervals of his labor, and several of them in foreign lands during the brief leisure afforded by halting upon a journey. Our spare hours are very short ones, but in these we have, to do all our work of this order, and hence we cannot round and polish our periods after the manner of those to whom literature is a profession. We value elegant writing; but while a thousand duties call us hither and thither, ours must remain rough-hewn. Such as it is, gentle reader, we present it to you, that it may amuse first, then suggest a holy or happy thought, and in all tend to edification. To this end may God grant his blessing on our pains, for in all things that is the first cause of success. Right truly did the devout Herbert say—

When Thou dost favour any action,
   It runs, it flies;
All things concur to give it a perfection.
   That which had two legs before,
When thou dost bless hath twelve,
   One wheel doth rise
To twenty then or more.

1

Honeywood Park;
or,
A Tale of My Grandfather

The recurrence of the name of a Tillage, a house, or a spot in one's family annals, interwoven with its most important events, is curious to observe. The superstitious imagine that a strange influence upon human destiny may be connected with peculiar places; we reject their theory, but all the more wonder at the facts upon which it is based. There is a spot in Essex, the name of which is as much associated with the life of my grandfather, now in heaven, as if providence had rooted him to it, and constrained him to live and die within its bounds. What I am about to write is; as nearly as my recollection serves me, the story as I had it from himself.

I had been preaching within twenty miles of Stambourne, where the good old man proclaimed the gospel for about sixty years; and I received a pressing letter from him, saying, that as he was now eighty-eight years of age, if I did not drive across the country to see him, we might never meet again in this world. Little did the grandson need urging to so pleasant a duty. Starting early I reached the village at eight in the morning, and found the venerable man on the look-out for his boy. He was remarkably cheerful and communicative, talking of his tutor at Hackney College, of his early life, his trials and his deliverances, the good men who had gone before him, and the occasions upon which he had met them. He then touched on what was evidently a favorite topic, and remarked that there was formerly a wood in what I think he called Honeywood Park, which was a very memorable place to him. In that wood he had groaned and wept before the Lord while under the burden of sin, and under a tree, an oak, then only a sapling, he had received the grace of faith, and entered upon the enjoyment of peace with God. It was a lonely spot, but henceforth it was to him "none other than the house of God, and the very gate of heaven." Often he resorted thither and praised the name of the Lord.

Some time after this happy event, having to go from Coggeshall to Halstead, his route was over the hallowed spot. On the night previous he dreamed very vividly that the devil appeared to him, and threatened to tear him in pieces if he dared to go along that footpath and pray under the oak as he had been wont to do. The evil one reminded him that there was another way through the farmyard, and that if ho took the farmyard path all would go well with him. When my grandfather awoke, the impression on his mind was overpowering, and he reasoned thus with himself. Whether it be a dream or really a temptation from Satan I cannot tell, but anyhow I will not yield to it, but will show the devil that I will not do his bidding in anything, but will defy him to his face. This was the good man all over. Like Luther, he had a vivid impression of the reality and personality of the great enemy, and was accustomed to make short work with his suggestions. One day when in the pulpit it came into his head that the place where the sand was kept for sanding the brick floor of his manse ought to be boarded in.

His next thought was, What business had the devil to make me think about the sand closet on a Sunday, and in the pulpit too? It shall not be boarded in at all. I will let Satan see that he shall not have his way with me. But to return to the story. My grandfather, then a young man, went on cheerily enough till he came to the stile where the two paths diverged, then a horrible fear came upon him, and he felt his heart beat fast. Suppose he really should meet the archfiend, and should find him too strong for him, what then? Better take the farmyard path. No, that would be yielding to Satan, and he would not do that for ten thousand worlds. He plucked up courage and tremblingly pressed on. The stile was leaped, the narrow track through the wood was trodden with resolution mingled with forebodings. The oak was in sight, the sweat was on his face, his pace was quickened, a dash was made, and the tree was grasped, but there was no Satan there. Taking breath a moment, the young man uttered aloud the exclamation, "Ah, cowardly devil, you. Threatened to tear me in pieces, and now you do not dare show your face."

Then followed a fervent prayer and a song of praise, and the young man was about to go on his way when his eye was caught by something shining on the ground. It was a ring, a very large ring, he told me nearly as large as a curtain ring, and it was solid gold; how it came there it would be hard to guess. Inquiries were made, but no claimant ever appeared, and my grandfather had it made into my grandmother's wedding ring, in memory of the spot so dear to him. Year by year he continued to visit the oak tree on the day of his conversion to pour out his soul before the Lord. The sapling had spread abroad its branches, and the man had become the parent of a numerous family, but the song of gratitude was not forgotten, nor the prayer that he and his offspring might forever be the Lord's; the angels of God, we doubt not, watched those consecrated seasons with delightful interest. The prayers offered there have been answered for sons, grandsons, and great-grandsons, who are now preaching the Gospel which the old man loved so well.

To add to the solemnity of the secluded wood, his father, while passing by the spot, was touched by the hand of God and suddenly fell dead. He could then feel even more deeply, "How dreadful is this place!" This made the annual visitations to the tree more deeply impressive, and we believe beneficial. They would have been continued till my grandfather's last year, were it not that the hand of modern improvement ruthlessly swept away tree and wood, and almost every relic of the past. His last prayer upon the dear spot was most ludicrously interrupted—as the wood was almost all felled, he judged by the pathway as nearly as possible where the long-remembered oak had stood; the place was covered with growing wheat, but he kneeled down in it and began to bless the name of the Lord, when suddenly he heard a rough voice from over the hedge crying out, "Maister, there be a creazy man a-saying his prayers down in the wheat over thay're."

This startled the suppliant and made him beat a hasty retreat. Jacob must wrestle somewhere else, for Jabbok was gone. The man of God looked at the spot and went his way, but in spirit he still raised an altar in that Bethel, and praised the God of his salvation. He has gone to his rest after having fought a good fight, but the prayers of Honeywood Park are blessing his children and his children's children to the third generation, and, through them, many thousands more. To them and all the world, his testimony is, "Resist the devil, and he will flee from you," and equally does he instruct us to "Bless the Lord, and forget not all His benefits." It were well if all of us were as decided to overcome temptation, let it come whence it may. To indulge in that which may even seem to be sin is evil; to strive against its very appearance is safety. Forgive, gentle reader, the egotism which made me think this odd story might have an interest beyond my own family circle; it is no small pleasure to remember such a grandsire, and to recall an incident in his life is pardonable.

2

Two Episodes in My Life

Superstition is to religion what fiction is to history. Not content with the marvels of providence and grace which truly exist around us, fanaticism invents wonders and constructs for itself prodigies. Besides being wickedly mischievous, this fabrication is altogether unnecessary and superfluous; for as veritable history is often more romantic than romance, so certified divine interpositions are frequently far more extraordinary than those extravaganzas which claim fancy and frenzy as their parents. Every believing man into whose inner life we have been permitted to gaze without reserve, has made a revelation to us more or less partaking of the marvelous, but has generally done so under protest, as though we were to hold it forever under the seal of secrecy.

Had we not very distinctly been assured of their trustworthiness, we should have been visited with incredulity, or have suspected the sanity of our informants, and such unbelief would by no means have irritated them, for they themselves expected no one to believe in their remarkable experiences, and would not have unveiled their secret *to us* if they had not hoped against hope that our eye would view it from a sympathizing point of view. Our personal pathway has been so frequently directed contrary to our own design and beyond our own conception by singularly powerful impulses, and irresistibly suggestive providences, that it were wanton wickedness for us to deride the doctrine that God occasionally grants to his servants a special and perceptible manifestation of his will for their guidance, over and above the strengthening energies of the Holy Spirit, and the sacred teaching of the inspired Word. We are not likely to adopt all the peculiarities of the Society of Friends, but in this respect we are heartily agreed with them.

It needs a deliberate and judicious reflection to distinguish between the actual and apparent in professedly preternatural intimations; but if opposed to Scripture and common sense, we must neither believe in them nor obey them. The precious gift of reason is not to be ignored; we are not to be drifted hither and thither by every wayward impulse of a fickle mind, nor are we to be led into evil by superstitious impressions; these are misuses of a great truth, a murderous use of most useful edged tools. But, notwithstanding all the folly of hair-brained rant, we believe that the unseen hand may be at times assuredly felt by gracious souls, and the mysterious power which guided the minds of the seers of old may, even to this day, sensibly overshadow reverent spirits. We would speak discreetly, but we dare say no less.

The two following incidents, however accounted for by others, have but one explanation to the writer; he sees in them the wisdom of God shaping his future in a way most strange. The first story needs a little preface to set it forth; pardon, therefore, gentle reader, trivial allusions. When I was a very small boy, I was staying at my grandfather's, where I had aforetime spent my earliest days, and, as the manner was, I read the Scriptures at family prayer. Once upon a time, when reading the passage in Revelation which mentions the bottomless pit, I paused and said, "Grandpa, what can this mean?" The answer was kind, but unsatisfactory: "Pooh, pooh, child, go on."

The child, however, intended to have an explanation, and therefore selected the same chapter morning after morning, and always halted at the same verse to repeat the inquiry, hoping that by repetition he would importune the good old gentleman into a reply. The process was successful, for it is by no means the most edifying thing in the world to hear the history of the Mother of Harlots, and the beast with seven heads, every morning in the week, Sunday included, with no sort of alternation either of psalm or gospel: the venerable patriarch of the household therefore capitulated at discretion, with, "Well, dear, what is it that puzzles you?"

Now the child had often seen baskets with but very frail bottoms, which in course of wear became bottomless, and allowed the fruit placed therein to drop upon the ground; here, then, was the puzzle—if the pit aforesaid had no bottom, where would all those people fall to who dropped out at its lower end?—a puzzle which rather startled the propriety of family worship, and had to be laid aside for explanation at some more convenient season. Queries of the like simple but rather unusual stamp would frequently break up into paragraphs of a miscellaneous length the Bible-reading of the assembled family, and had there not been a world of love and license allowed to the inquisitive reader, he would very soon have been deposed from his office. As it was, the Scriptures were not very badly rendered, and were probably quite as interesting as if they had not been interspersed with original and curious enquiries.

On one of these occasions, Mr. Knill, late of Chester, and now of the New Jerusalem, whose name is a household word, whose memory is precious to thousands at home and abroad, stayed at my grandfather's house on Friday, in readiness to preach for the London Missionary Society on the following Sabbath. *He* never looked into a young face without yearning to impart some spiritual gift: he was all love, kindness, earnestness, and warmth, and coveted the souls of men as misers desire the gold which their hearts pine after. He marked the case before him, and set to work at once. The boy's reading was commended—a little judicious praise is the sure way to the young heart; and an agreement made with the lad that on the next morning, being Saturday, he would show Mr. Knill over the garden and take him for a walk before breakfast: a task so flattering to juvenile self-importance was sure to be readily entered upon.

There was a tap at the door, and the child was soon out of bed and in the garden with his new friend, who won his heart in no time by pleasing stories and kind words, and giving him a chance to communicate in return. The talk was all about Jesus and the pleasantness of loving him, nor was it mere talk, there was pleading too. Into the great yew harbor—cut into a sort of sugar loaf—both went, and the soul-winner knelt down with his arms around the youthful neck, and poured out vehement intercession for the salvation of the lad. The next morning witnessed the same instruction and supplication, and the next also, while all day long the pair were never far apart, and seldom out of each other's thoughts. The Mission sermons were preached in the old Puritan meetinghouse, and the man of God was called to go to the next halting-place in his tour as a deputation from the Society, but he did not leave till he had uttered a most remarkable prophecy. After even more earnest prayer alone with his little *protégé* he appeared to have a burden on his mind, and he could not go till he had eased himself of it. In after years he was heard to say that he felt a singular interest in me, and an earnest expectation for which he could not account. Calling the family together, he took me on his knee, and I distinctly remember his saying, "I do not know how it is, but I feel a solemn presentiment that this child will preach the gospel to thousands, and God will bless him to many souls. So sure am I of this, that when my little man preaches in Rowland Hill's Chapel, as he will do one day, I should like him to promise me that he will give out the hymn beginning,

> God moves in a mysterious way
> His wonders to perform.

This promise was of course made, and was followed by another, that at his express desire I would learn the hymn in question and think of what he said. A sixpence was also given to me as a reward for the task, which was duly accomplished. The prophetic declaration was fulfilled, and the hymn was sung both in Surrey Chapel and in Wotton-under-Edge in redemption of my pledge, when I had the pleasure of preaching the Word of life in Mr. Hill's former pulpits. Did the words of Mr. Knill help to bring about their own fulfilment? I think so. I believed them, and looked forward to the time when I should preach the Word: I felt very powerfully that no unconverted person might dare to enter the ministry; this made me, I doubt not, all the more intent upon seeking salvation and more hopeful of it, and when by grace enabled to cast myself upon the Savior's love, it was not long before my mouth began to speak of his redemption. How came that sober-minded minister to speak thus of one into whose future God alone could see? How came it that he lived to rejoice with his young brother in the truth of all that he had spoken?

We think *we* know the answer; but each reader has a right to his own: so let it rest, but not till we have marked one practical lesson. Would to God that we were all as wise as Richard Knill, and habitually sowed beside all waters. On the day of his death, in his eightieth year, Elliott, "the apostle of the Indians," was occupied in teaching the alphabet to an Indian child at his bedside. A friend said, "Why not rest from your labors now?" "Because," replied the man of God, "I have prayed God to render me useful in my sphere, and he has heard my prayers; for now that I am unable to preach, he leaves me strength enough to teach this poor child his letters." To despise no opportunity of usefulness is a leading rule with those who are wise to win souls. Mr. Knill might very naturally have left the minister's little grandson on the plea that he had other duties of more importance than praying with children, and yet who shall say that he did not effect as much by that act of humble ministry as by dozens of sermons addressed to crowded audiences. At any rate, *to me* his tenderness in considering the little one was fraught with everlasting consequences, and I must ever feel that his time was well laid out. May we do good everywhere as we have opportunity, and results will not be wanting.

Those who are curious as to further evidence of this story will find it in the biography of Kichard Knill, though scarcely so fully told. No biographer was likely to know so much about it as myself, but yet the main facts are the same.

The second story is less remarkable, perhaps, but is not less true, nor less important in its bearing upon my life-course.

Soon after I had begun to preach the Word in the village of Waterbeach, I was strongly advised to enter Stepney, now Regent's Park, College, to prepare more fully for the ministry. Knowing that solid learning is never an encumbrance, and is often a great means of usefulness, I felt inclined to avail myself of the opportunity of attaining it: although I hoped that I might be useful without a college training, I consented to the opinion of friends that I should be more useful with it. Dr. Angus, the tutor of the College, visited Cambridge, and it was arranged that we should meet at the house of Mr. Macmillan, the publisher.

Thinking and praying over the matter, I entered the house exactly at the time appointed, and was shown into a room where I waited patiently a couple of hours, feeling too much impressed with my own insignificance, and the greatness of the tutor from London, to venture to ring the bell, and make inquiries as to the unreasonably long delay. At last, patience having had her perfect work, and my school engagements requiring me to attend my duties as an usher, the bell was set in motion, and on the arrival of the servant the waiting young man was informed that the doctor had tarried in another room until he could stay no longer, and had gone off to London by train. The stupid girl had given no information to the family that anyone had called, and had been shown into the drawing-room, and consequently the meeting never came about, although designed by both parties. I was not a little disappointed at the moment, but have a thousand times thanked the Lord very heartily for the strange providence which forced my steps into another path.

Still holding to the idea of entering the collegiate institution, I thought of writing and making an immediate application, but this was not to be. That afternoon, having to preach at one of the village stations of the Cambridge Lay Preachers' Association, I walked slowly in a meditative frame of mind over Midsummer Common to the little wooden bridge which leads to Chesterton, and in the midst of the common I was startled by what seemed a loud voice, but which may have been a singular illusion; whichever it was, the impression was vivid to an intense degree: I seemed very distinctly to hear the words, "Seekest thou great things for thyself? Seek them not!" This led me to look at my position from another point of view, and to challenge my motives and intentions. I remembered the poor but loving people to whom I ministered, and the souls which had been given me in my humble charge, and although at that time I anticipated obscurity and poverty as the result of the resolve, yet I did there and then solemnly renounce the offer of collegiate instruction, determining to abide for a season at least with my people, and to remain preaching the Word so long as I had strength to do it. Had it not been for those words, in all probability I had never been where and what I now am. I was conscientious in my obedience to the monition, and I have never seen cause to regret it.

Waiting upon the Lord for direction will never fail to afford us timely intimations of his will; for though the ephod is no more worn by a ministering priest, the Lord still guides his people by his wisdom, and orders all their paths in love; and in times of perplexity, by ways mysterious and remarkable, he makes them to "hear a voice behind them, saying, this is the way, walk ye in it." Probably if our hearts were more tender, we might be favored with more of these sacred monitions; but alas, instead thereof, we are like the horse and the mule, which have no understanding, and therefore the bit and bridle of affliction take the place of gentler means, else might that happier method be more often used, to which the Psalmist alludes when he says, "Thou shalt guide me with thine eye."

The two instances of divine guidance which we have given are specimens of those particular providences which are common in religious biographies.

Out of scores which start up in our memory, we shall select one from the eminently useful life of Peter Bedford, of Spitalfields.

"One summer Mr. Bedford and two of his nephews were staying for a fortnight at Ramsgate, enjoying the fine weather and the sea breezes. They had nearly spent their allotted term of holiday, which would expire on the Monday ensuing. But on the morning of the preceding Saturday Mr. Bedford woke very early, with a strong impression on his mind that he must return that day to London. Accordingly he rose at once, and, going to the bedroom of each of his nephews, informed them that he should have occasion to proceed to the city that morning. They at once ordered an early breakfast, settled accounts, and all went on board the first packet for the Metropolis.

"Mr. Bedford did not, however, know the particular object for his return, beyond the impulse of a strong and clear impression that it was his duty to do so.

"On arriving at his house in Stewart Street, Spitalfields, he found everything going on rightly; and the remainder of the day passed off quietly, as usual, and with no special occurrence whatever. He now began to feel suspicious that he had acted under a mistaken impression. Next day, Sunday, he attended worship as usual; both forenoon and afternoon passed, and still nothing particular took place. He now feared strongly that a delusion had actuated him.

"But in the evening, whilst sitting at the supper-table with two acquaintances, the door-bell rang violently, and a sudden conviction came into Mr. Bedford's mind that lie was about to learn the cause of his impression at Ramsgate. He rose from table, leaving his friends to themselves, and went to meet his visitor in a private apartment. A tall young man, pale and agitated, entered and threw himself on a sofa. He was greatly excited, but presently communicated to Mr. Bedford the information that a very near relative had just left his home and family under most painful circumstances, and with the intention of totally deserting them and at once going off to America. He besought Mr. Bedford to endeavour, by his personal influence, to prevent the accomplishment of this ruinous and desolating resolve.

"After going into the particulars of the case more fully, and ascertaining the most probable means of effecting the desired object, Mr. Bedford returned to his friends in the other room, and informed them that circumstances of urgent necessity compelled him to leave them immediately. He and the young man accordingly hurried off together to obtain an interview with another relative of the fugitive. They were able to make arrangements with this person, of such a nature as to preclude the accomplishment of the intended flight to America. The delinquent relative was persuaded to remain in England, and became penitent for what had happened, and eventually peace was restored to his family. Thus the sudden and unexpected impression made on Mr. Bedford's mind at Ramsgate was entirely justified and confirmed by its results, the appropriate test of the nature of such impulses. It is worthy of observation that these special interpositions of Providence generally appear unexpectedly, and as things not to be looked for, or waited for, to the interruption of ordinary life and its reasonable arrangements, but as afforded merely on exceptional occasions, and by a higher wisdom than any in our possession for daily use."

Our ordinary guides are right reason and the Word of God, and we may never act contrary to these, but still we accept it as a matter of faith and experience to us that, on exceptional occasions, special interpositions do come to our aid, so that our steps are ordered of the Lord and made to subserve his glory. Shepherd of Israel, guide thou us evermore.

3

Ten Thousand Skulls

The little village of Glys, at the commencement of the famous Simplon Road, has a church large enough to hold its inhabitants, should they all swell into Brobdignags, and occupy a pew each. When we passed the stone steps which lead up to the porch, they were strewn with boughs and blocked up with poles—the raw materials of the rustic finery to be displayed on the morrow, which was a high fête day. Inside the very clean and spacious edifice was an image of the Virgin Mary, very sumptuously arrayed, and placed upon a litter, so as to be carried about the streets in solemn procession; just as the heathen of old were wont to do with their gods. "They lavish gold out of the bag, and weigh silver in the balance, and hire a goldsmith; and he maketh it a god: they fall down, yea, they worship. They bear him upon the shoulder, they carry him, and set him in his place, and he standeth."

What made the travelers pause and enter the church? Certainly it was no respect for the idols or their shrines, but curiosity, excited by the grim information that here was *a charnel-house filled with skulls, ten thousand or more at a rough computation*. Now we had seen skulls and bones at Chiavenna, all clean and white and carefully placed, so as to form double-headed eagles, crowns, and all sorts of fanciful devices, and we had also passed bone-houses, where the heads of deceased villagers, all white as pipe-clay, were arranged in orderly rows upon shelves, labelled with their names and the dates of their decease; but ten thousand at once was a novelty of ghastliness not to be resisted. Was the information correct as to the number? Did it not sound like a gross exaggeration? It certainly struck us that we might allow a very liberal discount upon the sum total of horrors, and yet be perfectly content; but we had no necessity to make any deduction, for, like the heads of the sons of Ahab, they lay before us in two heaps, and were there in full number.

Under a chapel, which was decorated with scenery and flowers, not unlike a theatre, was the dreary home of the departed. From its unglazed windows, through the iron bars, peered out thigh bones and skulls—these were the rear ranks of the army of the dead. We entered the portal, and for a moment could see nothing but a few skulls on the floor; but when our eyes were accustomed to the gloom we saw plainly that on each side of a long chamber was a wall of grinning heads, with a leg bone under the chin of each. Here and there they had fallen down, and the wall was in need of the sexton's decorating hand; but for the most part the pile was complete from floor to ceiling, and was from six to eight feet thick.

A kneeling figure, in plaster, stuck up in the corner, half made us shiver, as it seemed to rise up from the floor of this hall of the dead like a sheeted ghost. At the far end were the usual appurtenances of Popish worship, and a comfortable place whereon to kneel amid the many remembrances of mortality. It was hard to avoid a sickening feeling in the midst of this mass of decay, but in our case this was overcome by wonder at the want of human tenderness in the religion which allows such needless and heartless exposure of the sacred relics of mortality. There they were, by dozens, on the floor, the skulls of old and young, male and female, and one could scarcely avoid kicking against them; while, by hundreds, the grim congregation grinned from the wall on either side. Abraham said, "Bury my dead out of my sight," and one feels that his desire was natural, decent, tender, and manlike; but of that horrible collection, open to the bat or the dog, or to every idle passer-by, what, could be said but that they were an abomination and an offence. As some years have passed since our visit, we hope that the march of improvement has closed the vault and buried the poor remains.

To what purpose have we brought our reader into this region of desolation? It is that he may ask, as we did, the question, "Who slew all these?" These thousands are but as the small dust of the balance, compared with the mountains of death's prey. These are but the ashes of the generations of one small hamlet—what vast mausoleum could contain the departed inhabitants of our great cities—the millions of Nineveh, Babylon, Rome, Pekin, London? What a mighty Alp might be formed of the corpses of the men of vast and populous empires, who these thousands of years have been born only to die! Surely the dust which dances in the summer's sun is never free from atoms once alive and human.

The soil we tread, the water we drink, the food we eat, the air we breathe, in all these there must, doubtless, be particles once clothing an immortal soul. In lovely flower, and singing bird, and flitting insect, there may be, perhaps, there must be, the constituents of human flesh and bone, new molded by the Master-hand. How perpetually does that question press itself upon us—Whence come the shafts which so surely reach the heart of life, and lay humanity in rotting heaps? Men of skeptical views have appealed to science, and have tried to show that death is an inevitable law of nature, and is to be viewed as a matter of course, having no more to do with sin or holiness than the fall of a stone by gravitation; but we are content with the divine teaching that "by man came death."

We confess that it is more than possible that creatures expired in agony and pain long before the time of man; but is it quite so clear that what may have occurred in periods before our age, upon animals alone, can be made to contradict a statement which relates to man, and to man only? From whatever cause animals may or may not die, the fact that *man* dies, as the result of Adam's sin, is not affected thereby. For aught we know, the law of mortality might have ruled over all non-intellectual creatures, and man-made in the image of his Maker might have remained immortal evermore had he never transgressed against the divine law.

Such a state of things was prevented by the fall, but it is enough for our enquiry that it might have been so, and that the supposition is not irrational. If it be contended that the condition of the animal creation is bound up with the state and position of man—without venturing into speculations, we are quite willing to accept the statement, and yet we are not at all perplexed by the apparent inconsistency of death before the fall, and the doctrine that death is the result of sin. He who foresees and foreordains all things may of old have constituted the creation upon the foresight of that death which he foresaw would reign, as the result of sin, over man and the creatures linked with him. Had not sin and death been foreseen, as part of the great epic of earth's history, it may be that there had been no brute creation at all, or else an *undying one*;

but since the existence of evil in man, and his consequent fall, was a portion of the great scheme of history which was always present before the divine mind, he made the world a fitting stage for the triumphs of his redeeming love by permitting the creation to groan and travail under subjection to vanity, in solemn harmony with the foreknown state of fallen man.

We are not disposed to accept all the statements of geologists as facts, but even if we were credulous to the last degree concerning their discoveries, we should still hold the Bible in its every jot and tittle with unrelaxing grasp, and should only set our brain to work to find ways of reconciling fact and revelation, without denying either. We unhesitatingly accept the inspired declaration, that "sin, when it is finished, bringeth forth death." What a view of the evil and mischief of sin have we here in this charnel-house! What a murderer is transgression! What a deadly poison is iniquity. Oh earth, earth, earth, scarce canst thou cover the slain! Thy caverns reek with death! And as for thee, Oh sea, thy waves are glutted with the bodies of the mariners, whom thou hast swallowed up! Sin is the great manslayer! Red-handed, with garments dyed in blood, sin stalks through the land, and leaves its awful tracks in tears, and pains, and graves, and charnel-houses, such as this. Would God it were no worse; but, alas, we must complete the picture, its trail is eternal damnation, it kindles the flames of Tophet, which burn even to the lowest hell. As Abraham got up early to the place where he was wont to commune with God, and looked towards Sodom and saw the smoke thereof going up like the smoke of a furnace, so may we look towards the place of torment and cover our faces with solemn awe.

A gleam of sunlight strays into the gloomy assembly of the dead, and as our eye drinks it in, our heart cheerfully hears another question? "Can these dry bones live?" So dry, so chalklike, so pierced by worms, so broken, so powdered, so scattered, so mixed up with other existences—blown by the winds, ground into dust, carried along by streams, lost, forgotten, unknown, can these dry bones *live*? As the top of one great mountain may be seen from another which towers to an equal height, so this one question may be breasted in all its greatness by another, and as the second enquiry deals with a familiar fact, it may ease the difficulties which faith and reason may find in the first: *Have these dry bones lived?* Is it possible that out of those sockets looked merry eyes, sparkling with laughter, or orbs of grief, flowing with tears? Did that hollow globe hold thought and emotion, love and hate, judgment and imagination? That yawning mouth, did it ever cry, "*Abba* Father," or chant the Morning Hymn, or utter discourses which thrilled the heart? How can it have been possible? How could mind be linked with such poor crumbling matter? How could this earthly substance which men call bone, be in intimate, sentient, and vital connection with a soul which thought and reasoned?

As well tell us that stones have walked, that rocks have danced, that mountains have fought in battle, as that spirits, fall of intellectual and emotional power, have once quickened this poor brittle clay; nay, more; walking, dancing, and fighting are actions which brutes might perform, for they involve no exercise of judgment and emotion, and therefore the wonder would not be so great as this before us, when we see the hollow circular box made of earth, and know that it was once essential to intellect and affection. Yet it is certain that these bones once lived; *why not again?* It is only because it is usual and common that life does not strike us as an equal miracle with resurrection. Let the wisest of our race attempt to animate the most accurate model which the most skilful anatomical modeler could prepare, and he would soon learn his folly. Omnipotence is needed to produce and maintain one life; granted omnipotence, and impossibility vanishes, and even difficulty ceases to exist: why cannot God give these bodies life again?

Believing that these shall live again, *what then?* In what body shall they come? What will be their future and where? Are these the bones of saints, and will they rise all fair and glorious in the image of their exalted Lord, just as the shriveled seed starts up a lovely flower, blooming and beautiful? Will they mount from the chrysalis of death into the full *imago* of perfection, just as you fly with rainbow wings has done? Will they march, like the ten thousand Greeks, in dense phalanx, from this their narrow city? And will they know each other in their new condition, and preserve a manifest identity, even as Moses and Elias did, when they appeared upon the mount? Many questions, both answerable and unanswerable, are suggested by these poor relics of humanity. They are great teachers, these silent sleepers! But it may be more profitable to leave them all, and our speculations too, and permit one reflection to abide with us, as we leave the close and dismal vault for the purer air without; that reflection is this, "*I, too, shall soon be as these are.*" It may be, through the care of kindly survivors that my body shall rest where no curious travelers shall gaze thereon; no moralist may muse on death with my skull in his hand; and yet I must be even as these are.

How vain, then, is life! How certain is death! Am I ready for eternity? This is the only business worthy of my care. Go, ye vanities, to those who are as vain as you are! Thoughtful men live solemnly, regarding this life as but the robing-room for the next, the cradle of eternity, the mold wherein their future must be cast. If we rightly think upon this well-known truth, it will have been a healthy thing to have visited the chambers of the dead. On the Sacro Monte, at Varallo, is a supposed imitation of the sepulcher of the Lord Jesus. It was a singular thing to stoop down and enter it, of course finding it empty, like the one which it feebly pictured. What a joyful word was that of the angel, which we saw written there, "He is not here!" Sweet assurance—millions of the dead are here in the sepulcher, thousands of saints are here in the grave, but HE is not here. If *he* had remained there, then all manhood had been forever imprisoned in the tomb; but he who died for his Church, and was shut up as her hostage, has risen as her representative, surety and head, and all his saints have risen in him, and shall eventually rise like him. Farewell, charnel-house, thou hast no door now, the imprisoning stone is rolled away.

"O death, where is thy sting? O grave, where is thy victory?"

4

The Dropping Well of Knaresborough

What the guide books have to say upon that most remarkable natural curiosity, called the Dropping Well of Knaresborough, we do not know; into the geology and chemistry of the wonder we have not enquired; we have only looked at it with the eyes of an ordinary sight-seer of a meditative turn of mind, and have been well repaid. A huge mass of rock has fallen from the face of the cliff, and seems ready to take a still further leap into the stream beneath. A constant drip of water flows over the front of this rocky fragment, whose face is polished as smooth as marble. The water apparently rises out of the rock itself and does not percolate from the cliff above, for between it and the rock there is a wide crack into which the visitor may easily pass. A perpetual shower of the coolest crystal descends into a little pool below, and looks as if nature had determined to outdo all artificial shower-baths with one of her own. Depending from the rock are miscellaneous articles, enduring the full force of the drip: hats, shoes, toy-houses, birds, birds' nests, and other objects, both elegant and uncouth, are hanging in the midst of the rainfall; they are all enduring the process of petrifaction, which the water accomplishes for them in a few months. Drop by drop the liquid falls, and leaves a minute deposit of stony matter every time; and thus slowly, but surely, the whole substance becomes coated and covered with lime, and absolutely transformed to stone.

The old fable of the foes of Perseus turned into stone might have been actually accomplished here if the hero's enemies could have been induced to remain long enough in the shower-bath. We have heard of a certain damsel who wished to be considered a fine lady, and declared herself, upon some great occasion, to have been quite *putrefied* with astonishment; she might here have putrefied in the most wholesome manner. A little museum in the inn contains a. small selection of petrifactions; these cariosities appear to command a rapid sale, for there were none to be disposed of, and many bespoken. It will amply repay anyone going north, to break his journey at York, and take a run to Knaresborough, where, in addition to this marvelous well, and the cave where Eugene Aram hid his victim, there is a view from the castle which is scarcely to be excelled in England.

If there be sermons in stones, surely there must be discourses in a stone-making well. Lot's wife, who may be said to have been petrified by a saline or bituminous shower, has been a standing illustration of the sad results of looking back to the sins and follies of a condemned world; she is God's great petrifaction, preaching evermore a divinely eloquent sermon. The reverse of this transformation, namely, the turning of stubborn, senseless stone into sensitive and tender flesh, is the Lord's enduring miracle of grace, by which he shows at once his wisdom and his power. To make flesh into stone is but a natural process, as this dropping well testifies; but to change stone into flesh is a divine act known to none but the Holy Spirit. May every one of us know by personal experience what the transformation means!

The method of moral and spiritual petrifaction is most instructively imaged by the objects at Knaresborough. Men and women are quite as capable of petrifaction as birds'-nests and old shoes, and they petrify in very much the same manner, with no other differences than those essential distinctions which must exist between a mental and a material operation. Let the world with its temptations, pleasures, and cares represent the spring, and the specimens of consciences, energies, affections, emotions, and a hundred matters petrified in it are endless, and to be met with everywhere. *Everything lifeless within range feels the stone-making influence of the world.* Men with consciences utterly impervious to truth, and hearts entirely unaffected by noble sentiments are, alas, all too plentiful! Ministers whose lifeless performances of heaven's work of mercy prove that their souls are passionless, and. hearers who hear as with "the dull, cold ear of death," are far from rarities. The current of the customs and pursuits of the world favors religious insensibility, and creates it on all sides. As everything beneath the dropping well feels the influence of the shower, so all men in all their faculties are more or less affected by the hardening influences of the world. Spiritual life alone effectually throws off the slimy incrustations of the earthly drip; but were it not for frequent removals from the evil element, life itself would be unable to bear up against it. Drip, drip, drip! The soul forever in it, and never alone with God in prayer, would sooner or later, according to circumstances, become a melancholy proof that friendship with the world is enmity against God. Preserving grace at frequent intervals withdraws the favorites of Heaven out of the deadly shower, and so prevents their ruin, or else Martha's being cumbered with much serving is clear evidence that even true lovers of Jesus in their very desire to serve him may get their thoughts sadly earth-bound.

The work is very gradual hut very constant. A day's deposit would scarcely be perceptible, and weeks would not complete the work; petrifaction is the achievement or innumerable drops following each other with unrelaxing perseverance. It could not be said of any one day's work that *it* petrified, or of any particular portion of the water that *it* wrought the change, but the whole together, throughout a long period, combined to effect the ultimate end. No one glaring sin may be adduced against the man whose heart is hardened, there may be no special season when he became incapable of feeling; but the whole course and tenor of his life in the world, and submission to its influence, must bear the blame of rendering his brow as brass, and his heart as a flint.

At the same time, the action of the world is never suspended, and all its customs, fashions, cares, and pleasures are but a continuance of the same hardening operation under varying forms. The ever-falling shower, which rustles amid the leafy groves upon the river's brink, pours forth its descending drops in unwearied armies, each drop bearing and depositing its burden of stone, and thus unceasingly petrifying everything within its range. Stars and sun alike see the well at its work. So both by night and by day, without fail or pause, carnal associations, and earth-born attractions stultify the mind, and render it unfit for the sacred sensibilities of fellowship with God.

Until we shall find the well of Knaresborough ceasing to petrify, we must not expect this present evil world to pause in its evil operations. The bands of Orion may be loosed, and the sweet influence of the Pleiades may be suspended, but the baleful effect of the world's evil eye can neither change nor cease. We need to watch against the honesties and graces of the world as well as against its rogueries and vices. Its influence is evil, only evil and that continually; and it has a power to penetrate the very soul of man and turn each bowel of compassion, each nerve of holy sensibility, each muscle of heroic energy into cold, cold stone; leaving the natural fashion and shape of manhood, but driving out from it everything warm and lovable; making the human form, a sarcophagus for the true man, and so bringing him back to the earth from which he came by a worse method than even death itself; and all this by degrees so slow that the victim is almost and sometimes altogether unable to perceive the change through which he is passing.

When accomplished the work is exceedingly thorough and unmistakeable. The substance is stone, clearly stone, and stone throughout, whatever it may have been before. We saw a raven whose glossy wings had often shone in the sunlight as he flew through the air, and there he was, a hard lump, utterly incapable of flight, although the wings were surely there, the very wings which once could mount so readily. Alas for the heavenward aspirations which once bade fair to elevate the youth to holiness; that earth-bound money-hunter knows nothing of them, and yet he is the same man with all his former faculties. A hare which had been under the spring had become so grotesque an object that one could hardly see in it the swift-footed creature which drinks the dew. Evil are the days which bring the zealous servant of God, who once ran in the ways of obedience, to become a mere stolid official, occupying a place which he cares not to use for its true ends.

Asahel was fleet as a roe, how comes he to be slower than Mephibosheth? Has the world turned the man into a statue? Has the child of Abraham been cast down and deadened into a stone! All that was raven and hare had become stone, and even so some men who once possessed hopeful qualities and redeeming characteristics, have become all worldliness, and moneygrubbing hardness, till there is not a soft; place in them, nor could a soul, as large as a pin's head, find a fleshy cavity in which to enshrine itself. It were better to grow poorer than Lazarus, and fuller of sores than he, than to be the willing subject of the tyranny of worldliness. Rich, famous, learned, powerful, a man may be, but he is an object for the deepest pity if he has sacrificed the tenderness of his conscience, and the gentleness of his heart. It is death above ground, it is the curse before hell, to be reduced to a mere lump of clay, or a senseless block of stone.

This curse of death in life has fallen upon whole families; hard maxims have stagnated the blood of a race, and made a house notorious for its grim worldliness. Nabal's heart became like a stone within him, but he appears to have died childless; other churls have unhappily left their like behind them, and a race of stone men has cursed generation after generation. A bird's-nest with petrified eggs, and the mother-bird lying in stone upon it, which we saw at the well, is a far more pleasant sight than a family tutored in selfishness, and educated in the unhallowed wisdom of greed.

Nor is the petrifying power of the world exercised only upon men themselves, but *matters which pertain to them are subject to the same power.* Gloves, stockings, and divers articles of apparel were shown us, no longer comfortable garments fulfilling a most useful purpose, but stone; as much stone as if they had been carved from a rock. Who has not seen petrified sermons? Hard, dry, lifeless, cold masses of doctrine cut into the orthodox shape, but utterly unfit for food for the children of God. Who has not heard of petrified prayers? Mere blocks of granite in which warmth and life were the last things to be looked for. Have not gospel ordinances themselves in the hand of formalists become rather the gravestones of religious enthusiasm than firebrands to kindle its sacred flame? Charity herself cannot deny that the world's great stumbling-block is a lifeless church, a powerless ministry, and formal ordinances. Life and its sensibilities of the highest spiritual order, are the mysterious powers by which true religion overcomes the world; take these away and it is not enough to say that the church is injured—it is destroyed outright. A worldly church makes sport for hell, wins scorn from the world, and is an abomination in the sight of heaven; and yet churches, like individuals, may in course of time succumb to the dangerous influences of worldliness, and religion may become a mere thing of stone, stately and tasteful, fixed and conservative, accurate and permanent, but inanimate and powerless; a record of the past rather than a power for the present.

It strikes the observer as he drinks of the apparently pure water of the Dropping Well, that *its actual operation is not one which would apparently have resulted from it.* Your usual experience of water leads you to look for softening rather than hardening, and in the case before you this is the immediate result, and, indeed, the real result too, for it is not the water which petrifies, but the substance which it holds in partial solution and deposits upon the object suspended. The water must not be blamed, it is softening enough in itself, but the foreign ingredient does the petrifying business. The world's trials ought to soften the heart and lead to holy sensibility; and its joys should evoke the tenderness of gratitude and hallowed softness of love; but sin is abroad, and the world is polluted thereby, and hence its outward circumstances operate far otherwise upon us than they would have done had transgression never entered.

It is not the scenery of this fair earth which is defiling, as some ultra-spiritual simpletons would have us believe; neither is there anything in a lawful calling which necessarily interferes with communion with the Lord Jesus; from man proceeds the vileness, it comes neither from hill nor dale, nor streaming river, nor even from the din of machinery and the hum of crowds; moral evil is the strange substance which poisons and pollutes, else earth might be the vestibule of heaven, and the labors of time a preparation for the engagements of eternity. Our gardens are still fair as Eden, and our rivers bright as the ancient Hiddekel; the same sun shines over the selfsame mountains, and the same heavenly blue canopies the earth, but the trail of the serpent is upon all things, and this is it which the spiritual have hourly cause to dread. The roses of Paradise are still with us, but we must beware of the thorns which sin has added to them.

Among the curiosities we did not see petrified hearts, but our anatomical museums frequently contain them, and the disease of a literal hardening of the heart is by no means rare. Spiritually, the petrifying of the heart by the removal of restraining grace is a most terrible judgment from God, and is the precursor of eternal destruction. Pharaoh is the type of a class who are given up to hardness of heart; the stubborn rebellion of their life forebodes their endurance of overwhelming wrath throughout eternity. A tender heart which trembles at God's word, is, on the other hand, a token for good; let those who have it go to Jesus with it, and trust in his blood to make them still more sensitive under the hand of God; and let those who have it not go to Jesus to obtain it, for the awakened conscience and the tender heart are as much HIS gifts as pardon and eternal life. It is doubtful whether Hannibal melted rocks with vinegar; it is certain that Jesus dissolves them with vinegar and gall, but these were his own potion upon the tree. The dropping well of Calvary softens all upon whom it rains its precious floods; happy those who leave the world's shower, and sit beneath the atoning drops, they shall feel the tenderness which is acceptable to God by Jesus Christ.

Leaving the well of Knaresborough we fell to rhyming, and here is the result:

> Though this well hath virtues rare
>   And excites a just surprise;
> There is yet a well more fair
>   And more wondrous in mine eyes.
>
> Blessed well on Calvary's mount,
>   Where the side of Jesus slain,
> Mercy's own peculiar fount,
>   Pours a *stone-removing* rain.
>
> See the heavenly blood-drops fall
>   On a heart as stern as steel!
> Though 'twas hard and stony all,
>   Lo, it now begins to feel!
>
> Legal hammers failed to break,
>   Flames of wrath could not dissolve,
> None the stolid soul could shake,
>   Fixed in fatal, firm resolve.
>
> But *the blood* performs the deed,
>   Softens all the heart of stone,
> Makes the rock itself to bleed,
>   Bleed for him who bled t'atone.
>
> As the crimson shower descends
>   All the stone is washed away;
> Stubbornness in sorrow ends,
>   And rebellious powers obey.

Hewn from out the pit of hell,
   And in Calvary's fountain laid;
By that sacred dropping-well
   Be my soul more tender made.

Till my heart contains no more
   Of the stone by which it fell,
But on Canaan's happy shore
   Sings the sacred dropping-well.

5

Voices from Pompeii

A rush of thought has hurried through our soul while traversing the streets of the long-lost city of Pompeii. Worn as its pavements are by the traffic of a thousand chariots in days of yore, it is all silent now, and its temples and palaces echo only to the footfalls of inquisitive visitors, who guess its life from its suggestive relics. The city was not destroyed by a fiery stream of molten lava, as is popularly supposed; but it would seem that first there fell a shower of ashes and cinders, with here and there a huge mass of volcanic matter; and then there followed torrents of liquid mud, which flowed over all and formed over the city a crust, preserving everything that remained from further injury or decay. Had the stream been burning lava it must have melted down the bronzes, calcined the marbles, and reduced all to one vast heap of molten matter; as it is, the most delicate frescoes remain uninjured, the most minute articles are found in their integrity, and even such readily combustible materials as thread and skeins of silk, are gathered from the ruined dwellings. We have seen a glass jar of oil still retaining its contents, delicate bottles of perfume apparently as fresh as when purchased at the shop, and amphora; of wine, with the age of the vintage as freshly marked thereon, as though but yesterday placed in the cellar. How marvelous does all this seem when we remember that the city was buried in A.D. 79, and, therefore, has lain in its grave for close upon eighteen hundred years.

Comparatively few human remains have been found in the excavations; for, although the inhabitants of Pompeii had but scant warning, it appears that the bulk of the population were, at the time of the eruption, assembled in the great amphitheater, which is outside the town; and, finding themselves cut off from the rest of the city by the falling ashes, they made their escape from the impending doom. All of them were not, however, so fortunate, for some six hundred skeletons have been exhumed, and as yet a bare half of the city has been uncovered. In the ear of our imagination have sounded voices from the dead in Pompeii, and in a hurried moment we sit down to record the impressions they have made.

The full chorus of the disinterred chants one solemn line, "Be ye also ready, for in such an hour as ye think not the Son of Man cometh." To many in that fair abode of luxury and vice the outbreak of Vesuvius appeared to be the end of all things. When the darkness which might be felt settled down upon them, when the earth rumbled and reeled beneath them, when the groaning waves of the tortured sea foamed beyond them; when the scorching glare of vivid lightnings flashed above them, and huge rocks blazing and hissing with fire fell all around them; they believed that the world's death had come—and so, indeed, in a manner it had come to them, but in a fuller and truer sense it hastens on for us!

Even now, while the ink is flowing from our pen, the Lord may be on his way, and may suddenly appear. In Pompeii's last tremendous hour the bread was in the oven, but the baker never saw it taken from it; the meat was seething in the pot never to be eaten; the slave was at the mill, the prisoner in the dungeon, the traveler at the inn, the money dealer in his treasury, but none of these saw aught of their labors, their pains, their pleasures, or their profits again. The burning dust fell over all, the poisonous vapors sought out every crevice, and the ocean of mud buried inhabitant and habitation, worshipper and temple, worker and all that he had wrought! Should a sudden overthrow come upon us also, are we ready? Could we welcome the descending Lord, and feel that for us his coming with clouds to recompense justice would be a joyful appearing, to be welcomed with exulting acclamation? The question is too important to be dismissed until honestly answered: may sincerity direct the examination it suggests.

A very large proportion of the dead were discovered in the barracks; thirty-four were found together, beyond all doubt the guard called out for the fatal night: discipline must have been powerful indeed to have kept men to their duty at such a time, especially when they were not far from the city gate.

It would seem that the officers' wives and children shared in the same spirit, and remained with the band, and with them those ever faithful friends of man, the dogs who had fed beneath their table. Soldiers are expected to endure hardness, and these Roman legionaries discharged their trust to the last. Christians are called soldiers of Christ: shall they be less firm, less bravely obedient, even unto death? Whoever flees in the evil day, a Christian must not. His it is to be at his post at all hazards, and faithless never. Christian and coward, saint and deserter, are words as much opposed as heaven and hell.

Everyone has heard of the lone soldier at the Herculaneum gate of Pompeii, who stepped under an arch to shelter himself from the hot ashes, and there remained close by the gate which he was set to guard, and was found there, spear in hand, faithful unto death. His martial voice rings in our ear, and bids us, even if alone, abide in our appointed place, come what may. It is ours not to consult personal ease or safety, but to abide where our great Captain has appointed our station till he himself shall release us from it. Like the dove which was found sitting upon her nest in the garden of Diomede, if we are entrusted with the care of others we must sooner perish than forsake our charge. If Jesus has said "feed my lambs," we must not flee when the wolf cometh, but must, under evil report and good report, "feed the flock of God which He hath purchased with His own blood." One of the first buildings seen by the traveler upon entering the excavations is the villa whose owner is supposed to have been named Diomede, because a tomb on the opposite side of the road bears that name.

In the ample cellars of this house seventeen persons were found huddled in a corner, who from their ornaments and dress are believed to have been females, and some of them the ladies of the house. Where was the father, the master, the husband of the family? Why did he not form the center of the group, and prove the mainstay of the tremblers in their hour of horror? A skeleton, believed to be that of the master of the house, was found near the garden gate, with the key of his villa firmly grasped in his hand; and behind him was an attendant with one hundred pieces of money in his girdle. What was he about to do? He was, doubtless, fleeing for his life and perished in the attempt; but why escape alone? It would have been useless to carry the key if the door remained unlocked. Had he, then, fastened in his family and left them all to die? Let us not judge even the dead severely; perhaps the timid females would not venture with him, and he went to discover for them a way of escape. The taking of a considerable sum of money with him does not give much countenance to the theory, but this much is clear—for some reason or other the strong man left his household behind him and sought safety for himself.

Meanwhile, outside his door, on the other side of the road, a lady stumbled through the heaps of small loose pumice stones which filled the roadway, and sought a shelter under the vault of the hemicycle, where many a traveler had rested before he entered the splendid city of pomps. She was not alone, but had two children clinging to her garments, and she carried another at her breast. Did she sever herself from the little ones? Did self-preservation drive her to drop her helpless burden? No; folded in each other's arms they fell into their last sleep, the mother still cherishing in death the children, about whose neck her love had hung pearls and finest gold while yet their days were happy. "Can a woman forget her sucking child, that she should not have compassion on the son of her womb?" Man is too often hard and selfish, but a mother's heart is tender, and her love makes sacrifices and counts them sweet.

In the Street of Abundance, in the house of a money-changer, in a dark vault-like room at the rear of the building, lies a skeleton upon a heap of rubbish, with outstretched arms and clutching fingers, as if he had been grasping at earth with his last life-throb. Near him the diggers found some 400 coins, mostly of silver, with quite a little fortune in rings and cameos. Was he a thief, and were these the spoils he had gathered and purchased with his life? Was he a money-lender, and were these his capital and his securities for loans? No man can answer these questions, but the blending together of death and gold in one story is no new thing; it is, indeed, but another among a thousand instances in which death has slain men with gilded darts. In another place was found an adventurous pilferer, who, after the destruction of the city, had marked the spot where stood a rich man's house, had burrowed down into it, and had met his end through the falling in of the earth upon him. He digged for treasure, and knew not that he had prepared his grave; fit warning to other earthworms among men that they also perish not in their grovelings, though it is to be feared the admonition is seldom heeded, and men continue to barter heaven for yellow clay. Less ignobly died the prisoners in their cells, and the soldiers in their stocks, for they were bound by no voluntary fetters, and may have been free in spirit while they lay in durance. Avarice both imprisons and degrades.

The skeleton in the large room behind the Temple of Isis reveals the overpowering energy of even a base animal appetite, for there it was found with bones of chickens, eggshells, fish bones, bread, wine, and a garland of flowers around it. He must have been a rare feeder who could find stomach for his meat amid such convulsions of nature; his worship of his belly had furnished him with a courage which far nobler devotions have not excelled. It shows how sottish he becomes who lives to eat instead of eating to live; he may one day die by his eating, and go from the banquets of Bacchus to the tortures of Tophet. Let all men beware of the tyranny of carnal passions, for no despots are so exacting as the appetites of the flesh. Suicide by one's own teeth is the meanest of deaths, and involves a man in everlasting contempt; the cruelest of tyrants have not demanded this of their victims. By all that we value for time and for eternity, let us conquer fleshly appetites, lest they conquer us.

Time would fail us to tell of the wretch who left his bones in a temple with all the evidence of his sacrilege about him. Will a man rob God? How will it fare with him should he perish in the act? Neither can we speak much of the gigantic personage, who with an axe had pierced a way through two walls of the Temple of Isis in his efforts to escape from the all-surrounding death. He at least was no sluggard or foolhardy glutton. He perished, but he made desperate efforts to be saved: many also will share this fate, in a spiritual sense, if they rely upon their own strength; but, blessed be God, none shall ever be left to die who labor against sin, trusting in the merits of the Redeemer.

Vain also would it be to conjecture who was the owner of that remarkable brain which once filled a skull of such striking conformation that it has excited the speculations of many phrenologists. He whose eyes looked out from under that overhanging brow was crushed beneath a falling column, literally severed in twain by the prostrate mass. Had he lived and thought for God, for truth, for man? Or was he some arch deceiver, a deluder of the multitude? Echo alone answers to our enquiries, and she by mocking them. The tomb is silent, and so also are those to whom sepulture is denied. But one thing is clear to the most superficial glance: these skeletons are the petrifactions of vitality, the abiding record of life's latest moments. As in the forum remain the half-finished columns, with the last mark of the sculptor's hand upon them; as in the chambers of the household remain the essences and rouge of ill-fated beauty; as in the bath remains the strigil, and in the hall the treasure-casket; so in the stone-like relics of the departed Pompeians abide the records of their concluding acts; they are the finis of their own history, observed by all men. Behold, at this hour our moral history is being preserved for eternity; processes are at work which will perpetuate our every act, and word, and thought; not alone the last line, but every word and letter of our actual history is being stereotyped for the world's perusal in the day which shall reveal the secrets of men. We are not writing upon the water, but carving upon imperishable material—the chapters of our history are "graven with an iron pen and lead in the rocks for ever."

Thus did we think amid the excavated streets of Pompeii, and if we have written to edification we are glad.

6

Ghost Stories for Christmas

We may be very wrong, but we confess a weakness for a ghost story, and cannot help listening to it, and all the more if it makes the blood curdle and blanches the cheek. It is a sort of stolen water, and that, as the wise man says, is sweet. We lived at one time among a people many of whom devoutly believed in apparitions, and wizards, and witches, and all that horrible rout, and often have we heard the most thrilling stories—stories, we believe, in more senses than one. We had sent us for review some little time ago a book upon apparitions, which claims to be a narrative of facts; and as we read it through we said, "Yes, these were facts *where they were done,*" and we put the book aside, to be looked up somewhat nearer the end of the year, when the Christmas number of our magazine might excuse our inserting one or more of the aforesaid *facts*. We are afraid our readers will think us rather a Sadducee, although we are nothing of the kind, nor a Pharisee either; but we do not believe that in nine out of ten ghost stories there is a ghost of truth, and we are not quite sure that we believe the tenth one.

The Wesley family undoubtedly were favored with a very noisy visitant of some sort, and we have no idea what it was, only there is no accounting for the noises which rats make in old houses any more than for the foul gases in new ones. When we meet with a thing which puzzles us we pry into the cause as far as we can, and generally find it out; and if we cannot read the riddle we lay it by to be solved another day, never flying to the old-fashioned resort of dragging in the supernatural. We traced a spirit song after much investigation to a foot-warmer filled with hot water, which was being used by an invalid. We sought out a band of celestial visitants, who whispered to us all night in a country house, and found them to be a nest of birds in a hole in the plaster of the wall at our bed head, which hole nearly came through into the room.

Nothing supernatural has ever been seen by our eyes, nor do we think we shall ever be blessed with such vision while in this body; for after seeing Robert Houdin and other wonder-workers we are case-hardened against the whole set of tricks and sham spirits, and these are the parents of most of the marvels which set silly people's hair on end. As a general rule, when we hear of an apparition, or anything of the kind, we do not believe it to be other than an illusion or a falsehood. The most wonderfully well-attested narratives seldom bear investigation, they are built up with hearsay and tittle-tattle, and will not endure a strict examination; like most rumors, they fall like card-houses as soon as the hand of truth touches them. Perhaps a few of them appear to be so far true that we may safely say that they are not yet accounted for except upon a supernatural hypothesis, but we should hesitate to say more. Some are evidently the result of strong imagination, and are true to the parties concerned, affecting their fears and stamping themselves upon their minds too firmly to allow them to doubt.

In many cases religious delusions and errors create a tendency to visions and the like, and the most vigorous repression should be exercised by ministers and other persons of influence. A woman once called upon us in great trouble, for she had seen a human form at the foot of her bed. We suggested that it might be her own gown hanging on a peg. No, that could not be, she believed it was either the Lord Jesus or Satan. We remarked it did not matter a pin which it was, for many saw the Lord when he was on earth, and were none the better, and our Lord himself saw the devil, and yet was none the worse. To her, however, it was a test matter, and she informed us that she should have known all about it *if she had seen its head*. We enquired how that was, and to our astonishment she told us that she had a likeness of the Savior, and she should have known him by it, and thereupon fetched out of her room a small woodcut which was supposed by her to represent the altogether lovely One.

Our reply was an urgent entreaty to burn the horrid thing at once, and to feel certain that if ever she saw anybody at all like that she might be sure that it was as likely to be Lucifer himself as the Lord Jesus. She was evidently greatly surprised, and we fell fifty per cent, in her estimation, for she had expected to have had the opinion of her own minister, a Methodist, contradicted by our authority. We told her that her minister was a very sensible man, and had dealt faithfully with her in telling her not to be deceived by optical delusions; we question, however, whether we shook her faith, for she had a budget of other wonders to tell us, only our declaration that they were "stuff and nonsense," and our plain statement of the spiritual character of true religion, made her cut the interview very short. Half-crazy people come to us in any quantity with such marvels, and we hope we have cured a good many by a little kindly raillery, but a considerable number leave us with the impression sadly confirmed in our minds that there are more lunatics outside of asylums than in them.

We do not affirm that ghosts have never been seen, for no one has any right to hazard so broad a statement; but all spirits, as such, must be invisible, and the two sorts of human spirits which we know of are both by far too seriously occupied to go roaming about this earth rapping on tables or frightening simpletons into fits. As for angels, though they also as spirits are not cognizable by the senses, no doubt they have been made visible to men, and there is no reason why they should not be made so now if God so willed it; it would certainly be a wonder, but we do not see that any of the laws of nature need to be suspended to produce it. We can readily believe that those messengers who keep watch around the people of God would be rendered visible to us and to others if some grand purpose could be accomplished thereby, and if the safety of the saints required it. Whether in these days angels or departed spirits ever do assume forms in which they can be seen is the question, and we have as yet *seen* nothing to lead us to believe that they do. Others assert that they have seen such things, but as they generally admit that they would not have believed unless they had seen for themselves, we hope they will allow us to exercise the same abstinence. Our two stories are so nicely balanced *pro* and *con*, that when they are read by the advocates of the positive and negative sides we hope they will admire our judicious impartiality. The first story is from "Apparitions: a Narrative of Facts," and it is entitled THE MYSTERIOUS HORSEMAN.

The *Tracthodydd*, or "Essayist," a Welsh quarterly periodical for 1853, contains a biographical memoir of the late Rev. John Jones, of Holiwell, Flintshire; and in that memoir there is an account of as remarkable an interposition of Providence by means of an *apparition*, which resulted in the preservation of life, as any on record.

I think it will be best to allow Mr. Jones to relate the incident in his own words, as he was often wont to do, merely premising that he was a minister of high principle and unblemished character, and renowned throughout the principality for his zeal and fervor as a preacher of the gospel, and one who showed by his life his just appreciation of what Plutarch has so finely said respecting—truth, than which no greater blessing can man receive or God bestow.

> One summer day, at the commencement of the present century, I was travelling from Bala, in Merionethshire, to Machynlleth, in the neighbouring county of Montgomery, in order to attend a religious meeting. I left Bala about 2 p.m., and travelled on horseback, and alone. My journey lay through a wild, desolate part of the country, and one which at that time was almost uninhabited. When I had performed about half my journey, as I was emerging from a wood situated at the commencement of a long steep decline, I observed coming towards me a man on foot. By his appearance, judging from the sickle which he carried sheathed in straw over his shoulder, he was doubtless a reaper in search of employment. As he drew near, I recognised a man whom I had seen at the door of the village inn of Llanwhellyn, where I had stopped to bait my horse. On our meeting he touched his hat and asked if I could tell him the time of day. I pulled out my watch for the purpose, noticing at the same time the peculiar look which the man cast at its heavy silver case. Nothing else, however, occurred to excite any suspicion on my part, so, wishing him a "good afternoon," I continued my journey.
>
> When I had ridden about half-way down the hill, I noticed something moving, and in the same direction as myself, on the other side of a large hedge, which ran nearly parallel with the road, and ultimately terminated at a gate through which I had to pass. At first I thought it an animal of some kind or other, but soon discovered by certain depressions in the hedge that it was a man running in a stooping position. I continued for a short time to watch his progress with some curiosity, but my curiosity soon changed to

fear when I recognized the reaper with whom I had conversed a few minutes before, engaged in tearing off the strawband which sheathed his sickle.

He hurried on until he reached the gate, and then concealed himself behind the hedge within a few yards of the road. I did not then doubt for a moment but that he had resolved to attack—perhaps murder—me for the sake of my watch and whatever money I might have about me. I looked around in all directions, but not a single human being was to be seen; so reining in my horse, I asked myself in much alarm what I could do. Should I turn back? No; my business was of the utmost importance to the cause for which I was journeying, and as long as there existed the faintest possibility of getting there, I could not think of returning. Should I trust to the speed of my horse, and endeavour to dash by the man at full speed? No; for the gate through which I had to pass was not open. Could I leave the road and make my way through the fields? I could not; for I was hemmed in by rocky banks or high hedges on both sides. The idea of risking a personal encounter could not be entertained for a moment, for what chance could I—weak and unarmed—have against a powerful man with a dangerous weapon in his hand? What course then should I pursue? I could not tell; and at length, in despair rather than in a spirit of humble trust and confidence, I bowed my head and offered up a silent prayer. This had a soothing effect upon my mind, so that, refreshed and invigorated, I proceeded anew to consider the difficulties of my position.

At this juncture my horse, growing impatient at the delay, started off: I clutched the reins, which I had let fall on his neck, for the purpose of checking him, when happening to turn my eyes, I saw to my utter astonishment that I was no longer alone. There, by my side, I beheld a horseman in a dark dress, mounted on a white steed. In intense amazement I gazed upon him; where could he have come from? He appeared as suddenly as if he had sprung from the earth. He must have been riding behind and have overtaken me. And yet I had not heard the slightest sound: it was mysterious, inexplicable. But the joy of being released from my perilous position soon overcame my feelings of wonder, and I began at once to address my companion. I asked him if he had seen any one, and then described to him what had taken place, and how relieved I felt by his sudden appearance, which now removed all cause of fear. He made no reply, and, on looking at his face, he seemed paying but slight attention to my words, but continued intently gazing in the direction of the gate, now about a quarter of a mile ahead. I followed his gaze, and saw the reaper emerge from his concealment and cut across a field to our left, resheathing his sickle as he hurried along. He had evidently seen that I was no longer alone, and had relinquished his intended attempt.

All cause for alarm being gone, I once more sought to enter into conversation with my deliverer, but again without the slightest success. Not a word did he design to give me in reply. I continued talking, however, as we rode on our way towards the gate, though I confess feeling both surprised and hurt at my companion's mysterious silence. Once, however, and only once did I hear his voice. Having watched the figure of the reaper disappear over the brow of a neighbouring hill, I turned to my companion and said, "Can it for a moment be doubted that my prayer was heard, and that you were sent for my deliverance by the Lord?" Then it was that I thought I heard the horseman speak, and that he uttered the single word, "*Amen.*" Not another word did he give utterance to, though I tried to elicit from him replies to my questions, both in English and Welsh.

We were now approaching the gate, which I hastened to open, and having done so with my stick, I turned my head to look—*the mysterious horseman was gone!* I was dumbfounded; I looked back in the direction from which we had just been riding, but though I could command a view of the road for a considerable distance, he was not to be seen. He had disappeared as mysteriously as he had come. What had become of him? He could not have gone through the gate, nor have made his horse leap the high hedges which on both sides shut in the road. Where was he? Had I been dreaming? Was it an apparition, a spectre which had been riding by my side for the last ten minutes? Could it be possible that I had seen no man or horse at all, and that the vision was but a creature of my imagination? I tried hard to convince myself that this was the case, but in vain; for, unless someone had been with me, why had the reaper resheathed his murderous looking sickle and fled? Surely no; this mysterious horseman was no creation of my brain. I had seen him; who could he have been?

I asked myself this question again and again; and then a feeling of profound awe began to creep over my soul. I remembered the singular way of his first appearance—his long silence—and then again the single word to which he had given utterance; I called to mind that this reply had been elicited from him by my mentioning the name of the Lord, and that this was the single occasion on which I had done so. What could I then believe?—but one thing, and that was, that my prayer had indeed been heard, and that help had been given from on high at a time of great danger. Full of this thought, I dismounted, and throwing myself on my knees, I offered up a prayer of thankfulness to Him who had heard my cry, and found help for me in time of need.

I then mounted my horse and continued my journey. But through the long years that have elapsed since that memorable summer's day I have never for a moment wavered in my belief that in *the mysterious horseman* I had a special interference of Providence, by which means I was delivered from a position of extreme danger.

Our second extract is from the "Christian at Work," a very lively, interesting, vigorously conducted paper, of which Mr. Talmage was the editor when I saw the story. It is entitled—A TRUE TALE OF A GHOST.

The first settlers of many of the New England towns laid out their graveyards at the centre of the town, and built up the village around the burying ground as if to keep in sight and have a tender and watchful care over their dead. Upon this public square—a part of which was consecrated to burial purposes—were usually erected all the public buildings.

About the time of which we write there was much being said and published about witches and ghosts in various parts of the country; very exciting accounts of their being seen and of their strange doings were told, until ghost stories became the topic of gossip in the shop, at the tavern, and at all the village gatherings by night and by day. About this time the ghosts made such a demonstration at Morristown, New Jersey, as to call forth a printed pamphlet of some fifty pages, giving the details of their midnight behaviour, etc., which was read and discussed by old and young, by mothers and grandmothers, until many actually became so timid that they dared not venture out after dark, and children would not go to bed alone. The more people talked about them, the more ghosts were seen; but always at night, and usually when it was very dark.

It was late in the month of November that some persons in Guilford, Conn., returning from a party one dark, dismal night—when the winds whistled and the signs creaked upon their hinges as they passed the graveyard—saw a large white object moving slowly about among the tombstones, and they all unhesitatingly pronounced it a ghost. It could be nothing else. Such an object in such a place, at such a time of night, must be a spirit of some departed one. Owing both to the fact of the parties being persons of character, and to the feverish state of the public mind, no small sensation was created in the usually quiet old town, and even the more intelligent people were made to wonder what it all meant. The next night it was seen again, and for several succeeding nights, by different persons, whose statements of the facts could not be questioned. At last curiosity ran so high, and the fact was so unquestioned, that there was a real live ghost to be seen every night about midnight in the graveyard, that several young men of respectability, who supposed they possessed courage, agreed to arm themselves with lanterns and clubs, and go out the next night and ascertain what it really was that had wrought up so many minds to such a degree of apprehension; and if it was the unquiet spirit of some departed one, to learn, if possible, what it wanted or what was its object in coming every night to disturb the peace and quiet of so many harmless people. They accordingly all met a little before midnight to carry out their plan, but seemed rather reluctant to set forth upon their desperate errand. However, they approached the graveyard; but they had not proceeded far when, sure enough, there was the very identical ghost confronting them, and slowly moving towards them. This brought them all to a halt, trembling with the cold chills of fear, in the stillness of midnight darkness, not a word spoken by any one. In a moment more they all simultaneously turned and fled.

The very next night after these brave young men had failed to communicate with the ghost, just at twelve o'clock, in the dead darkness of midnight, when the silence of the sepulchre brooded over the town, the people were aroused from their slumbers by the tolling of the bell high up in the belfry of the old "meeting-house," upon the other end of the public square. The next night the same thing occurred again, and, in connection with the current stories of the ghost, now began to excite no small degree of interest among all classes of the community. Several arose from their beds and went to the meetinghouse, and there called to the sexton to know what it meant. But they found the doors all locked and no sexton there. Was the town haunted? At last it was unanimously resolved that something must be done to unravel the mystery. So the next night six of the most resolute dare-devils in the town were bargained with to go into the graveyard and await the approach of the ghost, and when he appeared, to respectfully demand his business, and what his ghostship really wanted.

The night was fearfully dark and dismal, and when all the inhabitants had retired for the night—with not a light to be seen in any dwelling, and the profound stillness of midnight darkness spread over the borough—these six young fellows walked out and took a stand where the ghost had several nights been seen, and waited with no small degree of anxiety for nearly two hours, with their eyes turned in every direction, when, behold! in the dim distance was seen approaching a large white object moving slowly towards them, or towards the spot where they stood. They all watched with fearful tremor. They were near the centre of the grounds enclosed. No one spoke aloud or moved a limb. Some began to feel cold chills creep over them as they cast about in their own minds for a chance to retreat now, as the object, with a heavy tread, approached, and uncertainty began to take possession of them all. But here they were, and they had all sworn to see the end of this mystery or perish in the attempt: and the end seemed fast approaching that was to put their courage and manhood to the test.

The object on which all eyes were fixed, to discern through the darkness something more clearly, had now approached very near them, and as several were on the eve of turning to run, Fred Meigs, one of the party, who never knew fear under any circumstances, burst, out laughing, when they all stepped forward, and, behold! Mr. Lot Benton's old white mare, that for several nights had found her way out of the barn-yard nearby, and quietly walked out to graze on the high grass in the graveyard. And here was solved the puzzle of the ghost. But the bell tolling at midnight in a quiet old New England town for three successive nights, without the aid or knowledge of the sexton, yet remained an unsolved mystery. So the next day after the interview with the ghost, that matter was taken in hand, and with more boldness since the ghost had been discovered, when the fact was developed that a reckless fellow, who had become familiar with the excitement that had for some time existed concerning the ghost in the graveyard, had one night, after dark, undiscovered, climbed, by ways best known to himself, into the belfry, tied a twine string to the tongue of the bell, descended again to the ground and led the string to his chamber window, and there he sat for three nights fanning the excitement of the ghost stories by tolling the great church bell at midnight, until the whole town became alarmed or frightened with a superstitious dread of something—they knew not what. With these discoveries all interest in ghosts and witches ceased, and the people settled down into their usual quietness and sober orthodoxy.

Let the reader decide for himself whether ghost stories are all fudge or no; but in any case, if he be a Christian, let him never fear, for he spake truly who said, "Surely there is no enchantment against Jacob, neither divination against Israel." "Thou shalt not be afraid for the terror by night" is a divine promise which only needs faith in order to be realized by every child of God.

7

The Great Pot and the Twenty Loaves

"Set on the great pot ... Then bring meal. ... Give unto the people, that they may eat" (2 Kgs. 4:38–42).

We scarcely need go over the story. There was a dearth in the land; Elisha came to the college of the prophets, which consisted of about a hundred brethren, and found that they were in want, as the result of the famine. While he was teaching the young men he observed that they looked as if they needed food, and he found that there was none in the house. Elisha, therefore, ordered his servant to take the great pot, which generally stood upon long legs over the fire, and make a nourishing soup in it, True, there was nothing to put in the pot, but he believed that God would provide. It was his to set the pot over the fire, and it was the Lord's to fill it. Certain of the young men were not so sure as Elisha that God could fill it without their help, and one with great eagerness went out to gather something from the fields; his help turned out to be of small service, for he brought home poisonous cucumbers, and cut them up and threw them into the broth; and, lo, when they began to pour it out, it was acrid to the taste, gave them a terrible colic, and made them cry out, "There is death in the pot."

Then the prophet said "bring meal." This was put into the steaming cauldron, the poison was neutralized, the food was made wholesome, and the students were satisfied. This miracle was in due time followed up by another. A day or two afterwards the young prophets were still needing food, and the larder was again empty. Just at that time a devout man comes from a little distance, bringing a present for the prophet, which consisted of a score of loaves similar to our penny rolls. The prophet bids his servitor set this slender quantity before the college. He is astonished at the command to feed a hundred hungry men with so little, but he is obedient to it; and while he is obeying the little food is multiplied, so that the hundred men eat and are perfectly satisfied, and there is something left. I believe there are lessons to be learned from these two miracles, and I shall try to bring out these lessons in three forms. First, as they shall relate to *the present condition of religion in our land*; secondly, as they may be made to relate to *the condition of backsliders*; and thirdly, as they may afford comfortable direction *to seeking sinners*.

First, then, our text as in a parable sets forth in a figure OUR COURSE OF ACTION IN CONNECTION WITH RELIGION IN OUR OWN LAND.

And, first, there is a great need of the Gospel of Jesus Christ. We have not a hundred men famishing nowadays, but hundreds of thousands, and even hundreds of millions in this great world who are perishing for want of heavenly food. *The church must feed the people.* It is not for us to say, we hope they will be saved, and leave it there: or set it down as a work that cannot be done till the millennium, too difficult for us to undertake. Our business is in the strength of God to grapple with the present condition of things. Here are the millions famishing; shall we let them famish? I remember seeing a similar sentence under the likeness of the late Richard Knill. "The heathen are perishing! Shall we let them perish?" "But," says one, "how can we possibly supply them with food?" See what Elisha did: the people were hungry, and there was no food in hand, except a little meal, yet he said, "Set on the great pot."

Faith always does as much as she can: if she cannot fill the pot, she can put it on the fire, at any rate. If she cannot find meat for the pottage, she pours in the water, lights the fire, and prays and waits. Some have not this faith nowadays, and until we have it, we cannot expect the blessing. "Thus saith the Lord, enlarge the place of thy tent and stretch forth the curtains of thy habitation," Why? Because "thou shalt break forth on the right hand and on the left." What was the command on a great occasion when the host lacked water? Did not the prophet cry, "Thus saith the Lord, make this valley full of ditches"? They were to dig trenches before the water came, and thus show their confidence that the Lord would fill them. Few will regard such a summons as this. The feeble faith of our time finds it difficult to enlarge the tent even after the increase has come, and the people are there to fill it. Great faith would enlarge the tent before the necessity was apparent, and expect the Lord to keep his promise, and multiply us with men as with a flock. The church of God greatly needs, not foolish confidence in herself, which would lead her to be quixotic, but simple confidence in God, which would enable her to be apostolic, for she would then go forth believing that God would be with her, and great things would be accomplished by her. She would open her mouth wide, expecting that God would fill it, and fill it he would. Faith does what she can, and waits for her Lord to do what *he* can. Brother, what is your faith doing? Are you putting the great pot on the fire in expectation of a blessing?

"Set on the great pot," said the great prophet, "*and seethe pottage.*" He was not in jest; he meant what he said. Often when we get as far as setting on the pot, it is not for seething pottage. We feel the desire to carry out spiritual work, but we do not come to practical action as those who work for immediate results. Oh for practical common sense in connection with Christianity! Oh for reality in connection with the idea of faith! When a man goes to his business to make money, he goes there with all his wits about him; but frequently when men come to prayer and Christian service they leave their minds behind, and do not act as if they were transacting real business with God. Elisha, when he said, "Put on the great pot," expected God to fill it; he was sure it would be so, and he waited in all patience till dinner was ready. Oh church of God, set on the pot, and the great pot, too. Say, "The Lord will bless us." Get your granary cleaned out, that the Lord may fill it with his good corn. Put the grist into the hopper, and look for the wind to turn the sails of the mill. Oh ye doubters, throw up the windows, that the fresh breeze of the divine Spirit may blow in on your sickly faces. Expect that God is about to send the manna, and have your omers ready. We shall see greater things than these if we awake to our duty and our privilege. It is the church's business to feed the world with spiritual bread; she can only do so by faith, and she ought to act with faith in reference to it.

The faith of Elisha was not shared by all the brethren. There were some who must needs go and fill the pot, and they were in such a hurry that they gathered the gourds of the colocynth vine and poisoned the whole mess, and it became needful to find an antidote for the poison. Their unbelief made them catch at anything which came to hand, so that it seemed likely to fill up the cauldron; and, therefore, acting without discrimination, they had quantity but not quality, they had plenty of pumpkins, but death was in them. We here see our second duty—*the church must provide an antidote for the heresies and poisonous doctrines of the present age.* There has entered into the public ministry of this country a deadly poison. We may say of the church in general, "O thou man of God, there is death in the pot!" Zealous persons whose zeal for God is not according to knowledge, have gone about and gathered the gourds of the wild vine. I think I could tell you what kind of gourds they are; some of them are very pretty to look at, and they grow best on the seven hills of Rome—they are called "ritualistic performances"; these they shred into the pot. There are gourds of another kind, very delicate and dainty in appearance, which are known as "Liberal views," or "modern thought." As a philosopher once talked of extracting sunbeams from cucumbers, so these wild gourds are said to consist of "sweetness and light," but the light is darkness and the sweetness is deadly. They have shred these into the pot, and nobody can taste the doctrinal mixture which is served out from some pulpits without serious risk of soul-poisoning, for "there is death in the pot."

What scriptural doctrine is there which men do not deny and yet call themselves Christians? What truth is there which our fathers held which is endorsed by those who think themselves the leaders of advanced thought? Have they not polluted the entire sanctuary of truth, and lifted up their axes against all the carved work of the temple? On the other hand, have we not everywhere Christ put aside for the crucifix, and the blessed Spirit thrust into a corner by the so-called sacraments? Is not the outward made to drown the inward, and is not the precious truth of the gospel overlaid by the falsehoods of Rome? There is death in the pot: how is the church to meet it? I believe it will be wise if it follows the example of Elisha. We need not attempt to get the wild gourds out of the pot; they are cut too small and are too cunningly mixed up, they have entered too closely into the whole mass of teaching to be removed. Who shall extract the yeast from the leavened loaf? What then? We must look to God for help, and use the means indicated here. "Bring meal."

Good wholesome food was cast into the poisonous broth, and by God's gracious working it killed the poison: the church must cast the blessed gospel of the grace of God into the poisoned pottage, and false doctrine will not be able to destroy men's souls as it now does. We shall not do much good by disputing, and denouncing, and refusing to associate with people. I call such things *barking*, but preaching the gospel is *biting*. The surest remedy for false doctrine is preaching the truth. Christianity is the cure for Popery. Preach up Christ, and down go the priests; preach grace, and there is an end of masses.

I am more and more persuaded that the good old Calvinistic truths, which are now kept in the background, are the great Krupp guns with which we shall blow to pieces the heresies of the day, if once more they are plainly and persistently preached in harmony with the rest of revealed truth. Like ships of war in time of peace, the glorious doctrines of grace have been laid up in ordinary, but now is the time to bring them out to the fight, and if well managed they will pour red-hot shot into the enemy! The people need gospel teaching. "Bring meal," employ more and more the plain preaching of the gospel, and evils of all sorts will be overcome. Is the remedy very simple? Do not, therefore, despise it. God be thanked that it is simple; for then we shall not be tempted to give the glory to man's wit and wisdom when the good result is achieved.

In this work you can all help, for if only meal is needed a child may bring his little handful. One man may contribute more than another, but the humblest may put in his pinch of meal, and even the commonest servitor in the house may contribute a handful. Spread the gospel. Spread the gospel. Spread the gospel. A society for prosecuting Puseyites—will that do the work? Appeals to Parliament—will they be effectual? Let those who choose to do so cry to lawyers and to Parliaments, but as for us we will preach the gospel. If I could speak with a voice of thunder, I would say to those friends who are for adopting other means to stop the spread of error, "You waste your time and strength: give all your efforts to the preaching of the gospel. Lift up Christ, and lay the sinner low. Proclaim justification by faith, the work of the Holy Spirit in regeneration, and the grand old doctrines of the Reformation, and your work will be done; but by no other means." "Bring meal," said the prophet, and our word at this time is, "Preach the truth as it is in Jesus."

Some of the grossest errors of our own day may yet be overruled by God for the promotion of his truth. There are men who believe in sacramentarianism, who love the Lord Jesus very ardently. When I read some of the poetry of this school, I cannot but rejoice to see that the writers love my Lord and Master, and it strikes me that if the whole gospel could be put before them, we might expect to see some of them become noble preachers of the truth, and perhaps their influence might save the orthodox from dead dry doctrinalism by reviving a more direct devotion to the Savior. Perhaps they will not, after our fashion, talk often of justification by faith, but if they extol the merit of the precious blood and wounds of Jesus, it will come to much the same thing. For my part I care little for the phraseology, if essential truth be really taught, and the Lord Jesus be exalted; and hence the real piety which I see in some high churchmen makes me hope that God will prevent their errors from being so pernicious as otherwise they might be.

Some of the doubters, too—"thinkers," as they prefer to be called—if the Lord renewed them by his Spirit, might bring out the old truths with greater freshness than our more conservative minds are able to do. I love to hear those who have known the vanity of error speak out the truth. They put the old doctrines in new lights and call our attention to beauties which we had overlooked. They are more sympathetic towards the tempted, and are generally more conversant with the grounds of our faith.

Who knows? Who knows? I have a hope which may not prove a dream. I hope that thousands are feeling their way into light, and will come forth soon. Let us not despair, but keep to our work, which is gospel preaching, telling about Jesus and his dear love, the power of his blood, the prevalence of his plea, the glory of his throne; who knows, I say, but a multitude of the priests may believe, and the philosophers may become babes in Christ's school. "Bring meal," and thus meet the poison with the antidote.

Another lesson comes from the second miracle; let us look at it, and read from the forty-second verse.

> And there came a man from Baal-shalisha, and brought the man of God bread of the first fruits, twenty loaves of barley, and full ears of corn in the hush thereof. And he said, Give unto the people, that they may eat. And his servitor said, What, should I set this before an hundred men? He said again, Give the people, that they may eat: for thus saith the Lord, They shall eat, and shall leave thereof. So he set it before them, and they did eat, and left thereof, according to the word of the Lord.

The loaves brought to Elisha were not quarter loaves like ours, but either mere wafers of meal which had been laid flat on a hot stone, and so baked, or else small rolls of bread. The store was but little, yet Elisha said, "Feed the people," and they were fed. That is the third lesson: *the church is to use all she has, and trust in God to multiply her strength.* Nowadays individuals are apt to think they may leave matters to societies, but this is highly injurious; we should every one go forth to work for God, and use our own talents, be they few or many. Societies are not meant to enable us to shirk our personal duty, under the idea that our strength is small. Little churches are apt to think that they cannot' do much, and therefore they do not expect a great blessing. What can these few cakes do towards feeding a hundred men? They forget that God can multiply them. Ye limit the Holy One of Israel. Do you think he needs our numbers? Do you think he is dependent upon human strength?

I tell you our weakness is a better weapon for God than our strength. The church in the apostolic times was poor, and mostly made up of unlearned and ignorant men, but she was filled with power. What name that would have been famous in ordinary history do you find among her first members? Yet that humble church of fishermen and common people shook the world. The church is for the most part too strong, too wise, too self-dependent, to do much. Oh, that she were more God-reliant. Even those whom you call great preachers will be great evils if you trust to them. This I know, we ought never to complain of weakness, or poverty, or lack of prestige, but should consecrate to God what we have. "Oh, but I can scarcely read a chapter."

Well, read that chapter to God's glory. You who cannot say more than half-a-dozen words to others, say that little in the power of the Spirit, and God will bless the effort. If you cannot do more than write a letter to a friend about his soul, or give away a tract to a stranger in the streets, do it in God's name. Brother, sister, do what you can, and in doing this God will strangely multiply your power to do good, and cause great results to flow from small beginnings. Active faith is needed, and, if this be richly present, the Lord in whom we trust will do for us exceeding abundantly above all that we ask, or even think. Thus much concerning the passage in reference to the church of God.

Briefly, but very earnestly I desire further to speak TO BACKSLIDERS. In all our churches there are members who are no better than they should be. It is very questionable whether they ought to be allowed to be members at all; they have gone very far back from what they used to be, or ought to be. They scarcely ever join the people of God in public prayer, though they once professed to be very devout. Private prayer is neglected, and family prayer given up. Is it not so with some to whom I address myself? Have you not lost the light of God's countenance, and gone far away from happy communion with Christ? It is not for me to charge you; let your own consciences speak. I hope that you are now beginning to feel an inward hunger, and to perceive that your backslidings have brought famine upon you. What shall I bid you do? Go and attempt your own restoration by the works of the law? By no means: I bid you *bring your emptiness to Christ, and look for his fullness.* Yours is a great empty pot: set it on the fire, and cry to God to fill it. Jesus says to lukewarm Laodicea, "If any man hear my voice, and open the door, I will come in to him, and will sup with him." "Alas!" says the Loadicean, "I have nothing in the house." Your confession is true, but when our Lord comes to sup he brings his supper with him. He stands at the door of every backslider and knocks. Will you let him in? "Oh," say you, "I wish he would enter."

Dear brother, open your heart now, just as you did at the first, when as a poor sinner you went to him. Say unto him, "Blessed Lord, there is nothing in me but emptiness, but here is the guest-chamber. Come in all thy love and sup with me and let me sup with thee. I am nothing, come and be my all in all." "But," says the backslider, "may I really come to Jesus, just as I did at the first?" Listen. "Return, ye backsliding children, for I am married unto you, saith the Lord." He is married unto you, and though you have behaved badly, the marriage bond is not broken. Where is the bill of divorcement which he hath sued out? Is it not written, "he hateth putting away"? Come just as you are and begin anew, for he will accept you again. "But," say you, "alas for me, I have been gathering wild gourds!" What have you been doing, professor? You have left undone what you ought to have done, and you have done the things you ought not to have done, and therefore there is no health in you. You have been trying to find pleasure in the world, and you have found wild vines? You have been tempted by love of music, love of mirth, love of show, and you have gathered "wild gourds, a lap full," almost a heart full. You have been shredding death into the pot, and now you cannot feel as you used to feel, the poison is stupefying your soul. While God's people are singing you are sighing, "I want to sing as saints do, but there is no praise in me."

When you meet with a man who is mighty in prayer you say, "Alas, I used to pray like that, but my power is gone"—the poison is paralyzing you. If you are a worldling, and not God's child, you can live on that which would poison a Christian; but if you are a child of God you will cry out, "O thou man of God, there is death in the pot!" Some of you are rich, and have fallen into worldly, fashionable habits—these are the colocynth cucumbers which poison many.

Others of you are poor, and necessarily work with ungodly men, and perhaps their example has lowered the tone of your spirit, and led you into their ways. If you love this condition I grieve for you, but if you loathe it I trust you are a child of God, notwithstanding your decline. What are you to do who have in any way fallen? Why, *receive afresh the soul-saving gospel*. "Bring meal"—simple, nourishing, gospel truth, and cast it into the poisoned pottage. Begin anew with Jesus Christ, as you did at first; say to him, "Lord, be merciful to me a sinner." "Repent and do thy first works."

Do you not recollect the period when first your eyes lighted on his cross, and you stood there burdened and heavy-laden, fearing that you would sink to hell, until you read in his dear wounds that your sins were put away? There you found peace as you saw transgression laid on Jesus and removed from you. Oh, how you loved him. Come, brother, let us go tonight again to the cross, and begin to love him again. That will cure you of the world's poisonous influences, and bring back the old feelings, the old joys, the old loves, and take the death out of the pot. Backslider, you need now exactly what you needed at first, namely, faith in Jesus. Come repenting, come believing, to the Savior, and he will remove the ills which the gourds of earth's wild vines have brought upon you.

"Ah," say some of you, "we can understand how the Lord Jesus can fill our emptiness, and heal our soul's sicknesses, but how shall we continue in the right way? Our past experience has taught us our weakness, and we are now afraid that even the great pot will only last us for a little while, and then our souls will famish." Then remember the other part of our text, in which we read that when the few loaves, and the ears of corn in the husks, were brought to Elisha, the Lord multiplied them. Though you have very little grace, that grace shall be increased. "He giveth more grace." We receive grace for grace—daily grace for daily need. Between this and heaven you will want a heaven full of grace, and you will have it. No one knows what draughts you will make upon the sacred exchequer of the King of kings, but his treasury will not be exhausted. "Trust in the Lord, and do good; so shalt thou dwell in the land, and verily thou shalt be fed."

Our third and last word is TO THE SEEKING SINNER. Many of you, I trust, desire salvation. The subject before us has much comfort in it for you. You are hungering and thirsting after Christ, and have not yet found peace in him. You lament your own emptiness of all that is good. Then, poor soul, do just what the prophet bade his servant do—"set on the great pot"; that is, confess your emptiness unto the Lord. Tell the Lord what a sinner you are. I know not whether the story be true of Mr. Rowland Hill's leading the landlord of an inn to pray. Mr. Hill would have family prayer wherever he stayed, and if this was refused he would order out his horses and go on. On one occasion he is reported to have asked the landlord to act as priest in his own house, but the man replied, "I can't pray, I never prayed in my life." However, after a while Mr. Hill had him on his knees, and when the man said, "I cannot pray," Mr. Hill cried out, "Tell the Lord so, and ask him to help you." The man exclaimed, "O God, I can't pray, teach me." "That will do," said Mr. Hill, "you have begun." Whatever your state may be, if you desire salvation, go and tell the Lord your condition. Say, "Lord, I have a hard heart; soften it." If you cannot feel, tell him so, and ask him to make you feel. Begin at the root of the matter; set on the great pot, empty as it is. Be honest with the Most High; reveal to him what he so well knows, but what you so little know—the evil of your heart, and your great necessity. If you cannot come *with* a broken heart, come *for* a broken heart. If you cannot come with anything good, the mercy is that nothing good is needed as a preparation for Christ. Come just as you are. Do not wait to fill the pot, but set it on to be filled.

Do I hear you reply, "Ah, you don't know who I am! I have lived many years in sin." Yes, I know you: you are the young man that found the wild vine and went and gathered of its gourds a lapful—a horrible lapful. Some of you rebellious sinners have ruined yourselves, in body and in soul, and perhaps in estate as well, by your sins. We hear of people sowing their wild oats: that is a bad business. They had better never do it, for the reaping of those wild oats is terrible work. You have poisoned your life, man, with those wild gourds. Can the pottage of your life be made wholesome again? Yes, *you* cannot do it with your own efforts, but "bring meal," and it will be done. If thou believest on the

Lord Jesus he will be the antidote for deadly habits of sin. If thou wilt simply trust in him who bled for thee, the tendency of thy soul to sin shall be overcome, the poison which now boils in thy veins shall be expelled, and thy soul shall escape as a bird out of the snare of the fowler. Thy flesh upon thee, in a spiritual sense, shall become fresher than a little child's. Thou art full of the poison, till every vein is ready to burst with it: the great Physician will give thee an antidote which shall at once and for ever meet thy case. Wilt thou not try it? Incline thine ear and come unto him; hear, and thy soul shall live. May God put the meal of the gospel into the pot even now.

"Ah," say you, "but if I were now pardoned, how should I hold on? I have made a hundred promises and always broken them; I have resolved scores of times, but my resolutions have never come to anything." Ah, poor heart, that is when thou hast the saving of thyself; but when God has the saving of thee, it will be another matter. When we begin to save ourselves we very soon come to a disastrous shipwreck; but when God, the eternal lover of the souls of men, puts his hand to salvation-work, and Jesus puts forth the hand once fastened to the cross, there are no total failures then. He saves indeed, and saves to the end. The little grace received by the soul at first shall never be exhausted; it shall grow and grow so long as need remains. The barley loaves and the ears of corn in the husks shall be increased, and thou shalt have enough and to spare.

I have tried to preach a very simple sermon, and to say some earnest things; but it is likely I may have missed the mark with some, and therefore I will again draw the gospel bow in the name of the Lord Jesus. O Lord, direct the arrow. If God will bring souls to Jesus, I will bless his name throughout eternity. Poor lost souls, do you know the way of salvation, do you know how simple it is? Do you know the love of God to such poor souls as you are, and yet do you refuse to attend to it? Do you know that he does not exact any hard conditions of you, but he points to his Son on the cross, and says, "Look"? Can it be that you will not look? Does Jesus die to save, and do you think it is not worth your while to think about salvation? What is the matter with you? Surely you must be mad. When I look back on my own neglect of Christ, till I was fifteen years old, it seems like a delirious dream, and when I think of some of you who are thirty or forty, and yet have never thought about your souls, what can be invented to excuse you?

I see some of you with bald heads, or with the snow of wintry age lying upon them, and you have not yet considered the world to come; I would say to you, "Men, are you mad?" Why, ye are worse than mad, for if ye were insane, ye would be excused. Alas, the madness of sin has responsibility connected with it, and therefore it is the worst of all insanities. I pray you by the living God, you unsaved ones, turn unto the Savior at once. If you be saved or lost it cannot so much matter to me as it will to you. If I faithfully beseech you to look to Jesus, I shall be clear, even if you reject the warning: but for your own sakes, I beseech you to turn to Jesus. By death, which may be so near to you; by judgment, which is certain to you all; by the terrors of hell, by the thunderbolts of execution, by eternity, and better still, by the sweets of Jesus' love, by the charms of his matchless beauty, by the grace which he is prepared to give, by the heaven whose gates of pearl are glistening before the eye of faith, by the sea of glass unruffled by a single wave of trouble, where you shall stand for ever blest if you believe in Jesus, by the Lord himself, I entreat you, seek him while he may be found. May his Holy Spirit lead you so to do. Amen and Amen.

8

The Saint of the Smithy

Latter-day Saints are very objectionable people on account of their peculiar ideas upon marriage; but we have a great liking for *every-day saints*. The taste of the medieval ages was enchanted with holy men who could sail overseas upon outspread table-cloths, or fast for forty consecutive days, or carry their heads in their hands after decapitation, but such Specimens of sanctity, besides being in these degenerate times most hard to get at, are too unearthly, we mean too little human to enlist our sympathy. St. Francis, when described as so elevated by his devotions that his disciples could only kiss the soles of his feet as he floated in the air, is too ethereal for our liking, we want a little more gravity than this in a saint, peradventure it may turn out that a little more levity would do as well.

The grace which unfits a man for the duties of this present life is a doubtful blessing; in a romance your superfine mystic may have a conspicuous place allotted him, but in real life he is a nullity, a chip in the porridge, or worse. He who can pray like Elias is all the better an example for mankind if he avoids all affectation of superhuman refinement, and lets us see that, like the grand old prophet, he is a man of like passions with us. We admire Paul caught up into the third heaven; but those who were thrown into his company felt the power of his godliness all the more because he could make a tent or light a fire as occasion demanded. Holiness in white gowns or black silk aprons, or lace half-a-yard deep, reminds us of love in a valentine, very romantic, roseate, and all that, but quite another thing from flesh and blood affection. One longs to see the popular idea of holiness once for all dissociated from anything unreal and unpractical, and yoked with the common virtues of everyday life. The smashing up of the whole caravan of sanctified waxworks which, in years gone by, have attracted ignorant admiration, would be a special benefit to our race; and the exhibition of real, household, commonsense religion in its most vigorous form, would be under God one of the greatest blessings which our age could receive.

Our remarks will not, we hope, be misunderstood. Sanctification cannot be carried too far, holiness unto the Lord can never be too complete; the very highest forms of elevated character are to be our models, and we ought not to rest until we have equaled them; but we have lived long enough in this world to be afraid of squeamish and pretentious sanctity. The grossest hypocrites we have ever been deceived by were superfluously unctuous in expression; and the faultiest professors whose falls have saddened ns, were superlatively fastidious in their religious tastes. We have come to be afraid of gold that glitters too much, and bread that is too white. Men always will be imperfect, and when they profess perfection, and become too good to attend to their duties as husbands, or servants, or children, or parents, so as to make others happy, they prove themselves to be but "worse for mending; washed to fouler stains." If they could manage to be perfect without making everybody else miserable, they should have our reverent admiration, but while we can find in the life of the only truly perfect man so much that is genial and intensely human, we shall never enshrine mere unearthliness in the heavenly places.

Our Savior could not have been more a man had he been sinful; his humanity though immaculate was not effeminate, though without sin he was not therefore abridged of any essential attribute of everyday manhood; he was no walker on stilts, his holiness trod on *terra firma* with other men; he was no recluse, he ate and drank with the many; he was not even an ascetic, but was found at marriages and festivals. A man among men, nothing that concerned mankind was alien to him, no joy of humble men was to him ridiculous, no sorrow of mournful women contemptible. Give to the world an exhibition of such holiness on a wide scale, and while convents and monasteries would molder into ruins, the whole earth would be gladdened by a golden era worthy to match with the millennial glory. Let the parlor and the drawing-room be adorned with cheerful piety, let the kitchen and the scullery be sanctified with unobtrusive godliness, let the shop and the office, the shed and the factory, be perfumed with unassuming holiness; let forge and bench, and stall and lathe and spinning-jenny, all be holiness unto the Lord, and the better times long sighed for will have come at last. We do not mean that men should become abject slaves of mere external religiousness; far from it, the true piety of which we write will give them the fullest freedom; when hearts are right, wills are rectified, and goodness becomes the highest delight of the soul: the reign of righteousness will be the era of liberty and joy. Men will be all the more men when they become God's men; and even the peculiarities of their individual temper and constitution will not be extinguished, but made to subserve the glory of the Lord by exhibiting in charming variety the beauty of holiness.

Such thoughts came into our mind as we took up the memoir which we read years ago, and which we dare say some of our readers have even now fresh in their memories, we refer to the "Life of the Village Blacksmith," Samuel Hick, or more correctly, Sammy Hick. Sammy was a Yorkshireman, belonging to no readily specified order of men. If you sort and arrange mankind, he comes under no genus; he was one by himself, after his own order; he was—well, he was Sammy Hick, and nobody else. Simple, yet shrewd; bold, yet cautious; generous to a fault, thoroughly original, quaint to a proverb, humorous, devout, full of faith, zealous, sufficiently self-opinioned, humble, rough, gentle, pure, dogmatical, resolute—he was as a Christian a very remarkable amalgam of much gold and silver, with here and there a lump of iron or clay. Called by grace while wielding the hammer, he continued in his honest calling, and made his smithy the center of evangelical activities, which entirely changed the appearance of the society among which he moved. He was a man who could not be hid, and though poor and illiterate, the force of his character made him a power among all around.

Oh, that all our church members would make it their ambition to make their worldly avocations a vantage ground for fighting their Master's battles! While Sammy was yet a mere seeker, he showed the force of his nature by defending an open-air preacher against a clergyman. Just as his reverence was about to pull down the Methodist evangelist from the preaching-block, the youthful neophyte clenched his fists, and holding them in a menacing fashion before his face, accosted the surprised divine with the summary remark: "Sir, if you disturb that man of God, I'll drop you as sure as ever you were born." The emphasis of the words prevented the necessity of the blows, and having secured a hearing for his teacher, the muscular Christian subsided into the attentive listener. When at length led to the cross, and admitted into peace with God, Sammy thought that he could make all the world believe, and resolved to commence operations upon the landlady of an inn, which he had frequented in his unregenerate days. The woman was surprised to hear words of warning and instruction from such a mouth, and indignantly turned him out of her house. Having but lately proved the power of prayer on his own account, Sam withdrew to a quiet corner, and poured out his soul to God on her behalf. No sooner was the cry lifted up to heaven than it was heard: the woman, on his return to the house, begged his pardon for her rudeness, entreated him to kneel down and ask the Lord to save her, and lived and died a lover of the truths which she had once despised.

Thus encouraged, Hick became a leader among a zealous band of Wesleyans, who were incessantly seeking the conversion of souls; and so absorbed did he become in soul-winning, that one night, awaking suddenly from a dream, he aroused his wife, and accosting her by name, exclaimed, "Matty, I believe I am called to preach the gospel." Martha, who was his guardian angel, and an admirable make-weight in the direction of prudence, bade him go to sleep again, at the same time casting considerable doubts upon the authenticity of the call. His brethren in the circuit judged otherwise than Martha, and Sammy was allowed to deliver his singular but powerful addresses from the Methodist pulpits around his native village. His harangues would, doubtless, have been the reverse of edifying to our educated readers, but they created no small stir among the colliers and laborers of the district. Hick, as a preacher, was adapted to his hearers, a matter of the first importance; it is of no use to try to open oysters with a Mappin's razor, and, on the other hand, delicate surgery is not to be performed with a bill-hook; every instrument must be adapted to its end.

In so wide a world as this, it is a man's own fault if he does not find a sphere for which he is better fitted than any other man. Some of the quieter Methodists could not stand Samuel's noise; "But," said Samuel, "it was a mercy they went out, for it rid the place of a deal of unbelief, which they took away with them." No good man can hope to please everybody, and no brave man will break his heart when he finds that he has failed in this respect, as others have done before him. Our hero went on with his praying and preaching, and left others to criticize or censure who felt a leaning in that direction. His discoursings were once condemned as terribly rambling, and the good man, instead of denying the charge, claimed some sort of merit for it—"For," said he, "those who go straight on may perhaps hit one, but my talk, as it goes in and out among the crowd, knocks many down." His best preachings, however, were not from the pulpit, but by the smithy fire. Though he ranged his circuit with burning zeal, and had his name on two sets of plans, because, as he said, "There is no living with half work," yet it was at the forge that he dealt the heaviest strokes, there he melted the hardened, and riveted his life-work. A neighboring squire rode up to Sam's forge, upon a horse which had lost a shoe in the heat of the chase. His squireship commenced swearing at some other smith who had yesterday put on the shoe so clumsily; whereupon, without further ceremony, the worthy blacksmith quietly informed him that he paid the rent of the shop, and that while it was in his hands he would suffer no man to take God's name in vain within those walls, and that if he swore again, he would not set the shoe on. Many a man with a cleaner face would have hesitated before he so consistently maintained his Maker's cause. The rebuke was kindly taken, and when the horse was shod, a piece of silver was offered in payment, which he was expected to retain, but Sam, as honest as he was bold, returned the change, saying, "I only charge a poor man twopence, and I shall charge you, sir, no more." Shoeing must have been cheap in those days; but the return of the change has a nobility about it, grandly like the princely independence of Abraham, when he said to the king of Sodom, "I will not take from a thread to a shoe-latchet, lest thou shouldst say, I have made Abraham rich."

His rebuke of certain fox-hunting parsons was as clever as it was cutting. "They met *anent* (opposite) my shop," says Samuel, and stopped till the hounds came. Among the party were the Hon. C. C—, vicar of K—, the Earl's brother; the Rev. W—, rector of G—; the late Rev. C— vicar of A—; and Dr. E—, who followed the medical profession at K—. "It came into my mind," continued Samuel, "that the three clergymen had no business there." His movements generally corresponding with the rapidity of his thoughts, he instantly "threw down the hammer and the tongs," darted out of the shop door, and appeared in the midst of them with his shirt sleeves turned up, his apron on, his face and hands partaking of the hue of his employment, as fine game, in the estimation of some of them, to occupy the lingering moments, till other game should be started, as any that could present itself in human shape. "Most of them," says he, "knew me. I said to them, gentlemen, this is one of the finest hunts in the district. You are favoured with two particular privileges; and they are privileges which other districts have not." This excited curiosity, which was as quickly gratified; for the enquiry relative to *"privileges"* was no sooner proposed than the answer was given: "If any of you should happen to slip the saddle, and get a fall, you have a *doctor* to *bleed* you; and three *parsons* to *pray* for you: and what are these but privileges? THREE PARSONS! Oh! yes, there they are."

Methodists are great at begging, and our hero never flinched from his share of that hardest of labors. His success was remarkable, but his courage was more so. His begging was not confined within the limit which decorum usually suggests.

"I went to Ricall," says he; "and I purposed going to all the houses in the town; I thought there would be no harm in calling upon the church clergyman. I did so, and found him in his garden. I presented my book, which he gave me again, and looked at me." The look would have had a withering effect upon many of Samuel's superiors; but the same spirit and views which had emboldened him to make the application, supported him in the rebuff with which he met. "I am surprised," said the clergyman, "that you should make such a request; that you should ask me to support dissenters from the Church of England!" Samuel instantly interposed with, "No, sir, we are not dissenters; the church has *dissented* from us. The Methodists are good churchmen, where the gospel is preached. And as for myself, I never turned my back on a collecting paper when I went to church. I think there is no more harm in you helping to support us, than there is in us helping to support you." The clergyman here took shelter under the wing of the State—his only ground of defence—by replying, "You are obliged to support us; the law binds you to do it." Samuel, in return, resorted to the only code of laws with which he had any acquaintance, and which he consulted daily, the *Christian code*, saying, "Ours is a law of love; and if we cannot all think alike, we must all love alike."

Though foiled by the ecclesiastic, he succeeded better with the laity, and notably on the occasion when he carried a miser by storm. He had stated the needs of the Lord's work, but found his friend utterly immovable. Down on his knees fell Samuel, and commenced fervently pleading for the miserly soul, that God would forgive him for daring to plead poverty when he had thousands of gold and silver, and for venturing to profess to be a Christian while he worshipped his self. "Sam," cried the farmer, with great vehemence, "I'll give thee a guinea if thou wilt give over." This availed nothing, for the suppliant only began to plead with the greater fervor that pardon might be given to the miserly creature who could only give a single guinea towards the evangelization of the world, when the Lord had done so much for him. This last assault made the farmer alarmed lest he should be induced to give too much, and therefore he roared out, "Sam, I tell thee to give over: I'll give thee two guineas, if thou wilt only give it up." The two guineas were instantaneously secured, and borne away in triumph. Shockingly bad taste no doubt all this, but the man could no more help it than an eagle can help flying. His heart and soul were as red hot as his own coals when the bellows were going, and there was no room in his case for deliberations as to taste and propriety. His own giving was always beyond the point which prudence and Martha would have tolerated; he emptied his pockets on all missionary and collecting occasions, with far more glee than money grubbers feel when they are filling theirs. He had a right to fetch another man's ass for his Master, since he was delighted to put his own clothes upon it.

Sammy was great at a sick bed, though even there the eccentric element would occasionally crop out, as for instance, when upon going to visit a Roman Catholic, he was repulsed by the priest, but urged as a reason for admittance that he could help the priest, for "two are better far than one." Prayer was his delight, and his power in it with his God made many wonder. We personally know that prayer is a reality, and therefore we cast no doubts upon the recorded instances in which this childlike man prevailed in supplication. One of those most often caviled at is thus narrated by his biographer, Mr. Everett: Samuel was at Knottingly, a populous village in the neighborhood of Ferrybridge, in 1817, where he took occasion to inform his hearers that there would be a love feast at Micklefield, on a certain day, when he should be glad to see all who were entitled to that privilege. He further observed, with his usual frankness and generosity, that he had six bushels of corn, and that they should be ground for the occasion. These comprised the whole of the corn left of the previous year's produce.

When, therefore, he returned home, and named his general invitation and intention, Martha, who had as deep an interest in it as himself, enquired very expressively, "And didst thou tell them, when all the corn was done, how we were to get through the remainder of the season, till another crop should be reaped?" Tomorrow, alas! rarely entered into Samuel's calculations, unless connected with the church. The day fixed for the love-feast drew near—there was no flour in the house—and the windmills, in consequence of a long calm, stretched out their arms in vain to catch the rising breeze. In the midst of this death-like quiet, Samuel carried his corn to the mill nearest his own residence, and requested the miller to unfurl his sails. The miller objected, stated that there was no "wind." Samuel, on the other hand, continued to urge his request, saying, "I will go and pray while you spread the cloth." More with a view of gratifying the applicant than from any faith he had in Him who holds the natural winds in his fists, and who answers the petitions of his creatures, the man stretched his canvas. No sooner had he done this, than, to his utter astonishment, a fine breeze sprung up, the fans whirled round, the corn was converted into meal, and Samuel returned with his burthen rejoicing, and had everything in readiness for the festival. A neighbor who had seen the fans in vigorous motion, took also some corn to be ground; but the wind had dropped, and the miller remarked, "You must send for Sammy Hick to pray for the wind to blow again." We have more faith in this story than in all the Papist miracles put together, laugh who may.

His plain personal remarks to individuals were frequently the means of conversion. Would to God that we all were more skillful in the like means of usefulness. "A young lady, who had been known to him from her childhood, and whose palfrey had lost a shoe, called at his shop to have it replaced. She appeared delicate. He looked compassionately upon her, and asked, 'Do you know, *barn*, whether you have a soul?' Startled with the question, she looked in return; but before she was permitted to reply, he said, 'You have one, whether you know it or not; and it will live in happiness or misery forever.' These and other remarks produced serious reflections. Her father perceived from her manner, on her return home—her residence being not far from Samuel's dwelling—that something was preying upon her spirits. She told him the cause: 'What!' he exclaimed, 'has the old blacksmith been at thee, to turn thy head? But I will *whack* (beat) him.' So saying, he took up a large stick, similar to a hedge-stake—left the house—posted off to Samuel's residence—found him at the anvil—and without the least intimation, fetched him a heavy blow on the side, which, said Samuel, when relating the circumstance, 'nearly felled me to the ground,' adding, 'and it is not a little that would have done it in those days.' On receiving the blow, he turned round, and said, 'What are you about, man? what is that for?' Supposing it to be out of revenge, and that religion was the cause of it, he made a sudden wheel, and lifting up his arm, inclined the other side to his enraged assailant, saying, 'Here, man, hit that too.' But either the man's courage failed him, or he was softened by the manner in which the blow was received; beholding in Samuel a real disciple of him who said, 'Whosoever shall smite thee on the right cheek, turn to him the other also.' He then left him; and Samuel had the happiness of witnessing the progress of religion in the daughter.

Sometime after this, the person himself was taken ill, and Samuel was sent for. He was shown into the chamber, and, looking on the sick man, he asked, 'What is the matter with you? Are you *bown* to die?' He stretched out his arm to Samuel, and said, 'Will you forgive me?' Not recollecting the circumstance for a moment, Samuel asked, 'What for? I have nothing against you, *barn*, nor any man living.' The case being stated, the question was again asked, 'Will you forgive me?' 'Forgive you, *barn*? I tell you I have nothing against you! But if you are about to die, we will pray a bit, and see if the Lord will forgive you.' Samuel knelt by the side of the couch, and the dying man united with him: and from the penitence, fervor, and gratitude which he manifested, there was hope in his death. The daughter continued an object of his solicitude: she grew up to womanhood—became a mother, and he afterwards exulted to see her and two of her daughter's members of the Wesleyan Society. Four conversions are here to be traced in regular succession, and attributable apparently to a word fitly and seasonably spoken by one of the *weak things* of this world becoming mighty through God."

So accustomed to success was our friend, that when he was in London he felt an impulse to try his hand at the conversion of a Jew, who kept a silversmith's shop opposite his lodging. The result was such as one could have prophesied. Jacob eyed Samuel with keenness, thinking to himself, "Here is a greenhorn from the country, I will make some monish out of him." Samuel, on the contrary, with childlike simplicity, said within himself, "Here is a soul to be saved, I will tell him the blessed gospel." They exchanged looks, and Samuel opened fire. "Bless the Lord! Here is a fine morning!" Jacob replied, "It ish, it ish fery fine. Vat be the besht news in city?" "The best news that I can hear," replied Samuel, "is that Jesus Christ is pardoning sinners and sanctifying believers." "Poh, poh," rejoined Jacob, turning as red as scarlet, "tuff and nonshensh! It ish all telusion." Whereat Samuel replied with the testimony of his own experience of this *blessed* delusion, which for forty years had comforted and sanctified his soul: but Jacob had banged the shop door, and beaten a retreat into the little room, leaving Samuel to bless the Lord that he had not been left to be numbered with unbelievers. Such a man would beard the Pope himself, and tell the Grand Turk to his face, that in Jesus alone is salvation. The fact is, he lived an artless life; he believed unquestioningly, and was strong; he acted conscientiously, and had no need to fear; he served his Lord unwaveringly, and his reward was power both with God and men. The reader may enquire concerning his death, but we shall give no details; far more important is it to gather wisdom from his life. Like him we may expect to die, singing "Glory, glory, glory," if we have lived under the power of grace.

We should be sorry to see any man imitate Sammy Hick, the copy would be disgusting; but if all our working men and women who are saved by grace would in some such way as he did live and labor for the spread of the gospel, the day would soon break, and the shadows flee away. More genuine, simple, personal piety, and less burnish and mimicry of religion, and the world would behold the church as "terrible as an army with banners."

9

In A Fog

That Gog and Magog are legitimate sovereigns of our great city of London we will not venture to dispute; but there is a third potentate whose reign is far more real, and whose dominion is vastly more oppressive—his name is FOG. The other day we rode through London at noonday; through London we said; we meant through a mass of vapor looking almost as thick as melted butter,

>With a sordid stain
>   Of yellow, like a lion's mane,

A stinging savor of smoke made our eyes run with tears, and a most uncomfortable, clinging, cobwebby dampness surrounded us like a wet blanket, and sent a cold chill to the very marrow of our bones. Light had departed, and darkness, like a black pall, hung horribly over every street—a dense gloom which could not be cheered even by the lamps which in all the shops were burning as if night had set in. The fog sensibly affected all the organs of our body.

>Vapor importunate and dense,
>   It wars at once with every sense.
>The ears escape not. All around
>   Returns a dull unwonted sound.

Few were the passengers in the streets, and those few flitted before us like shadows, or passed shivering by us like wet sparrows looking out for shelter in a heavy rain. It was of no use to be wretched, and therefore we became thoughtful, and condensed a little of the black mist into drops of meditation.

Are we not all more or less travelling in a fog through this land of cloud and gloom? What is life? 'Tis but a vapor; and that vapor is often a thick, light-obstructing mist! Of the forms around us in God's fair universe have we much more discernment than a fog-picture? To some extent "a formless grey confusion covers all." Where we see one trace of our glorious God, do we not fail to perceive a thousand of the divine touches of his pencil? We may not dare to say even of earthly things that "we see," or those who have formed some guess of what true *seeing* means will soon declare us to be blind.

As to the revelation with which our heavenly Father has so graciously favored us, how little have we gazed upon it in the clear daylight of its own glory. Our prejudices, predilections, fancies, infirmities, follies, iniquities, unbeliefs, and vanities have raised a marsh-mist through which heaven's own stars can scarcely dart their cheering rays. There is light enough abroad if the dense fog would suffer it to reach us, but for want of the wind of heaven to chase away the obscuring vapors we walk in twilight and see but glimmerings of truth. We are proud indeed if we dream of attaining a clear view of heavenly things by our own carnal minds, while we grope under moral, mental, and spiritual glooms, which have made the best of men cry, "Enlighten our darkness, good Lord."

Well did Paul say, "Here we know in part," and, "here we see through a glass darkly." We have not yet attained face-to-face vision: happy day shall it be when we escape from this cloudland, and come into the true light where they need no candle, neither light of the sun. We who have believed are not of the night nor of darkness, but yet the smoke of things terrestrial dims our vision and clouds our prospect. When we think of the doctrines of grace, of the person of Christ, of the inward work of the Spirit—when we think of these simpler matters—to say nothing of the heaven which is to be revealed, of the prophetic apocalypse, or of the glorious coming of the Son of man, how great does our ignorance appear and how small our knowledge! Faith believes what her God has told her; but by reason of "the turbid air" in which we live, how little do we understand of what we believe! When our fellows boastingly cry,

"We see," how readily may we detect their blindness. Those men who claim to know all things—who are incapable of further enlightenment—whose creed is made of cast iron and can never be altered—these are the most blind of us all, or else they dwell amidst the thickest and densest mists. Surely, we are in a fog—the best of us feel the dread shadow of the fall hovering over us. O Sun of Righteousness, shine forth! Remove our darkness; in thy light let us see light. Then will our glad voices ring out thy praises, when we shall see thee as thou art, and shall be like thee! We would not give up what little we do see of our Beloved for all the world, for though it be but a glimpse, it is, nevertheless, a vision so blessed that it enables us to wait patiently until we shall see "the King in his beauty, and the land that is very far off."

Being once surrounded by a dense mist on the Styhead Pass in the Lake District, we felt ourselves to be transported into a world of mystery where everything was swollen to a size and appearance more vast, more terrible, than is usual on this sober planet. A little mountain tarn, scarcely larger than a farmer's horse-pond, expanded into a great lake whose distant shores were leagues beyond the reach of our poor optics; and as we descended into the valley of Wastwater, the rocks rose on one side like the battlements of heaven, and the descent on the other hand looked like the dreadful lips of a yawning abyss: and yet when one looked back again in the morning's clear light there was nothing very dangerous in the pathway, or terrible in the rocks. The road was a safe though sharp descent, devoid of terrors to ordinary mountain-climbers. In the distance through the fog the shepherd "stalks gigantic," and his sheep are full-grown lions. Into such blunders do we fall in our life-pilgrimage; a little trouble in the distance is, through our mistiness, magnified into a crushing adversity. We see a lion in the way, although it is written that no ravenous beast shall go up thereon. A puny foe is swollen into a Goliath, and the river of death widens into a shoreless sea. Come, heavenly wind, and blow the mist away, and then the foe will be despised, and the bright shores on the other side of the river will stand out clear in the light of faith!

Men often mistake friends for foes because of the fog in which they walk. Mr. Jay tells us of one who saw a monster in the distance. He was greatly afraid, but having summoned courage enough to meet it, the monster turned out to be his own brother John. We frequently keep aloof from the best of people for want of knowing them: if we could see them as they are we should love them.

The fog so marvelously magnifies faults and distorts peculiarities—we think men dragons, if not devils, in the distance, when a closer view assures us that they are saints and brethren. We all need to be cautioned against misjudging one another.

If the world-fog operates upon Christians who are the children of light, it is little wonder if it has a far worse influence *upon unconverted men*. They wander in a day of gloom and of thick darkness, in a "darkness which may be felt." Concerning them we may say that their mists shut out the sun. The mercy revealed in the gospel reaches not the sinner's eyes; his doubts, his sins, his follies keep it away from him. We have full often held up Christ crucified before the sinner, but he could not see him. We have preached a full salvation to the guilty one, but he could not discern it. The beams of gospel light are obstructed by the dense mist of carnality in which the worldling lives. Alas for the ungodly! Their state is one of such darkness that *they lose their way*. In the firm belief that they are travelling to heaven, they choose the path which leadeth to destruction. They go gayly on, dreaming that they shall reach the rest which remaineth for the people of God, but they stumble to fall forever. False teaching, sinful inclination, prejudice and predilection, cast a cloud over the sinner's reason, so that he chooses his own damnation. Even when partially convinced of sin he betakes himself to his own self-righteousness, and wanders like a blind man upon a vast plain, toiling hard to reach his destination but making no progress, for there is darkness over all his paths.

It is likely that in such a state as this *the sinner may be very near the home where there is rest to be had, and yet he may not know it*: in a dense fog it is no unusual thing for a person to be standing before his own door in total ignorance of his whereabouts. The sinner has heard the gospel preached, but he does not know it as good news for him. He has been present when the Spirit of God has been moving over the assembly, but he did not feel its power. When a mother's tears fell on his forehead he did not perceive that she was God's angel of mercy to him. When, afterwards, affliction came and he was laid on the bed of sickness to meditate, he did not know that God had designs of love towards him in bringing him low. Oh that the Spirit of God would dispel these soul-destroying clouds, and make the sinner see that the knocker of mercy's gate is near his hand, and that if he do but use it with earnestness the door will surely be opened, and he shall enter in to be housed, to be welcomed, to be feasted, to be blessed forever!

This darkness, if it continue always, *will lure the sinner on to his own destruction*. It makes him wretched now, for to walk in spiritual darkness is misery indeed. Our London fog finds its way through your clothing, your flesh, and your bones, right into your very marrow, there is hardly anything more cold and penetrating; and the sinner's life is very like it: he tries to keep out the feeling of despondency, and fear and apprehension, by a thousand inventions which the world calls pleasure, but he cannot do it. He is "without God," and he is therefore without hope; he is without Christ, and he is consequently without rest. He is well pictured by those poor shivering, hall-clad, hungry creatures whom we see in a foggy night hurrying on to get a cold seat on the workhouse doorstep. The worst of all is, that the sinner is hastening to his own destruction. He little knows what is before him. His last step was on the firm earth, but his foot now hangs over the jaws of perdition. Beware, O man. Beware, for you are on the brink of a precipice! The fog conceals your danger, but it is none the less real. Beware, for when that fatal plunge is once taken, remonstrances from friends and remorse from self will be all in vain!

* * *

To change our line of thought. Is there not a darkness which God sends on men,—not moral darkness, for "God is light, and in him is no darkness at all," but the gloom of adversity and affliction? The believer may be in thick darkness as to his circumstances, and as to his soul's enjoyment of the comforts of religion. Some Christians are favored with constant sunlight, but others, like nightingales, sing God's praises best in the night. How dense is this fog just now! Well, what about it? We do not recollect ever thanking God in family prayer for the light of the sun, but we will do so to-night right heartily, for the fog has taught us the value of sunlight. It may be that we should never value the sun it he did not sometimes hide himself behind a cloud. How thankful is the Christian for peace of mind when doubts and fears are gone! How grateful we are to God for prosperity when adverse days are over.

As one sees the lamps all lit, it strikes us that *the darkness makes us value the means of light*. On foggy nights every twopenny link boy is a jewel. He is of no use in the day; we drive the urchin away; but when it is very thick and foggy we are glad to see the blaze of his torch. When we are high and lifted up, and are marching on joyously, we are apt to despise the means of grace; but when we are troubled, the throne of grace, the prayer-meeting, and the preaching of God's Word are highly prized. Certain professors, who cannot hear anybody except their favorite minister, would be glad of consolation from any lip, if soul trouble should overtake them. The candle of the promise stands us in good stead when we walk in the shades of sorrow, and the Word becomes a lamp unto our feet, and a light unto our path.

When we are seeking our home in a fog *how we prize company!* When you do not know where you are going, and have only half an idea that you are steering right, how cheerfully you make a friend of any poor laboring man who is going your way! If it be a rough-looking navy, it does not matter, he is in the same distress, and you salute him. There is a close kinship in trouble. There are no gentlemen on board sinking ships: every man then is taken for what he is practically worth. When Christians are in the darkness of affliction, it is delightful to observe how "they that fear the Lord speak often one to another." Some poor old woman who knows the things of God by experience becomes of more value to you in your hour of grief than the dainty gentleman whose company bewitched you aforetime. Let all who are mourning open their hearts to true brethren, and in sympathy they will find solace.

We have harped long enough on this string, but we must strike it once more. When it is dark and misty abroad the traveler *longs the more earnestly to reach his home*; and it is one of the blessings of our heavy crosses, our sicknesses, and our troubles, that they set us longing for heaven. When everything goes well with us we exclaim, like Peter, "Lord, let us build three tabernacles, for it is good to be here." But the mists cover Tabor's brow, and we fear as we enter into the cloud, and long to be away where glooms can never come. After a long journey on a dismal, dreary, beclouded road, how delightful will it be when our Father shall shut to the door of his house above, and shut out every particle of darkness and sorrow for ever and ever.

Thus far we have thought of the believer's trials: but *those who are not saved may yet be caught in a fog of trouble.* We think we can see a lost one as we look into the haze around us. Yes—here is the picture. Up till lately he has always prospered. He was considered by all about him to be a knowing man; he knew "what's what," as the world says: he felt but little uneasiness of conscience or trouble of mind. All at once he has come into a state of doubt and distress. He is enveloped in a fog: he does not know which way to turn, he is *non-plussed*. He guided others, he wants a guide himself now, but dares not trust any man. All the old accustomed land-marks are gone from sight; whether to go this way or that he cannot tell. His health fails; he is depressed in spirits and feels broken down. A mighty one has taken the old lion by his beard, a mysterious influence has cowed the valor of the boaster. Man in the mist, we salute you, and are glad that you are where you are! Do not think that we rejoice in your sorrow for its own sake, but we hail it for its after consequences. We are rejoiced that your wisdom is turned to folly, for God's wisdom will now be displayed!

Now you are beginning to feel uneasiness in the world we are greatly in hopes that yon will give it up, and seek your lasting good elsewhere. O man in the mist! You have come to a dead stop; prudence has cried, "Halt!" While you are thus perplexed we pray that you may prayerfully consider your ways. You have been in a bad way up till now; for that road is always bad in which God is forgotten and Jesus slighted! You have had troubles and sicknesses, these have been mercy's fog signals laid down on your road, and they have startled you with their explosion; but you have gone on, and on, until you dare not proceed further, for yon cannot see an inch on either side.

Stop, poor friend, and listen to the voice of one who careth for the sons of men; "He that believeth on the Lord Jesus Christ shall be saved, but he that believeth not is condemned already, because he hath not believed in the name of the only-begotten Son of God." And, "Believe on the Lord Jesus Christ, and thou shalt be saved." When a ship is enveloped in fog, what can she do better than cast her anchor? But you have no anchor, for you are without hope in Christ. God give you of his grace to obtain the hope most sure and steadfast, and then your vessel shall ride at anchor and fear no ill. A simple reliance upon the work of Jesus brings salvation with it.

10

A Visit to Christ's Hospital

"Fools because of their transgression, and because of their iniquities, are afflicted. Their soul abhorreth all manner of meat; and they draw near unto the gates of death. Then they cry unto the Lord in their trouble, and he saveth them out of their distresses. He sent his word and healed them, and delivered them from their destructions. Oh that men would praise the Lord for his goodness, and for his wonderful works to the children of men! And let them sacrifice the sacrifices of thanksgiving, and declare his works with rejoicing" (Ps. 107:17–22).

It is a very profitable thing to visit a hospital. The sight of others' sickness tends to make us grateful for our own health, and it is a great thing to be kept in a thankful frame of mind, for ingratitude is a spiritual disease, injurious to every power of the soul. A hospital inspection will also teach us compassion, and that is of great service. Anything that softens the heart is valuable. Above all things, in these days, we should strive against the petrifying influences which surround us. It is not easy for a man, who has constantly enjoyed good health and prosperity, to sympathize with the poor and the suffering. Even our great High Priest, who is full of compassion, learned it by carrying our sorrows in his own person. To see the sufferings of the afflicted, in many cases, would be enough to move a stone, and if we go to the hospital and come back with a tenderer heart, we shall have found it a sanatorium to ourselves. I purpose at this time to take you to a hospital. It shall not be one of those noble institutions so pleasingly plentiful around the Tabernacle; but we will take you to Christ's Hospital, or, as the French would call it, the *Hôtel Dieu*, and we shall conduct you through the wards for a few minutes, trusting that while you view them, if you are yourself healed, you may feel gratitude that you have been delivered from spiritual sicknesses, and an intense compassion for those who still pine and languish. May we become like our Savior, who wept over Jerusalem with eyes which were no strangers to compassion's floods: may we view the most guilty and impenitent with yearning hearts, and grieve with mingled hope and anxiety over those who are under the sound of the gospel, and so are more especially patients in the Hospital of God.

We will go at once with the psalmist to the wards of spiritual sickness.

And, first, we have set out before us THE NAMES AND CHARACTERS OF THE PATIENTS. You see, in this hospital, written up over the head of every couch the name of the patient and his disease, and you are amazed to find that all the inmates belong to one family, and, singularly enough, are all called by one name, and that name is very far from being a reputable one. It is a title that nobody covets, and that many persons would be very indignant to have applied to them—"FOOL." All who are sick in God's hospital are fools, without exception, for this reason, that all sinners are fools.

Often, in Scripture, when David means the wicked, he says, "the foolish"; and in this he makes no mistake, for sin is folly. Sin is foolish, clearly, because it is a setting-up of our weakness in opposition to omnipotence. Every wise man, if he must fight, will choose a combatant against whom he may have a chance of success; but he who wars with the Most High commits as gross a folly as when the moth contends with the flame, or the dry grass of the prairie challenges the fire. There is no hope for thee, O sinful man, of becoming a victor in the struggle. How unwise thou art to take up the weapons of rebellion! And the folly is aggravated, because the person who is opposed is one so infinitely good that opposition to him is violence to everything that is just, beneficial, and commendable. God is love: shall I resist the infinitely loving? He scatters blessings: wherefore should I be his foe?

If his commandments were grievous, if his ways were ways of misery, and his paths were paths of woe, I might have some pretense of an excuse for resisting his will. But, O my God, so good, so kind, so boundless in grace, 'tis folly, as well as wickedness, to be thine enemy. Besides this, the laws of God are so supremely beneficial to ourselves that we are our own enemies when we rebel. God's laws are danger signals. As sometimes on the ice those who care for human life put up "DANGER" here and there, and leave all that is safe for all who choose to traverse it, so God has left us free to enjoy everything that is safe for us, and has only forbidden us that which is to our own hurt. If there be a law which forbids me to put my hand into the fire, it is a pity I should need such a law, but a thousand pities more if I think that law a hardship. The commands of God do but forbid us to injure ourselves. To keep them is to keep ourselves in holy happiness; to break them is to bring evil of all kinds upon ourselves in soul and body.

Why should I violate a law, which if I were perfect I should myself have made, or myself have kept, finding it in force? Why need I rebel against that which is never exacting, never oppressive, but always conducive to my own highest welfare? The sinner is a fool, because he is told in God's word that the path of evil will lead to destruction, and yet he pursues it with the secret hope that in his case the damage will not be very great. He has been warned that sin is like a cup frothing with a foam of sweetness, but concealing hell in its dregs; yet each sinner, as he takes the cup, fascinated by the first drop, believes that to him the poisonous draught will not be fatal. How many have fondly hoped that God would lie unto men, and would not fulfill his threatenings! Yet, be assured, every sin shall have its recompense of reward; God is just and will by no means spare the guilty. Even in this life many are feeling in their bones the consequences of their youthful lusts; they will carry to their graves the scars of their transgressions.

In hell, alas, there are millions who forever prove that sin is an awful and undying evil, an infinite curse which hath destroyed them for ever and ever. The sinner is a fool, because, while he doubts the truthfulness of God as to the punishment of sin, he has the conceit to imagine that transgression will even yield him pleasure. God saith it shall be bitterness: the sinner denies the bitterness, and affirms that it shall be sweetness. Oh fool, to seek pleasure in sin! Go rake the charnel to find an immortal soul; go walk in the secret springs of the sea to find the source of flame. It is not there. Thou canst never find bliss in rebellion. Hundreds of thousands before thee have gone upon this search and have all been disappointed; he is indeed a fool who must needs rush headlong in this useless chase, and perish as the result. The sinner is a fool—a great fool—to remain as he is in danger of the wrath of God. To abide at ease in imminent peril and scorn the way of escape, to love the world and loathe the Savior, to set the present fleeting life above the eternal future, to choose the sand of the desert and forego the jewels of heaven—all this is folly in the highest conceivable degree.

Though sinners are fools, yet there are fools of all sorts. Some are learned fools. Unconverted men, whatever they know, are only educated fools. Between the ignorant man who cannot read a letter and the learned man who is apt in all knowledge there is small difference if they are ignorant of Christ; indeed, the scholar's folly is in this case the greater of the two. The learned fool generally proves himself the worst of fools, for he invents theories which would be ridiculed if they could be understood, and he brings forth speculations which, if they were judged by common sense, and men were not turned into idiotic worshippers of imaginary authority, would be scouted from the universe with a hiss of derision. There are fools in colleges and fools in cottages.

There are also reckless fools and reckoning fools. Some sin with both hands greedily: "A short life and a merry one" is their motto; while the so-called "prudent" fools live more slowly, but still live not for God. These last, with hungry greed for wealth, will often hoard up gold as if it were true treasure, and as if anything worth the retaining were to be found beneath the moon. Your "prudent," "respectable" sinner will find himself just as much lost as your reckless prodigal. They must all alike seek and find the Savior, or be guilty of gross folly. So, alas, there are old fools as well as young ones. There are those who after an experience of sin burn their fingers at it still. The burnt child dreads the fire, but the burnt sinner lovingly plays with his sin again. Hoar hairs ought to be a crown of glory, but too often they are fools' caps. There are young sinners who waste the prime of life when the dew is on their spirit, and neglect to give their strength to God, and so miss the early joy of religion, which is the sweetest, and makes all the rest of life the sweeter: these are fools. But what is he who hath one foot hanging over the mouth of hell, and yet continues without God and without Christ, a trifler with eternity?

I have spoken thus upon the name of those who enter God's hospital; permit me to add that all who go there and are cured agree that this name is correct. Saved souls are made to feel that they are naturally fools; and, indeed, it is one stage in the cure when men are able to spell their own name, and when they are willing to write it in capital letters and say, "That is mine! If there is no other man in this world who is a. fool, I am. I have played the fool before the living God." This confession is true: for what madness it is to play the fool before the Eternal One, with your own soul as the subject of the foolery? When men make sport they generally do it with trifling things. A man who plays the fool, and puts on a cap and bells, is wise in comparison with him who sports with his God, his soul, heaven, and eternity. This is folly beyond all folly. Yet the sinner, when he is taken into God's hospital, will be made to feel that he has been such a fool, and that his folly is folly with an emphasis. He will confess that Christ must be made unto him wisdom, for he himself by nature was born a fool, has lived a fool, and will die a fool, unless the infinite mercy of God shall interpose.

Now, for a minute, let us notice THE CAUSE OF THEIR PAINS AND AFFLICTIONS. "Fools because of their transgression, and because of their iniquities, are afflicted." The physician usually tries to find out the root and cause of the disease he has to deal with. Now, those souls that are brought into grief for sin, those who are smarting through the providential dealings of God, through the strikings of conscience, or the smitings of the Holy Spirit, are here taught that the source of their sorrow is their sin. These sins are mentioned in the text in the plural. "Fools because of their transgression, and because of their iniquities." How many have our sins been! Who shall count them? Let him tell the hairs of his head first. Sins are various, and are therefore called "transgressions and iniquities." We do not all sin alike, nor does any one man sin alike at all times. We commit sins of word, thought, deed, against God, against men, against our bodies, against our souls, against the gospel, against the law, against the weekday duties, against the Sabbath privileges—sins of all sorts, and these all lie at the root of our sorrows. Our sins also are aggravated; not content with transgression, we have added iniquities to it. No one is greedier than a sinner, but he is greedy after his own destruction. He is never content with revolting: he must rebel yet more and more. As when a stone is rolled downhill its pace is accelerated the further it goes, so with the sinner, he goes from bad to worse.

Perhaps I speak to some who have lately come into God's hospital. I will suppose a case. You are poor, very poor, but your poverty is the fruit of your profligate habits. Poverty is often directly traceable to drunkenness, laziness, or dishonesty. All poverty does not come from that. Blessed be God, there are thousands of the poor who are the excellent of the earth, and a great many of them are serving God right nobly; but I am now speaking of certain cases, and probably you know of such yourselves, where, because of their transgressions and iniquities, men are brought to want. There will come to me sometimes a person who was in good circumstances a few years ago, who is now without anything but the clothes he tries to stand upright in, and his wretchedness is entirely owing to his playing the prodigal. He is one of those whom I trust God may yet take into his hospital. At times the disease breaks out in another sort of misery. Some sins bring into the flesh itself pains which are anticipatory of hell; yet even these persons may be taken into the hospital of God, though they are afflicted, to their shame, through gross transgression. Oh, how many there are in this great City of London of men and women who dare not tell their condition, but whose story is a terrible one indeed, as God reads it. Oh that he may have pity upon them, and take them into his lazar house, and heal them through his abundant grace!

In more numerous cases the misery brought by sin is mental. Many are brought by sin very low, even to despair. Conscience pricks them; fears of death and hell haunt them. I do remember well when I was in this way myself; when I, poor fool, because of my transgression and my iniquities was sorely bowed in spirit. By day I thought of the punishment of my sin; by night I dreamed of it. I woke in the morning with a burden on my heart—a burden which I could neither carry nor shake off, and sin was at the bottom of my sorrow. My sin, my sin, my sin, this was my constant plague. I was in my youth and in the heyday of my spirit; I had all earthly comforts, and I had friends to cheer me, but they were all as nothing. I would seek solitary places to search the Scriptures, and to read such books as Baxter's *Call to the Unconverted* and Alleyne's *Alarm*, feeling my soul ploughed more and more, as though the law, with its ten great black horses, was dragging the plough up and down my soul, breaking, crushing, furrowing my heart, and all for sin. Let me tell you, though we read of the cruelties of the Inquisition, and the sufferings which the martyrs have borne from cruel men, no racks, nor fire pans, nor other instruments of torture can make a man as wretched as his own conscience when he is stretched upon its rack. Here, then, we see both the fools and the cause of their disease.

Now, let ns notice THE PROGRESS OF THE DISEASE. It is said that "their soul abhorreth all manner of meat," like persons who have lost their appetite, and can eat nothing; "and they draw near unto the gates of death," they are given over, and nearly dead.

These words may reach some whose disease of sin has developed itself in fearful sorrow, so that they are now unable to find comfort in anything. You used to enjoy the theatre: you went lately, but you were wretched there. You used to be a wit in society, and set the table on a roar with your jokes; you cannot joke now. They say you are melancholy, but you know what they do not know, for a secret arrow rankles in your bosom. You go to a place of worship, but you find no comfort even there. The "manner of meat" that is served to God's saints is not suitable to you. You cry, "Alas, I am not worthy of it." Whenever you hear a thundering sermon against the ungodly you feel, "Ah, that is me!" but when it comes to, "Comfort ye, comfort ye my people," you conclude, "Ah, that is not for me." Even if it be an invitation to the sinner you say, "But I do not feel myself a sinner. I am not such an one as may come to Christ. Surely I am a castaway."

Your soul abhorreth all manner of meat, even that out of God's kitchen. Not only are you dissatisfied with the world's dainties, but the marrow and fatness of Christ himself you cannot relish. Many of us have been in this way before you. The text adds, "They draw nigh unto the gates of death." The soul is exceeding sorrowful, even unto death, and feels that it cannot bear up much longer. I remember using those words of Job's once in the bitterness of my spirit, "My soul chooseth strangling rather than life;" for the wretchedness of a sin-burdened soul is intolerable. All do not suffer the same strong conviction, but in some it bows the strong man almost to the grave. Perhaps, my friend, you see no hope whatever; you are ready to say, "There cannot be hope for me. I have made a covenant with death and a league with hell; I am past hope. There were, years ago, opportunities for me, and I was near unto the kingdom; but, like the man who put his hand to the plough and looked back, I have proved myself unworthy."

Troubled heart, I am sent with a message for you; "Thus saith the Lord, your covenant with death is broken and your league with hell is disannulled. The prey shall be taken from the mighty, and the lawful captive shall be delivered." You may abhor the very meat that would restore you to strength, but he who understands the human heart knows how to give you better tastes and cure these evil whims; he knows how to bring you up from the gates of death to the gates of heaven. Thus we see how terribly the mischief progresses.

But now the disease takes a turn. Our fourth point is THE INTERPOSITION OF THE PHYSICIAN. "Then they cry unto the Lord in their trouble, and he saveth them out of their distresses. He sent his word, and healed them, and delivered them from their destructions." The Good Physician is the true healer. Observe, *when* the physician comes in—"then they cry unto the Lord in their trouble." When they cry, the physician has come. I will not say that he has come because they cry; that would be true, but there is a deeper truth still—they cried because he came. For, whenever a soul truly cries unto God, God has already blessed it by enabling it to cry. Thou wouldst never have begun to pray, if the Lord had not taught thee. God is visiting a soul, and healing it when it has enough faith in God to cast itself, with a cry, upon his mercy. I cannot hope that there is a work of grace in thee yet, till I know thou prayest. Ananias would not have believed Paul to be converted, had not it been said, "Behold he prayeth!"

Note the kind of prayer here: it was not taken out of a book, and it was not a fine prayer in language, whether extempore or precomposed; it was a *cry*. You do not need to show your children how to cry: it is the first thing a new-born child does. It wants no schoolmaster to teach it that art. Our School Boards have a great deal to teach the children of London, but they need never have a department for instruction in crying. A spiritual cry is the call of the new-born nature expressing conscious need. "How shall I pray?" says one. Pour thy heart out, brother. Turn the vessel upside down, and let it run out to the last dreg, as best it can.

"But I cannot pray," says one. Tell the Lord you cannot pray, and ask him to help you to pray, and you have prayed already. "Oh, but I don't feel as I should!" Then confess to the Lord your sinful insensibility, and ask him to make your heart tender, and you are already in a measure softened. Those who say, "I don't feel as I should," are very often those who feel most. Whether it be so or no, cry. If thou art a sin-sick soul, thou canst do nothing towards thy healing but this—thou canst cry. He who hears thy cries will know what they mean. When the surgeon goes to the battle-field after a conflict, he is guided to his compassionate work by the groans of the wounded. When he hears a soldier's cry he does not enquire, "Was that a Russian or a Turk, and what does he mean?" A cry is good Russ, and excellent Turkish too; it is part of the universal tongue. The surgeon understands it, and looks for the sick man. And, whatever language, Oh sinner, thou usest, uncouth or refined, if it be the language of thy heart, God understands thee without an interpreter.

Note well, that as we have seen when the physician interposed, we shall see next *what he did.* He "saved them out of their distresses," and "delivered them from their destructions." Oh, the infinite mercy of God! He reveals to the heart pardon for all sin; and, by his Spirit's power, removes all our weaknesses, I tell thee, soul, though thou be at death's door at this moment, God can even now gloriously deliver thee. It would be a wonder if thy poor burdened spirit should within this hour leap for joy, and yet, if the Lord visit thee, thou wilt do so. I fall back upon my own recollection; my escape from despondency was instantaneous. I did but believe Jesus Christ's word, and rest upon his sacrifice, and the night of my heart was over: the darkness had passed, and the true light had shone. In some parts of the world there are not long twilights before the break of day, but the sun leaps up in a moment; the darkness flies, and the light reigns: so is it with many of the Lord's redeemed, as in a moment their ashes are exchanged for beauty, and their spirit of heaviness for the garments of praise. Faith is the great transformer. Wilt thou cast thyself now, whether thou live or die, upon the precious blood and merits of the Savior Jesus Christ? Wilt thou come and rest thy soul on the Son of God? If thou dost so, thou art saved; thy sins which are many are now forgiven thee. As of old, the Egyptians were drowned in a moment in the Red Sea—the depths had covered them, there was not one of them left; so, the moment thou believest, thou hast lifted a mightier rod than that of Moses, and the sea of the atoning blood, in the fullness of its strength, has gone over the heads of all thine enemies; thy sins are drowned in Jesus' blood. Oh, what joy is this, when, in answer to a cry, God delivers us from our present distresses and our future destructions!

But how is this effected? The psalmist saith, "He sent his word and healed them." *His word.* How God ennobles language when he uses it! The term *"word"* is uplifted in Scripture into the foremost place, and put on a level with the Godhead. THE WORD. It indicates a God-like personage, for, "in the beginning was the Word"; nay, it denotes God himself, for, "the Word was God."

Our hope is in the Word—the incarnate *Logos*, the eternal Word. In some aspects our salvation comes to us entirely through the sending of that Word to be made flesh, and to dwell among us. He is our saving health, by his stripes we are healed. But here the expression is best understood of the gospel, which is the word of God.

Often, the reading of the Scriptures proves the means of healing troubled souls; or else, that same word is made effectual when spoken from a loving heart with a living lip. What might there is in the plain preaching of the gospel! No power in all the world can match it. They tell us nowadays that the nation will go over to Rome, and the gospel candle will be blown out. I am not a believer in these alarming prophecies; I neither believe in the Battle of Dorking, nor in the victory of Pius the Ninth. Leave us our Bibles, our pulpits, and our God, and we shall win the victory yet.

Oh, if all ministers preached the gospel plainly, without aiming at rhetoric and high flights of oratory, what great triumphs would follow! How sharp would the gospel sword be if men would but pull it out of those fine ornamental, but useless, scabbards! When the Lord enables his servants to put plain gospel truth into language that will strike and stick, be understood and remembered, it heals sick souls, that else might have lain long at death's door! Still the word of God in the Bible and the word of God preached cannot heal the soul unless God *send it* in the most emphatic sense. "He sent his word." When the eternal Spirit brings home the word with power, what a word it is! Then the miracles of grace wrought within us are such as to astonish friends and confound foes. May the Lord, even now, send his word to each sinner, and it will be his salvation. "Hear, and your soul shall live." Faith cometh by hearing, and hearing by the word of God, and faith brings with it all that the soul requires. When we have faith, we are linked with Christ; and so our salvation is ensured.

This brings us to the last point—THE CONSEQUENT CONDUCT OF THOSE WHO WERE HEALED. First, *they praised God for his goodness*. What rare praise a soul offers when it is brought out of prison! The sweetest music ever heard on earth is found in those new songs which celebrate our late deliverance from the horrible pit and the miry clay. Did you ever keep a linnet in a cage and then bethink yourself that it was hard to rob it of its liberty? Did you take it out into the garden and open the cage door? Oh, but if you could have heard it sing when it had fairly escaped the cage where it had been so long, you would have heard the best linnet music in all the wood. When a poor soul breaks forth from the dungeon of despair, set free by God, what songs it pours forth! God loves to hear such music. Note that word of his: "I remember thee, the love of thine espousals, when thou wentest after me in the wilderness." God loves the warm-hearted praises of newly emancipated souls; and he will get some out of you, dear friend, if you are set free at this hour.

Notice that these healed ones praised God especially *for his goodness*. It was great goodness that such as they were should be saved. So near death's door and yet saved! They wondered at his mercy and sang of "his wonderful works to the children of men." It is wonderful that such as we were should be redeemed from our iniquities; but, our Redeemer's name is called Wonderful, and he delights in displaying the riches of his grace.

Observe that in their praises they ascribe all to God: they praise "*him* for *his* wonderful work." Salvation is God's work, from beginning to end. Their song is, moreover, comprehensive, and they adore the Lord for his love to others as well as to themselves; they praise him "for his wonderful works *to the children of men.*"

Forget not that they added to this praise *sacrifice*: "Let them sacrifice the sacrifices of thanksgiving." What shall be the sacrifices of a sinner delivered from going down into the pit? Shall he bring a bullock that hath horns and hoofs? Nay, let him bring his heart; let him offer himself, his time, his talents, his body, his soul, his substance. Let him exclaim, "Let my Lord take all, seeing he hath saved my soul." Will you not lay yourselves out for him who laid himself out for you? If he has bought you with a price, confess that you are altogether his. Of your substance give to his cause as he prospers you; prove that you are really his by your generosity towards his church and his poor.

In addition to sacrifice, the healed ones began to offer songs, for it was to be a "*sacrifice of thanksgiving.*" May those of you who are pardoned sing more than is customary nowadays. May we, each one of us, who have been delivered from going down to the pit, enter into the choir of God's praising ones, vocally singing as often as we can, and in our hearts always chanting his praise.

Once more, the grateful ones were to add to their gifts and psalms *a declaration of joy* at what God had done for them. "Let them declare his works with rejoicing." Ye who are pardoned should tell the church of the Lord's mercy to you. Let his people know that God is discovering his hidden ones. Come and tell the minister. Nothing gladdens him so much as to know that souls are brought to Jesus by his means. This is our reward. Ye are our crown of rejoicing, ye saved ones. I can truly say, I never have such a joy as when I receive letters from persons, or hear from them personally the good news, "I heard you on such-and-such a night, and found peace"; or, "I read your sermon, and God blessed it to my soul." There is not a true minister of Christ but would willingly lay himself down to die if he could thereby see multitudes saved from eternal wrath. We live for this. If we miss this, our life is a failure. What is the use of a minister unless he brings souls to God? For this we would yearn over you, and draw near unto God in secret, that he would be pleased in mercy to deliver you.

But, surely, if you are converted, you should not conceal the fact. It is an unkind action for any person who has received life from the dead through any instrumentality, to deny the worker the consolation of hearing that he has been made useful; for the servant of God has many discouragements, and he is himself readily cast down, and the gratitude of those who are saved is one of the appointed cordials for his heavy heart. There is no refreshment like it. May God grant you grace to declare his love, for our sake, for the church's sake, and, indeed, for the world's sake. Let the sinner know that you have found mercy, perhaps it will induce him to seek also. Many a physician has gained his practice by one patient telling others of his cure. Tell your neighbors that you have been to the hospital of Jesus, and been restored, though you hated all manner of meat, and drew near to the gates of death; and, may be, a poor soul, just in the same condition as yourself, will say, "This is a message from God to me."

Above all, publish abroad the Lord's goodness, for Jesus' sake. He deserves your honor. Will you receive his blessing, and then like the nine lepers give him no praise? Will you be like the woman in the crowd, who was healed by touching the hem of his garment, and then would fain have, slipped away? If so, I pray that the Master may say, "Somebody hath touched me," and may you be compelled to tell us all the truth, and say, "I was sore sick in soul, but I touched thee, O my blessed Lord, and I am saved, and to the praise of the glory of thy grace I will tell it; I will tell it, though devils should hear me; I will tell it, and make the world ring with it, according to my ability, to the praise and glory of thy saving grace."

Thus have we seen the patients in the hospital, and seen them coming forth from it, leaping and praising God, and now oar visit terminates as we breathe the prayer, "Heal us, O Lord."

11

St. Brelade's Bay

Never dispute about scenery. Besides the old rule which warns you against arguing upon matters of taste, there is the other—that it is better *not* to compare things which were not meant for comparison. We were one day at the Plemont Caves and the next in St. Brelade's Bay: the first, rugged and grand beyond description; the second, fair and beautiful. The question as to which was the finer scenery was suggested, but was dismissed as a topic not to be tolerated by sensible people. Each was, in its own way, surpassing; contrast was conspicuous, but comparison was absurd. You cannot take the fields all flower-bedecked, and the waves flashing and for ever changing, and the clouds fleecy, grey, or blazing with the red sunset, and say of them, "Here we have positive, comparative, and superlative." No, they are each and all superlative. God's works are all beautiful in their season, all masterpieces; there is nothing second-rate among them. Jersey may glory in Plemont and its other rugged headlands, and it may equally rejoice in the more quiet beauty of the bays of which St. Brelade's is the type.

The propensity to compare is frequently indulged in equally foolish and far more injurious ways. It cuts us to the heart when we hear excellent ministers decried, because they are not like certain others. Persons will actually discuss the graded rank and comparative merit of Punshon and Talmage, Landels and McLaren, forgetting that the men are different persons, and no more to be placed as first, second, third, and fourth, than cowslips and oysters, gazelles and dolphins. You cannot logically institute comparisons where they do not hold. Rugged Cephas has his place and order, and he is neither better nor worse, higher nor lower in value, than polished Apollos. No one enquires which is the more useful—a needle or a pin, a spade or a hoe, a wagon or a plough: they are designed for different ends, and answer them well; but they could not exchange places without serious detriment to their usefulness. It is true that A excels in argumentative power; let him argue then, for he was made on purpose to convince men's reason; but because B's style is more expository, do not despise him, for he was sent, not to reason, but to teach. If all the members of the mystical body had the same office and gift, what a wretched malformation it would be; it would hardly be so good as that, for it would not be a formation at all. If all ears, mouths, hands, and feet were turned into eyes, who would hear, eat, grasp, or move? A church with a Luther in every pulpit would be all fist; and, with a Calvin to fill every pastorate, she would be all skull. Blessed be God for one Robert Hall, but let the man be whipped who tries in his own person to make a second. Rowland Hill is admirable for once, but it is quite as well that the mold was broken. There is a great run just now for little Robertsons of Brighton, but there will soon be a glut in the market.

Why not appreciate the good in all true preachers of the gospel, and glorify God in each of them? Never let us say, "This is my man, and there is no other equal to him." It may be that our favorite is the most notable in his own peculiar order; but, then, other orders of men are needed and fulfil an equally important function. The sublime and commanding style of Isaiah should not put us out of patience with the plaintive tones of Jeremiah, nor with the homeliness of Hosea, or the abruptness of Haggai.

So much for moralizing on that point; we must make a halt, dismount, and come to closer quarters with this bay of St. Brelade.

What is to be seen? The guide-book tells of "a delicious little cove, with fantastic rocks and recesses, known as the *Creux Fantomes*, or Fairy Caves." Come along, worthy comrades, we will explore them first of all, and rest afterwards in some cool grot, where neither shall the sun light on us nor any heat. Shall we enquire the way? It may be as well; for where these fairy dwellings are we are only vaguely informed: they lie somewhere on the western side; but a mile or two more or less makes a difference to a limping traveler. Does anybody know of these wonders? It seems not. We get information at last about these "unknown, mysterious caves, and secret haunts"; but then we learn, also, that "there is no practicable way to them." Not the first things which we have desired to look into which have been beyond our reach. It is disappointing though! Instructive, at least; suggestive also. There are unapproachable men as well as caves. How many preachers have affected mystery and educated themselves into obscurity. They have become, by laborious art, little else than spiritual painted windows, which admit only a dim religious light. Few have the presumption to try to understand them. They do not claim to be infallible; but none would question their right, if they styled themselves "incomprehensible." Their thoughts may be as wonderful as these *Creux Fantomes*; but, alas, there is no path to their meaning which an ordinary understanding can follow. Their jargon, it is to be hoped, is to themselves its own exceeding great reward; to others, it is sound, and nothing more.

Adieu, then, to the fairies. Let us examine some more ordinary and accessible places. Here is the ancient church. Who was this Saint Brelade? Was he any relation of Ingoldsby's renowned St. Medard, who was so remarkably hard and solid about the parietal bone that his pate was not crushed even when the arch enemy of all saints hurled at it the weight of a great, big stone? We hope he was not at all of that breed, for we are not partial to those of whom the witty satirist sings:

> St. Medard, he was a holy man,
>   A holy man I ween was he,
> And even by day,
>   When he went up to pray,
> He would light up a candle that all might see.

Well, well, what matters who the good soul was? Here is his church, and a native ready to open the churchyard gate. Here on the left of the entrance is a good notion, a money-box for the poor, with an inscription in French: "*Jesus, étant assis vis-à-vis du tronc, regardait comment le peuple mettait de l'argent dans le tronc*" (Mark 12:41). A text even more suitable in French than in its English form: "Jesus sat over against the treasury, and beheld how the people cast money into the treasury." With that text before their eyes, surely many professing Christians would contribute more, and in a better spirit. We should be ashamed to give grudgingly, if we felt sure that Jesus looked on. This Scripture needs to be put over weekly-offering boxes, for it is generally neglected in the reading, all persons being in a hurry to get to the widow's mites. With all due respect to that most admirable widow, we are afraid that she has innocently been a shield for covetous hypocrites. Rich men contribute a guinea to some enterprise requiring tens of thousands, and they modestly say, "Put it down as the widow's mite." My dear sir, it was in the plural, two mites, so please make it two guineas, so as to be accurate in number, at any rate: and then remember that she gave all her living, and you defraud the woman if you call your donation by her name, and yet do not give a tenth nor a hundredth, nay, perhaps not even a thousandth part of your substance, to the Lord. It were to be wished that some minute subscribers out of magnificent incomes would become "widows indeed"; or, at least, give "widows' mites" indeed and of a truth.

The church—we are in it now—is a plain, decent, Christian place of worship, thoroughly well whitewashed. Capital stuff that lime-white to kill the Tractarian bug or worm, a pest very discernible in many of our parish churches, and about as destructive as the white ant in India. Churchwardens could not do better than try a coat of lime, at the same time remembering that the insect will cling to altar cloths, processional banners, or any other old rags which may be cumbering the place. If crosses, holy candlesticks, censers, and other trumpery to which these creatures attach themselves could be removed, it would be well; but we beg the purifiers not to carry these implements anywhere near dissenting chapels for fear the plague should spread there also. If a gracious providence should command a mighty strong east, west, north, or south wind to take away these creatures, we should greatly rejoice, for they cover the face of the earth, so that the land is darkened. There were other evidences of purity in St. Brelade's church besides the fair white upon its walls. There stood a plain communion table, with four legs, simple and unadorned, and over it, as usual, was the Apostles' Creed, Lord's prayer, and Decalogue. No frippery here. Moreover, there were suitable texts above and below each of these inscriptions; and we specially marked that over the creed were these words: "He that believeth and is baptized shall be saved," with this most appropriate text, by way of interpreter, beneath: "With the heart man believeth unto righteousness; and with the month confession is made unto salvation." We commend these parallel Scriptures to the careful and prayerful consideration of all our readers.

In the graveyard were the hillocks and stones which memorialize, not only the rude forefathers of the hamlet, but many from far and near, who came to

Jersey, saw it, and died. Inscriptions there were, English and French, a few in unmitigated doggrel, and many more of the usual rhymes of the sort, to which Pope's criticism might be applied:

> Where'er you find "the cooling western breeze,"
>   In the next line "it whispers through the trees;"
> If crystal streams "with pleasing murmurs creep,"
>   The reader's threatened, not in vain, with "sleep."

There surely should be some censorship of churchyard poetry, which ought to be elevating in sentiment and expression, but is too often neither. We were fortunate enough, however, to stumble on one epitaph which we copied eagerly, for it seemed to us, in its way, to be quite a gem:

> Weep for a seaman, honest and sincere,
>   Not cast away, but brought to anchor here;
> Storms had o'erwhelmed him, but the conscious wave
>   Repented, and resign'd him to the grave.
> In harbor, safe from shipwreck, now he lies,
>   Till Time's last signal blazes through the skies;
> Refitted in a moment, then shall he
>   Sail from this port, on an eternal sea.

The Eton boy's lines upon "The conscious water," which "saw its God and blushed," were evidently in the versifier's mind in line three; and the ring of some of the expressions reminds us much of Watts' Lyrics.

We looked into the very ancient building called the "*Chapelle des Pêcheurs*," or "Fishermen's Chapel," and marked the rude frescoes, now happily passing into well-deserved decay. What men of taste can see in the worse than childish daubs of the mediaeval times we know not; they are not merely grotesque, but comic, and in many cases revolting and blasphemous. Venerate the old if you will; but let old idols and abominations, "portrayed upon the wall round about," be devoured as speedily as possible by the tooth of time. We should like half an hour with a stout hammer and a ladder in several of our parish churches, and we would leave behind us improvements in architecture worthy of imitation by future architects.

> Reformations which another,
>   Hating much the Popish reign—
> Some faint, evangelic brother,
>   Seeing, might take heart again.

We certainly did not cross the Channel to spend our time inside a vaulty and dilapidated building; so away to the sea. What a splendid plain of sand; but see how it is stirred and moved by the wind. Such fine particles, in such constant motion, will assuredly blind us. Let us make a rush through it for the rocks, and then we can sit by the side of Mr. Disraeli's melancholy ocean; or, what Pollock calls the "tremendous sea." Judge our surprise when we find that the raging sandstorm reaches no higher than our knees, and all above is clear enough. Odd, very odd, to be beaten about the ankles by a torrent of blowing particles; and up here, in the region of breathing and seeing, to be serenity itself. If our daily trials could be kept under foot in the same manner, how happily might we live. The things of earth are too inconsiderable to be allowed to rise breast high. "Let not your heart be troubled." Out on the rocks, we enjoy the breeze and the view'; and, looking back on the bay of St. Brelade, half envy the cottagers whose profound quiet is unmolested by the shriek of locomotives, the roll of cabs, and the discord of barrel organs. By us, the blue wave must be left for the black fog, and the yellow sands for the dingy bricks; but there are souls to be won by thousands amid the millions of London, and, therefore, we will return to duty with willing step. With all the advantages of a country life—and they are many and great—the active servant of God will prefer the town, because there he sows in wider fields, and hopes for larger harvests.

Dr. Guthrie once said, "I bless God for cities"; and he rightly called them "the active centers of almost all church and state reforms, and the cradles of human liberty." We, also, bless God for cities, for there the willing crowds hang on the preacher's lips, there the laborious church is gathered, the student trained, the evangelist tutored, the mind inflamed by contact with mind, and the pulse of godliness quickened. We pronounce Raleigh's blessing on the country:

> Blest silent groves! O may ye be
>   For ever mirth's best nursery.

But we choose to spend our days where larger human harvests, white for the sickle, wait for the reaper's coming.

12

Sundew, A Strange Plant

In a swampy part of the New Forest, in Hampshire, we met with a plant which was quite new to us. To our unlearned eyes it looked like a lichen or a small red cactus, and yet it almost as much resembled a zoophyte; we did not know what to make of it, it was so old-world and weird-like. An abundance of red glandular hairs covered each leaf, and upon its surface glistened sparkling dew drops. To gather specimens and send them home by post in a box was a process suggested and carried out by a friend; our samples, however, did not endure the transit, and so we have not since seen our floral novelty. Upon making enquiry, the plant turns out to be the Sundew, or, as the learned call it, Drósera, from the Greek word *drosys*, dew. The older writers call it *Ros-solis*, which is but the Latin of its English name. From Anna Pratt's most interesting work, entitled, "The Flowering Plants, Grasses, Sedges, and Ferns of Great Britain," we have gathered several facts which may not unfitly be woven into parables, and made to illustrate truth.

Sundew is the tempting name of this plant, and what would seem more safe, attractive, and proper for an insect to light upon? Surely it might wisely sip the crystal drop and fly away refreshed: but "things are not what they seem," and there are lovely names which cover deadly evils. The gauzy-winged insect alights, drinks of the shining drops, and becomes henceforth a captive.

> For when there's moisture in the brake,
>   The clammy sundew's glistening glands
> 'Mid carmine foliage boldly make
>   Slaves of invading insect bands.

That dew was never born of the sun, neither was it exhaled by it; it is so viscid that when touched with the finger it will draw out in threads of more than an inch in length, and it is hardly possible that a small insect once caught by its glue can ever escape; in fact, the more it struggles the more it is covered with the clammy moisture, and the more surely it is held. It is too late now, thou pretty victim, thou hast been beguiled to an untimely fate, and escape is impossible. Like Jonathan, thou mayest complain, "I did but taste a little honey, and I must die"; only that which seemed a tempting sweetness to thee was not so, but acrid to the last degree, so that thou hast a double disappointment to bewail. Struggle thou mayest, but thy case is hopeless.

A watchful naturalist has seen the hairs upon the leaves close in upon the insect victim, and the edges of the leaf itself curl inwards, remaining in that condition long after the captive had died. The Sundew is an ogre towards flies, a cunning fowler among little winged wanderers, a vegetable spider, a deceiver and a devourer. Flies, much like our common house flies, have been seen to be captured by one of the leaves and held fast until the relaxing hairs of the plant have laid bare the blackened remains of their prey. One might naturally expect this from a plant bearing the name of Snapdragon, Catch-fly, or Swallow-wort; but who would have conjectured that Sundew would be the name of a deadly trap?

Yet all around us are such deluding names and flattering deceits. Do not men call unhallowed lust by the sacred name of love? Is not drunkenness spoken of as good cheer? Are not profligate habits labelled generosity? And is not slavery to the basest passions denominated free living? There is much in a name after all, as Satan knows full well, and well pleased is he to get a name, bright and fresh as that of Sundew, wherewithal to disguise the true character of his temptations. Fascinating are the counterfeit dews of youthful lusts; does it not seem a Puritanic harshness to deny them to the young? May they not taste and away? Nay, the dew is not dew, but clammy bird-lime for the soul; it will hold the youth and hold the man, and he will be utterly unable to escape, though he may become aware of his captivity and alarmed at the destruction which will follow upon it. The pleasures of sin cannot be enjoyed for a season and relinquished just when we will. We may say of them, as Virgil does of hell,

> Avernus' gates are open night and day,
>   Smooth the descent, and easy is the way;
> But to return to heaven's pure light again,
>   This is a work of labor and of pain.

True, the grace of God may interpose to rescue the prisoner from the fetters which he has forged for himself; but no man has a right to reckon upon such a deliverance, much less to tempt the Lord by plunging into enslaving habits on the ground that others have been, through infinite mercy, emancipated from them. Who in his senses would take poison because in some cases an antidote has been supplied before death has closed the scene? Who wishes to be plague stricken because a few survive amid the general mortality? Oh man, be wise, and shun the tempter and his honey-dew, lest thou be fatally ensnared and fastened down to certain ruin. Flies have no warning, but men have, therefore let them take it, and flee far away from the destroyer. Leave off vice before it be meddled with, is an allowable alteration of the wise man's proverb. Prevention is better than cure, abstinence is better than reformation. Touch not, taste not, handle not that Sundew which is not from heaven and prepares for hell.

We have not done with the singular tenant of the bog, but will use it for another purpose. Its flower is very seldom seen expanded. For some reason unknown to botanists, and apparently in no way dependent on the shining of the sun, this flower often remains closed during the greater part of its flowering season. One enquirer asks, "Has any person ever seen the blossoms of the round-leaved Sundew fully expanded? Wishing to obtain a specimen of this little plant in full bloom, to sketch from, I have visited in almost every hour of the day a bog traversed by a small rivulet, whose margin is thickly dotted with its glowing leaves, looking as if they had, indeed, impaled drops of the morning dew to cool them through the day. I have watched it from the time in which its slender scape first rises from amidst a bunch of circinate leaves to that in which it forms at top into a nodding raceme, but never have I seen its minute white flower-buds unclose."

Many other watchful observers declare that even in the fairest weather and brightest sunshine, they have looked in vain for opened flowers. Here and there a watcher has seen a flower unfold itself in the morning and close at noon to open no more, but the sight seems to be a great rarity even to the most attentive naturalists. One would not wish to follow the example of so rare a blooming, yet are there men of kindred spirit. They must surely have good times, seasons of affection, moments of generous impulse, when the soul reveals its best self; but those around them have looked in vain for such rare occasions. They are so miserly that seldom are they moved to pity and relieve the needy, so churlish that scarcely ever can they utter a kind encouraging word, so cold that never are they seen to warm into enthusiasm. Children of the marsh, they are damp even to the core, sunlight cannot woo them into blossoming, the genial influences which rule other hearts scarcely affect them for good.

Woe to those who are compelled to live with them; they watch in vain for sympathy or love. Unhappy is the Abigail who is married to such a Nabal. Perhaps now and then, to some favored companion, they become for the moment cordial, but they scarcely forgive themselves for the aberration, and relapse into the closed-up state again, to unfold their affections no more. Around them are men and women full of love, smiling and flourishing the various seasons through, perfuming their surroundings with kindly fragrance of good thoughts and deeds, yet do they abide shut up within themselves. May heaven pity them in boundless mercy, and save them from themselves. 'Twere better far to die of love than live without loving. Disappointment and heartbreak are infinitely to be preferred to selfishness and isolation; the one is an affliction which may happen to the noblest, the other is the vice of the base and groveling. Give the heart room to blossom like the rose, even though the hand of the cruel should pluck it; our nature sinks even below its natural depravity when we refuse to love. Be it ours to open wide our full soul beneath the smile of the Sun of Righteousness, and so to grow as the lily, and give forth a sweet smell as Sharon's ruddy flower; and never, never may we yield to the power of selfishness, which is as deadly to the heart itself as it is pernicious to those whom it despises.

Old writers highly praise the essence of the Sundew as a remedy for many diseases: it was celebrated under the name of *aqua rosæ solis*, or spirit of Sundew. One old herbalist declares that it is good for the lungs, and for nervous faintness, and, though it will raise blisters upon the skin, he considers it to be very useful inwardly, and puts it down as a great cordial. Ladies used it as a cosmetic, and perhaps do so still, but we are not learned in such matters; the country people use it to destroy warts and corns, so that after all it may have some good qualities, and perhaps this brief paper may conserve a measure of its virtues, to the benefit of manners and of men. Good lies latent in things evil, but the hand of wisdom extracts it: be thou thus wise, dear reader, and thy profiting shall be known unto all.

13

Two Sights Which I Shall Never Forget

I entered the town of Mentone just as the sun was going down, and I was struck by the number of persons who were congregated upon the beach, and along the road which skirts the sea. They were all gazing intently at a boat which was moving slowly, although rowed by several men. Evidently they were dragging a dead weight behind the boat, and one which needed to be tenderly towed along. Upon making inquiry, we learned that the corpse of a sailor had been met with, and they were bringing it on shore for burial. This information did not tempt us to remain a spectator, but hastened us into our hotel, wondering at the morbid curiosity which could be attracted by corruption, and find a desirable sensation in gazing upon a putrid corpse. From our window we saw a coffin carried down to the shore, and felt greatly relieved with the hope that now the poor drowned one would be quietly and decently laid asleep in the lap of mother earth.

As this occurred, as we have before said, just as we entered the place where we hoped to rest and recruit our health, it made a deep impression upon us. We are not in the least degree superstitious, and do not regard events as omens one way or another, but the incident was a sad one, and we were pensive; and therefore it cast a natural gloom over us, and at the same time engraved itself upon our memory. Unknown victim of the sea, thou hast a memorial in our heart!

The reflections which rushed upon our mind we have committed to paper, and here they are. Is not the church of God like that boat, and is she not encumbered by a mass of dead professors of religion who draw upon her strength, impede her progress, and spread around her an ill savor? Yes, it is even so, and our heart is heavy because we see it under our own eye every day. Persons have united themselves with the church who have neither part nor lot in vital godliness; they lend no assistance, they can lend none, for they have no spiritual strength, but they are a drag upon our energies, for we have to keep them in something like decent motion, and must carry them with us till they are laid in the grave.

The case is worse in reality than our picture represents, for the dead are in the boat with the living, and are thus able to cause greater grief of heart to the true saints of God. We are blamed for the actions of all our fellow members; their offensive worldliness both annoys us and renders us unsavory to others. It is a terrible thing to see one-half of a church praying and the other half trifling. We cannot soon forget our horror at hearing that while the Holy Ghost was visiting a church with revival, there were members in that very church who were engaged till far into the morning in worldly amusements. We did not believe our own ears; we should as soon have thought of hearing that the apostles sang profane songs at the time of the Pentecost. It was not that the season was untimely, we care little for that, but the act itself betrayed a taste which is not consistent with true religion.

Of course, the world laid this to the door of the church, and really devout people had to suffer for the sins of others, and God's Holy Spirit was grieved by such offences, which he saw, though the godly ones saw them not. The sincere and humble followers of Jesus in that church would hardly have believed such conduct possible had it come under their own eyes, and those who had the sorrow of knowing it to be true felt a depression of heart worse than any bodily sickness could inflict. If the church were unmixed and pure her growth would be far more rapid; for the tares, which we cannot uproot, weaken the wheat among which they live. The tone of spirituality is lowered throughout the whole body by the worldliness of the few. Sin outside the church is comparatively little harmful to her; she sees it and battles with it; but when the traitor is within her own gates the mischief which it works is terrible, Troy could not be taken by open assault, but the crafty scheme of the wooden horse filled with armed men worked the will of the Greeks. Once dragged within the walls, the warriors concealed within were able to open the city gates, and the foes soon swarmed in every street, and Troy fell to rise no more. Almighty watchfulness will avert such ruin from the church of God, but apart from the divine keeping the danger is quite as imminent.

We wish that every church member would recognize the fact that he either helps or hinders the church to which he belongs. Unless he adds to her actual fighting force he becomes a part of the *impedimenta* of the army, rendering its march the more laborious. He who prays, labors, and lives consistently with his profession, is an accession to her real power; he may be an obscure individual, endowed with but one talent, and most at home in the rear rank, and yet he may be of the utmost value to the whole host; and when the war is over he will share in the rewards of victory which will fall to the lot of the armies of the living God. On the other hand, if he be prayerless, idle, and worldly, no matter how rich, how well educated, or how respected he may be, he is a dead weight, a mere piece of baggage, a cause of non-success, an Achan in the camp of Israel. Which, dear reader, are you at this moment?

The second memorable sight which now rises before us was seen from the garden of that right worthy and renowned physician, Dr. Bennett, to whom Mentone owes its present prosperity. Looking out to sea beyond a headland we saw, when the doctor had pointed it out to us, a circle of commotion in the waters, as if a stream were boiling and bubbling from the bottom of the ocean. It was a spring of fresh water rising from the depths of the sea to the surface. There is a similar spring off the coast of Spezzia, which sends up an immense volume of sweet water, despite the overlying floods of brine. Such a phenomenon may appear to be impossible, but there it was before our own eyes, and very generally the traveler may see it for himself—a fountain of fresh water in the midst of the salt sea! Its force much depends upon the rainfall upon the mountains, and it therefore greatly varies, but it is often very manifest.

Have we not here a suggestive image of the power of divine grace? Coming down from the inexhaustible reservoir in which all fullness dwells, which is placed in the highest heavens, the blessed stream of grace has a forceful current which seeks to rise towards its own level, and therefore it wells up with matchless energy. It may be that the possessor of this inward spring has a thousand memories of sin, acquired habits of evil, and a dense mass of ignorance and prejudice overwhelming him; yet the new life must and will reveal itself; it forces its way, it rises to the surface, it clears an area for its own energies, it will not be choked up nor repressed. Or the illustration may refer to true religion in a neighborhood where everything is opposed to it, or in an age when the spirit of the many is in deadly hostility to it. Did not Christianity at its very beginning rise up like a spring from the dark floor of some lone ocean cave, far down below the bottom of the mountains? Did it not appear certain that the floods of heathenism would utterly swallow up a power so insignificant? How could it rise to the surface of human history? It might bubble on where obscure inferior creatures would be its sole observers, but the great sea of human affairs would utterly ignore its existence, its sweet waters would not even alleviate the saltiness of the brine. But what is the truth of the matter? Our holy faith burst through Judaism, philosophy, and idolatry, came into public notice, blessed the nations, and claimed for itself an ever widening sphere. Its fountain has risen through the salt waves of sinful society, and rises still, yea, it is transforming the waters and healing them: and through its influence there shall come a day in which there shall be no sea of sin and sorrow, for this "fount of every blessing" shall have made it a reservoir of the water of life.

A good man placed in a London court, or any of the slums of a huge city, labors under terrible disadvantages. All around him sin and ignorance abound. His religion is no sooner perceived than it is ridiculed, he becomes the butt of drunken jokes, the theme of riotous songs. Will he yield the point and cease from the fear of the Lord? He will if he be a hypocrite; on the other hand, if he be indeed a partaker of the living water which Jesus gives, it will be in him a well of water, springing up, and despite all opposition it must and will flow forth. At first in patience he will possess his soul and hold his own, by-and-by he will win respect and silence slander, next he will influence a few less evil than their neighbors, and in the end his vital godliness will subdue all things unto itself. One of the most cheering results of our ministry is the consistency of the extremely poor, whose testimony is borne in places which it is almost unsafe to traverse at night. Their honesty, sobriety and simple faith are sermons to the poor around them, which are not forgotten. Men are astonished when they see godliness under such circumstances, their attention is aroused, their wonder is excited, and in the presence of the strange sight they confess that this is the finger of God. The unconquerable energy of faith and love are the abiding miracles of the church, by which the candid are convinced and gainsayers are silenced.

Just now, what with ritualism and rationalism, it might have been feared that gospel life was smothered in Great Britain. The outbreak of the revival in many parts of the land has effectually banished all the fears of believers, and in a great measure stayed the boastings of skeptics. The living water welled up gloriously a few months ago. Yonder in Scotland it troubled the once calm surface of society! It boiled and bubbled up in Edinburgh and Glasgow! It made the sea of society to boil like a pot! Evermore in its own manner the sweet fountain rises to the surface. It pierces the overwhelming mass of sin, it clears its own channel, it rejoices to bless the sons of men. "Spring up, O well! Sing ye unto it!"

Dear reader, is there life of this order in you, or are you dead in sin? Look on this picture and on that: we have put before you death and life; which is most like your own condition? If compelled to condemn yourself, remember there is One near at hand of whom it is written, "In him was life, and the life was the light of men."

14

"Oh, You Wretch!"

I quite agree with the remark made by a cheerful believer, that the Christian life may be described as "good, better, best"—"the shining light, which shineth more and more unto the perfect day"; but close researches into our own heart lead us to apply very different adjectives to our own carnal nature, of which we feel far more inclined to say that, to our apprehension, it is bad, worse, worst. All is light in the Lord, but all is darkness in self; in the Lord Jehovah have we righteousness and strength: in ourselves nothing but sin and weakness.

>In him is only good,
>   In me is only ill;
>My ill but draws his goodness forth,
>   And me he loveth still.

I heard today from a friend an odd story, which has much amused me and something more. He kept a parrot of loquacious habits, and next door to him there lived a minister, who called upon him one morning and asked him to be so good as to remove the talkative bird, for it worried him exceedingly. It was not its noise, but what it said, which was the cause of annoyance. It did not swear like a trooper, or scream like a termagant, but still it disturbed the divine beyond all bearing. Its voice had not vexed his ears one-tenth so much as its utterance had rent and torn his conscience. My friend was anxious to know what dreadful words those might be which had thus transformed poor harmless Poll into a tormenting spirit, a very accuser of the brethren. It turned out that the bird, when he was hanging outside the window near to the preacher's study, had screamed out with all his might, "Oh, you wretch! Oh, you wretch!" "Just," said the minister, "when I am trying to prevail with God in prayer, or am endeavoring to confess my sins, a voice seems to mock me and sarcastically cry, 'Oh, you wretch!'" "And," said the good man, "it is so true; I feel it is so; it comes home to me; it makes me remember that I am not praying as I ought, nor laying hold upon the promise as I should, and it causes me to feel deeply ashamed of myself. When I am writing my sermon and preparing for the Sabbath, and am perhaps mourning over my cold-hearted and dilatory studies, the parrot calls out, 'Oh, you wretch!' and I think within myself, that is really just what I am. The parrot deeply distresses me by so continually bringing before my mind my shortcomings and unworthiness. It was all very well for a time, but it is now a perpetual blister to me." My friend vas very fond of his parrot, though he must have sadly neglected its education; but he parted with it to relieve his neighbor, hoping that he had thus given a cup of cold water to one of the Master's little ones.

I thought when I heard the story that I should like to have that parrot hung up in my study, but perhaps a little bird which lodges in my breast will do as well. My conscience softly moans to me like a turtle dove, "Oh, wretched man that I am!" and the note is so true that my heart repeats it again and again: the shadow of my infirmities is ever upon me. I dare not hold my head on high, for I am deeply conscious of the evil within my bosom. Nor do I desire to feel other than ashamed of myself, for I never pray better than when the mournful note of self-accusation is heard, and I never love Jesus more than when I feel my great need of his cleansing blood. So far as I can judge, I never quicken my pace so well in the spiritual pilgrimage as when my heart cries with all her might, "God be merciful to me a sinner." They run fastest home who most fear the storm; hence, "Blessed is the man that feareth alway." They carry most of Christ who have least of self, hence the richness of spiritual poverty.

As once a message from God came from the mouth of an ass, I shall borrow a text from a parrot, and use the words, "Oh, you wretch!" as a peg on which to hang a brief homily.

These words might be applied to some of us at sundry times and in divers places. For instance. Our Lord has been very gracious to us, and he has answered our prayers and fulfilled his promises times beyond number; he has brought us through six troubles, and in seven there has no evil touched us; we have been through fire and through water, and have been divinely shielded from every ill. If, in fresh trials, we grow unbelieving and desponding, what excuse can be made for us? Some of us have been preserved sixty or seventy years; others of us have been kept by all-sufficient grace, and have known the Lord now these twenty years, and have proved his faithfulness every moment during that long time. Now, when we begin to distrust and suspect the goodness of our God, our conscience might well say, "Oh, you wretch! Oh, you wretch!" What wretched creatures we must be so to dishonor our God, to question his immutable love, to doubt the veracity of his word, and suppose that he can change in his affection, or forget his people! How much more saintly to sing, "Away, distrust, my God hath promised: he is just!" Nothing degrades us more than unbelief. Nor is there any sin over which we ought to grieve with deeper anguish of repentance than mistrust of God. Oh, it is a high crime and misdemeanor to impute unfaithfulness to him who cannot lie! Wretch that I am, that I should thus insult my God! What fountains of evil must be in me when the streams are so polluted with unbelief of my faithful God!

To bring to remembrance another evil, let us reflect how often during the day we wander from God in heart; our love is fixed on an earthly creature, and images of jealousy are set up in opposition to the Well-beloved of our souls. Dagon is elevated hard by the ark. If it were not for grace, we should forsake our Lord, and, as it is, it almost comes to that; idolatry well nigh supplants our worship of God, and our love to the creature leads us to undervalue our Creator's goodness, and even to repine if the object of our overweening affection is removed. Then may we well chide ourselves—

> Wretch that I am to wander thus,
>   In chase of false delights!

We have been deceived so often by the dried-up brooks of earthly joy, why fly we to them again? We have been to the broken cisterns so many times, and found no water in them, why do we leave the everlasting spring to trust the leaking creatures?

So too, dear friends, such a word as that might be spoken to us by our conscience when we have been angry under provocation, so as to have spoken rashly with our lips. That may not be the temptation of some persons, but it is the besetting sin of not a few. Some believers soon lose their balance; they speak hard and biting words, and think very unholy things. How hardly and sharply may conscience cry, "Oh, you wretch!" When Christ has forgiven you all sin, to be so easily enraged and to find it so hard to forgive your offending brother! When the Great Creditor frankly forgave you ten thousand talents, what a wretch are you to think it so difficult to let your brother go who only owes you the hundred pence! What a wretch to have your hand upon your neighbor's throat with, "Pay me what thou owest." May we learn the mischief of an angry spirit, hate ourselves for ever yielding to it, and, by the softening power of the Holy Ghost, be preserved in patience and meekness, in imitation of our gentle Lord.

I need not mention the many, many times during the day in which such a cry as that of the poor imitating bird might be a needful reminder to us if a tender heart would but let us feel its power. Oh Savior in heaven, when we think of what we are in ourselves, we would lie in the very dust before thee. What is there in us that can recommend us to thee? How is it thou canst love us at all? It is a wonder of wonders that ever thy august and ennobling love should have been set upon us. We cannot see anything lovely in ourselves; what is there of attraction that thy far more observant eye can by any possibility discover? We are but wretched men, as the apostle saith, in ourselves, and yet for all that, such is the exceeding greatness and abounding fullness of the love and mercy of God, that we are as surely dear to Jesus as if we were perfect in the flesh, and as much beloved of him as if we had never sinned; yea, our sins have given opportunities for matchless and amazing displays of his love, which otherwise, so far as we can judge, had not been exhibited to the wondering gaze of principalities and powers. Loathsome as sin is, I am almost ready to agree with Augustine when, speaking of the fall, he said, *"Oh, beata culpa!"*—"Oh, happy fault!"—because it opened such room for redeeming love and divine compassion. Disastrous as was our first parents' sin, yet inasmuch as it made room for the wonderful display of the divine love to such sinners as we are, we can only magnify the depth of the wisdom, and the height of the grace, and the breadth of the love of God, in the way in which eternal mercy overcomes the evil which was permitted, doubtless, for that very end.

It is essential that we should always maintain in our inmost hearts a deep sense of the humbling truth that we are nothing but dust and ashes, sin and defilement; wretches in the worst sense if it were not for grace. When a man begins to think, "Well, there is something praiseworthy in my flesh after all," depend upon it, there is nothing in him of any real worth. I remember a friend of mine who, one morning, met in the market a deacon for whom up to that hour he had entertained the highest respect. This deacon said to my friend, "Friend So-and-So, I want you to do me a good turn." "Well," he replied, "I am sure I will if it is at all reasonable." Then said the other, "I want you to lend me a hundred pounds." My friend had it on his tongue to say, "Yes, I will write you a check at once," when the deacon said, "You can trust me, you know, I am perfectly safe; I am not like a young man, who may be led into doing wrong; I have been in the ways of the Lord for so many years, and have had so much experience, that I am past temptation."

"Past temptation!" muttered my friend. "Past temptation! I would not lend you the value of a sixpence." "Why not?" said the man, with surprise. "Because you say you are past temptation, and I distrust a man who is so confident in himself." I was gratified at the shrewd common-sense of my friend, and glad that he saved himself from losing one hundred pounds, for the boaster went to pieces and was in prison within a month of that time. Whenever we allow our hearts to dream that we are beyond the region of indwelling sin, we are encircled by its coils. Our congratulatory addresses to ourselves are the sure evidences of spiritual unsoundness. No slippery morass, or all-devouring bog, is more treacherous than a self-flattering estimate of human nature. Quaint Herbert says:

> Surely, if each one saw another's heart,
>   There would be no commerce,
> No sale or bargain pass; all would disperse
>   And live apart.

The poet does not tell us what a man would do if he could see his own naked self. It would be enough to drive him mad. Whenever we censoriously exclaim, "See how others behave! If I were in their position, I would do better," we are even then ready to slip with our feet. Ah, we do not know ourselves, my brethren, or instead of hearing laudatory words with pleasure, we should often shiver at the sound of a still small voice crying out, "Oh, you wretch!"

If you have a bird which cries, "Good master," wring its neck; but if it shrieks, "You wretch," be thankful that, if neither your own heart nor your neighbors are honest to you, there remains yet one truth-telling creature upon the earth.

The Lord keep us empty in ourselves and full of himself, so that though we may mournfully confess as David did, "So foolish was I, and ignorant: I was as a beast before thee"; yet with him we may add, "Nevertheless I am continually with thee: thou hast holden me by my right hand."

Book Four

The Mourner's Comforter

7 Discourses on Isaiah 61

Preface

Heavy heart, this book is meant for thee. He who sends forth this volume knows the heart of a mourner by a kindred experience, and is most anxious to be a "son of consolation" to the sorrowing. This little volume is meant to scare the night-raven, of which Milton tells us that it sits "where brooding darkness spreads his jealous wings." By most men it is known as Religious Melancholy, but we call it by the older and more scriptural name of Mourning in Zion. By whatever name it is called it is none the more pleasant, for truly—

> Its gloomy presence saddens all the scene,
>   Shades every flower and darkens every green;
> Deepens the murmur of the falling floods,
>   And breathes a browner horror on the woods.

To meet the sadness of the heart we have taken a prescription, not from Galen or Hippocrates, but from the great gospel prophet, Isaiah; and its one and only ingredient is Christ Jesus himself, who is anointed to comfort the distressed in heart, and fulfills his office by giving himself to them to meet all their needs. The sermons which make up this book are full of Christ Jesus, the consolation of Israel; and if, in any degree, they cheer the desponding, it will be entirely due to himself, their object and their theme. He is to mourning hearts—

> Sweet as refreshing dews or summer showers,
>   To the long parching thirst of drooping flowers.

No heart, however broken, needs any balm but Jesus to work its perfect cure. Sorrows, which like Noah's flood, drown all, are soon assuaged by a word from his lips. Get him and keep him, O bruised and bleeding heart, and thou art healed. For broken hearts the broken-hearted Savior died, and for them he lives and pleads. Look to him, mourner, and the black horror of despair shall end.

Thine heartily,

C. H. Spurgeon

1

The Anointed Messenger and His Work

"The Spirit of the Lord God is upon me; because the Lord hath anointed me to preach good tidings unto the meek; he hath sent me to bind up the broken hearted, to proclaim liberty to the captives, and the opening of the prison to them that are bound" (Isa. 61:1).

May a dew from the Lord rest upon us while we consider line by line this wonderful passage from what has been well called "the Gospel according to Isaiah," and may many mourners derive consolation from our meditations.

This Scripture is true if applied to every man whom God hath ordained to declare the glad tidings. It was true of Isaiah himself when he spoke as the great evangelical prophet, and it has been true of the apostles and of all those who have been enabled in the divine strength to proclaim the testimony of mercy. The text shows us that the great business of every true minister is to preach the gospel: there are other duties to be fulfilled, but this is the head and front of a minister's calling. Every minister should say, "this one thing I do: the Lord hath appointed me to preach good tidings unto the meek."

The preaching can, however, only be done in the power of a divine anointing. He that speaks for God should speak in God's strength, because the Spirit of God has come upon him, is moving him to speak, is helping him while speaking, and will make the word which he proclaims to be quick and powerful. To attempt to preach in any power but that of the Holy Ghost is to ensure failure. There can be no broken hearts bound up, or captives' set free, where the Spirit of God is not honored.

The preacher giving himself up wholly to his preaching, and discharging his work in the power of the Spirit, is to aim at the results which are mentioned in the text. He must pity broken hearts and endeavor to bind them up. He must remember the Lord's prisoners and seek their release. If he does not aim at these objects he forgets the design of true preaching, which is not for preaching's sake, much less for the preacher's sake; but all for the sake of the people of God, many of whom Satan holds in bondage under sin. He must never reckon that his preaching has succeeded unless he continually hears the joyful cries of liberated captives and the songs of mourners comforted.

But while it is true that the text has a meaning towards all God's servants, yet our Lord himself has told us that this passage is to be interpreted concerning himself. When he stood up in the synagogue of Nazareth and read from the roll these gracious words, he closed the book, gave it to the minister, and added, "This day is this Scripture fulfilled in your ears." That day in which he was present, preaching and teaching, was the time in which the text was fulfilled. The fullness of its meaning was turned into matter of fact, for there had come one who above all others was anointed of the Spirit of God that he might proclaim glad tidings to the meek. We shall, therefore, only consider the text as referring to our blessed Redeemer. We will allow all other teachers to vanish into him as the stars merge their light in the rising sun: Christ Jesus is he who comes to bind the broken hearts, and to break the iron chains.

Following our text closely, we shall first consider *our Lord's anointing*. He himself says, "The Spirit of the Lord God is upon me; because the Lord hath anointed me." Secondly, we shall dwell upon *our Lord's preaching*—"The Lord hath anointed me to preach good tidings unto the meek;" and then, thirdly, we shall dwell upon *our Lord's design and object*— "He hath sent me to bind up the brokenhearted, to proclaim liberty to the captives, and the opening of the prison to them that are bound."

I. First, let us contemplate OUR LORD'S ANOINTING.

The first remark under this head shall be this, that *it was very special*. He was anointed of the Spirit first in order, for he is first and chief. He is the head, and on him the sacred unction first descends and then to us. Even as upon Aaron's head the oil was poured, and then it flowed down to the skirts of his garments, so is the Spirit first, and originally, given to the Christ of God, and then through him it falls upon us. Our anointing is a secondary one: because he is Christ we are Christians—the Anointed is surrounded by anointed ones.

Our Lord was specially endowed with the Spirit at the first, for he was born supernaturally, according to the word of the angel to the highly favored virgin, "The Holy Ghost shall come upon thee, and the power of the Highest shall overshadow thee; therefore also that holy thing which shall be born of thee shall be called the Son of God." Mysteriously begotten, our Lord came into the world, and from his childhood manifested the special possession of the Spirit: for he was filled with wisdom, and the grace of God was upon him. His actual anointing took place at the time of his baptism. When he came up out of the water, John bare witness that he saw the Spirit descending like a dove and resting upon him. The Spirit has not in any visible form descended upon us. We, I trust, have received him, but not after that fashion. The manifestation was peculiar to him who came to baptize us with the Holy Ghost and with fire.

The specialty of his anointing lies also in the fact that "God giveth not the Spirit by measure unto him." To us the Spirit is given by measure according as our need requires. For quickening, for illumination, for sanctification, for the gift of utterance, and various necessary uses, according as we have capacity we receive of the Holy Ghost; but, having an infinite capacity, our Lord received an infinity of the Spirit of God.

Again, there was a specialty in this—that the Spirit, when he descended upon the Lord Jesus, "abode upon him" (John 1:32). He continueth not at all seasons with every child of God, for sometimes we grieve him, and he departeth from us. We have not always, at any rate, the conscious presence of the Holy Spirit, but John tells us, "He that sent me to baptize with water, the same said unto me, upon whom thou shalt see the Spirit descending, and remaining on him, the same is he which baptizeth with the Holy Ghost." So you see, dear friends, the anointing of our Lord has the special character of being without equal, without measure, and without withdrawal. Jesus is at no time more anointed than at another, but always full of the Holy Ghost. You and I have sometimes the fullness of the Spirit; at other times we are crying that his Spirit may return to us: but Jesus never grieved the Spirit, nor could do so, for in him is no sin.

Secondly, with regard to the possession of the Spirit by our Lord, it is special, because *it has ordained him to special offices*, upon which none of us can enter. There are three offices to which men were appointed of old by being anointed. First, the prophetical office was so received. We read of Elisha, that God said to Elijah, "Go and anoint Elisha, the son of Shaphat, that he may be prophet in thy stead." Priests, too, were anointed: you have a long series of rules given in the book of Leviticus as to the anointing of Aaron and of his sons with an oil that was made after the art of the apothecary, with choice spices mingled in a peculiar manner to make an oil which should never come upon the flesh of any man but the high priest. For him and for him alone was the oil of his anointing before God, and so the Lord Jesus is anointed as a priest with the oil of gladness above his fellows. Kings, too, were anointed. Saul was only anointed with a vial of oil, whereas David was anointed with a horn of oil, as if to mark the abundance of his kingdom and the favor in which he stood in the sight of God.

As for our most blessed Lord, he is called the Messiah, or the sent One, and that office comprehends priesthood, prophecy, and kingship, all in one, and in each of these offices he is plentifully anointed of God. Would you know the truth? Jesus can teach it to you. God has given him the Spirit to be a prophet among us. Would you be cleansed from sin? Christ can remove all impurity by means of his priestly office, for he has presented a complete sacrifice, and he can apply its cleansing power to your souls and make you know that as a priest the fullness of the Spirit dwells with him. Do you long to have sin conquered? Do you need the aid of supreme power to subdue your corruptions? Christ can exercise it, for he is anointed to be King in the hearts of men by the Holy Ghost. I delight to think of our blessed Lord in those three offices, each one of which we so much need. I delight to perceive the heavenly perfume which flows from his person and work, because of the holy oil of the Spirit which rests upon him.

Now *this produced in our Lord remarkable results*, worthy of being mentioned under this head. We noticed that the Spirit of God was upon Christ, that he might preach. To his preaching we must look for its effects, and we notice that his utterance as the result of the indwelling of the Spirit was surpassingly powerful. "Never man spoke like this man," said those who went to take him. Those who listened to him were charmed with his accents, and even the ministers of justice who were sent to seize him, and who are usually the last persons ever to be affected by oratory, nevertheless came under the spell of his words. I should suppose that a sheriff's officer who came to arrest a preacher would be the last person to be impressed by his sermon; but yet these men went back to those who sent them, and reported that they could not take him, for never man spoke as he did. He was a mighty preacher; he spoke as one having authority. All other speakers will do well to sit at his feet and learn their art from the great Master of it. Never man spoke like this man, because the Spirit of God rested upon him as it has never rested upon another.

The result was seen in his own spirit, for what a spirit was that which dwelt in Jesus Christ. So gentle; he was tender as a nurse with her child. So brave; he never feared the face of man. What strong words are his. How forcible! How courageous! He is a man to the very fullness of manhood, and yet he is always the holy child Jesus. His spirit was unselfish, for the Spirit of God consecrated him entirely to his work; he lived and died for it. He never thought of self at all, but the zeal of God's house did eat him up, and he was clothed with zeal as with a cloak. You never detect in his spirit the imperfections which are so palpable in us. He is never cold or indifferent; his words never freeze on his lips. He is never proud and lofty. You never find him using language which the poor could not understand; but you find him condescending to men of low estate as if it were no condescension at all. Above all, his spirit was saturated with love. He looked with love upon those who hated him, and even when at last he had to give them up to perish, his proclamation of the destruction of Jerusalem was wetted with his tears. He loved our guilty race as men never loved each other. He, the greatest of men, loved his ungrateful people with all his heart, and hence his preaching was so full of power.

And then as his utterance and spirit were thus full of the Holy Ghost his whole career became marvelous because of it: Jesus of Nazareth went about doing good, because he was a man filled with the Spirit of God. It was not only what he did and spoke in public, the Spirit of God was as conspicuous in his private prayers. The Spirit inspired not only his proclamations among the crowd, but his quiet and gentle teaching of the twelve in the lone places, where he told them the secrets of his heart. The man himself was power because of the Spirit. His thoughts, his words, his glances, his sufferings, everything about him through the power of this anointing became subservient to his great lifework. And hence it is that now, though Jesus has gone from us, there remains about his name a wondrous power; and about the truths which he reveals to us there is a sacred might. Since the Spirit of God still rests upon him, and upon his word, when he is preached his saving work is accomplished in them that believe.

This is the very joy and strength and hope of the church—that the Lord anointed Jesus to preach the gospel, and that his Spirit still goes forth with those who are sent in his name. The Spirit still rests upon the pages of the Bible, in each promise and precept and exhortation, making all to be instinct with life. He still comes upon the members of Christ's mystical body, and in his power that body remains unconquerable. All the multitudinous iniquities and grievous errors of this world shall yet yield before Christ, because the Spirit of God is almighty and he glorifies Christ. He that brooded over chaos broods over this disordered universe, and he will bring order out of confusion; therefore we look for a millennium from him. He that said "Let there be light," and caused light to spring forth, still lives, and he will still give light to the dark places of the earth, till over the new creation this glorious anointed Christ shall shine forth like the sun in his strength. He shall reign amongst his ancients gloriously, because the power of the Spirit is upon him.

II. Thus have I spoken upon the first head—the Lord's anointing; now, secondly, let us think of OUR LORD'S PREACHING. He says, "The Lord hath anointed me to preach good tidings to the meek."

First, then, *the anointing was with a view to preaching.* Such honor does the Lord put upon the ministry of the Word that, as one of the old Puritans said, "God had only one Son, and he made a preacher of him." It should greatly encourage the weakest amongst us, who are preachers of righteousness, to think that the Son of God, the blessed and eternal Word, came into this world that he might preach the same good tidings which we are called to proclaim.

We may profitably note how earnestly our Lord kept to his work. It was his business to preach, and he did preach, he was always preaching. "What," say you, "did he not work miracles?" Yes, but the miracles were sermons; they were acted discourses, full of instruction. He preached when he was on the mountains; he equally preached when he sat at table in the Pharisee's house. All his actions were significant; he preached by every movement. He preached when he did not speak; his silence was as eloquent as his words. He preached when he gave, and he preached when he received; for he was preaching a sermon when he lent his feet to the woman, that she might wash them with her tears and wipe them with the hairs of her head, quite as much as when he was dividing the loaves and the fishes and feeding the multitude. He preached by his patience before Pilate, for there he witnessed a good confession. He preached from the bloody tree: with hands and feet fastened there, he delivered the most wonderful discourse of justice and of love, of vengeance and of grace, of death and of life, that was ever preached in this poor world.

Oh, yes, he preached, he was always preaching; with all his heart and soul he preached. He prayed that he might obtain strength to preach. He wept in secret that he might the more compassionately preach the word which wipes men's tears away. Always a preacher; he was always ready, in season and out of season, with a good word. As he walked the streets he preached as he went along; and if he sought retirement, and the people thronged him, he sent them not away without a gracious word. This was his one calling, and this one calling he pursued in the power of the eternal Spirit; and he liked it so well, and thought so much of it, that he trained to the same work his eleven friends; and he sent them out to preach too; and then he chose seventy more for the same errand, saying, "As ye go, preach the gospel." Did he shave the head of one of them to make him a priest? Did he decorate one of them with a gown, or a chasuble, or a biretta? Did he teach one of them to say mass—to swing a censer, or to elevate the host? Did he instruct one of them to regenerate children by baptism? Did he bring them up to chant in surplices and march in procession?

No, those things he never thought of, and neither will we. If he had thought of them it would only have been with utter contempt, for what is there in such childish things? The preaching of the cross—this it is which is to them that perish foolishness, but unto us who are saved it is the wisdom of God, and the power of God; for it pleaseth God by the foolishness of preaching to save them that believe. As our Lord ascended he said, "Go ye into all the world, and preach the gospel to every creature." His charge in brief was—preach, preach even as I have done before you.

Now, as you have seen that our Savior came to preach, now notice *his subject*. "The Lord hath anointed me to preach *good tidings* to the meek." And what good tidings did he preach? Pardon, pardon given to the chief of sinners, pardon for prodigal sons pressed to their father's bosom. Restoration from their lost estate, as the piece of money was restored again into the treasury, and the lost sheep back to the fold. How encouragingly he preached of a life given to men dead in sin; life through the living water which becomes a fountain within the soul. You know how sweetly he would say, "he that believeth in me hath everlasting life." "He that believeth in me, though he were dead yet shall he live." "Like as Moses lifted up the serpent in the wilderness, even so must the Son of man be lifted up: that whosoever believeth in him should not perish, but have everlasting life." He preached a change of heart, and the need of a new creation. He said, "Ye must be born again," and he taught those truths by which the Holy Ghost works in us and makes all things new. He preached glad tidings concerning resurrection, and bade men look for endless bliss by faith in him. He cried, "I am the resurrection and the life: he that liveth and believeth in me shall never die." He gave forth precepts, too, and threatenings in their place—some of them very searching and terrible, but they were only used as accessories to the good news. He made men feel that they were poor, that they might be ready to be rich. He made them feel weary and burdened, that they might come to him for rest; but the sum and substance of what he preached was the gospel—the good spell—the glad news.

Brethren, our divine Lord always preached upon that subject, and did not stoop to secular themes. If you notice, though he would sometimes debate with Pharisees, Herodians, and others, as needs must be, yet he was soon away from them and back to his one theme. He baffled them with his wisdom, and then returned to the work he loved, namely, preaching where the publicans and sinners drew near together for to hear him. Our business, since the Spirit of God is upon us, is not to teach politics, save only in so far as these immediately touch the kingdom of Christ, and there the gospel is the best weapon. Nor is it our business to be preaching mere morals, and rules of duty; our ethics must be drawn from the cross, and begin and end there. We have not so much to declare what men ought to do, as to preach the good news of what God has done for them. Nor must we always be preaching certain doctrines, as doctrines, apart from Christ. We are only theologians so far as theology enshrines the gospel. We have one thing to do, and to that one thing we must keep.

The old proverb says, "Cobbler, stick to your last," and depend upon it. It is a good advice to the Christian minister to stick to the gospel and make no remove from it. I hope I have always kept to my theme, but I take no credit for it, for I know nothing else. I have "determined to know nothing among men, save Jesus Christ and him crucified." Indeed, necessity is laid upon me; yea, woe is unto me if I preach not the gospel. I would fain have but one eye, and that eye capable of seeing nothing from the pulpit but lost men and the gospel of their salvation: to all else one may well be blind, so that the entire force of the mind may center on the great essential subject.

There is, certainly, enough in the gospel for any one man, enough to fill any one life, to absorb all our thought, emotion, desire, and energy, yea, infinitely more than the most experienced Christian and the most intelligent teacher will ever be able to bring forth. If our Master kept to his one topic, we may wisely do the same, and if any say that we are narrow, let us delight in that blessed narrowness which brings men into the narrow way. If any denounce us as cramped in our ideas and shut up to one set of truths, let us rejoice to be shut up with Christ, and count it the truest enlargement of the mind. It were well to be bound with cords to his altar, to lose all hearing but for his voice, all seeing but for his light, all life but in his life, all glorying save in his cross. If he who knew all things taught only the one thing needful, his servants may rightly enough do the same. "The Lord hath anointed me," saith he, "to preach good tidings;" in this anointing let us abide.

But now notice *the persons* to whom he specially addressed the good tidings. They were the meek. Just look to the fourth of Luke, and you will read there, "The Lord hath anointed me to preach the gospel to the poor!" the poor, then, are among the persons intended by the meek. I noticed when I was looking through this passage that the Syriac renders it "the humble," and I think the Vulgate renders it "the gentle." Calvin translates it "the afflicted." It all comes to one thing. The meek, a people who are not lofty in their thoughts, for they have been broken down; a people who are not proud and lifted up, but low in their own esteem; a people who are often much troubled and tossed about in their thoughts; a people who have lost proud hopes and self-conceited joys; a people who seek no high things, crave for no honors, desire no praises, but bow before the Lord in humility. They are fain to creep into any hole to hide themselves, because they have such a sense of insignificance and worthlessness and sin. They are a people who are often desponding, and are apt to be driven to despair.

The meek, the poor—meek because they are poor: they would be as bold as others if they had as much as others, or as others think they have; but God has emptied them, and so they have nothing to boast of. They feel the iniquity of their nature, the plague of their hearts; they mourn that in them there dwells no good thing, and oftentimes they think themselves to be the off-scouring of all things. They imagine themselves to be more brutish than any man, and quite beneath the Lord's regard; sin weighs them down, and yet they accuse themselves of insensibility and impenitence.

Now, the Lord has anointed the Lord Jesus on purpose to preach the gospel to such as these. If any of you are good and deserving, the gospel is not for you. If any of you are keeping God's law perfectly, and hope to be saved by your works; the whole have no need of a physician, and the Lord Jesus did not come upon so needless an errand as that of healing men who have no wounds or diseases. But the sick need a doctor, and Jesus has come in great compassion to remove their sicknesses. The more diseased you are, the more sure you may be that the Savior came to heal such as you are. The more poor you are the more certain you may be that Christ came to enrich you; the more sad and sorrowful you are, the more sure you may be that Christ came to comfort you. You nobodies, you who have been turned upside down and emptied right out, you who are bankrupts and beggars, you who feel yourselves to be clothed with rags and covered with wounds, bruises, and putrefying sores, you who are utterly bad through and through, and know it, and mourn it, and are humbled about it, you may feel that God has poured the holy oil without measure upon Christ on purpose that he might deal out mercy to such poor creatures as you are. What a blessing this is! How we ought to rejoice in the anointing, since it benefits such despicable objects. We who feel that we are such objects ought to cry, "Hosannah, blessed is he that cometh in the name of the Lord."

III. We must now take the third head—OUR LORD'S DESIGN and object in thus preaching the gospel to the poor and the meek.

It was, you observe, first, that he might *bind up the broken-hearted*. "He hath sent me to bind up the broken-hearted." Carefully give heed, that you may see whether this belongs to you. Are you broken-hearted because of sin; because you have sinned often, foully, grievously? Are you broken-hearted because your heart will not break as you would desire it would break; broken-hearted because you repent that you cannot repent as you would, and grieved because you cannot grieve enough? Are you broken-hearted because you have not such a sense of sin as you ought to have, and such a deep loathing of it as you perceive that others have? Are you broken-hearted with despair as to self-salvation; brokenhearted because you cannot keep the law; broken-hearted because you cannot find comfort in ceremonies; broken-hearted because the things which looked best have turned out to be deceptions; brokenhearted because all the world over you have found nothing but broken cisterns which hold no water, which have mocked your thirst when you have gone to them; broken-hearted with longing after peace with God; broken-hearted because prayer does not seem to be answered; brokenhearted because when you come to hear the gospel you fear that it is not applied to you with power; broken-hearted because you had a little light and yet slipped back into the darkness; broken-hearted because you are afraid you have committed the unpardonable sin; brokenhearted because of blasphemous thoughts which horrify your mind and yet will not leave it?

I care not why or wherefore you are broken-hearted, for Jesus Christ came into the world, sent of God with this object—to bind up the broken-hearted. It is a beautiful figure, this binding up—as though the crucified One took the liniment and the strapping and put it round the broken heart and with his own dear gentle hand proceeded to close up the wound and make it cease to bleed. Luke does not tell us that he came to bind up the brokenhearted. If you examine his version of the text, you will read that he came *to cure* them. That is going still further, because you may bind a wound up and yet fail to cure it, but Jesus never fails in his surgery. He whose own heart was broken knows how to cure broken hearts. I have heard of people dying of a broken heart, but I always bless God when I meet with those who live with a broken heart, because it is written, "A broken and a contrite heart, O God, thou wilt not despise." If you have that broken heart within you, beloved, Christ came to cure you; and he will do it, for he never came in vain: "he shall not fail nor be discouraged." With sovereign power anointed from on high he watches for the worst of cases. Heart disease, incurable by man, is his speciality! His gospel touches the root of the soul's ill, the mischief which dwells in that place from whence are the issues of life. With pity, wisdom, power, and condescension he bends over our broken bones, and before he has done with them he makes them all rejoice and sing glory to his name.

The second object of his preaching is to proclaim *liberty to the captives*. Who are they? Captives were often persons taken in war and driven far away from home, as the Jews were in Babylon, where they wept, but could not sing. You that feel as if you were far off from God, far off from hope, far off even from fellowship with the Lord's people, you are the captives here meant—carried away against your will into the far off land of sin. Captives in their captivity were generally treated as slaves, and compelled to work very hard without wages. Perhaps that is your condition; you have been working for the flesh and the lusts thereof, working for the devil, working to please men and gratify your own pride, and you have had no better reward than the poor prodigal who was not even put upon board wages, but left to starve and envy the greedy swine.

Ah, sin is a bad master, and its wages are worse than nothing. You have spent your money for that which is not bread, and your labor for that which satisfies not. You have toiled and moiled till your soul is brought down with labor, and you fall down and there is none to help. Is that your case? Then the Lord Jesus is still the anointed of God to proclaim liberty to you. Behold, he will bring you back from banishment and bondage if you trust him. Are you one who is unable to do what you want to do? That is precisely the condition of a captive, he is in another's power and is not free to do his own will. You find sometimes that the will to do good is present with you, but how to perform that which you would you find not. You are in bondage, brought into captivity to the law of sin and death. You will think me cruel when I say that I am glad of it, yet I mean what I say, for it is for you captives, you far-away ones, you bond-slaves, you that cannot do what you would, that the Spirit of God rests upon Jesus on purpose that he may proclaim liberty to you.

There is an allusion here to the jubilee. "When the silver trumpet sounded in the morning because the fiftieth year had come, that moment every man who was a captive throughout Judea's land was free, and none could hold him in bondage. They began to sing—

> The year of jubilee is come,
>   Return, ye ransom'd captives, home.

That is the song I want my hearers and readers to sing even now. Jesus Christ proclaims it—*proclaims it*. Do you notice that? A proclamation is a message which all loyal subjects are sure to attend to. In this case it is headed, not with V. R., *Vivat Regina!* but *Vivat Rex Jehovah!* Long live Jehovah the King! He issues a proclamation from his throne, he bids his Son tell poor captive souls that Christ Jesus sets them free. Let them but believe him, and they shall rise to instant liberty. The Lord grant that many may accept this good news. We may expect it, for the Spirit of God rests upon the preaching of Christ.

Now, according to Isaiah, our Lord, came for a third matter—*the opening of the prison to them that are bound*. Kindly look at Luke and see how that evangelist words it: he puts it thus—"And recovering of sight to the blind, to set at liberty them that are bruised." They say that everything loses by translation—except a bishop; but here is a passage in which a text has greatly gained by translation, for, behold, it has doubly budded, and the one sentence is turned into two, and of the two each one is most precious. Nor is the Greek translation, quoted in Luke, incorrect, for there is a wealth of meaning in the original Hebrew, which runs thus—"to the bound open opening," and this includes both the eyes and the prison. A blind man is practically in prison. He is like a man shut up in a dark dungeon; his blindness is cell, and fetter, and closed door to him. Isaiah in our text promises an opening of eyes, and so of prison doors; it is a complete opening, a glorious liberation from darkness within and without. Who could bring this to us but a divine Messiah? O ye blind and bruised, hearken to this! Let Bartimeus hear that Jesus of Nazareth passeth by, and bids us bring the blind to him. You that see no light must not think that there is none, for the Sun of Righteousness has arisen; but, alas, you cannot see him, and so the gospel day is as midnight to your sightless eyeballs. You pine as in a dreary dungeon which you carry about with you; it is the atmosphere of unbelief, the dense fog of ignorance and fear. It all arises from your blind eyes; if these were opened, even the night would be light about you.

A blind man is the figure of one who cannot understand. You have heard the gospel hundreds of times, but you cannot grasp it, it remains a mystery to you. It has been put very plainly to you by minister, parent, teacher, and friend; you have read it in many simple books, but you have not found out its meaning yet. It is plain as the sun in the heavens, but you cannot see it. We may make a thing very clear, but a blind man cannot see it, and such is your case: but behold the Lord Jesus Christ has come on purpose to open your eyes. Do you know that you are blind? Then you have begun to see already. He who sensibly mourns that he is blind has some portion of sight. If you already feel the darkness of sin in which you are groping, and are beginning to cry, "Lord, open thou mine eyes," behold Jesus Christ stands before you, and says, "The Lord hath anointed me to give recovery of sight to the blind." Believe in the Messenger of the covenant and he will touch those eyes of yours, and light shall stream into your soul. He will do for you what he did for the man who was born blind, and you shall be a wonder unto many. I think I hear you say, "I understand it all now. However was it that I did not see it before?" You shall never be blind again, for when the Lord opens the eyes of a man Satan himself cannot shut them. The divine oculist does his work for eternity.

The last sentence, according to Luke, is—"*to set at liberty them that are bruised.*" This is an extreme case of sorrow where a man is entirely under bondage, as, for instance, bondage through fear of death, or bondage under an awful sense of the law of God—bondage under doubt, and an apparent inability to believe anything; bondage under heavy apprehensions of approaching judgment, bondage under the idea that you are forsaken of God, and that your conscience is seared; bondage under the notion of your having committed the unpardonable sin. And not only in bondage, but *bruised;* the fetters having hurt the limbs they bind, till the iron enters into the soul. You are suffering great spiritual pain, and it continues upon you from day to day. The chastisements of God leave bruises on your heart; you are so suffering that you write bitter things against yourself, and conclude that the bruises mean death.

Ah, poor bruised heart, there seems neither hope nor help for you; but it is not so, for according to the text Jesus Christ was anointed to set you at liberty. Oh, how happy you shall be if at this moment you can but trust the great Emancipator. Believe that if God anointed him to do it he can set even you at liberty, though you lie in the inner prison of despair with your feet bruised by the stocks of doubt. You who have been in bondage for years, you who have not dared to hope ever since you were a child, you who have given all up, you who consider yourselves to be already condemned, you who lie at death's dark door and seem already to feel the horrors of the bottomless pit—you most sad, most wretched of all mankind, daughters of sorrow, sisters of misery—

even to you is the gospel peculiarly sent. While it is to be preached to every creature under heaven, it is especially to be proclaimed to you. Here is comfort for all that mourn, for, behold, Jesus has come to proclaim liberty to such as you are, and to set free the braised ones. I feel an inward happiness at having such a gospel to preach, and my only sad thought is that so many will refuse it.

But, then, I am cheered with this—"The Lord knoweth them that are his." Those who are his sheep will hear his voice, and if ye believe not it will prove that ye are not of his sheep. All that the Father giveth to him shall come to him; and I will close with the other half of the verse, "and him that cometh to me I will in no wise cast out." May the Lord appear very graciously unto you, for Christ's sake. Amen.

2

The Proclamation of Acceptance and Vengeance

"To proclaim the acceptable year of the Lord, and the day of vengeance of our God; to comfort all that mourn" (Isa. 61:2).

We have already stated that this Scripture speaks concerning the Lord Jesus Christ. We say not this as if we relied upon our own opinion; for, as we noted in the previous sermon, we are assured of it by our Lord's own lips; since, reading this passage in the synagogue at Nazareth, he said, "This day is this scripture fulfilled in your ears." It is Jesus of Nazareth whom the Lord hath anointed to preach deliverance to the captives and recovering of sight to the blind, and he has also come to make a proclamation which ushers in the year of acceptance and the day of vengeance.

Notice well the expression, *to proclaim*, because a proclamation is the message of a king, and where the word of a king is there is power. The Lord Jesus Christ came into the world to announce the will of the King of kings. He saith, "I am come in my Father's name," and again, "My doctrine is not mine, but his that sent me." Every word of the gospel is hacked by the authority of "the King eternal, immortal, invisible," and he who rejects it is guilty of treason against Jehovah, God of all. The gospel is not of the nature of a commonplace invitation or human exhortation, which may be accepted or refused at will without involving guilt; but it is a divine proclamation, issued from the throne of the Eternal, which none can reject without becoming thereby rebels against the Infinite Majesty.

Now, if it be so, let us give the divine edict our most earnest attention, and take heed what we hear. When a proclamation is issued by the head of a state, all good citizens gather around to read what has been said to them, and to know what the supreme law may be: and so, when God proclaims his will, all right-hearted men desire to know what it is, and what bearing it has upon them, what the Lord demandeth or what the Lord promiseth, and what is their share therein. Listening to the gospel, then should always be very solemn work, since it is listening to the word of God. Though the voice is that of man, yet the truth is of God; I pray you, never trifle with it.

Nor let it be forgotten that a proclamation must be treated with profound respect, not merely by receiving attention to its contents, but by gaining obedience to its demands. God does not speak to us by his Son that we may be gratified by hearing the sound of his voice, but that we may yield to his will. We are not to be hearers only, but doers of the word. We should be quick in obedience to the command of the proclamation, swift in acceptance of its promise, and cheerful in submission to its demand. Who shall resist the proclamations of Jehovah? Is he not our Creator and King? Who is stubborn enough to refuse obedience? Or who hath brazen face enough to dispute his sway? Shall not he who made heaven and earth, and shaketh them when he pleaseth, and will destroy them at his pleasure, be regarded with reverential awe by the creatures of his hand?

O Son of God, since it is a divine proclamation which thou dost publish, send forth thy Holy Spirit that we may receive it with deepest reverence and lowliest obedience, lest, through our neglect, we do despite to thee as well as to thy Father. When a proclamation is not made by an ordinary herald, but when the Prince himself comes forth to declare his Father's will, then should all hearts be moved to sevenfold attention. It is the Son of God, anointed by the Spirit of God, who acts as herald unto us, and so by each Person of the divine Trinity we are called upon to bow a listening ear and an obedient heart to what the Lord proclaims. Attention, then! The Messenger of the Covenant makes proclamation! Attention for the King of kings!

With this as a preface, let me notice, that there are three points in the proclamation worthy of our best attention: the first is *the acceptable year*; the next, *the vengeance day*; and the third, *the comfort derived from both*—"to comfort all that mourn."

I. Jesus, in the first place, proclaims THE ACCEPTABLE YEAR OF THE LORD.

Take the expression to pieces and it comes to this—the year of the Lord, and the year of acceptance.

Now, what was *the year of the Lord?* There can be, I think, very little question that this relates to the jubilee year. Every seventh year was the Lord's year, and it was to be a sabbath of rest to the land; but the seventh seventh year, the fiftieth year, which the Lord reserved unto himself, was in a very marked and especial sense the year of the Lord. Now, our Lord Jesus has come to proclaim a period of jubilee to the true seed of Israel. The seed of Abraham now are not the seed according to the law, but those who are born after the promise. There are privileges reserved for Israel after the flesh, which they will yet receive in the day when they shall acknowledge Christ to be the Messiah; but every great blessing which was promised to Abraham's seed after the flesh is now virtually promised to Israel after the Spirit, to those who by faith are the children of believing Abraham.

Now, beloved, to all who believe, our Lord Jesus proclaims a year of jubilee. Let us dwell upon the four privileges of the jubilee, and accept with delight the proclamation which our Lord has made.

In the year of jubilee, as we read in the twenty-fifth chapter of Leviticus, there was *a release of all persons* who had sold themselves for servants. Pinched by great poverty, and unable to meet their debts, it sometimes happened that men were compelled to say to their creditor, "Take us and our wives and children, and accept our services instead of money. We have no goods or chattels, and our land has been mortgaged long ago, but here we are; we cannot pay in any other way—give us food and raiment and lodging, and we will put ourselves under apprenticeship to you." The law of Moses ordained that such persons were not to be treated harshly, nor regarded as slaves, but as hired servants; but still it must have been an unpleasant condition of servitude for a freeborn Israelite.

How happy then was the morning when the jubilee trumpet sounded, and the generous law came into operation which said, "He shall serve thee unto the year of jubilee, but then shall he depart from thee, both he and his children with him." From that moment he owed no more service, however great his debt might have been; he looked upon his wife and children and rejoiced that they were all his own and all free from the yoke, so that they could at once return to the possession of their fathers, all live in the cottage in which they formerly dwelt, and enjoy the piece of land which they had formerly called their own. Liberty, that gladsome sound, liberty had come to them; no matter that they had long been under obligations to the creditor, those obligations ceased on the sound of the sacred trumpet.

Beloved friend, proclamation is made to you in the Lord's name that if you are under bondage to sin and to sinful habits, there is liberty for you; faith in Jesus will set you free. If you are in bondage under justice and the broken law, there is deliverance, for Jesus has borne the penalty due for transgression. If you are under bondage through fear of death, or from the rage of Satan, our divine Lord and Master has come into the world on purpose to break those bonds in sunder. You need be bound no longer; if you believe in Jesus you *are* bound no longer, but you are set free from the servitude of the law, from the slavery of Satan and from the dread of death. Take the liberty which the great Lord freely presents to you, and be no longer a slave. Jesus has finished atonement, and brought in redemption, and believers are free; accept, I beseech you, his full emancipation, and rejoice therein.

The next jubilee blessing was *the redemption of alienated possessions*. Every man had his own plot of ground in the. Holy Land, but through the pressure of the times it sometimes happened that a man alienated his property: he was in need of ready money, his children wanted bread to eat, and he, therefore, parted with his land. It was gone: the vines and the fig trees, the corn and the oil, had passed over to another; but it was not gone forever, he had no power to sell beyond the year of jubilee. When the joyful morning dawned he went back to his family estate; it was all his own again, clear of all encumbrances; the little homestead, and the farmyard, and the fields, and the garden, all had come back to him, and none could dispute his right. Just so my Lord and Master declares to all who believe in him that the estate which Adam forfeited is restored to all for whom the Second Adam died. The alienated heritage is our own again. The great Father's love, and favor, and care, yea, all things, whether things present or things to come, or life or death, all are ours, and we are Christ's and Christ is God's. If we are believers, and are of the true seed of Israel, this day the Lord Jesus proclaims to us a restoration of all the lost privileges and blessings which originally belonged to manhood. Behold, believer, all covenant mercies are yours, rejoice in them! Partake of heavenly blessings freely. Let your soul rejoice in its portion, and delight itself in fatness.

It followed, also, as a third blessing of the year of the Lord that *all debts were discharged*. The man who had sold himself had, as it were, made a composition of his debts by the sale of himself, and this implied a full and final discharge at the jubilee. The person also who had mortgaged his land up to the jubilee year had discharged his debts thereby, and when the man received back himself and his property, no further liability rested upon him, he was cleared of all charges. The jubilee did not give the man back himself and his land under a reserve, but unreservedly. If debt had still been due the release would have been a mere farce, since he would have had to mortgage his land and sell himself again directly to meet the demand. No, there was a full discharge, a cancelling of all debts, a removal of all encumbrances upon the man and upon his estate, and he was free. What a joy this must have been! He who is in debt is in danger; an honest man sleeps on a hard bed till he has paid what he owes. He who is immersed in debt is plunged in misery, driven to his wits' end, not knowing what to do. Happy is he who has a discharge, full, free, and final, from all liabilities, once for all.

Now behold, O believer in Jesus, your innumerable liabilities are all met and ended; the handwriting that was against you is taken away and nailed to the cross, receipted in crimson lines by Jesus' precious blood. Being justified by faith you are clear before the sight of the Eternal; none can lay anything to your charge. What joyful notes are these! Jesus makes the proclamation; who will not believe it and be glad?

A fourth blessing of the jubilee trumpet was *rest*. They had their lands, but they were not to till them for a year. No more the spade and the plough, the sickle and the flail—they were to put away instruments of labor, and rest for twelve months. Think of a whole year of perfect repose, wherein they might worship and adore God all the week round, make every day a holy festival, and the whole year a Sabbath of Sabbaths unto the Most High. The Israelites had no small privileges under the ceremonial covenant, if they had lived up to it; but they failed to do so, for it has sometimes been questioned whether they ever kept a jubilee at all, and whether the Sabbath year was even once observed. If they had obeyed the Lord they would have been favored indeed; for in the matter of holidays and quiet resting times they were favored above all people. Think of one year in seven of absolute cessation from toil. What repose for them! And then they had also the year after the seventh seven, so that every man who reached the fiftieth year enjoyed two consecutive years of absolute rest from all labor, and yet knew no want, for the ground brought forth plentifully, and every man helped himself. Those who had land had a good store to last them through three years, and those who had none were fed by the spontaneous produce of the soil.

We live not under such laws, and if we did I am afraid we should not have the faith to trust in the Lord and avail ourselves of the divinely appointed holiday. But, beloved, we rest spiritually. He that believes in the Lord Jesus Christ has entered into rest. Now no more does he strive to work out a righteousness of his own, for he has already a divine one, and needs no other. It is his pleasure to worship God, but he no longer trembles beneath his wrath; it is his delight to do his commandments, but he toils and frets no longer as a slave under the law; he has become a free man, and a beloved child, and the peace of God which passeth all understanding keeps his heart and mind. Being justified by faith he has peace with God, and enjoys the influences of the divine Comforter whose indwelling gives rest to the soul.

The jubilee year, according to the text, was called *"the year of the Lord"* and the reason for all the four jubilee blessings was found in the Lord. First, the servants were set free because God said, "They are my servants, which I brought forth out of the land of Egypt" (Lev. 25:42). Ah, poor burdened soul, if thou believest in Christ thou shalt go free, for thou art the Lord's own—his chosen, his redeemed, and therefore he claims thee, and will suffer no other lord to have dominion over thee. The devil seeks to lay an embargo upon thee, and hold thee a slave, but Jesus saith, "Let go my captives, for I have redeemed them with my blood." Jesus claims thee, O penitent soul; he cries to sin as once the Lord said to Pharaoh, "Thus saith the Lord, let my people go." Jesus says of each repenting soul, "Loose him and let him go, for he is mine. My Father gave him to me—he is my chosen, my beloved. Neither sin nor Satan, nor death nor hell, shall hold him, for he is mine."

The land also was set free for this same reason, for concerning it the Lord said, "The land is mine" (Lev. 25:23). The freehold of the land was vested in Jehovah himself, consequently he ordained that no man should hold any portion of it by right of purchase beyond the fiftieth year, for the land was entailed and must go back to those for whom he had appointed it at the jubilee year. So the blessings of the everlasting covenant are God's, and therefore he appoints them unto you, poor believing sinner, and you shall have them, for the divine decree shall not be frustrated. As surely as he appointed Christ to reign, and placed him on the throne, so does he appoint you to reign with him, and you shall sit upon his throne though all the devils in hell should say you nay.

So, too, the debts were all discharged, because on the day before the jubilee the great atonement had swept away all transgression and indebtedness towards God, and he would have his people forgive all the debts of their fellow men. All things are the Lord's, and he exercised his crown rights on the day of jubilee so far as to declare all debts discharged. "The earth is the Lord's and the fullness thereof" was the motto of the jubilee, and sufficient reason for the cancelling of obligations between man and man.

As for rest, that came also, because it was God's year, and was hallowed unto the Lord. "A jubilee shall the fiftieth year be unto you: ye shall not sow, neither reap that which groweth of itself in it, nor gather the grapes in it of thy vine undressed. For it is the jubilee; it shall be holy unto you: ye shall eat the increase thereof out of the field." During man's years the earth brings forth thorns and thistles, and man must earn his bread with the sweat of his face; but when God's year comes, then the wilderness and the solitary place are glad, and the desert rejoices and blossoms as the rose. When the Lord's own kingdom cometh, then shall the earth yield her increase as she has never done before.

Dear friend, I trust you know the blessedness of living in God's year, for you live by faith upon his providence, casting all your care upon him, for he careth for you. This is the Sabbath of the soul, the counterpart of heaven. You behold the work of atonement folly accomplished on your behalf, and know yourself to be delivered from all servitude under the law, and therefore your heart leaps within you. You are clean delivered, set free, washed in the blood of the Lamb, and therefore do you come to Zion with songs and everlasting joy upon your head. But the text speaks also of the "*acceptable year of the Lord.*" Now, our Lord Jesus Christ has come to proclaim to sinners the Lord's acceptance of guilty men through his great sacrifice. Apart from the work of our Lord Jesus, men as sinners are unacceptable to God. Perhaps you are just now experiencing the misery of being in that condition, and the horror of conviction that the Lord is weary of you and your vain oblations. Since you have come in your own name and righteousness, God has not accepted you, neither has he heard your prayers nor listened to your cries, nor had respect unto your religious observances, for he saith, "Yea, when ye make many prayers, I will not hear."

If the Spirit of God has convinced you of your natural unacceptableness with God, you must have been brought into a very sad state indeed; for not to be accepted of God, and to be aware of it, is cause for intense sorrow. But now be sure, if thou believest in Jesus, that thou art accepted of God: notwithstanding thine infirmities and sins thou art "accepted in the Beloved," by him who hath said, "I will accept you with your sweet savor." And now, being thus accepted as to your persons, your petitions shall come up with acceptance before the Lord. As for your prayers, God heareth them; as for your tears, he putteth them into his bottle; as for your works, he counteth them to be fruits of his Spirit and accepts them. Yea, now that thou art accepted in Christ, all that thou art and all that thou hast, and all thou dost—the whole of thee is well pleasing to God through Jesus Christ our Lord.

Thrice happy am I to have such a subject as this. Art thou willing now to believe in Jesus? I tell thee this is the acceptable year of the Lord; God is reconciled, man is favored, blessings abound. Now is the accepted time, now is the day of salvation. Let sin be confessed and the confession shall be accepted, and thou shalt find forgiveness. Let transgression be repented of, the repentance shall be accepted and thou shalt hear a voice saying, "Go, and sin no more; thy sins, which are many, are forgiven thee." Hail! thou that art graciously accepted, blessed art thou among women! And thou too, my brother, remember the words of Solomon, "Go thy way, eat thy bread with joy, and drink thy wine with a merry heart; for God now accepteth thy works" (Eccl. 9:7.) Come to Jesus by faith, for though you come with a limping walk, and your faith is feeble, yet shall you be accepted. Come thou who hast a broken heart and a sorrowing spirit, thou who art downcast and darest not look up, this is no common time, the Lord Jesus has made it a red letter year for thee; for he proclaims a year of grace and acceptance. Behold in this *anno Domini*, or year of our Lord, we have a choice year of grace set apart for us. Who will not come to our gracious Prince, accept his mercy, and live?

Thus you see we get a double meaning from the text—the year of jubilee with all its accumulated privileges of free grace, and the year of acceptance in which whosoever will may come, and God will accept him if he cometh in the name of Jesus, trusting alone in the atoning blood.

II. May the Lord help us while we ponder the second part of the text: "THE DAY OF VENGEANCE OF OUR GOD." Does not the sound of vengeance grate upon your ear? Does it not seem discordant to the sweet tenor of the passage? Vengeance! Shall that happen side by side with acceptance? Yes, beloved, this is the mystery of the gospel; the system of redemption marries justice and mercy; the method of suretyship unites severity and grace; the economy of substitution blends acceptance and vengeance. This gospel mystery is to be published to every creature under heaven, for it is the power of God unto salvation to everyone that believeth. Now behold in the text you have the heart of God laid bare, for you have the year of acceptance coupled with the day of vengeance. Well and very sweetly has Dr. Watts expressed it:

> Here I behold his inmost heart,
>   Where grace and vengeance strangely join,
> Piercing his Son with sharpest smart,
>   To make the purchased pleasure mine.

Let us explain this strange commingling, and at the same time expound the text. In the first place, whenever there is a day of mercy to those who believe, it is always a day of responsibility to those who reject it, and if they continue in that state *it is a day of increased wrath to unbelievers.* It is not possible for the gospel to be without some effect. If it be a savor of life unto life to those who receive it, it must of necessity from its own intrinsic vigor be a savor of death unto death to those who reject it. To this sword there are two edges—one will kill our fears, or the other will surely kill our pride and destroy our vain hopes if we yield not to Christ. You may, perhaps, have noticed that when our Lord read this passage at Nazareth, he stopped short, he did not read it all; he read as far down as, "to proclaim the acceptable year of the Lord," and then he closed the book and gave it to the minister and sat down.

I suppose that at the commencement of his ministry, before he had been rejected by the nation, and before he had suffered for sin, he wisely chose to allude to the gentler topics rather than to the more stern and terrible ones; but he did not conclude his ministry without referring to the stern words which followed those which he had read. If you will turn to Luke's twenty-first chapter you will find him saying in the twenty-first and twenty-second verses, "Then let them which are in Judea flee to the mountains; and let them which are in the midst of it depart out; and let not them that are in the countries enter there into. For these be the days of vengeance, that all things which are written may be fulfilled." You know the story of the siege of Jerusalem, the most harrowing of all narratives, for the anger of God was concentrated upon that wicked city beyond all precedent. It was because they rejected Christ that vengeance came upon them. They filled up the measure of their iniquity when at last they disowned their King and cried out, "Away with him, away with him, let him be crucified."

Mark you then, dear friend, that if you have heard the gospel and rejected it, you have incurred great guilt, and you can never sin so cheaply as you did before; for you there will be a day of vengeance above the men of Sodom and Gomorrah, because you have perpetrated a crime which they were not capable of committing—you have rejected the Christ of God. The year of acceptance to believers will be a day of vengeance to those who obey not his gospel. Another meaning of the text comes out in the fact that *there is appointed a day of vengeance far all the enemies of Christ,* and this will happen in that bright future day for which we are looking. Not merely for rejecters of his gospel will there be vengeance, but for all men and fallen spirits who dare to oppose his sway. Behold he comes a second time; every winged hour hastens his advent, and when he comes it will be a great and a dreadful day to his foes. It will be to his saints the day of their revelation, manifestation, and acceptance, but to the ungodly "the day of vengeance of our God."

"Enoch, the seventh from Adam, prophesied of these, saying, Behold, the Lord cometh with ten thousands of his saints, to execute judgment upon all, and to convince all that are ungodly among them of all their ungodly deeds which they have ungodly committed, and of all their hard speeches which ungodly sinners have spoken against him." Paul also bears witness that the Lord Jesus shall be revealed from heaven with his mighty angels, "in flaming fire taking vengeance on them that know not God, and that obey not the gospel of our Lord Jesus Christ: who shall be punished with everlasting destruction from the presence of the Lord, and from the glory of his power; when he shall come to be glorified in his saints, and to be admired in all them that believe."

Note the vengeance and the grace combined. The prophet Isaiah saw our great Champion returning from his last fight, and thus spoke concerning him:

> Who is this that cometh from Edom, with dyed garments from Bozrah? this that is glorious in his apparel, travelling in the greatness of his strength? I that speak in righteousness, mighty to save. Wherefore art thou red in thine apparel, and thy garments like him that treadeth in the winefat? I have trodden the winepress alone; and of the people there was none with me: for I will tread them in mine anger, and trample them in my fury; and their blood shall be sprinkled upon my garments, and I will stain all my raiment. For the day of vengeance is in mine heart, and the year of my redeemed is come.

Observe, again, the connection between the day of vengeance and the year of the redeemed. At the Second Advent Christ will come to be glorified in his saints, and they shall be manifested in the fullness of their acceptance; but it will be an overwhelming day of vengeance for all those who have hardened their hearts and continued in their sins. "Behold, the day cometh, that shall burn as an oven; and all the proud, yea, and all that do wickedly, shall be stubble: and the day that cometh shall burn them up, saith the Lord of hosts, that it shall leave them neither root nor branch." However, I consider that the chief meaning of the text lies in this—that *"the day of vengeance of our God" was that day when he made all the transgressions of his people to meet upon the head of our great Surety*. Sin with many streams had been flowing down the hills of time and forming by their dread accumulation one vast and fathomless lake. Into this the sinner's Substitute must be plunged. He had a baptism to be baptized with and he must endure it, or all his chosen must perish forever. That was a day of vengeance when all the waves and billows of divine wrath went over his innocent head.

> Came at length the dreadful night;
> Vengeance with its iron rod
> Stood, and with collected might

> Bruised the harmless Lamb of God.
>   See, my soul, thy Savior see,
> Prostrate in Gethsemane!"

From his blessed person there distilled a bloody sweat, for his soul was exceedingly sorrowful even unto death. All through the night, with scourgings and buffetings and spittings of cruel men, he was tortured and abused; he was rejected, despised, maltreated, and pierced in his inmost soul by man's scorn and cruelty: then in the morning he was taken out to be crucified, for nothing could suffice short of his death. The outward sorrows of crucifixion may be known, but the inward griefs we cannot know, for what our Lord endured was beyond what any mortal man could have borne. The infinity of the Godhead aided the manhood, and I doubt not Hart was right in saying that he

> Bore all Incarnate God could bear
>   With strength enough, but none to spare.

It was an awful "day of vengeance of our God," for the voice cried aloud, "Awake, O sword, against my shepherd, against the man that is my fellow, saith the Lord of hosts." The doctrine that justice was executed upon our great Substitute is the most important that was ever propounded in the hearing of men; it is the sum and substance of the whole gospel, and I fear that the church which rejects it is no longer a church of Christ. Substitution is as much a standing or falling article in the church as the doctrine of justification by faith itself. Beloved, there would never have been an acceptable year if there had not been a day of vengeance. Be ye sure of this.

And now let us look at the instructive type by which this truth was taught to Israel of old. The year of jubilee began with the Day of Atonement. "Then shalt thou cause the trumpet of the jubilee to sound on the tenth day of the seventh month, in the Day of Atonement shall ye make the trumpet sound throughout all your land." "What did the high priest do on that day? Bead the seventeenth chapter of Leviticus. On that day he washed himself and came forth before the people, not wearing his breastplate, nor his garments of glory and beauty, blue and scarlet and fine linen; but the high priest wore the ordinary linen garments of a common priest. Even thus the Lord, who counted it not robbery to be equal with God, laid aside all his glory, and was found in fashion as a man. Then the priest took a bullock, and, having offered it, went within the veil with the censer full of burning coals of fire, and sweet incense beaten small, with which he filled the inner court with perfumed smoke. After this he took the blood of the bullock and sprinkled it before the mercy-seat seven times. Thus our Lord entered within the veil with his own blood and with the sweet incense of his own merits, to make atonement for us. Of the two goats, one was killed as a sin offering, and his blood was sprinkled within the veil, and the other was used for a scapegoat. Upon the head of the scapegoat Aaron laid both his hands, and confessed all the iniquities of the children of Israel, "putting them upon the head of the goat," which was then taken into the wilderness as the type of the carrying away of sin into oblivion.

Do you not see your Lord and Master bearing your sin away? "As far as the east is from the west, so far hath he removed our transgressions from us." Is there any wonder that a jubilee of peace should follow such a taking away of iniquity as our great High Priest has accomplished? Jesus is entered into the heavens for us, can we doubt of our acceptance with God? The bodies of the beasts whose blood was brought into the sanctuary for sin on the Day of Atonement were not suffered to remain in the holy place, but were carried forth without the camp to be utterly consumed with fire, in token that sin is loathsome in the sight of God, and must be put away from his presence. Even thus did our Lord suffer without the gate, and cry, "My God, my God, why hast thou forsaken me?" "Christ also hath once suffered for sins, the just for the unjust, that he might bring us to God." All this was absolutely needful to a jubilee. Without atonement, no rejoicing. Before there can be acceptance for a single sinner, sin must be laid on Jesus and carried away. The blood of Jesus must be shed, and must be presented within the veil, for "without shedding of blood there is no remission of sin;" for no man living under heaven can there be pardon or acceptance with God in any way but by the bloody sacrifice which our Redeemer offered when he bowed his head and gave up the ghost on Calvary. This great truth we must never becloud, nor ever cease to publish so long as we have a tongue to move.

The day of vengeance, then, is intimately connected with the year of acceptance; and mark, beloved, *they must be so connected experimentally in the heart of all God's people by the teaching of the Holy Ghost,* for whenever Christ comes to make us live, the law comes first to kill us. There is no healing without previous wounding. Depend upon it, there never will be a sense of acceptance in any man until first he has had a sense of the just and righteous vengeance of God against his sin.

Have you noticed that remarkable parallel to our text in the thirty-fifth chapter of Isaiah, where salvation and vengeance are so closely joined? There we read in the third verse and onward, "Strengthen ye the weak hands, and confirm the feeble knees. Say to them that are of a fearful heart, Be strong, fear not: behold, your God will come with vengeance, even God with a recompence; he will come and save you. Then the eyes of the blind shall be opened, and the ears of the deaf shall be unstopped. Then shall the lame man leap as an hart, and the tongue of the dumb sing: for in the wilderness shall waters break out, and streams in the desert."

O poor trembling, convinced sinner, God has come with vengeance to you, but his intent is to save you. Every soul that is saved must feel that wrath is deserved and that the death punishment is due on account of sin, and when this is known and felt, acceptance by faith will follow. There must be a death blow struck at all self-sufficiency and self-righteousness, and the man must be laid as dead at the feet of Christ before ever he will look up and find life and healing in the great atoning sacrifice. When our Lord puts on the helmet of salvation, he also girds about him the garments of vengeance, and we must see him in all his array (see Isa. 59:17). The day of vengeance is a needful companion to the year of acceptance; have they gone together in your experience?

III. The last point we propose to consider is THE COMFORT FOR THE MOURNERS DERIVABLE FROM BOTH THESE THINGS. "*To comfort all that mourn.*"

Now, I have no hope of interesting, much less of doing any good to, you, my dear reader, if you do not come under the description of a mourner. The sower's duty is to sow the seed everywhere, but he knows within himself that it will not take root anywhere except where the plough has been first at work. If the Lord has made thee a mourner, then this blessed subject will comfort thee; but the Lord never comforts those who do not want comfort. If you can save yourself, go and do it: if you are righteous, "he that is righteous let him be righteous still." I say it in sarcasm, as you perceive, for you cannot save yourself, nor are you righteous; but if you think so, go your way and try it—vainly try it, for surely when you have fanned your best works into a flame, and have walked by the light of the sparks of the fire which you have kindled, you shall have this at the Lord's hands—you shall lie down in sorrow and be astonished that you were ever so mad as to dream of self-salvation or of justification by your own works.

But oh, poor mourner, what joy is here, joy because this is the year of acceptance, and in the year of acceptance, or jubilee, men were set free and their lands were restored without money. No man ever paid a penny of redemption money on the jubilee morning: every man was free *simply because jubilee was proclaimed:* no merit was demanded, no demur was offered, no delay allowed, no dispute permitted. Jubilee came, and the bondman was free. And now, to-day, whosoever believeth in Jesus is saved, pardoned, freed, without money, without merit, without preparation, simply because he believeth, and God declareth that he that believeth is justified from all things from which he could not be justified by the Law of Moses. Dost thou believe? Then art thou of the house of Israel, and, thou hast God's warrant for it, thou art free. Rejoice in thy liberty! Surely this is sweet comfort for all that mourn. Look not for any marks and evidences, signs and tokens, look not for any merits or attainments, look not for any progress in grace or advancement in piety as a ground of salvation; listen only to the proclamation of the gospel, and accept the divine decree which ordains a jubilee. Art thou but of the chosen seed? Dost thou believe in Jesus? Then for thee it is an accepted year. Come, bring thy griefs and sorrows, and leave them at the cross, for the Lord accepts thee, and who shall say thee nay?

An equal joy-note, however, rings out from the other sentence concerning the day of vengeance. If the day of vengeance took place when our Lord died, then it is over. The day of vengeance was past and gone eighteen hundred years ago and more.

> Now no more His wrath we dread,
>   Vengeance smote our Surety's head;
> Legal claims are fully met,
>   Jesus paid the dreadful debt.

My heart, dost thou bleed for sin and mourn because of it? Be it so; but it has ceased to be, for Christ made an end of it when he took it up to his cross and bore it there in his own body on the tree. O believer, art thou bowed down and troubled on account of past sin? It is right thou shouldst repent; but still remember thy past sin exists no more, the pen is drawn through it and it is cancelled, for the day of vengeance is over. God will not twice take vengeance for the same sin. Either the atonement which Jesus offered was enough, or it was not; if it was not, then woe be to us, for we shall die; but if it was sufficient—if "It is finished" was not a lie, but a truth, then he hath "finished transgression and made an end of sin." The sin of the believer is annihilated and abolished, and can never be laid to his charge. Let us rejoice that the day of vengeance is over, and the year of acceptance has begun.

In another sense, however, it may be that some are mourning because of the temptations of Satan. Here, too, they may be comforted, for Jesus has come to take vengeance on the evil one, and the God of peace shall bruise Satan under your feet shortly. Are you afraid of death? Behold Christ has taken revenge on death, for he bids you cry, because of his resurrection, "O death, where is thy sting? O grave, where is thy victory?"

Are we mourning today because our dear ones are not converted? It is a good thing to mourn on that account, but let us take comfort, for this is an acceptable year; let us pray for them, and the Lord will save them. Are we mourning because sin is rampant in the wide world? Let us rejoice, for our Lord has broken the dragon's head, and the day of vengeance must come when the Lord will overthrow the powers of darkness. Have we been looking with mournful spirit upon old Rome, and the Mohammedan imposture, and the power of Buddhism and Brahminism and the sway of other ancient idolatries? Let us be glad. Behold the Avenger cometh! He comes a second time, and comes conquering and to conquer. Then shall the day of his vengeance be in his heart, and the year of his redeemed shall come. From the seven hills the deceiver shall be torn, no more to curse the sons of men with his pretensions to be the vicar of God. In blackest night shall set for ever the crescent of Mohammed, which already wanes; its baleful light shall no more afflict unhappy nations. Then shall fall the gods of the Hindus and the Chinese, broken like potters' vessels by the rod of iron which Jesus wields. At his appearing the whole earth shall acknowledge that he who was "despised and rejected of men" is "King of kings and Lord of lords." Behold, the day cometh on apace, let all that mourn be comforted. The day of vengeance, the full year of the millennial glory, the day of the overthrow of error, the year of the restoration of creation to all her former beauty, the age when God shall be all in all, is near at hand. Hasten it, O Lord. Amen.

3

Gracious Appointments for Zion's Mourners

"To appoint unto them that mourn in Zion" (Isa. 61:3).

In the last discourse we dwelt upon the singular conjoint mention of vengeance and acceptance in the second verse—"To proclaim the acceptable year of the Lord, and the day of vengeance of our God"; and we showed that there is a necessary connection between the two. We next observed that because God has executed vengeance upon Christ, and has now accepted his people, there is reasonable ground of comfort for all that mourn. The Savior came "to comfort all that mourn," and his sacrifice is for them a full fountain of hope. No mourner need despond, much less despair, since God has executed the sentence of his wrath upon the Great Substitute, that he might freely accept every sinner that believeth.

We are now going a step farther, and instead of reminding you that those who mourn may be comforted, we shall publish the loving-kindness of the Lord, and make it clear that God has a peculiar regard to mourners, and that he has appointed, provided, and reserved special blessings for them. "Blessed are they that mourn, for they shall be comforted": so runs the eternal purpose and so did our Lord declare in the opening of his Sermon on the Mount.

The anointed Savior came "to appoint unto them that mourn in Zion." Consider carefully four things; *What are they doing?* They mourn. *Where are they doing it?* In Zion. *Who thinks of them?* The Great God who here speaks about them. And *what is he doing for them?* His purposes are "to appoint unto them that mourn in Zion."

I. First, then, WHAT ARE THEY DOING—these people of whom the text speaks? They are *mourning*. Not a very cheerful occupation. Nobody will be very much attracted towards them by that fact. Most men choose lively, mirthful company, and mourners generally are left alone. Are they not to be greatly pitied? Reason thinks so; but faith has heard Jesus say, "Blessed are they that mourn"; and, therefore, she believes it to be better to be a mourning saint than a merry sinner, and she is willing to take her place on the stool of penitence and weep, rather than sit in the seat of the scorner and laugh.

Because these persons mourn, *they differ from other people*. If they are mourning in Zion their case is peculiar. There is evidently a distinction between them and the great majority of mankind, for men of the world are often lighthearted and gay, never thinking, or looking into the future. So unreal is their happiness that it would not bear the weight of an hour's quiet consideration, and so they make mirth in order to drown all thought of their true state. They are all for pastimes, amusements, gaieties: these are your lighthearted, jolly fellows, who drink wine in bowls and "drive dull care away."

It is greatly wise for a man to commune with his own heart upon his bed and be still; but these foolish ones never do this, and hence they flash with the effervescence of mirth, and sparkle with false joy. Those who mourn in Zion are very different from these giddy, superficial people; in fact, they cannot bear them, but are grieved with their foolish conversation, as any man of sense may well be. Who wants to have these blowflies forever buzzing about him? The gracious ones who mourn in Zion are as different from them as the lily from the hemlock, or as the dove from the daw. He who allows reason to take its proper place, and to be taught right reason by the word of God, from that time separates himself from the giddy throng and takes the cool sequestered path which leads to God.

Equally does this mourning separate the gospel mourner from the obstinate and the daring; for, alas, many are so wicked as to wear a brazen brow and exhibit a heart of steel in the presence of the Lord. They defy the divine wrath, and impudently scorn the punishment due to sin. Like Pharaoh, they ask, "Who is the Lord that I should obey his voice?" They despise death, judgment, and eternity, and set themselves in battle array against the Almighty. Those who mourn in Zion are not of this company, for they tremble at the word of the Lord. Their hearts are sensitive to the faintest sign of God's displeasure, and when they know that they have done that which is grievous in his sight, straightway their sorrow overflows; they deeply lament their provocations, and humbly pray that they may be kept from further offences.

Zion's mourners are also very different from the self-conceited who are puffed up with high notions of their own excellence. They are never known to assert that from their youth up they have kept all the commandments, nor do they even dream of thanking God that they are better than others. Room for boasting they find not; far rather do they abhor themselves in dust and ashes. Their sins, follies, and failings are a daily burden to them, and they loathe the very idea of self-satisfaction.

Those who mourn in Zion are not among those loud professors who glory in the abundance of their grace, and reckon that they are out of the reach of temptation. You will never hear them cry, "My mountain standeth firm: I shall never be moved;" but their prayer is, "Hold thou me up, and I shall be safe." Holy anxiety to be found sincere and acceptable with God prevents all self-confidence. I would not encourage doubts and fears, but I will go the length of the poet, and say—

> He that never doubted of his state,
>   He may—perhaps he may, too late.

I fear that not a few who dream that they possess strong faith are under a strong delusion to believe a lie; and instead of having the confidence which is wrought of the Spirit of God, which is quite consistent with holy mourning, they feel a false confidence based upon themselves, and therefore founded upon the sand. This puffs them up with a false peace, and makes them talk exceeding proudly, to the sorrow of the Lord's wounded ones. The Lord's people should prudently get out of the way of these lofty spirits, who grieve the humble in heart. They are the strong cattle, of whom Ezekiel speaks, which thrust with horn and shoulder, and despise the weak ones whom God has chosen. Lord, let my portion be with the mourners, and not with the boasters. Let me take my share with those who weep for sin, and weep after thee; and as for those who are careless, or those who are rebellious, or those who are self-righteous, let them take their frothy joy and drain the cup, for true saints desire not its intoxicating draught.

The mourners in Zion are not only different from other people, but they are also *much changed from their former selves.* They are scarcely aware of the great change which they have undergone, but even their mourning is an evidence of their being new creatures. The things wherein they formerly rejoiced are now their horror, while other things which they once despised they now eagerly desire. They have put away their ornaments: their finery of pride they have exchanged for the sackcloth of repentance; their noisy merriment for humble confession. They now wonder how they could have thought the ways of sin to be pleasurable, and feel as if they could weep their eyes out, because of their extreme folly. You would not think that they were the same people; in fact, to tell you the truth, they are not the same, for they have been born again, and have undergone a new creation, of which their humiliation before God is no mean sign. Their hearts of stone have been taken away, and the Lord has given them hearts of flesh, to feel, to tremble, to lament, and to seek the Lord. God's mourners also find themselves *different from what they are at times even now*; for they see themselves wander, and straightway they quarrel with themselves, and smite upon their offending breasts. Such occasions of self-abhorrence they find daily. The man who is satisfied with himself had better search his heart, for there are signs of rottenness about him. The man who is deeply discontented with himself is probably growing fast into the full likeness of Christ.

Do you, dear friend, feel that you could justify yourself as to all that you have done, or thought, or felt today from morning to evening—at home or abroad, in the shop or in the street? Oh, no; I am sure you will confess that in many things you have fallen short, and you will penitently grieve before the living God. You would not on any account do or say again all that you have done and said. You bless God who has sanctified you, and delivered you from the dominion of sin; but still you have to complain that sin has a fearful power to lead you into captivity, and therefore you are not pleased with yourself; and are more ready to join in a confession than in a hymn of self-glorifying. The text says of mourners of that kind, that God hath appointed great things for them, and therefore let us pray the Holy Ghost to work in us this morning.

Now, *this mourning,* of which we are speaking, *is part and parcel of these people's lives.* When they began to live to Christ they began to mourn. Every child of God is born again with a tear in his eye. Dry-eyed faith is not the faith of God's elect. He who rejoices in Christ at the same time mourns for sin. Repentance is joined to faith by loving bands, as the Siamese twins were united in one. The new birth always takes place in the chamber of sorrow for sin: it cannot be otherwise. The true Christian was a mourner at conversion, and since then he has been a mourner, even in the happiest day he has known. When was that? The happiest day I ever knew was when I found Jesus to be my Savior, and when I felt the burden of my sin roll from off me. "Oh, happy day! when Jesus washed my sins away"; but I mourned that day to think that I had been so greatly polluted, and had needed that my Lord should die to put away my sin. I mourned to think that I had not loved and trusted the Savior before; and ere the sun went down I was mourning to think that I did not even then love my Lord as I desired. I had not gone many paces on the road to heaven before I began to mourn that I limped so badly, that I travelled so slowly and was so little like my Lord; so that I know by experience that on the very brightest day of his spiritual experience a true believer still feels a soft, sweet mourning in his heart, falling like one of those gentle showers which cool the heat of our summer days and yield a pleasurable refreshment. Holy mourning is the blessed pillar of cloud which accompanies the redeemed of the Lord in their glad march to heaven.

Dear brethren, to some extent we live by mourning. Do not imagine we do not rejoice; for, in truth, "we rejoice with joy unspeakable and full of glory," but this is quite consistent with holy mourning. We sorrow every day that there should be any remains of sin in us, that we should still be open to temptation, and should have the slightest inclination to evil. We mourn that our eyes should look so longingly on vanity, and that our tongue should be so apt to speak unadvisedly. We mourn that our right hand should be so unskillful in holy service, and that we should be so apt to let it be seen of men when we are giving to the Lord. We mourn especially that our heart should still be unbelieving, unfeeling, and fickle. Yes, we are very happy, but we mourn to think that, being so happy, we are not more holy; that, being so favored, we are not more consecrated. We "rejoice with trembling." To the Lord's mourners, godly sorrow is so essentially a part of themselves that *they grow while they mourn*, and even grow by mourning. A man never becomes better till he is weary of being imperfect. He who is satisfied with his attainments will stay where he is; but he who mourns that he is not yet up to the standard will press forward till he reaches it. He that saith, "My faith is weak," is the man who will become stronger in faith. He who confesses that his love is not so intense as it ought to be, will have more love ere long. He who mourns daily that he has not attained that which he desires, is by that very agony of spirit approaching the goal. It will be well that mourning should be our companion till we come to the gates of paradise, and there we shall mourn no longer; but, I was going to say, so precious is the mourning which the Spirit works in us that we might almost regret parting with it. Rowland Hill used to say he felt half sorry to think that he must part with the tear of repentance at the gates of heaven; and he was right, for holy mourning is blessed, sweet, safe, and sanctifying. The bitterness is so completely evaporated that we can truly say,

> Lord, let me weep for nought but sin,
>   And after none but thee;
> And then I would—oh that I might!—
>   A constant weeper be.

Dear friends, *holy mourning is no mere melancholy or sickly fancy*; it has abundant reasons whereby to justify itself. We do not mourn because we give way to needless despondency, but we lament because it would be utter madness to do otherwise; we cannot help mourning. A Christian grieves over himself and his shortcomings, and this not from mock modesty, but because he sees so much to sigh over. He will tell you that he never thinks worse of himself than he ought to do; that the very worst condemnation he has ever pronounced upon himself was most richly deserved. If you praise him you pain him. If you commend him, he disowns your approbation, and tells you that if you knew him better you would think less of him, and you would see so much infirmity and imperfection within him, that you would not again expose him to danger by uttering flatteries.

A child of God also mourns because he is in sympathy with others. It is one part of the work of grace in the soul to give us considerateness for our afflicted brethren. Is a child of God himself prosperous? He recollects others who are poor and in adversity, and he feels bound with them. He is a member of the body, and hence he suffers with the other members. If each believer were distinct and separate, and kept his own joy to himself and his sorrow to himself, he might more often rejoice; but, being a member of a body which is always more or less afflicted, he weeps because others weep, and mourns because others mourn. The more sympathy you have in your nature the more sorrow you will experience. It is the unsympathetic man who laughs every day; but the friendly, tender, brotherly, Christ-like spirit must mourn; it is inevitable.

And chiefly do believers mourn because of the sins of others. This great city furnishes us with abundant occasion for deep concern. You can hardly go down a street but you hear such filthy language that it makes your blood chill in your veins. The sharpest blow could not cause us more pain than the hearing of profanity. And then the Sabbath, how little is it regarded; and the things of God, how little are they cared for! Everywhere a child of God with his eyes open must have them filled with tears, and if his heart be as it ought to be, it must be ready to break. Alas, the cause is frequently in the Christian's own family: he has an ungodly child or an unconverted wife. A Christian woman may have a drunken husband, or a godly daughter may have a dissipated father. These things make life gloomy beyond expression. Woe is me, cries the saint, that I dwell as among lions, with those that are set on fire of hell. Ill society makes a child of God sick at heart: as Lot was vexed with the filthy conversation of the wicked, and as David cried for the wings of a dove that he might fly away and be at rest, so do the saints pine in this world. Let such mourners take heart while they perceive in the text that Jesus has come to comfort all that mourn.

II. Now, secondly, let us note *WHERE THESE PEOPLE ARE MOURNING*. They are mourning *in Zion*. They could not carry their griefs to a better place. Sorrow is so common that we find mourners in Babylon, and Tyre, and even in Sodom and Gomorrah; but these are of a different order from the mourners in Zion.

If we are wearing our sackcloth in the house of the Lord, let us thank God, in the first place, that we are not mourning in hell. We might have been there, we should have been there if we had received our due; but we are mourning where mourning meets with acceptance from God. We are lamenting where a dirge can be changed into a song. I thank God also that we are not mourning as those do who fiendishly regret that accidentally they have done some good thing. You remember how angry Pharaoh was with himself because he had let Israel go, and I have known men who have never been penitent till they have by mistake done something good, or given too much away. They could gnaw their own hearts out for having done a good turn to another. God save us from such diabolical mourning as that; and yet it is not uncommon.

We have known some mourn, too, because they could not do others a mischief; because their hands were tied and they could not hurt God's people; like Haman, they have fretted because of Mordecai. They cannot endure the prosperity of the godly, but would fain take them for a prey and make them as the mire of the streets. That is a horrible mourning, which makes a man have fellowship with Satan.

Some even mourn because they cannot take their fling of sin. They would like to indulge every vile passion, have a mint of money at their command, and none to check them in any way; and they mourn because they are hedged up and hindered from destroying themselves. Such foolish ones mourn on the ale bench; they mourn in the synagogue of Satan; but as for God's people, they mourn *in Zion*.

Now let us indulge ourselves with a visit to the courts of Zion to see in what parts thereof the mourners may be found; for from her outer walls even to her innermost courts you will find her inhabited by them. Some of them mourn just hard by the walls of the holy city. Like the Jews of the present day, they have their wailing place under the walls of Jerusalem. Poor souls! They dare not enter into the holy place, and yet they will not, cannot go away. They wait at the gates of wisdom's house and they delight in the posts of her doors. They never like to be away when the saints assemble, yet they feel as if they had no right to be there. They are satisfied with any corner, and are content to stand all the service through. They take the lowest seats, and reverence the meanest child of God.

They sometimes fear that the good word is not for them, and yet like the dogs they come under the table, hoping for a morsel. If it is a sermon full of thunder, "Ay," they say, "the minister means me"; but if it is very sweet and full of comfort they say, "Alas, I dare not think that it is for me." They would not stop away from the holy congregation, for they feel that their only hope must lie in hearing the gospel, and they half hope that a word of comfort may be dropped for them, but yet they come trembling. They are like the robin redbreast in the winter time: they venture near the house and tap upon the window pane, and yet are half afraid to come in. When the cold is very severe and they are very hungry, they become daring, and pick up a crumb or two. Still, for the most part, they stand at the temple door and mourn. They are in Zion, and they sigh and cry because they feel unworthy so much as to lift their eyes towards heaven.

Ah, well, the Lord appoints great blessings for you; he is good to those who seek him; he hath regard to the cry of the humble, he will not despise their prayer. Now, if the arch-enemy should ever suggest to you that it is of no use for you to be found hearing the word, for you have heard the preacher so many times, and even for years have remained unblest, and therefore it is all hopeless, tell him he is a liar, be all the more diligent in your attendance, and strive to lay hold on what is preached. He will persuade you not to come when you are most likely to get a blessing. Whenever you feel as if "Really, I cannot go again; for I am so often condemned, and find no comfort," say to yourself, "Now, I will go this time with all the more hope. Satan is laboring to prevent my going, because he fears that Christ will meet with me." Oh, seeking mourner, forsake not the courts of Zion, though thou flood them with thy tears. Be found where the gospel note tells of Jesus. Be found at the prayer-meetings. Be found on your knees. Be found with your Bible open before you, searching for the promise, and above all, believe that Jesus came to save such as thou art, and cast thyself upon him.

Many ransomed ones have been enabled to enter the temple a little way. At the entrance of the holy place stood *the laver* full of water, where the priests were wont to wash themselves. He who frequents the courts of Zion will often mourn at that laver, for he will say, "Alas, that I should need such washing! Alas, that I should so frequently spot my garments and defile my feet! Cleanse thou me, O God. Wash me day by day. Dear Savior, cleanse thou me from secret faults." These mourners are deeply grieved at what others consider little spots, for sin hurts their tender consciences, and in the light of God sin is seen to be exceeding sinful in those whom God so highly favors.

Hard by the laver stood *the altar*, where they offered the victims. Now, he who sees the one great sacrifice by which sin was put away, while he rejoices in the finished atonement, also laments the sin which slew the Substitute. Many a time may you hear the plaintive song—

> Alas! and did my Savior bleed?
> And did my Sovereign die?
> Would he devote that sacred head
> For such a worm as I?

The surer we are of our pardon the more we mourn over our sin. We look on him whom we have pierced, and a mourning takes hold upon us like the mourning of Hadadrimmon in the valley of Megiddo when Judah lamented the best of kings and saw her sun go down in blood. Awakened souls mourn for Jesus as one that is in bitterness for his first-born. You can never stand at the altar and see Jesus bleed without your own heart bleeding, if, indeed, the life of God is in you. Can any but a heart of stone be unmoved at the sight of Calvary? Blessed are they who amidst their joy for pardoned guilt wash the pierced feet of Jesus with tears of love and grief.

Further on in the holy place, as you will recollect, there stood *the altar of incense*. It was placed before the veil which hid the holy of holies, but that veil is rent. Now, they who mourn in Zion often stand and weep as they think of him whose prayers are the incense which God accepts—even Jesus, by whose intercession we live. They think, "Alas! that I should be so cold in prayer when Jesus pleads so earnestly." They look over their own intercessions, and they see such faultiness, such wandering of thought, such coldness of heart, such forgetfulness, such pride, such want of faith, such utter unworthiness, that they cannot help deeply mourning. Besides, they remember when Satan desired to have them, and sift them as wheat, and would have destroyed them if Jesus had not prayed for them, and they mourn the state of heart which placed them in such jeopardy. As by faith they perceive how sweet the merits of Jesus are, they remember their own ill savor and begin anew to loathe themselves. Their very sense of acceptance in the Beloved fills them with humiliation; it seems too wonderful that Jesus should do so much for them, and make them so sweet to the Lord. Great love is a melting flame. When we nestle like doves in the bosom of our Lord we mourn like the loving turtle; we mourn because of the great love which makes us almost too happy. We rejoice with trembling, and feel both fear and exceeding great joy.

And then, those who entered the holy place would see a table covered with loaves of bread: it was called *the table of the shew-bread*. Our blessed Lord Jesus

Christ is that bread, and we feed on him, as the priests of old did on the shewbread; but I confess I never stand there myself, and think of how he feeds my soul with his own self, without mourning that I have not a larger appetite for him, and that I do not more continually feed upon him. I lament that ever I hoped to find bread elsewhere, or tried to feed on the swine-husks of the world. Oh, to hunger and thirst after Christ, for this is to be blessed! Oh, to feed upon a whole Christ, even to the full, for this is to be satisfied with royal dainties. We cannot feed on Jesus without mourning that others are starving, and that we are not more eager to bring them to the banquet; that we are not ourselves more familiar with heaven's bread, so as to know how to hand it out, that the dying multitudes of our great cities may be fed. Oh Lord, cause thy people more and more to lay to heart the sad fact that millions are famishing for want of the bread of heaven.

Within the holy place also stood *the seven-branched candlestick*, which was always burning and giving forth its pearly light; before it we also mourn. When we rejoice in the light of God's Holy Spirit we cannot help mourning over our natural darkness, and our former hatred of light. We mourn to think, also, that we ourselves shine with so feeble a ray that our light does not so shine before men as to glorify God to the fullest extent. We cannot enjoy the light of the divine Spirit without praying that we may have more of it. We acknowledge that if we have but little of it, it is our own fault, for he is ready to light us up with a splendor which shall make the sons of men to wonder whence such a luster came. We mourn, also, because the nations sit in darkness and death-shade, and refuse the heavenly light. And thus, you see, we mourn in Zion, from the entrance even to the innermost court.

Even when we pass through the rent veil, and stand at *the mercy-seat*, and enjoy the believer's true place and privilege, we still mourn. We think of the law, covered by the propitiatory, and we mourn our breaches of it. We think of the pot of manna, and mourn the days when we called the heavenly food "light bread." We remember Aaron's rod that budded, and say to ourselves, "Alas, it is a memorial of my own rebellion as well as of my Lord's power." We ask ourselves, "Where is my pot of manna of remembered mercy? Alas! my rod does not bud and blossom as it should, but often it is dry and fruitless. Alas! that law which my Lord hid in his heart, how little respect have I had for it, or remembrance of it." And then, looking at the golden mercy-seat, we wet it with our tears because here the blood-drops fell, by which we are brought nigh. The glory of Jehovah between the cherubim bows us down, and we cry, "Woe is me, for I have seen the King, the Lord of hosts." Our impurity prostrates us when like Esaias we behold the glory of the Lord. Is it not meet that it should he so?

Thus, you see, from the outer courts of Zion right into the Holy of holies, every spot suggests mourning, and true children of God yield to the influence thereof. In every place of mercy or privilege which they occupy they look down upon themselves with shame and confusion of face. Old Master Dyer used to say, "When the peacock shows his fine feathers he ought to recollect that he has black feet and a horrible voice"; and, so, truly, whenever we are full of divine graces and blessings it becomes us to recollect what we are by nature, and what there is of impurity still lurking within us, that we may be humble, and with our confidence in Jesus may mingle repentance of sin. Thus much upon where they mourn.

III. And now, thirdly, WHO THINKS OF THESE MOURNERS? Who appoints unto them that mourn in Zion? Who looks upon poor and needy souls? Very often their friends are shy of them: if they mourn much and long their friends shun their society, and their familiar acquaintances know them no more. There are places of worship where mourners in Zion might come and go by the year together, and no one would utter a sympathetic word; a broken heart might bleed to death before any hand would offer to bind it up. I love to see Christian people anxious after poor mourners, and eager to meet with penitent and desponding ones. It ought not to be possible, dear friends, in an assembly of believers for a mourning soul to come and go many times without some Barnabas—some son of consolation, seeking him out, and offering a word of good cheer in the name of the Lord. But mark this: Whoever forgets the mourner, the Lord does not. There are three divine persons who remember the mourner. The first is *the eternal Father*. Read the first part of the chapter. "The Spirit of the Lord God is upon me; because *the Lord* hath anointed me to preach good tidings unto the meek. *He* hath sent me to bind up the broken-hearted."

God, the ever blessed Father, pities his sorrowing children and has respect unto their prayers. Poor soul, you are deeply wounded because of your sin, and no one on earth knows it, yet your heavenly Father knows the thoughts of your heart, and he tenderly sympathizes with your anguish of mind. Where art thou standing, poor fretting Hannah? Thou woman of a sorrowful spirit, I come not, like Eli, to judge thee harshly and censure thee unjustly. Where art thou? Dost thou mourn and sigh after thy Lord? Then go in peace. The Lord grant thee thy petition. It shall surely be done unto thee according to thy faith. God, the eternal Father, first of all, remembers those who mourn. "I am poor and needy, yet the Lord thinketh upon me."

Moreover, *God the Son* has the same kind thoughts towards his mourners. What does the first verse say? "The Spirit of the Lord God is upon *me*"; and you know that it is Christ who speaks. "The Lord hath anointed *me*, to bind up the broken-hearted." Jesus, then, undertakes the cause of the troubled. He was a mourner all his days, and therefore he is very tender towards mourners.

> He knows what fierce temptations mean,
>   For he has felt the same.

"I know their sorrows," saith he. "In all their afflictions he was afflicted." He was made perfect through sufferings. Rejoice, O mourner, for the Man of Sorrows thinks upon thee.

And then *the Holy Spirit*—the third Person of the blessed Trinity—according to the text remembers mourners. "The Spirit of the Lord God is upon me," saith he, "because the Lord hath anointed me." Yes, thou blessed Spirit, thou art the Comforter, and whom canst thou comfort but mourners? It were useless to comfort those who never knew a sorrow: it were a superfluity to attempt to offer consolation to those who never were depressed. The Holy Ghost hovers like a dove over the assemblies of the Sabbath, and wherever he finds a heart which is broken with a sense of sin, he alights there and brings light and peace and hope. Be of good courage, then, ye mourners, for the three divine persons unite on your behalf: the One God thinks upon you, and the gentleness and tenderness of his almighty heart are moved towards you. Is not this good cheer?

IV. Our fourth and last point is this, WHAT DOES THE LORD DO FOR THEM? —"*To appoint unto them that mourn in Zion.*"

Let us take first the ordinary rendering of the text—"*To appoint* unto them." God makes appointments to bless mourners. It is his decree, his ordinance, his purpose to bless those who mourn in Zion. Some mourners are greatly frightened at predestination, they are afraid of the divine decrees. Be of good comfort, there is no decree in God's great book against a mourner. "I have not spoken in secret, in a dark place of the earth: I said not unto the seed of Jacob, Seek ye me in vain." God's terrible decrees are against the proud, whom his soul hateth, and he will break them in pieces; but as for the humble and the meek, his purposes concerning them are full of grace. Read the following verses and see—"To give unto them beauty for ashes, the oil of joy for mourning, and the garment of praise for the spirit of heaviness." It is registered in the record office above and stands in his eternal book, and so must it be, "Blessed are they that mourn, for they *shall be* comforted." When you think of the decrees remember this decree, and be of good comfort.

But an equally accurate rendering of the text is, "To provide for those that mourn in Zion." *To provide.* God not only purposes to bless, but he does bless his mourners. Our heavenly Father prepares good gifts for his mourning family. For whom did Jesus die but for mourners? For whom does he live but for mourners? For whom are the blessings of his coming but for mourners? Oh you that are troubled because of sin, and hate it, all God's heart goes out towards you, and all the riches of the everlasting covenant are yours. Make bold to take them, since for mourners they are provided. For whom are clothes but for the naked? For whom are alms provided but for the needy? For whom the bath but for the filthy? For whom the medicine but for the sick? For whom God's grace but for you that need it, and mourn because of your need? Come and welcome. The Lord bring you to himself at this very hour.

Last of all, the text may run thus, "*To arrange* for those that mourn." The Lord has arranged, settled, and appointed to bless those who mourn; his plans are laid for it, and the method and means are appointed. God hath made all things ready to bless you that mourn. The only actual preparation that is needed for Christ is that you should need him; and the only conscious preparation is that you should feel your need, or, in other words, should mourn. Christ is full: are you empty? Then there is room for you. Christ is generous: are you poor? Then you are the person on whom he will bestow his gifts. I think I see before me a beautiful tree loaded with fruit. Do you see it? There are the ruddy apples in profusion waiting to be gathered. The boughs are hanging down, they are burdened by the excess of fruit. The tree has a voice. I hear its leaves rustling with a request. If you could hear it speak, what would it say? "Baskets! Baskets! Baskets!" It is asking for baskets. Well, here are a number of baskets; and some of them are full; shall we bring them? No, they are of no use to the tree. But here is a poor basket which, if it could speak, would say, "I am utterly empty: I cannot be of any use to that beautiful tree which has such abundance of fruit upon it, while I have none." But, indeed, its use lies in its emptiness.

Now, my brother, the Lord Jesus is that loaded tree, and he asks you simply to be an empty basket into which he may put the rich fruits of his life and death. If you have a fullness of your own you may go your way; but if you have nothing whereof to glory, and if you desire to receive of his fullness, then you and the Lord Jesus are well met. Jesus Christ my Lord is willing to bestow his grace upon the guiltiest of mankind; even those that lie hard by the gates of hell Jesus is able to lift up to the gates of heaven. Only trust him, only trust him, ye that mourn. Only trust him, and ye shall be comforted; for he has appointed, provided, and arranged all good things for you. May his Spirit lead you at once to partake in the table which he has furnished for mourners in Zion. Amen.

4

Beauty for Ashes

"To give unto them [that mourn in Zion] beauty for ashes" (Isa. 61:3).

Again I would remind you that the mission of our Lord Jesus Christ related to mourners in Zion. He did not come into the world to exalt those who are high, to give greater power to the strong, or to clothe those who are already clad in their own righteousness. No, the Spirit of God was upon him that he might preach good tidings to the meek, that broken hearts should be bound np, captives redeemed, and prisoners released. He came with blessings for the poor, not with luxuries for the rich. This ought to be a very great subject of thanksgiving to those who are heavy of heart. Is it not sweet to think that the Anointed of the Lord came for your sakes, that you of the rueful countenance, whose eyelids arc fringed with beaded tears, you whose songs are dirges, you who dwell at death's door, may be brought forth into the sunlight? Most men choose cheerful company whereby they may be entertained, but the Lord Jesus evidently selects mourners, and delights in those whom he may encourage and cheer. Blessed be his name! How meek and lowly is he in all his ways! How forgetful of self and how thoughtful towards his poor servants. He looks upon them with a pitying eye, and makes untold blessings their portion.

Notice with pleasure that in dealing with mourners, according to the text before us, the Lord acts upon terms of exchange or barter. He gives them beauty for ashes, the oil of joy for mourning, and the garment of peace for the spirit of heaviness. It is a gracious exchange, but it is tantamount to everything being a free gift. "To give unto them beauty for ashes" is a free gift, because what he takes away is of no value, and they are glad to be rid of it. In condescending compassion he took our ashes upon himself. Ah, how they once covered his sacred head and marred his beauty! He took our mourning. Alas, how it made him the man of sorrows in the day of his humiliation! He took our spirit of heaviness; and as he lay prostrate in the garden beneath the load he was exceeding heavy and sorrowful even unto death. He took a loss to give us a gain, and so it is a barter in which there is a double profit upon our side. We lose a loss, and the gain is pure gain.

From our Lord the blessings of love are all of free grace, and therefore let him have all the praise. I am sure that no mourner would hesitate to deal with Jesus on these special terms, which only divine love could have thought of. If you have ashes, will you not be glad to exchange them for beauty? If you are mourning, will you not willingly cease from weeping to be anointed with the oil of joy? And if the spirit of heaviness presses upon you like a nightmare, will you not be glad to be set free, and to be arrayed in the glittering garments of praise? Yes, there could not be better terms than those which grace has invented; we accept them with delight. Poor mourner, they are specially ordained for you, that by a twofold grace in removing evil and bestowing good you might be doubly enriched and comforted.

In our present meditation I shall call attention, first, to *the lamentable condition* in which many of the Lord's mourners are found: they sit in ashes, expressive of deep sorrow. Secondly, we shall observe *the divine interposition* on their behalf, for the ashes are removed; and, thirdly, we shall notice *the sacred gift*—"Beauty for ashes."

I. Let us begin with THE MOURNER'S CONDITION—he is covered with ashes as the emblem of his sad estate. Let us now like Cinderella sit down amongst the cinders for a while, in order that we may come forth from the ashes with something better than glass slippers, adorned with a beauty which shall befit the king's courts. The fairy fable which has often made our childhood smile shall now be actually realized in our own souls, yea, we shall see how far truth outshines romance; how much grander are the facts of God than the fictions of men.

It seems, from the text, that *the righteous are sometimes covered with grief.* Orientals were always excessive in the use of symbols, and hence, if they were in sorrow, they endeavored to make their outward appearance describe their inward misery. They took off all their soft garments and put on sackcloth, and this they rent and tore into rags; and then upon their heads, instead of perfumed oil which they were so fond of using, they threw ashes, and so disfigured themselves, and made themselves objects of pity. Ashes were of old ensigns of mourning, and they continued to be so down to Popish times, of which we have a trace in the day called Ash Wednesday, which was the commencement of the time of fasting known as Lent. It was supposed that those who commenced to fast sat in ashes to begin with. Such symbols we leave to those who believe in the bodily exercises and outward rites of will worship. However, God's servants have their spiritual fasts, and their heads are metaphorically covered with ashes. I will not stop to read you the list of the occasions in which the princes of the blood royal of heaven are found sitting in the place of humiliation and distress. Suffice it to say that *they began their new life among the ashes*. Like Jabez who was more honorable than his brethren they were born in sorrow. Some of us will never forget our grief for sin: it was a bitterness with which no stranger could intermeddle. We shall never forget the anguish of our soul, and our deep humiliation, which no ashes could sufficiently symbolize. Like the patriarch of old, we cried, "I abhor myself, and repent in dust and ashes."

Repentance since then has always had a large degree of mourning connected with it: sorrow has salted all our penitential tears. It is right it should be so; and it is equally right that we should never leave off repenting. Repentance and faith are two inseparable companions, they flourish or decay together like the two arms of the human body. If faith could enter heaven, repentance would certainly pass the gate at the same time. That they will not both enter there, or something near akin to them, I will not venture to assert quite so confidently as some have done. Whether in eternity I shall regret that I have sinned and shall still believe in Jesus, and find my everlasting safety in so doing, I will not positively say; but if I so asserted who could refute the statement? Assuredly we shall mourn for sin as long as we are upon the earth, and we do not desire to do otherwise. Grief for sin and love to Jesus will endure through life; there will never come a time when we shall refuse to bathe with tears the pierced feet, and kiss them with warmest love.

> Sorrow and love go side by side;
>   Nor height nor depth can e'er divide
> Their heaven-appointed bands.
>   Those dear associates still are one,
> Nor till the race of life is run
>   Disjoin their wedded hands.

We have to mourn bitterly when we have fallen upon times of strong temptation, and, alas, of surprising sin. We grieve to confess the fact, but it is sadly true that faults have overtaken us. Who amongst God's chosen sheep has not gone astray? In consequence of such sin we have had to return to the sackcloth and the ashes, and our heart has sunk within us. By reason of our old nature we have transgressed like David, and then by reason of our new nature we have wept like David, and mourned our broken bones. If a foul spot has defiled our garments, we have been led by the Holy Ghost to go at once to Jesus, and, while he has washed it out with his blood, we have lamented our offence. Whenever believers permit the fires of sin to burn, they are made ere long to cast the ashes of repentance upon their heads and shrink into the dust.

Beloved friends, we have also covered our heads with ashes on account of the sins of others. Parents have been compelled to sorrow very grievously for their sons and daughters. The wail of David is no unusual sound. "O Absalom, my son, my son! Would God I had died for thee, O Absalom, my son, my son!" Many a woman sits in ashes half her life because of her ungodly husband, who makes her life bitter to her: many a loving sister pines inwardly because of a profligate brother who persists in ruining himself. The crimes of the world are the burdens of the saints. We cannot make the ungodly mourn for their guilt, but we can and do deeply mourn over their insensibility. How can we bear to see our fellow-men choosing everlasting destruction, rejecting their own mercies, and plunging themselves into eternal misery? If Hagar said, "Let me not see the death of the child," and if the prophet's eye ran with ceaseless tears over the slain of his people, shall not we mourn in dust and ashes the wilful soul-suicide of our neighbors, who perish before our very eyes with mercy at their doors?

Moreover, we pity the Christian who does not frequently mourn over the depravity of the times in which he lives. Infidelity has in these last days stolen the garb of religion, so that now we frequently meet with volumes in which the fundamentals of the faith are denied, written by ministers of churches whose professed creed is orthodox. Our grandfathers would have shuddered at reading from a disciple of Tom Paine sentiments which pretended ministers of the gospel have given forth to the world. Things have reached a painful pass when those who are called to office on purpose to proclaim the gospel are allowed to use their position to sow doubts about it, and sap and undermine all belief in it. Such conduct is meanness itself, and it is wonderful that the churches tolerate it.

Only Satan himself could have put it into a man's heart to become a salaried preacher of the gospel in order to deny its fundamental truths. He who does this is *Judas Redivivus*, Iscariot the second. God save us from all complicity with such practical falsehood and fraud! But when the child of God sees this, and sees besides ritualism and latitudinarianism spreading on all sides, he feels a sympathy with Mordecai of whom we read that "when he perceived all that was done, he rent his clothes and put on sackcloth with ashes, and went out into the midst of the city, and cried with a loud and a bitter cry." It were a happy omen if there were more of this, and especially if many could be found to imitate Daniel, who said, "I set my face unto the Lord God to seek by prayer and supplication, with fasting, and sackcloth, and ashes." We should soon behold the dawn of better days if such ashes were commonly found upon saintly heads.

Yes, the best of God's people must sometimes sit down among the ashes, and cry, "Woe is me." When the saints mourn, it will sometimes happen that they cannot help showing their sorrow; it is too great to be controlled or concealed. Usually a spiritual man tries to conceal his soul's distress, and he has his Master's command for so doing, for Jesus said: "Thou, when thou fastest, anoint thine head and wash thy face, that thou appear not unto men to fast." In personal trouble we would rather bear our burden alone than load others with it, and therefore we endeavor to maintain a cheerful manner even when our heart is sinking like a millstone in the flood. As to spiritual depressions, we cannot show these to men who know nothing about them, and in the presence of the ungodly we are dumb upon such topics; but there are sorrows which will have a tongue, concerning which we may even be bidden to speak; as saith the prophet, "O daughter of my people, gird thee with sackcloth, and wallow thyself in ashes." At such times we must express our inward grief, and then the men of the world begin to ask, "What ails him?" and jeeringly to cry, "He is melancholy: religion has turned his brain."

Note that mourning young woman. Her mother said only the other night, "What makes Jane so sorrowful?" She did not know that her girl was under a sense of sin. Your workmates asked you, my good friend, the other morning, "What makes you so dull?" They did not comprehend that their vile language had helped to vex your heart, and had wounded you so that your heart was bleeding inwardly. As we have joys that worldlings cannot share, so have we sorrows which they cannot comprehend; and yet we are obliged now and then to let them see that we are cast down, even though this brings us new reproach. The ashes must sometimes be upon our head, and we must cry, "They have heard that I sigh; all mine enemies have heard of my trouble."

Do not, therefore, beloved friends, when you see a mournful believer, condemn him, nor even depreciate him, for his sorrow may be a necessity of nature, yea it may even be a direct result of his eminence in grace. He may, perhaps, love the souls of men more than you think; he may have a more tender sense of the sinfulness of sin than you have; and, perhaps, if you knew his family trials, and if you knew the jealousy of his walk with God, or if you knew how the Lord has hidden his face from him, you would not wonder at his rueful countenance. You might even marvel that he was not more cast down, and you might be ready to give him your pity, and even your admiration, instead of your cold censure. Be sure of this, that some of the holiest of men have mourned as David did: "I have eaten ashes like bread, and mingled my drink with weeping."

Next let us note that *such grief disfigures them*. I gather that from the contrast intended by the words of our text—"Beauty for ashes." Ashes are not beautifiers, and mournful faces are seldom attractive. A believer when he is in a mourning frame of mind wears a marred countenance. He is disfigured before his friends: he makes bad company for them, and they are apt to see his weak points. He is disfigured before his fellow Christians: they delight to see a brother rejoicing in the Lord, for this is a manifest token of favor, but sorrow of heart is often contagious, and therefore it is not admired. The mourning Christian is especially disfigured in his own esteem. When he looks in the glass and sees his rueful visage he cries to himself, "Why art thou cast down, O my soul? Can all be right within? If it be so, why am I thus?" He questions, upbraids, and condemns himself. If his eyes were not so weakened by tears he might see a beauty in his sorrow, yet just now he cannot, but views himself as a mass of uncomeliness: nor is he altogether in error, for generally with spiritual mourning there is a measure of real disfigurement. Unbelief, for instance, is a terrible blot upon any man's beauty. Distrust of God is a horrible blotch. Discontent exceedingly injures mental and spiritual loveliness. We are not lovely when we are unbelieving, petulant, envious, or discontented. We are not beautiful when we are distrustful and suspicious, self-willed and rebellious; yet these evils often go with soul sorrow, and we may truthfully say that some Christians are not only at times very sorrowful, but their beauty is marred by their misery.

The grief of good men's hearts *is often a very expressive one*, as the language before us suggests. When sorrow puts ashes on its head, what does it say? It makes the man eloquently declare that he feels himself to be as worthless as the dust and ashes of his house. "I cover my head," saith he, "with ashes to show that the very noblest part of me, my head, my intellect, is a poor fallen earthly thing of which I dare not boast: I count the best thing there is in me to be but dust and ashes fit only to be cast away." You mourners often thus despise yourselves.

Well, if it is any consolation to you to know it, I know a minister of Christ who the longer he lives thinks less and less of himself, and utterly abhors himself before God. It is a wonder of divine grace that the Lord should ever have loved us at all, for there is nothing in our nature that is lovely. Through our fall there is everything in us to be hated by his pure and holy mind, but nothing to esteem; and the best of the best, when they are at their best, are poor creatures. "Lord, what is man that thou art mindful of him?" If the righteous Judge had swept the whole race away at the first with the besom of destruction, he would still have been as great, and glorious, and blessed as he is; he only spares us because he is infinite in mercy.

When Abraham said, "I have taken upon me to speak unto the Lord, I that am but dust and ashes," he had not too lowly an opinion of himself, for even the father of the faithful, though a prince among men, was nothing in himself but a son of fallen Adam, and nothing but undeserved mercy made him to differ from the idolatrous race out of which he was chosen and called. "Earth to earth, ashes to ashes," is our last memorial, and all along we are tending that way by nature, for we are of the earth earthy. When we put ashes on our head we do but confess ourselves to be what we really are.

The use of ashes would seem to indicate that the fire is out. Men would not place burning coals upon their heads, but, when they cast ashes there, they mean to say, "These ashes from which all fire is gone are like ourselves: we too are spent, our fire of hope has burned out, our joy, our confidence, our strength have all departed from us, and left us only the black ashes of despair." Is not this suggestive of a state of feeling common enough to truly humbled men? Let me ask my brethren: Have you never felt as if your coal were quenched in Israel? Have you not owned that, apart from any salvation which might come to you from your dear Lord and Savior, you had no hope whatever? Have you not felt as if every spark of faith, and love, and gratitude, and all that was good, was gone out in darkness? Some of you young Christians have never yet stumbled into that slough, and I hope you never will; but if you ever do it may console you if I let you know that older saints have been there before you, and have had to cry to the strong for strength or they would have perished. Some of us know what it is to feel as if we had not even a spark of grace left. We cry,

> If aught is felt,
>   'Tis only pain to find we cannot feel.

At such times we have felt that if there was any prayer in us it was only a prayer to be helped to pray, or to be helped to mourn that we could not pray, for our stock was lying dead, and our poor husbandry yielded us no increase, for want of dew from above. Our soul has been in a state of drought, the rain from heaven has been withheld, and the earth has broken and chapped beneath our foot, devouring rather than nourishing the seed. God's children have their droughts and famines, and then dust and ashes are fit emblems of their dry and dead condition.

Ashes, too, as the symbol of sorrow, might also indicate having passed through the fire of trial, even as these ashes have been burned. Truly, some of God's best servants have been most often through the furnace, and have been so long in the heat that strength faileth them, and hope well-nigh expires. They cry to God for patience to endure all his holy will, but they feel that their own power is as much spent as if they were burnt to nothing but ash, and there was nothing more left of them upon which the fire could kindle. Is it not a mercy that the Lord looks upon such as these—the utterly spent ones who are ready to be blown away, and to perish, even as smoke and dry ashes are borne away by the wind and lost? You who are at ease in Zion know little about these terrible feelings, but you should be grateful to God and sympathize with those who are more exposed to tribulation. Join with them in magnifying the Lord because he promises beauty instead of these ashes of the furnace.

Ashes, also, as you know, are the emblem of death. The Romans placed in sepulchral urns the ashes of the dead. We say "Dust to dust, ashes to ashes," when we bury the departed. It is no uncommon thing for tried saints to complain that they are brought into the dust of death by a faintness of mind which renders life a difficulty. We come to look upon the grave as a refuge and a relief. "Ah," cries one, "they may as well bury me, for I am more dead than alive. Well may I heap ashes on my head." Like Elias they say, "Let me die, for I am no better than my fathers." To such depths of grief the best of men have sometimes descended; many of the most peaceful and joyous spirits have joined in David's description of himself—"I am as a man that hath no strength: free among the dead, like the slain that lie in the grave, whom thou rememberest no more: and they are cut off from thy hand."

But enough of this dolorous ditty, let us now change the subject. We have shown you the believer in the ashes, let us now rejoice that some better thing is in store for him.

II. Secondly, there is *A DIVINE INTERPOSITION*. The Lord himself breaks in upon the mourner's misery, and makes the most gracious arrangements for his consolation. When a man is in sore trouble he naturally begins to look this way and that way for deliverance, and thereby much of the man's mind and heart are made manifest. You may readily judge whether you are a child of God or a hypocrite by seeing in what direction your soul turns in seasons of severe trial. The hypocrite flies to the world and finds a sort of comfort there, but the child of God runs to his Father, and expects consolation only from the Lord's hand. True grace abides with God and submits itself to his will. This is always good for us. Brother, if the Lord make thee sick, remain sick till the Lord restore thee, for it is dangerous to call in any other physician to thy soul but thy Lord. If the Lord frown do not ask others to smile, for you can derive no joy from that source. If it be God's wrath that breaks thee, let God's love mend thee, or else remain broken.

> I will not be comforted
> Till Jesus comfort me—

is a sweet resolve of a truly penitent soul, for hath not the Lord said, " I kill, and I make alive; I wound, and I heal. I the Lord do all these things." Wilt thou take the healing and the making-alive out of Jehovah's hand? God forbid! Where thou hast received thy smart there get thy sweet. Where thou dost drink the gall of sorrow there drink the wine of joy, for in the Lord's hand there is abundant mercy to be found, and he will end thy misery.

According to the text, the way in which believers rise out of their mourning is through, *the coming of Jesus*. Read the chapter again. What does the Lord say? "The Spirit of the Lord is upon me, because the Lord hath anointed me." Yes, beloved, our hope lies in the mission of Christ, in the person of Christ, in the work of Christ, in the application of the blood of Christ to our hearts. We turn our eyes evermore towards the hills whence cometh our help. Look thou, Oh sinner, always to the brazen serpent whatever serpent bites thee. Whether it be the old serpent himself, or some smaller serpent of the same brood, which lurks in the way and bites at the horse's heels, still look to the one appointed cure. Never speculate in healing drugs, but keep to the one antidote which never fails. Jesus is the consolation of Israel, and let not Israel place her hope elsewhere.

And, mark you, it is Jesus coming *in the gospel* which is the mourner's hope: for this coming of the Lord is to preach good tidings to the meek, and so to bind up the broken-hearted. I have little confidence in those persons who speak of having received *direct* revelations from the Lord, as though he appeared otherwise than by and through the gospel. His word is so full, so perfect, that for God to make any fresh revelation to you or me is quite needless. To do so would be to put a dishonor upon the perfection of the sure word of testimony. In "the most sure word of testimony" there is a release from every difficulty, a plaster for every sore, a medicine for every disease. My dear sorrowing friend, it is very dangerous to look for consolation from dreams, or from the opening of the Bible upon certain texts, or from fancied voices, or from any other of those foolish superstitions in which weak-minded persons seek for comfort. Go you to what God has said in the Scriptures, and when you find your character described, and promises made to such a character as your own, then take them home, for they are plainly spoken to you. Go not about to look for comfort in the cloud-land of fancy or the moonshine of superstition, but believe in the Lord Jesus, who comes to bless broken hearts in no other way than by preaching to them the glad tidings of his grace. You are not to expect the Lord Jesus to speak with you in any other way than by the written word applied to the soul by the Holy Ghost.

Look for no new revelation; drive out the very idea as deceptive. If an angel were to come to my chamber and inform me that he brought a message from God which would tell me more than is written in the scriptures of truth, I would not listen to him for a moment, but say, "Get thee behind me, Satan. The end of these manifestations has come: the stars no more appear for the sun has risen." Our heavenly Father has already sent the Lord Jesus, and it is written, "last of all he sent his Son." In Christ Jesus there is such a fullness of truth and grace that all the angels combined could not increase it. He who looks for more revelation should beware lest he receive the curse with which the Bible concludes, which will certainly come upon any who either add to, or take from the inspired words of God. The sum of the matter is this—if there be any comfort to be received, it is in Christ, and if there be any ashes to be taken away, and any beauty to be given, it will be through the Lord Jesus in the preaching and reading of the word. This much by way of protest against the superstitions of weak minds.

But now I want you to notice a something which does not appear in our English version, but is clear in the Hebrew. It is that *the Lord very easily makes a change in his people's condition*, for the word in the Hebrew for ashes is *peer*, and the word for beauty is *peer*. The change is very slight in the original. Some idea of the similarity of the words may be given you in English if I quote from Master Trapp. "The Lord promises to turn all their sighing into singing, all their musing into music, all their sadness into gladness, and all their tears into triumph." Perhaps I may myself give you a closer imitation still, and more after the Hebrew model, by saying, he turns our mourning into morning. In the case before us we might say, "He gives us splendors for cinders," beauty for ashes. Now, as readily as we change a word by a single letter, so easily doth the God of all comfort alter the state of his own people. With him nothing is hard, much less impossible. From the cross to the crown, from the thorn to the throne, from misery to majesty is but a hand's turn with the Lord. Often doth he call his people like Mordecai from sitting at the gate to riding upon the king's horse, like Joseph from lying in the dungeon to ruling in the land, like Job from the dunghill to double wealth, like David from the caves of Engedi to the palace in Jerusalem. This he doth both suddenly and easily, as when a man lights a candle and the darkness departs at once. How charming and astonishing the change: to pass in a moment from winter into summer, from midnight into noon, from storm into profound calm! This is the finger of God, and it is often seen. Many have been able to join in the song of the psalmist.

> All through the night I wept full sore,
>   But morning brought relief;
> That hand, which broke my bones before,
>   Then broke my bonds of grief.
>
> My mourning he to dancing turns,
>   For sackcloth joy he gives,
> A moment, Lord, thine anger burns,
>   But long thy favor lives.

When you are at your lowest do not conclude that it will be months before you can rise. Not so. From the nadir to the zenith you will spring at a single leap when the Almighty Helper girds you with power. David in the psalms describes the Lord coming to his rescue in baste most marvelous. Out of the depths he was snatched by the flash of Jehovah's power.

> On cherub and on cherubim
>   Right royally he rode,
> And on the wings of mighty winds
>   Came flying all abroad.
>
> And so deliver'd he my soul:
>   Who is a rock but he?
> He liveth—Blessed be my Rock!
>   My God exalted be!

How joyously he sings! And well he may after so special a rescue. There is no slow travelling with God when his people are in sorrow. Before they have time to call he answers them; while they are yet speaking he hears their requests. He hears them chanting "*De Profundis*," and he lifts them to sing aloud, "*Gloria in Excelsis*": from "Out of the depths" their tune changes to "Glory in the highest." Nor are there slow pauses of weary hope, but the Lord worketh a world of wonders in the twinkling of an eye.

Thus we see how our Lord giveth beauty for ashes.

III. We now turn to the last point, which is, WHAT HE BESTOWS INSTEAD OF THE ASHES—beauty. All disfigurement is removed. The ashes had made the person to be defiled uncomely to others and unpleasant to himself; but all this is removed. Beauty is given, and his countenance is not marred with dust and grime. His face is bright with joy and beaming with hope. No more unpleasant to the eye, the person has even become attractive and delightful. The original Hebrew implies that occasions for joy and emblems of joy are also given, for it might be read, "A chaplet for ashes." The ashes were on the head, and now a crown is placed there. The allusion is to the nuptial tiara which men wore on their marriage day. The Lord's mourners arc to be decked with crowns of delight instead of being disfigured with ashes of grief. When does that happen to us? Do you recollect when you first obtained a sense of forgiveness? How gloriously were you then arrayed! When the father said of his prodigal son, "Bring forth the best robe and put it on him, put a ring on his hand, and shoes on his feet," that was a high day; and so was it with us when we also were delivered from our filthy rags and clothed in righteousness divine. Our ashes were gone, then, and a crown adorned our heads. Forgiven! It was a joy of joys. Even now as we look back upon it we begin to sing again—

> Happy day! Happy day!
>   When Jesus washed my sins away.

We went a little farther on in spiritual life, and then we discovered that we were the children of God. We did not at first know our adoption: but it burst gloriously upon us like a newly kindled sun. Do you recollect when you first learned the meaning of the word, and perceived that adoption secured eternal salvation? For the heavenly Father does not cast his children away, nor can they cease to be the objects of his love. How can any child be unchilded? And, if still a child, he must be still beloved, and still an heir. When you once drank consolation from that doctrine, did you not receive a tiara for ashes? How lovely a thing it is to be a child of God! "Behold, what manner of love the Father hath bestowed upon us, that we should be called the sons of God!"

We lived a little longer, and we began to understand the doctrine of vital union with Christ. We had not dreamed of it at the first. We discovered then that there is a vital, actual, conjugal union between us and Christ—that we are married to him. It is a great mystery, but yet it is a great truth. It is all but inconceivable that we should be members of his body, of his flesh, and of his bones; and yet it is even so. That was a heavenly day wherein we perceived that we were one with Jesus—"by eternal union one." Then we rejoiced as wearers of a marriage crown, and we sang, "My Beloved is mine and I am his."

Since then we have learned other truths, and on each occasion of being thus taught of the Lord we have again obtained a crown for ashes; another and yet another chaplet has adorned our brow. We have felt ourselves to be made priests and kings unto God, and the beauty of the Lord our God has rested upon us. All glory be to his name!

But, beloved, reading the word as our own version does, our God has given us "beauty for ashes." Every child of God has the beauty of the imputed righteousness of Jesus Christ, and at this moment he is all fair as he is viewed in him who is altogether lovely. Washed in Jesus' precious blood we are without a stain, and clothed in his righteousness we are accepted in the sight of God. Oh justified man, think of thine ashes as a condemned sinner, and now think of the beauty which the righteousness of Christ has put upon thee, and be astonished and ravished with delight.

Besides that, the Holy Spirit has given us a measure of sanctification or beauty of character. We know that we are not what we used to be, and though we are not what we want to be, or what we shall be, yet there is a beauty about us now in the fact of our being at heart wholly consecrated to God, and in the repentance of sin and the desire after holiness which the Holy Spirit has created in us. Even the beginnings of holiness are beauty before God.

Then, brethren, we know there is a beauty put upon us by virtue of our union with Christ, for every member of Christ must be beautiful. See how even the spouse of the Old Testament, as she sang her canticle of love, though she could not have had a very clear sight of him in those dim days of types, which were only like a golden candlestick compared with the sun which shines on *us*, yet even she was enraptured with him. She sings of him with unqualified admiration. From head to foot she delights in him, she perceives the very locks of his head, and the sandals of his feet to be beautiful, and she cries in rapture, "Yea, he is altogether lovely." If, then, thou art a member of Christ, however lowly a part thou art of him, thou art well pleasing and delightful in the sight of God. Did you ever drink into your soul that amazing text, "Thou art all fair, my love; there is no spot in thee"? (Song. 4:7.) It is the voice of the Bridegroom to the church he loves, and to the soul which is espoused to him. As for myself, I appear to my own conscience to be spotted and defiled all over, and yet by faith I know that in Christ Jesus I am made to be spotless before the throne of God. Concerning myself I cry, "Look not upon me, for I am black, because the sun hath looked upon me"; I am become like a bottle in the smoke, my beauty hath consumed away like a garment eaten of the moth; and yet in Christ Jesus, together with the rest of his saints, I know that comeliness is put upon me,

> Though in ourselves deformed we are,
>   And black as Kedar's tents appear,
> Yet when we put his beauties on,
>   Fair as the courts of Solomon.

Blessed is he that understandeth this beauty which the Lord hath given us instead of ashes!

Let us remark that the contrast of our text is peculiarly suggestive, because it is not quite what we might expect. The Lord takes away our ashes, but what does he give in exchange? The natural contrast would be *joy*, but the Lord bestows that which is better, namely, *beauty*, because that is not only joy to ourselves but to others. "A thing of beauty," as we say, "is a joy forever." A beautiful person gives pleasure to all around. Now, child of God, you are not only to have those ashes taken away which have hitherto disfigured you, but you are actually to become the source of joy to others. How pleasant that will be for you who have so long touched the mournful string that you have distressed your family.

Yes, young friend, you are to make your mother rejoice by telling her that you have found peace with God. You are yet to cheer your father's heart, young woman, when you shall say to him, "Father, I have found him in whom you trust, and I am trusting in him too." Yes, poor mourner, you will yourself be comforting other mourners one of these days. You who have been in Giant Despair's castle shall help in pulling down the monster's den. You can hardly believe it, but so it shall be.

In the sense of being a joy to others many of the Lord's people are very beautiful indeed: you cannot help being charmed with them, especially with those of deep experience. Good men are glad of the company of those to whom the Lord has given the beauty of grace. Even the ungodly, though they do not confess it, have a respect for the majesty of holy characters. There is a charm about beauty which makes her ride as on a lion through the midst of her foes; every man's hand is bound to defend her, and none dare to injure her. The beauty which the Lord gives to his people is as a queen among all beauties, and swayeth a potent scepter.

Yes, and when the Lord makes his people beautiful they are a delight even to God himself, for the Lord rejoices in his works, and his grace-works are the noblest labor of his hands, and as being fullest of grace are most graceful. The Lord delights in his people. We read of the Lord Jesus, that his delights *were* with the sons of men, and even now, though angelic harps ring out his praises, he loves to be here in our churches, and to commune with us as a man speaks with his friend. Beloved, cultivate his society: abide with him, and if he can find any cause of delight in you, which is a wonder of wonders, put all your delight in him.

Let us have this gracious beauty about us, and even our heavenly Bridegroom will have to say, "Turn away thine eyes from me, for they have overcome me. Thou hast ravished my heart with one of thine eyes." May we be kept from marring this beauty, and be forever so fair that even our Lord himself may look and love. Amen.

5

The Oil of Joy for Mourning

"The oil of joy for mourning" (Isa. 61:3).

Mourners in Zion ought to be doubly comforted, for here is a second gift of love to them, a second exchange of loss for gain. The varied expressions of this choice Scripture show the manifold loving-kindnesses of the Lord to his afflicted, and the plentiful devices of wisdom by which he ministers consolation. It was not enough to give the sorrowing ones "beauty for ashes"; he must needs add an oil with which to enhance the beauty, and take away, not only the ashes, but the mourning which lay beneath them. This, also, illustrates the exceeding fullness of the blessings which are stored up in the Lord Jesus: in him we have everything which heart can wish, a rich variety of joyful blessings never to be exhausted. It shows us also the marvelous fitness of our Lord Jesus, since solely because of his coming as the anointed of the Lord there is healing for the wounded, liberty for the captives, eyes for the blind, comfort for mourners, beauty for the disfigured, and oil for fading countenances. He meets every want of the soul, and fills the heart to overflowing with contented gratitude. Let it be repeated, and gratefully remembered, that all these good things come by the anointed Savior alone. There can be no traffic with heaven except by the crimson road of the atoning blood; no channel for divine favor except by the Christ of God, on whom the Spirit of the Lord forever rests. To him be glory forever. Blessed be his name, he is the channel of grace, and in him is no straightness or shallowness. A divine riches of glory flows to us by Christ Jesus.

"Immortal joys come streaming down, Joys, like his griefs, immense, unknown."

If our Redeemer were not what he is, what should we do? But being what he is, there is no necessity which he cannot supply, there is no grief which he cannot assuage, and there is no right desire which he cannot satisfy. Let us drink of the river of his fullness and sing to his praise.

Notice, also, at the outset of our present meditation, the effectual way in which the blessings which Jesus brings are bestowed upon mourners. We have often heard doubting ones say, Yes, there are promises, but we cannot reach them. We know that there are abundant consolations, and comforts rich and free, but we do not feel their power, nor dare to take them to ourselves. Now, in this place we see the condescending Lord himself applying the oil of joy in exchange for mourning. His own right hand pours the precious oil upon the bowed head; he himself causes the face to shine and banishes woe. A man may lie bleeding on the battlefield, and there may be liniments close at hand, but in his weakness and agony he may be quite unable to bind up his own wounds, or reach the cordials; he may die because he is not able to stretch so much as a finger to help himself to remedies which lie by his side. It is an unspeakable mercy that our Lord gives his grace to us in such an effectual manner that his mourners actually obtain the help they need. He is a very present help, a real Comforter; the oil of joy is not shown us in an unbroken alabaster vase, nor merely offered to us in a vial, but it is actually and effectually applied to the soul.

Let us now come to the consideration of this second of the three great blessings bestowed upon the mourners in Zion, and may we all enjoy a portion thereof while we meditate thereon.

In working out the metaphor we shall observe that OUR LOVING LORD BRINGETH HIS MOURNERS TO SIT AT A FEAST.

This is clearly intended, for oil was largely used by Orientals upon festive occasions. The oil which maketh man's face to shine was associated with the bread which strengtheneth man's heart, and the wine which maketh glad the heart of man (Ps. 104:15), because these are the chief provisions of a banquet. Before the feast, or during the entertainment, the guests were refreshed with perfumed oil, which would be either poured upon the head, or furnished for anointing the face. It was part and parcel of a great feast. Hence we read of those who "drink wine in bowls, and anoint themselves with their chief ointments." Therefore, our first thought is this, that the Lord Jesus brings mourning souls to a feast of love, at which they sing, "Thou preparest a table before me in the presence of mine enemies, thou anointest my head with oil." How great will be our joy if we can feel that our Lord has brought us into his banqueting house, and that we are now reclining there. Now to all believers this is truly the case. Our hunger now is assuaged, for he satisfies our mouth with good things. That fierce, wolf-like hunger, which we once felt, is gone for ever; for it is written, "He that eateth of this bread shall never hunger." Our craving, all-consuming thirst is ended; for he that drinketh of the water which Jesus gives him shall never thirst. Many of Zion's mourners are sitting under the Word, longing for divine provision, and praying, "Lord, evermore give us this bread." The bread is theirs, and a voice cries to them, "Eat, O friends; drink, yea drink abundantly, O beloved." Your deadly famine of heart is gone, and the spiritual hunger which you now feel is a pleasant appetite, which gives a zest to heavenly food—an appetite which you long to have increased to the utmost.

Even at this moment, though you feel a blessed hunger and thirst after righteousness, you are filled with royal dainties. You are no longer starving in the streets, nor famishing under the hedges and in the highways, but by divine grace you have been sweetly compelled to come in, and you are at this moment the guests of the table of boundless mercy, where the name of Jesus is as ointment poured forth, so that all around you the oil of gladness is shedding a divine perfume. You are no longer feeding the swine, but resting at the Father's table: the oxen and the fatlings are killed, and you are actually at the supper. Believe this, and act accordingly.

And what a feast it is! For who is your host? The Lord of life and glory himself ordains "the feast of fat things, of fat things full of marrow, of wines on the lees well refined." "The King sitteth at his table." It is his table, and he sits at it. It is a great thing to dine with a king, but what must it be to be daily eating bread at the table of the King of kings? Let the joy-bells ring in your soul at the very thought, for you are already come to the great feast which the King hath made for his Son; he cometh in himself to see the guests.

It is *the* feast of the universe. There never was such another, and there never can be its like. It is the antepast of the great supper of the Lamb. What provisions are put upon the table! Men do eat angels' food when they come hither. Yea, they eat viands better than the bread of angels, for the body of Christ has become the meat and the drink of his mourners. Poor souls, you feast upon incarnate deity. Speak of oxen and of fatlings? These are poor types compared with the wondrous provision of celestial grace with which the infinite Jehovah has loaded the table of the covenant. And all these things are yours. You may have as much as you will. There remains no need to eat bread by weight, or to drink water by measure; but he will satiate your soul with fatness, and nothing shall be withheld from you. Ought you not to bless him that you are now a guest at such a table, and that such food is at this very moment spread before you?

Think of your fellow guests. Look around you and inspect the company. Remember where you were a little while ago; you were strangers and foreigners, yea, you were as dogs in the street. Where are you now? You are permitted to sit with the children of God, with the saints of the Most High. Does it not bring the water into your eyes to think that you—you who long refused to come, and despised the feast of grace—are, at last, brought in? Nay, not only with God's people here are you sitting at the feast of love, but the saints above are your comrades now: for "ye are come to the general assembly and church of the firstborn, which are written in heaven, and to God the Judge of all, and to the spirits of just men made perfect." We sup with the glorious company of the apostles, the goodly fellowship of the prophets, the noble army of martyrs, and the holy church throughout all the world.

Now also have we fellowship with angels. We have come unto Mount Zion and to an innumerable company of angels. Better still, we have fellowship with Jesus. "Jesus the Mediator of the new covenant" is the center of the whole. It is his wedding feast, and we are glorifying him by partaking of his Father's bounty. We cannot at this moment actually put our heads upon Jesus' bosom as John did, nor need we wish for that visible and physical delight, but our heart rests upon his breast, and enjoys a bliss unspeakable in so doing. Jesus, Immanuel, we are safe in thine arms, and our heart is at perfect rest in thee. We are even now abiding in thee, while at thy Passover we keep the feast. We are feasting with the great Father himself; for, beloved, when the glorious sacrifice becomes a meat offering, God himself delights therein and partakes with us in the satisfaction made by his Son. Oh, the satisfaction which God the Father finds in Jesus! It is a theme upon which we dare not attempt to expatiate; but this we know: the Lord rests in his love. He smells a sweet savor in the person and work and sacrifice of his dear Son. If we love Jesus, so does the Father, and if we rest in Jesus, so does he, and if we would fain glorify Jesus, so would the Father. Thus are we brought to feast with God the Judge of all, when we come to "the blood of sprinkling, which speaketh better things than that of Abel." Here the oil of joy is most befitting. Is it not most natural and proper that it should be poured out at such a festival?

We cannot linger, but must pass to the next observation, which is this: that BEING AT A FEAST, IT IS BECOMING THAT WE SHOULD HAVE PRESENT JOY. Hence the text speaks of "the oil of joy for mourning:" the mourning was present enough, the joy should be equally so. At feasts, the perfume poured upon the heads of the guests was a seemly and appropriate thing. It suited the feast, it made the guests feel at home, and it gave refreshment all around as the delicious perfume sweetened the air. Come, beloved, we have at this moment reason for joy, and let us use it. Let every child of God feel that he has the oil of joy, in the fact that he possesses present blessings. Our best things lie on the other side of the Jordan: we are looking for our full bliss at the coming of our Lord, but we have much in the present. The oil of joy is on our faces now, our locks are even now bedewed with the sacred anointing, and it will be well for us to turn our thoughts towards that truth.

For, first, let all believers recollect that we have to-day the joy of the atonement. "By whom also," saith the apostle, "we have received the atonement." The atonement will be no more ours in heaven than it is now. "We have redemption by his blood." Our sin will be no more put away in glory than it is at this moment, for our iniquity is even now cast into the depths of the sea. Our Substitute hath finished transgression and made an end of sin, and having believed in him we know that for us the full atonement is already made and the utmost ransom for ever paid. "It is finished" (John 19:30). "Therefore being justified by faith, we have peace with God" (Rom. 5:1). "There is therefore now no condemnation to them which are in Christ Jesus" (Rom. 8:1). Having believed, we know that our sin is as far removed from us as the east is from the west. We know also that the righteousness of Christ is imputed to us and that it covers us from head to foot. This is a divinely sweet ingredient of the oil of joy, which now distils upon us from the head of our glorified Aaron, and perfumes even those who are as the skirts of his garments.

Besides that, my brother, at the present moment you live in the love of God. It may not be at this moment sensibly shed abroad in your heart by the Holy Ghost, but still "the Father himself loveth you." If you are a believer in Christ he will *not* love you more when you are in heaven than he loves you now, for he loves you infinitely at this instant. You are even now "accepted in the Beloved." "Beloved, now are we the sons of God." Infinite love, eternal love, unchanging love, almighty love, is the present possession of the children of God. Hence comes our safety, hence comes the certainty of the supply of all our wants; hence, indeed, flow all our joys. At this moment, despite our spirit depression and soul battling and heart strife, the Lord hath set his love upon us and rests in that love. Should not this make our faces to shine?

At this time, too, we possess the divine life within us. Having believed, we have been regenerated and the Spirit of God dwelleth in us. Yes, within these mortal bodies doth the Godhead dwell. He hath made our bodies to be the temples of the Holy Ghost. And what a favor is this; for this indwelling is the witness of the Spirit within us, the perpetual seal of grace. God has put into us a new life, a life like his own; he has created in us a superior principle, unknown to flesh and blood, for we are not born again of the will of man, nor of the will of the flesh, but of the will of God. A supernatural life has been implanted in us which cannot die, because it is born of God. *We* have this and we know it; and because of it we greatly rejoice.

And not only so, but because we are the sons of God, we are heirs according to the promise, since it is written, "If children, then heirs; heirs of God, and joint-heirs with Christ." Is not this oil to make the face shine? What better delights can your imagination conceive than the divine joys of adoption? O ye mourners, have ye not here the oil of joy?

Further, we have the present joy of a high calling, involving the exercise of sacred functions. You are at this hour, beloved, as many of you as believe in him, made kings and priests unto God. You are consecrated to the service of him who has bought you with a price. The mark of the blood is upon you, and "ye are Christ's." At this moment you are a living sacrifice bound with cords to the horns of the altar. Your Lord has sent you into the world, even as the Father sent him into the world, to proclaim his truth and to do his will among the sons of men. Is not this cause for delight? Does not your divine vocation anoint you with the oil of gladness?

With this we have special privileges. There is one privilege I prize at this moment: I cannot tell you how much. It is this—the liberty to pray, the power to pray, the promise that I shall be heard. Take the mercy-seat from me, and poverty, faintness and anguish would seize my soul! As long as there is a mercy-seat, and a rent veil, and the voice that bids me draw nigh, and tells me that if I wait upon the Lord I shall renew my strength, I have a joy worth worlds. What, have you lost a child? Is your property melting before your eyes? Does health decline? Do friends forsake? Yet the throne of grace is accessible; fly thither and lose your griefs. There burdens are light, there crosses bud with crowns, and tears sparkle into diamonds. Come hither, ye mourners, even with the load of your doubts and fears; supplication will quicken you, and for mourning you shall obtain the oil of joy.

Time would fail me if I were to go through the whole catalogue of the sources of the Christian's present joy. Ah, you worldling, you know, and we confess it is true, that our chief joys are yet to come; but notwithstanding we have enough today to make us more than a match for you. You may display your present mirth and carnal delight if you will, and laugh at us who weep now; but we can endure your ridicule with calm complacency because we have a secret peace and a deep fathomless repose of heart, which make us even now as far from envying you as an angel from envying a mole. We are not of all men the most miserable, but of all men the most blessed. Our eternal hopes revive us amid the sorrows of this fleeting life; the harvests of heaven shale out and drop golden grain from above, upon which we feed even now. To have Jesus for our Brother, God for our Father, and the Spirit to be our Comforter is a better portion than the richest, the proudest, or the most famous of worldlings can possibly possess. The oil of joy is not made in the presses of earth, it drops upon us through the golden pipes of the sanctuary, flowing from the sacred olive trees which the Lord hath planted.

Passing on from that observation we would offer a third, which is implied in the text, namely, that THIS JOY COMETH OF THE HOLY GHOST. This is clear, since evermore when we read of oil we have before us in Scripture the divine influence of the Holy Spirit. The first part of the chapter before us runs thus: "The Spirit of the Lord God is upon me, because the Lord hath anointed me."

The oil with which Christ was anointed was the Holy Ghost; and the oil of joy with which we are anointed is the same Spirit. It is he who gives us joy in the Lord.

The Holy Spirit brings joy to believers thus: first, he clears the understanding, and enables us to comprehend the deep things of God. Many poor souls know but little of the precious boons which the Lord has bestowed upon them. As yet, though they be the Lord's elect, they are not aware of it. Though they be the redeemed of the Lord, they perceive it not. There is light about them, and yet they cannot see, for their eyes are not yet opened beyond the power to see men as trees walking. Let us be grateful if we have passed beyond this stage. Through infinite mercy the Holy Spirit has visited some of us, and while he has painfully made us see our ruin, he has also most blessedly led us to comprehend something of the remedy, and has enabled us to understand with all saints what are the heights and depths, and to know the lore of Christ which passeth knowledge. We have an anointing so that we know all things. Now are the mysteries opened, and the hidden things laid bare; and, therefore, we have joy in the Lord, for our renewed understanding floods our heart with rivers of delight.

The Holy Spirit also gives us joy, by enabling us to exercise an appropriating faith. You that have faith, do you bless God sufficiently for it? Do we not fail to adore the divine mercy which has wrought this grace in us? We ought to blame ourselves when we find our faith to be weak, but we must never commend ourselves when faith is strong. The weakness of faith is ours, but the strength of faith comes of the Holy Spirit, and of him alone. Let us bless him that he has enabled us to take to ourselves what the Lord Jesus has provided, so that now we do not only see is grace to be excellent, but we grasp it as our own. Here is oil of joy for us indeed.

The Spirit also, very graciously, sanctifies us, and this is joy. It is a part of his work to discover sin in us, and to excite a holy hatred of it. He burns in our soul like flames of fire consuming evil. Now, the destruction of sin is the destruction of sorrow; and as a child of God grows in likeness to Jesus he grows in solid peace of mind. If you will follow your doubts and fears to their roots you will find that they grow from the dunghill of your sins; and when the Lord cleanseth out the evil of our hearts, and creates a new spirit within us, the oil of joy perfumes the soul, and we are glad in his salvation.

Moreover, the Holy Spirit graciously quickens his people; and what a wonderful effect quickening has upon our joy! Whenever we are slothful in the things of God, we miss the delights of healthy spiritual life, and ere long we mourn; but when the Holy Spirit comes and makes us feel lively and energetic and sensitive, then we begin, also, to rejoice in the Lord; and the power of his might within us works in us a leaping of holy joy. Those who not only have life, but have it more abundantly, are a highly favored people, and know how to exult in the Lord. Beloved, long for no joy but that which the Holy Spirit gives you. Thank God for the comforts of this life, but do not let them become your idols, as they will be if they become your exceeding joy. Draw from the upper fountains, fill your pitcher at the eternal springs; ask neither for the cinnamon nor camphire of this world's gardens, but let your chief spices be the fruit of the Spirit, which are joy and peace through believing.

We may now, in the fourth place, remark that THE JOY WHICH THE HOLY SPIRIT GIVES US IS A GREAT PRESENT BOON. I once heard a person say, very wickedly indeed, as I thought, and still think, that sin could do the believer no harm; but he added, "Except that it destroys his comfort." I thought, "Well, that is a terrible 'exception' indeed; that surely is quite enough to fill us with holy fear. If anything robs the Christian of his joy, surely the loss is great enough to set him upon his watch tower." Yet I fear that many Christians do not consider this. They dream that it can be well with their souls when the joy of the Lord is gone; but, brethren, it is not so; the healthy condition of a child of God is a state of peaceful rest in the Lord. It is wonderful how full Scripture is of comfort for mourners, because the Lord's object is that the mourner maybe comforted. "Comfort ye, comfort ye my people, saith your God. Speak ye comfortably to Jerusalem." Our Lord desired that we might have his joy fulfilled in ourselves, and he said, "Let not your hearts be troubled." "Rejoice in the Lord alway," said the apostle; and as if that were not enough he added, "and again I say, rejoice."

Hear me, ye mourning ones—the maintenance of a cheerful, happy frame of mind is of the utmost importance to you, and that for many reasons which may be drawn from the metaphor of oil.

Oil is refreshing, and so is holy joy. It puts new life into the soul, and renews its youth like the eagle's. When the man is faint with long pursuing, he revives if he perceives he already possesses present blessings in which he may rejoice. The joy of the Lord is our strength.

Oil was intended also to make each guest agreeable to his neighbors. When his head was anointed with the sweet perfume, those round about him were gratified. Happy Christians are pleasing to those about them; and thus they become a means of attracting souls to Jesus. We ought to be so happy that others ask, "Whence have these men their joys?" If so, you can clearly see why we should exchange our mourning for the oil of joy. It would be ill to frighten men from the glad tidings by drawing long faces, and using doleful tones.

Besides, brethren, you all know how weak you are in the service of God if your heart runs down into despondency; but when holy joy comes back you feel that you could face a lion, or the old roaring lion himself. Joy makes us brave. "The spirit of a man will sustain his infirmity, but a wounded spirit who can bear?" Give me the joyful Christian for his Master's service, for he will break through a troop and leap over a wall.

How gloriously doth sacred joy lift you up above the sorrows of the world! Yea, more, how it lifts you up above earth's joys! The man who has once drunk the old wine of the kingdom does not desire the new and sour wine of earth. He who knows the joy of the Lord will despise the joy of the world. Earthly comforts are small concerns to the heavenly mind. He receives them gratefully as matters of ordinary gift from his Father's hand; but his heart cries, "The Lord is my portion, saith my soul." He who has eaten the white bread of heaven has his mouth put out of taste for the brown bread of earth. He who has feasted at God's table, and had the oil of joy poured upon his head by the Holy Ghost, has risen above the fascinations of the hour. What can charm a man who has gazed on the beauties of Jesus? What can delude us into idolatry when we have once beheld the glory of the Lord? The joy of the Lord is a grand safeguard.

Earnestly could I wish that all God's people were flooded with it; there would then be no fear of angry tempers, harsh speeches, or murmuring words. Full of the joy of the Lord, deeds of injustice in trade or of grasping at the world would be disdained by you; suffering would be endured with patience, and labor performed with diligence; railing would never be returned for railing, nor proud looks given to the poor. The joy of the Lord makes a man so calm, so quiet, so heavenly that he lives above the world. What a grand life is that of Abraham. He has his trials, and some of them are intense, but he walks along the road of history with an almost noiseless tread, gliding along as though all were smooth. The record says, "It came to pass that the Lord had blessed Abraham in all things"; and yet in the previous pages we read of trials with Lot, with Hagar and Ishmael, and the grand ordeal with Isaac. Faith made his trials blessings, and his inward joy, like Aaron's rod, swallowed up all the rods of his afflictions. The same road is open to us, and we have the same reasons for walking in it, since the God of Abraham is our God for ever and ever. He who can live by faith shall have a constant supply of the oil of joy poured upon him by the Holy Spirit, and his mourning shall flee away.

Our last observation is, THE JOY WHICH GOD GIVES HIS PEOPLE IS BEST SEEN, AND FREQUENTLY BEST FELT, IN FELLOWSHIP. We began with noting that oil is connected with festivity; sweet spices are for banquets, where men feast together. Oh mourners, you will often find your souls made joyous when you assemble with your brethren. Bread eaten in secret is sweet, and morsels behind the door are delicious; but still the choicest and most abundant provisions are brought forth when the king's household gather around his table, and realize that "they being many are one bread." Speaking personally, my happiest times are spent with my brethren and sisters in Christ in the high festivals, when the multitude keep holy day. Draw a circle around my pulpit, and you have hit upon the spot where I am nearest heaven. There the Lord has been more consciously near me than anywhere else; he has ravished my heart while I have been trying to cheer and comfort his mourners.

Many of you can say the same of your pew where you are wont to sit: it has been a Bethel to you, and the Lord Jesus has revealed himself to you in the midst of his people. Let us remember what delightful times we have had in prayer together. We have come into the sanctuary heavy of heart, and while one brother after another has approached the throne of grace for us, we have been unburdened and helped to joy in God till the prayer-meeting has seemed to be a heaven below, an antepast of the eternal meetings above. Thus the oil of joy is poured out in the assembly of fellowship. Ofttimes, also, when we have been singing together some delightful hymn, in lively, feeling manner, we have felt as if we could leap with delight, and so the oil of joy has streamed upon our heads. Have you not often cried with the poet:

> I would begin the music here,
>   And so my soul should rise;
> Oh for some heavenly notes to bear
>   My passions to the skies.

Yes, that is the oil of gladness given at the festival of praise among the sons of God: who would not be there?

A joyous influence has also been within the house when believers have met to talk with one another concerning the things of God in simple, pious conversation. Alas, how little is there of such speaking one to another, especially among wealthy Christians. A Christian man remarked to me the other day that when he was a boy the good old Christian people were constantly talking upon the doctrines of grace and other things which concern the kingdom of God, but there is little of this now. The staunch old men of the last generation knew what they believed, and discerned between things that differed; they were, perhaps, a little too severe in their judgments; but still they did converse on divine things and were refreshed thereby. But now we are so very charitable that we are afraid to talk to one another about the things of God, for fear we should differ. It should not be so, for when Christ is the subject, and God's people converse together, their hearts burn within them with sacred delight, and the oil of gladness is poured upon their heads. Holy fellowship brings heavenly joy: the converse of saints with each other is the source of unnumbered delights.

Lastly, the communion table has been to many of us, above all other places in the world, the palace of delight. There are certain of us who never forget the ordinance for a single Lord's Day, and years of experience bear witness to the value of this means of grace. It is marvelous that so few even among Christians are regular in their attendance at that thrice blessed supper. A young girl said to me the other Sabbath, "Jesus seems so near when we are at the table;" and she was quite right. The emblems used at the supper so vividly bring our Lord before us that we think only of his passion, of the blood that was shed, and of the body which was made to suffer for our sins. Then are we borne away with grateful emotion and feel as if we had reached the very gate of heaven. While we drink the wine and eat the bread the oil of gladness is poured upon us by our Lord himself. You who neglect that ordinance are losing a great privilege, and besides that you are neglecting a solemn duty. May the Lord convince you of your negligence and bring you to delight in that ordinance which is the joyful means of communion with himself.

Now all this while I have been talking to God's people, and you will say, "Have you not a word to say to the sinner?" Well, I have all the while been speaking to the sinner, too, because all this is for you if you repent of sin and believe in the Lord Jesus Christ. If you will come and have it, the table is spread and loaded for you; nay more, "the word is nigh thee, even in thy mouth." What! Is the bread of life *in your mouth*, and will you not eat it? Poor, hungry, empty, needy sinner, can you reject what God himself puts into your mouth? If angels will rejoice when you repent, depend upon it there is joy in store also for you. Come then to Jesus just as you are. Bring no money with you, bring no fitness with you, bring no fancied goodness with you; bring your undesert and sin, and lay them before your Lord. Bring your hard heart, your want of feeling, your want of grace, and just come and find all that you want in Christ, who is waiting to bless you.

When I was a child I remember how at a school festival the children were instructed to bring their own mugs with them. Now that showed the poverty of those who gave the treat; but my Master does not want you to bring anything; he supplies everything. Come as you are, with nothing about you except your needs and your willingness to be saved. When an empty, guilty, lost, undone, ruined creature is coming to a great, blessed, and mighty Savior, all he has to think of is the love which invites him and the greatness of the Redeemer who will receive him. Come hither, then, all ye who mourn for sin, or mourn that you cannot mourn, and by believing in Jesus you shall obtain the oil of joy, and the days of your mourning shall be ended.

6

The Garment of Praise

"The garment of praise for the spirit of heaviness" (Isa. 61:3).

Not yet have we exhausted the list of comforts which the Anointed has prepared for his mourners. He seems as if he delighted to give "according to the multitude of his tender mercies" a very cloud of blessings. This is the third of his sacred exchanges—"the garment of praise for the spirit of heaviness": grace, like its God, delights to be a trinity. This is also the broadest of the blessings; for whereas the first adorned the face with beauty, and the second anointed the head with joy, this last and widest covers the whole person with a garment of praise. Man's first vesture was of his own making, and it could not cover his shame; but this garment is of God's making, and it makes us comfortable in ourselves, and comely in the sight of God and man. They are better adorned than Solomon in all his glory, to whom God giveth the garment of praise. May the blessed Spirit sweetly help us to bring out the rich meaning of this promise to mourners; for again I must remind you that these things are only given to them, and not to the thoughtless world.

We have noticed already the variety of the consolation which Jesus brings to mourners; the Plant of Renown produces many lovely flowers with rich perfume, and a multitude of choice fruits of dainty taste. Now we would call your attention to their marvelous adaptation to our needs. Man has a spirit, and the gifts of grace are spiritual; his chief maladies lie in his soul, and the blessings of the covenant deal with his spiritual wants. Our text mentions "the spirit of heaviness," and gives a promise that it shall be removed. The boons which Jesus gives to us are not surface blessings, but they touch the center of our being.

At first we may not perceive their depth, but only know that beauty is given instead of ashes: this might seem to be an external change. Further on, however, joy is given instead of mourning, and this is inward; the thought has advanced, we are getting nearer the heart: but in the words before us the very spirit of heaviness, the fountain whence the mourning flows, the hearth whereon the ashes are burned, is dealt with and taken away, and instead thereof we receive the garment of praise.

What a mercy it is that the blessings of the everlasting covenant belong to the realm of the spirit; for, after all, the outward is transient, the visible soon perishes. We are grateful for the food and raiment which our bodies require; but our sterner need is nourishment, consolation, and protection for our spirits. The covenant of grace blesses the man himself, the soul, which is the essence of his life. It puts away the sordid sackcloth of despondency, and robes the spirit in royal garments of praise. Judge ye your state by your estimation of such favors, for if ye have learned to prize them they are yours. The worldling cares nothing for spiritual blessings; his beauty, and joy, and praise are found in things which perish in the using; but those who know their preciousness have been taught of God, and since they can appreciate them, they shall have them. Soul-mercy is the very soul of mercy, and he whom the Lord blesses in his spirit is blessed indeed.

I want you still further to notice how these blessings grow as we proceed. At first, out of the triplet of favors here bestowed there was beauty given instead of ashes. There is much there: beauty of personal character before God is no mean thing; yet a man might have that, and by reason of his anxiety of heart he might scarcely be aware of it. Doubtless many who are lovely in the sight of God spend much of their time in bewailing their own uncomeliness. Many a saint sorrows over himself while others are rejoicing in him; therefore the next mercy given to the mourner in Zion is the oil of joy, which is a personal and conscious delight. The man rejoices. He perceives that he is made beautiful before God, and he begins to joy in what the Lord has done for him, and in the Anointed One from whom the oil of gladness descends. This is an advance upon the other, but now we come to the highest of all: seeing that God has made him glad, he perceives his obligations to God, and he expresses them in thankfulness, and so stands before the Most High like a white-robed priest, putting on praise as the garment in which he appears in the courts of the Lord's house, and is seen by his brethren. As you advance in the divine life the blessings you receive will appear to be greater and greater. Some promising things become small by degrees and miserably less; but in the kingdom of heaven we go from strength to strength. The beginning of the Christian life is like the water in the pots at Cana, but in due time it blushes into wine. The pathway which we tread is at the first bright as the dawn; but if we pursue it with sacred perseverance its refulgence will be as the perfect day. There shall be no going down of our sun, but it shall shine with increasing luster till it shall be as the light of seven days, and the days of our mourning shall be ended.

I beg you also to mark that when we reach the greatest mercy, and stand on the summit of blessing, we have reached a condition of *praise*: praise to God invests our whole nature. To be wrapped in praise to God is the highest state of the soul. To receive the mercy for which we praise God is something; but to be wholly clothed with praise to God for the mercy received is far more. Why, praise is heaven, and heaven is praise! To pray is heaven below, but praise is the essence of heaven above. When you bow lowest in adoration you are at your very highest. The soul full of joy takes a still higher step when it clothes itself with praise. Such a heart takes to itself no glory, for it is dressed in gratitude and so hides itself. Nothing is seen of the flesh and its self-exaltation, since the garment of praise hides the pride of man. May you all who are heavy in spirit be so clothed upon with delight in the Lord, who hath covered you with the robe of righteousness, that you may be as wedding guests adorned for the palace of the King with glittering garments of adoring love.

Looking carefully into the words before us, we will dwell, first, upon *the spirit of heaviness*; secondly, upon *the promise implied in the text—that this shall be removed*; and then, thirdly, upon *the garment of praise which is to be bestowed*.

I. First, let us muse upon THE SPIRIT OF HEAVINESS. We would not make this meditation doleful; and yet it may be as well to set forth the night side of the soul; for thus we may the better show a sympathetic spirit and come more truly home to those who are in heaviness through manifold temptations. Some of us know by experience what the spirit of heaviness means. It comes upon us at times even now. There are many things in the body, there are many things in the family, there are many things in daily life which make us sad. Facts connected with the past and with the future cause us at times to hang our heads. We shall just now dwell upon those former times when we were under the spirit of heaviness on account of unpardoned sin. We cannot forget that we were in bondage in a spiritual Egypt. We would awaken our memories to remember the wormwood and the gall, the place of dragons and of owls.

Observe that this heaviness is an inward matter, and it is usually a grief which a man tries to keep to himself. It is not that he is sick in body, though his unbelieving friends fancy that he must surely be ailing, or he would not seem so melancholy. "He sitteth alone and keepeth silence," and they say that he has a low fit upon him, and they invite him out into company, and try if they can jest him out of his distress. The fact is, that sin is pressing upon him, and well may the spirit be heavy when it has that awful load to carry. Day and night God's hand also is heavy upon him, and well may his spirit be loaded down. Conviction of sin makes us as a cart that is loaded with sheaves; but it is intensely inward and therefore not to be understood of careless minds. "The heart knoweth its own bitterness, and a stranger intermeddleth not therewith."

I have known persons who have been the subject of this heaviness most sedulously endeavor to conceal from others even the slightest appearance of it; and I cannot say that there has not been some wisdom in so doing, for ungodly men despise those who tremble at the word of God. What do they care about sin? They can sin and rejoice in it as the swine can roll in the mire and feel itself at home. Those who weep in secret places because the arrows of the Lord have wounded them are shunned by those who forget God, and they need not be sorry for it, since such company can furnish no balm for their wounds.

Mourner, you are wise to keep your sorrow to yourself so far as the wicked are concerned; but remember, though perhaps you think not so, there are hundreds of God's children who know all about your condition, and if you could be bold enough to open your mind to them and tell them of your heaviness of spirit you would be surprised to find how thoroughly they would sympathize with you, and how accurately some of them could describe the maze through which you are wandering. All are not tender of heart, but there are believers who would enter into your experience, and who might by God's blessing give you the clue to the labyrinth of your grief. The Lord comforted Paul by Ananias, and you may be sure that there is an Ananias for you. If you feel, as many do, that you could not unburden your soul to your parents or relatives, go to some other experienced believers, and tell them as far as you can your painful condition. I know, for I have felt the same, that all hope that you shall be saved is taken away, and that you are utterly prostrate; but yet there is hope.

While this heaviness is inward, notice in the next place that it is *real*. Heaviness of spirit is one of the most terribly true of all our griefs. He who is cheerful and light-hearted too often contemns and even ridicules him who is sad of soul. He says that he is "nervous," calls him "fanciful," "almost out of his mind," "very excitable," "quite a monomaniac," and so on. The current idea being that there is really no need for alarm, and that sorrow for sin is mere fanaticism. If some persons had suffered half an hour of conviction of sin themselves they would look with different eyes upon those who feel the spirit of heaviness; for I say it, and know what I am saying, that next to the torment of hell itself there is but one sorrow which is more severe than that of a broken and a contrite spirit that trembles at God's word, but does not dare to suck comfort out of it. The bitterness of remorse and despair is worse; but yet it is unspeakably heart-breaking to bow at the mercy-seat and to fear that no answer will ever come; to lie at the feet of Jesus, but to be afraid to look up to him for salvation. To be conscious of nothing but abounding sin and raging unbelief, and to expect nothing but sudden destruction—this is an earthly Tophet. There are worse wounds than those which torture the flesh, and more cruel pangs arise from the broken bones of the soul than from those of the body. Sharp is that cut which goes to the very heart and yet does not kill, but makes men wish that they could die or cease to be. There is a prison such as no iron bars can make, and a fetter such as no smith can forge. Sickness is a trifle compared to it—it is to some men less endurable than the rack or the stake. To be impaled upon your own sins, pilloried by your own conscience, shot at by your own judgment as with barbed arrows—this is anguish and torment.

This heaviness of spirit puts a weight upon the man's activity, and clogs him in all things. He is weighted heavily who bears the weight of sin. You put before him the precious promises, but he does not understand them, for the heaviness presses upon his mental faculties. You assure him that these promises are meant for him, but he cannot believe you, for heaviness of spirit palsies the grasping hand by which he might appropriate the blessing. "Their soul abhorreth all manner of meat, and they draw near to the gates of death." Troubled minds at times lose all their appetite. They need spiritual food, and yet turn from it. The most wholesome meat of the gospel they are afraid to feed upon, for their sadness makes them fearful of presumption. Heaviness brings on amazement, and this is but another word for saying that the mind is in a maze, and cannot find its way out.

They are weighted as to their understanding and their faith, for "the spirit of heaviness" presses there also. Their memory, too, is quick enough at recollecting sin, but to anything that might minister comfort it is strangely weak; even as Jeremiah said, "Thou hast removed my soul far off from peace: I forget prosperity." Indeed, David was more oblivious still, for he says, "My heart is smitten and withered like grass, so that I forget to eat my bread." All the faculties become dull and inert, and the man is like one in a deadly swoon. I have heard persons under conviction of sin say, "I seem absolutely stupid about divine things." Like one that is stunned by a severe blow, they fall down, and scarcely know what they feel or do not feel. Were they in their clear senses we could set the gospel before them, and point out the way of salvation, and they would soon lay hold of it; but, alas, they seem to have no capacity to understand the promise or to grasp its consolation!

I remember once speaking to a captain in distress of mind as we were sailing down a river, and when I spoke about the many promises of the word he replied, "You see those great mooring-posts along shore?" "Yes," I saw them clearly enough. "Well," he said, "it is a very easy thing, you know, to moor a ship when you once get the rope round those posts, but I cannot throw the line or fasten the hawser, and so I drift down the stream. I know the promises would hold me well enough, but I cannot hitch the rope round one of them." Yes, there is the difficulty. When men reel to and fro, and stagger like a drunken man, and are at their wits' end in the midst of a sea of soul trouble, you may tell them, "There is the harbor," but they are befogged, and cannot see it. You ask them if they cannot see the red lights? Yes, they can, but they appear to dance before their eyes, and they cannot put the ship about. Alas, for this heaviness of spirit!

Now, this heaviness of spirit also renders everything around the man heavy. The external is generally painted from within. A merry heart maketh mirth in the dull September fog under a leaden sky, but a dull heart finds sorrow amidst May blossoms and June flowers. A man colors the world he lives in to the tint of his own soul. "Things are not what they seem;" yet what they seem has often more influence upon us than what they are. Given a man, then, with heaviness of spirit, and you will find that his sorrows appear to be greater than he can bear. The common-place worries of life which cheerfulness sports with are a load to a sad heart; yea, the grasshopper is a burden. The ordinary duties of life become a weariness, and slight domestic cares a torture. He trembles lest he should commit sin even in going in and out of his house. A man who bears the weight of sin has small strength for any other load. Even the joys of life become somber. It matters not how much God has blest a man in his family, in his basket, or in his store; for as long as his heart is oppressed and his soul bowed down with sin, what are the bursting barns, and what are the overflowing wine vats to him? He pines for a peace and rest which these things cannot yield. If the eye be dark the sun itself affords no light.

There is one thing, however, which we would say to mourners pressed down with guilt: whatever heaviness you feel it is no greater heaviness than sin ought to bring upon a man, for it is an awful thing to have sinned against God. If the sense of sin should drive you to distraction—and cavilers often say that religion does this—it might reasonably do so if there were no other matters to think upon; no forgiving love and atoning blood. That which is the result of sin ought not to be charged upon religion; but true religion should be praised, because it brings relief to all this woe. Sin is the most horrible thing in the universe, and when a man sees how foully he has transgressed it is no wonder that he is greatly troubled.

To think that I, a creature that God has made, which he could crush as easily as a moth, have dared to live in enmity to him for many years, and have even become so hardened as to forget him, and perhaps defy him. This is terrible. When I have been told of his great love I have turned on my heel and rejected it. Yes, and when I have even seen that love in the bleeding body of his dear Son, I have been unbelieving and have done despite even to boundless grace, and gone from bad to worse, greedy after sin. Is it marvelous that, when they have seen the guilt of all this, men have felt their moisture turned into the drought of summer and cried in desperation, "My soul chooseth strangling rather than life"? However low you are, beloved mourner, you are not exaggerating your guilt. Apart from the grace of God your case is indeed as hopeless as you suppose. Though you lie in the very dust and dare not look up, the position is not lower than you ought to take. You richly deserve the anger of God; and when you have some sense of what that wrath must be, you are not more fearful of it than there is just need to be; for it is a fearful thing to fall into the hands of the living God. "He toucheth the hills and they smoke."

> The pillars of heaven's starry roof
> Tremble and start at his reproof.

What will his wrath be when he puts on his robes of justice and comes forth to mete out justice to the rebellious? Oh God, how terrible is thy wrath! Well may we be crushed at the very thought of it.

Another reflection we would suggest here; and that is, that if you have great heaviness of spirit on account of sin, you are by no means alone in it; for some of the best servants of God have endured hard struggling before they have found peace with God. Read their biographies, and you will find that even those who have really believed in Christ have at some time or other felt the burden of sin pressing with intolerable weight upon their souls. Certain of them have recorded their experience in terrible sentences, and others have felt what they have not dared to commit to writing. "Weeping-cross," as the old writers call it, is a much-frequented spot; many roads meet at that point, and most pilgrims have there left a pool of tears.

There is this also to be added. Your Lord and Master, he to whom you must look for hope, knew what heaviness meant on account of sin. He had no sin of his own, but he bore the iniquity of his people, and hence he was prostrate in Gethsemane. We read that "he began to be sorrowful and to be very heavy." The spirit of heaviness was upon him, and he sweat as it were great drops of blood falling to the ground. This same heaviness made him cry upon the tree, "My God, my God, why hast thou forsaken me?" Jesus was sore amazed and very heavy; and it is to him as passing through that awful heaviness that I would bid you look in your hour of terror, for he alone is your door of hope. Through his heaviness yours shall be removed, for "the chastisement of our peace was upon him, and with his stripes we are healed."

II. So much, then, concerning heaviness of spirit. And now, secondly, let us see THE HEAVINESS REMOVED, for of this the text contains a divine promise: the anointed Savior will take it away. Only a word or two upon this.

Brethren, do you enquire how does Jesus remove the spirit of heaviness? We answer, he does it thus—by revealing to us with clearness and certainty that our sin is pardoned. The Holy Ghost brings us to trust in Christ, and the inspired word assures us that Christ suffered in the room, place, and stead of all believers, and therefore we perceive that he died for ns, and also that nothing remains for us to suffer, because sin having been laid upon the Substitute, it is no more upon us.

We rejoice in the fact of our Lord's substitution, and the transfer of our sins to him. We see that if he stood in our place we stand in his; and if he was rejected we are "accepted in the beloved." Then straight away this spirit of heaviness disappears, because the reason for it is gone.

> I will praise thee every day!
>   Now thine anger's turn'd away,
> Comfortable thoughts arise
>   From the bleeding sacrifice.

Moreover, in the new birth the Holy Spirit infuses into us a new nature, and that new nature knoweth not the spirit of heaviness. It is a thing of light and life and joy in the Holy Ghost. The newborn nature looks up and perceives its kinship with God. It rejoices in the favor of the Holy One, from whom it came. It rests in the Lord, yea, it joys and rejoices in him; and, whereas, the old sin-spirit still sinks us down according to its power, there being in us still the evil heart of unbelief, this new life wells up within us as a living fount of crystal, and buoys us up with the peace and joy which cometh of the Holy Ghost's indwelling.

Thus the inner life becomes a constant remedy for heaviness of spirit.

And faith, too, that blessed gift of God, wherever it resides, works to the clearing away of heaviness; for faith sings, "All things are mine, why should I sorrow? All my sin is gone, why should I pine and moan? All things as to the present life are supplied me by the God of providence and grace, and the future is guaranteed to me by the covenant ordered in all things and sure." Faith takes the telescope and looks beyond the narrow range of time into the eternal heavens, and sees a crown laid up for the faithful. Ay, and her ears are opened so that she hears the songs of the redeemed by blood before the throne, thus she bears away the spirit of heaviness.

If I see no joy with these poor optics, faith has other eyes with which she discovers rivers of delight. If flesh and blood afford me nothing but causes for dismay, faith knows more and sees more, and she perceives causes for overflowing gratitude and delight. Hope also enters with her silver light, borrowed from faithful promises. She expects the future glory, at which we hinted just now, and begins to anticipate it all; and so, again, she drives away the gloom of the heart. Love, also, the sweetest of the three, comes in and teaches us to be resigned to the will of God, and then sweetly charms us into acquiescence with all the divine purposes; and, when we reach that point, and so love God that whatever he may do with us we are resolved to trust him, and praise his name, then the spirit of heaviness must vanish.

Now, beloved mourners, I trust you know what this great uplifting means. It is a work in which the Lord is greatly glorified when he raises a poor, begrimed soul out of the sordid potsherds among which it has lain, and gives it to soar aloft as on the silver wings of a dove. Some of us can never forget the hour of our great deliverance; it was the day of our espousals, the time of love, and it must forever remain as the beginning of days unto us. All glory be to him who has loosed our bonds and set our feet in a large room.

III. But now we come to the third, and most prominent, point of the text;

Which is THE GARMENT OF PRAISE BESTOWED, which takes the place of the spirit of heaviness. We suppose this may mean, and probably does mean, that the Lord gives us a garment that is honorable and worthy of praise: and what is this garment but the righteousness of our Lord Jesus Christ? The Lord arrays his poor people in a robe which causes them to be no more worthy of shame, but fit to be praised. They become unblameable in his sight. What a blessing this is! Did not the father when he received the prodigal say, "Bring forth the best robe and put it on him"? That was a praiseful garment instead of the spirit of heaviness; and whenever a child of God begins to perceive his adoption, and to say, "*Abba*, Father," then he puts on a fit garment for a child to wear, an honorable dress, a garment of praise. When we realize that Christ has made us priests unto God, and we therefore put on the priestly garment of sanctification by beginning to offer the sacrifice of prayer and praise, then, again, we wear a praiseful garment. When we exercise the high prerogative of kings, for we are kings as well as priests, then, again, we wear not a sordid vesture of dishonor, nor the costume of a prison-house, nor the rags of beggary, nor the black robe of condemnation, but a garment of honor and of praise. Every child of God should be clothed with the garments of salvation: his Savior has prepared them for this end, and let him wrap them about him and be glad, for these garments make him beautiful in the sight of God.

But I choose, rather, to follow the exact words of our version tonight, and speak of the garment of praise as meaning gratitude, thanksgiving, and adoration. The anointed Comforter takes away the spirit of heaviness, and he robes his people in the garment of praise.

Now, this is something outward as well as inward. A wise man endeavors to hide the heaviness of his spirit; but when the Lord takes that away he does not wish to conceal his gratitude. I could not help telling those I lived with when I found the Lord. Master John Bunyan informs us that he was so anxious to let someone know of his conversion that he wanted to tell the crows on the ploughed land all about it. I do not wonder. It is a piece of news which it would be hard to withhold. Whenever a man's inward heaviness is graciously removed he puts on the outward manifestation of joy, and walks abroad in the silken robes of praise.

As we have already said, a garment is a thing which covers a man; so when a man learns to thank God aright, his praise covers him: he himself is hidden while he gives all the glory to God. The man is seen as clothed in praise from head to foot. Many persons very unfairly judge Christians when they begin to speak of the love and mercy of God to them, for they cry out that they are egotistical; but how can it be egotistical to talk of what the Lord has done for you? If you speak with any sort of confidence captious individuals say that you are presumptuous. How can it be presumptuous to believe what God himself declares? It is presumptuous to doubt what God says, but it is no presumption to believe God; neither is it egotism to state the truth. If I were to say that God has not blest me abundantly, the pulpit on which I stand would cry out against me. Shall I conceal the mercy of God as if it were stolen goods? Never; but the rather will I speak the more boldly of the measureless love which has kept my soul from going down to the pit. "Him that glorieth, let him glory in the Lord." Bless the Lord, O ye saints of his, and give thanks to his holy name. Show forth his salvation, compel men to see it, gird it about your loins, and wear it for your adorning in all companies.

While speaking of this garment of praise, let us enquire *what it is made of*.

Is not praise composed in a large measure of an attentive observation of God's mercy? Thousands of blessings come to us without our knowledge: we take them in at the back-door and put them away in the cellar. Now praise takes note of them, preserves the invoice of favors received, and records the goodness of the Lord. Oh friends, if you do this you will never be short of reasons for praise. He who notices God's mercy will never be without a mercy to notice. This is the chief material of the garment of praise: attentive consideration of divine grace is the broadcloth out of which the garment of praise is made.

The next thing is grateful memory. Very much that God does for us we bury alive in the grave of oblivion. We receive his mercies as if they were common trash. They are no sooner come than they are gone, and the proverb saith true, "Bread eaten is soon forgotten." Why, my brethren, the Lord may give you a thousand favors, and you will not praise him, but if he smites you with one little stroke of the whip you grumble at him. You write his mercies on the water and your own trials you engrave on granite: these things ought not to be. Maintain the memory of his great goodness. "Forget not all his benefits." Call to remembrance your song in the night; and remember the loving-kindnesses of the Lord. In this also we find rich material for the garment of praise.

We are further aided by rightly estimating mercy. Is it not a great mercy to be alive, and not in hell; to be in your senses, and not in the lunatic asylum; to be in health, and not in the hospital; to be in one's own room, and not in the workhouse? These are great favors, and yet, perhaps, we seldom thank God for them. Then count up your spiritual mercies, if you can. Remember on the other hand what you deserved, and what it cost the Savior to bring these blessings to you, how patient the Lord has been with your refusal of his love, and how continuously he has loaded you with benefits. Weigh his mercies as well as count them, and they will help you to put on the garment of praise.

It is the telling out of the divine goodness which largely constitutes praise: to observe, to remember, to estimate, to prize, and then to speak of the Lord's gracious gifts—all these are essential. Praise is the open declaration of the gratitude which is felt within. How greatly do many fail in this: if you visit them, how readily they enlarge upon their troubles; in five minutes they have informed you about the damp weather, their aching bones, and their low wages. Others speak of the bad times and the decline of trade, till you know their ditty by heart. Is this the manner of the people of God? Should we not regale our visitors with something better than the bones of our meat and the hard crusts of our bread? Let us set before them good tidings, and cheerfully tell of the divine goodness to us, lest they should go away under the impression that we serve a hard master. It would create an almost miraculous change in some people's lives if they made a point of speaking most of the precious things and least of the worries and ills. Why always the poverty? Why always the pains? Why always the dying child? Why always the husband's small wages? Why always the unkindness of a friend? Why not sometimes—yea, why not always—the mercies of the Lord? That is praise, and it is to be our everyday garment, the livery of every servant of Christ.

Secondly, *who ought to wear this garment?* The answer may be suggested by another—whom does it fit? Truly there is a garment of praise which exactly suits *me*, and I mean to wear it on my own person. It is so capacious that some of my brethren would wonder if they could see it spread out. I am so much in debt to my God that, do what I will, I can never give a fair acknowledgment of it. I freely confess that I owe him more than any man living and am morally bound to praise him more earnestly than anyone else. Did I hear some of you claiming to be equal debtors? Do you demand to be allowed to praise him more than I? Well, I will not quarrel with you. Let the matter stand; and if you will excel me I will praise my Lord for it. I once in preaching remarked that if I once entered heaven I would take the lowest place, feeling that I owe more to God's grace than anybody else; but I found when I left the pulpit that I had several competitors who would not yield the lowest place to me. They were each one ready to exclaim—

> Then loudest of the crowd *I'll* sing,
>   While heaven's resounding mansions ring
>   With shouts of sovereign grace.

Blessed be God, this is the only contention among the birds of paradise—which owes the most, which shall love the best, which shall lie lowest, and which shall extol their Lord the most zealously. Charming rivalry of humility!

Let us have more of it below. I again say there is a garment of praise that fits me. Brother, is there not one which fits you, exactly suiting your state and condition? If you are an heir of heaven there is, there must be, a garment of praise which will rest most becomingly upon your shoulders and you should put it on at once.

Thirdly, *when shall we wear it?* We should certainly appear in it on high days and holidays. On Sabbath days and communion seasons the hours are fragrant with grateful memories. I heard of someone who did not attend public worship because his clothes were not fit to come in, and I replied, What can he mean? Does the Lord care for our outward dress? Let him put on the garment of praise, and he may come and welcome. The outer vestments matter little indeed, all garments of that sort are only proofs of our fall, and of the need to hide our nakedness for very shame. Fine dress is unbecoming in the house of God, especially for those who call themselves "miserable sinners." The best adornment is humility of spirit, the robe of thanksgiving, the garment of praise. The Lord's Day should always be the happiest day of the week, and the communion should be a little heaven to our souls. "Call the Sabbath a delight, the holy of the Lord, honorable."

These garments of praise should be our continual clothing. If we only praise God on high days and public occasions we do no more than hypocrites and Pharisees. Even publicans and sinners will give God a good word when their days are bright; but we must bless him when the tempest threatens. They will say, "Thank God," when they have fine weather for their pleasures, or count up a good day's takings in their shop; but only the child of God will praise the Lord in the dark, while smarting under his rod. It is the peculiar privilege of the true believer to say, "Though he slay me, yet will I trust in him"; "The Lord gave and the Lord hath taken away, blessed be the name of the Lord." There was grand music in such speech when Job first uttered it. I do not think the angel Gabriel can put so much praise into his song as Job put into that heroic word. He was covered with sore boils and blains, his children were dead, his wife was grieving him, and his friends tormenting him, yet he cried, "Blessed be the name of the Lord." Oh keep to that, ye mourners; it is music to the ear of your God. To wear the garments of praise when the cupboard is empty, when the little grave is being dug, when the head is aching and the heart is throbbing, when the ship is sinking, or trade is failing—this is the fruit of grace, and is well pleasing unto the Lord.

We should wear the garment of praise on the most commonplace of days. It should be the peasant's frock, and the merchant's coat, the lady's dress, and the servant's gown: it is the best for wear, for comfort, and for beauty, and it never gets out of fashion. I once knew an old saint, a Methodist, a very quaint, original, rustic old man, who was celebrated for happiness. When he went out to day labor early in the morning, he was always singing as he went along the road. The country people used to call it "tooting to himself." Quietly he hummed a bit of a hymn wherever he was. When he used his spade or his hoe, he worked to the music of his heart, and never murmured when in poverty, or became angry when held up to ridicule. I wish we were all as spiritually minded and as full of praise as he. Bless the Lord! Bless the Lord! When should we not bless him? We will praise him when our beds refresh us: blessed be he who kept the night watches. When we put on our clothes in the morning we will bless his name for giving us food and raiment. When we sit down to break our fast, we will bless the love which has provided a table for us. When we go forth to our work, we will bless the Lord who gives us strength to labor. If we must lie at home sore sick, with fierce pain or slow decay, let us praise him who heals and sanctifies all our diseases. Let us endeavor to display the sweet spirit of thankfulness from the rising of the sun to the going down of the same. Every moment may suggest a new verse of our life-psalm, and cause us to magnify him whose mercy endureth forever.

Now, lastly, *why should we wear the garment of praise?* We should wear it as we wear other raiment, to keep us warm and comfortable, for there is no such vesture in the world as that of praise: it warms the inmost heart, and sends a glow through the whole man. You may go to Nova Zembla and not freeze in such a robe; in the worst cases, and in the most sorrowful plights, be you where you may, you are proof against outward circumstances when your whole being is enwrapped in praise. Wear it because it will comfort you. Wear it also because it will distinguish you from others. It will be livery to you, and men will know whose servants you are; it will be a regimental dress, and show to which army you belong; it will be a court dress, and manifest to what dignity you have attained. So arrayed you will bear the tokens of your Lord, who often in the days of his sorrow lifted his eye and heart to heaven and thanked the great Father for his goodness.

You should wear the garment of praise because it honors your Lord, especially if you put it on in the time of trouble, for then even ungodly men enquire, "What makes him so calm, so resigned, so happy? There must be something worth having in the religion which he professes." Therefore wear the garment of praise, and never take it off till, having ad it cleansed, and renewed, and made completely new, you shall wear it in the courts of heaven for ever and ever, adoring, magnifying, and praising him who has delivered you from the spirit of heaviness and clothed you with the garment of praise.

May some poor burdened soul lose its heaviness while thinking over our text, and henceforth wear this kingly robe—the garment of praise. Amen.

7

Trees of Righteousness

"That they might be called trees of righteousness, the planting of the Lord, that he might be glorified" (Isa. 61:3).

We have now come to our last discourse upon this choice passage: may those who have been mourning enter into the spirit of the text and forget themselves in the glory of God. This is the near way to the surest comfort. When our one all- absorbing desire is the glory of God we rise out of ourselves, and sorrow grows light. May the Holy Ghost, the Comforter, raise us to this state of heart.

The main end and object of the whole system of grace-is that the Lord might be glorified. This will be the ultimate result of all that God has planned and wrought for the salvation of men. Throughout the whole dispensation of love his attributes shine forth in their meridian splendor: his mercy in forgiving the guilty, his justice in the death of their Substitute, his truth in fulfilling his threatening, and his faithfulness in keeping his promise,—all will be made manifest to the admiring eyes of the intelligent universe. The brightest beams of Jehovah's perfect nature might never have been perceived if sin had not entered upon the scene; but Eden's fall and Calvary's redemption have given scope and occasion for the display of divine pity, mercy, justice, and truth. The Lord has an eye to this fact. Since no motive could be found in us, the Lord dealeth well with us for his own sake, to manifest his own glory. For this end he hath chosen his people: "Having predestinated us unto the adoption of children by Jesus Christ to himself, according to the good pleasure of his will, to the praise of the glory of his grace, wherein he hath made us accepted in the beloved"; for this he hath called them, "that he might make known the riches of his glory." For this he preserves, upholds, sustains, sanctifies, and perfects all those whom his sovereign grace has favored: "To the intent that now unto the principalities and powers in heavenly places might be known by the church the manifold wisdom of God."

The passage before us declares that to glorify Jehovah the Spirit of God rested upon our Lord, and for this cause mourners are the objects of his mercy, and prisoners and brokenhearted ones the witnesses of his saving power. Let us now consider that when the saved ones are delivered from their sorrows and so filled with grace that they are called "trees of righteousness, the planting of the Lord," it is still with this in view, "that he might be glorified."

I. In the first place, much of the glory of grace is seen in the choice of such lowly persons to become partakers of heavenly blessings. THEIR HUMBLE ESTATE commends the love which chose them to be made "trees of righteousness." The choice of men from the dungeon and the ash pit displays the absolute sovereignty and boundless pity of the Lord. Well may we feel, in thinking it over, as our great Lord and Master did when he said, "I thank thee, O Father, Lord of heaven and earth, because thou hast hid these things from the wise and prudent, and hast revealed them unto babes. Even so, Father: for so it seemed good in thy sight." The Lord might have chosen to execute his works of grace upon the kings and princes of the earth; but instead thereof he poureth contempt upon princes. As one and another of the Alexanders and Caesars pass before us we hear a voice, saying, "Look not on his countenance or on the height of his stature, because I have refused him." Had these been the sole objects of election, human pride would have imputed their salvation to the superiority of their descent, or the loftiness of their rank: therefore this shall not be. If the Lord had chosen sages and philosophers, if it had been necessary to pass through various grades of scholarship in order to obtain the favor of God, then human learning would have been reckoned the cause of holiness, and the university would have monopolized the glory: this also shall not be. Neither can riches sway the choice of heaven, nor personal beauty, nor courage, nor favor among men: grace, and grace alone, must reign and lift the mourners from the dunghill, while the haughty sons of pride are passed by.

Moreover, the Lord has not made his selection according to natural character, for if he had in every case chosen those who have been excellent in morals from their youth up, then the honor would have been ascribed to good works, and grace would have been elbowed out of the throne. If the good Shepherd had come only to watch over the ninety and nine that went not astray, and not to seek lost sheep, then it would have been said, "After all, these saved ones owe but little to mercy, for their admirable character lies at the root of it all. It is all very well to talk of grace, but what sort of grace is that which comes only to the most deserving?" In such a case the mercy of God would have received honor; but now as we read the passage before us we see that the choice of God was not directed by any consideration of personal deservings, and we are led to adore the Lord in his condescending love. The divine choice is not such as to manifest the goodness of man—alas! Where is it? Nor the wisdom of man—what is it? Nor the greatness of man—where can it be found? But to manifest the greatness, the wisdom, and the grace of God, that thereby "he might be glorified." What a mine of comfort is hidden in this fact! Mourners in Zion who lament their own unworthiness should remember this and be encouraged.

Now, note well, that the anointed Savior came to bless those who are *of a meek and unpretending spirit*—"The Lord hath anointed me to preach good tidings unto the meek," which Luke renders, "unto the poor." Both expressions point at the same class of persons: those who are despised by others, and look upon themselves with small esteem; persons who have lowly thoughts, and consider themselves to be quite unworthy of a glance from the eye of God. These meek ones of the earth never think of standing in the center of the temple to thank God that they are not as other men, but take their places in any out-of-the-way corner, and smite on their breasts and confess that they are sinners. These lowly-minded ones our Savior came to bless, because he knows that they will never advance a claim to the honor of their own salvation. They know themselves too well to dream of boasting, and nobody in the world will ever think of rendering honor to them, for they are despised of their fellows. In the choice of such the Lord's end is answered, "that he might be glorified."

Furthermore, the Lord has chosen those *who are broken-hearted*. When persons are very low in circumstances they may, nevertheless, possess great force of character and wonderful courage, by means of which they may force their way to the front: but the persons who are interested in the blessings which Jesus came to bestow are not described as being of this brave and resolute race; for it is written, "He hath sent me to bind up the broken-hearted": he is sent to encourage those whose spirit fails them. As for the self-confident, who say, "I may be very poor in spiritual matters, but I can soon make myself better, and lay up a heap of religious wealth," nothing whatever is promised to them; but the broken-down ones, who are crushed in spirit and wounded in heart, are specially spoken of. These are they who feel that if they ever rise it must be God alone who can raise them, for they have no strength left, and these are among the first to own that if ever they are brought to heaven it will be a miracle of divine power and grace. As for themselves, each of these broken hearts cries, "My strength is dried up like a potsherd. I scarcely feel power to pray, or even to think a good thought. Where shall I find foundation for hope? What can I expect but wrath?" Such broken-spirited ones as these the Lord Jesus is anointed to bind up, and from their grateful hearts he will derive unmingled praise, since their natural condition is such as to exclude all boasting, and their deep and conscious obligations to grace will ensure their magnifying the Lord so long as they have any being.

> Perish each thought of human pride,
>   Let God alone be magnified;
> His glory let the heavens resound,
>   Shouted from earth's remotest bound.

If a poor man has but little spirit, yet there is always hope for him while he has his liberty; but those whom the Lord blesses *are in bonds*. A brave heart says, "Set me free, and I will hope for some turn of the tide"; but what shall he do who is a captive? There are, doubtless, men who believe that they are by nature morally free. They are always glorying in the freedom of their wills. They do not believe for a moment that free-will is a slave, as some of us know it to be; but they glory in the dignity of their nature, and the soundness of their judgment, and they are persuaded that they are able, whenever they think fit, to climb to any moral or spiritual elevation they may desire. These are not the persons, however, whom the Anointed comes to bless, for they are described as captives and as bound in prison. The objects of divine grace feel that when they would do good evil is present with them; they own that they dare not trust to their own understanding, for it is too much a captive to ignorance and prejudice; neither dare they obey their own will, for it is obstinate and perverse; nor may they indulge their own heart, for it is naturally enthralled by sin and Satan, and even when delivered carries about with it the marks of its fetters. These are the people to whom our Lord proclaims liberty, in order that when they are emancipated they may not be able to glory in themselves even in the slightest degree; for they cannot pride themselves in their freedom, since it was a pure gift procured for them by another's hand when they themselves could not move hand or foot to procure it, seeing that they were bound in chains which they could not break. In their case also the design of God's grace is answered, "that he might be glorified."

Besides that, these people whom the Lord chose to glorify him were *bowed down with sorrow*. They are described as having ashes on their heads and heaviness in their hearts. These feel the burden of sin, and are crashed under a sense of the wrath of God which they have consciously deserved, and if through rich mercy they at length find forgiveness they are certain to ascribe the work of salvation to God alone. They will be clear and sound upon the doctrines of grace. We have almost wished that certain preachers who are very indistinct in their teachings as the grace of God had suffered some little of the self-abasement and self-despair which have fallen to the lot of many saints.

Lack of law-work in the heart is at the bottom of much mingle-mangle doctrine; if cloudy teachers had felt more of the plague of their own hearts they would be more clear in their declaration that we are saved by grace "through faith, and that not of ourselves, it is the gift of God." Salvation is of the Lord from first to last. It is not of man, neither by man; it is not of the will of man, nor of blood, nor of birth, nor of outward ordinances, nor of anything, but of the sovereign will and power of God alone. What does the Scripture say? "I am the Lord; that is my name, and my glory will I not give to another." Let me, therefore, beseech all who have tasted the love of God to make this point clear as the sun whenever they speak to others, and to make it plain to their own hearts; since to roll God of his honor is treason-felony against the majesty of heaven. As for myself, I protest that I cannot put my finger upon anything in my whole life for which I dare take the least credit before God. Truly, if in any of us there has been any virtue, if there has been any praise, if there has been anything honest or of good repute, if there has been any power in prayer, or usefulness, or consecration, or likeness to Christ, all the honor thereof must be rendered unto the Lord alone. "Not unto us, O Lord, not unto us, but unto thy name give glory, for thy mercy, and for thy truth's sake." This is the spot of God's children; they all, without exception, render all the honor of their salvation, heartily and unreservedly, to the Lord alone, thus is the end of eternal love secured," that he might be glorified." Mourning friend, what say you? Is not this method of grace as suitable to you as it is glorifying to the Lord, and do you not cheerfully accept it? I know you do.

II. Compelled by our space to be brief, we now note, secondly, God is glorified in THEIR AFTER CHARACTER; for those poor, humbled, downcast souls become so remarkable in character that the text says, "They shall be called trees of righteousness, the planting of the Lord." Holy Scripture is very fond of comparing good men to trees. In this place it seems to be a somewhat incongruous metaphor; but this may be intentional, in order to call us away from the letter to the inward sense, which is spiritual. If the meaning had been natural, and moral, no doubt the figures would have run on in a connected series; but here we leap from one to another, as if to show that the outward and external cannot fully set forth the inner and spiritual.

Let us look into the expression, "Trees of righteousness." When men, whom God has loved, are saved, they are saved in a righteous way, they are "trees *of righteousness*, the planting of the Lord." True, they are saved by sovereign grace, but yet in a righteous way. They are saved by mercy, but they are not called trees of mercy, because righteousness is the greatest marvel in their salvation, and to compass this the utmost wisdom has been exercised. In a previous sermon I tried to show you how in the life and death of Christ mercy proclaimed acceptance and yet justice meted out vengeance; and therefore we see that those whom grace redeems are so saved that they glorify the divine righteousness more than any other beings. It is a wonderful thing that a sinner should be saved righteously! That God should be "just and yet the justifier of him that believeth!" The grand fact of the substitution of Christ for his people, so that mercy could be exercised without eclipsing justice, is the marvel of eternity. Men may cavil at it, but angels admire it. All adown eternity there will be mighty spirits, educated in heaven itself, who will, notwithstanding their lofty powers, be lost in wonder at the righteous salvation of God. The redeemed shall forever be signs and wonders to the whole intelligent universe—

they shall "be called trees of righteousness," the grandest of all exhibitions of the righteousness of God. There was a tree of knowledge, and by that we fell; there is a tree of life by which we rise; and we ourselves are now trees of righteousness, the immortal embodiments of the rectitude of our glorious God.

The text, however, means something more: God is glorified in the character of his people, because they become righteous in their lives. It is no small wonder when a great sinner becomes a great saint. Nothing is more interesting or surprising than the phenomenon of conversion: I am sure we do not make enough of it in answering the worldling. He sneeringly enquires, "Where is your God?"

Our answer may well be—"Here we see him divinely transforming the nature of men." We have seen hundreds, if not thousands, converted, in whom there has been a change so extraordinary that they themselves would not have believed that such a transmutation could have been accomplished. The work of conversion in many has been so marked that it the men had actually died and risen again from the dead they could not have been more completely different from their former selves. We have seen the unchaste become delicate in modesty, the thief scrupulous in honesty, the blasphemer devout in heart, and the man of fierce, impetuous temper meek as a lamb. Surely "this is the finger of God." All things do not continue as they were, for here is a new creation going on before our eyes every day. The Lord makes the saved ones to be temperate, upright, and gracious, so that men who look on them are compelled to exclaim, "This is the planting of God, and these are trees of righteousness." Those who profess to be converted should remember this, and in all things adorn the doctrine of their God and Savior "that he may be glorified."

But what is meant by the expression, "trees of righteousness"? Does it not assure us that the poor and broken-hearted when renewed by grace shall flourish like the trees of the wood? They were like the heath in the desert before, or like a tree cut down whose stump alone is left; but when Jesus visits them they exhibit new life and beauty, and rise to a prominence and continuance which are very wonderful. "He shall be as a tree planted by the rivers of water." "As the days of a tree are the days of my people." There is joy in their face, rest in their heart and peace in their life: the barren soul is revived; in holiness it grows and in hope it buds.

Does not the expression teach us, also, that those whom Jesus comforts become fixed and established? You could move them about at your pleasure before, for they were likened to "a rolling thing before the whirlwind"; but now they have roots, which hold them firmly, like the oak or the cedar. Rough winds of trial do but strengthen their hold, and the jests and slanders of a cruel world cause them to adhere all the more closely to the truth with the very roots of their soul. What a mercy it is when God gives his people fixity and stability! so that men may call them trees of righteousness. When the saints abide in their steadfastness to the Lord, then is the design accomplished, "that he might be glorified."

Now, also, like trees these renewed ones yield a pleasant shade of gracious influence over others. Under a tree one shelters himself from the burning heat; and God worketh so graciously in believers that the poor soul that was once so broken-hearted as to need comfort from others, now becomes himself a son of consolation. As a tiny plant he needed to be sheltered with care, but now he has become a tree and the birds of the air come and lodge in his branches. Young saints gain knowledge, and tried saints obtain consolation from those very persons who a little while ago sat in ashes, bowed down with heaviness. We may think of them while we remember what the poet said of the trees:

> And ye are strong to shelter all meek things;
>   All that need home and covert love your shade;
> Birds of shy song, and low-voiced quiet springs,
>   And nun-like violets, by the wind betray'd.

Now when the Lord does all this, then he is greatly glorified. When the Lord brings his mourners to be like the blessed man in the first Psalm, "a tree planted by the rivers of waters," then he is had in honor. Never does a growing, flourishing, established, useful believer extol himself; but he lives to show forth the praises of the Lord, to whose right hand planting he owes everything.

III. We must further observe that the text says, "They shall be *called* trees of righteousness": they not only are so, but they shall be called by that name. This also honors God when his people obtain PUBLIC RECOGNITION of their righteous character both from the willing and the unwilling who observe them. Possibly this may aid us in seeing the suitableness of the figure, for certain trees have become famous in connection with events and qualities as "the oak of weeping," because there Deborah was buried, and the Gospel Oak, under which the gospel was preached in the days of the reformers. Christian men have sometimes become as famous as celebrated trees. For instance, trees have been *landmarks*; the county terminates at the great oak, or the parish boundary is fixed by the ash-grove. In history trees have been landmarks: the tree of knowledge of good and evil marks the fall, the olive marks the assuagement of the deluge, the tree in Mamre notes the era of Abraham, and the palms of Elim record the age of Moses. You may divide the ages, if you like, by memorable trees, and evidently after the like manner you may name succeeding periods by good men who have thus become "trees of righteousness." Eras may be dated from Adam to Enoch, from Noah to Abraham, from Jacob to Moses, from Joshua to David, and so on. May our Lord take some of you who are broken-hearted and sore afflicted and make you so eminently gracious that you may be the landmarks of your age; or at least landmarks in the history of one and another who shall date their new birth from the hour when you conversed with them.

Some trees are *centers of attraction*. That great tree at Mamre under which God met with Abraham, has for ages been the center of a fair; and even so there are some Christians under whose branches their fellow Christians hold high holiday and commerce. I have known aged and afflicted believers to whom the saints of a whole region have gone to hear their goodly words, and observe their Christian patience. Scarcely can you go into one of our villages but you will hear of some gracious man or woman in whom all believers take pleasure. Happy are they who do not divide and scatter, but become rallying points for the faithful, and so "trees of righteousness." Would you have thought that mourners in Zion could ever have risen to such importance? See what the Holy Spirit has done that the Lord might be glorified. Courage, ye mourners, the like shall be done with you.

Trees frequently become *marvels of grandeur*. In the New Forest I have wondered as I have measured the girth of the grand old giants—both among beech and oak—that have braved for ages the changeful climate of our isle. There they stand, covering many a rood with their shade. What a history is embodied in those gnarls and knots and twisted branches! How they tell of stormy nights and days of heavy snow! All over the bark and the boughs time has with his pencil written records of sunshine and tempest. Now, such is a

Christian when God makes him rich in grace: if you could but know him and read him he is a mass of history. His virtues are the results of severe trial, and the records of sublime joys. All the lines of his face mean something; there is not a scar upon his soul, or a dark memory upon his spirit, or a bright recollection in his mind but what it redounds to the glory of God. He is a wonder unto many, and will be such even among the angels of God. As monuments of the power of spiritual life to endure all kinds of trials, believers shall be called "trees of righteousness."

Trees, also, are often *pictures of beauty*. Nothing more adorns a landscape than its trees. If you were to cut down every grove and wood, you would produce a horrible dead level. A tree, symmetrical from its root to its highest branch, awakens in the mind of the tasteful observer high delight. Such is the beauty of the Christian character. If you draw near to one who lives near to God, you will be struck with his loveliness; he is the noblest work of God.

> Green as the leaf, and ever fair,
>   Shall his profession shine;
> While fruits of holiness appear
>   Like clusters on the vine.

All saints are not alike, but they are all beautiful, for as Dr. M'Cosh observes, "One tree differs from another tree in glory. There is one glory of the oak, which has faced a hundred storms and is ready for as many more; another glory of the sycamore, that 'spreads in gentle pomp its honey'd shade;' another glory of the birch, so graceful in the midst of its maiden tresses; another glory of the elm, throwing out its wide arms as if rejoicing in its strength; and another glory of the lime, with its sheltered shade inviting us to enter and to linger." All these differ, but they all agree in displaying the glory of their Creator.

May such beauty yet adorn every mourning soul, that God may be glorified.

IV. Lastly. It is said in the text that God is glorified, because they are not only called "trees of righteousness," but "the planting of the Lord": this marks THEIR EVIDENT ORIGIN. Men will say, "This is God's work: we know what they once were, and we now see what they have become, and therefore we are sure that the Lord has been at work upon them." I have known persons so desperately bad, so outrageously wicked, that, when they have been converted, their neighbors have said, "Do you mean to say that *he* is a Christian? Then miracles will never cease." As one said of his old father, "I have scarcely known him a day sober since I was born, and if he has become a sober, praying man, then there is something in religion, I am sure." When the Lord chooses a ringleader among sinners, and saves him, his power and grace are undeniably demonstrated. When the proud man is humbled, when the careless boaster becomes serious, when the argumentative infidel prays, when the persecutor preaches, then men say, "This is the planting of the Lord," and the Most High is glorified. And, dear friends, when Christians rise to a high degree of grace, and exhibit a gracious character in the common walks of life—especially in times of temptation and trial—then, again, men say, "These are trees of the Lord's planting." When a man discovers that you will not yield to temptation though you might be a great gainer by it, when he sees that you do not lose your temper, but are patient under insult, when he sees you do what it is not ordinary for human nature to do, then lie is convinced, and in his conscience praises God. I pray you, then, beloved, if you are indeed the elect of God, in all things endeavor to show the power of the grace which dwells in you. Compel the world to glorify the Lord, who has done such great things for you. You have the promise that you shall accomplish this; rest not till it is fulfilled.

Thus have we seen the mourner led on from step to step till he becomes a grand living monument to the glory of God. Will it be your case, O troubled one? Why should it not be? You are now a mere bramble or thorn, but grace can make you into one of the trees of the Lord, planted in the courts of our God. Why should it not be sought and found by you *there* and *now?* There is nothing in the word of God to forbid your coming to God in Christ Jesus, but everything to invite and encourage you. Why not come at this moment, and commit your soul to him who is sent and anointed to save the mourning one? In the name of Jesus I entreat you at this moment to yield yourself unto God and trust in his Son. Do so, and the work of grace is begun in you, and ere long you also shall be called one of the "trees of righteousness, the planting of the Lord, that he might be glorified."

Book Five

The Bible and the Newspaper

Preface

"I read the newspaper," said John Newton, "that I may see how my heavenly Father governs the world"; a very excellent reason indeed. We have read the newspaper during the last three months that we might find illustrations of the teaching of our heavenly Father's word; and we think we have not read in vain, for we have gathered instances in proof, and facts in explanation, which we have jotted down in these pages. The worlds of nature and of providence are full of parallels to things moral and spiritual, and serve as pictures to make the written book of inspiration more clear to the children of God. The Bible itself abounds in metaphors, types, and symbols; it is a great picture book; there is scarcely a poetical figure which may not be found in the law and the prophets, or in the words of Jesus and his apostles. The preacher is bidden to speak as the oracles of God, and consequently he should imitate their illustrative method, and abound in emblems and parables. A sermon which is full of "likes" is full of windows to enlighten the mind, and hands to hold it captive. Discourses decked with similes will not only give pleasure to the children, but persons of riper years will be charmed and instructed thereby.

Time does not allow us to read the papers with the searching glance which would readily have discovered hundreds of emblems, we have had to give a hasty look as best we could, and hence our harvest is not so rich as that of a more quiet eye. A sense of leisure and of rest is needed if one is to follow the trails of nature, and listen to all her echoes. Not idleness but amplitude of space for thought is a requisite for the weaving of allegory and the fashioning of similitudes. Lacking these essentials, amid the hum of London and the whirl of the wheel of daily duty, we have produced a little home-spun where others might have woven tapestries of golden thread.

The things which we have seen and noted we now give our readers, not merely for their entertainment, but that we may encourage in them the habit of looking for emblems and analogies. It is a mental exercise as profitable as it is pleasant. Sunday-school teachers and all other servants of the great parable-making Master would find it an improving occupation to walk abroad in the garden and the field, and resolve to find some instructive similes before they returned home; and it would be almost as helpful to them if they stayed at home and did with the newspaper what we have done. This might be done by Bible classes and other associations of young men, very much to the development of a happy faculty. In a short time they might produce far more excellent specimens than those which are here presented. When they become practiced fishermen their nets would probably draw to shore much more precious fish than we in our haste have been able to capture.

Reader, may the good Lord speed us in this and in every other good design.

Thine to help,

C. H. Spurgeon

1

A Voice from the Sea

"Yea, it shall be at an instant suddenly" (Isa. 29:5).

"The Lord sent out a great wind into the sea" (Jon. 1:4).

About four o'clock in the afternoon of Lord's-day, March 24th, the inhabitants of London were startled by a sudden hurricane which all at once brought with it darkening clouds of dust, and for a short season raged furiously. Sitting in our study in quiet meditation, we were aroused and alarmed by the noise of doors and windows, and the terrible howling of the blast as it swept upon its headlong course. Unhappy were travelers across heath and moor who were overtaken by such an overwhelming gust, for it gave no warning, and allowed no time to seek a shelter. It was soon over, but it was followed by cold and dreary weather, and it would seem to have been a token that winter meant to make another struggle to assume his ancient throne. His Parthian arrow was driven forward with intense force, and left its mark in ruin and death.

Just at the moment when landsmen were terrified by the threatening storm, her Majesty's training ship "Eurydice," which had returned from a cruise to the West Indies, was rounding Dunnose headland, off the Isle of Wight, with all plain sails and also her studding sails set. Those on board were all naturally anxious to reach their homes, and having only to round the coast and to anchor off Spithead, they were making the best of the wind. The noble frigate was plainly seen from the lovely village of Shanklin; but one who was watching the fine vessel suddenly missed it and wondered why. She was hastening along with all sails set except her royals, and her ports open, when in a moment the fierce wind pounced upon her. It was in vain that the captain ordered sail to be shortened; the ship lurched till her keel was visible, and, in less time than it takes us to write it, the ship capsized, and more than three hundred brave seamen perished. Well might her Majesty's telegram speak of "the terrible calamity of the 'Eurydice.'" What mourning and lamentation had that one cruel blast scattered over the land! How swift is the swoop of death! How stealthy its step! How terrible its leap! *In the midst of life we are on the verge of the sepulcher.* This lesson is preached to us by those three hundred men who lie enshrouded in the all-devouring sea, with a gallant ship as their mausoleum.

> Toll for the brave!
> The brave that are no more!
> All sunk beneath the wave,
> Fast by their native shore!

Great is the peril of the ocean, but there are also dangers on the land, and at any moment we also may be summoned to appear before our God. Since this cannot be questioned, let each prudent man foresee the evil and prepare himself for it.

Another lesson which lies upon the surface of this sad event is this—*never feel perfectly safe till you are in port*. Many awakened souls are almost within the haven of peace, and are at this time rounding the headland of thoughtfulness, with the sails of earnest enquiry all displayed to the breeze. Their condition is very hopeful, but it is not satisfactory to those who are anxious about their eternal welfare, nor should it be satisfactory to themselves. They are steering for the harbor, they enjoy favoring winds, they have all sails set, but still they have not quite believed in Jesus, nor surrendered themselves to his grace. We who watch them can see that their ports are open, and we dread lest they should be overtaken by a sudden temptation and should suddenly be overturned at the very moment when our hopes are at their best. Is the reader in such case? Then let us beseech him not to be content till he has found Christ, and so by faith has anchored in the harbor of "eternal salvation."

Do not be happy, dear friend, till you are moored to the Rock of Ages, under the lee of the everlasting hills of divine mercy, through the atoning blood.

It seems very wonderful that a ship which had been to sea so many times and had just completed a long winter's cruise in safety should at last go down just off the coast in a place where danger seemed out of the question. It is doubly sad that so many men should be within sight of a shore upon which they must never set their foot. To perish in mid ocean seems not so hard a lot as to die with the white cliffs of Albion so near: to die with the gospel ringing in our ears is still sadder. Never reckon the ship safe till it floats in the haven: never reckon a soul safe till it is actually "in Christ." The "almost persuaded" are often the last to be fully persuaded.

Aroused, impressed, and moved to good resolutions, to tears, and even to prayers, yet men postpone decision, and by the force of Satan's arts are lost— lost when we all hoped to see them saved. O that seekers were wise enough to be distressed until they are thoroughly renewed. Any position short of regeneration is perilous in the extreme. The manslayer would have been cut down by the avenger had he lingered outside the walls of the refuge city; it would have been all in vain for him to have touched its stones or sheltered near its towers: he must be within the gates or die. Seekers after salvation, you are not safe till you actually close in with Jesus, place all your confidence in him and become forever his. Shall it be so *now*, or will you abide in death? Rest not an hour. Trifle not for another moment; for death may seize you, or a spiritual lethargy may come over your soul from which you may never again be aroused. Give no sleep to your eyes, nor slumber to your eyelids, till your anchor has entered into that within the veil and you are saved in Christ Jesus.

A further lesson should be gleaned from the scant wreckage which as yet has floated up from the sunken vessel. Let us all take warning, and remember that *we cannot tell when fierce temptations may assail us.*

> Be watchful, be vigilant, danger may be,
> At an hour when all seemeth securest to thee.

As the wind bloweth where it listeth, and we cannot tell whence it cometh, our want of foresight keeps us in constant jeopardy, and should therefore induce unceasing watchfulness. The gale may burst upon us either from the north or from the south, and if we make ready for an easterly breeze we may be assailed from the westward instead. He who has sailed upon the sea never trusts it; he who has been at the mercy of the wind never depends upon it.

Beloved believer, you have had a long stretch of fair sailing; let a brother whisper in your ear, "Keep a good lookout." Those who are familiar with spiritual navigation know that there is never more likelihood of storm than when the barometer stands at "set fair."

> Whene'er becalm'd I lie,
>   And storms forbear to toss;
> Be thou, dear Lord, still nigh,
>   Lest I should suffer loss:
> Far more the treacherous calm I dread,
>   Than tempests bursting o'er my head.

The danger of a foreseen tempest is comparatively little, for your ship with close-reefed sails, and bare poles, is ready for whatever comes; but the perils of the calm lie in the temptation to security, and the liability that sudden temptation may find us unprepared. "What I say unto you I say unto all, Watch": for if the good captain of the ship had known at what hour the storm would come he would have lowered all his sails, and have weathered the gale. He did all that a brave man could do, but all was little enough, for the huge ship was tossed over and sucked down, and but two remained to tell the tale. Be ye always ready, for in such an hour as ye think not the danger will be upon you.

One other warning let us collect from the wreck while yet it lies beneath the wave. *Always be most afraid of sudden temptation when all sails are filled with a fair wind.* Personal experience teaches some of us that our gladdest times attract perils to us. The temper of the placid may readily be ruffled when they have newly come from solitary communion with God: the rude shock of the world's rough speech tells most upon a mind which has been bathed in heaven. Even the love of Jesus may lead us in the heat of our spirit to wish that we could invoke fire from heaven on his foes. Great power in prayer, unless we guard ourselves well, may be followed by a fit of depression, even as Elijah fled from Jezebel very soon after his wrestlings upon Carmel. High and rapt enjoyment may be followed by fierce temptation, for the enemy watches for loaded vessels when he allows the empty bark to escape. Even our Lord found but a short interval between the testimony from heaven at his baptism and the temptation from hell which beset him in the wilderness. Our full sails tempt the prince of the power of the air to rage with more than his usual malignity. It is right that all sail should be set when the wind is favorable. Why should we not avail ourselves of everything which may speed us on our way? Still, let us never forget to watch unto prayer, or our happiness may be our danger. Brother, mark well your steps in coming down from the mount of communion, for at the foot of it you may meet mocking Pharisees, dispirited disciples, and perhaps one possessed of an evil spirit of the kind which goeth not out save with prayer and fasting.

Let the self-exalting professor specially beware; but remember, dear brother, that you may soon become such a character. When your sails are big with the wind, and you are flying over the waves, clap your hands if you please, and hope soon to have perfected your voyage; but take care to have all hands ready for an emergency. Perhaps one of the best things that could happen to you would be that when you are sailing along so bravely, confident and at ease, your topsails of pride should be carried away; you would be all the better for losing such lofty gear. Plenty of ballast must be stowed away, or our royals may be our ruin. Better have our glory rent to ribbons by the gusts than for the ship itself to be blown over.

Mark this: Are you prospering in business? Keep your eye on the weather, and expect a change. Is all going well with your family? Be grateful, but rejoice with trembling. Is every desire gratified? Thank God, but do not suffer the watch to go below. Are you progressing in the spiritual life? Doubtless Satan has told you that you are somebody now, strong in faith, exceedingly earnest, wonderfully busy, and quite an example to others! Do you not see that the storm-fiend is near you? What a wind he can raise! He slew Job's children by a wind which smote all the four corners of the house, and he reserves those four-cornered hurricanes for men in high estate as Job was; therefore beware.

Brother, reef sail, for the weather is dirty, and cannot be relied on for five minutes. As you dread shipwreck, cultivate holy jealousy, maintain godly fear, and evermore look to him that keepeth Israel. He never slumbers, for he knows that his children always need his watchful eye.

2

Calling Out the Reserves

"Reserved against the time of trouble, against the day of battle and war" (Job 38:23).

"Proclaim ye this among the Gentiles; Prepare war, wake up the mighty men, let all the men of war draw near; let them come up: beat your plowshares into swords, and your pruning hooks into spears: let the weak say, I am strong" (Joel 3:9, 10).

On the evening of April 1, the Lord Chancellor read a message from the Queen, stating that: "Her Majesty has thought it right to communicate to the House of Lords that her Majesty is about to cause her Reserve Force and her Militia Reserve Force, or such part thereof as her Majesty shall think necessary, to be forthwith called out for permanent service."

Might not some such message from the King, who is in the midst of Zion, be just now very seasonable, if the Holy Spirit should convey it to all the churches? There should be no reserves in the hosts of the Lord; but alas, through the lukewarm condition of many, *these reserves form a numerous part of our membership*, and need a great many calls from their officers before they will obey. Perhaps if they felt that the King himself ordered that they should be "forthwith called out for permanent service," the love of Christ would constrain them, and we should see them marching forth to war. "I pray thee have me excused" has been upon their lips for a long time, or else they have said, "I go, sir," but they have not gone. The word of Moses to the children of Gad and Reuben is exceedingly needed by many at this time: "Shall your brethren go to war, and shall ye sit still?"

The reserved forces are so terribly numerous as compared with the active army of our great King that our holy war is sadly hindered and the Canaanites are not subdued. Among these inactive professors there are many who are commonly known as "very reserved people." These must no longer sit at ease, but must summon up courage enough to come up to the help of the Lord against the mighty, lest the curse of Meroz fall upon them. Others are idle, and allow their armor and their weapons to rust. Many are busy here and there about inferior things, but forget their allegiance to their Lord. Very much time, talent, and opportunity is held in reserve for various reasons, and ought at once to be brought forth and consecrated actively to the Lord.

What meanest thou, O sleeper? What aileth thee, O sluggard? There is much to be done; why doest thou not thy part? Every man has a place appointed him in the battle; what excuse can be accepted for those who are at ease in Zion, and stir not a hand for their Master and his cause? Nor is it in men alone that a sinful reserve is made, but great treasures of gold and silver belonging to Christians are laid by to canker, while the Lord hath need of them. Men talk of loving Jesus so as to give him all, and in their hymns they say that if they might make some reserve, and duty did not call, their zeal would lead them to a total sacrifice, and yet the *financial* reserve of the church of God is probably a hundred times as great as that which is expended in the Lord's service. Your own judgments will confirm this statement. The funds actually in the hands of professed believers are immense, for many Christians are enormously rich, and yet we hear daily appeals for money, till one might conclude that all professors of the Christian faith were as poor as Lazarus, and that nowadays no holy women were able to minister to the Lord of their substance, and such persons as Joseph of Arimathea were no longer disciples of Jesus.

There is a great deal of reserve *time*, and reserve *talent*, and reserve *energy* and *fire*, and we would in the name of Jesus call it out. Why, some men when engaged in the service of God seem to be only the tenth part of men compared with their zeal in their business pursuits. It would take nine of some church members to make one real praying man, and twice that number of some preachers to make a downright earnest minister of the gospel. Is this judgment too severe? Are not some men mere apologies for workers, even when they do pretend to be up and at it? Verily it is so. Oh, if they would but be aroused; if all their manhood, all their heart, and soul, and mind, and strength, were truly engaged, how differently they would act; and if they sought strength from on high, what grand results would follow! I long to see the Holy Spirit filling us all with ardor, and causing every man and woman among us to yield himself or herself fully unto the Lord.

When the reserves are called out, matters look very serious, and we expect to see war. Every lover of peace shuddered as he read the Queen's message, for he felt that at last war was really threatened. God grant it may not be so. But with regard to the church of Christ, when the reserves are called out, the world believes that it really means war for Christ. At present the world despises many a church for its inactivity; but when *all* Christians come forth it will know that we are in earnest. While the regular workers are marching to and fro like a standing army, going through its regular drill, very little is done beyond mere defense, but when the reserves are called out, it means *defiance*, and the gauntlet is thrown to the foe.

Our Lord would have us fight the good fight of faith, and go forth in his name conquering and to conquer; but the elect host is hampered and hindered by the sutlers and camp-followers who hang about us and work us serious ill. If all this mixed multitude could be drilled into warriors, what a band would the Son of David lead to the war! Once get the reserved members of the church praying, working, teaching, giving, and the enemy would soon know that there is a God in Israel. There is too much playing at religion nowadays, and too little of intense, unanimous, enthusiastic hard work.

A part of the church is all alive, but a far larger portion is as a body of death, by which the life of the church is held in bondage. Once find the whole body tingling with life from head to foot, from heart to finger, and then you shall have power over the adversary and prevalence with God. When all the people shout for joy and long for the battle, the Philistines will be afraid, and cry out, saying, "God has come into the camp." O that my eyes could once perceive the signal! Zion travailing is the sign by which those who know the times will be able to prophecy concerning Zion triumphant. O for the universal agony, the inward throes of deep compassion and consuming zeal; for when these are felt by the whole body, the joyous hour is come.

The Queen's message reminds me of a great and comforting truth. *God himself, blessed be his name, has forces in reserve which he will call forth in due time*. Remember the Lord's own language in the book of Job: "Hast thou entered into the treasures of the snow? or hast thou seen the treasures of the hail, which I have reserved against the time of trouble, against the day of battle and war?" He represents himself, in the language of his servant Joel, as calling out innumerable locusts as a part of his host: "The Lord shall utter his voice before his army; for his camp is very great." The hiding of his power we cannot estimate, but we know that nothing is impossible to him. Whatever the church may have seen and experienced of divine power, there is yet more in reserve, and when the fit moment shall come all restraint shall be withdrawn, and the eternal forces shall be let loose to rout every foeman, and secure an easy victory. For the moment, our great Captain puts his hand into his bosom and allows the enemy to exult; but he is not defeated, nor is he in the least disquieted.

"He shall not fail, nor be discouraged." His time is not yet, but when the time comes he will be found to have his reward with him and his work before him. Let us never be daunted by the apparent failures of the cause of God and truth, for these are but the trial of patience, the test of valor, and the means to a grander victory. Pharaoh defies Jehovah while he sees only two Hebrews and a rod, but he will be of another mind when the Lord's reserves shall set themselves in battle array and discharge plague upon plague against him. Even the doubling of the tale of bricks, and the wanton cruelty of the tyrant, all wrought towards the divine end, and were no real hindrances to the grand design; nay, they were reserved forces by which the Lord made his people willing to leave Goshen and the fleshpots.

Today, also, the immediate present is dark, and there is room for sad forebodings; but if we look a little further, and by faith behold the brilliant future which will arise out of the gloom, we shall be of good cheer. My eye rests at this moment somewhat sorrowfully upon the battlefield of religious opinion; truly, there is much to rivet my gaze. It is a perilous moment. The prince of darkness is bringing up his reserves. The soldiers of the devil's old guard, on whom he places his chief reliance, are now rushing like a whirlwind upon our ranks. They threaten to carry everything before them, deceiving the very elect, if it be possible. Never were foes more cunning and daring. They spare nothing, however sacred, but assail the Lord himself: his book they criticize, his gospel they mutilate, his wrath they deny, his truth they abhor. Of confused noise and vapor of smoke there is more than enough; but it will blow over in due time, and when it is all gone we shall see that the Lord reigneth, and his enemies are broken in pieces.

Let us watch for the coming of recruits divinely prepared. Let us be eager to see the reserves as they come from the unlikeliest quarters. There may be sitting even now by some cottage fireside, all unknown, the man who shall make the world ring again with the gospel, preaching it with apostolic power. The orthodox advocate, born to cope with subtle minds and unravel all their sophistries, may even now be receiving his training in yonder parish school; yea, and even in the infidel camp, like Moses in the palace of Pharaoh, there may dwell the youth who shall act the iconoclast towards every form of skepticism. Jabin and Sisera may reign, but there shall come a Deborah from mount Ephraim, and a Barak from Kedesh-naphtali. Let the Midianites tremble, for Gideon who threshes wheat in the winepress will yet beat them small. The Ammonites shall be smitten by Jephtha, and the Philistines by Samson: for every enemy there shall be a champion, and the Lord's people shall do great exploits. I for one believe in Omnipotence. All other power is weakness; in God alone is there strength. Men are vanity, and their thoughts shall perish; but God is everlasting and everliving, and the truth which hangs upon his arm, like a golden shield, shall endure to all eternity. Hither come we, then, and bow before the face of the Eternal, who reserveth wrath for his enemies and mercy for them that seek him; and as we lie at his feet we look up right hopefully, and watch for the moment when all his reserves of grace, and love, and glory shall be revealed to the adoring eyes of his chosen people world without end.

3

Ladies' Dress

"Be clothed with humility" (1 Pet. 5:5).

"I will that women adorn themselves in modest apparel, with shamefacedness and sobriety" (1 Tim. 2:8, 9).

On the 11th of April, in the course of an action brought by the well-known *modiste*, "Madame Rosalie," against a gentleman of property to compel him to pay a debt contracted by his wife, it was stated in evidence that from £500 to £2,000 a year might be considered a reasonable sum for a lady moving in good society to expend on dress. The gentleman's wife, in the witness-box, repudiated with lofty scorn the idea that the former amount was sufficient. The lady is an invalid, has never been presented at court, and is not called into company, and yet was indebted for millinery to a very large amount.

Is it, then, a fact that so large a sum is considered needful for the clothing of one human form? Surely the luxury of the old Roman Empire is infecting our beloved country: may God grant that it may not, in our case, also be a sign of the decay of the nation. Women should be too considerate of the needs of the sick and suffering to spend their money so wastefully. A blanket placed on the bed of a poor old woman would be a better ornament to a lady's character than all the lace a dukedom could purchase. Yet so it is, but tell it not in Gath, a lady cannot be dressed under £2,000 a year!

Are we wrong if we place side by side with this modern fact, a description of the follies of women of the olden times? "Moreover the Lord saith, Because the daughters of Zion are haughty, and walk with stretched forth necks and wanton eyes, walking and mincing as they go, and making a tinkling with their feet: Therefore the Lord will smite with a scab the crown of the head of the daughters of Zion, and the Lord will discover their secret parts. In that day the Lord will take away the bravery of their tinkling ornaments about their feet, and their cauls, and their round tires like the moon, The chains, and the bracelets, and the mufflers, The bonnets, and the ornaments of the legs, and the headbands, and the tablets, and the earrings, the rings, and nose jewels, the changeable suits of apparel, and the mantles, and the wimples, and the crisping pins, the glasses, and the fine linen, and the hoods and the vails" (Isa. 3:16–23).

What a contrast is the teaching of the apostle Peter, in his First Epistle, at the third chapter. "Whose adorning let it not be that outward adorning of plaiting the hair, and of wearing of gold, or of putting on of apparel; But let it be the hidden man of the heart, in that which is not corruptible, even the ornament of a meek and quiet spirit, which is in the sight of God of great price. For after this manner in the old time the holy women also, who trusted in God, adorned themselves, being in subjection unto their own husbands." Peter sends the ladies to a wardrobe better than any which the frivolous possess, and to a jewel-case richer than ever belonged to the rain and showy; but, alas, the mass of women do not care to adorn themselves in this right royal fashion. Pride of dress is so childish that one wonders to see it in grown-up people. The old proverb speaks of being twice children; but fops and dandies of either sex are always children. Archbishop Leighton has well said, "It is strange upon how poor things men and women will be vain, and think themselves somebody; not only upon some comeliness in their face or feature, which, though poor, is yet a part of themselves, but of things merely without them; that they are well lodged, or well mounted, or well appareled, either richly, or well in fashion. Light, empty minds are like bladders, blown up with anything."

The only excuse we can think of for some dressy women is that they think themselves very ugly. What deformity must exist if it needs two thousand a year to cover it. If these persons accurately gauge their lack of personal charms, they must be suffering under a fearful measure of uncomeliness. Why, ten or twenty families could be reared in comparative comfort upon the amount thus expended in wastefulness; and as matters go with the agricultural laborers in many of the shires, forty of the families owned by Hodge and his companions, including all the father Hodges and their wives, could be decently provided for upon two thousand a year. It will not bear thinking of!

Yet many women professing godliness are shockingly extravagant, and can never be happy till their heads are tricked out with strange gear and their bodies with fashionable millinery. They little think how much they degrade themselves and grieve the Spirit of God. A forgiven sinner decked out in the flaunting garments of a worldling, casts suspicion upon her own pardon; if she had ever been renewed in heart, would she, could she, adorn herself after the manner of a Jezebel? It is hard to think of a disciple of the Lord wasting her substance upon personal decoration. Does the lowly Jesus keep company with persons who spend hours at the glass, adorning, if not adoring, their own flesh? Can extravagance and fashionableness be pleasing to the Lord? No. Assuredly not.

We are not judging that "neat handsomeness" which George Herbert says: "doth bear the sway," but we are sorrowful when we see those who set themselves up as examples, and move in a position where no outward show is required, going beyond ordinary worldly women in extravagance. It is the bane of society, and the disgrace of religion.

We wonder how much of the extravagance of female dress could be traced to the man-millinery of Anglican priests. Church congresses have been edified by exhibitions of ecclesiastical finery, in which were seen robes and vestments of the costliest material and the gaudiest colors. We have read of altar frontals which have taken years to finish, and are valued at more than £500. All this to deck out a table; no wonder that it costs so much to dress a woman. When men, and even ministers, take to resplendent trappings, who can wonder that the weaker sex exercise a larger liberty? For shame, ye so-called priests, put away your baby garments and quit yourselves like men.

4

The Deceiver and the Victim

"Behold, ye trust in lying words, that cannot profit" (Jer. 7:8).

"Though thou rentest thy face with painting, in rain shall thou make thyself fair" (Jer. 4:30).

"After I had used the wash for some time an eruption came on my face. I think it was in December, 1877, that this occurred. At this time I had paid the defendant altogether about £20, and when I found the rash come out on my face I went to the defendant, and she said that I was in a terrible state, all the pores of my skin were opened, and that unless I let her finish me at once I should be disfigured for life."

These are reported as the words used in evidence concerning a certain Madame who pretends to make ladies "beautiful forever." The date was about the same with the last incident. Willing dupes ask for her famous cosmetics, washes, and drugs, and beg to be enameled that their charms may conquer all who gaze upon them, and before long they find themselves in the deceiver's toils, their hopes all disappointed, and themselves compelled to pay continually, lest some worse thing should happen unto them. Now this is an admirable parable, and full of detail which a wise man may work out to edification. We will only use it as a caution. Before we commit ourselves into the hands of any of the fair-speaking generation we had better look about us. Loan offices profess to help the needy with great generosity and then devour them with unsparing ferocity. Companies inveigle unwary shareholders, and then strip them of every feather. *Beware!* is a warning much needed on all hands.

In spiritual matters we have many flattering deceivers concerning whom we have need to be on our guard. Peter speaking of false teachers says, "Through covetousness shall they with feigned words make merchandise of you," and Paul says, "Of this sort are they which creep into houses and lead captive silly women." These are the people whom the apostle calls "grievous wolves." Woe unto any unsuspecting sheep if they come in their way; for nothing but almighty grace can rescue them from their jaws.

Yet these flattering teachers who are to do such wonders for their dupes are deceivers all. As the aged pretender, mentioned in the newspaper, was not herself preserved in beauty by her own oriental balms, and yet boasted of her power to conserve the radiance of youth in others, so Peter says again, "While they promise them liberty, they themselves are the servants of corruption." Still, though the fraud is transparent, custom begets a facility in deception, and there are ungodly men and women of whom again the apostle says that "they cannot cease from sin; beguiling unstable souls; an heart they have exercised with covetous practices; cursed children."

Satan is an arch-deceiver in the line of the pretended beautifier. He told our mother Eve that if she would follow his directions she should be as God, and when instead thereof she found herself covered with shame, he knew that he had her in his power. Young men are flattered by the promise of pleasure until they follow after the strange woman to the ruin of both body and soul, and to their own bitter disappointment as to the very pleasure which sin had promised them. "With her much fair speech she caused him to yield"; but shall he win the bliss which she has promised? Ah, no! "A wound and dishonor shall he get, and his reproach shall not be wiped away."

Self-righteousness also commends itself to men as a choice beautifier, and they spend their money to be enameled therewith; but ere long it covers them with the purple rash of shame, and their comeliness is turned into corruption. Trust no deceitful word, but seek unto him who is truth itself, who can make us comely with the true comeliness which he alone can put upon us.

5

Floods in the Streets

"Rivers of waters in the streets" (Prov. 5:16).

"Let judgment run down as waters, and righteousness as a mighty stream" (Amos 5:21).

On Thursday morning, April 11th, when we reached the Tabernacle, at eleven o'clock, we found the rooms of the basement covered with water, so that they could not be occupied. Our Conference was unable to meet for dinner in the schoolroom, and was obliged to adjourn to another building. The papers, among many accounts of the flooded districts, thus speak of our near neighbors in the somewhat aristocratic region of Brixton:

> The easterly gale which had been blowing since Sunday morning subsided on Wednesday night, and was followed by such a downpour of rain as seldom occurs in this latitude except in connection with summer thunderstorms. It was very heavy all through the night, and continued yesterday without much abatement through the early hours of the forenoon, until more rain had fallen in a few hours than the average rainfall for a month. At Brixton there was a serious flood, caused by the inability of the Effra River, which is nothing better than a covered sewer, to carry off all the water. It burst forth at all openings, and even forced itself upward in jets which are compared to the spoutings of a whale. The water rising with much rapidity, the inhabitants, who in most cases were sitting down to or preparing for breakfast, had barely time to escape from their breakfast-rooms, when the water was upon them. Snatching

up what came first to hand, they made the best of their way upstairs, and finding all efforts to save their property futile, gave up the attempt in despair. In Brixton Road, not alone the carriage-way, but the footpaths were submerged, and in some places the flow of water was so great that the roadway and pavement were broken up by the rushing waters seeking to find an outlet, and in some instances the pavements were actually washed away. The main road itself was like a quickly flowing river, and many of the side roads were also flooded. The water was in most places upwards of a foot in depth, and in many nearly two feet. Locomotion was exceedingly difficult, vehicles of all descriptions having to be drawn through the flood, with the horses nearly up to their knees in water, while with the tram-cars the water reached up to the steps, and an extra horse was necessary to draw the car.

When the Lord is pleased to open the windows of heaven and refresh the thirsty earth with plentiful showers, man in his boasted wisdom has so arranged the cities where he dwells that there is no room for the divine bounty, and a benison becomes a danger. His careful preparations in blotting out rippling brooks and watercourses begirt with willows, and burying in the earth beneath arches of brick the once silvery streams, are all sources of peril to him; peril, too, from that which should have been his greatest blessing. The rain is good, but we have not room enough to receive it; we have space for our own filthiness if the heavenly rains will let us alone, but for "showers of blessings" our arrangements have left no receptacle, and they must drown us out, and stop our traffic, to gain even a temporary lodging-place. Time was when the Effra River would have carried the water down to the Thames without any greater inconvenience than a flooded meadow, or a garden swamped for an hour or two.

Some living persons remember the Effra as a pretty brook with a charming walk by its side and overhanging trees. We have seen some pretty bits of scenery which an artist copied from this rural streamlet of days gone by. There were little rustic bridges here and there, and many a nook where lovers of quiet could sit down and meditate; but now there is no sign of the brook until you pass into Dulwich; almost throughout its entire length our modern civilization has transformed it into a covered drain. Confined within a dark arch of brick, the stream forgets its sunny days, and, like a prisoner urged along the corridor of an underground dungeon, pursues its dreary way. Alas, that man should have made human life to be so much after the same manner. Of green fields and fresh breezes how little do the multitudes of our toilers ever see or feel; of cheerfulness and content how little do many of our merchants and traders understand; and of sacred joy and consecrated delight the bulk of men know nothing whatever. Life comes to us, but too often we will not allow it to flow freely in holy content and joy, where the trees are flourishing and the birds singing among the branches, but we compel it to grovel underground in anxiety and unbelief.

Yet heavenly life cannot always be made to abide among the dead, just as the Effra when fed by showers from heaven would no longer brook its prison. It burst forth wherever a vent existed, and forced ways of escape for itself where there were none before. Every now and then this happens in spiritual affairs, and men behold the phenomenon with wonder and even with alarm. It was so in the age of Whitefield and Wesley, when the Lord opened the windows of heaven upon our land. What an outbreak there was! What a commotion and upheaval! The old pavements of conventionality were torn away, and the floods burst up through them. Attempts were made to stop the stream, persecution was tried against the Methodists, they were denounced from the pulpit, threatened by mobs, and ridiculed as modern enthusiasts and madmen, and regarded as the off scouring of all things; but all this availed nothing, omnipotence was at work, and malice could not hinder. The sacred flood would not be denied a channel, but found free course, and God was glorified. Of course it stirred the mud and raised the foulness of the community to most offensive rage; but it cleansed as it rushed forward, and swept away the accumulated vices of dreary years. May the like happen again in our times; indeed, we are not altogether strangers to such burstings forth of the living waters even now.

It were well if in individuals there were such floodings of the soul with the grace of God, that the divine life would break forth everywhere—in the parlor, the workshop, the counting-house, the market, and in the streets. We are far too ready to confine it to the channel of Sunday services and religious meetings; it deserves a broader floodway, and must have it if we are to see gladder times. It must burst out upon men who do not care for it, and invade chambers where it will be regarded as an intrusion; it must be seen by wayfaring men streaming down the places of traffic and concourse, hindering the progress of sinful trades, and surrounding all, whether they will or no. We want another universal deluge, not of destruction, but of salvation, so that the knowledge of the Lord shall cover the earth as the waters cover the sea.

Would to God that religion were more vital and forceful among us, so as to create a powerful public opinion in behalf of truth, justice and holiness. It will be a blessed day when all the streets of our land shall be flooded with grace. Amos, in the text which we have quoted, bids us aim at this, in the name of the Lord. The formalities of religion are of little worth compared with this; for the Lord says, "I hate, I despise your feast days, and I will not smell in your solemn assemblies." And, "Though ye offer me burnt offerings and your meat offerings, I will not accept them: neither will I regard the peace offerings of your fat beasts. Take thou away from me the noise of thy songs; for I will not hear the melody of thy viols. But let judgment run down as waters, and righteousness as a mighty stream."

He would have us exhibit a life which would purify the age, and sweep before it every obstacle; a life to be seen even in the streets, where men care least to have it. It is much to be desired that the Christian church may yet have more power and influence all over the world for righteousness and peace. Something of it is felt even now, but not enough. The Church of Christ in England has more power to-day than it ever had before. Our country would have been plunged into war months ago (May, 1878), if it had not been for Christian men who have been the backbone of the opposition to the war party. Peace would not have been kept unbroken so long as it has been had it not been earnestly promoted by the prayers and labors of those who worship the Prince of Peace. In other matters, also, of social reform, and moral progress, the influence of true religion is felt, and it will be yet far mightier.

May the day come when the Spirit of righteousness shall have complete control over those who govern and direct our affairs, then shall "judgment run down as waters, and righteousness as a mighty stream." All will not go pleasantly even then, for many will be greatly vexed by such prevalence of right principles: their craft will be in danger, they will be greatly inconvenienced in their sins, they will be upon their knees in an element which they do not relish, and they will rave against it; but, for all that, it will be a blessing if God sends us such showers of grace as to become an irresistible flood. Come, mighty stream. Send it, we beseech thee, O Lord: and let us live to see Ezekiel's vision fulfilled. "Then said he unto me, These waters issue out toward the east country, and go down into the desert, and go into the sea: which being brought forth into the sea, the waters shall be healed. And it shall come to pass, that every thing that liveth, which moveth, whithersoever the rivers shall come, shall live: and there shall be a very great multitude of fish, because these waters shall come thither: for they shall be healed; and every thing shall live whither the river cometh."

6

The Race and Its Spectators

"Wherefore seeing we also are compassed about with so great a cloud of witnesses, let us lay aside every weight, and the sin which doth so easily beset us, and let us run with patience the race that is set before us" (Heb. 12:1).

I n an article upon the University Boat race of April 13, the *Times* alludes to the dense throngs upon the bank of the river, and to the interest which everybody seemed to feel in the struggle, and it then very truthfully adds—

> Nor do the competitors themselves fail to gain much from the sight of the vast crowds which attest the strength of the popular interest. The rivalry would hardly be so keen if the race were to be rowed amid the comparative privacy of a provincial stream or lake. Some years ago this was kept out of sight in a high and mighty way by the suggestion that, to prevent the contest from being vulgarized, or for some other reason, it ought to be held at some quieter place than the neighborhood of London. Loch Maree, in the wilds of Ross-shire, would afford charming tranquility and a few scores of cool spectators. But the stimulus of a great public competition would be gone, and, if we may venture to assume that undergraduates are made of the same stuff as other human beings, that stimulus is essential to such muscular exertion as we see at Oxford and Cambridge.

This excellently illustrates the meaning of the apostle when he represents believers as running for a prize, with saints, apostles, and martyrs looking on.

The stimulus communicated by spectators is his prominent idea. No doubt the young oarsmen find a stimulus in every eye that gazes upon them, and if the crowd were thinned they would take less interest; in their task. The crowds which line the Thames may well be compared to clouds, so completely do they darken the banks from end to end of the course; and much more may those who gaze upon the Christian's life be thus spoken of. Myriads lean from heaven, or look from earth, or peer upwards from the pit. Holy men of all ages, now with God, join with a great host still abiding here below. Angels, and principalities, and powers, unite as one vast army and observe ns intently; and frowning demons of the pit in their dread array all gaze with interest upon the Christian's work and way. Should not every glance animate us to do our utmost? And what eyes there are amongst those who observe us. Had the Queen been present, we could imagine the young athletes straining themselves even more than they had done, for the glance of royalty quickens energy to the utmost.

In our case, the King of kings looks down upon us, and the Prince of Life with tender sympathy watches our progress: what manner of race should ours be under the Lord's own eye? Competitors of former years were at the boat-race to see whether the new-comers would maintain the honor of their University. Even so the worthies of ancient times, who counted not their lives dear unto them, take pleasure in the efforts of those who to-day are wrestling for victory, as they themselves did in ages past. The approving glances of prophets and apostles may well stir our souls. Dear ones who have gone before also mark our behavior in the race: a mother in heaven takes delight in the ardor of her son; brothers "gone over to the majority" are serenely glad as they see their brothers pushing forward in the noble cause. Our leaders in the faith, oarsmen who taught us how to fly over the waves, regard us with anxious interest and joy in our successes. These things should quicken us, and lend us arguments for unabated energy.

Of course the apostle was not alluding to a boat race, but to the Olympian Games. Those games furnish a suggestive figure which we leave the reader to work out at leisure when we have given him a glimpse at the race from the window of good Dr. John Brown.

At Olympia, a town of Elis, games were celebrated in honor of Jupiter once every five years. An almost incredible multitude from all the states of Greece and from the surrounding countries attended these games as spectators. The noblest of the Grecian youths appeared as competitors. In this race a course was marked out for the candidates for public fame, and a tribunal erected at the end of the course, on which sat the judges—men who had themselves in former years been successful competitors for Olympic honors. The victors in the morning contests did not receive their prizes till the evening; but after their exertions they joined the band of spectators, and looked on while others prosecuted the same arduous labors which they had brought to an honorable termination.

It is a fine thought that those honorable men in the church of God who have themselves behaved worthily, take the deepest interest in the young men who have newly set out upon the race: let the youngsters so behave themselves that the veterans may never fear for the cause of God. We know that a great deal of anxiety is felt just now, for the rising race shows signs of being unstable, and superficial; but we hope for better things, and even trust that the men of the coming age will outstrip their predecessors, and draw forth the approving shouts of the encompassing cloud of witnesses.

7

Double-Minded

"They feared the Lord, and served their own gods" (2 Kgs. 17:33).

"Them that worship and that swear by the Lord, and that swear by Malcham" (Zeph. 1:6).

"Out of the same mouth proceedeth blessing and cursing" (Jas. 3:10).

The New York *Examiner and Chronicle*, of April 13, says, "Luke, Mr. Tweed's attendant, states that the first thing he did on rising in the morning was to read the Bible; then he had breakfast, and after that read the papers and settled down to write. He spent his time thus until dinner was ready, and after eating, read the Bible again, and a third time before going to rest at night. If anything went wrong with him, or any annoying circumstance occurred at any time, he always had recourse to the Book. His temper was cheerful and even, as a role; but he did not conquer his old habit of swearing, and would, upon provocation, look up from the pages of the Bible and swear at his servant in good set terms. It was, however, but an evanescent irascibility, and in a moment he was good-natured again."

Whether this statement is true or false, it may serve as a somewhat exaggerated picture of the condition of many men. They have enough religion to observe its outward forms, but not enough even to improve their language, much less their hearts. Like the Pharisees of old, they are attentive to the exterior rites of religion, and yet such is their enmity to Christ that they are ready to cry, "Crucify him, crucify him," when that voice will serve their turn. Their piety is a thin coat of whitewash daubed over a leprous wall: they are mere players, with religion as the farce in which they act—a farce which will turn to a tragedy before they have done with it.

To unite Bible-reading and swearing is rather too clear an inconsistency for most men; but very many go in the like direction, and try both to hold with the hare and run with the hounds. They love the wages of unrighteousness and yet maintain a form of godliness. Such men make religion ridiculous in the eyes of their more honest companions; and if they take to Bible-reading, they cause the Word of God to become contemptible; whereas the ridicule is deserved by their own meanness, and the contempt should be poured upon their base hypocrisy. We would say to every man who makes the slightest claim to honesty, "Be one thing or another; if Jehovah be God, serve him; if Baal be God, serve him." Don't try to cheat the devil by shamming to serve God. No possible advantage can accrue to the double-minded man by his pretense of godliness; it can only serve to increase his condemnation. Of all sons of perdition Judas is the worst, for he betrayed the Lord and yet kissed him.

8

A Fox in the Pulpit

"Take us the foxes, the little foxes, that spoil the vines" (Song 2:15).

"O Israel, thy prophets are like the foxes in the deserts" (Ezek. 13:4).

A short letter which appeared in *The Bock*, April 18th, is well worth preserving in connection with the above texts. It is to be feared that the writer might have pointed to not a few Nonconformist pulpits and might have made the same remark concerning their occupants, "Duty requires that they should be taken out and kept out."

> A FOX IN THE PULPIT.—Sir, a singular circumstance took place at Hever, in Kent, on Saturday last. A fox, hard pressed by the huntsmen, leaped the churchyard wall and disappeared. The hounds and huntsmen were searching and wondering, when an old woman came out from a back door of the church which happened to be open, with the exclamation, *"Here he is, in the pulpit"*; and, sure enough, poor Reynard had slipped in at the open door and sought sanctuary, curled up in a corner of the pulpit. Of course, he was soon ejected. To my friend, who had witnessed the scene and described it very vividly, I observed that it reminded one of certain sly foxes in the Church of England, who get into our pulpits and think they are safe there. Duty requires that they should be taken out and kept out.—I am, *&c*, W. J. B.

This is written by a Church of England man, and published in a sound Church paper, and so it is no violation of charity to repeat it, especially as we quite agree with every word of it. We wish that all the Popish foxes could be ejected from the National Establishment, for they do more mischief than tongue can tell.

> The fox that steals the lamb so tender,
>   Can never be the fold's defender,
> He's but a base and sly pretender.

The difficulty seems to be to get these foxes out and keep them out. Once in the pulpit, they know how to hold their position; you may dig out a fox, but you cannot dislodge a Romanizing priest. Acts of Parliament altogether fail, because such things are meant for men, and foxes dexterously evade them. Reynard's imitators have many knavish tricks, and know how to twist and turn, and so they escape statutes and laws, and still pursue their evil business. In the reforming times a popular caricature represented a priest as a fox preaching to an assembly of geese from the text, "How earnestly I long for you all in my bowels." The drawing would not be out of date if it were published today. How silly must the geese be who yield themselves heart and soul to such foxes! Yet there are flocks of them.

9

The Evil Wrought by One Man

"One sinner destroyeth much good" (Eccl. 9:18).

"That man perished not alone in his iniquity" (Josh. 22:20).

An American paper contains the following paragraph: "An oil train of forty oil-tanks ran into a heavy freight train near Slatington, Pa. The engineer of the latter train had been compelled to stop to cool off a hot 'journal,' but the conductor had sent no one back to warn following trains of danger. Several persons were killed and about forty injured—the result of one man's carelessness."

Amid the blaze of the oil, the screams of burning men and women, and the charred remains of the unhappy victims, we see how great a calamity may arise out of a little neglect, and how much the destiny of others may hang upon the acts of one man. Have we a due sense of our own personal responsibility? Have we ever reflected that our own conduct may influence others for good or evil throughout eternity? We may have no wicked intent, and yet our carelessness and indifference may be as fatal to immortal souls as if we had been profane or profligate. Moral virtues apart from religion may suggest to our children that godliness is needless; was not their father an excellent man, and yet he was unconverted?

Thus may generation after generation be kept in spiritual death by an argument fetched from the irreligion of one who was in other respects a model character. Who among us would desire this?

Even if we hope that we are ourselves saved, it should cause us grave question if we are not bringing others to Jesus.

A destroyer of souls will have an awful doom at the last, and he who failed to do his best to save his fellows will not be held guiltless before the Lord.

10

Sympathy Created by Kindred Experience

"I am as ye are" (Gal. 4:12).

"Who can have compassion on the ignorant, and on them that are out of the way; for that he himself also is compassed with infirmity" (Heb. 5:2).

The present week (the close of April, 1878), witnesses an extensive strike among the Lancashire operatives, who strongly resist a reduction of wages, which the masters declare to be absolutely necessary. There appears to be a hope that the dispute may be speedily ended, and the *Daily Telegraph* mentions one element of the question which is exceedingly encouraging. It says,

> There is one characteristic which distinguishes the present from all previous strikes in the same trade. Lancashire artisans are in some cases now able to look at the difficulty from exactly the same point of view as the masters, being, in fact, masters themselves. In the many co-operative spinning concerns, the shareholders are nearly all artisans and small tradesmen. The managers are all practical men, and every economy or improvement is carefully utilized. Hence, if the business can be made to pay at all, these mills should leave a profit. It happened, however, that all last year the results of the working of joint-stock companies became more and more unfavorable; and the first quarter of the present year was worse still. The decline has been gradual, but constant. Of nearly thirty such undertakings within a given radius, fully half were found to return

a loss at the beginning of this month, and none of the remainder showed what could fairly be called a working profit. It is not, therefore, a mere accident that the Amalgamated Association of Operative Cotton Spinners and Weavers of Lancashire and the adjoining counties has, after a long discussion, recommended the men to accept the ten per cent reduction for the present. Being to a certain extent employers and capitalists themselves, they understand the crisis with a clearness enlightened by self-interest. This advice cannot fail to have a great effect on many wavering operatives.

No one understands another so as to enter into his case unless he has been himself in a like position. Even our Lord could not become perfect as the Captain of our salvation without enduring hardness as all his followers must do. He must needs be found in fashion as a man, and be tempted in all points like as we are ere he could be touched with a feeling of our infirmities. To us it must ever be a source of abounding joy that our Lord Jesus wears our nature and intensely sympathizes in our experience.

This is one reason why the Lord's ministers have such a fight of outward afflictions and inward temptations. How else could they enter into the experience of the tried people of God? Luther placed affliction among the three essential things for a good minister; but we would enlarge the area of expression, and say that experience of all kinds must be the preacher's school. He must know how to be full and to be empty, how to abound and how to suffer loss. Like the psalmist David, the preacher must be a man of ups and downs, rising till he reaches *in excelsis*, and sinking till his note is *de profundis*. All their varied moods are meant to qualify men of God to sympathize with the afflicted. "For whether we be beside ourselves, it is to God: or whether we be sober, it is for your cause."

Our own personal obligation to sympathize with others and have patience with them arises out of our being in the same nature and partakers in the like perils. We are to weep with those that weep, and to rejoice with those that do rejoice, because we are followers of the same Savior, and carry the same cross. It is not always true that "a fellow-feeling makes us wondrous kind," but it ought to be so. The apostle says, "Remember them that are in bonds, as being bound with them; and them which suffer adversity, as being yourselves also in the body," and again he writes, "Considering thyself, lest thou also be tempted." Yet this argument is often slighted till it is brought home to us in actual life. The workman cannot feel for the employer till he becomes a master himself, and the child does not appreciate a father's love till he is himself a parent. A master would probably be all the more considerate for his men if he took a turn at their labor, and shared their domestic trials; and hearers would treat their ministers differently if they were themselves occasionally called upon to preach. This is no doubt the reason why some Christians have to pass through so checkered a career—they are to learn how to see out of other men's eyes, and judge matters from other men's points of view. The lesson is worth learning, cost what it may.

Should the operatives prove to have learned nothing by their own experience, the fact will be in opposition to the old proverb, *experientia docet* (experience teaches), and it will not be the only time in which we have seen that to learn by experience a man must be wise to begin with, and that is not the case with all.

11

The Morning Drummer and the Preacher

"Their line is gone out through all the earth, and their words to the end of the world" (Ps. 19:4).

"And this gospel of the kingdom shall be preached in all the world for a witness unto all nations; and then shall the end come" (Matt. 24:14).

In the *Daily Telegraph*, of May 1, we read:

> The real essence of Exeter-Hallism just now is missionary zeal. The British Empire is wide, and we often quote the orator who spoke of the morning drum of the British army making the circuit of the world as our earth lifts up each section of its surface in turn to be bathed in the light of the sun. But something British besides a drummer w seen and heard in succession as daybreak follows daybreak round the globe. A most unsuccessfully attired Englishman, with clothes that, as a rule, are neither fashionable, well-made, suitable, nor picturesque, is heard and seen with an open Bible in his hands reading or expounding it. 'There is no land where their voice is not heard'; there is hardly a known tongue that has not its version of a Book which owes more of its circulation to English money and agency than to any other international means.

This is not exactly worded as one might desire. Perhaps a suppressed sneer is perceptible; but yet, taking it from whence it comes, it is a valuable testimony; indeed, all the more valuable because the witness is not biased in favor of the fact which he asserts. We only wish that it were still more evidently true, and that worldlings were oftener compelled to admit its power, even if they did so in an almost scornful manner. The duty of the church is to keep her herald side by side with that drummer who is said to wake the morning all round the globe. The fashionableness of his clothes is too small a matter to be worthy of notice; but the best of books in his hand must always be his noticeable mark and sign; thank God that in any measure it is so.

Encouraged by some measure of success in sounding forth the word of God, let all who love our Lord Jesus arouse themselves to do the work yet more thoroughly. When a certain chaplain asked the Duke of Wellington whether he thought it was worthwhile to teach the gospel to the Hindus, the man of discipline is reported to have replied, "What are your marching orders?" These are clear enough, "Go ye into all the world and preach the Gospel to every creature"; what remains but to obey? Once the sneer was directed against consecrated cobblers, but now the lack of fashionable tailors appears to be the point of remark. What matters it? Let the men be sent, and if they be "clad with zeal as with a cloke," they will be fashionable in heaven. May the Holy Spirit rest upon them, and they will be a power in the earth to whom even the most worldly shall yield a silent homage.

> Nor shall the spreading gospel rest,
>   Till round the earth its course has run,
> Till Christ has all the nations blest,
>   That see the light or feel the sun.

12

Have to Have More

"For whosoever hath, to him shall be given, and he shall have more abundance: but whosoever hath not, from him shall be taken away even that he hath" (Matt. 13:12).

"A wise man will hear, and will increase learning; and a man of understanding shall attain unto wise counsels" (Prov. 1:5).

The *Times*, May 8th, speaking of the Exhibition of the Royal Academy Bays, "No doubt people ought to bring to a collection of pictures, or other works of art, as much knowledge as possible, according to the old saying that if we expect to bring back the wealth of the Indies, we must take the wealth of the Indies out with us. Learning and progress are continual accretions." This witness is true. He who studies the works of art in an exhibition of paintings, being himself already educated in such matters, adds greatly to his knowledge, and derives the utmost pleasure from the genius displayed. On the other hand, he who knows nothing at all about the matter, and yet pretends to be a critic, simply exhibits his own ignorance and self-conceit, and misses that measure of enjoyment which an entirely unsophisticated and unpretending spectator would have received. We must bring taste and information to art, or she will not deign to reveal her choicest charms.

It is so with all the higher forms of knowledge. We were once in the fine museum of geology and mineralogy in Paris, and we noticed two or three enthusiastic gentlemen in perfect rapture over the specimens preserved in the cases; they paused lovingly here and there, used their glasses and discoursed with delighted gesticulations concerning the various objects of interest; they were evidently increasing their stores of information. They had, and to them more was given. Money makes money, and knowledge increases knowledge.

A few minutes after, we noticed one of our own countrymen, who appeared to be a man of more wealth than education. He looked around him for a minute or two, walked along a line of cases, and then expressed the utmost disgust with the whole concern: "There was nothing there," he said, "except a lot of old bones and stones, and bits of marble." He was persuaded to look a little further, at a fine collection of fossil fishes, but the total result was a fuller manifestation of his ignorance upon the subjects so abundantly illustrated, and a declaration of his desire to remain in ignorance, for he remarked that "He did not care a rap for such rubbish, and would not give three half-crowns for a wagonload of it." Truly, in the matter of knowledge, "Unto every one that hath shall be given, and he shall have abundance; but from him that hath not shall be taken away even that which he hath."

The same principle holds good in matters of religion: he who has love to Christ, and a spiritual appetite, enjoys the word of God, and finds it to be marrow and fatness; but he who has no spiritual perception turns away from the most instructive doctrine, rejecting it, even as the full soul loatheth the honeycomb. Such a hearer is no gainer by the gospel, and though it may seem to be a contradiction that he who had nothing should have something taken away from him, yet so it is: the unspiritual man is frequently a loser by the gospel which he hears, he loses that curiosity which at first induced him to listen, that measure of interest which in some degree aroused his attention, and that slender sense of ignorance which remained in him so long as he did not even know what the gospel was.

Henceforth, he has heard all that the preacher has to say, he thinks he knows all that the Bible can teach him, and any little hope that there may have been for him is greatly diminished. There must be life in us, or we cannot feed on the food around us; there must be an eye in the body, or light will be in vain; there must be some grace within the soul, or else all the grace in means and ordinances cannot enrich us. When the soil is made good the good seed yields a harvest; but often the barren soil devours all that the husbandman can put into it and is none the better. We ought to go to public worship with an earnest desire to obtain a blessing, a willing heart to receive it, and a sense of our need of it, and then we shall not hear in vain. If, beyond this, our soul is in actual fellowship with our Lord already, we shall find that his paths drop fatness. "To him that bath shall be given."

Remember, too, that a religious profession requires grace to sustain it. A company which begins business without cash will soon lose even its nominal capital, will in fact lose what it never had; thus thoroughly illustrating the words of our Lord, and, as in a parable, setting before us the result of pretending to be Christians if we have no grace. If we have no oil in our vessels with our lamps, the lamps themselves will go out and leave us in total darkness.

On the other hand, where there is grace already more grace will be given. As riches make riches, and knowledge acquires knowledge, so doth spiritual life grow, and add to itself gifts and virtue by which it is greatly enriched.

13

Conscientious Separation

"A conscience void of offence toward God, and toward men" (Acts 24:16).

"If the Lord be God, follow him: but if Baal, then follow him" (1 Kgs. 18:21).

The *Daily News*, of May 8th, in an article on Lord Carnarvon's resignation, says,

> Mr. CARLYLE, wearied with much eighteenth century talk about virtue, somewhere requests the talker, with a strong adjuration, to "be virtuous and have done with it." Too much praise of what is after all but the carrying into statesmanship of the laudable but not marvelous practice of common honesty might lead the hearer to express a similarly petulant prayer. It is not at all desirable that a politician should be perpetually interrogating his conscience to see what its opinion may be as to this tax on tobacco and that alteration in the bankruptcy laws. Such a practice could only lead to very considerable public inconvenience, and in the case of the individual practicing it, to something not very different from hypocrisy. But occasions may and do arise when a policy or an individual measure commends itself to the majority of a Ministry which seems morally wrong or politically unadvisable to some member thereof. When this is the case, ought he to put his convictions in his pocket, and salve his conscience with the theory of party allegiance, or ought he to go out from those respecting whom he feels that he is not of them? No one will in words profess the former doctrine, but many

will act upon it. Lord Carnarvon has acted upon the latter doctrine, which everybody professes, but many set aside in practice. Of course it is important that the conscience appealed to should be a healthy conscience, not given to unnecessary questioning and quibbling.

Not only do we admire the consistency of Lord Carnarvon, but we wish we saw a little more of it among professing Christians. We know some ministers who do not believe the doctrines of the church to which they belong, and yet for reasons best known to themselves they remain in that community, and undermine the very foundations of the faith which they profess to preach. How this can be made to be in accordance with morality we know not. Surely it would be more like common honesty if they would at once show their colors, and no longer pretend to be what they are not. Some Christians, too, who never enter a pulpit, are equally guilty, for they are recognized as members of churches against whose teaching they frequently protest. They support evil systems and know them to be evil. They dissent in their hearts, but yet consent by their actions: for fear of giving offence to men, they are constantly offending God and their own consciences. Whatever their excuses may be, are they not resolvable into doing evil that good may come?

Of course it is not to be desired that men should be perpetually vexed with scruples upon minor points, and ready to quarrel about anything or nothing, because their conscience is morbidly sensitive; but surely it cannot be right for a truthful man to be a member of a church from whose confession he widely disagrees; his position is a protest against his own convictions, and his convictions make his profession a falsehood. We ought to be intensely anxious to be so clear in the whole of our religious standing that under the light of the day of judgment no glaring contradictions shall be discovered in our lives; otherwise we may not only be guilty of "something not very different from hypocrisy," but we may fall into hypocrisy itself. A little tampering with conscience is a very dangerous thing, it is very like the dropping of a stitch which may lead to the unravelling of all the work. We used to say in our childhood—

> He who steals a pin,
>   Will live to steal a bigger thing.

The rhyme was bad, but the doctrine was true. If we violate conscience, even upon the smallest matter, we may come at last to have no conscience at all.

Mr. Carlyle's advice is thoroughly sound, and his adjuration is none too strong, "Be virtuous and have done with it:" speak the truth and stand to it, profess the faith which is revealed in the Scriptures, and neither by word of mouth, nor by act, nor by association, nor even in thought, contradict the eternal verities of God. We have had too much of concession in order to win a hollow peace from philosophic Rationalists on the one hand, and superstitious Romanizers on the other. The thing will not work, and if it would, it is wrong, and ought not to be attempted. Who gave us the right to yield an atom of truth? Are the doctrines of God's word yours or mine to do as we like with, to give up this and modify that? Nay, verily: we are put in trust with the gospel, and it is at our peril that we dream of compromising the least of its teachings. A straightforward, decided line of testimony is the best, is most consistent with true charity, and in the end will most promote peace.

The trimming, hesitating policy of many reminds us of Luther's words to Erasmus: "You desire to walk upon eggs without crushing them, and among glasses without breaking them!" This is a difficult game to play at, and one which is more suitable for a clown at a theatre than a servant of Christ. When you are attempting a compromise, you have to look around you and move as cautiously as a tight-rope dancer, for fear of offending on one side or the other. A little too much this way or that and over you go. A cat on hot cinders is in an enviable position. No true-hearted man will ever bear such wretched constraint for any length of time, or indeed at all. Think of being able to go no further than the aforementioned timorous, time-serving Erasmus, who said, "I will not be unfaithful to the cause of Christ; *at least, so far as the age will permit me.*" Out upon such cowardice: life is too dear when bought at such a price.

> I cannot tell what you and other men
>   Think of this life; but for my single self,
> I had as lief [gladly] not be, as live to be
>   In awe of such a thing as I myself.

14

On Exposing Others to Peril

"When thou buildest a new house, then thou shall make a battlement for thy roof, that thou bring not blood upon thine house, if any man fall from thence" (Deut. 22:8).

"Thou shalt not kill" (Ex. 20:13).

The morning papers of May 9 have the following humiliating paragraph,

> An acrobat, named Gilfort, was performing at the Dublin Exhibition Palace, at a height of no less than forty feet from the ground. He was going through the 'acts' usually done by Blondin—lying down on the rope, sitting astride it, pretending to slip from it, balancing himself on it in a chair, and so forth. Suddenly one of the supports by which the fabric was steadied gave way, and the rope jerked violently towards the left, throwing Gilfort off his equilibrium. The unfortunate man made a desperate effort to save himself, clutching at his perch with both arms and legs. The attempt failed, and he fell a sheer distance of forty feet, with his balancing-pole still in his hand. The pole was splintered into fragments by the violence of the fall. Gilfort himself struck the ground heavily, rebounded from it, and was picked up severely crushed and bruised. Immediate assistance was, of course, rendered to him, and at first it seemed hardly possible that he could survive his injuries. He lay delirious, unconscious of what had happened, and terribly maimed.

Even if the unfortunate acrobat had not fallen, we conceive that attendance at such a performance was in itself an immoral act. The pleasure derived by the spectators arose in a great measure from the extreme danger to the individual. His skill might equally well have been exhibited upon a rope near the ground, or at some small distance above the spectators' heads; but this would have been unattractive; the forty feet, and the danger of a fall, gave a horrible interest to the exhibition, and collected the multitude. This, we say, is immoral and degrading: the commandment which forbids us to kill practically prohibits our placing another where his life is in danger, and forbids our doing anything which would lead to his exposing himself by attempting a perilous feat without justifiable cause.

When dangerous deeds must be done, we are bound to provide every possible safeguard; but to induce a man unnecessarily to risk life and limb, and to omit precautions, is essentially murder, and every person who by his subscription assisted, or by his presence encouraged, such a risking of life, was guilty of the violation of the commandment, "Thou shalt not kill." If we are bound to guard against common accidents such as the fall of a person from a roof, by placing a battlement that none might step over unawares, we are equally bound to keep people out of danger as much as we can. We ought not to need a law to prohibit these horrible exhibitions; there ought to be enough of humanity in the world to lead every human being to denounce the proposal that a fellow creature should run the risk of falling from a terrible height to be dashed in pieces merely to gratify a vulgar curiosity.

Yet may we not all have been more or less guilty of such conduct in a moral and spiritual sense? May we not by smiling at the wit of a doubtful story have encouraged the teller to repeat the wicked jest? May we not have introduced others into doubtful questions which have proved too high for them, and have led to their faith staggering, and their minds falling into unbelief. Some writers and preachers greatly encourage tight-rope speculations upon mysterious subjects, and cause no end of mischief. A skeptical remark repeated in the pulpit has placed many a youth upon a dizzy height, and caused his ruin; the man who uttered it had no idea of doing harm, but he ought to have remembered that positions which are safe for practiced judgments may be deadly to the inexperienced.

May we not, by our lukewarmness in matters of religion, have tempted others to remain careless and indifferent while their souls are in jeopardy? Do not many professors tempt sinners to delay by their own dilatoriness in divine things?

Is it not very possible that some strong minds may, by their example, induce the weaker sort to do that which is eminently hazardous to them? Who among us can plead entire innocence? For the future let us be careful not to lead the feebleminded into slippery places by going there ourselves.

Another phase of the same subject deserves a passing word. If at any time we join in the popular admiration of men because they are successful and raised to high positions, although their characters are evil, and their conduct more than questionable, are we not acting like those who lift up their shouts of applause when the acrobat is pacing along a slender line at a giddy height? It is the part of a Christian to applaud nothing but virtue. Let the world give its acclamations to its heroes as they move aloft, and salute its conquerors with paeans as they look down upon them; as for us, let humble piety and quiet excellence engross the whole of our admiration. We have something else to do besides encouraging men in walking in a way which is contrary to the mind of God. They may be very clever, and display wonderful skill; but that is nothing to us if they are doing that which tends to the destruction of their souls. We foresee the awful fall which must end the scene, and we feel more like weeping than shouting.

15

Want of Light

"Seek ye first the kingdom of God, and his righteousness; and all these things shall be added unto you" (Matt. 6:33).

"Ye pay tithe of mint and anise and cummin, and have omitted the weightier matters of the law, judgment, mercy, and faith" (Matt. 23:23).

A correspondent of a newspaper, dated May 9th, writes as follows: "The arrangements in the French galleries are so imperfect that in many cases the lower portions of the pictures are in a full glare, while the upper are in comparative darkness. The artists are loud in their complaints."

Yet this is by no means an uncommon arrangement in far greater matters than pictures, for the lesser and lower concerns of life are generally set in full glare, while the greater and higher matters of consideration are left in comparative darkness. The title-deeds of an estate are made as secure as law can make them, but the eternal inheritance is utterly neglected. Honesty towards man is made a prime virtue, while God is robbed, and his claims are rejected. Concern to be respectable is often greater than anxiety to be useful, and to be a gentleman is more the subject of care than to be a Christian. The body is dressed, and the soul is left naked; the mouth is fed with the bread of earth, but the heart knows no hunger for the bread of heaven; all things are prepared for this life even to a superabundance, and the life to come is disregarded as if it were a mere fiction. Many men spend more thought over shirt-collars than over their souls. Dogs and horses are more the themes of meditation than heaven and hell; and the next race, or ball, or kettle-drum calls forth more thought than the coming of the Lord, or the Day of Judgment. Is this according to sound reason?

Oh that men were wise, and could see eternal things in the full noontide of God's countenance, then would there be a balanced light upon the whole of life, and men would find "the promise of the life that now is" to be wrapped up in preparation for the life which is to come. Alas, it is not so: "What shall we eat, and what shall we drink, and wherewithal shall we be clothed?" These make up the trinity of questions which still engross the heart of the multitude. "After all these things do the Gentiles seek." The angel holds the crown over the worldling's head, but he is looking downward, busy with the muckrake, scraping together earth's trifles, and so he has neither eye nor heart for immortal glory. "Oh that they were wise, that they understood this, that they would consider their latter end!"

More light for the upper portion of the picture is greatly to be desired.

16

Tale-Bearing

"Thou shalt not raise a false report: put not thine hand with the wicked to be an unrighteous witness" (Exod. 23:1).

"Thou shall not go up and down as a talebearer among thy people" (Lev. 19:16).

"Keep thee far from a false matter" (Exod. 23:7).

The *Boston Weekly Advertiser*, May 9th, says:

> We have often heard the conundrum, "Which is the mother of the chickens, the hen that lays the eggs or the hen that hatches them?" and now it is gratifying to have a legal decision of this vexed question of agricultural equity. A resident of West Stratford, Conn., owned a hen of a fancy breed that strayed upon a neighbor's premises and laid a nest full of eggs. Another hen belonging to the owner of the land took possession of the nest and hatched the eggs. Then the two neighbors got into a wrangle about the chickens. They were sold by No. 2 to a third party, whereupon No. 1 got out a writ of replevin, and the case was tried a few days ago with able counsel and many witnesses. The court decided that the hen that hatched the eggs was the legal mother, and dismissed the replevin suit.

It may be regarded as equally settled by the court of common sense that a person who repeats a slanderous tale is as much the parent of it as the first inventor—the hatcher is as bad as the layer, if not worse.

He who first forges the lie is assuredly guilty; but little or no harm would come of his deed if there were not persons willing to hear and to believe the calumny; and even then the mischief would be slight unless there were ready tongues to convey the story from place to place and so spread the evil. If it is true that the receiver is as bad as the thief, he who believes a lie is guilty as well as the man who utters it; how much more then is he an accomplice in the crime who repeats the falsehood, and finds it currency. Yet this is done very thoughtlessly, and when the slander is refuted, men seldom repent of having repeated it, though it is a sin for which they will have to answer before the Judge of all.

If I did not make the dagger, yet if I stab a man with it I am guilty of murder; if I did not concoct the accusation, yet if I injure my neighbor's character by repeating it, I am a partaker in the crime. To save ourselves from falling into this evil the safest course will be to be extremely incredulous of all libelous reports, and never under any circumstances to become tale-bearers. There are dogs whose delight it is to fetch and carry, and there can be no need that we should degrade ourselves by undertaking such an errand.

Plautus would have tale-bearers and tale-hearers alike punished by hanging, the one by the tongue and the other by the ears: we should soon be short of timber for gibbets if this witty sentence were carried out, but there is no need that any one of us should earn the right to swing among the company. If telephones and microphones are carried much further we shall have enough of hearing and over-hearing, and it will be wise for us to cultivate deafness when others are chattering. There would be very little lost if we were all to turn our vowels into mutes, and conclude our table-talk with a full stop.

The next time the black hen lays an egg let her sit upon it herself and bring out her own chicks. No sensible being would wish to stand step-father to a lie, or to be a cat's-paw to the devil when he chooses to roast good men in the fire of slander. The town-crier of the City of London has an honorable office, but to be common crier for the town of Falsehood is not desirable; the work ranks next to that of common informer.

17

Tempting Temptation

"Blessed is the man that walketh not in the counsel of the ungodly, nor standeth in the way of sinners, nor sitteth in the seat of the scornful" (Ps. 1:1).

"Lead us not into temptation" (Matt. 6:13).

The *Rock* of May 10, speaks of foxhunting parsons, and remarks:

> To come down to modern times, the late Rev. Joseph Berington, Roman Catholic chaplain at Buckland, Berks, and a writer on history, was fond of a run with the hounds. When visiting his patron's family, the Throckmortons, of Weston Underwood, Bucks, he was in the neighborhood of two packs, and did not neglect the opportunity. He did not actually go 'to cover,' but rode out in the direction the hounds might take, and thus fell in with the hunt, and got half-a-day's sport without appearing to seek it. This was playing the politician to gratify his inclination. This anecdote was learned at a table where he has often dined, from personal friends of his own.

Why could not the man have hunted openly or not at all? If he felt ashamed of it, why did he do it? Thoroughbred fox-hunters must have despised him. The policy of the Rev. Joseph is followed by a great many in daily life; they complain of being tempted, and yet they carefully put themselves in the way of temptation; they profess to have been grievously misled by evil company, and yet they continue to stand in the way of sinners, and to delight themselves with their evil conversation. They express the greatest grief if they fall into drunkenness, and say that they have been "overtaken"; but notwithstanding this they carefully ride along the road which drunkenness is known to pursue, and, under the name of moderation, drink themselves fully up to the boundary line. They do not actually go "to cover," but they ride out in the direction which the hounds always take. They profess to be averse to frivolous amusements, to feasting, rioting), and the like, but they are pretty careful to call upon their friends when such things are going on, and so get half-a-day's sport without appearing to seek it. They are averse to infidelity, and yet peruse skeptical reviews; they dislike licentiousness, and yet spend hours over doubtful novels. They tempt the devil to tempt them, and go into dark lanes in order to be beset by their favorite sins.

Thus to excuse sin as many do is mere nonsense, or worse; such fooling may amuse conscience, and prevent its plainly speaking the truth; but it is altogether unworthy of an honest man. Excuses which hold no water are caught up under the notion that a bad excuse is better than none; the fact being that a bad excuse is worse than none, for it proves that the man has not the courage to defend what he has the audacity to do, nor the common honesty to take the responsibility of his own act and deed. Let us follow the advice of Solomon: "Enter not into the path of the wicked, and go not in the way of evil men. Avoid it, pass not by it, turn from it, and pass away." We pity a man who catches an infectious disease, but we should cease to do so if we heard that he purposely went down to the fever hospital or wilfully rode in the small-pox carriage. If you go to live with a sweep you ought not to blame him if your linen loses its whiteness, or, if you do so, everyone will see through your inconsistency. If it be true that when you go to Rome you must do as Rome does, then do not go to Home at all, and no such necessity will arise.

It is wonderful how circumstances appear to help a man when he wants to do wrong, and some there are who even dare to quote the fact as a reason why they ought not to be blamed. "They happened to be on the spot or they would never have thought of it"; thus they are profane enough to hint that providence itself misled them. This is only a repetition of Adam's plea, "The woman whom thou gavest me, she tempted me, and I did eat." Alas, the vile attempt to father sin upon the Lord himself is often made, but it is none the less horrible. Let us abandon such blasphemous endeavors to shift the responsibility of our actions, and give our consciences a fair chance of being heard.

18

Review at Aldershot

"Thou hast given a banner to them that fear thee, that it may be displayed because of the truth" (Ps. 60:4).

"Terrible as an army with banners." (Song. 6:4).

The *Daily News*, of May 14, in its report of the Review at Aldershot before the Queen, mentions—"The 49th, whose color-party bore the tattered green flag that floated on the heights of Alma and over the trenches in front of Sebastopol, and served as a rallying point amid the mists of Inkerman; and the gallant 52nd, whose history has been untarnished from the first campaign in Hindostan, through all the Peninsular wars, beginning at Vimiera and ending at Waterloo, down to the conquest of Delhi." Soldiers appear to have an almost religious attachment to the colors of the regiment, and the more tattered they become the more they value them; and well they may, for they are in fact the materialized history of the host. They tell of the cruel rain of shot and shell, the dust and smoke of the conflict, and the battle, "with confused noise, and garments rolled in blood,"—terrible records truly, but as long as there are warriors, and courage in fight is valued, banners and standards must always be prized.

The sacramental host of God's elect bears the standard of the truth, and has borne it these thousands of years, and the truth has become endeared to every soldier of the cross by all the conflicts through which we have borne it. Heresies and skepticisms have raged around the banner, but from the first campaign even until now it has gone on from victory to victory. The very thought of it stirs enthusiasm in the hearts of the warriors of Christ. Shall we ever desert it? Shall we suffer it to be trailed in the mire? God forbid. We will uplift it, and display it in the face of the enemy until the last great battle shall be fought, and we shall hear the triumphant shout, "Hallelujah! Hallelujah! The Lord God omnipotent reigneth."

It has of late been proposed that the army of Christ should march without its banner, or that all the banners of philosophic skeptics should be stitched together and uplifted in its place. To this we solemnly demur. We will march under the old ensign; of the new ones we know nothing, except that they will lead us to defeat. Faith has won all her victories under the standard of revelation, and she expects to win all her future glory under the same unaltered and unalterable flag. Let others do as they will; as for us, the old, old gospel shall be our rallying point amid the mists of modem thought, and we hope to bear it from land to land throughout the whole campaign of this dispensation, till we shall see it borne aloft at the coronation festival of our triumphant Lord.

> Stand up, stand up for Jesus,
>   Ye soldiers of the cross;
> Lift high his royal banner,
>   It must not suffer loss.
>
> From victory unto victory
>   His army shall he lead,
> Till every foe is vanquish'd,
>   And Christ is Lord indeed.

19

"Quis Separabit?"

"Who shall separate us from the love of Christ?" (Rom. 8:35).

Another incident of the Review before the Queen, at Aldershot, is thus described by the *Daily News*: "The 86th (County Down) Regiment, with Lieutenant-Colonel Adams at its head, went by with a firm, elastic tread, never wavering as they passed the saluting point, but preserving the touch as if the old motto, '*Quis separabit?*' had been instilled into every man."

We can scarcely credit that their motto, which is in somewhat questionable taste, can have any influence upon the 86th, but we are quite sure that it ought to operate very strongly upon those to whom it properly belongs. The question, "Who shall separate us from the love of God, which is in Christ Jesus our Lord?" should bind us first of all to the great Captain of our salvation. If he himself by inspiration forbids the fear of separation from himself, let us not act as if such a division were possible, but cling to him with all the tenacity of vital union. Shall the member be cut away from the body? The thought is too painful. Shall the branch be torn from the vine? The result would be deadly. Shall the stone be rent from the foundation? The overthrow would be terrible. Shall the bride be divorced from her husband? The consequences would be dishonor, poverty, destruction.

No force of persecution shall ever drive us from our Lord through fear, and no fascination of pleasure shall tempt us from him through selfish hope. Closer and closer let us cling to him who is our one and only hope for time and for eternity. Defying things present and things to come, and the great master power of evil, let us cry "*Quis separabit?*" and march on our way to the marriage supper of the Lamb, through all the opposing hosts of the world, the flesh, and the devil.

Equally influential should this motto be with regard to our union with our fellow-Christians. The church is one and indivisible: imperfections and infirmities are frequent causes of discord; but where charity rules, they cannot create disunion: the existence of the old man is a dividing power, but the new man is ever one, and draws and attracts to itself all life of the same kind. We will not leave our brethren because we cannot agree with them in sentiment in all respects, but we will endeavor to keep the unity of the Spirit in the bonds of peace. We will not forsake our brethren because they are in poverty or disgrace, but we will regard them as suffering members of the one body. We will not even believe that death can separate, but our faith and love shall follow to the skies the members of the general assembly and church of the first-born who have taken wings for the seats above. Our hearts are gladdened while we sing,

> One family we dwell in him,
> > One church above, beneath;
> Though now divided by the stream,
> > The narrow stream of death.

Our love takes a sweep which, in its circle, includes all who are one in Christ, whether in heaven or in earth. It shall be ours throughout life to promote the visible union of the people of God, and never will we lend a hand to tear the seamless vesture of our Lord. Sinking selfishness, and cultivating ever the mind which was in Christ Jesus, we will labor to carry out the spirit of our great Master's prayer, "That they all may be one; as thou, Father, art in me, and I in thee, that they also may be one in us." So will we challenge the dispersing influences of sin and the world with the grand question, "*Quis separabit?*" never wavering as we pass the saluting point, but preserving the touch as if the old motto had been instilled into every man.

Reader, are you a peace-maker or are you a divider? Search your heart and see; for it is an important enquiry. The divider of churches will have hard work to prove himself a Christian, since it is written, "Though I bestow all my goods to feed the poor, and though I give my body to be burned, and have not love, it profiteth me nothing." More love would enable us to work in harmony with those who are now the victims of our dislike. Unity in error and in sin is increase of evil; but unity in the truth and in good works is so desirable that woe is unto that man by whom the offence cometh.

"*Quis separabit*" it seems is the motto of an order of knighthood, that of St. Patrick. The nationality indicated does not suggest the most united and peaceable of the human race, but the question suggests such a determined unity that we would urge each Christian church to write it upon its walls. When will true brotherhood become so strong among us that nothing can rend our churches, but all men shall exclaim, "See how these Christians love one another"?

20

Life Versus Machinery

"God is a Spirit: and they that worship him must worship him in spirit and in truth" (John 4:24).

The *Daily News* describing the "Dreadnought" says:

> The system of auxiliary engines, which is met with at every turn, engines for pumping, ventilating, feeding, starting, steering, &c, has been finished and tested, but their maintenance in a serviceable condition will be obviously one of the chief cares of the engineers on board. In a word, the Dreadnought is an example of the most modern battle-ship in which cranks and pistons, valves and cylinders, take the place of the bone and muscle of our Blue jackets. Whether it is wise thus to dispense entirely with human energy and substitute for it pulseless mechanism is, of course, a moot point, for if machinery cannot be wounded, it is obvious that a gunner is more easily replaceable in action than a broken chain or leaky valve. Fortunate it is for ns that we do not rely alone upon clockwork ships, like those of the Dreadnought and Thunderer class.

Assuredly there is sound common sense in this, and it is applicable to other matters besides ships of war. There is in human nature a tendency to permit religion itself to become mechanical: priests, temples, sacraments, the performing of services, organs, choirs, all go towards the making up of a machine which may do our worship for us, and leave us all our time to think about bread and cheese and the latest fashions. As cranks, pistons, valves, and cylinders take the place of bone and muscle on board ship, so millinery, bellows and ritual take the place of hearts and spirits in the place of worship. Certain outward appliances may be well enough in their place, but they too easily become substitutes for real heart-work and spiritual devotion, and then they are mischievous to the last degree. The preacher may use notes if he needs them, but his manuscript may steal from him that which is the very essence and soul of preaching, and yet his elaborate paper and his elegant reading may conceal from him the nakedness of the land.

Praise may be rendered with musical instruments, if you will; but the danger is lest the grateful adoration should evaporate, and nothing should remain but the sweet sounds. The organ can do no more than help us in noise-making, and it is a mere idol, if we imagine that it increases the acceptance of our praises before the Lord. Outward ordinances may be very properly used, and two of them at least are solemnly enjoined; but human nature is apt to forget the substance in the shadow, and in such a case the good is turned into evil, the road is regarded as the end, and the symbol is made to rival the truth which it sets forth. It were almost better for us to be placed where outward signs were out of reach, provided that the inner fellowship were more valued and more directly sought from the Holy Spirit.

The Lord never intended that religion should be a performance to be done for us, or a business to be carried out by mechanical actions; it is an inward matter and requires the life of love, the vigor of consecration, and the intense energy of zeal.

In the service of the Lord everything should be hearty and voluntary, and nothing should be mechanical and perfunctory. Hireling worship is never worth that which is paid for it. Religion provided by authority and carried on without the choice of the people is a mockery. When the ark was put upon a new cart, we read that "the oxen shook it," and very soon the entire proceedings were marred and stopped by the breach which the Lord made upon Uzzah. The primary fault lay in using bullocks which needed to be driven: the divine ordinance was that the ark should be carried upon the willing shoulders of faithful men, whose honor and privilege it was thus to wait upon the Lord. It was not a service which brute force could properly perform: it needed that chosen bearers should reverently carry the sacred token of Jehovah's presence, praying and praising while they bore along their sacred load. No church can possibly prosper unless its work is carried on by holy, devout, willing men, full of divine life, moving cheerfully in their work because they love it with their whole hearts. The laborer is worthy of his hire, and ought to have it, but he must not labor *for his hire*, but for love of his Master, or else his work will be an abomination in the sight of God. Nothing will ever compensate for personal enthusiasm: this we must have, or the work of the Lord among us will flag. Those who preach or teach as a matter of course, much in the same way as a piston moves, or a valve opens, or a wheel revolves, are not acceptable in the sight of God. "God is a spirit: and they that worship him must worship him in spirit and in truth."

Are we not all in danger of trusting to religious machinery, and leaving the work of the Lord to be done by secretaries, committees, missionaries, and so forth, whom we half regard as substitutes; for ourselves? No doubt they will do the work, and do it tolerably well, as the engines do on board the "Dreadnought"; but if anything is to be accomplished which will last in the day of trial, we must, every one of us, be ready to take our part in the great battle of the Lord. At present the most of professors suppose that a good work is going on, but they do not seem to know how or when; they leave God's work to anybody or nobody. It will be an evil day when the servants of Christ cease to take a *personal* interest in the work of winning souls: societies may come to grief, broken chains and leaky valves will occur in such machinery, and what then? We shall censure our substitutes, but the burden of blame will not thus be shifted. We must all appear before the judgment seat of Christ, and every man must bear his own burden before the Lord.

Fortunate is it for the true church of God that she does not rely upon clockwork service, but through divine grace has at her command faith, love, courage, heroism, and consecration: above all, the Spirit of God dwells in her, and furnishes her with life, wisdom, and strength, so that in the day of battle she will utterly defeat her foes. We see this life and force breaking out in many places in new works for the Lord Jesus, and frequently it takes very irregular forms, greatly to the distress of spiritual Tories, who must have all things cut and dried after the most ancient fashion. We confess that we, also, are somewhat perplexed at certain of the more outrageous forms of religious energy, and we are sorry to see so manifest a tendency to work apart from recognized organizations. We should rejoice to see intense zeal in continuous exercise, in fine order for immediate service, but working daily in the regular service of the church of God. The blue-jackets are just as much under command as the pistons and valves, and so should the living and earnest among us learn discipline, and act in harmony with the churches to which they belong. We want more of those men of Zebulon who were expert in war, *and could keep rank*. But even if there should be occasional irregularity it is better than the monotony of mere mechanism. No doubt the eccentricities of life are sometimes troublesome, but they are nobler than the regularities of dead formality: give us life under law to Christ, and there can be no doubt about it, we shall then have found the noblest form of force—that manifestation of power by which the Holy Spirit delights to work.

21

Homesickness

"When shall I come and appear before God?" (Ps. 42:2).

"By the rivers of Babylon, there we sat down, yea, we wept, when we remembered Zion" (Ps. 137:1).

The *Globe* has a paragraph upon home-sickness worth preserving, and, as the Puritans would say, improving.

> Among minor maladies of the sentimental order is one from which probably a good many of our army-reserve men are suffering more or less severely just now. "Homesickness" is usually regarded as something altogether peculiar to schoolboys. According to Dr. H. Rey, who calls it nostalgia, and who has just written an interesting article on the subject, this is by no means the case. He considers it a form of insanity from which grown men often suffer severely, and of which they sometimes die. He gives particulars of his observations among the French soldiery, where it is of very frequent occurrence, more particularly among the infantry. The cavalry man, he thinks, is less liable to suffer in this way, probably because he has less leisure time on his hands. It is the young foot soldier who is most prone to pine for his native place, and this is pre-eminently the case with the men of Bretagne, among whom he has observed more instances than in those from all parts of France together. The young conscript, he says, becomes gloomy and taciturn, loses his

appetite, is fond of solitude, and often gives way to tears. Then follow evident effects of this upon his general health. He suffers from incessant headache, and is unable to sleep, and after a while, unless he can be aroused and interested in his surroundings and distracted from his dreams of home and friends, gradually becomes the victim of general prostration, followed by delirium, and sometimes by death. Dr. Rey believes that children do not often suffer in this way, nor do very old persons; and women, he has observed, are less liable to it than men, especially men who have been transported from quiet country scenes, town men for the most part forming new associations far more readily than the natives of a country place.

If these men, the most of whom were born in some poor village, by no means remarkable either for architecture or for scenery, pine for their homes, how much more may those who have a mansion above, a house not made with hands, eternal in the heavens. Born from above, our native country is heaven itself and sometimes the longing to be there steals over us. It is no insanity, but it is a panting which the ungodly cannot comprehend. We grow weary of the temptations, the disquietudes, and the failures of earth, and sigh for the fair city within whose gates there shall never enter anything that defileth: our heart goes out towards the Lord Jesus, who is altogether lovely, and then we pant for the day when we shall see the King in his beauty, and the land that is very far off. The more we love, the more we long to be with the object of our affection. It is not that we are miserable here below, for godliness hath the promise of the life which now is, and we have foretastes of glory even now; but still the Father's house is very dear to the loving child, and the sight of the heavenly Bridegroom is longed for by his expectant spouse. When shall the marriage supper be set, and the guests be invited? It seems a long and weary time since he went up to prepare a place for us. Has he not finished that work ere this, and will he not soon come according to his promise to receive us unto himself, that where he is there we may be also? It is no marvel if a believer has to describe himself as Samuel Rutherford did, as "a man often borne down and hungry, and waiting for the marriage supper of the Lamb." Very naturally do saintly souls sing—

> With hope deferr'd, oft sick and faint,
>   "Why tarries he?" I cry:
> Let not the Savior chide my haste,
>   For then would I reply:
>
> "May not an exile, Lord, desire
>   His own sweet land to see?
> May not a captive seek release,
>   A prisoner to be free?
>
> A child, when far away, may long
>   For home and kindred dear;
> And she that waits her absent lord
>   May sigh till he appear.
>
> Ah, leave me not in this base world,
>   A stranger still to roam;
> Come, Lord, and take me to thyself,
>   Come, Jesus, quickly come!"

Do my readers confess that such a feeling never affects them? Does that homesickness never come over you at all? Let the fact cause you great searchings of heart, for surely something is amiss. Have you a home above? Are you quite sure? If so, if you never sigh to enter it, are you not rooting yourself too closely to the world? "Ah," said one, when he looked upon a friend's house and gardens, "these are the things that make us loth to die!" Wealth, or even moderate comfort, will often act like birdlime and hold the birds of Paradise prisoners to carnal joys. When the nest is well lined men do not wish to quit it; they dread the very thought of dying, and have no desire to depart and to be with Christ. It should not be so: if this world of vanity seems better to you than the realm of glory, your judgment is diseased, and the carnal nature is sadly hindering the aspirations of the divine life.

Still, we may not allow home-sickness to unfit us for present duty, or cause us in any way to desert our colors. *It is wrong to pine to be in heaven because we are growing idle.* A laborer who is always longing for Saturday night, or watching for the time to leave off work, is a sorry specimen of the British workman;

a gardener was overheard to say that the days were not long enough for him, for so much needed doing. This was more like the true spirit; but there are not many of his stamp. Many do as little as ever they can, and would welcome any sort of excuse for seceding from the busy throng, and living for ever with Lord Do-no-more.

Of the service of our great Master it is wicked to grow weary. Because we are not successful in preaching, or because we cannot win every child in our Sunday school class to Jesus, shall we become sluggards, and sigh for the wings of a dove that we might fly away and be at rest? While there are souls to be won for Jesus here below by our means we are not wanted in heaven, nor should we be welcome there if we could go. We should evidently be out of sympathy with the heavenly host, who never indulge the thought of escaping from their Master's service. Shall heaven be a rendezvous for runaways, a shelter for idle heads? Is it not written that the glorified serve the Lord day and night in his temple? How would this suit the deserter? He dreams of flowery mounts and seas of heavenly rest, but there are no such things in heaven or earth for those who are unfaithful to their Lord. Did Jonah find rest when he fled from the presence of the Lord to go unto Tarshish? Did he not many a time wish himself at Nineveh rather than in the depths of the sea? As long as there are poor people to be comforted, ignorant children to be instructed, desponding spirits to be lifted up, so long as God has any work for us to do, let us stand to our guns and never dream of going home.

Neither may we whine out a desire to go to heaven because we are in a spiritual pet. There are some who do this; they become sulky and disagreeable with everybody and everything. Nothing suits them; the church, which appears to others warmhearted, they denounce as having neither love nor life in it; and the service, in which others find pleasure, has grown flat, stale, and unprofitable to them. The world is a howling wilderness to them, and they take care to keep up the howling themselves; the church is cold and lifeless, and they seem anxious to be in their own souls fair samples of it, and then they cry, "Woe is me," and wring their hands and wish to be gone. They prognosticate terrible calamities, and to save their own skins they pray it may not be in their days, but that they may be taken from the evil to come. Worse than this, they even quarrel with their Lord. They have served him these many years, and yet he has never given them a kid that they may make merry with their friends; they rebel against their afflictions, and, by kicking against the pricks, they drive the goad further into their flesh, and then sigh to be gone from this weary world. Like naughty little children, who will not play anymore because they cannot have everything their own way, they want to leave the engagements of life and go they scarce know whither. If we are homesick for this reason, we may depend upon it that we shall not at present go home to heaven, for we are not in a fit state for that holy region. They do not want rebellious spirits and sulky souls up yonder, for there the will of the Lord is the joy of all his servants.

When faith and love and hope produce the feeling, it is well to be in a strait betwixt two, willing to depart, but yet feeling that to abide in the flesh is more needful for the good of some whom we would benefit for Christ's sake. It is the sign of a right state of heart when this home-sickness comes upon us, not because we are tired, nor because we are angry, but simply because we long to be rid of infirmity and imperfection, because we desire to escape from temptation and from the filthy conversation of the wicked, that we may see the face of our Lord, and bow before his glorious majesty. In such a spirit we may cry with Rutherford—"O when will we meet? Glorious Lord Jesus take wide steps! O, my Lord, come over the mountains with a stride! O, fairest among the sons of men, why stayest thou so long away? O heavens, move fast! O time, run, run, and hasten the marriage day!"

22

Religious Sluggards

"Their nobles put not their necks to the work of their Lord" (Neh. 3:5).

"Slothfulness casteth into a deep sleep" (Prov. 19:15).

"Let us not sleep, as do others" (1 Thess. 5:6).

An American paper has the following in its corner of wit and anecdote: "A Sunday-school boy at Maysville, Ky., was asked by the superintendent the other day if his father was a Christian. 'Yes, sir,' he replied, 'but he is not working at it much.'"

In too many cases the same statement might be made, for multitudes have a name to live and are dead, and the love of many has waxed cold. Religion is a profession with them, but it is not accompanied by practice. Now, of all pursuits in the world the Christian profession requires the most energetic action, and it utterly fails where diligence and zeal are absent. What can a man do as a farmer, a merchant, a carpenter, or even as a beggar unless he follows up his calling with activity and perseverance? A sluggard desireth and hath nothing, whatever his trade may be. What then can he hope to win who calls himself a Christian and neither learns of Christ as his teacher, nor follows him as his Master, nor serves him as his Prince? Salvation is not by works, but it is salvation from idleness; we are not saved because we are earnest; but he who is not earnest has great reason to question whether he is saved.

Do you know a Christian who never attends week-day services, and only comes to public worship once on the Sunday? "He is not working at it much."

Do you know a professor who is not engaged in the Sabbath School, the Visiting Society, the Tract Association, or in any other form of usefulness? "He is not working at it much." Do you know a man who gives little or nothing to the work of the Lord, neglects family prayer, never says a word for Jesus, and never intercedes for perishing souls? "He is not working at it much." Perhaps he is the best judge of his religion and does not think it worth being diligent about. We heard of one who said his religion did not cost him a shilling a year, and a friend observed that he thought it was more than it was worth; and in the present case we may conclude that a man's religion is a very poor affair when "he does not work at it much."

Our Lord does not set before us the Christian life as a dainty repose, but as a warfare and a struggle. He bids us "strive to enter in at the strait gate," and never suggests to us that we can enter into his rest if we are not willing to wear his yoke. Faith saves us, but it is the faith which worketh by love; all our salvation is wrought in us by the Lord both as to willing and doing, but yet we are to work it out with fear and trembling; which also by his grace we will henceforth do.

> Sure I must fight if I would reign;
>   Increase my courage, Lord!
> I'll bear the toil, endure the pain,
>   Supported by thy word.

23

The Withering of Unbelief

"Let them all be confounded and turned back that hate Zion. Let them be as the grass upon the housetops, which withereth afore it groweth up: wherewith the mower filleth not his hand; nor he that bindeth sheaves his bosom" (Ps. 129:5–7).

"Nothwithstanding the humidity of the season, the grass crop on Wandsworth Bridge will not be submitted to tender this year." This witty paragraph, taken from the *South London Press*, an interesting local paper, of May 25, refers to a bridge upon which there is little traffic. Of course the grass will not be mown, for it has no depth of earth to grow upon, and is of no value.

The text which we hare quoted here finds an illustration. It is true a bridge is not a house-top, but in scantiness of soil it is much the same. The opponents of the gospel are very numerous, but they never come to anything; they are always confounded before they can well establish their theories. Various orders of infidels have sprung up suddenly, and have almost as suddenly disappeared, and even those which have endured for a longer season have ultimately passed away, leaving scarcely any memorial behind them. Unbelief is an unhealthy and unsatisfactory plant; there is nothing in it; it yields neither seed for the sower nor bread for the eater; it is not even good enough to fodder the cattle with; the very lowest of mankind find it unsatisfactory meat. Rationalists should never be too confident of their favorite scheme, for it is only one of a long series of short-lived weeds, and will be sure to wither before long and to be denounced by some other order of advanced thinkers. Infidelity like Canaan of old under the Hivites and the Jebusites, is a land which eateth up the inhabitants thereof. Skepticism derives most of its life from opposition, it has no natural stamina, and is rather a negative than a real existence. Little cause can there be for the citizens of Zion to be afraid of such adversaries; instead of dismay we may even breathe defiance. "The virgin daughter of Zion hath despised thee, and laughed thee to scorn; the daughter of Jerusalem hath shaken her head at thee." It were well if this sacred confidence were more common among us; for it is to be deplored that, as each crop of the housetop grass of unbelief springs up, much unjustifiable alarm is manifested, and this does most of the mischief. There is really no cause to fear things so essentially feeble and self-destructive as systems of unbelief. The wooden guns of the Chinese are not more ridiculous than the philosophies of infidels.

> Ashamed they fly, they start aloof,
>   Each foe of Sion flies;
> They are as grass upon the roof,
>   That ere th' uprooting dies;
>
> Where no glad store may reaper find
>   To fill his gathering hand,
> Nor high their bosom heap, who bind
>   The sheaves in wreathed band.
>
> Where never traveler as he past,
>   Did prayer or greeting frame,
> Or say, "God's blessing o'er thee last
>   We bless you in God's name."

24

Sympathy

"Touched with the feeling of our infirmities" (Heb. 4:15).

"The king also himself passed over the brook Kidron" (2 Sam. 15:23).

"The queen and Mr. Bright.—Yesterday Her Majesty the Queen sent from Windsor Castle a telegraphic message to Rochdale, expressing her deep sympathy with Mr. John Bright in the irreparable bereavement he is now sustaining. Mr. Bright acknowledged Her Majesty's kind consideration."—*Daily News*, May 15.

It is thought to be a great honor to receive royal sympathy; how much greater to enjoy continually the sympathy of the King of kings! Our Lord whose diadem was made of thorns has secret ways of communing with his tried servants, and assuring them that in all their afflictions he is afflicted. A mysterious telegraph works between the courts above and the mourner here below, and the message is quietly sent—"When thou passest through the waters I will be with thee."

No doubt the fact that the Queen herself has experienced a never-to-be-forgotten bereavement has made her heart tender towards those who suffer in like manner; she understands the sadness of a lonely heart through having lost the well-beloved partner of her life. We all of us learn sympathy by being made familiar with suffering. The same truth holds good in the higher sphere of the perfect human nature of our Lord Jesus Christ. He was in this respect made perfect through suffering, and consequently he hastens to send by his Spirit assurances of sympathy to all his afflicted people, assurances which shall be a sacred balm for their sorrows, and 'cause them to find a honeyed sweetness in their caps of gall.

> There is no heart like the heart of Jesus,
>   Filled with a tender lore:
> Not a throb or throe our hearts can know,
>   But he suffered before.

How greatly these kindly deeds of her Majesty tend to secure the loyalty of her subjects and to set her on high in the estimation of her people. Thoughtful people are not fascinated by the pomp of royalty, they look to the character of the monarch, and are far more charmed by generous acts than by diamonds and gold. Our own Lord and King above is exceeding glorious, but his conquering glory lies in his superlative love and matchless tenderness. He hath remembered our souls in adversity, and therefore is he very glorious in our eyes; we praise him without ceasing because he abounds towards us in lovingkindness, and his mercy endureth forever.

> Let his dear love our hearts inflame,
>   That perfect love which faileth never;
> And sweet Hosannas to His name
>   Through Heaven's vast dome go up for ever!

25

Benefit of Trial

"Patience worketh experience, and experience, hope" (Rom. 5:4).

"Thy servant slew both the lion and the bear: and this uncircumcised Philistine shall be as one of them" (1 Sam. 17:36).

The *Times*, May 23rd, says:

> Experiments are to be resumed at Shoeburyness for the purpose of gaining information as to the penetrative power of steel and wrought-iron projectiles and the resistance of specially prepared targets. Some of the results already obtained have produced most unexpected and surprising experiences, the most remarkable being found during a trial of a composite steel and iron target. When fired against the steel face of the target, the projectiles broke up badly, but when the target was reversed the shot not only penetrated the softer wrought iron, but went clean through the steel as well. This is theoretically accounted for by the supposition that in passing through the wrought iron the metal of the projectile gets set up in a more compact body, and is therefore better able to endure the shock of the heavier impact.

If this theory be correct, it is clear that passing through one form of opposition prepares the projectile to pass through a yet sterner one; and here we have an illustration of the beneficial influence of affliction upon the child of God. He is materially strengthened by the trials through which he passes; he is braced up, consolidated, and, in a right sense, hardened by what he undergoes. If the believer had to meet at first the severest of his troubles, like the shot striking upon the steel face of the target, he might be unequal to the task; but those trials which he has already undergone, like the shot's passage through the iron, are so arranged by providence that they harden him for those which are to follow. We should naturally have thought that the shot would lose its force in passing through the wrought iron, and so we might have imagined that believers would lose their strength and patience while enduring a series of troubles; but instead thereof, as the projectile by its passage through the iron is prepared to pass through the steel, go the earlier trials of the believer render him capable of enduring those which are yet more terrible. Sanctified trials are not our destruction but our instruction, not our breaking but our making.

There are great wonders in the material world, and there are equal marvels in the spiritual world. Only by experiment do the gunners at Shoeburyness come to understand the results of their science, and only by experience can believers understand the influence of trials when God sanctifies them by his grace. Often are the engineers surprised by their discoveries, and even more often is this the case with experimental Christians. It would seem possible to drive a shot through anything whether it be iron or steel, and so all things are possible to him that believeth; yet the projectile can do most when it has become most compact, and so can the believer when he is most consolidated by trial. A hard target can be penetrated by a still harder shot, and when we meet with great difficulties we must pray for a great heart; firm opposition must be overcome by a firm will, and hard trials by a harder resolve. Perhaps we shall never reach this state of compacted manhood except by stern adversity: we shall not be able to face the Philistine until we have first slain both the lion and the bear. Weapons intended for stern battles must be annealed in the fire; guns must go to the proof-house before they are trusted in action, and vessels which are to ride Atlantic billows must bear many a thousand blows from the hammer before they are launched. In all bur trials, when truly sanctified, growth is the result, and by bearing we learn to bear more. Through affliction patience must have her perfect work, that we may be perfect and entire, wanting nothing.

26

Watching

"We made our prayer unto our God, and set a watch against them day and night" (Neh. 4:9).

"I will stand upon my watch" (Hab. 2:1).

"Behold, I come as a thief. Blessed is he that watcheth, and keepeth his garments" (Rev. 16:15).

The *Daily News*, May 27, in speaking of the border countries, says:

> Every parish and township in old times had its watchers of the forts and passes. In the *Leges Marchiaram*, compiled by William Nicholson, Bishop of Carlisle, we can read the names of the fords and the appointed sentinels. "First, the watch along the water of Warn, from Warn-mouth to Doxford Burn, William Maners to set one watchman between his house and the Blake dyke," and so forth. The statesman had to keep a keen eye on the beacon where the fire shone out, when the Scots or Armstrongs crossed the march. "And whosoever bydes from the fray, or turns again while the beaken burns, shall be holden as partaker to the enemies." Then there was quick mounting on horse, tufts of lighted straw were fastened on the spearheads, and the slot dogs were set on the trail.

In this manner alone could the inhabitants of the border hold their lands or even their lives, and their condition is a striking picture of the spiritual position of every child of God while yet he sojourns here below. We are in an enemy's country, and that enemy may at any moment pounce upon us to kill and to despoil. We never know at what hour temptation may come, hence we must sleep in armor, and never neglect the watch for a single hour. Each man must watch his own heart, and keep the door of his lips, for it is written, "What I say unto you I say unto all, Watch."

United watchfulness for the protection of the church, as to its purity, its doctrines, its prosperity, should never be neglected, although it is to be feared that it is seldom thought of. Few seem to keep their eyes open to the general good of the church, but most men leave it to the ministers. It should not be so, but each man should himself be the "watchman between his house and the Blake dyke," pacing to and fro upon his beat, with sleepless vigilance, ready to sound an alarm at any moment. When the enemy draws near, believers should never "byde" from the fray, but each one should take his part in the struggle, like a good soldier of Jesus Christ: and so long as the controversy lasts he must not shun the field, or turn again "while the beacon burns," lest he be "holden as partaker with the enemies." This is a time in which sentinels are peculiarly necessary, and in which sleeping at the post is a seven-fold treachery. "Let us not sleep as do others, but let us watch and be sober." The love of peace throws many off their guard. They close their eyes to the errors and sins which are invading the church, and so secure a name for being *charitable*, but surely it is ill to receive praise for negligence, and obtain favor by compromising truth. If damage be done by our fear of being charged with bigotry, our Lord will call us to account, and it will be a poor consolation to be able to remember that we thereby earned the praises of men. It is no recommendation to a warrior when the king's enemies are enraptured with him, and in our own case f here is double reason to watch our ways when the world speaks well of us. Watch your friends as well as your enemies, for our worst foes dwell at home.

> Watch, for the time is short;
>   Watch, while 'tis called to-day;
> Watch, lest temptation overcome;
>   Watch, Christian, watch and pray!

Watch, for the flesh is weak;
    Watch, for the foe is strong;
Watch, lest the Bridegroom knock in vain;
    Watch, though He tarry long!

Chase slumber from thine eyes;
    Chase doubting from thy breast;
Thine is the promised prize
    Of heaven's eternal rest.

Watch, Christian, watch and pray;
    Thy Savior watched for thee,
Till from His brow the blood-sweat poured
    Great drops of agony.

27

Moore's Remonstrance

"Should such a man as I flee?" (Neh. 6:11).

"He that endureth to the end shall be saved" (Matt. 10:22).

On Tuesday, May 28th, Earl Russell died. In biographical notices given by most of the papers allusion is made to the proposition of Lord John Russell to retire from public life while yet a young man in consequence of some serious discouragement which he had received. It is stated that he was deterred from so doing by the expostulations of Thomas Moore, and quotations are made from the "Remonstrance" which that sparkling poet addressed to him. On reading the poem it struck us at once that many of the remarks would apply in other and higher senses to any Christian who should be tempted to withdraw himself from the service of his Lord. The first three verses of the poem we will quote at length:

> What *thou*, with thy genius, thy youth, and thy name—
>   Thou, born of a Russell—whose, instinct to run
> The accustom'd career of thy sires, is the same
>   As the eaglet's to soar with his eyes on the sun!
>
> Whose nobility comes to thee, stamp'd with a seal
>   Far, far more ennobling than monarch e'er set,
> With the blood of thy race, offer'd up for the weal
>   Of a nation, that swears by that martyrdom yet!

> Shalt *thou* be faint-hearted and turn from the strife,
>   From the mighty arena where all that is grand
> And devoted, and pure, and adorning in life,
>   'Tis for high-thoughted spirits like thine to command?

Born from above, and bearing the name of Christian, shall the child of God cease to battle for that which is good? Conscious of a sacred instinct which impels him onward and upward, shall he sit down in despair or retire into inglorious ease? Serving a Lord who spared not his heart's blood for man's redemption, and following in the track of thousands of martyrs who counted not their lives dear unto them, shall we selfishly shun self-denial and avoid reproach? No, by God's grace, let us never dream of timorous silence, nor think for an instant that our light can be spared from the darkening horizon of our times. We may have neither eloquence nor genius, but such as we have we will consecrate to the last moment of our lives to him who hath bought us by his precious blood. We may address to every timorous heart the closing verse of Tom Moore, altered to suit the case.

> Thus ransomed, thou never canst sleep in the shade;
>   If the stirrings of impulse, the terror of fame,
> And the charms of thy cause have not power to persuade,
>   Yet think how to Jesus thou'rt pledged by thy name.

He who wears the name of Christian is sworn to sustain the cause of God and truth with the last drop that warms his veins.

28

H. C. Wants Money

"Be began to be in want" (Luke 15:14).

"The Lord is my Shepherd; I shall not want" (Ps. 23:1).

The *Times*, of May 29, has the following advertisement: "H. C. Wants Money." So do a great many more, but everybody does not publish the fact, for it would not alter it to make it known. We suppose that H. C. has some person in his eye who will read the advertisement, and send on the ready cash; and if so, it is very wise on his part to make his need known. There is a secret understanding between H. C. and some unknown friend, and these few words will be understood by the person to whom they are addressed. It is a happy circumstance for all believers that they also can make known their requests with certainty that there is One who will supply their needs. "Be careful for nothing; but in everything by prayer and supplication with thanksgiving let your requests be made known unto God." Our petitions will be understood by our Father who seeth in secret, for he has appointed prayer to be the means of communicating with himself. H. C. would be very foolish not to advertise if by so doing his poverty can be supplied: is it not the height of folly to restrain prayer before God? Who would not ask, when it is written—"Ask and ye shall receive"?

"H. C. wants money." Of this he seems to be well aware; but there is another deeper and more pressing want which belongs to all men, and yet very few persons appear to be conscious of it. The great want of the soul is Christ: to obtain an interest in Jesus and his salvation is the one thing needful, but men let this go and put a very secondary matter into its place: hence H. C. wants money, and all the other letters of the alphabet want this also. Money is called by many "the needful," and the getting of it is styled "minding the main chance." Many men will continue to want money to the end of the chapter; but he who wants grace may have it for the asking. Happy are we that in spiritual things our wants are already supplied in Christ Jesus, and no man need long advertise that he wants grace. It would, however, be a happy sign if we could hear that H. C. and millions more were earnest in declaring that they want mercy.

"H. C. wants money." How comes he to want it? Has he been spending too freely, or is he out of a situation, or does he lie sick? If he wants money, and is in good health, why does he not earn it himself? Why does he degrade himself by begging? A host of questions arise, which it would not be easy to answer. When we are in want of necessary temporal things we should ask ourselves the reason why; for often we may be helped to shape our course by the answer which truth compels us to give. God has usually some design when he allows us to suffer poverty. Birds and beasts are tamed and trained by hunger, and men are instructed by their wants. May H. C. become a wiser and a better man through being in present need, and whenever we are in a like case may our want of money make us rich.

"H. G. wants money." Possibly his desires need cutting down, and if he could be contented with what he has his wants would vanish. We know many whose means are very slender, whose property might all be tied up in a handker-chief, and yet they do not want, for they live upon the perpetual supplies of the Great Lord of providence, and they hear him saying, "Trust in the Lord and do good; so shalt thou dwell in the land, and verily thou shalt be fed." True riches belong to those who have God for their portion. Between the words *God* and *Gold* there is but little difference in letters, but an infinite difference in sense. Gold in millions can never fill the heart of man, but God is able to make the heart supremely blessed even when no outward possessions are within reach. Reader, do not be a gold worshipper, "for the love of money is the root of all evil"; be a worshipper of God, for the love of God is the source of all good.

A word in the ear of those who want to make their fortunes. The Bible tells you how your fortune can be made. It will do you good to look out the passage for yourself, especially if you follow its golden advice. See Matthew 6:33.

29

Sinking of the Ironclad

"How are the mighty fallen, and the weapons of war perished" (2 Sam. 1:27).

"Ye see my casting down and are afraid" (Job 6:21).

The newspapers, of June 1st, contained paragraphs similar to the following:

> Three ironclad ships—the Grosser Kurfurst, Koenig Wilhelm, and Preussen, left Wilhelmshafen for Plymouth, on Wednesday night, and were reported off Dover, at 8 a.m. on Friday morning, May 31st. The weather was calm and a slight wind blowing, when about five miles due south of Sandgate Castle, the Koenig Wilhelm ran into the Grosser Kurfurst and sank her. The ship went down in a few seconds with the larger part of her crew.

We mourn over this sudden wreck and the dreadful loss of life, and then we take breath and moralize. Peace has its dangers as well as war. No enemy had ever fired a shot at the huge ironclad, but it perished by a friend, and that not by treachery but by pure mischance. There was scarcely a ripple upon the waters, but the smoothness of the sea did not secure the proud vessel from sinking into the deep; the air was clear, the accident was not occasioned by a fog, but no result came from this circumstance except that the destruction was the more visible to the astonished spectators. Thus too have men who seemed capable of great deeds perished before our eyes by the hand of one of their own comrades, and that not by wicked intent but by an unwise movement never meant to involve such ruin. A hasty word has been spoken, evil feelings have been aroused, and the injured man has no longer been numbered with the professing people of God. We never dreamed that such a result could happen, and yet it has occurred when all has been apparently going well: there has been no persecution, no heresy, no schism, but the man has been offended, and has passed away. It seemed as if none could injure the ironclad professor, and yet in an instant he has ceased to be a member of the squadron. We have looked on awe-stricken as we have seen the apparently sound professor suddenly sink in the deep waters of sin never to be heard of again.

Keep us, O Lord, yea, keep us every moment, lest we come to an untimely end. Even in the company of our own brethren we are in danger unless thou thyself shalt be on board our vessel and preserve it from itself.

There is another aspect of this occurrence which has somewhat impressed us. This was the "German Squadron of Evolution;" fit name, and fit country to remind us of the school of modern-thought who proudly float upon our seas at this time and threaten the peace of our churches. These philosophers are all ironclads, and cannot be touched by the heaviest guns of those poor simple souls who believe in the Bible and its plenary inspiration. Nevertheless we need not fear them, for happily they destroy one another, and that very readily, as if they were created on purpose for this and nothing else. A little change in the steering and they ram each other to the bottom. As it was of old so is it now, "the children of Ammon and Moab stood up against the inhabitants of Mount Seir, utterly to slay and destroy them: and when they had made an end of the inhabitants of Seir, every one helped to destroy another." One school of unbelief effectually sweeps away another. So let it be. In perfect peace the true believer may, "stand still and see the salvation of God." Already over scores of ironclad infidelities we may sing, "the depths have covered them, they sank into the bottom, like a stone."

The fishing boats in the neighborhood of the huge monitors did admirable service by rescuing many of the drowning sailors, and so may true-hearted men hover around the huge infidelities of the period, and snatch here and there a sinking doubter from destruction. It would be idle for smacks and luggers to attack an ironclad; they can far better distinguish themselves by coming to the rescue in the hour of distress; and in the same way simple-minded believers, who know nothing of controversy, can do a vast amount of service by bringing salvation to those who are ready to perish. Let us not argue, but let us love. We will not confront the skeptical with reasoning, but, by God's Spirit, we will save them by the gospel and by believing prayer.

30

Test for Diamonds

"The Lord trieth the righteous" (Ps. 11:5).

"Try my reins and my heart" (Ps. 26:2).

The following letter suggests thought:

To the Editor of the Times.

Sir—Already a panic seems to have been created by the report in the *Times* of today of frauds in connection with imitation jewelry and diamonds known as the "Waterkloof." It may allay much misapprehension if those of your readers who have recently purchased diamonds of which they have any doubt would submit them to a very simple test—viz., the file. By drawing across the surface of any imitation diamond a small steel file, an effect is produced as highly detrimental to the spurious as it is satisfactory to the genuine article. To the uninitiated no better test presents itself.

Your obedient servant,
F. W. Streeter.
New Bond Street, June 6.

True faith in God is a gem more precious than the diamond, but alas, among his many inventions, man has found out how to imitate faith, and he has done it so well that to the external observer it is difficult to tell the spurious article from the faith of God's elect. It can however be known by trial, and the great owner of all the true faith in the world is very careful to apply fitting tests in due time. So sure is he to put all grace to the proof that experienced men have made bold to say that untried faith is not faith at all.

Sometimes the small steel file which the Lord uses is *the preaching of the word*. Searching doctrines unpalatable to the unrenewed mind are brought forward, and the mere pretender is offended. Our Lord on one occasion uttered certain hard sayings, and the file operated so effectually that many went back and walked no more with him: but his true disciples did not go away, for they said "To whom shall we go? Thou hast the words of eternal life." The preaching of a faithful minister will act as a file discerning between the true and the false, as it is written, "If thou take forth the precious from the vile, thou shalt be as my mouth."

False doctrine acts in an opposite way, but with the same result. The superficial professor, whose knowledge is altogether of the head is carried away with plausible arguments and bewitching words, while the man who is taught of God rejects falsehood with prompt decision. The evil teachers of the age would, if it were possible, deceive even the very elect, and as this is not possible, the elect remain in their steadfastness, and the mere pretenders are driven hither and thither.

The file of *persecution*, which was more largely used in ages past, is still in its measure employed by the great discerner of spirits. Under biting sarcasms and cutting jests, base-born professors soon show that they are made of yielding stuff; their piety is scratched and defaced, and they cease to be numbered among the jewels of the Lord: on the other hand, true faith "endureth all things," and even derives benefit from that which is so detrimental to the hypocrite. The more the genuine child of God is reproached and despised the more docs he shine with the brightness of the terrible crystal, and the more fully is he recognized by the eyes of the watchers, and the holy ones, as being precious in the sight of the Lord.

The *common temptations of life* are another file, and in the hand of God serve valuable purposes as tests. The cares of this world, the deceitfulness of riches, the passions of the flesh, and the suggestions of Satan, soon detect the paste gem, while none of these things operate to the destruction of the real diamond of God. He is of a nature which through divine grace defies the file; he cannot sin, because he is born of God; the evil one toucheth him not. An inward loathing of iniquity, a fear of himself, and a watchfulness wrought in him by the Holy Spirit, enable the Christian to resist the assaults of temptation, and to come off more than conqueror. "This is the victory that overcometh the world, even our faith."

The ordinary trials of daily life suffice to detect the counterfeit faith of some men. So far from "resisting unto blood striving against sin," they are not able to endure losses and crosses of the most ordinary kind; but the rebellion of their heart is displayed, and they cast off their pretended allegiance to God because they think that he deals hardly with them. Not so the true believer; he endureth trial, for "many are the afflictions of the righteous, but the Lord delivereth him out of them all"; and his beauty is not marred by his adversities, but he comes from under the file altogether unscathed.

Death will operate terribly upon all the imitation jewelry of false religion, utterly destroying its luster and discovering its worthlessness. The nearness of eternity to the ungodly turns his doubt into despair; apprehension of judgment causes the faith of the hypocrite to give way, and his hope is crushed and utterly ruined; and yet this self-same ordeal only serves to perfect the adamantine solidity of the faith of God's truly regenerate ones. Some of the brightest flashes of the Lord's jewels are seen in the darkest hour, and their reality and infinite worth are proven in the presence of the solemnities of eternity. Then doth the Lord discern between him that feareth him and him that feareth him not. Exulting songs of triumph stand out in solemn contrast to the trembling and alarm of the detected formalist.

Do any of our readers question their salvation? Do they desire that their apprehensions may be allayed? Let them apply the file of *self-examination*. Taking the word of God in their hand, and observing carefully the marks and evidences of the child of God, let them see if their spot is the spot of God's children. Let them enquire whether their faith is resting alone upon the blood and merits of the Lord Jesus Christ; whether it is simple and undivided, having no lingering or hankering after legal hope and carnal confidence. Let them examine whether their faith works by love and purifies the soul; whether it leads them to desire communion with God, and likeness to him, and whether it enables them to seek the glory of the Most High rather than their own selfish ends and aims. Such questions as these will be like the use of the file, and will soon discover the stuff which we are made of. "Examine yourselves," says the apostle, "whether ye be in the faith; prove your own selves. Know ye not your own selves, how that Jesus Christ is in you, except ye be reprobates?"

No man should hesitate to apply this file with solemn earnestness; if he dreads the test, his hesitation may suggest a solemn suspicion to his heart. Are you afraid to try yourselves? It is more than probable that you have grave cause for the fear. But are you willing to be tested, and, lest your own test should be insufficient, do you cry, "Search me, O God, and know my heart, try me, and know my thoughts, and see if there be any wicked way in me, and lead me in the way everlasting"? Then the very desire to be searched by the omniscient God may foster the comfortable conviction that you are sincere in heart. Blessed is he who in answer to his Master's question, "Lovest thou me?" can answer with Simon, son of Jonas, "Yea, Lord, thou knowest all things, thou knowest that I love thee."

31

A Path Strewn with Blessings

"I will save you, and ye shall be a blessing" (Zech. 8:13).

"When the ear heard me, then it blessed me; and when the eye saw me, it gave witness to me: because I delivered the poor that cried and the fatherless, and him that had none to help him" (Job 29:11, 12).

The *Sussex Daily News*, of June 6th, has the following quotation and remark: "'The path of a Pope must be strewn with blessings.' Such is the neat and appropriate sentiment attributed to Leo XIII."

So far as the history of a Pope has come under our own observation it has rather been strewn with curses than with blessings. Pio Nono (Pius IX) at any rate appeared to be exceedingly voluble when delivering a tirade, and could fulminate an anathema as neatly and appropriately as any other dealer in strong language. Happily we have reason to believe that his denunciations were not much more effectual than his benedictions. If either the one or the other had any effect at all it would appear to have operated by the rule of contrary: for those whom he cursed most prospered best, and those whom he blessed had cause to cry "save us from our friend." We believe that as a matter of fact his fulminations were so barren of all results that we may apply to them the lines of "Ingoldsby Legends," which describe the cardinal in his great red hat when he had lost his costly turquoise ring:

> The Cardinal rose with a dignified look,
>   He call'd for his candle, his bell, and his book!

> In holy anger and pious grief,
>> He solemnly cursed the rascally thief!
> He cursed him at board, he cursed him in bed;
>> From the sole of his foot to the crown of his head;
> He cursed him in sleeping, that every night
>> He should dream of the devil, and wake in a fright;
> He cursed him in eating, he cursed him in drinking,
>> He cursed him in coughing, in sneezing, in winking;
> He cursed him in sitting, in standing, in lying;
>> He cursed him in walking, in riding, in flying,
> He cursed him in living, he cursed him in dying!
>> Never was heard such a terrible curse!!
> But what gave rise
>> To no little surprise,
> *Nobody seem'd one penny the worse!"*

True, there was a certain thievish jackdaw which began to pine and lose its feathers, but we do not believe that Pio Nono ever managed to injure even a sparrow or a spider with his bulls and excommunications.

Let us hope that Leo XIII intends to abound in benisons, but even if he does so we suspect that nobody will seem one penny the better. However it will be all the better for Leo himself if he will learn to lie down with the lamb.

If from the quotation we take out the word "Pope," and write "Christian," the sentiment will be more neat and appropriate than ever—"The path of a Christian must be strewn with blessings." God has blessed him unspeakably in Christ Jesus, and he should therefore bless God with all his heart and soul. The promise is "I will bless thee, and thou shalt be a blessing," and every child of believing Abraham should endeavor to be a blessing to all those that are round about him, according to that ancient covenant promise. Like David, the believer should bless his household; nay, more, like the high priest of old he should bless all the people.

His words should impart the blessing of instruction and his life should confer the blessing of holy example. His private prayers should bring down innumerable blessings from heaven, and his public acts abounding with pity and love should bless the poor and needy of earth. The sick, the afflicted, and the desponding should hail his presence, and find in him a tender friend. He should go about doing good. As there is a promise that his path like the shining light shall increase in splendor so also should he increase in the warmth and light of love and kindness, bearing life and joy and healing to the sons of men. May the blessed God reveal himself in his blessed people, that in them and in their seed all the nations of the earth may be blessed.

32

The Fickleness of Mankind

"Unstable as water, thou shalt not excel" (Gen. 49:4).

"Surely men of low degree are vanity, and men of high degree are a lie" (Ps. 62:9).

The *Times*, June 10, has the following from its correspondent at St. Petersburg on public opinion in Russia:

> A well-known Russian journalist, who has had abundant opportunities of observing and studying the consecutive changes of public opinion among the educated classes of his countrymen during the last two years, has just published the following results of his observations:—
>
> July, 1876.—Wild enthusiasm. Complete enchantment with the Servians. Desire for war.
>
> October, 1876.—Despondency. Disenchantment with regard to the Servians; hostility towards them, and regret for what has been done for them.
>
> November, 1876.—Enthusiasm for a war in the interest of the Bulgarians. Pity for and sympathy with them.
>
> April, 1877.—Complete ecstasy. Brotherly love for the Bulgarians. Dissatisfaction with the Servians.
>
> August and September, 1877.—Despondency in consequence of failures (before Plevna and elsewhere). Silent irritation against the Bulgarians. Readiness to abandon the whole thing if only a way could be found out of it.

December, 1877.—Intoxication from success. Desire to carry the thing out to the end. Bad feeling towards the Bulgarians.

February. 1878.—Wild delight at the peace and the yielding disposition of Turkey. Sympathy with Turkey and corresponding coolness towards the Bulgarians. Passionate determination to insist on the acquisition of Batoum. Consciousness of the necessity of this acquisition. Indifference to the question of England and Austria.

May, 1878.—Complete disenchantment on the score of the Bulgarians. Suspicions of insincerity on the part of the Turks. Talk about Batoum not being so necessary for us as it had formerly seemed. Something like disgust with the Eastern Question. Talk about getting the thing finished anyhow.

This curious laconic register, though far from complete, is pretty correct so far as it goes.

We insert this as a curious instance of the fickleness of the popular mind. He who lives to win the approbation of the public, even should he gain it, should set but small store by it, for it is as changeful as the wind and altogether as unsubstantial. The multitude one day cried, concerning our Savior, "Hosanna, Hosanna," and before the week was ended they as lustily shouted, "Crucify him, crucify him." The apostles at Lystra found themselves at one moment in danger of being worshipped as gods, but the mistake did not last long, for the people stoned them before the sun had set. The many-headed cry first this thing, and then another: "unstable as water," they rush to extremes. The war upon which they enter with enthusiasm will either close with curses at the bloodshed it has entailed, or else it will end with illuminations intended to welcome the return of peace which they broke with so light a heart.

Let those who pride themselves upon the applause of the multitude see the worthlessness of the mere vapor for which they spend themselves. Blessed is he whose life is ruled by the will of God, and whose highest ambition is acceptance with the Most High through Jesus Christ his Son. His is an immortal and immutable inheritance, a crown of life which fadeth not away. Is the reader living wholly unto God? Then he shall not know the disappointment of those who put their trust in the sons of men, in whom is no strength. But hunters after popularity and aspirants for fame will do well to consider whether the mirage is worth their notice, or the will-o'-the-wisp worthy of their pursuit.

33

Pearls

"No mention shall be made of coral or of pearls: for the price of wisdom is above rubies" (Job 28:18).

"Who, when he had found one pearl of great price, went and sold all that he had, and bought it" (Matt. 13:46).

The Paris correspondent of the *Daily News* of June 11, writes: "The French have grown so clever at imitating pearls, that a jeweler in this Exhibition shows a necklace which purports to be a mixture of true pearls and false, and he challenges his customers to single out the real ones if they can. Nobody had yet succeeded when I myself made an ineffectual attempt." The art of pearl-making is by no means a new discovery; by various methods imitation pearls have been manufactured in various countries for many years. The French have, however, proved themselves superior to all competitors. Specimens of their artificial productions exhibited at the Exposition of 1867 could neither in their luster nor color be distinguished from oriental pearls, even when the genuine and the sham were laid side by side. We are told that there is only one way by which they can be detected, and that is by their specific weight, they are much lighter than the real pearls.

There is "one pearl of great price" about whose genuineness there can never be a question, but all the goodly pearls which this world can yield need to be weighed before we may conclude them to be of any great value; indeed, the choicest pearls of earth are insignificant in price compared with him who is more precious than rubies, and of whom it is written, that "all the things thou canst desire are not to be compared unto him." Even real pearls, the best of them, fit to adorn an emperor's crown, and to heighten the beauty of the fairest of maidens, have been known to sicken and die and vanish in a day. Every now and then we hear of magnificent ancestral pearls, the pride of noble families, turning of a sickly color and crumbling into dust. Not long ago the crown-jeweler of France solemnly applied to the Academy of Science for the means of preventing the decay and corruption of the precious gems in the royal crown. No satisfactory answer was given, and many highly-prized jewels have since then passed away. "Behold, all is vanity and vexation of spirit."

In a work entitled *The Wonders of the Deep*, Maximilian Schele de Vere tells us the following story, of which we leave our readers to draw the moral for themselves:

> A dusky fisherman in the far-off seas of India once found a pearl in an oyster. He had heard of such costly gems, and sold it to an Arab for a gold coin which maintained him for a whole year in luxury and idleness. The Arab exchanged it for powder and shot furnished him by a Russian merchant on board a trading vessel, who even yet did not recognize the dirty, dust-covered little ball as a precious jewel. He brought it home as a present for his children on the banks of the Neva, where a brother merchant saw it and bought it for a trifle. The pearl had at last found one who could appreciate its priceless value, The great man—for it was a merchant of the first class, the owner of a great fortune—rejoiced at the silent fraud by which he had obtained the one pearl of great price, without selling all and buying it fairly, and cherished it as the pride of his heart. Visitors came from all parts of the world to see the wonder. He received them in his merchant's costume in a palace plain without but resplendent inside with all that human art can do to embellish a dwelling, and led them silently through room after room, filled with rare collections and dazzling by the splendor of their ornaments. At last he opened with his own key the carved folding-doors of an inner room which surprised the visitor by its apparent simplicity. The floor, to be sure, was inlaid with malachite and costly marble, the ceiling carved in rare woods, and the walls hung with silk tapestry; but there was no furniture, no gilding, nothing but a

round table of dark Egyptian marble in the center. Under it stood a strong box of apparently wonderful ingenuity, for even the cautious owner had to go through various readings of alphabets, and to unlock one door after another, before he reached an inner cavity, in which a plain square box of Russia leather was standing alone. With an air akin to reverence, the happy merchant would take the box and press it for a moment to his bosom, then devoutly crossing himself and murmuring an invocation to some saint, he would draw a tiny gold key, which he wore next his person, from his bosom, unlock the casket, and hold up his precious pet to the light that fell from a large grated window above.

It was a glorious sight for the lover of such things. A pearl as large as a small egg, of unsurpassed beauty and marvelous luster. The sphere was perfect, the play of colors, as he would let it reluctantly roll from his hands over his long white fingers down on the dark table, was only equaled by the flaming opal, and yet there was a soft, subdued light about the lifeless thing which endowed it with an almost irresistible charm. It was not only the pleasure its perfect form and matchless beauty gave to the eye, nor the overwhelming thought of the fact that the little ball was worth any thing an emperor or a millionaire might choose to give for it—there was a magic in its playful ever-changing sheen as it rolled to-and-fro—a contagion in the rapt fervor with which the grim old merchant watched its every flash and flare, which left few hearts cold as they saw the marvel of St. Petersburg. For such it was, and the Emperor himself, who loved pearls dearly, had in vain offered rank and titles and honors for the priceless gem.

A few years afterwards a conspiracy was discovered, and several great men were arrested. Among the suspected was the merchant. Taking his one great treasure with him, he fled to Paris. Jewelers and amateurs, Frenchmen and foreigners, flocked around him, for the fame of his jewel had long since reached France. He refused to show it for a time. At last he appointed a day when his great rival in pearls, the famous Dutch banker, the Duke of Brunswick, and other men well known for their love of precious stones and pearls, were to behold the wonder. He drew forth the golden key, he opened the casket, but his face turned deadly pale, his eyes started from their sockets, his whole frame began to tremble, and his palsied hand let the casket drop. The pearl was discolored! A sickly blue color had spread over it, and dimmed its matchless luster. His gem was diseased. In a short time it turned into a white powder, and the rich merchant of St Petersburg, the owner of the finest pearl known to the world was a pauper! The pearl had avenged the poor Indian of the East, the Arab, and the poor traveler, and administered silent justice to the purchaser who paid not its price.

34

Safe—Not Saved

"They that are whole have no need of the physician, but they that are sick" (Mark 2:17).

"Thou sayest, I am rich, and increased with goods, and have need of nothing; and knowest not that thou art wretched, and miserable, and poor, and blind, and naked" (Rev. 3:17).

The morning papers of June 13th, contained an account of the suicide of a French nobleman, the Count Aubriet de Pévy, who drowned himself in the Thames. A letter was found in his clothes on the bank, headed "Last Impressions of Count Aubriet." He had resolved to die, the world was but a kind of experimental hell, he hoped for a better world, in which, immediately after, he should appear in an ethereal body. He had great respect for Jesus of Nazareth, but this was the only resurrection. He had a firm belief that he was safe—"saved," was ridiculous.

Count de Pévy has only a little more plainly than usual expressed the sentiment of multitudes. They are so good, so amiable, so religious, that to speak of their being lost appears to them to be a ridiculous misuse of terms; and salvation for them is an insulting superfluity. They are "safe" and need not to be "saved." They thus shut themselves out of all the benefit of the mission of the Savior, since he came to save, and his work has to do with *the lost* and no others. It is pitiful to see a sinner so proud that he bars the door of mercy against himself by his own deliberate act and deed in order to maintain a fictitious claim to personal excellence. Here is a poor soul about to commit the horrible crime of self-murder and yet he calls himself "safe," and ventures to insult the Christ of God by offering him his "respect"—the respect of a suicide. Think of a criminal honoring his judge with a declaration that he respects him! A patient expressing his respect for a physician whose skill he rejects with ridicule! He who feels his guilt and his need of salvation is not content with cold respect, but loves and adores his Savior. O that this poor child of Adam had but seen his real state and had sought after the salvation which he despised. Let him serve as a warning to many who are wrapped in the same deadly daydream. May God arouse them from it, or it will be their ruin. Many are the mighty ones who have fallen down, slain by self-righteousness:

>Though various foes against the Truth combine,
>>Pride above all opposes her design;
>Pride, of a growth superior to the rest,
>>The subtlest serpent with the loftiest crest,
>Swells at the thought, and kindling into rage,
>>Would hiss the cherub Mercy from the stage.

35

Diplomacy & Duplicity

"Not double-tongued" (1 Tim. 3:8).

"Putting away lying, speak every man truth with his neighbor" (Eph. 4:25).

The *Daily News*, June 15th, commenting on the reply of the Chancellor of the Exchequer to a question concerning the Berlin Congress, says: "We seem, in fact, to be gliding into the use of two tongues, one for the ordinary business of life, and one for diplomacy."

Surely this gentleman has forgotten the well-worn description of an ambassador, as a gentleman who is sent abroad to tell lies for the good of his country. Diplomacy from time immemorial has used words rather to conceal its meaning than to express it. In the high quarters where state-craft is carried on, the dictum of George Herbert is utterly rejected—"Dare to be true, nothing can need a lie." Lies seem to be about the most necessary stock-in-trade of the managers of foreign politics. Our book of synonyms has a very suggestive list—"*finesse*, trick, dodge, ruse, diplomacy."

It is earnestly to be hoped that the contagion of political example will not spread through other classes of the community, and yet there is great fear that it has already done so. Among the clergy there has been no little talk of words used in a natural and non-natural sense, and many labored treatises hare been compiled to explain away the self-evident meaning of language. In polite society it used to be customary to deny one's self, and "not at home" was a fashionable mode of lying. This habit has we trust come to an end, but many of the compliments still exacted by etiquette may come under the same censure.

Men who hate each other are full of "My dear Sir," and call themselves "the obedient servants" of persons whom they regard with supreme contempt. These are mere straws, but they show how the wind blows.

However much falsehood may be tolerated by society, it is none the less loathsome to every pure-minded man; and it is not one whit the less abominable in the sight of God because men combine to keep it in countenance. Its most horrible form is seen when professing Christians become double-tongued and have one voice in religion and another voice in common conversation. Who is not disgusted with lips candied with affected love, and yet bitter with malicious hate? It is dreadful to speak like a saint at one time and like a devil at another. We have known persons who have talked so unctuously of divine things in religious meetings that they have won a high repute for godliness out of doors, while at home, under the little provocations of common life, they have habitually stormed and raved, and led their children and servants a sorry life. This thing deserves no quarter. Occasionally we hear of fictitious experience, and listen to wonderful narratives of events which never occurred: this also is execrable.

Actions have as plain a voice as words, and there is a duplicity of life which is quite as evil as verbal falsehood. Many characters are double-tongued. Spence said of Lady Wortley Montague that she was a shining character, "but like a camel she is all irregularity, and always wandering." "He calls her the most wise, most imprudent, loveliest, most disagreeable, best natured, cruelest woman in the world." Other forms of practical contradiction are common; some are intolerantly liberal, others are ferocious advocates of peace, or intemperate upon intemperance. We have known persons who were rashly slow, and imprudently wise. Hot and cold in five minutes. You would think the man to be two persons till you revised your opinion and reckoned him to be nobody at all because one side of his character neutralized the other. Nothing is sadder than to see that things do not tally in a man's character. We have known great pleaders for generosity who were themselves miserably stingy. We have heard of persons who have been wonderful sticklers for "the truth," meaning thereby a certain form of doctrine, and yet they have not regarded the truth in matters of buying and selling, or with regard to the reputations of their neighbors, or the incidents of domestic life. "These things ought not so to be." If by speaking the truth we shame the devil, we must be consistent in it as long as we live, or surely the devil will shame us.

36

Labor in Vain

"The people shall weary themselves for very vanity" (Hab. 2:13).

"By the works of the law shall no flesh be justified" (Gal. 2:16).

The *Daily News*, June 18th, has the following:

> The man in the old legend set out to sail to the happy islands. He encountered many storms, lost many companions, and was worn and weak before he landed, and then he found that he had only come back to his starting point, the island where his home was. He had sailed round the world for that. He was not praised as a navigator or a philosopher.

This legendary personage accurately symbolizes those who start upon the adventurous voyage of salvation-by-self. They are lured onward by a vain imagination, and they enter upon an enterprise which will utterly exhaust them, and bring them no desirable result. In their laborious efforts to discover a righteousness of their own they will see many companions wrecked at their side, and if they themselves are fortunate enough to sail onward along the track of morality, bearing aloft the flag of respectability, they will nevertheless find little comfort therein. If at all enlightened by divine grace they will remain as dissatisfied as ever after all their doings and feelings, worshippings and pleadings and almsgivings; despite their self-reliant diligence they will have made no progress towards the desired haven. Like Vanderdecken in his endless sailings, they are doomed to a fruitless toil. It must be so. Beaten back after all his efforts the moralist makes no headway.

Why is this? Let Scripture answer: Because they seek it not by faith, but as it were by the works of the law. Paul in his day bore witness of many self-righteous persons that they had a zeal for God, but not according to knowledge. "For they being ignorant of God's righteousness, and going about to establish their own righteousness, have not submitted themselves unto the righteousness of God." Successors to these persons are still among us, rolling up-hill the stone of Sisyphus with no more success than he.

The most earnest self-savers will come back to their starting-point disappointed and despairing. What a pity it is that they should be so infatuated as to go far to seek after that which lies so near at hand! The Holy Spirit says, "The word is nigh thee, even in thy mouth, and in thy heart." What can be possibly nearer than that which is absolutely in the mouth? Let no man be so set on mischief, so desperately resolved to destroy his own soul, as to reject that heavenly bread which almighty grace puts into his mouth. Wherefore attempt to climb to heaven or to descend into the deep? Why practice penance or pursue a weary round of ceremonies? Why despond and look within, and argue and despair? Is not the gospel message clear enough? "Believe on the Lord Jesus Christ, and thou shalt be saved."

> Hard lot of man—to toil for the reward
>   Of virtue, and yet lose it! Wherefore hard?—
> He that would win the race must guide his horse
>   Obedient to the customs of the course;
> Else, though unequall'd to the goal he flies,
>   A meaner than himself shall gam the prize.
> Grace leads the right way, if you choose the wrong,
>   Take it and perish, but restrain your tongue;
> Charge not, with light sufficient and left free,
>   Your willful suicide on God's decree.

37

Chaotic Theology

"Desiring to be teachers of the law; understanding neither what they say, nor whereof they affirm" (1 Tim. 1:7).

"Be not carried about with divers and strange doctrines. For it is a good thing that the heart be established with grace" (Heb. 13:9).

A correspondent of the New York *Examiner and Chronicle*, June 20, writing from West Virginia, says:

> Of course, things here are in a measure in a *formative state*—even the capital itself is not regarded as fully and finally located. It is now said to be "on a steamboat somewhere between Wheeling and Charlestown." The last vote of the legislature on it decided the latter place to be the location hereafter.

In much the same condition are the minds of many who claim to be preachers of the gospel of "the advanced school." There is no telling what they say nor whereof they affirm. They believe nothing and therefore they speak. Their creed is in "a formative state"—nebulous, cloudy. They know not what they believe: it is a question whether they believe anything at all. One of them informed us that he held his mind in a receptive condition, and revised his creed every week at the least—a human jelly-fish, or something more gelatinous still. We fear that even the main and fundamental points of the atonement of Christ, and his divine person, are unsettled with some of the Broad School. Their capital is on a steamboat somewhere between Unitarianism and Pantheism. The sooner they fix its location the better. It would probably be less injurious to those around them, if they were to become downright atheists than that they should remain in their present loose and skeptic-making condition. Their manifest indecision for truth is a clear gain to the side of unbelief. These rolling stones in the road cause many to stumble who else would have held on their way. With their cloudy speculations they throw an air of uncertainty over the most settled truths. They cause faith to dwindle into mere opinion and throw thousands into a condition of miserable suspense.

Elijah would long ago have said to them, "How long halt ye between two opinions? If the God of Israel be the Lord, serve him;" and if "cultured thought" is to manufacture a god of its own, finish the article and let us know what it is like. One would think from the talk of some men that the promises of the gospel were made to doubt and not to faith. Their sympathies are all with the infidel, whose doubt is decorated as "honest" and "thoughtful." Their anathemas are reserved for the orthodox, who are always prejudiced, narrow-minded, and stunted. Their charity pours its oil upon all except those horrid beings who adhere to the creed of the Puritans: as for those fellows, they despise them with all the Cavalier's contempt for psalm-singing Roundheads. Nevertheless, we pray for all true brethren, that the God of all grace may stablish and settle them, and we desire to be numbered with those who can say, "We believed, therefore have we spoken." "That which we have seen and heard declare we unto you."

38

Want of Stamina

"Ye did run well; who did hinder you?" (Gal. 5:7).

"If thou faint in the day of adversity, thy strength is small" (Prov. 24:10).

Out of the lion Samson took an abundance of honey, and we also may learn something from an evil business.

The *Daily News*, June 21st, in an article upon horse-racing, says: "It is in regard to stamina that the French racehorses distinguish themselves the most. While the English thoroughbreds can nearly always hold their own against the French over short courses, they are year by year less able to maintain their former supremacy over long distances."

And this is exactly the point where many men fail in the race of life. There is no stay in them, they make a rush of it at the first, but they cannot maintain the pace or persevere to the end; and all because they lack stamina. Hence the great importance of maintaining the inward strength: he who would run well must first have the strength to run with. Vital godliness is the chief consideration, because out of it must come all practical godliness. It is clear that nothing can come out of a man which is not in him; if therefore grace be at a low ebb his life will be shallow, but if the life of God in his soul be deep and vigorous, his action will be correspondingly forcible and energetic. Stimulants are of doubtful value at best, but in religion stimulants have too often been resorted to, and spiritual intoxication has been mistaken for heavenly strength. Attempts have been made at making men strong by setting them strong men's work, but common sense tells us that you cannot turn a dwarf into a giant by dropping him into the big man's boot.

What is needed to render men capable of great deeds is a great nature. The heart must be full or the streams of life will be shallow. The matter of stamina is too often overlooked, but we are obliged to observe it when we come to the actual work of the Christian life, and to the long stretch of it which opens up before us as life is lengthened. We must have stamina or we shall be poor workers. No man would think of going to Brompton Hospital, selecting a company of consumptives who could scarcely walk across the room, and sending them forth to excavate a tunnel, or to heap up an embankment. These pining patients have no stamina, and therefore they must be excused from the sterner toils of life, for they cannot rightly discharge them. If they are driven to engage in heavy labor they will disappoint their employers. A contractor selects fine robust sons of toil, with broad chests and brawny arms, and giving them the mattock and spade and barrow, he sees the mountains fly before them, and the valleys quickly disappear.

While so many Christians are weak and sickly among us it is but little wonder that the Lord's cause is hindered. The pining sickness is upon many, and they can do nothing. Worse still, the lean kine eat up the fat kine, and so the strength of the church is devoured. When we shall ourselves and all our fellow Christians become strong in the Lord and in the power of his might, then we shall do marvels by the aid of his divine Spirit, but till then the work of the Lord will languish.

Continuance in holy service is the test of spiritual energy; many run well for a time, and it is not the pace which kills them, but the length of the course draws upon their slender store of energy, and by and by they drop from the front, and are found far back in the rear, utterly beaten. Well did the Savior say to his disciples, "He that shall endure unto the end, the same shall be saved." Nothing but the unfailing power of God himself can enable the believer to keep up the pace from the beginning to the end of his Christian life. Happy is he who is enabled to do this, yea, blessed is he who shall at the last be able to exclaim with Paul, "I have finished my course, I have kept the faith: henceforth there is laid up for me a crown of righteousness, which the Lord, the righteous Judge, shall give me at that day: and not to me only, but unto all them also that love his appearing."

To obtain stamina we must be more real and intense to begin with, we must resort more continually to the source of strength, we must feed more eagerly upon the soul-sustaining word, and we must be much more abundant in prayer. No time will be lost which shall be spent in obtaining more inward power. Tarrying at Jerusalem till the Spirit is given is no loss of time, but true diligence. It will be the most economical thing in the long run if we sit with Mary at the Master's feet awhile, even though Martha should be pressingly urging us to help her at the table. We must see to the condition of our souls. If the fire burns low the engine will lose its propelling power, if the secret fountain dries the stream will dwindle, if spiritual stamina declines the evil result will be seen somewhere or other, and especially in the want of power to hold on and hold out to the end.

39

Blasting Prohibited

"Ye strain at a gnat, and swallow a camel" (Matt. 23:24).

The *Times*, June 22nd, reports a speech of Mr. Burt in the House of Commons, which contains the following:

> He thought that in certain parts of the country it might be desirable to abolish blasting in coal mines altogether, and, as a general rule, blasting should be entirely prohibited wherever it was absolutely necessary that the safety-lamp should be used. It was absurd to hedge about a small flame of less than one inch and to deal recklessly with a flame which might be hundreds of times as great.

We are entirely of Mr. Burt's opinion; there cannot be a second judgment upon it. We would carry the same thought into morals and religion, for there are persons who think a great deal of trifling offences against the rules of society, and are quite indifferent concerning the alienation of the heart from God: an unimportant violation of propriety in religious worship shocks them, but they can sin against the Most High at a sad rate, and yet their conscience is by no means affected. They are punctilious concerning the ritual of outward ceremonies, but indifferent to the evils of the heart. They tithe mint and anise and cummin, and neglect the weightier matters of the law, judgment, mercy, and truth. There is a story told of a Spanish bandit who had killed many persons without compunction, but was struck with alarm because a little of the blood of one of his victims had spurted upon his lips on a Friday, and thus he had been guilty of tasting animal food on a fast day. Not long ago our police made great efforts to put down the sin of gambling as it displayed itself in a few boys playing pitch and toss with halfpence, but it never occurred to the authorities to interfere with Tattersall's and the almost universal gambling connected with Epsom and Newmarket. Should a poacher steal a goose from a common, he would be prosecuted with the utmost rigor of the law, but lords of the manor have stolen the common from the goose, and no law has been able to reach them. We still strain at gnats and swallow camels.

Conscience, which some cry up as God's vicegerent in the heart of man seems to be a very imperfect monitor in the case of many persons; it lays on its strokes heavily concerning a minor offence, and flogs with a feather when the transgression is really great in the sight of God. The fact is that when conscience is unenlightened its judgment is misleading, and it will make more of a mote than of a beam.

A little of Mr. Burt's common sense would be invaluable both to moralists and religionists. They look to outward actions and neglect the heart. Yet acts are but as the flame of one inch in the miner's Davy and the depravity of the heart is a flame a thousand times more dangerous. What is the filth upon the outside of the cup and platter compared with that which lies within? The interior to anyone who uses the cup is vastly the more important. So too, an ill word which grates upon a single ear is instantly condemned, but a false doctrine which may slay a thousand souls is allowed to spread, and to protest against it is accounted bigotry. We have heard of ministers whose speculations in theology are no better than so many firings of shots in dangerous mines; their blasts are ruinous to multitudes of young men, and yet they are tolerated and even esteemed.

If these divines were heard to swear a profane oath, or known to pick a pocket, they would be scouted from society, but they are doing worse, and yet retain their position. Little do they consider what harm their vagaries cause among the younger and weaker part of their hearers. O that the grace of God would make them wise enough to desist from such perilous operations. At any rate their churches should look to it, and deal with them honestly if they will persist in their murderous romancings. If a man will play with powder and shot he must be kept out of the way, for we cannot afford to risk hundreds of lives for the amusement of a so-called "thoughtful man." Let him play off his gunpowder "thinkings" and his dynamite "culture" in some other sphere, but not among subjects which concern eternity, immortality, glory, and perdition.

40

Deserters

"Will ye also go away?" (John 6:67).

"Demos hath forsaken me, having loved this present world" (2 Tim. 4:10).

The *Daily News*, of June 22nd, in an article upon the character of the men in the British army, says:

> One great cause of misconduct is that few men enlist deliberately, but rather take the shilling as a means of escaping temporary trouble of some sort. Either a man is temporarily out of work, or he has a quarrel with his sweetheart, or he wishes for a while to keep out of the way of the police. Comparatively rarely does he become a soldier from a conviction that it is an honorable mode of earning a living, and that there are some extremely good prizes to be won. Hence speedy repentance, and if he is unable to purchase his discharge he will frequently in desperation steal, so openly that he must be discovered, some, to him, useless article, such as a broom or one boot.

It seems then that very much depends upon the manner of the enlistment of soldiers, and we are quite sure that with young converts everything depends upon the reason for their enrolment in the army of Christ. If they merely come to Christ because they are under some temporary alarm of soul, and not because they are heartily convinced of the error of their ways, they will probably desert from the standard of the cross as soon as the temporary pressure of natural conviction is removed. The awakening sermon is forgotten, the alarming providence is over, the eloquent revivalist has gone to another town, and the superficial converts regret that they ever made a profession of religion, and under one pretext or another they slide away. How well it is that our young friends should count the cost and understand what they are doing, and then should deliberately and heartily cast in their lot with the people of God. They must be convinced that to be a Christian is right, and honorable, and for their own eternal good, they must also be assured that the cause is one of truth and righteousness, and that in it lies all their hope of eternal salvation: they must in a word be renewed in the spirit of their minds, or they will soon be the prey of temptation, and the church will be filled with alarm at the large number of deserters.

Our Lord was always anxious that men should be saved, but he was never in a hurry to gather nominal disciples. When the scribe said to him "Master, I will follow thee whithersoever thou goest," he did not reply, as many of us would have done, with a pressing invitation, and an enthusiastic welcome, but he was far more wise in his procedure, for he replied, "The foxes have holes, and the birds of the air have nests; but I, the Son of man, have not where to lay my head." He put before him the poverty of the Captain and the hard fare of the soldier. When the multitude thronged around him, he did not commence taking their names, enrolling them as his converts, and counting heads in order to publish astounding statistics, but on the contrary he sifted them with words like these: "Verily, verily, I say unto you, Ye seek me, not because ye saw the miracles, but because ye did eat of the loaves, and were filled."

The recruiting sergeants of her majesty's army are so anxious to get hold of the men that they are not scrupulous as to the arguments they use; drink is freely given, the soldier's condition is set forth in rosy colors, and the young man is cajoled and seduced into a way of life which he would not have thoughtfully chosen: but it must not be so among us. We may not repel any man who wishes to join our ranks, but we may not persuade men and women to make a hasty profession, and take the name of Christian upon them to please their friends. The door must not be closed with lock and key, but there must be a porter to open it in order that the sheep, and not the goats, may go in and out and find pasture. Since the porter himself may be readily deceived, it is every man's personal responsibility to see that he enters with his heart and soul into the church of God, if he does enter at all; and it is at his own peril that he dares to intrude unworthily or insincerely into the fold of Christ.

A profession carelessly made will soon be dishonorably abandoned. We know who it was that said: "They went out from ns, but they were not of us; for if they had been of us, they would no doubt have continued with us: but they went out, that they might be made manifest that they were not all of us." He who wrote these words was of a loving nature, and never formed a harsh judgment, and therefore from his verdict we conclude that the backslidings and apostasies which weaken the visible church of Christ are caused by a want of reality at the commencement of the religious life. There was no root, and therefore the plant withered when the sun was risen with burning heat. There was no call to the soldier's life, or the reputed warrior of the cross would not have so shamefully deserted the colors. Hence the stern necessity of our being careful in examining all candidates, and honest in warning them of their responsibilities.

> Have ye counted the cost?
>   Have ye counted the cost,
> Ye warriors of the Cross?
>   Are ye fixed in heart, for your Master's sake,
> To suffer all earthly loss?
>   Can ye bear the scoff of the worldly-wise,
> As ye pass by pleasure's bower,
>   To watch with your Lord on the mountain-top,
> Through the weary midnight hour?
>   Do ye answer, "We can,"
>   Do ye answer, "We can,"
> Thro' his love's constraining power?
>   But do ye remember, the flesh is weak,
> And shrinks in the trial-hour?
>   Yet yield to his hand, who around you now,
> The cords of a man would cast!
>   The bands of his love, who was smitten for you,
> To the altar binding you fast.
>   In the power of his might! In the power of his might!

Who was made through weakness strong,
    Ye shall overcome in the fearful fight!
And sing his victory song!
    But count ye the cost; yea, count ye the cost—
The forsaking all ye have!
    Then take up your cross and follow your Lord,
Not thinking your life to save!

41

Blame the Scale-Maker

"The woman said. The serpent beguiled me, and I did eat" (Gen 3:13).

"Every man shall bear his own burden" (Gal. 6:5).

The South London Press, June 22nd, reports the following, among a number of other cases of unjust weights and measures:

> A.B., cheesemonger. One machine. *Defendant said he paid a scale-maker 10s. 6d. to attend to it, and the neglect was his.* The chairman said one of the first things defendant should have attended to was the correctness of his scales and weights. Fined £1. Defendant thought the scale-maker ought to pay the fine. The Clerk: We look to you; we have nothing to do with the scale-maker.

National law is based upon the principle of personal responsibility, and it will not allow a transgressor to escape by pleading that he has shifted the burden of duty upon another. If in any cases responsibility could be transferred, it surely should be under the circumstances before us; but the law knows nothing of scale-makers, it deals with traders, and if anything be wrong with scales or weights it does not hold the shopkeeper guiltless, but visits the wrong upon him, even though he may have employed a person to keep his weights in order. This course appears to be severe, but it is both just and necessary; there would be no security for the purchaser, nor indeed for government itself, if the essential principle of personal responsibility could be departed from. Every man *must* bear his own burden.

Yet this truth is too often put into the background. In religion men have often acted as if they had altogether forgotten that it must of necessity be strictly personal. We hear of sponsors promising and vowing no end of things, and of priests performing service and doing the devotions of others. Proxies however in such matters are a sheer delusion, all true religion is a personal thing; men sin personally, and they must personally repent of that sin, or personally bear the guilt of it. No man can receive the new birth on behalf of another, nor can another man's faith excuse ns from believing in Jesus. Sanctification is not a boon to be vicariously received, any more than heaven can be vicariously enjoyed. A man may fancy that he pays a priest or a minister to do his religion for him, just as the tradesman paid the scale-maker, but the law does not recognize the transaction, it deals with principals only. We cannot leave our heavenly business in the hands of a clergyman as we place our secular concerns in the hands of a lawyer, we must believe in Jesus Christ on our own account or judgment will go against us. It is true that in the matter of our justification before God we have been redeemed by the blood of our Substitute and are accepted in his imputed righteousness, but in the practical application of the blessings thus procured everything must be direct and personal. Another may procure us food, but he cannot eat or digest it for us: Jesus has become our bread from heaven, but we must individually partake of him if we would live forever. Another may bring us a candle, but we cannot see the light except with our own vision, nay more, even the Sun of Righteousness makes no man to see except by his own eyes.

Never then let us leave our doctrinal views to be settled for us by the church, but let us search the Scriptures for ourselves; let us not derive our peace and confidence from the good opinion of our pastor and the deacons, but aim at attaining a full assurance of our calling and election by the seal of the Spirit upon our own hearts; neither let us leave the work of the Lord to be discharged by others, but honestly render our fair share of the service. We must ask for grace to see to our own scales, and cease to leave to the scale-maker a matter which is altogether our own concern.

42

Spurious Imitations

"Beloved, believe not every spirit, but try the spirits whether they are of God" (1 John 4:1).

"Be not deceived" (Gal. 6:7).

Several papers contain an advertisement commencing as follows: "BEWARE OF SPURIOUS IMITATIONS."

This is very useful and necessary advice, and we cannot do better than urge people of all ranks and ages to follow it.

Beware of spurious imitations of the gospel. There are several of them now on sale. One especially is much in vogue in these days, and secures a vast amount of patronage: it is the ritualistic gospel, in which Christ is displaced by the priest, and the work of the Spirit by sacramental efficacy. Instead of faith in the atoning blood we are taught confidence in the parish priest, and instead of regeneration by the Holy Ghost we are told of a new birth through the operation of water applied by a clergyman. In order to sell this article it is done up in tasteful mediaeval wrappers, and warranted to be the old original primitive mixture; but it is a base cheat. With half an eye you can see that it is not fine flour, but Roman cement, the old Popish mixture which has ruined such multitudes and will certainly destroy all who place their confidence in it. Of all cheats it is one of the most impudent, but the pretty wrappers entice buyers by the thousand.

Beware of spurious wisdom, for there is much abroad in the world of "science falsely so called." Hypotheses are invented, and facts are manufactured, or at least colored, to sustain them, and then for a season the learned world goes mad upon its new theory, and we are solemnly warned that we must not oppose ourselves to the spirit of the age, to scientific development, and to the astonishing results of modern culture.

However, in a short time, a fresh hypothesis shoves the former one from its perch, and the wisdom of yesterday is turned into foolishness, to be used as a foil for the infallible wisdom of today, which also in its due time will be exploded, and go into the limbo of the ten thousand equally absurd infallibilities which have preceded it. We are ready to accept all that science teaches us when it has made up its mind what it is. We never despise knowledge, but on the contrary seek after it as for hidden treasure; but we do not want to be duped by conjectures and fooled by speculations. We are glad to receive all that the observation of intelligent minds can discover for us concerning the wonderful works of the Lord, but we must beware of spurious imitations. There are learned men—and learned men. One class of savants mistakes assertion for proof, and sneering for logic; from such we turn away. It is written of certain persons, "professing themselves to be wise, they became fools," and we know the family is not extinct; therefore we would look before we leap.

Beware also of spurious holiness: a holiness which has ceased from conflict with sin, which knows nothing of inward corruption, has no transgressions to confess, and has no need of watchfulness and holy anxiety. It is very easy to amass a great fortune in Russia just now if you will accept paper rubles, and reckon them at their nominal value, and it is equally easy to be eminent in the higher life if you take your emotions to be facts and your conceits to be realities. Grow in grace, strive after holiness, watch unto prayer, humble yourselves before the Lord, and seek to be perfect even as your Father which is in heaven is perfect, but beware of spurious imitations.

Beware of spurious imitations of the Christian graces, for they are very easily concocted, and are exceedingly plentiful. There is a faith which is not the faith of God's elect, for it is rather grounded upon fancy than upon the Word of God. It rests upon impressions and not upon the testimony of the Most High, it puffs up with presumption, but does not build up with the solid work of the Spirit of God. The faith which looks to God alone as he manifests himself in Christ Jesus is the only faith which will save the soul. Dreams, excitements, visions, and groundless assurances, are all to be avoided as spurious imitations.

Hope may be counterfeited, for there is a false hope; and love may be mimicked, for there is such a thing as attachment to Christ for the sake of the loaves and fishes which he distributes to the multitude. Courage may be counterfeited by rashness, and patience by sullenness. We have known impudence to be mistaken for fidelity, and mere cant for holy unction. We fear that the solid silver plate of true grace is going out of fashion, and everything is German silver nowadays; a very thin deposit being quite sufficient to electro-plate the basest substance into the likeness of the genuine metal. We have lately read in the newspapers of violet powder which has poisoned little children by the arsenic mingled with it, and the parallel of this is to be met with every day. Who could have suspected death in the puff-box? It is where we least look for it that the greatest deception will be found. Therefore prove the spirits whether they be of God, and beware of spurious imitations.

It is almost necessary to say, *beware of spurious revelations*, for nowadays there is much talk of spiritual manifestations, and strange doctrines are foisted upon the world as the utterances of beings from the mysterious land of the departed. It is forbidden to all the followers of Jehovah to have dealings with necromancers, yet some religious professors must needs pry into the devil's den of deceit. Hath net the Lord said unto his people, "There shall not be found among you a charmer, or a consulter with familiar spirits, or a wizard, or a necromancer. For all that do these things are an abomination unto the Lord." To believe what is declared to be said by spirits will be to accept the imitation of a revelation. It is a thorough imposture, and not even what it pretends to be. If men were not such idiots as to doubt God, they would never sink so low as to believe in spiritualism.

To close, let us *beware of everything deceptive in religion*. Let us not be among those who have the form of religion but deny the power thereof, from these we are bidden to turn away. Let us not offer spurious worship like those of old, of whom the Lord wrote through Isaiah, "This people draw near me with their mouth, and with their lips do honor me, but have removed their heart far from me, and their fear toward me is taught by the precept of men." Let us beware of spurious hearing, lest we be as those in Ezekiel's day, of whom the Lord complained, "They come unto thee as the people cometh, and they sit before thee as my people, and they hear thy words, but they will not do them: for with their mouth they show much love, but their heart goeth after their covetousness." There are such things as spurious prayers, like those of the Pharisee, who praised himself under pretense of praying to God. We have need to be on our watch against spurious revivalists, of whom Paul would have said, "They zealously affect you, but not well," and against spurious "missions," to whose agents may be applied the language of the Savior, "Woe unto you, scribes and Pharisees, hypocrites! for ye compass sea and land to make one proselyte, and when he is made, ye make him twofold more the child of hell than yourselves." Nothing but truth will be acceptable with the Most High; nothing but sterling grace will bear even the test of time, much less the trying fires of the coming judgment. Wood, hay, and stubble are now made up into forms which liken them to solid stones fit for the builder's use, and for this reason we must the more carefully avoid all spurious imitations, lest we suffer loss in the day of Christ's appearing. Oh, for the abiding teaching of the Holy Spirit that we may always be able to discern at once between the true and the false!

To many, life is all deception; they walk as in a vain show. They dwell as if in an elfin palace, where everything is the fabric of a vision, and yet seemeth to be substantial. The walls are of such stuff as dreams are made of, yet they account them to be built of hewn stone; they are hung with tapestries and arras, so the inhabitants dream, yet are they of the spider's spinning, and are cobwebs all. A breath would lay the card-house low, and annihilate its mimic splendors. The joy of these poor dupes, who live for this present life alone, is a mere Venice glass, soon to be dashed to shivers, or as the frozen drops which diamond the brow of winter, speedily to melt and to disappear forever. O that men were wise enough to have done with the world and its enchantments, for they must soon be taken from them! Why will they clutch imaginary treasure, and spend their souls to gather that which lasts for so short a space? Will they never seek true happiness? If they will, there is One who serenely looks upon them and beckons them to look on him, for saith he, "I am the way, the truth, and the life."

43

The Watch Tower

"Looking diligently ... lest any root of bitterness springing up trouble you" (Heb. 12:15).

"Behold, how great a matter a little fire kindleth!" (Jas. 3:5).

The *Sussex Daily News*, describing the new chief fire brigade station of London, says:

> A prominent and important feature in the building is the watch-tower, which is about 70-feet high, upon the top of which a man is to be on duty day and night, and is to be provided with a speaking-tube communicating with the engine-room, so that the reflection of a sudden outburst of fire within sight will at once be reported, that when the call is received the horses and men may all be in readiness.

This is an admirable emblem of the watch which should be maintained by every Christian pastor, and indeed by every instructed believer. We should watch day and night lest the fire of sin should break out in the midst of the community, and on its first appearing we should be ready at once to quench it with the water of life. Our eye should carefully mark the first uprising of the fires of strife, lest anger and ill-will should mar the union of the church of Christ, and thereby many should be offended. It may not be our house which burns, nor may the flames be apparent in our quarter of the sky, but anything which concerns any part of the church concerns us all. Knowing how great a matter a little fire kindleth, we should all be eager in the spirit of love to quench

BOOK FIVE: *The Bible and the Newspaper*

the tiniest spark, which may become the mother of a flame. There are many ways in which the fire of evil may break out besides that of strife, such as doctrinal error, fanaticism, worldliness, or sin; but if the evil be speedily detected the outburst may be kept within limits, and stopped before it leads to a general conflagration. Since we never know when evil may come we must always watch unto prayer. The horses must stand ready harnessed to the fire-engine, to dash to the scene of danger at an instant's notice. Before the cry is heard, "Fire! Fire!" we must be already on the road to it.

Alas, too many seem to be of a very different mind, for they are amusing themselves with spiritual-dreaming and worldliness while the fires are raging all around them, and men are perishing in them. Like Nero they sit fiddling on the top of the tower while the city is burning; they are indifferent to the mischief which ought to arouse all their zeal. "Woe unto them when HE cometh who hath said," If thou dost not speak to warn the wicked from his way, the wicked man shall die in his iniquity; but his blood will I require at thine hand." O believer, stand upon thy watch-tower, and weary not in doing sentry's duty. Blessed is the servant who shall be found watching when the Master cometh.

We had come to the end of this passage when our mind persisted in an odd association. We recollected some who watch with all diligence to keep out of the way of anything like hard work. They climb the tower, like the firemen of London, but it is to observe carefully where a fire may be that they may travel in another direction. If there is any honor to be had they are to the front, but if labor must be expended and money given, where are they? The brave Mr. C. during the old French war, when the militia papers were left at his house, regularly inserted in the column of exemptions, "old, lame, and a coward" and returned it to the proper officer within an hour of his haying seen it. Some of our friends without being able to say that they are old or lame, might, without the slightest untruthfulness, claim to be cowards, and so excuse themselves from fire or fray. Some of them, we doubt not are looking out even now; they are valiantly upon their guard against certain of those "many calls" which break their hearts, but which will never break their banks.

As the New England goose always went into the woods at Michaelmas, so are they sure to be absent when they might be called upon for any sort of self-sacrifice. Theirs is a saving faith, for if it does not save their souls it saves their coppers. When anything is to be done or given these brethren beat a hasty retreat. Well, we must let them go; perhaps they would do more mischief if they stayed.

44

Battered Scripture

"He that hath my word, let him speak my word faithfully" (Jer. 23:28).

"Ye shall not add unto the word which I command you, neither shall ye diminish ought from it" (Deut. 4:2).

The London correspondent of the *Deal Telegram*, June 29, calls attention to the mutilation of the inscriptions on the wall of the Beauchamp Tower, which, he says, is being carried on so rapidly that, if the present practice continues, the touching memorials of illustrious prisoners will be completely obliterated in less than a year. He specially points out that it is not the visitors to the Tower of London who are guilty of the "barbarity"; it is the huge Beefeaters who are the vandals. In going their rounds to point out the chief objects of interest, they are provided with short sticks, and with these they rap, tap, strike, and poke the time-honored inscriptions as they explain their meaning, and the correspondent says that fresh marks, showing where the stone has been bruised by this shameful maltreatment, are to be seen on the very inscriptions themselves.

We do not know how far the unfortunate Beefeaters deserve this censure, but if they be indeed guilty, it is a great pity that valued inscriptions should be destroyed by their guardians during the process of exhibition. This singular piece of mischief has its precise parallel, and therefore may serve as a warning. Texts of Scripture are rapped and tapped, poked and smitten by preachers who are endeavoring to call attention to them and are at the same time misrepresenting them. How often is a text explained away, or expounded into confusion, or spiritualized into nonsense! Scripture probably suffers more from the hands of its friends than its foes. Great bruises remain upon some passages of scripture, and these will never be effaced, for the shameful maltreatment has not only fixed itself upon the memory, but affected the judgment of the hearer. Parson Pound-text is by no means a fictitious personage.

True reverence for the inspired word should lead a man to guard carefully the most delicate shades of meaning; the mind of the Spirit should be carefully ascertained, and then as carefully declared to the people. There should be no forcing of meanings, no twisting of words, no concealment of evident teachings. The word was written by God and not by man, and therefore it deserves to be protected even at the cost of life if need be; never under any circumstances should it be made the martyr of prejudice, or the victim of learned wrestings, or the slave of ignorant misrepresentation.

When atheists and infidels batter the word of God we can very well understand their object, but it is grievous when a man of God in order to call attention to a passage darkens its meaning, and in order to show his esteem for every letter smites it with an exaggerated emphasis which utterly mars it. When we visited the Golden House of Nero at Rome, the custodian showed us the frescoes upon the ceiling of the corridor by means of candles raised aloft upon a long rod. The colors were fresh after all these hundreds of years, and so far as the wear and tear of weather were concerned were quite uninjured; but we noticed, with regret, that the smoke of the candles was sadly disfiguring them and even coating them with soot. It will be a sad thing for us if, while we are endeavoring to exhibit divine truth, we at the same time destroy or becloud its loveliest tints with our ignorance or prejudice. Our candles had better be put out rather than they should do permanent damage to the glorious doctrines of grace, which are the masterpiece of Infinite Wisdom.

45

The True Wrestler

"So fight I, not as one that beateth the air" (1 Cor. 9:26).

"Beware ye of the leaven of the Pharisees, which is hypocrisy" (Luke 12:1).

"Thou hast a name that thou livest, and art dead" (Rev. 3:1).

A local newspaper complains of the modern circus. We scarcely know so much about it as Paul did concerning the Olympic Games, but we will take it for granted that the gentleman is correct in his descriptions:

> Everything, with the exception of simply dangerous feats, is so strangely artificial. It is all sham. Our old friends "the riders" are dexterous and graceful enough, going through their conventional business more or less satisfactorily; but there is no dash, no daring, nothing desperate or manly about it. The spangled youth, with the scarlet fillet about his carefully-oiled locks, who trips in with the dancing-school bow, and springs gracefully upon the back of the Wild Horse of the Pampas, which urges on its mad career at the rate of a couple of miles an hour, might, for any peril he encounters, be taking a ride in a sedan chair. There is nothing of the skill which can "catch the wild goat by the hair," which can "leap the rainbows of the brooks," or of the daring which snatches triumph from peril. As to the gymnasts, they simply fail to satisfy any of the conditions of the gymnasium. They are all show, and posture, and grimace. The acrobat is the substitute for the gymnast. We ask for muscle,

and they give us attitude. We look for the highest training of the schools, and they offer us tricks and contortions. We are sick of somersaults, and human pyramids, and sham gladiators, and pseudo-Roman brothers. It is quite time that all this trumpery were swept aside—or reserved for the delectation of the youngsters—and that we had a circus suited to a day of popular gymnastic and athletic training.

We fear that many of these criticisms will apply to the arena of spiritual conflict. Sham is abundant there. Many sermons are "dexterous and graceful," but they do not boldly rebuke sin, nor aim at the human heart. Many public prayers are far removed from the wrestlings of prevailing Israel. Much of professed piety is more careful of show and posture than of heart-work and vital godliness. "We ask for muscle, and they give us attitude." Power from on high is lacking, but the magicians work their feats with their enchantments as in the days of Moses. There is little striving against sin, and decided battling with iniquity. Evil is talked against rather than lived down; worldliness is condemned and practiced; the higher life is mimicked, but not practically exhibited; outward worship consists too much of fine music and elaborate singing, too little of deep devotion and praying in the Holy Ghost. Church membership is frequently a mere name, and discipline a farce. The form of godliness is everywhere, but where is the power? What the world really needs is the old-fashioned Christian, who "wrestled not with flesh and blood, but against principalities, against powers, against the rulers of the darkness of this world, against spiritual wickedness in high places."

46

The Best Preparation for the Second Advent

"Let your loins be girded about, and your lights burning; and ye yourselves like unto men that wait for their Lord" (Luke 12:35, 36).

The *Daily Telegraph*, has a leading article commencing as follows:

> There is a well-known story in New England which relates that, about a century ago, a day of remarkable gloom and darkness overspread the States of Massachusetts and Connecticut—a day still spoken of in local histories as "the dark day," when the light of the sun was slowly extinguished as if by an eclipse. The Legislature of Connecticut happened at that moment to be in session, and, to quote an American writer, "As its members saw the unexpected and unaccountable darkness coming on, they shared in the general awe and terror.
>
> It was supposed by many that the Last Day—the Day of Judgment—had come, and, in the consternation of the hour, some member moved the adjournment of the House. Then straightway there arose an old Puritan legislator, Davenport of Stamford, and said that if the Last Day had come, he desired to be found in his place and doing his duty; for which reasons he moved that candles should be brought, so that the House might proceed with its debate."

This Davenport of Stamford was a wise man. What could the other senators have suggested which would be equally suitable for the occasion? If it had been the Last Day, would they have been more ready for it if they had gone to their homes, and waited there in idleness? Would it have been more seemly to have rushed into the street, and to have stood there with gaping mouths looking upward to the sky? What was better than being ready for whatever might happen, and waiting at the post of duty? We believe firmly in the second advent of Christ, and in the grand fact that he may come at such an hour as we think not, but what of that? What is the practical use of the revelation? Are we to forego matters of immediate concern in order to pry into the impenetrable darkness of the future? Are we to make ourselves into mere star-gazers and prognosticates? Are we to spend our time in idle wonder, concluding that every time we hear of wars and rumors of wars, and read of earthquakes in divers places, it is an infallible token that the end of the world is near?

Why, there have been wars and rumors of wars and all the other signs a score of times, and yet the world wags on at its usual rate. No, rather let us give ourselves up more entirely to the pressing demands of our Lord's household, let us bring out of his storehouse things new and old, continue to feed our fellow-servants and welcome home the wanderers, and then, whether the Master come at cockcrow or at midnight, it will signify little enough to us. We shall welcome him whenever he comes, and he will meet us with joy, for "Blessed is that servant, whom his Lord when he cometh shall find so doing." Master Davenport of Stamford doubtless had a solid confidence in the Lord Jesus, his faith had fixed itself upon his first advent, and received the salvation which Jesus came to bring, and therefore, delivered from all trepidation and alarm, he did not share in the general terror, nor draw inferences of alarm from the unexpected and unaccountable darkness. The heavens might fall, but he dwelt above the heavens, and in quietness and assurance was his strength.

Moreover, the good man possessed a faith which manifested itself by works; his business was his religion, and religion was his business. He believed he was called of God to sit in the legislature of Connecticut, and therefore there he sat; he only wanted candles that he might see what he was at. He was doing what was right, he was there to vote for justice and truth, and if his Master had come, he would have risen from his seat and said, "Here I am, in the place thou wouldst have me to occupy." We remember once calling upon one of our members, a sister who managed her household with discretion. She was in humble circumstances, and when we stopped opposite her house she was whitening the front steps. She rose from her pail, and apologized for being found with her sleeves up; but we begged her to make no excuse, for she was doing her duty, and we earnestly hoped that when our Lord should come he would find us in the same condition. If she had known we were coming, it is just possible she would have put on her best gown, and have been waiting in the little parlor, but we should not have been one half as charmed with her prepared appearance as with the exhibition of her everyday industry. The most fitting condition for death and for judgment is to be diligent in the Master's business, fervent in spirit, serving the Lord. The times are very dark, bring in the candles, and let the house proceed with the present business.

* * *

Thus we bring our little book to a conclusion, only wishing our readers to remember the words of him who so shortly shall appear—"Behold, I come quickly; and my reward is with me, to give every man according as his work shall be. I am Alpha and Omega, the beginning and the end, the first and the last. Blessed are they that do his commandments that they may have right to the tree of life, and may enter in through the gates into the city."

Book Six

Eccentric Preachers

Preface

I have published this little volume very much in self-defense. Some years ago I delivered a lecture on "Eccentric Preachers," and a reporter's notes of it were published in one of the newspapers. These, like all such things, were mere pickings and cuttings, and by no means the lecture itself. Gentlemen of the press have an eye to the amusement of their readers, and make selections of all the remarkable anecdotes, or odd sayings, used by a speaker, and when these are separated from their surroundings the result is anything but satisfactory. No man's speeches or lectures should be judged of by an ordinary newspaper summary, which in any case is a mere sketch, and in many instances is a vile caricature.

I thought no more of my lecture till the other day I found the mere rags and bones of the reporter set forth in America as an address by myself, worthy to be bound up with my book upon "Commenting and Commentaries." Those notes were all very well for a newspaper, but I altogether disown them as my production. It amazes me that the American editor should not have corrected the more obvious mistakes of the reporter, such as calling Peter Cartwright Peter *Garrett*, and Lady Ann Askew Lady *Askayne*. Peter Cartwright was an American backwoods preacher, and his name should have been familiar to the American editor, but some publishers are so intent upon getting out their books that they cannot afford time for correction.

Finding that I had by me the whole of the mutilated lecture, I thought of printing it, to show what I had really spoken; but upon looking it over, I judged it to be better to expand it and make it into a small book. I hope the reader will not be a loser by my resolution.

I desire by this little volume to plead against the carping spirit which makes a man an offender for a word, and the lying spirit which scatters falsehood right and left, to the injury and grief of the most zealous of my Master's servants. Many hearers lose much blessing through criticizing too much, and meditating too little; and many more incur great sin by calumniating those who live for the good of others. True pastors have enough of care and travail without being burdened by undeserved and useless fault-finding. We have something better to do than to be forever answering every malignant or frivolous slander which is set afloat to injure us. We expected to prove our ministry "by evil report and by good report," and we are not therefore overwhelmed by abuse as though some new thing had happened unto us; and yet there are tender, loving spirits who feel the trial very keenly, and are sadly hindered in brave service by cruel assaults. The rougher and stronger among us laugh at those who ridicule us, but upon others the effect is very sorrowful. For their sakes are these pages written; may they be a warning to wanton witlings who defame the servants of the Most High God.

As ministers we are very far from being perfect, but many of us are doing our best, and we are grieved that the minds of our people should be more directed to our personal imperfections than to our divine message. God has purposely put his treasure in earthen vessels that the excellency of the power should be ascribed to himself alone: we beseech our hearers not to be so occupied with the faults of the casket as to forget the jewel. Wisdom is justified of her children, and grace works by such instruments as it pleases. Reader, be it yours to profit by all my Master's servants, and even by

Yours truly,
C. H. Spurgeon

1

What is Eccentricity?

Ought I not to be very timid in speaking upon eccentric preachers when I am somewhat sarcastically requested by an anonymous letter writer to *look at home*? I do look at home, and I am glad that I have such a happy home to look at. Trembling has not seized upon me upon receiving my nameless friend's advice, for two reasons; first, because I am not horrified by being charged with eccentricity, and secondly, because I do not consider myself to be guilty of that virtue or vice, whichever it may be. Years ago I might have been convicted of a mild degree of the quality, but since so many have copied my style, and so considerable a number have borrowed my discourses, I submit that I am rather the orthodox example than the glaring exception. After having lived for a quarter of a century in this region, I am not now regarded in London as a phenomenon to be stared at, but as an old-fashioned kind of body, who is tolerated as an established part of the ecclesiastical life of this vast city. Having moved in one orbit year after year without coming into serious collision with my neighbors I have reason to believe that my pathway in the religious heavens is not eccentric, but is as regular as that of the other lights which twinkle in the same sky. I have probably done my anonymous correspondent more honor than he deserves in taking so much notice of him; indeed, I only mention the man and his communication that I might bear witness against all anonymous letters. Never write a letter to which you are ashamed to put your name; as a rule, only mean persons are guilty of such an action, though I hope my present correspondent is an exception to the rule.

Be so eccentric as to be always able to speak the truth to a man face to face. And now to our subject.

It is not the most profitable business in the world to find fault with our fellows. It is a trade which is generally followed by those who would excuse themselves from self-examination by turning their censures upon others. The beam in their own eye does not appear to be quite so large while they can discover motes in other men's optics, and hence they resort to the amusement of detraction. Ministers are the favorite prey of critics, and on Sundays, when they think it right to talk religion, they keep the rule to the letter, but violate its sense by most irreligiously overhauling the persons, characters, sayings and doings of God's servants. "Dinner is over. Bring the walnuts, and let us crack the reputations of a preacher or two. It is a pious exercise for the Sabbath." Then tongues move with abounding clatter; tales are told without number, and when the truth has been exhausted a few "inventions" are exhibited.

One saw a preacher do what was never done, and another heard him say what was never said. Old fictions are brought up and declared to have happened a few days ago, though they never happened at all, and so the good people hallow the Sabbath with pious gossip and sanctimonious slander. There is a very serious side to this when we remember the fate of those who love and make a lie; but just now we will not dwell upon that solemn topic, lest we should be accused of *lecturing* our audience in more senses than one. So far as I am personally concerned, if the habit we are speaking of were not a sin, I do not know that I should care about it, for after having had more than my fair share of criticism and abuse, I am not one jot the worse for it in any respect; no bones are broken, my position is not injured, and my mind is not soured.

From the earliest period it has been found impossible for the messengers whom God has sent to suit their style of utterance to the tastes of all. In all generations useful preachers of the gospel have been objected to by a portion of the community. Mere chips in the porridge may escape censure and mildly win the tolerance of indifference, but decided worth will be surrounded with warm friends and red-hot foes. He who hopes to preach so as to please everybody must be newly come into the ministry; and he who aims at such an object would do well speedily to leave its ranks. Men must and will cavil and object: it is their nature to do so. John came neither eating nor drinking; he was at once a Baptist and an abstainer, and nothing could be alleged against his habits, which were far removed from the indulgences of luxury: but this excellence was made his fault, and they said, "He hath a devil."

Jesus Christ came eating and drinking, living as a man among men; and this which they pretended to desire in John became an offense in Jesus, and they libeled him as "a drunken man and a wine-bibber, a friend of publicans and sinners." Neither the herald nor his Master suited the wayward tastes of their contemporaries. Like children playing in the market-place, who would not agree about what the game should be, so were the sons of men in that generation. They rejected the messengers because they loved not the God who sent them, and they only pretended to object to the men because they dared not avow their enmity to their Master. Hence the objections were often inconsistent and contradictory, and always frivolous and vexatious.

Filled with the same spirit of contrariety, the men of this world still depreciate the ministers whom God sends them and profess that they would gladly listen if different preachers could be found. Nothing can please them, their cavils are dealt out with heedless universality. Cephas is too blunt. Apollos is too flowery. Paul is too argumentative. Timothy is too young. James is too severe. John is too gentle. Nevertheless, wisdom is justified of all her children. At this time, when God raises up a man of original mind who strikes out a course for himself and follows it with success, it is usual to charge him with being eccentric. If his honesty may not be suspected, nor his zeal questioned, nor his power denied, sneer at him and call him *eccentric*, and it may be the arrow will wound.

Let us now pay our attention to this dreadful word *eccentric*, and then see by what means it has been fixed upon certain preachers of the gospel, and those not the least in usefulness.

What is it to be eccentric? The short and easy method for determining the meaning of a word is to go to the dictionary. Dr. Samuel Johnson, what say you? The sage replies, "It signifies deviating from the center, or not having the same center as another circle." The gruff lexicographer proves his definition by quoting from an astronomer who charges the sun with eccentricity. "By reason of the sun's eccentricity to the earth and obliquity to the equator, it appears to us to move unequally." Eccentric preachers are evidently in brilliant society. Now I am free to admit that the word has come to mean singular, odd, whimsical, and so forth; but by going a little deeper into its etymology, we discover that it simply means that the circle in which an eccentric man moves is not quite coincident with that which is followed by the majority: he does not tread the regular ring, but deviates more or less as he sees fit. It would be easy to prove that a movement may be eccentric, and yet quite regular and effective. Every man who has to do with machinery knows what it is for one wheel to be eccentric to another, and he knows also that often this may be a needful and useful arrangement for the purpose of the machine. It does not seem so very horrible after all that a man should be eccentric.

I suppose the popular meaning is that a man is off the circle, or in more vulgar phrase, "off the square." But the point is, who is to tell us what the square is, and who is to decide which circle a man is bound to follow? True, this second circle is not concentric with the first, but it is not therefore more eccentric than the first, for each one is eccentric to the other. It may be that 'A' is eccentric to 'B,' but 'B' is quite as much eccentric to 'A.'

A man called me a Dissenter the other day, and I admitted that I dissented from him, but I charged him with being a Dissenter because he dissented from me. He replied that I was a Nonconformist, but I retorted that he also was a Nonconformist, for he did not conform to me. Such terms, if they are to be accurately employed, require a fixed standard; and in the case of the term "eccentricity" we need first to settle a center and a circumference, from which we may depart. This will be no easy task: indeed, those who attempt it will find it to be impossible in matters of taste and deportment, according to the old adage, "*de gustibus*, etc.," (concerning matters of taste it is idle to dispute), and the well-worn proverb, "every man to his taste."

In morals conscience has fixed the center and struck the ring; and in religion revelation has used the compasses and given us a perfect sphere. God grant that we may not be eccentric towards God, either as to holiness or truth, for that were fatal: but when fashion and custom mark out ill-proportioned imitations of the circle of perfection, or even dare to impose curves of their own, it may be grandly right to be eccentric, for an eccentric path all the saints have trodden as they have tracked the narrow way in the teeth of the many who pursue the downward road.

From such consecrated eccentricity come martyrs, reformers, and the leaders of the advance guard of freedom and progress. Breaking loose from the shackles of evil customs, such men first stand alone and defy the world; but ere long the great heart of manhood discerns their excellence, and then men are so eager to fall at their feet that the idolatry of hero-worship is scarcely escaped. To us the men seem grander in their solitary adherence to the right, and to the true, than when they become the centers of admiration: their brave eccentricity is the brightest gem in their crown. The slavery of custom is as hard and crushing as any other form of human bondage, and blessed is he who for the truth's sake disdains to wear the galling chain, preferring rather to be charged with singularity and held up to ridicule. It is clear, then, that eccentricity may in certain cases be a virtue. When it touches the moral and the spiritual it may be worthy of all honor.

As to preachers and their mode of procedure, what is eccentricity? Who is to fix the center? I say to all those professed critics who tell us that certain preachers are eccentric—"Who is to fix the center for them?" Shall this important task devolve upon those gentlemen who buy lithographed sermons and preach them as their own? These men are in no danger of violating propriety in the excess of their zeal, for their discourses are cut and dried for them at wholesale establishments. Do you ask, "Is this true?" I answer, undoubtedly; for the other day, to test the matter, I sent my secretary to a certain bookseller's, and he brought home to me specimens of these precious productions, lithographed or written by hand, at prices descending from a shilling to sixpence each: a choke variety, believe me. Some of these invaluable discourses are carefully marked in places to indicate the degree of emphasis to be used, and spaces or dotted lines are employed to indicate the pauses and their suggested length.

No one calls the users of these pretty things eccentric; are we, therefore, to regard them as the model preachers to whom we are to be conformed? Are we all to purchase spiritual food for our flocks, at the liberal rate of half a guinea a quarter for thirteen sermons, to be exchanged at Lady-day, Midsummer, Michaelmas, and Christmas? If these things be so, and this trade is to be continued and increased, I suppose that we who think out our own sermons, and deliver them fresh from our hearts, will be regarded as odd fellows, just as Mr. Wesley was stigmatized as eccentric because he wore his own hair when all the fashionable world rejoiced in wigs.

Well, my brethren, if it should ever be the fashion to wear wooden legs I shall be eccentric enough to keep to those which nature gave me, weak as they are, and I trust that the number of eccentric people will be sufficient to keep me in countenance.

Who is to fix the center of the circle? Shall we give the compasses into the hand of the high-flying brethren whose rhetoric towers into the clouds and is shrouded and lost in them? Certainly these do the business very grandly, dealing in the sublime and beautiful quite as freely as Burke himself. No common man understandeth or so much as dareth to attempt understanding these gentlemen of the altitudes and profundities. Their big words are by no means needful on account of the greatness of their matter, but seem to be chosen upon the principle that the less they have to say the more pompous must be their phrases. In their magniloquence they:

> Set wheels on wheels in motion—such a clatter—
>   To force up one poor nipperkin of water!
> Broad ocean labors with tremendous roar,
>   To heave a cockle-shell upon the shore.

Mr. Muchado is still engaged in whipping his creams into a froth of the consistency of half a nothing; and we may hear the Rev. Mr. Pretty-man in many a pulpit exercising the art of spread-eagle to a coterie who do not suspect him of eccentricity, but consider him to be the model divine.

Not in words only are the high-fliers comparable to masses of floating cloud, but in doctrine they are equally beyond all comprehension. They are philosophical gentlemen, superior persons of special culture, though what has been cultivated in them, except an affectation of learning, it would be hard to say. They confuse those whom they ought to confirm, and stagger those whom they should establish. Bishop Blomfield tells us that a certain verger said to him, "Do you know I have been verger of this church fifty years, and though I have heard all the great sermons preached in this place I am still a Christian." Now, are these dealers in words and dreams to fix the center? If so, we intend to be eccentric; and blessed be God we are not alone in that resolve, for there are others who join with us in the opinion that to be studying the prettinesses of elocution, and the fancies of philosophy, while men are perishing around us is the brutal eccentricity of a Nero, who fiddled while Rome was burning and sent his galleys to fetch sand from Alexandria while the populace died for want of bread. If the center is to be up in the clouds, let a few of us who care for something practical stop down below and be regarded as eccentric. It is an odd thing that some men prefer to speak upon topics of which they know nothing, and from which no benefit can possibly arise, while themes which might edify are disregarded. Timbs tells us of an eccentric "Walking Stewart," who had perambulated half the world but would never talk of his travels, preferring to descant upon "The Polarity and Moral Truth," whereon he spoke so wildly that no one could make head or tail of it. Like this departed worthy, certain men are most at home when they are all abroad, and most important when their subject is insignificant. We do not choose their center, for it is far more suitable for will-o'-the-wisps than ministers of the eternal word. When all souls are saved and all mourners comforted we may venture to discuss recondite theories, but not while graveyards are filling with those who know not God.

Where, then, is the center to be found? Am I directed to yonder vestry? I beg pardon—sacristy. If you will open that door, you will perceive a considerable number of cupboards, presses, and recesses. Where are we? Is this a milliner's shop, or a laundry, or both? Those linen garments reflect great credit upon the washerwoman and ironer; but the establishment is not a laundry, for here hang black gowns, and white gowns, and raiment as fine as Joseph's coat. And what a variety! Here, young man, fetch the ecclesiastical dictionary! Here we have an alb and an amice, a cope for the parson, and a corporal for the bread and wine, and—well, there's no end of the concerns! We are not well instructed in the terminology of these drapery establishments, but we are informed that these things are not to be treated with levity, seeing that therein abideth much grace, which ministereth to the establishment of the saints.

In truth, we have small care to linger among these resplendent rags, but assuredly if the center of gravity lies with gentlemen who thus bedizen their corporeal frames, we prefer to be eccentric, and dress as other male humanities are wont to do. It has seemed to us to be needful to discard even the white necktie. While it was the ordinary dress of a gentleman, well and good; but as it has grown to denote a personage of the clerical sort, or in other words, has become a priestly badge, it seems best to abjure it. This may be done the more readily because it is also the favorite decoration of undertakers and waiters at hotels, and one has no wish to be taken for either of these deserving functionaries. Some young preachers delight in cravats of extreme length, and others tie them with great precision, reminding us of Beau Brummel, who produced miraculous ties, because, as he said, he gave his whole mind to them. I was much aided in the summary dismission of my tie by an incident which happened to me when I first came to London. I was crossing the river by a penny steamboat, when a rude fellow said to me, "How are you getting on at Hitchcock's?" I could not imagine what he meant; but he explained that he supposed I was in the drapery line, and was probably at that eminent firm. He tried hard to find out where I was serving, and when I gave him for answer that I knew none of the houses in the City, and was not in the drapery, "Then," said he, "you're a Methodist parson"; which was a better shot by far, and yet not quite a bulls-eye. Having no desire to be lifted into the clerical order, or to claim any distinction above my fellow church members, I dress as they dress, and wear no special distinguishing mark. Let men of sense judge whether this is one-half so eccentric as arraying one's self so that it is hard for spectators to guess whether you are a man or a woman, and very easy to say that your garnishing is not manly, but ostentatious, and oftentimes meretricious and absurd. The center is not here. They that wear soft raiment are in king's houses, but the King of kings cares nothing for the finery and foppery of ecclesiastical parade.

According to common talk, the center of the circle is fixed by the dullest of all the brotherhood, for to be eccentric means with many to have anything over half a grain of common sense, or the remotest favoring of humor. Have anything like originality, anything like genius, anything like a sparkle of wit, anything like natural whole-souled action, and you will be called eccentric directly by those who are used to the gospel of Hum-drum. The concentric thing with many is to prose away with great propriety and drone with supreme decorum. Your regular man says nothing which can by any possibility offend anybody, and nothing which is likely to do anyone good. Devoid of faults, and destitute of excellencies, the *proper* preacher pursues his mechanical round, and shudders at the more erratic motions of real life. Far be it from us to depreciate the excellent brother, his way is doubtless the best for him, yet are there other modes which are quite as commendable though more likely to be censured. If you will be as dry as sawdust, as devoid of juice as the sole of an old shoe, and as correct as the multiplication table, you shall earn to yourself a high degree in the great university of Droneingen, but if you wake up your soul and adopt an energetic delivery, and a natural, manly, lively, forcible mode of utterance, all the great authorities of that gigantic institution will say, "Oh dear, it is a pity he is so eccentric." Common sense decidedly objects to have the center for an eagle fixed by an owl, or the circle for a waxwork figure forced upon a living man.

As to this supposed center of the circle, which we have tried in vain to settle, it may be as well to remark that it is not fixed, and never can be fixed; for climes and times and circumstances involve perpetual change. Some hundred or more years ago Mr. John Wesley stood on his father's grave to preach in Epworth churchyard, and he was thought very eccentric for proclaiming the gospel in the open air; as for Mr. Whitefield, he was considered to be demented, or he would never have taken to the fields. Our Lord and his apostles had long before preached under the open heavens, and, persecuted as they were, no one in those days called them eccentric because of that particular practice; and, to show how the ideas of men have changed again, no one is now considered to be eccentric for open-air preaching, at least, not in these regions.

I might preach standing on a gravestone tomorrow, and none would blame me. Yes, I forgot, it must not be in a national graveyard, or I should be liable to something dreadful. We must neither stand on an Episcopal tombstone nor be laid under one with our own funeral rites. Those orthodox worms which have fattened on correctly buried corpses so long, would be taken ill if they fed on bodies over which the regular chaplain has not asked a blessing. This care for the worms is to my mind rather eccentric, but let that pass, it will soon be numbered among the superstitions of a dark age. As times roll on, that which is eccentric in one era becomes general and even fashionable in another. The costume and general cut of a preacher of Queen Elizabeth's day would create a smile if it should be copied under the reign of Queen Victoria, and even the knee breeches, silk stockings, and silver buckles which I have myself seen upon my venerated grandfather would create many a smile if they were to reappear at the next meeting of the Congregational Union. "The nasal twang learned at conventicle" was once regarded as the holy tone of piety, and yet the man who should use it now, if he were an Englishman, would be thought an odd being. Indeed, much of the oddity of the famous Matthew Wilks lay in that particular habit; he made you smile, even when speaking with all solemnity by the strangeness of his voice, and yet I never heard that our Puritanic ancestors were otherwise than grave while listening to the same peculiar form of utterance. Time was when it was accounted one of the outrageous deeds of a certain Jack Hanway, that he actually walked down a street in London on a rainy day, carrying a new-fangled kind of round tent to keep off the wet; yet no one quotes this action now as a proof of extreme eccentricity, for umbrellas are as common as mushrooms.

The following incident, which happened to myself, will show the power of race and climate in producing the charge of eccentricity. A Dutchman, who from the very orderly style of his handwriting, and the precision of his phrases, should be a very exemplary individual, once wrote me a sternly admonitory letter. From having read my printed discourses with much pleasure he had come to consider me as a godly minister, and, therefore, being in London, he had availed himself of the opportunity to hear me. This, however, he deeply regretted, as he had now lost the power to read my sermons with pleasure any more. What, think you, had I said or done to deprive me of the good opinion of so excellent a Hollander? I will relieve your mind by saying that he considered that I preached exceedingly well, and he did not charge me with any extravagances of action, but it was my personal appearance which shocked him. I wore a beard, which was bad enough, but worse than this, he observed upon my lip *a moustache!*

Now this guilty thing is really so insignificant an affair that he might have overlooked such an unobtrusive offender. But, no, he said that I wore a moustache like a carnal, worldly-minded man! Think of that. Instead of being all shaven and shorn like the holy man whom he was accustomed to hear, and wearing a starched ruffed collar all round my neck, about a quarter of a yard deep, I was so depraved as to wear no ruff, and abjure the razor. His great guy of a minister, with ruff and bands and gown, and a woman's chin was *not* eccentric, but because I allowed my hair to grow as nature meant it should, I was eccentric and frivolous and carnal and worldly-minded, and all sorts of bad things. You see, what is eccentric in Holland is not eccentric in England, and *vice versa*. Much of the eccentric business is a matter of longitude and latitude, and to be quite correct one would need to take his bearings, and carry with him a book of costumes and customs, graduated according to the distance from the first meridian.

Moreover, we may not forget that as in religion there have been times of persecution, and times of toleration, so has it been with the pulpit. At one date propriety ruled supreme, and men were doomed to instant ostracism if they passed beyond the settled line; while at another date a sort of Eccentric Emancipation Act is passed, and every man does what is right in his own eyes. At the present moment great latitude is allowed, and several persons are now saying and doing very remarkable things, and yet are escaping the charge of eccentricity. It is well for them that some of us lived before them, and for far smaller liberties were set in the pillory. For myself, I venture to say that I have been severely criticized for anecdotes and illustrations of the very same kind which I meet with in the very excellent discourses of my friend, Mr. Moody, whom I appreciate probably more than anybody else.

Many dear, good souls who have heard him with pleasure would not have done so twenty years ago, but would have regarded him as very eccentric. As to Mr. Sankey's singing, of which I equally approve, would not that have been unpardonable even ten years ago? Would Ned Wright and Joshua Poole, and brethren of that order, have been tolerated in 1858? According to the rules which judged Rowland Hill to be eccentric, I should say that these brethren are quite as far gone, if not further, and yet one does not hear an outcry against them for eccentricity. No, the bonds are relaxed, and it is just possible that they are now rather too slack than too tight. It is, however, very curious to watch the moods of the religious public and see how what is condemned today is admired tomorrow. Such an observation has a great tendency to make a man rise superior to the verdict of the period, and choose his own path. To promote a manly, courageous course of action in such matters is our main object in delivering this lecture.

Let us, if we are ministers, do that which we believe to be most likely to be useful, and pay little heed to the judgments of our contemporaries. If we act wisely we can afford to wait; our reward is in a higher approbation than that of men; but even if it were not, we can afford to wait. The sweeping censures of hurried critics will one day be blown away like the chaff of the threshing-floor, and the great heart of the church of God will beat true to her real champions, and clear their reputations from the tarnish of prejudice and slander.

The eccentricity of one century is the heroism of another; and what is in one age cast out as folly may be in the next revered as a wisdom which lived before its time. Well said the apostle, "With me it is a very small thing that I should be judged of you, or of man's judgment: yea, I judge not mine own self."

To return to our circle and concentricity: It would be a very great pity if the center of the circle could be fixed by a decree like that of the Medes and Persians, which altereth not. If we could settle once for all what is concentric and what is eccentric, it would be a very serious evil, for the differences of utterance and modes of address among God's ministers serve a very useful purpose. When Dr. John Owen said that he would give all his learning to be able to preach like the tinker, John Bunyan, he spake not wisely, unless he meant no more than to extol honest John; for Owen's discourses, profound, solid, weighty, and probably heavy, suited a class of persons who could not have received Bunyan's delightfully illustrated preaching of the plain gospel.

No, Dr. Owen, you had better remain Dr. Owen, for we could by no means afford to lose that mine of theological wealth which you have bequeathed to us. You would have looked very awkward if you had tried to talk like the marvelous dreamer, and he would have played the fool if he had imitated you. It is pitiful to hear comparisons made between the different servants of the same Lord. They were made by their Master, the one as well as the other, and set in different spheres to answer his own designs, and the same wisdom is displayed in each. I heard the other day of a discussion which may have answered its design in educating youthful powers of debate, but intrinsically it was an idle theme; it was this—does the world owe most to the printing press or to the steam engine? The machines are alike useful for the purposes intended, and both essential to the world's progress, why contrast them? Why not as well raise a controversy as to the relative values of needles and pins? Robert Robinson, of Cambridge, had a terse, vigorous, and somewhat homely style of preaching, and I heard it asserted that it was more effective than that of Robert Hall, by whom he was succeeded, who was grandly rhetorical and overwhelming. Who is to judge in such a matter? Who in his senses would even tolerate the question? We claim for Robert Hall a master's seat in the assembly of divines, nor would we place Robert Robinson below him, for each man suited the condition of the church. We admire every man in his own order, or even in his own disorder, so long as it is really his own. He has some end to serve in

God's eternal purpose, let him answer that end without carping criticism from us. Who are we, that we should even condemn what seems to us odd and singular?

How many souls were won to God by Mr. Rowland Hill's "eccentricities," as they called them, the judgment day alone will reveal. You have, doubtless, heard of the young man who was about to go to India, and a pious friend was very anxious that he should not leave the country in an unconverted state. He induced this young man to stay a week with him in London, and took him to hear a minister of much repute, a very able man—a man of sound argument and solid thought, in the hope that perhaps something which he said would lead to his friend's conversion. The youth listened to the sermon, pronounced it an excellent discourse, and there was an end of it. He was taken to hear another earnest preacher, but no result came of the service. When the last night came, the godly friend, in a sort of desperation, ventured with much trembling to lead his companion to Surrey Chapel, to hear Mr. Hill, praying earnestly that Mr. Hill might not say any funny things; that he might, in fact, preach a very solemn sermon, and not say anything whatever that might cause a titter.

To his horror, Mr. Hill that night seemed to be more than ever lively, and he said many quaint things. Among the rest he said that he had seen a number of pigs following a butcher in the street, at which he marveled, inasmuch as swine have usually a will of their own, and that will is not often according to their driver's mind. Mr. Hill, upon inquiring, found that the aforesaid pigs followed the leader because he had peas in his pocket, and every now and then he dropped a few before them, thus overcoming their scruples and propensities. Even so, said Mr. Hill, does the devil lead ungodly men captives to his will, and conduct them into the slaughterhouse of everlasting destruction, by indulging them in the pleasures of the world. The sober gentleman who had brought his friend to the chapel was greatly shocked at such a groveling simile, and grieved to think of the mirth which his young friend would find in such a dreadful observation. They reached the door, and to his surprise the youth observed, "I shall never forget this service. That story about the pigs has deeply impressed me, for I fear it is my case." A happy conversion followed, and the critic could only retract his criticism in the silence of his own grateful heart. Well, then, let each servant of God tell his message in his own way. To his own Master he shall stand or fall.

If God moves a Rowland Hill to speak of pigs, it will be better than if he had descanted upon purling brooks, or blue-eyed seraphim. Taste may be shocked, but what of taste when men are to be aroused from the fatal slumbers of indifference! If you are living without Christ in the world, your state and condition are far more shocking in themselves than any arousing words can possibly be. It is sin which is vulgar and in bad taste; so they think who best can judge—the purest of our race and the angels in heaven. It disgusts me to see a man whom God's word declares to be "condemned already" giving himself airs, and affecting to be too delicate to hear a homely sentence from one who desires to save him from eternal wrath. He is coarse enough to despise the altogether lovely One, brutal enough to reject the gospel of love, and base enough to rebel against his Creator and Preserver, and yet forsooth he is a connoisseur in religion, and picks over every word which is spoken to him for his good! This spiritual prudery is sickening to the last degree.

I have given the story of Mr. Hill because it is a type of many which are considered to be eccentric and coarse, but which are not so at all, except to shallow minds. There is nothing essentially vulgar in an allusion to pigs any more than to any other animals, for our Lord himself spoke of "casting pearls before swine," and the apostle Peter alluded to the sow that was washed wallowing in the mire. Nor is there anything essentially coarse in the simile of the hogs following the butcher; in fact, it is less coarse than Peter's metaphor which we have quoted, especially when coupled with the dog's returning to his vomit. No creature, truly represented, is common or unclean. It is only a sort of Pharisaism of taste which makes it so. Real vulgarity lies in foul allusions and indelicate hints, and these are to be found among men of dainty speech, such as Laurence Sterne, and not among holy and homely minds after the order of Rowland Hill.

Tinge your stories or your figures with dirt, Mr. Slopdash, and we abandon you: nothing which is indelicate can be endured in the service of a holy God. Come home to the heart in your own genial, home-spun manner, and I, for one, will delight in you, Mr. Slapdash, and bid you God speed. So much difference is there between *slop* and *slap* that it might furnish a theme for a lecture, and yet there is only the change of a vowel in the words. So may disgusting vulgarity and homely force wear the same aspect, and yet they differ as much as black and white. There is a charming poetry in many a simple figure which unsophisticated minds delight in. If a smile is raised it only shows that the soul is awake, and is pleased to be taught so plainly. Critics may take out their penknives to gore and gash, but honest hearts delight in the natural expressions, the instructive comparisons, and the heartfelt utterances of the earnest man whom the world sets down as *an eccentric preacher*.

2

Who Have Been Called Eccentric?

In the previous lecture we gained some little light upon the true meaning of eccentricity, and we discovered it in certain quarters where it is little suspected, while we saw many to be free from it who have been popularly charged with it. Let it not, however, be supposed that we shall attempt the justification of all eccentrics. We are sorrowfully compelled to concede to critics of the ministry that persons have entered it who have sadly disgraced our high calling. Men in all denominations have earned notoriety by being out of center morally and spiritually: these have deserved to be called eccentric in the worst sense. Now, while we stand up for the apostles, we expressly exclude Judas Iscariot. Find us a man who tries to attract attention by the affectation of oddity, who is a mere mountebank or mimic, and we have not a word to say in his defense, but we give him over as a dead horse to the dogs of criticism. They may rend him in pieces, and devour him if so they desire, for impostors and pretenders deserve the critic's sharpest teeth. Find us a preacher who obtains notoriety for himself by descending to buffoonery, and who goes out of his way to say smart things, and make jokes on sacred subjects, and we decline to be his advocate.

Natural humor may possibly be consecrated and made to wear the yoke of Christ, but he who apes it is no true man. If you find us a man who has any object in this world in what he says but the glory of God, and the winning of souls, he is the man who is out of center, and into his secret may we never come. And furthermore, if you discover a preacher who is indelicate, and causes the cheek of modesty to tingle, let him be cast out of the pulpit, and the door locked against him. We have known men of the Slopdash order who would have been nothing if they had not been outrageous, and of these it may be said that they were worse than nothing when they followed their own style. There was nothing in their absurdities to excuse them, for they were not carried away by zeal, nor did the excellence of their matter make up for the ridiculousness of their manner. Of such men we will neither be defender nor judge.

We do not care whether he performs in the parish church or hangs out at a little Bethel, the man who shocks decency and plays the fool with solemn truths is unworthy of his office. I have heard that a certain preacher finding himself in Northamptonshire, among the shoemakers, in order to draw a congregation, gave notice in the morning that he would in the evening tell them the quickest way to make a pair of shoes. When they crowded the place, he bade them *take a pair of boots and cut the tops off*. If this was really done, then I say, let this wit among cobblers live and die at his trade, but let him not again go beyond his last. I had my doubts about this story, for I found it told both of Henley and of Hill, and I was morally certain that at least the second edition of it was an old tale new vamped; but I am sorry that I have met with an advertisement by Orator Henley which proves that he actually did this, not in Northampton, but in London, and headed his announcement with a Latin sentence signifying that the greater includes the less. We shall have more of this Orator Henley directly.

In my youth I remember the eccentric fame of a clergyman who lived near my father's house. He found himself at church one Sunday morning with a political pamphlet in his pocket instead of his sermon, and throwing it down into the churchwarden's pew, he bade him read a bit of it while he went home for his discourse. Many very questionable deeds were done by this parson of the old fox-hunting school, and his general manners fully entitled him to be called eccentric. It would be a pity to revive the stories told in many an Essex village thirty years ago of parsons and clerks of a race which ought to be speedily forgotten. Methodists and Ranters have been the song of the drunkard and the target of many fiery arrows, but never has anything been imputed to the indiscretion of their zeal which has been one-tenth as mischievous as were the evil lives of those who opposed them. I care not to say more; no section of the church can afford to throw stones, for no department has been free from unworthy ministers, adventurers, hypocrites, and downright fools.

Moderation is not the virtue of many. If one man casts a sprinkling of the salt of wit into his sermon straightway some half idiotic brother must set the people grinning all the sermon through. If one, to whom it is natural, is so carried away by his earnestness that his action becomes at times highly dramatic, instantly a certain crew fall to mouthing and posturing as if these things were the great power of God. If one man occasionally spiritualizes, but keeps within the bounds of discretion, they must needs indulge all sorts of fancies till one might say of them as a foreigner said of King James's favorite preacher, "He playeth with his text, patting it to and fro, as a cat doth a mouse." They put the wise man's wig upon their little skulls, and fancy that they have become as great as he. These hangers-on of useful men have not even the virtue of being the genuine article, they are counterfeits in which are exaggerated all the imperfections of the original, while all the excellencies are omitted.

One can hardly tell at this distance of time what to believe, and what to reject, of the character of Orator Henley, who flourished some hundred and thirty years ago in Butcher Row, Newport Market. If the representations of historians are correct he was an eccentric man of the class which disgusts all godly minds. He announced himself as "the restorer of ancient eloquence," and selected for his themes subjects religious, political, and personal. He was frequently prosecuted for libel, and never seemed to bridle his tongue on that account, but with low ribaldry and buffoonery he pursued the golden object which he had set before him. In an unfortunate moment he attacked the poet Pope, who in revenge held him up to scorn in his "Dunciad":

> Imbrown'd with native bronze, lo Henley stands,
>   Tuning his voice, and balancing his hands,
> How fluent nonsense trickles from his tongue!
>   How sweet the periods, neither said nor sung!
> Still break the benches, Henley, with thy strain,
>   While Sherlock, Hare, and Gibson preach in vain.
> O great restorer of the good old stage,
>   Preacher at once and zany of thy age!

I say again that there is no knowing how far Henley deserved all this, but if report speaks truly he was a mournful instance of talent perverted to evil uses, and of self-conceit blown up to an amazing pitch. To such men the whip of scorpions, which Pope could handle so skillfully, was well applied.

Creatures of Henley's kind existed among the friar-preachers of the mediaeval period, whose ignorance and cunning were equally the ridicule of their contemporaries; though even among them there were true-hearted men whose singularities arose out of their zeal to do good. The genus of religious mountebank is not quite extinct at the present day, though seldom seen in such full development as in the friar period. Men of this order are generally known and read by the Christian public, and seldom gain either profit or honor from their wretched adventure; it were a pity that they should.

The miserable instances alluded to are often used as stones to throw at really gracious men, and the attempt to prove that all preachers are alike is repeated in the face of a thousand facts. Because some charlatans have been eccentric, therefore all eccentric men must be mere impostors; and this being taken for granted, the next thing to be done is to represent really sober-minded men as wild and singular, that so they also may be regarded as deceivers.

A reputation for eccentricity has been unjustly fastened upon many men by persistent falsehood. Throw enough mud and some of it will be sure to stick: upon this theory have good men been assailed. Whatever of originality and quaintness they have possessed has been grossly caricatured; and silly tales, the worthless legends of remote periods, have been revived and fathered upon them. It is interesting to trace the pedigree of a pulpit story, though it is not often possible to discover its actual parent: in fact, we believe that, like Topsy, many of these tales have no father nor mother, but may say of themselves, "'specs I growed." The rise and progress of a current falsehood, if well studied, would reveal a sad page in human history. The same anecdotes occur from age to age, but they are tacked on to different men.

In the days when hour-glasses were affixed to many pulpits, to suggest a limit to long-winded discourses, it was natural that wags should invent humorous stories concerning them. One of them is set forth in a print which represents Hugh Peters preaching, and holding up an hour-glass as he utters the words, "I know you are good fellows, so let us have another glass." It is probable that Peters never said this, and more than probable that if he did say something like it, the connection in which it was spoken set it in quite another light.

However that may be, it was too good a story to be allowed to go out of use, and therefore it came to pass that in due time it was told with slight variation of Daniel Burgess, a celebrated Nonconformist divine, whose vigorous speech frequently made him enemies. Nor was this enough, for a very similar anecdote turned up a third time in a neighboring country, and this time it was a Presbyterian clergyman who used the expression, "Let us have another glass, and then"—when preaching before the High Commissioner. Happily for Rowland Hill and Matthew Wilks the hourglass was out of date in their day, or else they would have been represented as saying the same thing. Liars ought to have good memories that they may recollect that they have already assigned a story to someone else. A particle of creative genius might also render their work a little less monotonous.

I remember reading with some amusement of Lorenzo Dow, who is reported some sixty years ago to have slipped down a tree in the backwoods, in order to illustrate the easiness of backsliding. He had previously pulled himself up with extreme difficulty, in order to show how hard a thing it is to regain lost ground. I was all the more diverted because it has so happened that this pretty piece of nonsense has been imputed to myself. I was represented as sliding down the banisters of my pulpit, and that at a time when the pulpit was fixed in the wall and was entered from behind! I never gave even the remotest occasion for that falsehood, and yet it is daily repeated, and I have heard of persons who were present when I did so, and, with their own eyes, saw me perform the silly trick. It is possible for a person to repeat a falsehood so many times that he at length imposes upon himself and believes that he is stating the truth. Here is the original tale, extracted from Mr. Taylor's *Model Preacher*:

> A man once went to Vincennes, in the United States, to hear Lorenzo Dow preach on backsliding. He said, "An immense concourse of people assembled in the woods, and waited for Dow's arrival. Finally he made his appearance, and at the time all expected the sermon he arose, climbed up a smooth sapling, and cried out, 'Hold on there, Dow; hold on.'" He soon slid down to the ground, and put on his hat and left. That was all the sermon we heard that day.

If this was all the sermon it certainly left a great deal for the hearer to work out, and it reminds us of the Welsh preacher who, with almost as little speaking, forcibly brought a great question before his people. He ascended the pulpit on the Sunday morning, looked around him and said, "My brethren, I shall ask you a question which neither you nor I can answer—'What shall it profit a man if he gain the whole world and lose his own soul?'" When he had thus spoken he left the pulpit, walked down the aisle, and went home. If the hearers did not think that morning it was no fault of his. I wonder that someone has not told this story of me; perhaps they think it too good.

It was reported of Mr. Rowland Hill that on one occasion having saved up sufficient money to buy a chest of drawers his wife appropriated the amount to purchase therewith a new bonnet. To punish her for this misappropriation of household goods Mr. Hill is described as having exclaimed on the following Sunday, "Here comes Mrs. Hill with a chest of drawers on her head." It is truly marvelous that this anecdote should have lived even for an hour, for Mr. Hill was of honorable family, and possessed considerable property. The purchase of any number of chests of drawers or bonnets would have been a matter of small consequence to him; and besides, he was so attached to his wife, and a man of such excellent breeding, that no such language could have been used by him under any supposable circumstances.

When Mr. Hill heard of the story he said, "It is an abominable untruth, derogatory to my character as a Christian and a gentleman: it would make me out a bear." Across many of the stories which were printed concerning himself he wrote with his own hands the words, "A lie"; and truly there are others of us who might wear out our pencils in doing the same. What need is there of all this invention? We have faults enough without imputing to us more than we have committed. Men who are really eccentric furnish quite enough remarkable and singular incidents in the course of their lives, and if the actual singularities were criticized there would be no room for complaint; but wherefore all this delight in lies?

A minister who is much before the public has need to be thick skinned, and to exercise to a very high degree the virtue of longsuffering. It may help him if he will remember the conduct of good Cotton Mather, a man remarkable for the sweetness of his temper. On one occasion, having taken a prominent interest in the political concerns of his country, he received a large number of abusive letters. All of these he tied up in a packet, and wrote upon the cover, "Libels. Father, forgive them." No man of God need be astonished at slander, as though some strange thing had happened unto him, for the best servants of God have been subject to that trial. Mr. Whitefield truly said, "Thousands of prayers are put up for us, and thousands of lies are spread abroad against us." Of himself, concerning his tour in Scotland, they said, "Wherever he went he had a gaping crowd around him, and had the address to make them part with their money. He was a pickpocket, and went off to England with a full purse, but with a ruined reputation among all except his bigoted admirers." This was falsehood itself.

I commend to young preachers when they are tried in this fashion the wise and weighty words of Thomas A'Kempis:

> My son, take it not grievously if some think ill of thee, and speak that which thou wouldest not willingly hear.
>
> Thou oughtest to be the hardest judge of thyself and to think no man weaker than thyself.
>
> If thou dost walk spiritually, thou wilt not much weigh fleeting words.
>
> It is no small wisdom to keep silence in an evil time, and in thy heart to turn thyself to God, and not to be troubled by the judgment of men.
>
> Let not thy peace depend on the tongues of men; for whether they judge well of thee or ill, thou art not on that account other than thyself. Where are true peace and true glory? Are they not in God? And he that careth not to please men, nor feareth to displease them, shall enjoy much peace.
>
> From inordinate love and vain fear ariseth all disquietness of heart and distraction of the mind.

Dr. Campbell once told me the following story: On one occasion, when Mr. Wesley was preaching, he said, "I have been falsely charged with every crime of which a human being is capable, except that of drunkenness." He had scarcely uttered these words before a wretched woman started up and screamed out at the top of her voice, "You old villain, and will you deny it? Did you not pledge your bands last night for a noggin of whisky, and did not the woman sell them to our parson's wife?" Having delivered herself of this abominable calumny the virago sat down amid a thunder-struck assembly, whereupon Mr. Wesley lifted his hands to heaven, and thanked God that his cup was now full, for they had said *all* manner of evil against him falsely for Christ's namesake. After this we feel reconciled to the idle tales which buzz about us, annoying us for a small moment, but doing no great damage.

I would gladly hope that some untruthful representations of good men are the accidental results of misreports. In these days when reporters must furnish brief accounts of public speeches, it is almost impossible for them to do the speakers justice, for in their hurry they hear inaccurately, and in their brevity they give of necessity but a partial report. Now, the omission of a single sentence may make a speaker appear very absurd and eccentric. Of this we have a notable instance in the case of our beloved friend Mr. C. A. Davis, of Bradford. His is a sweet, poetical, well-balanced mind, and yet one would not think so from the newspaper report of a late speech at our College meeting. He is reported to have said of us, "May every hair of your head be a wax candle to light you into glory, and may you be in heaven ten minutes before the devil knows you are dead."

Assuredly this looks very outrageous as it stands; but let me personally vouch for its connection. Our friend said that he wished that he was able to express his love to us, and his hearty desires for us, and that he envied the enthusiastic ingenuity of a poor Irish woman who in thanking her benefactor exclaimed, "May, etc." Now, the reporter in this case was a friend to us all, but probably the exigencies of the printing office knocked out the previous sentences, and there stood the Catholic benediction in all its exuberance. I am somewhat amused that certain papers should abuse my brother Davis for this, for he is one of the most quiet, orderly, and correct speakers that I know of, and I congratulate him upon gaining a reputation for eccentricity by mere accident.

Do you not think it very hard that some of us can never utter a playful sentence without being criticized? Often would I speak familiarly to my dear friends, and unbosom myself, as a man might in the midst of his family, but

> A chiel's amang ye takin' notes,
> And faith he'll prent it.

This is a sore oppression to a true-hearted man who does not care to be forever under restraint. I sympathize thoroughly with Archdeacon Tillorson when he said, "It is surely an uneasy thing to sit always in a frame, and to be perpetually on your guard; not being able to speak a careless word, or to use a negligent posture without observation and censure. Nothing but necessity, or the hope of doing more good than a man is capable of doing in a private station, can recompense the trouble and uneasiness of a more public and busy life." The injustice of the matter is that what a man does but once in a playful moment—and what poor slave among us does not sometimes play?—is bandied around as if it were a fair specimen of his whole life. A man in a walk chases a rare butterfly, and straightway is regarded as a mere boy who wastes his time in catching flies. But is this fair? Is it not a practical lie? For my own part, I have so long lived under a glass case, that like the bees that I have seen at the Crystal Palace I go on with my work, and try to be indifferent to spectators; and when my personal habits are truthfully reported, though they really are not the concern of anybody but myself, I feel utterly indifferent about it, except in times of depression, when I sigh for a lodge in some vast wilderness, where rumors of newspaper men and interviewers might never reach me more. Would not some of our hearers be rather more eccentric than their ministers if they were hunted and reported as we are? May heaven spare them the affliction.

Here I take leave to say that there should be greater caution in believing silly stories about ministers of the gospel, and a far greater reluctance to repeat them. They have enough to bear without being made a laughingstock before the world, for matters of which they are perfectly innocent. Taken as a body, they are probably less guilty of anything *outré*, than any other set of men; in fact, they are too apt to freeze into a cold, professional propriety: and therefore it is on all accounts unwise by exaggeration and falsehood to damp exceptional fervor because it may be attended with vivacity of spirit and originality of style.

Still there have been eccentric men, and names occur to us with which the epithet is fitly connected. Who are they? I will not dwell on Robert South, a masterly preacher, some of whose pungent expressions are almost as forcible as they are ferocious. I shall do no more than mention such personages as Dean Swift and Laurence Sterne, and I shall only allude to that witty and worthy person the Reverend Sydney Smith, for these gentlemen, with all their genres, were not overdone with gospel, and would scarcely care to be mentioned in connection with the worthies whom I shall more largely speak upon. Neither will I dwell upon the eccentric persecutors who roared and raved against Methodists and revivalists from their pulpits, except that one of them deserves "honorable mention."

"Samuel Roe, a Bedfordshire clergyman in the last century, and vicar of Stoffold, in that county, was a specimen of that inconsistent, but not uncommon character, an enthusiast against enthusiasm. Without any extraordinary capacity or attainments, he might have lived without notice, and have died without remembrance, had he not signalized himself by a proposal for preventing the further growth of Methodism—a proposal as full of genius as it was of humanity. But this amiable and benevolent man shall be heard in his own words: 'I humbly propose to the legislative powers, when it shall seem meet, to make an example of the tabernacle preachers, by enacting a law *to cut out their tongues*, as well as the tongues of all field teachers, and others who preach in houses, barns, or elsewhere, without apostolical ordination or legal authority.'" [Larwood's Book of Clerical Anecdotes.]

I shall almost entirely confine myself to good men and true, who have really edified the church of God and led sinners to repentance.

To begin at the Reformation period, I should single out first and foremost grand old Hugh Latimer. The miter upon his head did not quench either his zeal or his wit. Is there any reformer whose name strikes with such a homely sound upon the English ear as that of Latimer? We admire Cranmer and Ridley and Hooper, and the rest of them, but we love Latimer. There is something so genuine, and as we proudly say, so thoroughly English about that honest servant of God, that whether he kisses the stake in death or rebukes kings in his life, our hearts go out towards him. Yet he was not only homely, but at times so odd and quaint in his speech that for a bishop he must be regarded as very eccentric. Did he not talk of that woman who could by no means be made to sleep till she begged them to take her to the parish church, where she had so often slept the sermon through, for she felt sure she should sleep there? Did he not tell his hearers a queer story of the countryman who thought that Tenterden steeple was the cause of the Goodwin Sands? Listen to such talk as this:

> I will tell you now a pretty story of a friar to refresh you withal. A preacher of the Gray Friars preached many times, and had but one sermon at all times, which sermon was of the Ten Commandments. And because this friar had preached this sermon so often, one that heard it before told the friar's servant that his master was called *Friar John Ten-Commandments*; wherefore the servant showed the friar his master thereof, and advised him to preach of some other matters; for it grieved the servant to hear his master derided. Now, the friar made answer saying, "Belike, then, thou knowest the ten commandments well, seeing thou hast heard them so many a time." "Yea," said the servant, "I warrant you." "Let me hear them," saith the master. Then he began—"Pride, covetousness, lechery," and so numbered the deadly sins for the Ten Commandments. And so there be many at this time which be weary of the old gospel; they would fain hear some new things; they think themselves so perfect in the old, when they be no more skillful than this servant was in his Ten Commandments.

More homely still, if possible, is his talk about the various cheats of his own day:

> I will tell you of a false practice that was practiced in my country where I dwell. But I will not tell it you to teach you to do the same, but rather abhor it, for those who use such deceitfulness shall be damned world without end. I have known some that had a barren cow, and they would fain have had a great deal of money for her, therefore they go and take a calf of another cow and put it to this barren cow, and so come to the market, pretending that this cow hath brought that calf, and so they sell their barren cow six or eight shillings dearer than they should have done else. The man which bought the cow cometh home; peradventure he hath a many of children, and hath no more cattle but this cow, and thinketh he shall have some milk for his children; but when all things cometh to pass, this is a barren cow, and so this poor man is deceived. The

other fellow which sold the cow thinketh himself a jolly fellow, and a wise merchant, and he is called one that can make shift for himself. But I tell thee, whosoever thou art, do so if thou list, thou shalt do it of this price; thou shalt go to the devil, and there be hanged on the fiery gallows world without end. I tell you another false deed: I know that some husbandmen go to the market with a quarter of corn. Now, they would fain sell dear the worst, as well as the best, therefore they use this policy, they go and put a strike of fine malt or corn in the bottom of their sack, then they put two strike of the worst they had, then a good strike aloft in the sack's mouth, and so they come to the market. Now, there cometh a buyer, asking, "Sir, is this good malt?" "I warrant you (saith he) there is no better in this town"; and so he selleth all the malt or corn for the best, when there is but two strike of the best in the sack. The man that bought it thinketh he hath good malt, he cometh home. When he putteth the malt out of the sack, the strike which was in the bottom covereth the ill malt which was in the midst, and so the good man shall never perceive the fraud till he cometh to the occupying of the corn: the other man that sold it taketh this for a policy, but it is theft afore God, and he is bound to make restitution of so much of those two strikes which were nought [and] were sold too dear. So much he ought to restore, or else he shall never come to heaven, if God be true in his word. I could tell you of another falsehood, how they make wool to weigh much, but I will not tell it you.

Fancy the flutter among the lawn sleeves if a right reverend father were to talk in that fashion in these days. "Shockingly eccentric," would be the verdict of Canterbury and Winchester, and even of Sodor and Man.

Taking a great leap and coming down to modern times, we note the great religious revival under Whitefield and Wesley, and we ask—who is the eccentric man here? The answer is that several might be so named, but among them all the chief would be John Berridge, of Everton. What a lump of quaintness that man was; but who thinks of him at the present moment without admiration? His portrait forces you to smile, and you cannot read his letters without laughing; but what a power was upon him to stir the souls of men and lead them to the Savior's feet. Mr. Thornton seriously admonished Mr. Berridge for asking in his prayer at Tottenham Court Road that the Lord would give his people no stale bread, but that which was baked in the oven that day. I fail to see the very serious impropriety of the prayer; but when Thornton says, "You once jocularly informed me that you were born with a fool's cap on; pray, my dear sir, is it not high time that it was pulled off?" I agree with the question. Still I have more sympathy with Berridge's answer: "A fool's cap is not put off so readily as a night cap; one cleaves to the head and the other to the heart. Odd things break from me as abruptly as croaking from a raven." Berridge could not have lived if he had not found a vent for his spirits in witty sayings. He would seem to have had a fine, frank soul, which acted upon its impulses without the fear of what observers might say. Yet was he ever ready to confess his fault in the direction of excessive mirth, and on one occasion he traces it to his not being in the best physical condition. This may seem very absurd, but it is not: I have known seasons when suffering from neuralgia or depression my only hope of speaking at all has been found in taking off all the brakes, and allowing my mind to have full swing. The more my head has ached the more have I indulged in humor, or I should not have been able to speak at all.

Here is the passage which I referred to, it is from one of Berridge's letters: "Laughter is not found in heaven; all are too happy there to laugh; it is a disease of fallen nature, and as such infested me sorely *when sunk into the lowest stage of a nervous complaint.* It forced itself on me without provocation, and continued with such violence as quite to overwhelm me; and nothing could check it but choking it, viz.—filling my mouth with a handkerchief." Such fits were not frequent with him, although he was always radiant with smiles. I rather admire the pluck of the man that he could laugh when he was suffering so severely. The effect which the sight of Berridge produced upon the very sober mind of Andrew Fuller is well worth mentioning. He says: "I greatly admired that divine savor, which all along mingled itself with Mr. Berridge's facetiousness, and sufficiently chastened it. His conversation tended to produce a frequent, but guileless smile, accompanied with a tear of pleasure. His love to Christ appears to be intense. The visit left a strong and lasting impression on my heart of the beauty of holiness, of holiness almost matured."

When I remember that there is credible information that in the space of about twelve months some four thousand souls were brought to Christ by his preaching, and that in the region wherein he labored his name is still mentioned as that of a great saint, I feel that there was nothing in the eccentricity of Berridge of which he needed to be ashamed.

Mr. Hill, whom Berridge calls "Dear Rowley," was hard at work for his Master when the old vicar was going off the stage, and well did he carry out the old man's advice, "Study not to be a fine preacher: Jerichos are blown down with rams' horns. Look simply unto Jesus for preaching food, and what is wanted will be given, and what is given will be blest, whether it be a barley or a wheaten loaf, a crust or a crumb. Your mouth will be a flowing stream or a fountain sealed, according as your heart is. Avoid all controversy in preaching, talking, or writing; preach nothing down but the devil, and nothing up but Jesus Christ."

With Rowland Hill we naturally associate Matthew Wilks, who kept the Tabernacle full while Mr. Hill crowded Surrey Chapel. Of both of these we hope to speak more fully further on. America in the time of her first formation produced back-woods' preachers of a rarely eccentric order, such as Jacob Gruber, William Hibbard, James Oxley, Peter Cartwright, and others of a brave fraternity of men who labored with the axe in their hands and the gospel on their ready tongues. The same country also gave us Father Taylor, the sailor preacher of Boston. However grotesque some of these men may seem we cannot but admire their readiness for service and their unconquerable courage. Think of going to a charge where the people write, "Be sure and send us a good swimmer, for he will have to cross no end of rivers." "George," said Bishop Asbury to George Roberts, "where are your clothes?" "Bishop, they are on my back." This man carried needle and thread in case of accident to his one set of garments. We cannot countenance the propensity of Cartwright for physical warfare. We trust it will remain a peculiarity confined to America for a preacher to be equally ready to fight or to preach. Some men may be all the better for being knocked down, but the knocker down will surely be all the worse. However, these members of the church militant were rough men dealing with rough men, and we are glad that we are not tempted in the direction of fisticuffs.

The Baptists among many others of lesser note have had Robert Robinson, of Cambridge, of whom Robert Hall said that he could say "what he pleased, when he pleased, and how he pleased," and John Ryland, of Northampton, whose force and naturalness sometimes carried him into eccentric regions.

Among the Methodists have sprung up William Dawson, Gideon Ousely, Squire Brooke, and others whose names will not soon be forgotten. Now, it strikes me that if we were bound to make out a short list of earnest and successful soul-winners we might be content to take the list which we have already made out. To say the least, it is remarkable that eccentricity and usefulness often go together. These wicked eccentric people, who are so frequently condemned, have nevertheless, it turns out, been among the most useful men of their times. Matthew Wilks' way of meeting objections to his whims and oddities was not a bad one. I am told that a deputation of his friends waited upon the old gentleman to expostulate with him for his irregularities of utterance; he was shocking many good people, and his advisers hoped that he would endeavor to amend. He said, "Well, gentlemen, if you have said what you have to say, I will get you to wait just a minute or two while I run up stairs." Mr. Wilks went upstairs, and brought down a long roll of paper, which he unfolded with due dignity. "Look at that." Yes, they looked at it. "Do you see the number of names?" "Yes." "Here is another roll for you. Look at this! Count those names! Here is number three, look at this! Now, gentlemen," he said, "you see all these names? Well, then, all these precious souls profess to have found the Savior and everlasting life through what you are pleased to call my whims and oddities; and if you will find a longer roll in the hands of those who have no such whims and oddities I will try and alter my ways to please you; but until then I shall certainly follow my own course." Common sense declares Mr. Wilks to have been right. We do not say that the end justifies the means, but we would venture to hint that means which have such an end need very little justifying.

Let those whose barren ministries are as proper and decorous as a row of gravestones complain of the oddities of those who bring thousands to Christ: as for us, we have no heart for fault-finding, and only wish, without imitating their eccentricity, to find out the secret of the success of these men, if by any means we might save some. Eccentric or not eccentric will be a small matter with us if men are delivered from the wrath to come and led to trust in Jesus by the word which we preach.

3

Causes of Eccentricity

We have continued talking about eccentric men, but we have not yet decided what it is which makes a man eccentric. Let us now come to the point. Some ministers have been reckoned eccentric simply and only because *they have been natural.* They have been themselves, and not copies of others: what was in them they have not restrained, but have given full play to all their powers. Take for instance John Berridge. Berridge was quaint by nature. In the former lecture I quoted purposely from his letters rather than from any of his sermons or didactic works, because in a letter you see a man at ease. Berridge could not help being singular, for the form of his mind led him in that direction, and his bachelor life helped to develop his idiosyncrasies. His quaintness was all his own, and you see it in his household arrangements, as, for instance, when he says to a friend:

> I am glad to see you write of a visit to Everton; we have always plenty of horse provender at hand; but unless you send me notice beforehand of your coming, you will have a cold and scanty meal; for we roast only twice in the week. Let me have a line, and I will give you the same treat I always gave to Mr. Whitefield, an eighteen-penny barn-door fowl; this will neither burst you nor ruin me; half you shall have at noon with a pudding, and the rest at night. Much grace and sweet peace be with yourself and partner; and the blessing of a new heart be with your children. With many thanks, I remain your affectionate servant, J.B.

Nor is it less manifest in his hymns, even the most sober of them, as for instance in the well-known verse where he speaks of the saints in heaven and cries—

> Ah, Lord, with feeble steps I creep,
>   And sometimes sing and sometimes weep;
> But strip me of my house of clay,
>   And I will sing as loud as they.

We are not likely to censure the good man for his oddities more severely than he does himself, for in another of his pieces he writes—

> Brisk and dull in half an hour,
>   Hot and cold, and sweet and sour,
> Sometimes grave at Jesus' school,
>   Sometimes light and play the fool.
>
> What a motley wretch am I,
>   Full of inconsistency!
> Sure the plague is in my heart,
>   Else I could not act this part.

Rowland Hill, again, was odd by nature, and though he put great constraint upon himself his oddity would break out. On one occasion he preached in Dr. Collyer's chapel at Peckham, where everything was of the most stately order. He spoke for twenty-five minutes in a strain of deepest solemnity, but at last the real man broke out, and for the next quarter of an hour quaintness came to the front. In the vestry, at the close, he observed that he had over and over again resolved to utter no expression which could excite a smile, but, said he, "I find it's of no use. Though my very life depended upon it, I could not help myself." He never went out of his way for odd and striking sayings, he even strove to avoid them, but they were natural to him, and he was not himself without them. Do we blame the man for being himself? We blame him not, but commend him. Originality is not to be censured, but encouraged. Sir Joshua Reynolds says of painters, "Few have been taught to any purpose who have not been their own teachers." It was the excellence of Gainsborough that he formed his style for himself in the fields, and not in the studios of an academy. "The methods he used for producing his effects had very much the appearance of an artist who had never learned from others the usual and regular practice belonging to the art; for still, like a man of strong intuitive perception of what was required, he found out a way of his own to accomplish his purpose." We need in the pulpit more Gainsboroughs, for we have quite enough of the academy men of this school and the other.

Cold-hearted professionals follow each other in one line, like those caterpillars which I have seen at Mentone, which make a procession head to tail in a straight line, till you half fancy it is only one single insect; but the man who serves his God with his whole heart is apt to forget his surroundings, and to fling himself so completely into his work that the whole of his nature comes into action, and even his humor, if he be possessed of that faculty, rushes into the battle.

Some men have been dubbed eccentric because *they have been more truthful than their fellows*. Exact truth-speaking is none too common in our country. Few say that they are busy and cannot see those who call on them, but they are "not at home." Writing to persons whom they hate, many begin with, "My dear sir"; and to persons for whom they have no respect they subscribe themselves, "Your obedient servant." These are only quoted as feeble specimens of genteel falsehood; but like straws they show how the wind blows. Now there are a few men who are called eccentric because they do not believe in etiquettical lying, but speak the truth whether they offend or please. A gentleman not long ago was set down as very eccentric because being asked whether the tea was to his taste, he replied that it was not, for it was very weak and nearly cold. Others had equivocated, or had expressed themselves delighted with the nauseous decoction, and none of these were set down as eccentric. The more's the pity! Where truth is thought to be eccentric, the age itself is out of gear.

Father Taylor presided at a prayer meeting among his sailor converts, and a great man from the City came in to honor the poor people with his presence and to patronize their missionary. He made a speech, in which he extolled the kindness of the wealthy Christian people of Boston in helping to build Mr. Taylor's chapel, and assisting in his support. He praised these superior people for their great consideration of poor degraded sailors; and he gave the audience a sufficient allowance of condescension to last them for the next six months at the least. As soon as the great man had finished, Mr. Taylor quietly asked, "Is there any other old sinner from up town who would like to say a word before we go on with the meeting?" The eccentricity of that expression lay in the truthfulness which thus rebuked the impertinence of the speaker.

Good Mr. Grimshaw of Haworth once displayed his eccentricity when Mr. Whitefield was preaching in his church. Whitefield in his sermon having spoken severely of those professors of the gospel who, by their loose and evil conduct, caused the ways of truth to be evil spoken of, intimated his hope that it was not necessary to enlarge much upon that topic to the congregation before him, who had long been privileged to listen to the earnest addresses of such an able and faithful preacher. Up gets Mr. Grimshaw and says in a loud voice, "Oh sir, for God's sake, don't speak so; I pray you do not flatter them. I fear the greater part of them are going to hell with their eyes open." Very different this from the smooth-spoken flatterer who did not desire the visit of an evangelist, because such people were only fit to preach to the wicked, and he was not aware that there was one such person in his parish.

Mr. Hill once rebuked an Antinomian who was in the habit of drinking. The man replied with a knowing look, "Now, do you think, Mr. Hill, a glass of spirits will drive grace out of my heart? "No," said the faithful old gentleman, "for there is none in it." This was putting the truth pretty clearly, and for that very reason it is spoken of as eccentric.

Matthew Wilks was remarkable for hatred of the flattering terms which certain unctuous brethren would every now and then lavish upon him. "There," said he, "I have been much pleased with my people's prayers tonight. No stuff, no flattery, no speaking of me as a dear, venerable saint, until I almost go into hysterics. Saint, indeed! A poor worm! I can scarcely refrain from speaking aloud, when such language frets my ears." To a wealthy man who had headed a subscription list for an excellent institution with a very small sum, he said, "I will have nothing to do with it since you do so little for it. You have strangled the child in its birth, when you should have nourished and cherished it until you had set it upon its feet."

Now, in these cases the eccentricity lay in plain speaking, and this is an order of eccentricity of which we cannot very well have too much, if it be accompanied by sincere affection and tempered with gentleness. But of this I feel quite sure, that if any man will make up his mind that he will only say what he believes to be strictly true, he will be thought odd and eccentric before the sun goes down.

Certain preachers have been very eccentric because *they have been manly*, too manly to be hampered by the customs and manners of the period. They have broken through one and another of the rules which have been constructed for the propping up of manikins, and have behaved themselves as men. Mr. Binney was often thought eccentric for nothing else but his boldness and freedom from pulpit affectations. Why, sirs, there are places where it would be eccentric to speak so as to startle the drowsy; eccentric to illustrate your words by suitable action; eccentric to use a simple illustration: in fact, eccentric to utter anything more striking than the polished nullities of Blair. True-hearted men are not readily held in by the cramping-irons of childish fashion, but they are of the mind of Matthew Wilks who said, "Flesh will cry out, 'What will men say?' but a sanctified conscience will cry, 'What will God say?'" Egyptian art was reduced to an unvarying ugliness by laws which fixed the form of every feature and limb of its statues: the artist who should have anticipated the graceful life of Grecian sculpture would have been condemned by his nation as grievously eccentric, and yet unbiased ages would have exonerated the innovator from any fault; the case is the same with preachers who break through artificial rules, and boldly refuse to be mere copyists of the regulation patterns. In some places the style has been fixed by some venerated pastor who has gone to his rest; his threadbare mantle, which was excellent wear for him, is supposed to be the exact garment for his successor, and the old women of both sexes cry out against any who choose to wear their own clothes.

It is easy enough among Dissenters to find regulations as rigid as could be invented by any bench of bishops; you may not vary the length of the hymn or the order of the service by a hair's breadth, or you will sin against your own reputation and the feelings of the conservative portion of the congregation. There are few of such places now, but quite enough and, where the evil rules, the good folks are as tenacious of their established nonsense as ever the Church of England can be of her printed prayers and rubrics; and the preacher must submit to all the regular fudge as if it were Scripture itself, or be pronounced eccentric and wanting in decorum. A man that *is* a man will yield for peace sake as far as his soul is unhampered, but beyond that he will ask, "Who makes these regulations, and to what end are they made?" Finding them to be worthless and injurious, he will put his foot through them, and there will be an end of the rubbish. Some congregations are dying of dignity, and must be aroused by real life. People said that Mr. Hill rode on the back of order and decorum, and therefore he called his two horses by those names, so that if he could not ride on the back of them he might make the saying nearly true by being dragged behind them. Order and decorum, in some of our churches, have manifested themselves to be deadly sins; dead and burying the dead. Some congregations are so very orderly that they are like a vault in which the corpses lie, each one in due place, and none dares to move or lift a voice loud enough to be called a chirp. This will not do. Bring the trumpet! Sound a blast and wake the sleepers! Eccentric! Yes, eccentricity, if you like to call life by that name. Heaven knows it is sadly wanted.

After all, the eccentricities of manly life never equal those of the wretched dance of death, or sleep of death, which is so dear to mere routine. Think of such an event as the following happening among your orderly readers of other men's discourses, for the like has happened and must have happened many times. A certain preacher delivered a discourse in which occurred such a passage as this: "On account of your sins, and your neglect of the house of God, your wantonness and your gluttony, the anger of the Most High is provoked, and therefore is this great plague come upon you, and death is raging in every street." When the sermon was finished the officials of the township came to know where this plague was, and what deaths had happened; indeed, all the congregation were anxious to know where this dreadful disease was raging.

"Oh," said this orderly reader of sermons, "I do not know where it is, but it was in my sermon, and so I was obliged to read it to you." It would be easy enough to enlarge upon the accidents which must occur where borrowed, or rather stolen, sermons are preached; but this is not my point, I merely mention this as one instance of the way in which prosy routine becomes itself ludicrous. To me it seems always ludicrous if looked at through the glass of truth. Primness, fashionableness, and dignity are but little separated from the ridiculous; at their very best there is but one step between them, and that step is often taken with grave obliviousness that it is so.

I make bold to say that some men have been styled eccentric because *they are really in earnest*, and earnestness defies rules. I do not believe that it is possible for a man in downright earnest to be always "proper." I suppose there is a proper way of getting a lady out of her bedchamber when her house is on fire, but doubtless our firemen often violate the proprieties when they have such a thing to do. They have to rush in anyhow to save life, and they cannot stay to make apologies. The flames are urgent, and so must the rescuer be, or life will be lost. I suppose there is a proper way of pulling persons out of the water when they are drowning, but I have known brave fellows drag them out by the hair of their heads: this was rough and rude, but it answered the purpose.

Did anyone ever blame the doer of the deed for his roughness? Is not the soul more precious than the body, and who would suffer it to be lost for the sake of etiquette? A man may go into the pulpit as prim as you please, and he may even wear tight-fitting lavender gloves, such as I have heard of; but let him feel an inward anguish for the souls of men and he will forget his dignity and burst his gloves, and in all probability never buy a second pair. A man may be stiffly proper, and even elegant and delicate till he comes to real grips with men's consciences, and then, like the soldier at Waterloo who wished to be in his shirt-sleeves, he will feel hampered by his buckram and his starch, and speak like a man to men, and then some booby or other will hold up his hands and cry, "Dear me, how dreadfully eccentric!"

A few divines have seemed to be eccentric because of *the wealth of poetry which dwelt in their speech.* Men of the prosaic school are quite startled by expressions which to poetical minds are natural enough, and by no means singular. It needs genius in the hearer to enjoy genius in the preacher. One of my personal friends, whose sermons are essentially poems, laughed the other day right heartily at the expression of an admiring hearer, who did not at one time appreciate him. "Ah," said the good man, "I am very sorry that I was so foolish as to leave your ministry for a time; but then, you see, *I used to hear you with a jaundiced eye!*" It is this jaundiced eye of cold matter-of-fact which is unable to perceive the beauty of sparkling metaphors and images, and therefore sees instead mere eccentricity. In my earlier days I have heard rustic prayers which thrilled *me*, not only with their spirituality, but with their poetry, and yet I heard others exclaiming against the extravagance of the language. One whom many regarded as eccentric in his preaching was a great favorite with me, and I remember now his striking sayings, his choice aphorisms, and his rare imagery, while other sermons have faded from my memory, because they never touched my heart. I could have said of him what John Bradford said of Latimer, "I have an ear for other divines, but I have a heart for you." Doubtless there are many others who are condemned for their eccentricity by the simpletons around them, because they have wealthy creative minds, and scatter pearls with both their hands.

Eccentricity has also been charged on *men of shrewd common sense.* They have baffled those who sought to entrap them, and, in revenge, their adversaries have dubbed them eccentric. They were not quite so easily gulled as their contemporaries, but leveled a little mother-wit at cants, and hypocrites, and deriders, and so they must be libeled as odd fellows. As this is a point which I do not intend to dwell upon at any length, I will only illustrate it by the story of the eccentric shepherd, and remark that similar shrewdness on the part of ministers is of the utmost value, but is pretty sure to incur the charge of eccentricity. Here is the story.

> An exceedingly proud clergyman, riding over a common, saw a shepherd tending his flock, and wearing a new coat. The parson asked in a haughty tone who gave him that coat. "The same people (said the shepherd) that clothe you—the parish." The clergyman, nettled a little, rode on murmuring a considerable way, and at length sent his man back to ask the shepherd if he would come and live with him, for he thought of keeping a fool. The man went to the shepherd accordingly and delivered his master's message, imagining that his master really wanted a fool. "Are *you* going away then?" said the shepherd. "No," answered the other. "Then you may tell your master (replied the shepherd) that his living won't maintain *three* of us."

Such crushing replies Rowland Hill and others were quite capable of giving to hypocrites and mockers, and they did well thus to silence them, but it earned them the title of eccentric.

Some men have been eccentric on account of *the vast amount of dramatic energy with which they have been endowed.* Certain persons when they talk suit the action to the word from the force of nature and habit. It is in their way to be dramatic. Look at a Frenchman, how he speaks with his hands, his shoulders, his eyebrows, his feet, and his whole body. Very few Englishmen are thus dramatic, but here and there we meet with persons who are as energetic in that direction as the liveliest of our Gallic neighbors. And why not? The famous William—or as the public delighted to say, "Billy"—Dawson, was nothing if not dramatic. I have heard a well-known minister tell that Dawson was once preaching about Noah's ark, and finding himself boxed up in the pulpit he said, "This won't do." He opened the pulpit door and he came down the stairs to the bottom of the pulpit, and there he began to fell trees and cut and saw them, and then he seemed to be hammering away to make the ark, which was represented by the pulpit. This ark was made before them all, the people being worked up to an extreme excitement while Dawson continued to cry, "There is a flood coming, I am making this ark for the saving of my house; there is no hope for anybody but those who come into the ark." Then he seemed to be boiling a great cauldron of pitch, until he took his long brush and pitched the ark within and without, and when all was done there was his ship on the dry land, and like Noah he turned round and asked the people once again whether they would come into it and be saved. They would not come in, and so he declared he would go in alone. He went up into the pulpit and shut the door with the words, "And the Lord shut him in." Then came the flood, and our informant said that he felt as if the floor of the chapel burst up and the water began bubbling from below, while great water-floods poured from above in mighty torrents; and there was Dawson, another Noah, all alive and safe, crying out that it was now too late, for the door was shut.

All were awed and filled with breathless attention while he bade them remember that such would soon be the case, and preached unto them Jesus as the only salvation. None of us would attempt this, but I would not have laid a finger on Dawson. Why should he not depict the scene in his own way? If God gave him the histrionic faculty, why should he not use it to impress his hearers? Perhaps he knew that those who were around him could not be impressed in any other way. This was he who on another occasion described David and Goliath. He represented David coming forth with his sling, and the giant boasting that he would give his flesh to the fowls of the air and to the beasts of the field, and so on; but David replies, "Thou comest to me with a sword, and with a spear, and with a shield; but I come to thee in the name of the Lord of hosts." He laid his stone carefully in the sling, whirled the sling in the air, and you could hear the stone whizzing towards the giant's brow. Just then Sammy Hick, the village blacksmith, who was sitting near the preacher, rose up under tremendous excitement and cried, "Now then, Billy, off with his head!"

For my part, I like this dramatizing kept within check and thoroughly well done. You have, probably, seen Mr. Gough do that sort of thing admirably in his orations. Have I not seen him walk what seemed to me miles while he was delivering one of his addresses, rushing over the plains and through the rivers, and at last up the sides of Vesuvius after a bubble? I think I see him now, with his feet sinking in the hot ashes, struggling in vain and perishing before our eyes. It was grandly done, and no one had a right to object to it. Gough has caught Garrick's idea, and speaks of truths as truths, making them visible before our eyes. I know the criticisms which are so easy to make about histrionic displays, theatrical action, miracle plays, and so forth, and I know also the real dangers which surround the practice; but I would far rather incur all the supposable perils than altogether banish such an awakening force from the pulpit.

Sometimes men have been regarded as eccentric because *they have been practical*. The occasion has demanded what in other circumstances would have been unjustifiable, and others not knowing the peculiar conditions have set their words and actions in another light, and made them seem objectionable. They meant to save men's souls somehow, by the blessing of God, and therefore they resolved to do anything and everything by which they could get at the stolid, ignorant, and indifferent; and hence the things which they did have been *outré* and striking, but not more so than the need required. Such singular words or acts have been divorced from the circumstances out of which they grew, and put aside from the connection; the design of the preacher has been forgotten, and then the thing which has been done has seemed to be eccentric at least, if not censurable; though, mark you, had you yourself been there, and had you possessed the preacher's ready wit and intense earnestness, you could scarcely have done better. Let me give you one or two instances, and the first is from Mr. Grant's sketch of Rowland Hill in "The Metropolitan Pulpit"; it is told in a somewhat wordy style, but the change from my more abrupt manner may be a relief:

A pious woman, a member of Surrey Chapel, was married to a husband who, though kind to her, had no sense of religion, but delighted in spending the hours in swilling beer which she spent in attendance on the preaching of the gospel. It so happened that the couple, through some disappointment in business, had been unable to pay their rent on a particular quarter day. The consequence was that a distraint on their furniture was put into their house, and a party was employed, as the technical phrase has it, "'to take possession." After turning over every scheme in their minds which could suggest itself for extricating themselves from the difficulties in which they were involved, they were about to despair, when the idea occurred to the wife of submitting the circumstances of the case to Mr. Hill. She accordingly proceeded to his house, at once got access to him, and with no small degree of tremor made a short and simple representation of the state of matters.

"How much would you require to save your furniture and get rid of the person in possession?" enquired Mr. Hill.

"Eighteen pounds, sir, would be quite sufficient for the purpose," answered the poor woman, with a palpitating heart.

"I'll let you have the loan of twenty, and you can repay me at your convenience. Send your husband to me on your return home, and I will have two ten pound notes ready by the time he arrives. I wish to give the notes to him rather than to you."

Mrs. D— quitted Mr. Hill's house and hurried home with light foot, but with a still lighter heart. Having communicated to her husband what had passed between herself and her minister, it is unnecessary to say that he lost no time in proceeding to the house of Mr. Hill. The latter received him with much kindness of manner.

"And so," said he, "you are so unfortunate as to have a person in possession."

"We unfortunately have, sir."

"And twenty pounds will be sufficient to get rid of him and restore your furniture to you?"

"It will, sir."

"Well, then," said Mr. Hill, pointing to the table, "there are two ten pound notes for you, which you can repay when you are able. Take them."

The other advanced to the table, took the notes, and was in the act of folding them up, at the same time warmly thanking Mr. Hill for the act of friendship he had done him, and expressing a hope that he would soon be able to pay the amount back again, when the reverend gentleman suddenly exclaimed, "Stop a little! Just lay the notes down again until I ask a blessing on them."

The other did as he was desired, on which Mr. Hill, extending both his arms, uttered a short prayer to this effect: "O Lord, who art the Author of all mercy and the Giver of every good and perfect gift, do thou be graciously pleased to bless the sum of money which is given to him who is now before thee, that it may conduce to his present and eternal welfare. For Jesus Christ's sake."

"Now sir," said Rowland Hill, as he finished his brief supplication, "now, sir, you may take the money."

The party a second time took up the two ten pound notes, and was in the act as before of folding them up, when Mr. Hill interposed, by reminding him that he had forgotten one thing. It may be easily supposed that by this time he was a good deal confused. His confusion was increased a hundredfold when Mr. Hill remarked, "But, my friend, you have not yourself asked for a blessing on the money. You had better do it now."

"Sir," faltered out the other, scarcely able to support himself, "sir, I cannot pray. I never prayed in all my life."

"You have the more need to begin now," observed the reverend gentleman, in his own cool yet rebuking manner.

"I cannot, sir; I do not know what to say."

"Try, try and thank God and ask his blessing, however short your prayer may be."

"I cannot, sir! I cannot say a single sentence."

"Then you can't have the money. I will not lend twenty pounds to a prayer-less man."

The other hesitated for a moment, and then with dosed eyes, and uplifted hands, he said with great earnestness, "O Lord, what shall I say to thee and to Mr. Hill on this occasion?" He was about to begin another sentence, when the reverend gentleman interrupted him by observing, "That will do for a beginning. It is a very excellent first prayer, for it is from the heart. Take the money, and may God's blessing be given along with it." As he spoke, Mr. Hill took up the two ten pound notes, and transferring them to the half-bewildered man, cordially shook him by the hand, and wished him good morning.

It only remains for me to mention, that not only did the husband and wife become prosperous in secular matters, but the incident made so deep an impression on the husband's mind as to end in his conversion to God.

It was strange thus as it were to drive a man to pray, but who shall say it was wrong? My second incident is even more wild, and I give it as I recollect it; if I err in accuracy I shall be sorry, but I will tell it as nearly as I remember it. A Methodist preacher went to a certain town in the north, but found hardly anyone to hear him, and he preached a while with no stir appearing among the dry bones. One Sunday morning he said, "I tell you what it is, friends. This town is responsible to God for the possession of the means of grace, which it does not use. I cannot get the people to hear, but I can remove some of their responsibility by destroying the pulpit which they despise, and the place of worship which they will not enter. Here is a beginning; we will break the desk to pieces at once, and then if no one comes we will clear out the pews and everything else, and leave the chapel a wreck. The people shall not perish with the gospel so close to them. The candlestick shall be taken away since they refuse the light." He commenced by laying his axe at the pulpit, and in part demolishing it, before the eyes of the few who were present. "Now," said he, "tell your friends that there is part of the responsibility gone, and the rest will follow." The astonished folks went home and spread the amazing news, and in a very short time the place was thronged. You say, "This *was* an eccentric man." Well, I do not justify his proceedings, but I judge that he knew his own way about better than I could have shown it to him. After all, he was only sacrificing a few boards; and at that small cost he broke through that indifference which more costly methods might have failed to touch. Within a little time Methodism lifted up its head in the town, and the forlorn meeting-house rang with songs of praise. Why, dear me, if the Tabernacle were empty, and we could not fill the house without doing or saying something striking, I think we might, if it were for the first time in our life, run the risk of being thought eccentric.

Everything looks ridiculous or not according to its surroundings. Wisdom and wit may become folly and even falsehood, if they are severed from the occasion which called them forth. Listen to an ancient tale of a traveler who reported that he had seen a cabbage so large that a whole regiment of soldiers took shelter under it from a shower of rain. To him another, who was no traveler, asked if they would believe him if he told them that on the very day in which this cabbage was seen he had himself passed by a place where four hundred braziers were making a cauldron—two hundred of them hammering outside, and two hundred inside fastening the rivets! The traveler eagerly inquired of what use such a cauldron could be, and received the following answer: "Sir, it was to boil your cabbage." Now, if this second person's story was repeated away from its connection, and its form slightly altered, a richly deserved rebuke would be made to look like an attempt to exceed in lying. Many a word spoken or the principle of answering a fool according to his folly has been quoted against a wise man, and the folly has been laid at the wrong door.

There is an extraordinary story of Father Andre, a French preacher of great repute, for what was called eccentricity. He was preaching one afternoon to a congregation or persons who disregarded religion both as to themselves and their families, and he wished both to convict them and to upbraid them for the bad way in which they were bringing up their little ones. He first asked the children questions from the Catechism, and obtained no replies; and he then shook his sleeve, and out there flew a pack of cards. The people were shocked with him, of course, but he quietly looked down and said to one of the children, "Boy, bring me a card. You boy, bring me another. You girl, another, and come here with them!" They gathered around the pulpit, and he asked of one, "What is this card, my child?" The boy answered at once. The next, a girl, came up, and she also knew her card. He continued his questions till he had gone far into the pack, and received correct answers all round. "Ah," he says, "I see how you are training your children. You teach them to know all the cards, but you do not instruct them in the faith. Are you not ashamed of yourselves?" Here I pronounce no verdict, I could not have done it myself, nor should I like to hear of any friend of mine doing the like; but I cannot tell what was good for Catholics in France so long ago.

Lassenius, a Dutch court preacher, in the end of the seventeenth century, had been greatly vexed by seeing a considerable part of his congregation going to sleep. One day he suddenly stopped, and pulling out a battledore and shuttlecock, began playing with them. Of course, the sleepers all awoke directly; the wakeful ones jogging their neighbors to share in their astonishment. Then Lassenius turned upon them with a severe rebuke. "When I announce to you serious and important truths, you are not ashamed to go to sleep; but when I play the fool you are all eye and ear." Sharp medicine this for a desperate disease, and the physician who administered it was in grievous danger of injuring himself. I do not think that I can justify this procedure, but I do not know the Dutch people as well as Lassenius did, and my own people never go to sleep, and so I do not pretend to form an opinion one way or the other. Certainly it must, be very provoking to see people sleeping, and yet it is not so very wonderful that they should do so when we consider the drowsy sounds to which they are doomed to listen. "I feel very tired with preaching," said a young bombastic preacher. "O man," said a shrewd old hearer, "did you say you were tired? If you are only half as tired of it as I am, I pity you." I am afraid that this side of the question is too often forgotten.

The following story is worth recording. I do not hesitate to say that I should have done the same, and should have felt justified in thus practically rebuking a miserable people for leaving their place of worship in such a shameful condition.

> The Rev. Zabeliel Adams at one time exchanged with a neighboring minister—a mild, inoffensive man—who knowing the peculiar bluntness of his character, said to him, 'You will find some panes of glass broken in the pulpit window, and possibly you may suffer from the cold. The cushion, too, is in a bad condition; but I beg of you not to say anything to my people on the subject; they are poor, and sensitive!" "O no! O no!" said Mr. Adams, "You may trust me to be very quiet about such things." But before he left home he filled a bag with rags and took it with him. When he had been in the pulpit a short time, feeling somewhat incommoded by the free circulation of the air, he deliberately took from the bag a handful of rags, and stuffed them into the windows. Towards the close of his discourse, which was more or less upon the duties of a people

towards their minister, he became very animated, and purposely brought down both fists upon the pulpit cushion with tremendous force. The feathers flew in all directions, and the cushion was nearly emptied. He checked the current of his thoughts, and simply exclaimed, "Why, how these feathers fly!" and then proceeded. He had fulfilled his promise of not addressing the people on the subject, but had taught them a lesson not to be misunderstood. On the next Sabbath the window anti cushion were found in excellent repair.

I have talked to you thus cheerfully about eccentric preachers, but I would not have you forget the serious side of the matter. If I were addressing a congregation I would say to them: If you knew how we desire to lay hold of your minds for Christ, and how willingly we would be as solemn as death itself if we thought that this would win your hearts, you would not so much blame our occasional sallies. If you knew how little we desire notoriety, and how much we desire to save your souls, you would commend our object and excuse our style. We ramble because you ramble. O that we could seize the wandering sheep, and bring them home to the true fold. I say, if you knew the desire we have to bring men to Christ, you would not be so ready to catch at every little thing which violates the canons of taste. Besides, we are not bound to abide by your judgments. May it not be possible that we know what we are at as well as you do? Will you take our work and do it better? If so, we are ready to learn by your example. Judge the preacher if you like, but do remember that there is something better to be done than that, namely, to get all the good you can out of him, and pray his Master to put more good into him. What if the man be odd and strange, yet, as men take pearls out of oyster shells, so may you be willing to accept from God whatever of precious truth he sends you. Despise not the heavenly treasure because of the earthen vessel. Lose not an opportunity of being enriched because the gold lies in connection with common earth.

And, oh, dear brothers, who are engaged in winning souls, let me say to you, by the memories of all these good men who have gone before you, and who were counted eccentric, fear no man's frown, and court no man's smile, but say the right thing and the true, and say it as best you can, and ask God's help that you may say it so that you may make men feel it, even though you sting them into anger; for blessed shall that man be who has discharged his conscience before the living God. Do not sacrifice your hearers' souls to your own reputations. Be fools for Christ's sake, if need be, that you may gain the careless ones. The curse of the age is the unearthly ministry which mocks it. I say "unearthly," but I do not mean heavenly, I mean unpractical, unhuman— a thing which does not come home to men, or arouse the slightest interest in their minds. Do you believe that our working men would, as a rule, shun the churches of London if they were there regaled with hearty, homely discourses such as they could understand, and such as would touch their everyday life? I, for one, have reason to speak to the contrary, and that without a shadow of a doubt. Do you think that England would be so ready to be enticed back to Rome if all her ministers were preaching the gospel as they ought to be? With such a company of preachers discoursing twice every Sunday, besides the weekday exercises, ought not our island to be illuminated, as by the sun at noon, so that it would be impossible for the Roman darkness to return. Things would have been very different if there had been more love, more earnestness, more passion for souls in the pulpit; but then I greatly fear that there would also have been more eccentric men. Do you dread the evil? I share not your fear, but say, God send it, so that is be an outgrowth of true life.

4

Hugh Latimer (1480–1555)

Popish historians have not hesitated to describe Latimer as extremely eccentric. Lingard says, "His eloquence was bold and vehement, but poured forth in coarse and sarcastic language, and seasoned with quaint low jests and buffoonery." This accusation is evidently made for the purpose of whitewashing Popery and blackening the Reformation. It is with pleasure that we read it, because it enables us to entail the bishop amongst the noble army of the slandered servants of God. We have no wish to deny that Latimer was exceedingly quaint, and intermingled flashes of pleasantry with his earliest exhortations and serious arguments; but it was always with the view of confounding error and reaching the hearts of his hearers.

Here is an example of his shrewdness. Dr. Buckingham, one of the Black Friars, undertook to confute Latimer, and in his sermon said among other remarkably wise things that the reading of the Scriptures in the vulgar tongue would cause people to leave their vocations, and run into all sorts of extremes. "Thus," said he, "for example, the ploughman, when he heareth this in the gospel, 'no man that layeth his hand on the plough and looketh back is meet for the kingdom of God,' will peradventure upon this cease from his ploughing. Likewise the baker, when he heareth that 'a little leaven corrupteth the whole lump of dough,' may perchance leave our bread unleavened, and so our bodies be unseasoned." Latimer heard this sermon, and engaged to answer the arguments, which he did from the same pulpit in the afternoon, Dr. Buckingham sitting opposite to him with his Black Friars' cowl upon his shoulders. After discoursing upon the figurative phrases of Scripture, Latimer said that such metaphors were commonly used and were well understood in all languages, "as for example," observed he, looking towards the place where the friar sat, "when the painters represent a fox preaching out of a friar's cowl, no one is so weak as to take this for a real fox, but only as a figure of caution to beware of that hypocrisy, craft, and dissimulation which lie hid many times under those cowls."

The general preaching of Latimer before and after he became a bishop was very plain and homely, and exactly suited to the manners and tastes of the people to whom he spoke. His sermons should be read by every lover of racy English. We have only space for one extract, which will show how very plain and colloquial he could be. "A good fellow on a time had another of his friends to a breakfast, and said, 'If you will come, you shall be welcome; but I tell you aforehand, you shall have but slender fare, one dish, and that is all. What is that?' said he. 'A pudding, and nothing else.' 'Marry' (said he), 'you cannot please me better; of all meats, this is for mine own tooth; you may draw me round about the town with a pudding. These bribing magistrates and judges follow gifts faster than the fellow would follow the pudding.'" Latimer wanted his words to be remembered so as to work reform, and he did well to put them in such a shape that they would ring over the land. We will warrant that this pudding story of his did more for justice than a dozen refined orations. His was practical preaching, and it dealt with the sins of the great as well as with those of the common people, in tones too honest to be very polite.

The dauntless courage of this noble servant of God was seen in his conduct towards Henry VIII. One New Year's day, instead of carrying, according to the custom of that age, a rich gift to the king, he presented him with the New Testament, a leaf of which was turned down at this passage, "Whoremongers and adulterers God will judge." This might have cost him his life; but bluff Hal, instead of being angry, admired the good man's courage. Upon a certain occasion, when preaching before Henry, Hugh, as was his wont, spoke his mind very plainly, and the sermon displeased his majesty; he was therefore commanded to preach again on the next Sabbath, and to make an apology for the offense he had given. After reading his text, the bishop thus began his sermon: "Hugh Latimer, dost thou know before whom thou art this day to speak? To the high and mighty monarch, the king's most excellent majesty, who can take away thy life if thou offendest; therefore take heed that thou speakest not a word that may displease! But then consider well, Hugh, dost thou not know from whence thou comest; upon whose message thou art sent? Even by the great and mighty God! Who is all present! And who beholdeth all thy ways! And who is able to cast thy soul into hell! Therefore, take care that thou deliverest thy message faithfully." He then proceeded with the same sermon he had preached the preceding Sabbath, but with considerably more energy. The sermon ended, the court were full of expectation to know what would be the fate of this honest and plain-dealing bishop. After dinner, the king called for Latimer, and with a stern countenance asked him how he durst preach in such a manner. He, falling on his knees, replied, his duty to his God and his prince had enforced him thereto, and that he had merely discharged his duty and cleared his conscience by what he had spoken. Upon which the king, rising from his seat, and taking the good man by the hand, embraced him, swing, "Blessed be God, I have so honest a servant."

Under Edward VI Latimer had great influence, but the return of Mary soon called him to severer conflicts. Dauntless, honest, and simple-hearted, Latimer rejoiced when he was called upon to lay down his bishopric; and when he was summoned to be tried for his life the old man hesitated not to appear and defend our holy faith to the death. His words at the stake were characteristic of the man. Addressing Bishop Ridley, who was to die with him, he said, "Be of good comfort, Master Ridley, and play the man. We shall this day light such a candle by God's grace in England as I trust shall never be put out." *And by God's grace it never shall be.*

5

Hugh Peters (1599–1660)

The most slandered man of his times was Hugh Peters, who was executed at the Restoration as a ringleader in the so-called Great Rebellion. He is usually set down as a wretched jester, and traduced as a mountebank, whereas there is far more evidence to show that he was a zealous preacher of the gospel. We give him a place here, not because we altogether admire him, but as a matter of justice to one who has been falsely accused.

In his unconverted life he was a daring sinner; but after he was converted he became a powerful preacher of the word. At St. Sepulchre's Church his preaching was very popular, and, better still, it was made useful in the conversion of hundreds. Having in a prayer for the queen uttered words which were taken to imply that she was in need of repentance, as in all probability she was, he was imprisoned by Laud. He ultimately fled the country, and became a pastor, first in Holland, and then in America. His reputation was so great that his brother colonists sent him home as a mediator upon important business. Here he was detained by the breaking out of the civil wars, during which he became an army chaplain, was present at many great battles, and was frequently sent up to the parliament to report progress.

Peters was at one time secretary to Oliver Cromwell. Carlyle quotes his description of the taking of Basing House, and speaks of him as "a man concerning whom the reader has heard so many falsehoods." The utmost malice of the Cavaliers was expended in blackening this man's character with the view of excusing his execution by Charles II, which was nothing better than a judicial murder. A respectable biographer says of him, "Peters was not a wise man in all things; he was forward and hasty of speech, but he was a true and sincere man; a man of unblemished reputation in circles where nothing foul or mean was tolerated, and a man who in every respect was immensely the superior of those who traduced him."

It was the common expression of those days that the saints should have the praises of God in their mouths and a two-edged sword in their hands, and this was far too prominently the case with Peters. He was "the fighting parson" of his day; but like the Ironsides among whom he ministered he was a devout soldier, and was made a soldier by his devotion. Our views and sympathies do not run in that direction, but we are too much indebted to the warriors of the commonwealth to be in a hurry to condemn them. There was an intense earnestness about Hugh Peters, and as his sermons were meant for soldiers, and had relation to stormy politics, they were in all probability rough-hewn, and by no means pleasant in the ears of cavaliers; but the coarse jests which were imputed to him were evidently none of his, since they were current long before he was born. Some studious owner of the little volume in the British Museum which records these vile witticisms has annotated it in such a way as to prove that the larger number of the anecdotes are fabrications. Thus, "Jest 1: This is a Norman tale of the twelfth or thirteenth century. Jest 14: Taken from Taylor, the water poet's works," etc.

Nevertheless, such stories as the following may have some truth in them: "Praying in a village, he espied in the church the king's arms, whereupon he brought in these words, *Good Lord, keep us from the yoke of tyranny*; and spreading his hands towards the king's arms, saith he, *Preserve thy servants from the paw of the lion and the horn of the unicorn.*

Discoursing of the advantage Christians have above heathens, and showing that the heathen are guided by a natural instinct, but we have the word preached to us; and indeed, saith he, the gospel hath a very free passage amongst us, for I am confident it no sooner enters in at one ear, but it is out at the other.

Mr. Peters espying a friend of his, deeply cut in the head, through having engaged in a foolish fray, he began to check him for his indiscretion. But, saith he, 'tis too late now to give you counsel; come along with me to a surgeon, and I'll see you drest. Where being come, the surgeon begun to wash away the blood, and search for his brains, to see if they were hurt. At which Mr. Peters cries out,' What a mad man are you to seek for any such thing; if he had possessed any brains he would never have ventured into so foolish a contest.'"

Hugh Peters sinned against the whole party of Church-and-King by his zealous defense of the Parliamentary cause, and at the same time he shocked the Presbyterians by pleading for A TOLERATION OF ALL SECTS, and this was reckoned to be the very worst of crimes. Men who are in advance of their age are abused for principles which in due time become accepted. A man who was secretary to Oliver Cromwell, who had Philip Nye and Goodwin for intimate friends, and Milton for his apologist, was not a bad man: this is morally certain. His peculiarities arose out of his passionate enthusiasm for the cause of liberty, and the remarkable combination in his person of soldier and preacher.

In the works of Hugh Peters there are no indications of his being a jester, but abundant evidence of his genius and fertility of mind. The little book entitled *A Dying Father's Last Legacy to an only Child* was written by his own hand just before his execution, and is rich in holy instruction. Here are extracts:

"He that sets up religion to get anything by it more than the glory of God and the saving his own soul will make a bad bargain of it at the close."

"Make Christ your wisdom. Oh that you were thus wise! Much of wit must be pared off before it will be useful. I have seen the ways of it though I never could pretend to much of it: but this I know, that being unsanctified, wit is a sword in a madman's hand. It spends itself in vanity, foolish jesting, and abuse of those who are weaker than ourselves, yea, it often leads men to play with the blessed word of God."

"If I go shortly where time shall be no more, where neither cock nor clock distinguishes hours, sink not, but lay thy head in his bosom who can keep thee, for he sits upon the waves."

6

Daniel Burgess (1645–1713)

The name of Daniel Burgess is usually associated with jesting, but this is another instance of the way in which worthy men have been held up to ridicule. He was a Dissenter, and a man of great courage and boldness of speech; he was also a quaint and attractive preacher, and so the word went forth from the evil one that he should be denounced as a buffoon. In those days there was no law to protect the Dissenter, or at least no officer who cared to put it in force, and so Mr. Burgess and his congregation were shamefully annoyed by persons of the baser sort; but when he was urged to prosecute these disturbers he only replied, "No, I have freely forgiven them, and shall never meditate revenge." These are not the words of a buffoon.

His hearers procured for him a meeting-house in Brydges Street, Covent Garden, where a large congregation always gathered. "Being situated," says one of his biographers, "in the neighborhood of the theater, and surrounded by many who were fools enough to mock at sin and religion, he frequently had among his hearers those who came only to make themselves merry at the expense of religion, Dissenters, and Daniel Burgess. This his undaunted courage, his pointed wit, and ready elocution turned to great advantage: for he frequently fixed his eye on those scoffers, and addressing them personally in a lively, piercing, and serious manner, was blessed to the conversion of many who came only to mock."

He continued as pastor over this congregation for thirty years, during which a new place of worship was built by them in Carey Street, and when this was utterly wrecked by Sacheverell's mob, it was repaired at the expense of the government; but the expense and trouble to which they were put seriously burdened his people. He died January 1712–13, in the sixty eighth year of his age, and was buried at St. Clement Danes, Strand. A writer says, "It has escaped the notice of his biographers, that the celebrated Lord Bolingroke was once his pupil, and the world has to regret that his lordship did not learn what Daniel Burgess might have taught him; for Daniel, with all his oddities, which made him for so many years the butt of Swift, Steele, and the other wits of the time, was a man of real piety."

One story which is told of him may have possibly been true, but we are not sure. When treating on the robe of righteousness, he said, "If any of you would have a good and cheap suit, you will go to Monmouth Street; if you want a suit for life, you will go to the Court of Chancery; but if you wish for a suit that will last to eternity, you must go to the Lord Jesus Christ, and put on his robe of righteousness." This is probably a garbled quotation. The reader may accept it *cum grano salis*.

Although it pleased the graceless witlings of his day to father silly stories upon Burgess, it is clear to all impartial persons that he was a man of mark, and of deep piety. When the Society for the Reformation of Manners was instituted he was selected to preach the first sermon. This was published under the title of "The Golden Snuffing," and is a proof of how the good man was vilified; for a critic describes it as "replete with forced puns," and we therefore procured it, but cannot find a pun in it, and scarcely anything quotable for special quaintness, unless it be the following passage: "Christ's ministers are your souls' physicians. We are not fiddlers to tickle your ears, nor confectioners to please your palates, but physicians to cure your diseases, and if you nauseate our most needful medicines we dare not withhold them, and gratify you with sugared poisons." We are sure that the critic never saw the sermon, but judged it from the title alone. The first choice of the preacher by a society which commanded the ablest ministers would not have fallen on a mere buffoon.

Our best evidence that Daniel Burgess was a good man and true is found in the facts that he was thought worthy by his contemporaries to preach one of the sermons in the famous series of "Morning Exercises," that he was much beloved by the excellent Dr. Bates, and that Matthew Henry preached a funeral sermon for him, wherein his homely speech is admitted and abundantly justified. With an extract from this sermon our brief notice must conclude:

> He often said he chose rather to be profitable than fashionable in his preaching, and that he thought it cost him more pains to study plainness than it did others to study fineness; and he would be willing to go out of the common way to meet with sinners, to persuade them to return to their God. "That is the best key (said he) that fits the lock, and opens the door, though it be not a silver or a golden one." Many have acknowledged that they came to hear him at first only to scoff at him, and make a jest of what he said, but went away under such convictions about the concerns of their souls and another world, as, it was hoped, ended in a happy change of their spirits.
>
> In his preaching he insisted mostly upon the first great principles of religion, which all good Christians are agreed in; and one who was a very competent judge told me, he thought he had as good a faculty in demonstrating them, and making them plain and evident, as most men he ever heard. He much lamented and vigorously opposed the growth of deism and infidelity among us, saying he dreaded a "Christless Christianity." He meddled not with party matters, or matters of doubtful disputation, but plainly made it his aim to bring people to-believe in Jesus Christ, and to live in all godliness and honesty. He was particularly careful to explain the two covenants of works and grace, and to guard against the two rocks of presumption and despair. He now and then used some plain similitude's or surprising turns of expression, or little stories, such perhaps as we find Bishop Latimer's sermons full of, which by some were turned to his reproach; but it is certain many particular stories were maliciously fathered on him, that were abominably false, and raised by a lying spirit only to obstruct his usefulness; and in the general he was industriously misrepresented by many, who it is to be feared therein discovered no kindness for serious godliness. A gentleman having once the curiosity to go to hear him, when he had done, could scarce be made to believe that this was Mr. Burgess; for, said he, "I never heard a better sermon in my life!"

7

John Berridge (1716–1793)

John Berridge, the Vicar of Everton, was commended by John Wesley as one of the most simple as well as most sensible of all whom it pleased God to employ in reviving primitive Christianity. He was a man of remarkable learning, being as familiar in the learned languages as in his mother tongue, and well instructed in theology, logic, mathematics, and metaphysics: he was not, therefore, eccentric because he was ignorant. He possessed a strength of understanding, quickness of perception, depth of penetration, and brilliancy of fancy beyond most men, while a vein of innocent humor ran through all his public and private discourses. His biographer tells us that this softened what some might call the austerity of religion, and rendered his company pleasant to people of a less serious habit; and yet he adds, "It is very singular that it never overcame his own gravity; he remained serious himself while others were convulsed with laughter."

Before he was converted he preached mere morality, but after he was called by the Holy Spirit he was zealous for the doctrines of sovereign grace, and preached the gospel in the clearest possible manner. In his ministry he was diligence itself, journeying through the counties of Cambridge, Bedford, Hertford, and Huntingdon continually, preaching upon an average from ten to twelve sermons a week, and riding from place to place on horseback. He wrote to a friend:

> I fear my weekly circuits would not suit a London or a Bath divine, nor any tender evangelist that is environed with prunello. Long rides and miry roads in sharp weather! Cold houses to sit in, with

very moderate fuel, and three or four children roaring or rocking about you! Coarse food and meager liquor; lumpy beds to lie on and too short for the feet; and stiff blankets like boards for a covering. Rise at five in the morning to preach; at seven breakfast on tea that smells very sickly; at eight mount a horse, with boots never cleaned, and then ride home, praising God for all mercies.

A complaint was lodged against him, and the bishop sent for him and reproved him for preaching "at all hours and on all days." "My lord," said he, modestly, "I preach only at two seasons." "Which are they, Mr. Berridge?" "In season and out of season, my lord."

The revival which resulted from his efforts was remarkable for depth and continuance, and for the personal persecution which it brought upon the good man. The clergy and gentry made common cause with the lowest mob against him. "*The old devil*" was the only name by which he was distinguished for between twenty and thirty years: but none of these things moved him. Crowds waited upon him wherever he journeyed, and his own church was crammed, we had almost said up to the ceiling, for we have heard of men clambering up and sitting upon the cross-beams of the roof, while the windows were filled within and without, and even the outside of the pulpit, to the very top, so that Mr. Berridge seemed almost stifled. There is no wonder that the people thronged him, for his style was so intensely earnest, homely, and simple, that every ploughman was glad to hear the gospel preached in a tongue which he could understand, and with an earnestness which he could not resist.

His discourses were not after a set fashion, and were frequently well-nigh impromptu. Mr. Berridge says that sometimes on entering the pulpit he found himself unable to exercise his thoughts on his subject, and felt himself to be "like a barber's block with a wig on"; but his hearers did not think so, for they were excited to a passionate fervor by his words. On one occasion, while mounting the stairs of the pulpit at Tottenham Court Road, his memory seemed to fail him, and he commenced his sermon by saying, "I set out to this place to-night with a sack well filled with well-baked wheaten bread, which I hoped to set before you, but the bottom came out of the sack as I walked upstairs, and I have nothing left for you but five barley loaves and a few small fishes. You will have those loaves hot from the oven; may they be food convenient for your souls."

His voice was loud, but perfectly under command; ten or fifteen thousand persons frequently composed his congregation in the open air, and he was well heard by all. People came to hear him from a distance of twenty miles, and were at Everton by seven o'clock in the morning, having set out from home soon after midnight. In the early years of his ministry he was the witness of strange scenes, when the revival took the same form as it did a few years ago in certain parts of the north of Ireland, and was accompanied by physical manifestations. The phenomena then presented were very remarkable, but we must confess that we have no faith in their *spiritual* character, and are sorry to hear of their occurrence. After a while the shoutings and contortions came to an end, and the work proceeded steadily and after the usual fashion. Amid all the excitement Berridge never lost his head or became a fanatic, neither was he exalted above measure, but remained one of the humblest and most genuine of men.

There is no doubt that his style was very remarkable, and entirely his own. In one of his letters he writes:

> I have been recruiting for Mr. Venn at Godmanchester, a very populous and wicked town near Huntingdon, and met with a patient hearing from a numerous audience. I hope he also will consecrate a few barns, and preach in them to fill up his fold at Yelling; and sure there is a cause when souls are perishing for lack of knowledge. Must salvation give place to a fanciful decency, and sinners go flocking to hell through our dread of irregularity? While irregularity in its worst shape traverses the kingdom with impunity, should not irregularity in its best shape pass without censure? I told my brother he need not fear being slandered for sheep-stealing while he only whistles the sheep to a better pasture, and meddles neither with the flesh nor the fleece, and I am sure he cannot sink much lower in credit, for he has lost his character right honestly by preaching the gospel without mincing it. The scoffing world makes no other distinction between us than between Satan and Beelzebub; we have both got tufted horns and cloven feet, only I am thought the more impudent devil of the two.

Little cared Berridge if the wicked world treated him as it did his Master, he only longed to save those who loved to revile him. His works are published in an accessible form, and all that we know of his life will be found in the memoir which precedes them; there is therefore no reason for us further to enlarge.

8

Rowland Hill (1744–1833)

It is not our design to write a life of Rowland Hill, but merely to sketch an outline portrait from the "eccentric" point of view. As a preacher Mr. Hill was the child of John Berridge, whose church he attended while he was a student at Cambridge, riding over to Everton every Sabbath to hear him. From that veteran he no doubt learned that freedom and simplicity of language which always distinguished him. He also associated much with John Stittle, one of Berridge's converts, and a man of very marked individuality, who preached in Green Street, Cambridge for many years. Their intimacy may be gathered from the incident recorded by William Jones:

> On one occasion, when Mr. Hill was on his way to Duxford, to preach for the Missionary Society, he suddenly exclaimed, "I must go to Cambridge, and see the widow of an old clergyman, who lives there, for I have a message to leave with her." He was urged not to go, but he was firm to his purpose. He spent a short time with the venerable widow, and reached Duxford just before evening service. On entering his friend Mr. Payne's house he said, "Dear me, I quite forgot to leave the message with the widow," and seemed almost determined to return to Cambridge. He, however, remained during the service, and on being asked whether the message he had forgotten was important he replied, "Yes, sir, I wanted the old lady, who will soon be in heaven, to give my love to Johnny Stittle, and tell him I shall soon see him again."

Mr. Hill's first preachings were of an itinerant character. He was glad of a church, and equally delighted with a meeting-house; but the village green, a barn, an assembly room, or a hovel were all used as they were offered. He was not reared in the lap of luxury as a preacher, nor was he surrounded by the society of unmingled aristocracy, so as to be guarded from every whiff of the air of common life. He mingled so thoroughly with the people that he became the people's man, and forever remained so. With all the high-mindedness which ought to go with nobility he mingled an unaffected simplicity and benevolence of spirit, which made him dear to persons of all ranks. He was thoroughly a man, thinking and acting for himself with all the freedom of a great emancipated mind, which bowed only at the feet of Jesus; but he was essentially a child-man, a Nathanael in whom was no guile—artless, natural, transparent, in all things unaffected, and true. He once said of a man who knew the gospel but seemed afraid to preach it, "He preaches the truth as a donkey munches a thistle—*very cautiously*:" this was exactly the opposite of his own way of doing it.

His fixed places of ministry were Surrey Chapel, and Wotton-under-Edge. He facetiously styled himself "Rector of Surrey Chapel, Vicar of Wotton, and Curate of all the fields and lanes throughout England and Wales." Surrey Chapel was called by many "The Round-house," and it was reported that its form was chosen by Mr. Hill that the devil might not have a corner to hide in. The locality is described by Berridge "as one of the worst spots in London, the very paradise of devils." It was hard by the assembling ground of Lord George Gordon's Protestant rowdies, and was in many respects an unsavory spot, and therefore so much the more in need of the gospel The spacious structure was the center of philanthropic, educational, and religious work of all kinds, and it would be difficult to find a building from which more beneficial influences have emanated.

At Wotton, Mr. Hill lived in what he called "a paradisiacal spot," having his house near the chapel, and lovely scenery all around. He says of the village, "This place, when I first knew Gloucestershire, was filled with brutal persecutors; since they have been favored with the gospel they have been wonderfully softened." We visited the place with great interest, and were taken to the spot where dear old Rowland would sit with his telescope and watch the people coming down the neighboring hills to the meeting, and would afterwards astonish them by mentioning what he had seen. Both in London and in the country he was the universal benefactor, and mixed with all sorts of people. In London he might be teen in the streets with his hands behind him, gazing into the shop windows, and in the country the cottages and the cornfields were his study. A friend told me an anecdote which I have not met with in print. When at Wotton he heard of a woman who was noted for her sausages, and therefore called in upon her, and bought a supply. "Now, my good woman," said he, "how is it that you make such good sausages?" "Why, sir," said she, "I think it is a gift from the Almighty." Mr. Hill shook his head at this, and began to repent of his bargain, as well he might, for the articles turned out to be stale. He told the story afterwards as an instance of how people try to pass off their bad goods by canting talk, and as a proof of the fact that fanaticism is often in alliance with knavery, "A gift from the Almighty!" said he, "and yet the produce of this precious gift is good for nothing." We give this as an instance of the manner in which he turned every little incident to good account.

Our friend Mr. Charlesworth, of the Stockwell Orphanage, has written a life of Rowland Hill, which in our judgment surpasses its predecessors in giving a full length portrait of the good man, and as this is readily to be had, we refer our readers to it. We remember reading an article in one of the reviews of the day in which Mr. Hill is abused after the manner of "the Saturday." It did us great good to see how those who were before us endured the tongue of malice and survived its venom. It is clear from many remarks made by contemporary writers, and especially from the way in which one of his biographers has tried to take the very soul out of him by toning down his wit, that he was regarded by many serious people as a good brother whose infirmity was to be endured, but to be quietly censured.

Now, we are not at all of this mind. Mr. Hill may have allowed his humor too much liberty, perhaps he did, but this was better than smothering it and all his other faculties, as many do, beneath a huge feather-bed of stupid formalism. When we hear our long-visaged brethren condemning all mirth, we remember the story of holy Dr. Durham, the Scotch divine, who wrote a commentary upon Solomon's Song, and another upon the Revelation. His biographers say of him that he was so grave at all times that he very seldom smiled, much less laughed, at anything. We wonder if he had any children. What kind of father must he have been? But here is the story in the old-fashioned language in which we find it. The Rev. Mr. William Guthrie, minister at Finwick, met with Mr. Durham at a gentleman's house near Glasgow, sometime before his last sickness, and observing him somewhat dull, endeavored to force him to smile and laugh, by his facetious and pleasant conversation. Mr. Durham was somewhat disgusted at this innocent freedom of Mr. Guthrie, and displeased with himself that he was so merry. When Mr. Guthrie, according to the laudable custom of that family, and at their desire, prayed, he showed the greatest seriousness, composure, and devout liveliness. When he rose from prayer, Mr. Durham tenderly embraced his friend, and said to him, "O William, you are a happy man; if I had been so merry as you were before you went to pray, I should not have been serious, or in a frame for prayer, or any other religious exercises for two days." This occurrence led Mr. Durham to judge more leniently of his lively brethren, and our trust is that it may have the like effect upon any sour person who may chance to read this little book.

Mr. Hill's name is very sweet in South London, and if you chance to meet with one of his old hearers, it will do your heart good to see how his eyes will sparkle at the bare mention of his name. He made religion a delight and the worship of God a pleasure; yea, he made the very memory of it to be a joy forever to the hearts of the aged as they recall the days of their youth when Rowland Hill—dear old Rowland Hill as they like to call him—was in his glory.

9

Matthew Wilks (1746–1829)

What Rowland Hill was on one side of the Thames Matthew Wilks was upon the other. He came to London in 1775, and John Berridge took part in his ordination over the Tabernacle churches which had been gathered by Whitefield. He was a person of commanding appearance, of great shrewdness, and special singularity, and, like other worthy men, he has been much belied because a vein of humor was manifest in him. This matters little, since the good man led multitudes to Jesus, and was a faithful pastor to the flock which he gathered. He was one of the fathers of the London Missionary Society, the Evangelical Magazine, the Irish Evangelical Society, the Bible Society, and the Religious Tract Society in fact, from his great practical wisdom, he was called upon to be a leader in all kinds of Christian work.

Many an odd thing has fallen from his lips; as for instance when he wished to explain the text, "See that ye walk circumspectly," he pictured a cat walking upon the top of a high wall covered with bits of glass bottles. We have heard this illustration quoted with ridicule, but we fail to see any objection to it. Let anyone watch a cat in such circumstances, and then find a better instance of circumspect walking if he can. We do not believe the tradition that he rebuked the head-dresses of the day by preaching upon "top (k)not come down," which is a cutting from the text, "Let him that is upon the house top not come down": but we have met a gentleman who said that he saw him hold up a small pair of scales when preaching from "Thou art weighed in the balances." We do not wish to doubt our informant, but we think it probable that no actual scales were present, but that Wilks so imitated the holding up of balances and the act of weighing that in after years the memory became a little aided by the imagination, and actual scales and weights were supplied in the narrator's mind.

Mr. Wilks' anniversary sermon for the London Missionary Society was a very striking one. Certainly the text was remarkable enough. "The children gather wood, and the fathers kindle the fire, and the women knead their dough, to make cakes to the queen of heaven, and to pour out drink offerings unto other gods, that they may provoke me to anger" (Jer. 7:18).

> When the text was announced, in the midst of a crowded assembly, every eye seemed to express astonishment at the preacher's choice. He had not proceeded far, however, in his undertaking, when the feeling of astonishment gave place to pure delight, when all seemed convinced that though the text was uncommon, it was by no means inappropriate. Having glanced at the idolatrous worship of the queen of heaven, the ardor of the worshippers, and the persons employed in it; he then said, "I will *contrast* your objects, *compare* your ardor, and *muster* your agents." The appeal was admirably directed, and energetically sustained, and from the hearing and perusal of that part of it which referred to the agents, viz., *the men, women, and children,* arose the system of auxiliary institutions which now pervades the whole country, and combines in its support young and old, rich and poor; such an extraordinary effect has seldom, perhaps, sprung from the preaching of a single discourse. Irrespective, however, of its impression as delivered from the pulpit, it possesses considerable merit, as an argument and as a composition.

Beyond a wretched little memoir and a few mere outlines of sermons, nothing remains of all the great and good things which were spoken by Mr. Wilks, and the stories told of him relate to him rather as a man than as a preacher. My venerable friend Mr. George Rogers has given me the following note:

> Matthew Wilks was very comic in his appearance, in his voice, and in his language. Like Mr. Hill, he was sound in is gospel views, was very useful, and deservedly popular. He has called upon me, and frequently engaged me to preach for him at "both Tabs.," as he

called them. He had a stern aspect, but a tender heart. Two incidents I may mention, which I received from a mutual friend of myself and Mr. Wilks, and which I believe to be authentic. When John Williams was recommended to the London Missionary Society, and nearly all the directors were opposed to him, he found a determined supporter in Mr. Wilks, who even went so far in pressing the point as to be charged with being overbearing. When the debate was over, Mr. Wilks went into the room where Mr. Williams was waiting for the decision of the committee and said, "Well, young man, you have been accepted, but if it, had not been for my overbearing disposition you never would have got in." This was Williams the martyr at Erromanga.

A minister from the West of England having called upon Mr. Wilks, and informed him that he was in great distress of mind on account of debt; Mr. Wilks said, "You are a great fool; you ought not to get in debt." "Oh," he replied, "it gradually accumulated, and I could not help it. My wife was ill, and some of my children died, and my income is very small." "How much do you owe?" "About £70?" "Then you are a great fool. I want you to preach at Greenwich next Sunday." "Oh, I am too much dejected." "But I say you must go, and I will send a note to the gentleman with whom you must dine." Returning to Mr. Wilks on Monday morning, he told him the gentleman with whom he dined gave him £10. "Well," said Mr. Wilks, "but you are a fool for getting into debt for all that." He then produced another £10, and said he had obtained that from another gentleman for him. Observing him to be much affected by this, Mr. Wilks added, "Still you are a great fool." He then produced another £10, called him a fool more vehemently than before, and thus continued to put £10 before him again and again and to scold him until the whole £70 was produced; and then he said, "Now go home, and don't be such a fool as to get into debt again." This showed a great knowledge of human nature, for he thus kept the good man from being overwhelmed by the great and unexpected relief.

But Mr. Wilks could be fearfully severe, and when he had doubts about the ability or character of a candidate for the ministry he showed no mercy.

On one occasion he had badgered and brow-beaten a young man to such a degree that he was scarcely able to answer a single question. "Man," said Mr. Wilks, "you'll never be fit for the ministry: you seem to know nothing at all: can you tell the difference between me and Moses?" "Hoot, toot, Mr. Wilks," interposed good Dr. Waugh, anxious to release the young victim, "you should na' put such a question as that to the lad; but if you like I'll tell you the difference between Moses and you: *Moses was the meekest of men.*"

More genial was his mode of finding a wife for a brother minister. He sent him to the lady's house with this laconic note:

> My dear madam, Allow me to introduce to you my worthy friend, the Rev. Mr. A—
>
> > If you're a cat,
> > You'll smell a rat!
>
> Yours truly,
> > Matthew Wilks.

The lady found it needful to request the gentleman to explain the letter; this led them into pleasant conversation, and into mutual admiration, which ended in marriage. The mystery of the cat and the rat was thus solved.

We may not imitate his drollery, but it would be a happy circumstance if all ministers as diligently read the Bible as he did, for he read it through carefully four times in the year. He was careful that his co-pastors and assistants were well remunerated, but he would only receive £200 a year himself, and of that he gave £100 away. He loved the poor, and his poor people loved him. His power over his members was very great, for it was founded in love. The common people heard him gladly, and among them he enjoyed a long and fruitful ministry. The works which he commenced have been perpetuated, especially the societies which he helped to inaugurate. The Lord has thus enabled his work to endure the fiery ordeal of time, which is a severe test, causing many pretentious ministries to pass away as smoke. Call him eccentric if you please, but our prayer shall be to the Lord that we may share in the blessing which rests on the labors of Matthew Wilks. "Establish thou the work of our hands upon us; yea, the work of our hands establish thou it."

10

William Dawson (1773–1841)

Mr. William Dawson, the Yorkshire farmer and Methodist preacher, should be mentioned among the eccentrics, but not on account of any great use of wit in his preaching. Gross falsehoods were forged concerning him, and he was made to appear as a mere comic actor by the ribald world, but there was nothing about his preaching to deserve it. He was apt at repartee, and there was a slight mixture of drollery in his sermons, but he was mainly distinguished for his wonderful dramatic power, by which he made everything stand out before the people's eyes, and thus created the deepest impressions. In a note from Dr. Osborn to us, that gentleman says: "Wit was not Dawson's specialty, it was the intense activity and fervor of his imagination, with a basis of sound doctrine and sound character, which was the source of his power, and a mighty power it was." In a brief sketch of Mr. Dawson, by Mr. R. A. West, we read the following description of his outer man, which lets us see the farmer and the preacher combined:

> I first heard Mr. Dawson from the pulpit in the year 1828. His apparel and demeanor struck me as unclerical. True, he wore a black coat and vest, and a white neck-cloth, but his lower extremities were encased in a pair of drab breeches, and he wore what are technically called "top boots," such as are, and were at the time, universally worn in England by substantial farmers as a part of their Sunday or market-day attire. He crossed the floor of the chapel on his way to the pulpit with a rolling gait, as though he were traversing a

ploughed field, with a hand in each pocket of his drabs, half whistling, half humming the air of a good old Methodist tune. Of this he was apparently unconscious, for his eyes were turned downward in a reverie, and he seemed shut in from all surrounding objects. In all my subsequent knowledge of him I never saw a repetition of the mood.

He was always natural and farmer-like; the smell as of a field that the Lord had blessed was upon him, and the multitude delighted to hear him. His power in setting an illustration before his hearers will be seen from the following:

> Preaching on the returning prodigal, Mr. Dawson paused, looked at the door, and shouted out, after he had depicted him in his wretchedness, "Yonder he comes, slipshod! Make way—make way—make way, there." Such was the approach to reality that a considerable part of the congregation turned to the door, some rising on their feet, under the momentary impression that someone was entering the chapel in the state described. In the same sermon, paraphrasing the father's replying to the son that was angry, and would not go in, he said: "Be not offended; surely a *calf* may do for a *prodigal*, *shoes* for a *prodigal*, a *ring* and a *robe* for a *prodigal*, but ALL I have is THINE." As to the more striking effect, when pointing to the door, similar results were produced when referring to the Witch of Endor. His picturing took such hold on the imagination that on exclaiming, "Stand by! Stand by! There she is!" some of the poor people inadvertently directed their eyes downward, where his own eye was fixed, and the spot to which he was pointing, as if she were about to rise from beneath their feet, and become visible to the congregation.

The next extract is part of a peroration of a sermon from Revelation 6:7, 8, "And when he had opened the fourth seal, I heard the voice of the fourth beast say, Come and see," etc. "'Come and see,' then, the awful condition of an unsaved sinner. Open your eyes, sinner, and see it yourself. *There* he is in the broad road of ruin; every step he takes is deeper in sin; every breath he draws feeds his corruption; every moment takes him farther from heaven and nearer hell. Onward, onward he is going—death and hell are after him quickly, untiringly they pursue him—with swift but noiseless hoof the pale horse and his pale rider are tracking the godless wretch. See! See! They are getting nearer, they are overtaking him." At this moment the stillness of the congregation was so complete that the ticking of the clock could be distinctly heard in every part of the chapel. Upon this, with a facility peculiarly his own, he promptly seized, and without seeming interruption. Leaning over the pulpit in the attitude of attention, and fixing his keen eye upon those who sat immediately before him, he continued in an almost supernatural whisper, "Hark! Hark! That swift rider is coming, and judgment is following him. That is his untiring footstep! Hark!"—and then imitating for a moment or two the beat of the pendulum, he exclaimed in the highest pitch of his voice,

> Lord, save the sinner! Save him! Death is upon him, and hell follows! See, the long arm is raised! The final dart is poised! O my God, save him—save him—for if the rider overtakes that poor sinner, unpardoned and unsaved, and strikes his blow, down he falls, and backward he drops—hell behind him, and as he falls backward, he looks upward, and shrieks—"Lost! Lost! Lost! Time lost; Sabbaths lost; means lost; soul lost; heaven lost! ALL LOST, and lost forever!" Backward he drops; all his sins seem to hang round his neck like so many millstones as he plunges into the burning abyss. "Come and see." Lord, save him! O my God, save him! "Come and see." Blessed be God! The rider has not overtaken him yet; there is time and space yet for that poor sinner: he may be saved yet—he has not dropped into hell. "Come and see." The horse and the rider have not overtaken you yet; there is, therefore, an "accepted time," there is a "day of salvation!" "Come and see." There is God the Father inviting you; God the Father commanding you; God the Father swearing he has no pleasure in your death, but in your life. There is Jesus Christ come to seek you. He has travelled thirty years to save you. He is dying on the cross. With his outstretched arms he says, "Come unto me, and I will give you rest." "He that believeth in me shall never die!"

The effect was so overwhelming that two of the congregation fainted, and it required all the preacher's tact and self-command to ride through the storm, which his own vivid imagination had aroused.

Those must have been stirring services in which his hearers audibly responded to his appeals. On one occasion when he exhorted his hearers to give their hearts to the Lord, he added, with his hand on his breast and his eyes towards heaven, "Here's mine." A voice from the gallery called out, "Here's mine, too, Billy!"

Preaching at Ancoats, Manchester, on Judges 8:4, "Faint, yet pursuing," every eye seemed at one time suffused with tears; and when people and preacher were craned up to the highest pitch of feeling, a momentary pause ensued, during which the clock struck *twelve*, and broke the stillness that reigned, like the hammer on the bell at a watch night, on the departure of the old year. In an instant he darted his eyes to the front of the gallery, and personifying the timepiece, said, "You may speak, clock, but I am not done yet." Though no apparent expectation existed on the part of the auditory that he would close his discourse with the hour, yet it had all the effect of reviving disappointed hope, and threw a gleam of sunshine into every countenance.

William Dawson was a man by himself. When nature formed him she broke the mold, but we could have wished that she had given us at least another after his manner and order. Of his power in witty answers we will only give one specimen, and then close our notice. The following dialogue was held between Dawson and a fault-finding gentleman.

Gentleman. "I had the pleasure of hearing you yesterday."

Mr. Dawson. "I hope you not only heard but profited."

Gent. "Yes, I did; but I don't like those prayer-meetings at the close. They destroy all the good previously received."

Mr. D. "You should have united with the people in them."

Gent. "I went into the gallery, where I hung over the front, and saw the whole, but I could get no good; I lost, indeed, all the benefit I had received during the sermon."

Mr. D. "It is easy to account for that."

Gent. "How so?"

Mr. D. "You mounted the top of the house; and on looking down your neighbor's chimney to see what kind of a *fire* he kept, you got your eyes filled with smoke. Had you entered by the door, and gone into the room, and mingled with the family around the household hearth, *you* would have enjoyed the benefit of the fire as well as they. Sir, you have got the smoke in your eyes."

11

Jacob Gruber (1778–1850)

When the population of the United States was sparse and widely scattered, the public services of religion could not have been maintained at all if the Lord had not raised up a race of zealous itinerants, who passed rapidly from one hamlet or homestead to another, and by their intense earnestness kept alive the sacred fire. We allude to a period ranging from one hundred years back to within half-a-century of the present date. The men of that time were necessarily strong physically, or they could not have borne the hardships of their wandering mission, and they were also sturdy mentally, and needed to be so, for they met with people who required vigorous handling. Of course they were rough and unrefined—what could they have effected had they been other-wine? Of what use would a razor be in clearing a forest? Very frequently they were wildly humorous as well as vehemently zealous; but probably this play of their spirits was needful to keep them from sinking down under the burdens of their uncomfortable and trying circumstances. At any rate, they did the work which God gave them to do, and left America a Christian instead of a heathen country, which last it might readily have become had it not been for their efforts. We do not commend all that they did, much less hold them up for imitation; but we think it profitable to see how others did their work, and therefore we would describe Jacob Gruber, of whom his contemporaries said, "He is a character, and copies no man." We shall do little more than give extracts from a biography written by W. P. Strickland, which has not been published in this country. We shall make a long chapter of this, because we shall regard Gruber as a sort of specimen American evangelist of the backwoods' order.

At the beginning of the present century there appeared at the seat of the Philadelphia Conference a young man who was impressed with the conviction that it was his duty to preach. His parents were of German descent, and had been brought up in the faith of the great leader of the Reformation. The German Reformed Church for many years had the exclusive control of the religious interests of the neighborhood. The time, however, came when this quiet was broken. Two itinerant Methodist preachers had divided up the country into circuits, and, claiming to be successors of the apostles, thought it no robbery to imitate them in traversing the country, and preaching the gospel wherever they found an open door. The strangeness of their manner, and the wonderful earnestness of their preaching, attracted the attention of the people, particularly the younger portion, and the cabins and barns where they held forth were crowded.

Young Gruber listened to these circuit preachers with amazement; and though they were denounced by the staid and sober Reformers as wild and fanatical, he nevertheless felt strangely drawn to their meetings. There was such a fervor in their prayers, such a zeal and earnestness in their preaching, and such a power in their songs, that he was entirely fascinated, and soon became convinced of the need of conversion. His prayers for a change of heart were soon answered, and with gladness he went with his parents to the place of meeting, and with them joined the Methodist church.

That the reader may have a correct description of the religious condition of this particular neighborhood, we give an account prepared by Gruber himself. He says: "The Methodist preachers came into the neighborhood, and held several meetings. As the result of their labors a revival commenced, and quite a number of persons were converted, and professed a knowledge of sins forgiven." Some of the members of the German minister's church went to the old gentleman, expressing a desire to know something about this new doctrine. In reply to their inquiries about the knowledge of forgiveness, he said: "I have been a preacher more than twenty years, and I do not know my sins forgiven, and indeed it is impossible that anyone should know it." It was not considered very wonderful by some that this preacher should be in darkness on that subject, as he frequently became intoxicated. An aged woman, a member of the German church, at one of the revival meetings where some were praising God for having pardoned their sins, stood thoughtfully shaking her head and said, "It could not be, for if they had to answer a hundred and sixty questions, as she had before she got religion, they would learn that it could not be obtained in such quick time."

Among the early itinerants who visited Pennsylvania about this time was the eccentric Valentine Cook. He was fresh from the halls of Cokesbury College, and perhaps the first native college-bred preacher that had appeared in the American Methodist church. When Cook made his appearance, and it was rumored that he was a graduate of a college, he attracted general attention. The German Reformed, like several other churches we could name, entertained the idea that no man could possibly be qualified to preach who had not received a classical education; and hence vastly more respect was paid to Cook than to any of his colleagues in the ministry. His learning, however, did not always avail to insure him respect, as the following incident will show: After travelling a whole day without refreshment in a region where he was not known, he halted in the evening at the house of a German, and asked if he could obtain feed for his horse and something for himself to eat. Being a tall, rough-looking specimen of humanity, the good woman, who was engaged in spinning, took him to be an Irishman. She was not at all favorably impressed with his appearance, but at her husband's request she procured a lunch for him and returned to her wheel, saying to her husband somewhat petulantly in German, she hoped the Irishman would choke in eating. After Cook had finished his repast he asked the privilege to pray, which being granted he knelt down and offered up a fervent petition in German. In his prayer he besought the Lord to bless the kind woman at the wheel and give her a new heart, that she might be better disposed towards strangers. Such a personal reflection was more than the good woman could stand,

and she left her wheel and ran from the house overwhelmed with chagrin at her wicked wish.

We mention these incidents for the propose of giving the reader some idea of the times in which young Gruber commenced his religious career. Being a sprightly lad, he was soon called out to exercise his gifts in public prayer and exhortation. As usual in such cases, a storm of persecution arose, not only from those who were outside the church and the family, but from his own household. Father, mother, brothers, and sisters, as if by one consent, rose up against the young exhorter, and he was obliged to leave home and seek more congenial quarters elsewhere. Some of the more zealous Methodists interpreted this differently from what young Jacob had imagined, and persuaded him that it was a clear indication of Providence that it was his duty to abandon everything for the exclusive work of the ministry. This interpretation of Providence was soon after verified. As he went on his way afoot and alone to the town of Lancaster he met one of the itinerants, who in a short conversation convinced him of the duty of entering upon the ministry, and sent him to an adjoining circuit to fill a vacancy. He accordingly procured a horse and went to the appointment.

As the conference embraced sickly regions in its territory, he knew not but he might be sent by the intrepid Bishop Asbury to some one of these localities, if for no other propose than to try his mettle. Many a young man has finished his course in one year's service; but it was not to be so with Gruber. He had a powerful constitution, an iron frame capable of enduring an amount of hardship, labor, and fatigue which made him the wonder of all his ministerial companions.

The second year of our young itinerant's ministry was spent where vast tracts of wilderness interposed between the appointments, and new hardships were to be endured. Nothing daunted, he scaled the mountains, penetrated the woods, and sought the cabins nestling among them, that he might preach the gospel to their inmates. Here he labored with the most unremitting zeal and diligence. Through his fervent appeals many were awakened and converted.

At a certain place on this circuit there lived a man who had been in great distress of mind, bordering on despair. He wept much and prayed almost constantly, but found no relief. He was visited by Gruber, who conversed with him for a considerable length of time, quoting such passages of the Bible as were applicable to his case. He could not, however, be persuaded that any promise was for him, as he believed his day of mercy and hope was gone forever. The following colloquy then ensued between Gruber and the despairing man:

"What will become of you?" "I shall be lost." "Where will you go?" "To hell." "But if you go there you will have it all to yourself." "What do you mean?" "I mean just what I say: if you go to hell weeping and praying, you will scare all the devils away, for I never heard or read of one going to hell weeping and praying." At this a smile came over his face like sunshine on a cloud; his despair was gone, and hope full and joyous sprang up in his soul.

At the next conference Gruber was sent to the Winchester circuit, having for a colleague a young man by the name of Richards. This young itinerant in a great measure destroyed his usefulness by getting the crotchet into his head that, to maintain ministerial dignity, he must put on extra airs of reserve and sanctity. A "sad countenance," as our old English version has it, in the description of the Pharisees in the days of the Savior, is not a true index of spirituality. One of the old preachers who had outlived his day, and was constantly harping upon one string—"Ye are fallen! Ye are fallen!" remarked on a certain occasion that he wished some of the old preachers were as solemn as that young man. Bishop Asbury, who was present when this remark was made, smilingly said: "Do you make any allowance for solids and fluids?" We recollect a reply once made by a lighthearted, joyous, talented young preacher to a pious lady, who reprovingly said to him, "I wish you would be as serious as Brother C." "Ah!" said the young brother, laughingly, "when I get the dyspepsia as bad as he has it, I will, no doubt, be equally serious."

He had now been six years in the work of the ministry, and had exhibited such good proof of his fidelity and success that the good Bishop Asbury deemed him qualified for the more responsible post of presiding elder, and accordingly, in the year 1807, he was appointed to the presidency of Greenbrier district. It embraced a wild region of country in Virginia, said to be the roughest in the bounds of the Baltimore Conference. To use his own language, he had "hard work, rough fare, and bad roads;" but by way of offset to these disadvantages he had "great meetings." Towards the close of the year camp-meetings were held on every circuit, and hundreds were converted. Indeed, a camp-meeting in those days without numerous conversions and large accessions to the church would have been a great wonder.

At that time even a quarterly meeting was considered dull and profitless unless souls were converted and added to the church, and a revival inaugurated for the coming quarter. In describing these camp-meetings, Gruber said: "Some complained about too much wildfire, and called the preachers the fire company; but we wanted fire that would warm and melt, not tame-fire, fox-fire, and the like." During the three years on this district he experienced many hardships. In describing his labors he says: "One very cold night in the winter I took a path for a near way to my stopping-place, but got out of my course, wandered about among the hills and mountains, and went to the top of one of them to see clearings, or hear dogs bark, or roosters crow, but all in vain. After midnight the moon arose; I could then see my track. The snow was knee-deep, and I went back till I got into the right course, and reached my lodgings between four and five o'clock in the morning. The family was alarmed, and said I was late, but I called it early. After lying down and sleeping a little I arose, and getting breakfast departed on my day's journey, filling two appointments."

At the end of his first year on the district he had a line of appointments reaching to Baltimore. On his route he passed through a wild, mountainous region, traversed by a dim path. Not a single cabin was to be found in a distance of twenty miles. He struck for the path on the mountain about ten o'clock, but, had not proceeded many miles before he found it covered up knee-deep in snow, and not a single track to be seen. He picked his way, however, as best he could, and traveled on. During the day it began to rain, which rendered his journey still more uncomfortable. At length he reached Cheat River, and found it considerably swollen, with ice in the middle. When he reached the ice it was with difficulty he dismounted, and then making his horse leap upon it he again mounted. The ice did not break, and he was enabled to reach the other shore. He traveled on in the woods until night overlook him, when he lost his path and became entangled in the forest. The rain, which had been pouring down, now changed into snow, and the wind blew furiously.

Besides all this, it was becoming increasingly cold. What to do he knew not, except to pray. The night was spent sitting on his horse. Above the roar of the storm he could hear the scream of the panther and the howl of the wolf. It was a dreadful night; but morning came, and with it he found the path, and in a short time found himself at the house of a friend. The family were alarmed at seeing him, and expressed their surprise at his undertaking so perilous a journey, as no person had been known to pass through that portion of the wilderness before in winter. Neither he nor horse had tasted a morsel of food since they started, but riley were both inured to hardships, and suffered but little in consequence. After obtaining some refreshment, he started to his appointment, thankful for his escape from the dangers through which he had passed.

Gruber gives several incidents that occurred at camp-meetings. "In one camp," he says, "some bold sinners came to fight for their master, the devil; but our captain, Immanuel, made prisoners of them, and then made them 'free indeed.' One fine, strong, good-looking young man among the mourners was in great distress, and found no relief until he drew a large pistol out of his pocket, with which he intended to defend himself if anyone should offer to speak to him on the subject of religion. When he laid it on the bench beside him the Lord blessed him, and gave him a great victory over his foes."

Gruber was dreadfully severe upon all worldliness, and especially upon foppishness in dress, which he denounced and ridiculed. A little of his healthy banter might be useful in these dressy days.

While preaching in a certain place on one occasion an unusually tall lady entered. On seeing her he stopped preaching and said: "Make room for that lady; one might have thought she was tall enough to be seen without the plumage of that pird in her ponnet." Some days afterward the lady met Gruber and complained that he had treated her rudely. "O sister," he replied, "was that you? Well, I did not know it was you; I thought *you* had more sense."

At a camp-meeting on a certain occasion, where considerable difficulty was experienced in getting the people to observe order, from the number of young persons who were walking about, collecting in groups, and engaged in conversation, the presiding eider, in the most respectful and courteous terms, requested them to be seated. Not seeming to understand, or not caring to comply with the request, the young people paid no attention whatever to what was said, but kept up their walking and talking. Gruber, who was present, felt greatly aggrieved, and rising in the stand he roared out, "Mr. Presiding Elder, you called those young folks gentlemen and ladies, and they did not know what you meant!" He then added, "Boys, come right along and take seats here," pointing to the right; "and you, gals, come up and take your seats here on the left." Earnest and peremptory as he was, yet so comical was his manner that their attention was at once arrested, and they came smilingly forward and took their seats.

To us this mode of address would have seemed rude and irritating, and very unlikely to secure the desired end, but Jacob knew the people he had to deal with, and how to handle them. To some persons a polite address sounds like affectation, and, taking it to mean nothing, they let it go in at one ear and out at the other; a plain, blunt, commanding mode of speech they see to be earnestly intended, and yield to it. Very much depends upon the character of the persons to whom we speak, and something also upon our own age and position: it would never do for a young minister fresh from college to address those of his own age as girls and boys, neither would such a style of admonition be acceptable to our educated young people even if the oldest divine so accosted them. The practical lesson is to have the thing done somehow, if it is right, and to use just such a method of speaking as will be best calculated to secure it. The dread of sinning against etiquette is as much to be avoided as the vulgarity which causes needless offense. The case in which Gruber acted so oddly will perhaps never occur to us, and, if it does, we must use our best judgment, and hope to succeed as he did.

"At a camp-meeting near Baltimore, after the trumpet had been blown announcing the time for closing the exercises in the praying circles, one of them, unwilling to stop, kept on singing and praying. Gruber, somewhat impatient, shouted out at the top of his voice, 'That's right, brothers, blow all the fire out.'" Often has the same thought occurred to our mind when we have seen unwise brethren ranting on long after the "spirit of supplication" has been fully exhausted. Long prayers and long addresses blow out the fire which they are intended to increase.

Gruber's later years were more calm and quiet, but they were not quite devoid of stirring incident. The sinners of his day were as eccentric as the preachers who sought to win them. If they were assailed from the pulpit with rough weapons, they knew how to be vigorously offensive in return. Gruber says—

> I was sent a second year to Dauphin circuit. Nothing extraordinary took place, only some fellows of the baser sort made an attempt to blow up our meeting-house in Harrisburg. On a Sunday night after preaching they got in at a window, put something under the pulpit with powder in it and a match. It made a report like a cannon, tore up the pulpit, and broke the glass out of some of the windows. We soon, however, had all repaired, and pursued our course. My colleague this year was a poor thing hunting a fortune. He found out who was rich; but the girls found out that he was lazy, so he had little success in winning souls, and none in getting a wife. Some young men think if they can only get married (the sooner the better) they will be at once in paradise; and some young women have an idea that if they can only get a preacher they will have an angel for certain; but more than one has been disappointed very much.
>
> While in attendance at conference in Philadelphia, in 1830, he was appointed to preach in his old charge, St. George's. He took for his text Psalm 84:4: "Blessed are they that dwell in thy house,

they will be still praising thee." Retaining a keen sense of the unkind manner in which he was treated by some of the members of that charge, which resulted in his removal at the end of the first year, he felt disposed to let his hearers know it by witty and cutting allusions. Under the head of "The Character of those who dwell in the House of the Lord," he mentioned three characteristics,

1. They were a *humble* people, willing to occupy a humble place in the church; indeed, any place so that they might be permitted to abide in the church; but there were some people who were so proud and ambitious that, unless they could be like the first king of Israel, from the shoulders up higher than everybody else, they wouldn't come into the house at all, but hang about the doors.

2. They were a *contented* people. If everything did not exactly suit them, they made the best of it, and tried to get along as well as they could; but there are many who are so uneasy and fidgety that they can't *dwell* in the church, but are continually running in and out, disturbing themselves and everybody else.

3. They were a *satisfied* people, always finding something good, and thankful for it. Let who would be their preacher they could always get something that would give them instruction and encouragement. But some people are never satisfied, but are always finding fault with their preacher; some preach too loud, and some too long, and some say so many hard and queer things, and some are so prosy and dull that they can't be fed at all and are never satisfied. If the multitude that were fed by the Savior had been like these people they never would have been fed. If one had cried out, "John, you shan't feed me, Peter shall"; and another had said, "Andrew shall feed me, but James shan't"; and another, "I want all bread and no fish"; and others, "I want all fish and no bread," how could they have been fed? Such dissatisfied people cannot dwell in the house of the Lord. If they are not turned out they will soon die out: they can't live.

Though he was sometimes severe in his criticisms on young preachers, he always entertained for them a fatherly affection, and sought only to correct their errors: but we cannot think he was justified in publicly rebuking a foolish stripling who had attacked

Methodism, by asking the Lord, "to make his heart as soft as his head, for then he might do good."

A young preacher, desirous of improving his style as a pulpit orator, and having great confidence in Father Gruber, wrote to him for advice. The young man had contracted the habit of prolonging his words, especially when under the influence of great excitement. Deeming this the most important defect in his elocution, Gruber sent him the following laconic reply—

"Dear Ah! Brother Ah!—When-ah you-ah go-ah to-ah preach-ah, takeah care ah you-ah don't-ah say-ah Ah-ah! Yours-ah, JACOB-AH GRUBER-AH."

But one of the oddest reproofs I ever knew him to administer was on a larger scale, and proved not less effectual. In a certain church the congregation had an unseemly practice of turning their backs on the pulpit during a certain portion of the singing. One Sabbath Mr. Gruber conducted the service, and, as usual, the whole congregation simultaneously turned round, presenting their backs to the preacher. Instantly the preacher, to be even with them, turned round also, presenting his back to the congregation. When the time for prayer came, at the close of the hymn, the congregation were astonished to find the preacher turned from them and gazing at the wall. The hint was enough; they did not repeat the objectionable practice."

Mr. Martin thus describes the closing scene of Gruber's life:

He was taken suddenly worse on the evening of the twenty-third of May, having several attacks of fainting or swooning. He gradually grew weaker and weaker, until forty-eight hours afterwards the scene closed. He was conscious that his end was rapidly approaching, and sighed for the happy release. He requested brother Blake, if it could be ascertained when he was about to die, to collect a few brethren and sisters around him, that they might (to use his own words) '*See me safe off*; and as I am going, all join in full chorus and sing: "On Jordan's stormy banks I stand."

A few hours before he died he asked Brother Blake whether he could stand it another night, and was answered that in his judgment he could not. "Then," said he, "tomorrow I shall spend my first Sabbath in heaven! Last Sabbath in the church on earth, next Sabbath in the church above!" and with evident emotion added—

"Where congregations ne'er break up,
And Sabbaths have no end."

Brother Blake, perceiving that he was fast sinking, in accordance with his request, the hymn he had selected was sung; but ere it was concluded his consciousness was gone. The singing ceased, a deathlike stillness reigned, only broken by his occasional respiration. An overwhelming sense of the presence of God melted every heart. A minute more and his happy spirit winged its way to its long-sought rest. He died in the seventy-second year of his age.

If any judge too severely the personal peculiarities of such a man, we would urge them to do better; but to us it seems more than probable that were preachers more in earnest we should see more of what are called eccentricities, which are often only the ensigns of real zeal, and the tokens that a man is both natural and intense. If a fisherman can catch fish with silk lines and artificial bait, let him be thankful; but if with a superior tackle he is unsuccessful, it shows a very proud spirit if he indulges in harsh criticisms of the style and manner of brethren who succeed better than himself in the gospel fishery. "Every man in his own order" is a good rule. Apollos may be polished and Cephas blunt, but so far as they are honest, prayerful, and true to the Gospel, God will bless them both, and it ill becomes them to pick holes in each other's coats. We would never say to a man, "Be eccentric"; but if he cannot help being so, we would not have him otherwise. The leaning tower of Pisa owes much of its celebrity to its leaning, and although it certainly is not a safe model for architects, we would by no means advise the taking of it down. Ten to one any builder who tried to erect another would create a huge ruin, and therefore it would not be a safe precedent; but there it is, and who wishes it were other than it is? Serve the Lord, brother, with your very best, and seek to do still better, and whatever your peculiarities, the grace of God will be glorified in you.

12

Edward Taylor (1793–1871)

We would now introduce "Father Taylor," the Sailor-Preacher of Boston. Not Father Taylor of California, who is a younger man, but Edward Taylor, of the Bethel—the man whom Charles Dickens thus described in his "American Notes":

> The only preacher I heard in Boston was Mr. Taylor, who addresses himself peculiarly to seamen, and who was once a mariner himself. I found his chapel down among the shipping, in one of the narrow, old, waterside streets, with a gay blue flag waving freely from its roof. The preacher looked a weather-beaten, hard-featured man, of about six or eight and fifty; with deep lines graven as it were into his face, dark hair, and a stern, keen eye. Yet the general character of his countenance was pleasant and agreeable. His text was, "Who is this that cometh up from the wilderness, leaning upon her beloved?"
>
> He handled this text in all kinds of ways, and twisted it into all manner of shapes; but always ingeniously, and with a rude eloquence, well adapted to the comprehension of his hearers. Indeed, if I be not mistaken, he studied their sympathies and understandings much more than the display of his own powers. His imagery was all drawn from the sea, and from the incidents of a seaman's life; and was often remarkably good. He spoke to them of "that glorious man, Lord Nelson," and of Coilingwood; and drew nothing in, as the saying is, by the head and shoulders, but brought it to bear upon his purpose, naturally, and with a sharp mind to its effect.

Sometimes, when much excited with his subject, he had an odd way of taking his great quarto Bible under his arm and pacing up and down the pulpit with it; looking steadily down, meantime, into the midst of the congregation. Thus, when he applied his text to the first assemblage of his hearers, and pictured the wonder of the church at their presumption in forming a congregation among themselves, he stopped short with his Bible under his arm and pursued his discourse after this manner:

"Who are these, who are they, who are these fellows? where do they come from? Where are they going to? Come from! What's the answer?" leaning out of the pulpit, and pointing downward with his right hand: "From below!" starting back again, and looking at the sailors before him: "From below, my brethren, from under the hatches of sin, battened down above you by the evil one. That's where you come from!" a walk up and down the pulpit: "and where are you going?" stopping abruptly; "where are you going? Aloft!" very softly, and pointing upward: "Aloft!" louder: "Aloft!" louder still: "That's where you are going, with a fair wind, all taut and trim, steering direct for heaven in its glory, where there are no storms or foul weather, and where the wicked cease from troubling and the weary are at rest." Another walk: "That's where you're going to, my friends. That's it. That's the place. That's the port. That's the haven. It's a blessed harbor—still water there, in all changes of the winds and tides; no driving ashore upon the rocks, or slipping your cables and running out to sea, there: Peace, peace, peace, all peace!" Another walk, and putting the Bible under his left arm: "What! these fellows are coming from the wilderness, are they? Yes. From the dreary, blighted wilderness of iniquity, whose only crop is death. But do they lean upon anything—do they lean upon nothing, these poor seamen?" Three raps upon the Bible: "Ah, yes. Yes. They lean upon the arm of their beloved," three more raps: "upon the arm of their beloved,"—three more, and a walk: "Pilot, guiding star, and compass all in one, to all hands—here it is"—three more: "Here it is. They can do their seaman's duty manfully, and be easy in their minds in the utmost peril and danger, with this"—two more: "They can come, even these poor fellows can come, from the wilderness leaning on the arm of their beloved, and go up—up—up," raising his hand higher and higher, at every repetition of the word, so that he stood with it at last stretched above his head, regarding them in a strange rapt manner, and pressing the book triumphantly to his breast, until he gradually subsided into some other portion of his discourse.

We are not so enamored of Charles Dickens as to consider his verdict upon a preacher to be of any material consequence with reference to the man's real usefulness: but as a judge of vivacity of manner, and power of style, no better critic could be found.

Mr. Taylor's first regular recognized official holding-forth was before a quarterly Methodist Conference, assembled to test his qualifications. It has been reported that upon this occasion he had the coolness to select as his text the words, "By the life of Pharaoh, surely ye are spies;" but his biographer says that although those words might have been worked into the sermon, the real text was a more humble but equally singular one, "I pray thee, let me live." He adds, that the triers saw that his fervor and talents were more than an offset for his defects; and in answer to his prayer, they "let him live." We do not see how they could have done otherwise, for no Conference would have been strong enough to kill him.

After itinerating for some few years, the man and his mission met, and Father Taylor took up his abode in Boston, as a minister of the Methodist Episcopal Church, specially set apart to labor among sailors. His chapel, at first, held about five hundred hearers, and was immediately filled to its utmost capacity. He began in 1828 in full revival vigor, frequently preaching four times a day. To him it never occurred to polish his style, and prune away its power: he spoke as his heart prompted him, and worked as the Holy Spirit moved him. He did work enough for two men, and had a double blessing upon it. In a very short time Boston felt his power, and its wealth and its culture were at his feet as well as its poverty and roughness. A noble Bethel was built for him, a house of large dimensions, a fit sphere for his operations, and by his soul-stirring ministry he made "the Bethel" famous in all lands.

It was not at all wonderful that sailors especially, and other classes of the community in proportion, should flock to hear Mr. Taylor, for he was a man of great human sympathies, manly, bold, honest, childlike and outspoken;

and, withal, a man on fire with love to Christ and perishing souls. His preaching never could be dull, the intense white heat of his nature prevented that. He was terribly in earnest, and commanded the attention of all around him for that very reason.

No ideas of propriety, or notions of delicacy, hung about him like fetters: he spoke to sailors, not to squeamish pomposity's, and to "the sons of Zebulon" he poured out his great heart in a homely eloquence, which was all on flame. One who heard him in 1835 said of him—

> His eloquence was marvelous: his control over the audience seemed almost absolute. Tears and smiles chased each other over our faces, like the rain and sunshine of an April day. He had one of the most brilliant imaginations that ever sparkled and burned. His sermon was all poetry, though it came in bursts and jets of flame. It was like the dance of the aurora, changing all the while from silver flame to purple, and back again. But the secret of his magnetic power lay in his overflowing sympathies, that leaped over all barriers, and had no regard for time or place. There was no wall of formality between him and his hearers, any more than if he were talking to each one of us in a private room. He would single out a person in his audience, and talk to him individually, with the same freedom as if he met him in the street. "Ah! my jolly tar," turning to a sailor who happened at that moment to catch his eye, "here you are, in port again; God bless you! See to your helm, and you will reach a fairer port by-and-by. Hark! Don't you hear the bells of heaven over the sea?"

The ludicrous was allowed considerable play in his discourses, and we think rightly so. To the pure mind, none of the powers of our manhood are common or unclean. Humor can be consecrated, and should be. We grant that it is a power difficult to manage; but when it is under proper control, it more than repays for all the labor spent upon it. Children do sad damage with gunpowder; but what a force it is when a wise man directs its energy. Mr. Taylor made men laugh that they might weep. He touched one natural chord, that he might be able to touch another; whereas, some preachers are so unnatural themselves, that the human nature of their hearers refuses to subject itself to their operations. O ye who are evermore decorously dull, before ye judge a man whose loving ministry conducted thousands to the skies, think how immeasurably above you all he soared, and remember that with all his violations of your wretched regulations, he was one whom the Lord delighted to honor. Farthing candles rail at the sun for his spots, while they cannot be sure that those spots are not excessive light; and may be quite sure of another thing, that, spots or no spots, ten thousand such glimmers as theirs are not worthy to be compared with the stray beams of the great orb of day.

At the prayer-meetings Father Taylor, like a father in his family, cast off all restraint, and unveiled his inner nature with childlike unguardedness. One of his most remarkable displays of this kind was after an address by a visitor, who related the death of a very wicked man, who was blown up a few days before in a powder mill at Wilmington. He came down crushed and mangled, and gave his heart to God; and now who would not say with the holy man of old, "Let me die the death of the righteous, and let my last end be like his?" Father Taylor rose at once. "I don't want any trash brought unto this altar. I hope none of my people calculate on serving the devil all their lives and cheating him with their dying breath. Don't look forward to honoring God by giving him the last snuff of an expiring candle. *Perhaps you never will be blown up in a powder-mill.*" "That holy man," he continued, "that we heard of was Balaam, the meanest scoundrel mentioned in the Old Testament or the New. And now I hope we shall never hear anything more from Balaam, *nor from his ass.*"

His own prayers were more like the utterances of an Oriental, abounding in imagery, than a son of these colder western dimes. Think of his prayer at the dedication of a new church: "If any man attempts to sow heresy in this pulpit, or to preach aught but Christ and him crucified, Lord drive him out of the house *and sweep his tracks off the floor.*" The Sunday before he was to sail for Europe, he was en-treating the Lord to care well for his church during his absence. All at once he stopped and exclaimed, "What have I done? Distrust the Providence of heaven! A God that gives a whale a ton of herrings for a breakfast, will he not care for my children?" and then went on, closing his prayer in a more confiding strain.

His work in one peculiar field is not, generally known. Living at the North End, near the lowest haunts of vice, he was often called to attend the death-beds of abandoned women. Protected by his eccentricity and his purity alike from any shadow of suspicion, he always obeyed such a summons. At all hours of the day or night he visited the foulest haunts of crime in this noble service; never with one harsh word for the fallen, never with any apology for their crime. He received many warnings against venturing on such errands. The only notice that he ever took of them was to lay aside his cane, which was elsewhere his constant companion, but which he never took with him when he visited the cellars and garrets of North Street. This was simple courage in the Christian soldier; but it was also the wisest prudence.

It grieves one's heart to relate that after many years of glorious service Father Taylor faded away by degrees during ten long years, losing slowly all his powers. It was as the Lord would have it; but to drift about as a poor hulk, with the armament removed, and the light in the binnacle extinguished, was very grievous both to the old man and to his friends.

So passed away one whom Emerson called one of the two greatest poets of the United States. He was a Paedobaptist, an Arminian, and a man of a thousand divergences from our line of things, which we believe to be more scriptural than his; but, for all that, upon the coffin of a good man and true, with no grudging hand we cast a funeral wreath, and say, "Would God there were others to fill his place!"

13

Edward Brooke (1779–1871)

Our Wesleyan brethren have lately lost from their ministry an eminently useful preacher, who was the last survivor of a little band of simple-hearted and downright earnest men, who in their day were mighty winners of souls, but had the reputation of "being somewhat eccentric." William Dawson and Samuel Hick were worthily perpetuated in Squire Brooke, who entered into rest in January, 1871. We must not be supposed to endorse all his theology, or to hold up to admiration all his modes of procedure; but we have no patience with those who imagine that you cannot admire a man's character unless you agree with him in every doctrinal sentiment. Mr. Brooke was soundly abused in his day, and certain scurrilous papers imputed the most outrageous conduct to him; but, in truth, he was only a homely and somewhat quaint preacher of the old, old gospel, and his Master clothed him with great power.

Squire Brooke came of a substantial Yorkshire family, which possessed a considerable estate among the wild moorlands of the North. His parents belonged to the Established Church while Edward was in his boyhood, but were brought to know the Lord in after years by the preaching of their zealous son. Edward was not sent to Eton or Harrow, as he should have been; but following the bent of his inclination he was allowed to remain upon the farm, to fish, and hunt, and shoot, and to develop a fine constitution and an original mind. Amid the rocks and the heather, the forest trees and the ferns, Edward Brooke, with his dogs and his gun, found both sport and health; or dashing over the country after the hounds, he enjoyed exhilaration and trained his courage in the hunt.

Up to the age of twenty-two he seems to have been devoid of religious thought; but as we Calvinists are wont to put it, the time appointed of the Lord drew near, and sovereign grace issued its writ of arrest against him, resolving in infinite love to make him a captive to its power.

Early in the year 1821, Edward Brooke rose one morning, intent on pleasure. Equipped for his favorite sport, with gun in hand and followed by his dogs, he was crossing the Honley Moors, when a lone man met him with a message from God. The man was a Primitive Methodist preacher, named Thomas Holladay, one of those strong-minded, earnest evangelists, the validity of whose orders is disdainfully denied by many, but who, judged by the results of their ministry, hold a commission higher than bishops can bestow—a commission signed and sealed by him who is "head over all things to his church."

Intent upon his Master's work, "in season and out of season," Holladay was prompt to seize an opportunity of usefulness. Passing the young sportsman, he respectfully saluted him, and said, with pitying earnestness, "Master, you are seeking happiness where you will never find it." On went the man of God, perhaps little dreaming that the arrow thus shot at a venture had pierced the joints of the armor encasing the young sportsman's heart. Yet so it was.

Home went the wounded sportsman, the words of Holladay still sounding in his ears, "Master, you are seeking happiness where you will never find it." The time was opportune. It was a day of visitation for that neighborhood. The Spirit of God was moving upon the population. A great revival was in progress. It commenced at Thong, and spread from house to house, till nearly every family felt its power. On every hand sinners were strangely affected by a sense of their guilt and danger, as transgressors of the law of God, and exclaimed, "Men and brethren, what must we do?" Many believed on the Lord Jesus Christ and found peace through believing; their altered and happy life proclaiming them to be new creatures in Christ Jesus. Drunkards became sober, and abodes of misery were transformed into homes of peace.

The awakened young gentleman began to attend cottage prayer-meetings and to converse with the godly men of the neighborhood, and thus his anxiety was greatly deepened, and his desire for salvation inflamed.

> It was the day of his sister's wedding. Ill-prepared to join in the festivities of the occasion, because of the sorrow of his heart, Edward Brooke spent the previous night hours in reading his Bible and wrestling with God for salvation.
>
> > All night the lonely suppliant prayed,
> > All night his earnest crying made.
>
> About four o'clock in the morning, whilst kneeling by the old arm-chair in his father's kitchen, still pleading for mercy through the mediation of Jesus, his soul grew desperate, and like Jacob wrestling with the angel till the break of day, he resolved, "I will not let thee go except thou bless me."
>
> That mighty importunity was the manifestation of true faith. He was enabled to receive Jesus as his Savior, and believing with the heart unto righteousness, these words were applied to his heart, as distinctly and impressively as though spoken by a voice from heaven: "Thy sins which are many are all forgiven thee, go in peace and sin no more." All fear and sorrow vanished, and, believing, he rejoiced with joy unspeakable and full of glory.
>
> Exulting in his wonderful deliverance, his first impulse was to make it known. He hastened to his sister's chamber and told her the glad news that Christ had saved him—a glorious announcement on her bridal morn: then, early though it was, he ran out into the village and roused a praying man called Ben Naylot, whose heart he knew would be in sympathy with his, and told him how he had found the Lord; and they two called up a third, named Joseph Donkersley, to share their joy; and from the rejoicing trio up went a song of praise, the jubilant and sweet notes of which were music in God's ear, and woke up the songs of angels, and gave new impulse to the happiness of heaven, "for there is joy in the presence of the angels of God over one sinner that repenteth."

From that moment Edward Brooke was what he would have called "a brand new man." He could do nothing by halves, and therefore he renounced once for all his former course of life, and finding field sports to have too great a charm for him, he gave them up in the most resolute manner. "Sir," said he to a Christian friend, "I found that the gate was strait, and so I pressed into it myself, and left my horses, and dogs, and the world outside." In his zeal to be quit of what he felt to be a temptation, he gave orders to have his dog kennels pulled down, on hearing which, his father interposed and countermanded the instructions, saying, "I hope Edward will want the kennels again"; but it was in vain, the die was cast, the camel had gone through the needle's eye, and could not come back through so narrow a passage. Edward Brooke frequented cottage prayer-meetings, talked with the workpeople at the mill, exhorted in his father s kitchen, and instructed wayfarers by the roadside; he began, in fact, to put himself in training to become "a mighty hunter before the Lord," a consecrated Nimrod whose game would be the souls of men.

Mr. Brooke's early career illustrates the great usefulness of small meetings in rooms and cottages, where the uneducated, the poor, and raw beginners may feel at home in their first attempts at speaking. Had it not been for such gatherings he might have remained silent, for he could not have dared to make his first essays before a large congregation. Our author wisely remarks that

> the cottage prayer-meeting is certainly one of the best training schools for the development of Christian gifts. In some of our town-circuits, where chapels are few and large, and the pulpits invariably supplied by ordained ministers, and where Sunday afternoon services have been discontinued, and no rooms or cottages are opened for mission work, what opportunity have those whom the Spirit moves to preach his word, to test their call by actual experiment, and to develop their preaching power by frequent practice?
>
> In such meetings, Edward Brooke first ventured to deliver the message of salvation, which was as a burning fire shut up in his bones, till he was weary with forbearing and could not stay; and there he found encouragement and strength for further service.

After prayerful consideration and consultation with Christian friends, it was arranged that Edward Brooke should submit his convictions of duty to the judgment of others, by preaching in James Donkersley's chamber, a large room which answered the threefold purpose of a workshop, a bedroom, and a place where the neighbors might gather to worship God. The service was duly announced, and great interest awakened in the young squire's first appearance as a preacher. The chamber was thronged, and many a heart uplifted in earnest prayer that God would encourage and help his young servant in this first trial of his pulpit gifts. The preacher took for his text a passage in harmony with his intense convictions: "The wicked shall be turned into hell." Acting upon a sense of duty, and humbly relying on God, the preacher was divinely assisted, and the effort was a success.

The news that the young squire had begun to preach soon spread through the neighborhood and district, and created no small sensation. Opportunity to exercise his gifts offered on every hand, which he accepted as a call from God. Those who had known the squire in his wild days, and those who had heard of his remarkable conversion, all flocked to hear him. The announcement that Squire Brooke would preach, not only drew young squires, but emptied the public houses far and near, and was the signal for many an old poacher, dog-fighter, pigeon-flyer, drunkard, and habitual Sabbath-breaker, to find his way to the house of God. The squire attracted congregations such as no other man could get, comprising the fast men, the publicans and harlots, the roughs and outcasts of society, the sight of whom, in the house of God, must have made the heart of the preacher leap for joy, and carried him out of himself.

Influenced by the strange character of the congregations which thronged to hear him, and by the fact that many heard him, to whose untaught, sensual minds, theological terms and doctrinal definitions conveyed no meaning, and ordinary preaching was unintelligible, he, of set purpose, renounced the style of his first sermon in favor of another, which but for the preacher's motive and exceptional position, might be open to criticism, and which, in a copyist, would be most reprehensible.

We cannot pretend to give even an outline of Mr. Brooke's long and useful life, but must content ourselves with citing incidents which illustrate both his eccentricity and fervor. He gradually relinquished all his secular pursuits for the sake of soul-winning, and having an ample fortune he traveled far and wide, bearing his own charges, and preaching the gospel without money and without price, a mode of life which we both admire and envy. In his rambles, and at other times, he was always on the look-out for individual cases, with which he dealt in his own fashion, and with remarkable success. Note the following:

One of the members of the Sheepridge Society unhappily tampered with strong drink, till his enemy got the advantage of him. He was found one day, in a public-house, indulging in free potations; and his wife's persuasions failing to bring him out, she came to the squire to ask his interference.

> Away went the squire forthwith, conducted by the sorrowing woman, and, reaching the house, he walked straight into the bar, where a number of old topers were soaking according to their custom; and there, in their midst, was the fallen man. "What art thou doing here?" said the squire, fixing his eyes upon the poor back-slider, "This is no place for thee." Disconcerted by Mr. Brooke's unexpected appearance, and conscience-stricken, the man gave no reply, and seemed as though he would fain have dropped through the floor to escape the terrible gaze of the squire's reproving eyes. "Come out with me and come home with me," said the squire, and as the culprit still kept his seat, he seized him by his coat collar and pulled him out into the street.
>
> The topers, exasperated by such infringement of the "liberty of the subject," sprang to their feet and rushed to the rescue. The squire turned himself about, looked his opponents in the face, and raising his big, powerful arm, said, "There is not a man in the lot dare lay a finger on me." He then walked off his captive, gave him good counsel, and there is reason to believe that he never fell into the snare again.
>
> Driving to an appointment on a flue Sabbath morning in spring, with Mr. D. Smith, a Sheffield local preacher and a colleague in labor, Mr. Brooke suddenly said, "Pall up, Smith." Mr. Brooke then

stood up in the conveyance and shouted to a man in a distant part of a field by the wayside, who was gathering nettles, "Here, I want thee," beckoning with his hand at the same time for the man to come to him, When he came up to the fence, Mr. Brooke said, "Thou poor foolish sinner, art thou going to sell thy precious soul to the devil on a Sunday morning for a few paltry nettles!" And looking earnestly into his face, he prayed with great solemnity, "The Lord have mercy on thy soul. Amen." Then, quick as thought, he said, "Drive on, Smith." When fairly on the way again, he said, "I could not let that man sell his soul for nettles without warning him."

Driving to some village in Derbyshire, where he was expected to preach in the after part of the day, the squire pulled up at a wayside inn. Having seen his horse fed, he ordered his usual refreshment of ham and eggs. A fine, healthy-looking young countryman entered the room and sat down to rest. The squire made some friendly observations, and when his repast was spread, invited the young man to join him. The offer was gratefully accepted. Whilst enjoying their savory dish the youth's heart opened, and there was a pleasant flow of conversation. "We are expecting a very strange preacher," said he, "at our village tonight. He is a great man for prayer-meetings, and tries to convert all the folks into Methodists."

"Indeed," replied the squire, with evident interest in the topic, "Have you ever heard him?" "No, I haven't," said the youth, "but my brother has." "Well, what did your brother say about him?" enquired the squire. "Oh, he told me he never heard such a queer chap in his life; indeed, he didn't know if he were quite right in his head; but," said the young man, "I intend to go and hear for myself." "That is right, my lad," said the squire, "and get your brother to go too, he may have a word to suit you both."

They did go, and greatly to the young man's surprise, as the preacher mounted the pulpit, he recognized his friendly entertainer at the wayside inn. As the squire proceeded with the service the young man's heart was touched, and his brothers also. At the prayer-meeting they were found amongst the penitent seekers of salvation, and were both converted not merely into Methodists, but into Christian believers.

Here is a specimen of his characteristic letters: brief, but all on fire:

> DEAR JOHN—In reply to yours, I beg leave to say that our labor at Honley was not in vain. A new class has been formed, and about a dozen have gone to it. Two found peace. Praise the Lord! We shall rise. All hell is on the move, but we must go round about the bulwarks of our Zion, and mark well her palaces, and we shall ultimately and finally triumph over all. I say all. Go on, John, in the work. Live near to God. Be a giant in religion; one of the first and best men in your day. Plead with God. Live in the glory. "Advance" is the Christian's motto. Onward to certain victory over sin, the world, and hell. Trample down worldly, fashionable conformity; know the will of God, and do it. Do it heartily, cheerfully, fully, eternally, and heaven will be your guide, defense, and all in all. Our kind respects.
> And in your prayers, remember
> EDWARD BROOKE.

We take farewell of Squire Brooke with regret, as we copy the last entry from his diary:

> "In returning and rest shall ye be saved: in quietness and in confidence shall be your strength."—"Thou shalt see greater things than these."—"Thou preventest him with the blessings of goodness."—"I will do better unto you than at your beginnings."—"My soul is even as a weaned child." And then, possibly to express his fuller apprehension of the infinite mercy of his covenant God, and a firmer trust than he had heretofore exercised, he writes with a trembling hand that was soon to forget its cunning, "Never before."

We do not wonder that his memoir is in the fourth thousand ("Squire Brooke," by the Rev. J. H. Lord. Hamilton, Adams and Co.); it is exceedingly well written, and we congratulate Mr. Lord upon his spirit and ability.

14

Billy Bray: The Uneducated Soul-Winner

Many Chritians who are prepared to tolerate, and even to admire considerable diversities of character, have yet, unconsciously to themselves, laid down in their own minds very fixed and definite limits within which those diversities shall range. So far they are still looking for a measure of uniformity, and will probably require several more or less violent wrenches of their propriety before they will be able to admit within the circle of their sympathy sundry eccentric and erratic forms of genuine spiritual life, which, nevertheless, have had their uses, and have brought no small glory to God. We are most of us somewhat tolerant of well-educated eccentrics; we almost reverence the oddities of genius, but we are squeamish if we see singularities combined with ignorance, and idiosyncrasies prominent in men who cannot even spell the word.

What in a gentleman would be a peculiarity, is reckoned in a poor man to be an absurdity. Such slaves are most men to kid gloves and good balances at the banker's, that they toady to aristocratic whims, and even affect to admire in my Lord Havethecash that which would disgust them in poor Tom Honesty. This partiality of judgment, in a measure, affects even Christians, who, beyond all other men, are bound to judge things by their own intrinsic value, and not according to the false glitter of position and wealth. We claim for uneducated Christian men as wide a range for their originality as would be allowed them if they were the well-instructed sons of the rich; we would not have a shrewd saying decried because it is ungrammatical; nor a fervent, spiritual utterance ridiculed because it is roughly expressed. Consider the man as he is; make allowances for educational disadvantages, for circumstances, and for companionships, and do not turn away with contempt from that which, in the sight of God, may be infinitely more precious than all the refinements and delicacies so dear to pompous imbecility.

With this long-winded preface we now introduce a few notes upon William Bray, of Cornwall, for several years a local preacher among the Bible Christians: we beg his pardon for calling him by a name which he never used, and introduce him a second time, with due accuracy, as *Billy Bray*. This worthy was once a drunken and lascivious miner, but grace made him an intensely earnest and decided follower of the Lord Jesus. His conversion was very marked, and was attended with those violent struggles of conscience which frequently attend that great change in strong-minded and passionate natures.

His actual obtaining of peace brought the tears into our eyes as we read it, and made us remember a lad who, more than twenty years ago, found the Lord in a somewhat similar style; it also reminded us of George Fox the Quaker, and John Bunyan the Baptist, when undergoing the sacred change. Children of God are born very much alike; their divergences usually arise as a matter of after years. In their regeneration, as in their prayers, they appear as one. Bray was assailed by the fierce temptation that he would never find mercy; but with the promise, "Seek, and ye shall find," he quenched this fiery dart of the wicked one, and in due time he learned, by blessed experience, that the promise was true. Beautifully simple and touching are his own words:

> I said to the Lord, "Thou hast said, *They that ask shall receive, they that seek shall find, and to them that knock the door shall be opened,* and I have faith to believe it." In an instant the Lord made me so happy that I cannot express what I felt. I shouted for joy. I praised God with my whole heart for what he had done for a poor sinner like me: for I could say, the Lord hath pardoned all my sins. I think this was in November, 1823, but what day of the month I do not know. I remember this, that everything looked new to me; the people, the fields, the cattle, the trees. I was like a man in a new world. I spent the greater part of my time in praising the Lord. I could say with David, "The Lord hath brought me up out of a horrible pit, and out of the miry clay, and set my feet upon a rock, and established my goings, and hath put a new song in my mouth, even

> praise unto my God." I was a new man altogether. I told all I met what the Lord had done for my soul. I have heard some say that they have hard work to get away from their companions, but I had hard work to find them soon enough to tell them what the Lord had done for me. Some said I was mad; and others that they should get me back again next pay-day. But, praise the Lord, it is now more than forty years ago, and they have not got me yet. They said I was a *mad*-man, but they meant I was a *glad* man, and, glory be to God! I have been glad ever since.

No sooner was Billy saved than he began at once looking after others. He prayed for his work-mates, and saw several brought to Jesus in answer to his prayer. His was a simple faith; he believed in the reality of prayer, and meant to be heard, and expected to be answered whenever he supplicated for the souls of his comrades. He was a live man, not a dummy. In his own simple style he did all that he did with rigor, physical vigor being more than sufficiently conspicuous in his shouting and leaping for joy.

> He tells us, soon after his conversion, "I was very happy in my work, and could leap and dance for joy underground as well as on the surface."
>
> Bray began publicly to exhort men to repent, and turn to God, about a year after his conversion. Towards the end of 1824 his name was put on the Local Preachers' Plan, and his labors were much blessed in the conversion of souls. He did not commonly select a text, as is the general habit of preachers, but he usually began his addresses by reciting a verse of a hymn, a little of his own experience, or some telling anecdote. But he had the happy art of pleasing and profiting all classes, the rich as much as the poor; and all characters, the worldly as much as the pious, flocked to' hear him. He retained his popularity until the last. Perhaps no preacher in Cornwall ever acquired more extensive or more lasting renown, and the announcement of his name as a speaker at a missionary meeting, or on any special occasion, was a sufficient attraction, whoever else might or might not be present. Sometimes his illustrations and appeals made a powerful impression. I remember once hearing him speak with great effect to a large congregation,

principally miners. In that neighborhood there were two mines, one very prosperous, and the other quite the reverse, for the work was hard and the wages low. In his sermon he represented himself as working at *that* mine all the week, but on the "pay-day" going to the prosperous one for his wages. Had he not been at work at the other mine? the manager inquired. He had, but he liked the wages at the good mine the best. He pleaded very earnestly, but in vain, and was dismissed with the remark, from which there was no appeal, that he must come there to work if he came there for his wages. And then he turned upon the congregation, and the effect was almost irresistible, that they must serve Christ here if they would share his glory hereafter, but if they would serve the devil now, to him they must go for their wages by-and-by. A very homely illustration certainly, but one which convinced the understanding and subdued the hearts of his hearers.

There was excitement in some of his meetings, more than sufficient to shock the prejudices of highly-sensitive or refined persons. Some even who had the fullest confidence and warmest affection for Billy could not enjoy some of the outward manifestations they occasionally witnessed to the extent that he himself did. Billy could not tolerate "deadness," as he expressively called it, either in a professing Christian or in a meeting. He had a deeper sympathy with persons singing, or shouting, or leaping for joy, than he had with

The speechless awe that dares not move,
    And all the silent heaven of love.

Methodism is the mother church of Cornwall, and Bray was a genuine though uncultivated child of her heart. As John Wesley always associated the grace of God with the penny a week, so Bray's religion was not all shouting; it had an eminently practical turn in many directions. Billy was quite a mighty chapel builder; he began by getting a piece of freehold from his mother, which he cleared with his own hands, and then proceeded to dig out the foundations of a chapel which was to be called *Bethel*. Under great discouragement's, both from friends and foes, mostly, however, from the first, he actually built the place, working at it himself, and at the same time begging stone, begging timber, and begging money to pay the workmen. His little all he gave, and moved all around, who had anything to spare, to give likewise. On-lookers thought Billy to be silly, and called him so; but, as he well remarked, "Wise men could not have preached in the chapel if silly Billy had not built it." Almost as soon as one building was finished, he was moved to commence another. It was much needed, and many talked about it, but nobody had the heart to begin it but Billy Bray. He begged the land, borrowed a horse and cart of the giver; and then after doing his own hard day's work underground in the pit, and providing for five small children, he and his son worked at raising stone and building the walls; frequently working twenty hours of the twenty-four. He had a hard struggle over this second chapel; but his own account is best.

> When our chapel was up about to the door-head, the devil said to me, "They are all gone and left you and the chapel, and I would go and leave the place too." Then I said, "Devil, doesn't thee know me better than that; by the help of the Lord I will have the chapel up, or lose my skin on the down." So the devil said no more to me on that subject. Sometimes I had blisters on my hands, and they have been very sore. But I felt I did not mind that, for if the chapel should stand one hundred years, and if one soul were converted in it every year, *that* would be a hundred souls, and that would pay me well if I got to heaven, for they that "turn many to righteousness shall shine as the stars for ever and ever." So I thought I should be rich enough when I got there. The chapel was finished after a time; and the opening day came. We had preaching, but the preacher was a wise man, and a dead man. I believe there was not much good done that day, for it was a very dead time with the preacher and people; for he had a great deal of *grammar*, and but little of *Father*. "It is not by might, nor power, but by my Spirit, saith the Lord." If it was by wisdom or might, I should have but a small part, for my might is little and my wisdom less. Thanks be to God, the work is his, and he can work by whomsoever he pleases. The second Sunday after the chapel was opened I was "planned" there. I said to the people, "You know I did not work here about this chapel in order to fill my pocket, but for the good of the neighbors, and the good of souls; and souls I must have, and souls I will have." The Lord blessed us in a wonderful manner. Two women cried to the Lord for mercy;

and when I saw *that* I said, "Now the chapel is paid for already." The good Lord went on to work there; and the society soon went up from fifteen members to thirty. You see how good the Lord is to me; I spoke for one soul a year, and he gave me fifteen souls the first year. Bless and praise his holy name, for he is good, and his mercy endureth forever, for one soul is worth a thousand worlds. Our little chapel had three windows, one on one side, and two on the other; the old devil, who does not like chapels, put his servants, by way of reproach, to call our chapel *Three-Eyes*. But, blessed be God, since then the chapel has become too small for the place; and it has been enlarged; now there are six windows instead of three; and they may call the chapel *Six-Eyes* if they will. For, glory be to God, many that have been converted there are now in heaven; and, when we get there, we will praise him with all our might; and *he shall never hear the last of it.*

No sooner was this second house finished, than he began a third and larger one, and in this enterprise his talent for collecting, as well as his zeal in giving and working, were well displayed. He had high—and as we believe proper—ideas of his mission, in gathering in the subscriptions of the Lord's stewards. "A friend who was with Billy on a begging expedition, suggested, as they were coming near a gentleman's house, and Billy was evidently making for the front door, that it would be better if they went to the back door. 'No,' said Billy, 'I am the son of a King, and I shall go frontways.'" "At one time, at a missionary meeting, he seemed quite vexed because there was something said in the report about money received for 'rags and bones.' when he rose to address the meeting he said: 'I don't think it is right supporting the Lord's cause with old rags and bones. The Lord deserves the best, and ought to have the best.'" Well done, Billy! This is right good, and sound divinity.

Billy knew how to fight the devil and his agents with their own weapons. Returning late from a revival meeting, on a dark night in a lonely road, "certain lewd fellows of the baser sort," tried to frighten him by making all sorts of unearthly sounds; but he went singing on his way. At last one of them said, in the most terrible tones, "But I'm the devil up here in the hedge, Billy Bray." "Bless the Lord! Bless the Lord!" said Billy, "*I did not know thee 'wust' so far away as that.*" To use Billy's own expression, "What could the devil do with such as he?"

One of the most blessed results of his deep piety was his unfeigned humility, and his continual sense of dependence upon God. The Lord's servants without the Lord's presence are weak like other men, like Samson, when he lost his locks. Here is one experience of Billy's: "When I was in the St. Neot's Circuit, I was on the plan; and I remember that one Sunday I was planned at Redgate, and there was a chapel full of people, and the Lord gave me great power and liberty in speaking; but all at once the Lord took away his Spirit from me, so that I could not speak a word: and this might have been the best sermon that some of them ever heard. What! you say, and you looking like a fool and not able to speak? Yes, for it was not long before I said, I am glad I am stopped, and that for *three* reasons. And the first is, To humble my soul, and make me feel more dependent on my Lord, to think more fully of the Lord and less of myself. The next reason is, To convince you that are ungodly, for you say we can speak what we have a mind to, without the Lord as well as with him; but you cannot say so now, for you hear how I was speaking, but when the Lord took away his Spirit I could not say another word; without my Lord I could do nothing. And the third reason is, That some of you young men who are standing here may be called to stand in the pulpit someday as I am, and the Lord may take his Spirit from you as he has from me, and then you might say, it is no good for me to try to preach or exhort, for I was stopped the last time I tried to preach, and I shall preach no more. But now you can say, I saw poor old Billy Bray stopped once like me, and he did not mind it, and told the people that he was glad his Lord had stopped him: Billy Bray's Lord is my Lord, and I am glad he stopped me too, for if I can benefit the people and glorify God, that is what I want. I then spoke a great while, and told the people what the Lord gave me to say."

Preaching in such a spirit Bray was sure to have a blessing, and a blessing he had. Many orators and doctors in divinity look very small by the side of Billy Bray, if we estimate ministries by their results in soul-winning, and they will look smaller still when the souls saved by poor humble speakers shall shine forth like stars, and their own rhetorical fame and boasted learning shall be as darkness.

We say no more, but refer the reader to the memoir of Billy Bray, written by Mr. F. W. Bourne, and published at the Bible Christian Book Room, 57, Fairbank Street, East Road.

15

In Conclusion

All these eccentric preachers were in downright earnest, and because they were so their humor sometimes came to the front. Had their consecration to their work been less complete they would have taken more thought of public opinion, and have been more fearful of incurring reproach; but they were so set upon their one object of sending home the truth to the consciences of their hearers that they forgot their own reputations, and spoke with boldness.

Had these men been triflers with holy things, or jesters upon sacred topics, they would have been worthy of all the censure which has been poured upon them; but they were nothing of the kind. Among the earnest they were the most earnest; no one can doubt that. This, indeed, lay at the bottom of the opposition which they aroused. Had they been mere jesters the world would not have hated them so much as it did, for it loves those who make it sport. Had they cultivated a prim feebleness, or had they been content to discharge their office with the lifelessness of routine, they would have run no risk of standing in the pillory of scorn, for men may be as dull and as powerless as they please in the ministry without fear of being called eccentric.

If all men were right-minded they would be willing to listen to the message of salvation, even if it were couched in the driest terms of technical theology; but men are so careless about all the matters of their souls that we have not only to preach to them, but to induce them to hear us. A great part of our labor lies in seeking out attractive illustrations, parables, and choice sayings, by which we may coax men to attend to their own interests; and even then we fail unless a higher power intervenes. We would be content to preach didactic truth with unvarying solemnity if the multitude would but hear us, but they will not. What then? If the healing medicine is nauseous to the child, we must sweeten the draught or gild the pill. If our words will not run by themselves, we must put them on wheels and so set them in motion. Our object is—if by any means we may save some; and since men will not believe without hearing, and will not hear unless we make the word pleasant and attractive to them, we dare not do otherwise than indulge them in this respect, and woo them to instruction as children are enticed to learning by stories and pictures.

This little book is not written to inculcate eccentricity, or even to excuse all its displays; but, if possible, to take the edge from the scalping knife of slanderous misrepresentation and carping censure. Fair and honest criticism is not to be deprecated; it may be useful if honestly and kindly spoken. No Christian minister in his right mind wishes to shield himself behind his office, nor does he desire to be regarded as infallible; but what we do request is that our hearers' thoughts should not be diverted from our subject by the little details of our style and manner. These are trifles, but our message is a matter of life and death.

Reader, if you are brought to believe in the Lord Jesus Christ you will find rely little fault with the ministry which has led to so desirable a consummation; and if you are a hearer of the gospel and still reject the Savior, you will not be able to make an excuse for your unbelief out of the singularity of the preacher, for in these days if one man cannot profit you it is easy for you to find another, and there is no law to prevent your going where you are most benefited. Better shift your seat than waste your Sabbaths.

To all wise and candid believers we commend the language of the apostle—as the Lord gave to every man?" They are not to be pitted one against another, as if they were rivals engaged in fighting for the belt, they are to be loved, helped, and prayed for as fellow-helpers of our faith. "Therefore let no man glory in men, (or despise them either,) for all things are yours, whether Paul, or Apollos, or Cephas, or the world, or life, or death, or things present, or things to come; all are yours; and ye are Christ's; and Christ is God's."

Book Seven

Be of Good Cheer

The Savior's Comforting Exhortations Enlarged Upon

Preface

This little work is sent forth at the close of a long illness by one who has had great need to hear the Master say, "Be of good cheer." It comes to the reader as a dove which has been wearily flying over leagues of cheerless ocean; but not in vain, for at length she has plucked off an olive leaf, which she brings home with her. Comfort is to be found even in this troubled world; the floods do not cover all high hills, the waters are assuaging, hope rules the hour.

The words, "Be of good cheer," "Be of good comfort," occur at least seven times in the New Testament, according to the following list:

Be of good cheer—"He calleth thee" (Mark 10:49). "Thy sins be forgiven thee" (Matt. 9:2).

"Thy faith hath made thee whole" (Matthew 9:22). "It is I; be not afraid" (Mark 6:50). "I have overcome the world" (John 16:33). "As thou hast testified of me in Jerusalem, so must thou bear witness also at Rome" (Acts 23:11). "For I believe God, that it shall be even as it was told me" (Acts 27:25). Upon these texts as a backbone the body of this book has been fashioned: may the Spirit of God graciously put life into it.

The words of the Lord Jesus are spirit and life, and we are never so likely to obtain enduring consolation as when we sit at his feet and receive truth directly from his own mouth. The words of *the Word* are more than words: there is a power in them which proves them to be the children of the Omnipotent. When Jesus consoles, it is always with sure effect. He practices even now the art of wiping all tears from his people's eyes. His "Cheer up," or "Be of good comfort," banishes melancholy and begets joy. Many afflicted saints can bear witness to this; for they know the charm of his voice, and they testify to the mystic energy which dwells in it, turning sorrow into joy. Did any merely human sentences ever rival for a moment the peace-creating power of the fourteenth chapter of John? Let those speak whose weary brain has been only able to bear a few minutes' reading, even in the tender tones of an affectionate wife; let them be witnesses that there is a soft, sweet, soothing power about the language of Jesus which may be enjoyed, but cannot be described.

> All his words are music, though they make me weep,
> Infinitely tender, infinitely deep.

It is of the utmost importance that Christians should be happy. The joy of the Lord is your strength. Depression is a leak through which the soul's force wastes itself drop by drop. Peace is the condition of a healthy soul, and when it is broken it should cause deep concern. Some speak lightly of a believer's comfort, but God thinketh not so, for he cries, "Comfort ye, comfort ye, my people." Losing peace, the believer misses the spring and enthusiasm by which he runs unweariedly in the way of the commandments, and the heroic valor by which he leaps over the wall of difficulty. He is but half a man who is habitually a downcast man. Our Lord would have his joy fulfilled in us that our joy may be full.

Yet is it no easy task to be always calm and cheerful. In pain, and poverty, and loneliness dark thoughts are bred, which flit like bats and owls over the darkened soul, and unless we let in the blessed light of heaven we shall soon find them taking up their abodes within us. These children of darkness are very apt to return again and yet again, however earnestly they may be driven out. Perseverance must never tire of expelling them, for they must not dwell within the temples of the Holy Ghost. If we give way to gloomy feelings they will multiply; darkness will settle upon us like a heavy pall, and we shall become confirmed mourners. Up, then, in the name of him who saith, "Be of good cheer," and cry, "Rejoice not against me, O mine enemy; when I fall, I shall arise."

C. H. Spurgeon

1

Good Cheer from Christ's Call and From Himself

"And they came to Jericho: and as Jesus went out of Jericho with his disciples and a great number of people, blind Bartimaeus, the son of Timaeus, sat by the highway side begging. And when he heard that it was Jesus of Nazareth, he began to cry out, and say, Jesus, thou son of David, have mercy on me. And many charged him that he should hold his peace: but he cried the more a great deal, Thou son of David, have mercy on me. And Jesus stood still, and commanded him to be called. And they call the blind man, saying unto him, Be of good comfort, rise; he calleth thee. And he, casting away his garment, rose, and came to Jesus. And Jesus answered and said unto him, What wilt thou that I should do unto thee? The blind man said unto him, Lord, that I might receive my sight. And Jesus said unto him, Go thy way; thy faith hath made thee whole. And immediately he received his sight, and followed Jesus in the way" (Mark 10:46—52).

The blind man described in the gospel narrative printed above is a picture of what I earnestly desire that every reader of this book may become. In his first condition Bartimaeus was a type of what the sinner is by nature—blind, hopelessly blind, unless the healing Savior shall interfere, and pour in upon him the light of day. It is not, however, to this point that we shall now turn our thoughts; but to his conduct while seeking sight. This man, by God's great mercy, so acted that he may be held up as an example to all who feel their spiritual blindness, and earnestly desire to see the light of grace.

Several of the blind men of Scripture are very interesting individuals. There was one of them, you remember—the man born blind—who baffled the Pharisees by answering them with cool courage mixed with shrewdness and mother wit. Well might his parents say that he was of age, for he had all his wits about him. Blind as he had been, he could see a great deal, and when his eyes were opened he proved beyond all dispute that his questioners deserved the name of "blind Pharisees" which the Lord Jesus gave them.

Bartimaeus, the son of Timaeus, is a notable character. There is a sharp-cut individuality and crispness of style about him which makes him a remarkable person. He is one who thinks and acts for himself, is not soon daunted nor soon swayed, makes sure of what he knows, and when he is questioned gives a clear reply. I suppose that, as he sat in the midnight darkness which was his perpetual lot, he thought much; and having heard that from the seed of David there had arisen a great prophet who wrought miracles and preached glad tidings to the poor, he studied the matter over, and concluded that his claims were true. A blind man might well see that fact, if at all familiar with Old Testament prophecy; and as he heard more and more of Jesus, and compared him with the prophetic description of the coming King, he felt convinced that Jesus was the promised Messiah. Then, he thought within himself, "If he were ever to come this way, I would announce myself to be one of his followers. I would proclaim him, whether others acknowledged his royalty or not. I would act as a herald to the great Prince, and shout aloud that he is the son of David." Then he further resolved to seek the pity of the Messiah, and beg for his sight, for it was foretold that the Messiah would come to open blind eyes. This resolution he had so long dwelt upon that when the time did come, and he heard that Jesus passed by, he immediately availed himself of the opportunity, and cried out with all his might, "Pity me, thou son of David." O that you who read these lines would think over the claims of Jesus, and come to the same conclusion as the blind beggar of Jericho.

Learn a simple lesson from this man, I pray you. He made use of what senses he had. He could *hear* if he could not see. We have heard persons talk about their natural inability to perform gracious acts, and we have not answered them because it will be time enough to talk of what they cannot do when they have done what they can do. There are some things which we are sure they can do, and these they have neglected; it is mere hypocrisy, therefore, for them to be pleading want of power, when they do not use the strength they have. They do not constantly hear the gospel, or, if they do, they do not listen with attention, and, consequently, they do not get faith, for "faith cometh by hearing." In the case of Bartimaeus, everything was honest and sincere: the man had no eyes, but he had ears and a tongue, and he took care to use the faculties which remained to him, so that when the Savior passed by he cried to him with all his might; he made his confession of faith, and offered, at the same time, a personal petition for mercy as he cried aloud, "Thou son of David, have mercy on me."

I wish to drive at one point only, which will stand out clearly before my reader's eye when this chapter is ended; but I must go a little round about to compass my design. May the Holy Spirit dictate every word.

My first remark is that this man is a pattern for all seekers, because HE SOUGHT THE LORD UNDER GREAT DISCOURAGEMENTS.

He cried to the Lord Jesus so loudly, so unceremoniously, and at so unseasonable a time, as others thought, that they checked him, and bade him hold his peace; but this was like pouring spirits upon a fire, and it only made him the more intense in his pleading.

Notice his first discouragement: *no one prompted him to cry to Christ*. No friend lovingly whispered in his ears, "Jesus of Nazareth passeth by. Now is your opportunity: seek his face!" Possibly you, dear reader, may have been so neglected that you have sighed out, "No man careth for my soul." Then yours is a parallel case to that of Bartimaeus. Very few can fairly thus complain if they live among lively Christians, for in all probability they have often been invited, entreated, and almost compelled to come to Christ. Some even complain of Christian importunity, and are weary of it, not liking to be spoken to about their souls. "Intrusion" it has been called by some cavilers; but indeed it is a blessed intrusion upon a sinner, slumbering in his sin over the brink of hell, to disturb his slumbers, and arouse him to flee for his life. Would you not think it very ridiculous, were a house on fire, if the fireman declined to fetch anybody out of the house because he had not been introduced to the family? Must he send his card up, and obtain leave to enter? I reckon that a breach of courtesy is often a most courteous thing, when the desire is the benefit of an immortal soul. If in this book I should say a very personal thing, and it should arouse my reader to seek and find salvation, I know he will never blame me on that score.

Still, a person may reside where there is no one to invite him to seek Jesus, and, if so, he may recall the example of this man, who, all unprompted, sought the Savior's aid. He knew his need without telling, and, believing that Jesus could give him his eyesight, he did not need pressing to pray to him. He thought for himself, as all ought to do. Will not you do the same, my dear reader, especially on a matter so weighty as your own soul? What if you have never been the subject of friendly importunities and entreaties, yet you ought not to require them. You are possessed of your reason: you know that you are already sinful, and will be lost forever unless the Lord Jesus saves you: does not common sense suggest that you cry to him at once? Be at least as sensible as this poor blind beggar, and let the voice of your earnest prayer go up to Jesus the son of David.

The discouragement of Bartimaeus was still greater, for when he did begin to cry, *those around discouraged him*. Read the 48th verse: "*Many* charged him that he should hold his peace." Some for one reason, and some for another, charged him that he should hold his peace. They did not merely advise him, but they "*charged* him." They spoke like people in authority. "Be quiet, will you? Be still! What are you at?" Judging him to be guilty of a grave impropriety in disturbing the eloquence of the great Preacher, they would have hushed him to silence. Those who do not smart under a sense of sin often think awakened sinners are out of order and fanatical when they are only in earnest. The people near the blind beggar blamed him for his bad taste in shouting so loudly, "Thou son of David, have mercy on me." But he was not to be stopped.

On the contrary; we are told that he cried *the more*, and not only the more, but "the more *a great deal*" so that it was time wasted to try to quiet him. One man thought that surely he would put him down, and therefore spoke most peremptorily; but he gained nothing by the effort, for the blind man shouted still more lustily, "Thou son of David, have mercy on me." Here was an opportunity for having his eyes opened, and he would not miss it to please anybody. Folks around him might misjudge him, but that would not matter if Jesus opened his eyes. Sight was the one thing needful, and for that he could put up with rebuffs and reproaches. To him, discouragements were encouragements; and when they said, "Be silent," he cried the more a great deal. His manhood and determination were developed by opposition. Friend, how is it with you? Can you defy the opinion of ungodly men, and dare to be singular that you may be saved? Can you brave opposition and discouragement, and resolve that, if mercy is to be had, you will have it? Opposers will call your determination obstinacy; but never mind, your firmness is the stuff of which martyrs are made. In a wrong cause, a strong will creates incorrigible rebels, but if it be sanctified, it gives great force to character, and steadfastness to faith. Bartimaeus must have sight, and he will have sight; and there is no stopping him; he is blind to all hindrances, and pushes through. He had been begging so long that he knew how to beg importunately. He was as sturdy a beggar with Christ as he had been with men, and so he followed up his suit in the teeth of all who would stave him off.

There was, however, one more discouragement that must have weighed on him far more than the want of prompting and the presence of opposition: *Jesus himself did not answer him at first.* He had evidently, according to the run of the narrative, cried out to Jesus many times, for how else could it be said "he cried the more a great deal"? His cry had waxed stronger and stronger, but yet there was no reply. What was worse, the Master had been moving on. We are sure of that, because we are told in the 49th verse that Jesus, at length, "stood still," which implies that, before this time, he had been walking along, speaking as he went to the crowd around him. Jesus was passing away—passing away without granting his desire—without giving a sign of having heard him.

Is my reader one who has cried for mercy long and found it not? Have you been praying for a month, and is there no answer? Is it longer still? Have you spent weary days and nights in waiting and watching for mercy? There is a mistake at the bottom of the whole affair which I will not explain just now, but I will tell you how to act. Even if Jesus hear you not, be not discouraged, but cry to him "the more a great deal." Remember, he loves importunity, and sometimes he waits a while on purpose that our prayers may gather strength, and that we may be the more earnest. Cry to him, dear heart. Be not desponding. Do not give up in despair. Mercy's gate has oiled hinges, and it swings easily; push at it again. If you will use the knocker long enough, the porter will open to you, and say, "Come in, thou blessed of the Lord. Wherefore standest thou without?" Do have the courage of this poor blind man, and say, "Though for a while he hear me not, yet still will I confess him to be the son of David, and so avow that he is able to save me, and still will I cry to him, 'Thou son of David, have mercy on me.'"

Note, then, that this blind man is an example to us, because he did not take much notice of discouragements, whatever they were. He had within himself a spring of action which none could dry up. He was resolved to draw near to the great Physician, and put his case into his hands. O, dear reader, let this be your firm determination and you shall yet be saved.

II. Observe, in the second place, that there came a change over the scene. "Jesus stood still, and commanded the man to be called." Here we see him under a warmer and brighter light for a moment; and we remark that AFTER A WHILE HE RECEIVED ENCOURAGEMENT. The encouragement was not given him by our Lord, but by the same persons who had formerly rebuked him. Christ did not say to him, "Be of good comfort," because the man was not in need of such a word. He was by no means backward or disconsolate, or staggered by the opposition he had met with. Jesus Christ said, "Be of good comfort" in the case of the poor paralytic man who was let down by cords from the roof, because he was sad at heart; but this man was already of good courage, and therefore the Savior gave him no superfluous consolation. The onlookers were pleased with the hope of seeing a miracle, and so offered their encouragements, which were not of any great worth or weight, since they came from lips which a few minutes before had been singing quite another tune.

At this time I wish to give my anxious readers, who are trying to find their Savior, some little word of cheer, and yet I warn them not to think too much of it, for they need something far better than anything that man can say. The comfort given to Bartimaeus was drawn from the fact that Christ called him. "Be of good comfort, rise; *he calleth thee*" to every sinner who is anxious to find Jesus this is a note from the silver trumpet. You are invited to Jesus, and need not therefore be afraid to come. In one sense or another, it is true of all who hear the gospel, "He calleth thee," and therefore to every one we may say, "Be of good cheer."

First, it is true that Jesus calls each one of us by *the universal call* of the gospel, for its message is unto all people. Ministers are bidden to go into all the world, and preach the gospel to every creature. You, my friend, are a creature, and, consequently, the gospel has a call for you—"Believe in the Lord Jesus Christ, and thou shalt be saved." We are bidden to preach the gospel of the kingdom throughout all nations, and to cry, "Whosoever will, let him come and take of the water of life freely." "Whosoever." There is no limit to it, and it would be a violation of our commission if we should attempt to enclose what God has made as free as the air, and as universal as manhood. "The times of this ignorance God winked at; but now commandeth all men everywhere to repent." This is the universal call—"Repent ye, and believe the gospel." In this there is comfort of hope for all who desire to come to God.

> None are excluded hence but those
> Who do themselves exclude;
> Welcome, the learned and polite,
> The ignorant and rude.

But there is more comfort still in what, for distinction's sake, we will name the *character-call*. Many promises in the Word of God are directed to persons of a certain character. For instance, "Come unto me, all ye that labor and are heavy laden, and I will give you rest." Do you labor? Are you heavy laden? Then Christ specially calls you, and promises rest *to you* if you come to him. Here is another, "Ho! Everyone that thirsteth, come ye to the waters." Are you thirsting after something better than this world can give? Then the Lord bids you come to the waters of his grace. "And he that hath no money, let him come." Is that you? Are you destitute of merit—destitute of everything that could purchase the favor of God? Then you are the person whom he specially invites. We find a very large number of invitations both in the Old and New Testament addressed to persons in certain conditions and positions, and when we meet with a person whose case is thus anticipated we are bound to bid him be of good cheer, because the Lord is plainly calling him.

Next, there is *a ministerial call*, which is made useful to many. At times the Lord enables his servants to give calls to people in a very remarkable way. They describe the case so accurately, even to the little touches, that the hearer says, "Somebody must have told the preacher about me." When personal and pointed words are thus put into our mouths by the Holy Spirit we may give our hearer comfort, and say, "Arise, he calleth *thee*" What said the woman of Samaria? "Come, see a man which told me all things that ever I did: is not this the Christ?" When your inmost secrets are revealed—when the word of God enters you as the priest's keen knife opened the sacrificial victim, laying bare your inward and secret thoughts and intents, you may say, "Now have I felt the power of that word which is quick and powerful. O that I might also know its healing power." When a call to repentance and faith comes on the back of a minute personal description, you may assuredly gather that the Lord has sent this message especially to you, and it is yours at once to feel the comfort of the fact that Jesus calls *you*, "To you is the word of this salvation sent."

Yet there is another call, which overtops these three, for the universal call and the character-call and the ministerial call are none of them effectual to salvation unless they are attended with the Holy Ghost's own personal and *effectual call*.

Dear friend, when you feel within yourself a secret drawing to Christ which you do not understand, but yet cannot resist—when you experience a tenderness of spirit, a softness of heart towards the Lord—when your soul kindles with a hope to which it was a stranger, and your heart begins to sigh and almost to sing at the same time for love of God—when the Spirit of God brings Jesus near you, and brings you near to Jesus—then we may apply to you this comfort, "Be of good comfort; rise, he calleth thee."

III. Thus have I tried to set this man before you as receiving comfort; but we shall see that HE OVERLEAPED BOTH DISCOURAGEMENT AND ENCOURAGEMENT AND CAME TO JESUS HIMSELF.

Bartimaeus did not care one whit more for the comfort than he did for the rebuffs of those around him. This is a point to be well observed. You who are seeking Jesus must not rest in *our* encouragements, but press on. We would cheer you, but we hope you will not be satisfied with our cheering. Do what this blind man did. Let us read the text again: "Jesus stood still, and commanded him to be called. And they called the blind man, saying unto him, Be of good comfort; rise, he calleth thee. But (it should be 'but' and *not* 'and') he, casting away his garment, rose, and came to Jesus." He did not give them a "thank you" for their comfort. He did not stop half-a-minute to accept or to reject it. He did not need it: he wanted Christ, and nothing else.

Dear reader, whenever any man, with the best intentions in the world, tries to comfort you before you believe in Jesus, I hope you will pass him by and press to the Lord himself; for all comfort short of Christ himself is perilous comfort. You must come at once to Christ. You must hasten personally to Jesus, and have your eyes opened by him. You must not be comforted till he comforts you by working a miracle of grace. I fear we pamper you too much in unbelief, applying balm that does not come from the mountains of myrrh, nor from the sacrifice of our redeeming Lord. I fear that we talk as if there were balm in Gilead; but there is none anywhere except at Calvary. If there be a balm in Gilead, the Lord enquires, "Why then is not the health of the daughter of my people recovered?" The ointment of Comfort-apart-from-Christ has been tried long enough, and has healed none: it is high time to point you to Christ Jesus himself. Even the consolation to be drawn from the fact of a man's being called requires much caution in its use, lest we do mischief with it. The true eye-salve is with Jesus himself, and unless the soul comes actually into personal contact with Christ, no other comforts ought to satisfy it, for they cannot save. Note with admiration, then, that this man did not content himself with the best comforts that friendly lips could utter, but he was eager to reach the Son of David.

We read first that *he arose*. He had been sitting down before, wrapped up in his great cloak, in which he had often sat begging; and now that he heard that he was called, he, according to some versions, "leaped to his feet." The expression may be, perhaps, too strong; but at least he rose up eagerly, and was no laggard. His opportunity was come, and he was ready for it, nay, hungering for the boon. Now, dear reader, I pray you, let neither discouragements nor comforts keep you sitting still, but rise with eagerness. Oh be stirred up to seek the Lord. Let all that is within you be aroused to come unto the Savior. The blind man was on his feet in far less time than it takes to tell; and as he rose *he flung off his old cloak*, which might have hindered him. He did not care what he left or lost so long as he found his sight. His mantle had, no doubt, been very precious to him many a time when he was a poor beggar; but now that he wanted to get to Jesus he flung it away as if it were nothing worth, so that he might get through the throng more quickly and reach the one in whom his hopes centered.

So, then, if anything impedes you in coming to your Savior, fling it off. God help you to be rid of self and sin, and everything that is in the way. If any ill company you have been accustomed to keep, if any bad habit into which you have fallen, if anything dear as life, hinders you from simple faith in Jesus, regard it as an evil to be renounced. Off with it, and make a rush to him who calls you. Now, even now, draw near, and cast yourself at the Redeemer's feet. Say within yourself, "Encouraged or discouraged, I have weighed the matter, and I perceive that faith in Christ will save me. Jesus Christ will give me peace and rest, and I mean to have him at once, whoever hinders or helps."

Then we are told that *he came to Jesus*. He did not stop half-way, but, emboldened by Christ's call, he came right up to him. He did not stay with Peter, or James, or John, or any of them, but he came to Jesus. Oh that you, my reader, may have faith in Jesus Christ, and trust in him at once, putting your case by a distinct and personal act into Jesus Christ's hands that he may save you.

Our Lord was well aware that this man knew his name and character, and so without giving him further instruction he addressed him in these words, "What wilt thou that I should do unto thee?" Our Lord's addresses to persons were usually based upon their condition. He knew that this man very clearly understood what he wanted, and so he put the question that he might openly give the answer. "What wilt thou that I should do unto thee?" "Lord," said he, "that I might look up," or as our version has it, "that I might receive my sight." Go, dear friend, to Jesus, whether comforted or discouraged, and tell him what ails you. Describe your case in plain words. Do not say, "I cannot pray. I cannot find language." Any language will do if it be sincere. In the matter of speech Jesus does not want hyacinths from a conservatory, he is delighted with field flowers plucked from any hedge where you can find them. Give to him such words as come first to hand when your desires are fully awake. Tell him you are a wretch undone without his sovereign grace. Tell him you are a sinner worthy of death. Tell him you have a hard heart. Tell him you are a drunkard, or a swearer, if such be the case. Tell him all your heart, as the woman did of whom we read in the gospel. Then tell him that you need forgiveness and a new heart. Speak out your soul, and hide nothing. Out with it, reader! Out with it! Do not stay listening to sermons or consulting with Christian friends, but get to your chamber and speak with Jesus. This will do you good. It may be well to go into an enquiry-room to be helped by an earnest evangelist, but it is infinitely better to make your own chamber your enquiry-room, and there enquire of the Lord himself on your own account. May the divine Spirit lead you to do this *now*, if you have never before accepted Jesus.

So when Bartimaeus had stated his case in faith he received more than he had asked for. He received salvation—so the word may be rendered.

He was made whole and so saved. Whatever, therefore, had caused his blindness was entirely taken away; he had his sight, and he could look up, a saved man. Do you believe that Jesus Christ is as able to save souls as he was to heal bodies? Do you believe that in his glory he is as able to save now as he was when he was a humble man below? Why, if there be any difference, he must have much more power than he had then. Do you believe that he is the same loving Savior now as he was when here on earth? O soul, I pray you argue this out with yourself, and say, "I will go to Jesus straight away; I will go before I put down this book. I never find that he cast out any. Why should he cast out me? No bodily disease baffled him, and he is master of the soul as well as the body; why should my soul-disease baffle him? I will even go and lie at his feet and trust him, and see whether he will save me or not. Discouraged or encouraged, I will have done with men and I will go to the Savior." That is the lesson which I would have my reader learn before he leaves this chapter: I would have him go beyond the outward means of grace, to the secret fountain of grace, even to the great sacrifice for sin. Go to the Savior himself, whether others cheer you or frown upon you. Dejected, rejected, neglected, yet come to Jesus and learn that you are elected to be perfected in him.

One thing more, and I have done. I want this man to be an example to all of us, if we get a blessing from our Lord and are saved. *Having found Christ, he stuck to him.* Jesus said to him, "Go thy way." Did he go his way? Yes; but what way did he choose? Read the last sentence: "He followed Jesus in the way." The way of Jesus was *his* way. He in effect said, "Lord, I do go my way when I follow thee. I can now see for myself, and can therefore choose my way, and I make this my first and last choice, that I will follow thee in every pathway which thou dost mark out."

Oh that everyone who professes to have received Christ would actually follow him! But, alas, many are like those nine lepers who received healing for their bodies, but only one of them returned to praise him. Great numbers, after revival services, are like the nine lepers: they declare that they are saved, but they do not live to glorify God. How is this? "Were there not ten cleansed?" In great disappointment we enquire, "Where are the nine?" Alas, we ask with bleeding hearts, "Where are the nine?" They are not steadfast in our doctrine and fellowship, or in breaking of bread; they are neither active in service nor exemplary in character. Where are they? Where? Echo answers,

The Shilling Series

"Where?" But this man was of a nobler breed; immediately he received his sight he followed Jesus in the way.

He used his sight for the best of purposes: he saw his Lord, and kept to his company. He determined that he who gave him his eyes should have his eyes. He could never see a more delightful sight than the Son of David who had removed his blindness, and so he stopped with him that he might feast his eyes upon him. If God has given your soul peace and joy and liberty, use your new-found liberty in delighting yourself in his dear Son.

Bartimaeus became Christ's avowed disciple. He had already proclaimed him as the royal son of David, and now he determines to be one of David's band. He enlists under the Son of David, and marches with him to the conflict at Jerusalem. He stayed with our great David in the hold, to share his persecutions, and to go with him to death itself. We are told that he went with Jesus in the way, and that way was up to Jerusalem, where his leader was soon to be spit upon and to be mocked and to be crucified. Bartimaeus followed a despised and crucified Christ; reader, will you? Will you fare as he fared and endure reproach for his sake? Brave men are wanted for these evil times; we have too many of those thin-skinned professors who faint if society gives them the cold shoulder. Power to walk with a crucified Lord into the very jaws of the lion is a glorious gift of the Holy Ghost; may it rest on you, dear reader, to a full degree. May the Spirit of God help you.

This Bartimaeus, the son of Timaeus, is a fine man. When he is once really aroused you can see that he possesses a firm, decided, noble manhood. Many nowadays bend to every breeze, like the osier by the stream, but this man held his own. Most men are made of soft material, which will run into every mold, but this man had stern stuff within him. When he was a blind man he cried till he received his sight, though Peter, and James, and John forbad him; and when he became a seeing man he followed Jesus at all costs, though shame and spitting lay before him. It is our impression that he remained a steadfast and well-known disciple of Jesus, for Mark, who is the most graphic of all the gospel writers, always means much by every stroke of his pen, and he mentions him as Bartimaeus, whose name signifies "son of Timaeus," and then he further explains that his name really has that meaning. A name may not be actually correct, for many a Johnson is not the son of John, many a Williamson is not the son of William, and so there might possibly have been a Bartimaeus who was not the son of Timaeus; Mark, however, writes as if Timaeus was very well known, and his son was known too. The father was probably a poor believer known to all the church, and the son made his mark in the Christian community. I should not wonder if he was what we call "a character" in the church; known to everybody for his marked individuality and force of mind.

If, my reader, you have been long in seeking salvation and have become discouraged, may the Lord give you resolution to come to Jesus Christ this very day. Bring that firm, steadfast mind of yours, and bow it to Jesus, and he will accept you, and end your darkness. Under his teaching you may yet become a marked man in the church, of whom in after years believers will say, "You know that man—that grievous sinner while he was unsaved, that eager seeker when he was craving mercy, that earnest worker after he became a believer: he will not be put back by anybody. He is a true man, and gives his whole heart to our Lord." I shall be delighted beyond measure if my reader should be such a convert—a man who will not need looking after, but a determined man, resolute to do right, cost what it may. Such persons are a great gain to the good cause: gently would I whisper to you while your eyes follow these lines: *Will you not be one of them?*

2

Good Cheer from Forgiven Sin

"And, behold, they brought to him a man sick of the palsy, lying on a bed: and Jesus seeing their faith said unto the sick of the palsy; Son, be of good cheer; thy sins be forgiven thee" (Matt. 9:2).

"And they come unto him, bringing one sick of the palsy, which was borne of four. And when they could not come nigh unto him for the press, they uncovered the roof where he was: and when they had broken it up, they let down the bed wherein the sick of the palsy lay. When Jesus saw their faith, he said unto the sick of the palsy, Son, thy sins be forgiven thee" (Mark 2:3–5).

"And, behold, men brought in a bed a man which was taken with a palsy: and they sought means to bring him in, and to lay hint before him. And when they could not find by what way they might bring him in because of the multitude, they went upon the housetop, and let him down through the tiling with his couch into the midst before Jesus. And when he saw their faith, he said unto him, Man, thy sins are forgiven thee" (Luke 5:18–20).

This man was paralyzed in body, but he was very far from being paralyzed in mind. From the little we know of him, he would appear to have been earnest, resolute, energetic, and persevering. You very seldom find persons attempting more for you than you yourself desire; and if the four men who carried this paralytic person were so zealous in getting him under the Lord's notice, we may be morally certain that he, himself, was even more set upon it. His bearers would never have gone the length of breaking up the roof and letting him down upon the heads of the crowd unless he had urged them so to do. He was something more than passive under such heroic treatment. If he did not suggest the plan he evidently entered into it most willingly.

Suppose it to be your own case, my dear reader. Are you not persuaded that if, broken in spirit, you were to say to your friends, "Let me alone, my case is hopeless," few would dream of exciting themselves to desperate efforts on your behalf, but would let you lie still in your apathy, according to your request? It is a rule that you must yourself be energetic if you are to make other people energetic on your behalf; and therefore it seems to me that this man had a resolute and intense spirit, and had such influence over his friends that he inspired them by his eagerness, having first won them by his importunity. He besought them to aid him in what had become a necessity of his life; he must see Jesus. He must be brought before the great Healing One, somehow or other; and because of his personal eagerness and pressing importunity, his friends made up their minds to help him.

We may yet discover a little more about this palsied man, and it will not be mere conjecture; for by certain rules established by observation and experience we may often learn much of character from very small circumstances. Our Lord Jesus was accustomed to address the persons who came to him very much according to their mental condition. When one poor man half imbecile in spirit was brought to him, he asked him, "Wilt thou be made whole?" He was so listless as barely to have the will to be restored, and Christ's saying, "Wilt thou be made whole?" is evidence to us that even the poor creature's wishes had begun to slumber. Take it as a general rule that, while Christ regarded the onlookers and spoke with some view to them, yet in the main his first thoughts were towards his patient, and he generally spoke with an eye to that patient's case. I gather therefore from the fact that Jesus said to this man, "Son, be of good cheer," that he was very greatly depressed in spirit and unhappy; and when he added, not "Thy palsy shall be removed," but "Thy sins be forgiven thee," we are quite safe in concluding that the cause of the man's sadness was his sin, for which beyond all things else he desired pardon. Our Lord went straight to the roots of the mischief: the man was sad, and he cheered him; the man was sad about his sin, and so he granted him forgiveness. His palsy would secondarily be a fountain of bitter grief to the sick man, and therefore the Savior dealt with it in the second place; but, first and foremost, over and above all grief for his infirmity, was his painful sense of unforgiven sin. It is not likely that he told his bearers about that, for they might not have been able to sympathize with such a spiritual necessity; to them he spoke of his affliction, and not of his repentance, for while they would pity him for his palsy, they might have ridiculed him for his guilty conscience. The Lord, however, knew the heart's grief without telling; he read it in the sufferer's looks. The great Sin-Forgiver knew right well that earnest gaze which meant, "Be merciful to me a sinner"; and he met that wistful glance with a smile and the cheering words, "Son, thy sins be forgiven thee."

I suppose that the patient was a young man, for the word "son" would hardly have been spoken by our Lord to a man older than himself. I gather that he was a man of childlike faith, for Jesus did not call people his "sons and daughters" unless there was something of the childlike spirit about them. He was evidently a man of simple-hearted faith, who fully believed that Christ could forgive his sin; and so it happened to him, after the rule of the kingdom—"According to thy faith, so be it unto thee."

The case stood thus: The paralyzed man was burdened with sin, weighed down and oppressed in conscience. This urged him to seek the Savior. "I must see the Christ," said he. His passionate earnestness extracts a promise from the neighbors that they will take him to Jesus. He begs them to do it *now*. But the Lord could not be got at, for a dense crowd shut him in. "I must see Jesus," cries the man. His friends reply, "You cannot rise from your bed." "Carry me upon it," cries he. "But we cannot get in." "Try," says he. They reached the door, and they cried, "Make room. Here is a man sick of the palsy, who must see Jesus." They are gruffly answered, "Plenty of other poor men want to see him. Why should everybody give place to you? What is the use of pushing? There is no room for that bed here! What folly to drag a sick man into all this pressure and heat. The prophet is speaking: you will interrupt him. Away with you!" The bearers cannot enter. They plead and they push, but all in vain. "Then," cries the resolute man, "take me up the back stairs. Get me to the top of the verandah, and let down the bed through the ceiling. Run any risk; for I must get to Jesus." Possibly, his friends demur, and state the difficulties of the procedure suggested. "Why," says one, "you will be hanging over the people's heads, for there will be no room for you when we let you down." "Try it," cries he. "If I am let down from the top, there will be no fear of my reaching the ground; they cannot push me up again, or keep me on their heads. They must make room for me." His earnestness having been ingenious, now becomes infectious. His bearers smile at his eagerness, and enter into it with zest. He will give them no rest till his desire is accomplished; and so they break up the tiling, and let him down before Jesus, with the glad result described in the gospel: "Jesus said to him, Son, be of good cheer; thy sins be forgiven thee."

We have before us, first, *a doctrine*. The doctrine that it is one of the grandest comforts in the world to have your sins forgiven you. "Son, be of good cheer; thy sins be forgiven thee." Secondly, we have before us *a question*. May every reader have the honesty to put it, and to answer it in his own case: the question, Have I my sins forgiven me? For, if so, I have a right to be of good cheer, and to be as merry as the birds in spring. But, if not, I am destitute of the greatest comfort which Christ himself can speak to a sinner's heart.

I. Dear reader, let us give our hearts at once to THE DOCTRINE. It is plainly taught us here that the pardon of sin is one of the richest comforts which the Lord can give to a man.

It is so, first, because *the pardon of sin removes the heaviest sorrow which a man can feel.* Some know little about this grief. May the Lord cause them to mourn with broken hearts, or they will perish in their sins. Those of us who have known the burden of sin can tell you that it is a crushing load. Thoughtful persons who have seen things in their true light, honest persons who refuse to be flattered, pure-minded people, who long to be right with God—all these will tell you that a sense of sin is of all miseries the most sharp and disquieting. To know that you have sinned against light and knowledge with special aggravations is as a hot iron to the flesh, and as a serpent's venom in the blood. There is no rest day or night to a soul which carries this hell within it.

I write what I do know from personal experience, and I only write what many a reader knows, too, within his own soul. Once let conviction flash in upon the soul, and the world loses its fascinations, the music hall, the ballroom, and the theatre are robbed of their enchantments; even business wearies, and domestic joys are deprived of sweetness; for a sense of sin spoils all. Guilt on the conscience hangs over everything like a funeral pall, it drowns all music with its prophetic knell, and withers every green herb beneath its burning feet.

Sin, sin—what direr ill than thou art can even Satan himself beget? A man infected with a deadly disease is never at ease; whatever garments he may put on, or at whatever tables he may feast, he is still unhappy, because he has the arrows of death sticking in him. Such is a man conscious of sin. Nothing can please him, nothing can ease him, till his sin is removed. But when sin is gone—when he knows that he is pardoned, he is as a bird set free from its cage.

A great fire raged one night in a village, and a large thatched mansion in which a man of God resided caught fire. It blazed furiously, but he and his wife and the most of his children escaped. Judge of their horror when they counted them over to discover that one little one was missing. Nothing would content them while that dear child was in the burning house. "Mr. Wesley," his neighbor might say to him, "we have saved your chest of drawers. We have saved your valuable books from the house." "Ah, but," the good man would have said, "my boy is in danger." What his wife thought of it when she recollected that little John would be burned to death, I need not tell you; but when, at last, he was lifted out of the window, and brought to his parents' arms, then be sure the good man would gather his whole family about him and bless the Lord, even though all his substance was consumed. Now, when a sensible man's soul is in danger nothing can content him. He prospers in business, his happy children play around him; but what of these while his soul remains in deadly peril? When once, through pardoned sin, his soul becomes like a brand plucked from the burning, then his daily troubles lose all their weight and his heart is full of joyful song.

It is clear to every experienced man that the pardon of sin is an immense comfort, because it removes the bitterest cause of distress and alarm.

Next, forgiveness of sin is a comfort of the first order, for, indeed, *it is altogether indispensable.* You may possess every luxury, but you cannot be solidly happy until sin is forgiven. "Why?" says one, "I am really happy, and yet I am not pardoned." Yes, but it is a remarkable thing that happy people of your kind are never pleased while they are quiet; they must get up an excitement, and dance, or fiddle, or drink, or play the fool in some sort, or they are not happy. I call that real happiness which I can enjoy by the hour together in my room alone, calmly looking into things, and feeling content. I call that real joy which I feel when I wake up at night, and, though full of pain, can lie still and bless God for his goodness. It was said of old, "Philosophers can be merry without music"; and so can the saints of God; but the ungodly, as a rule, cannot enjoy themselves without external objects to raise their spirits. The truly happy man is satisfied from himself. A spring within him of living water quenches his thirst, so that he never feels the drought.

A man cannot be really happy till his sin is pardoned, because sin brings, more or less, to men a sense of condemnation. Picture a man in the condemned cell. Try to make him comfortable. We provide him with a dainty supper, we sing him gladsome glees, we exhibit fine pictures; but he is condemned to die to-morrow, and he loathes our feast and our fineries. Bring in a thousand pounds, and make him a present of it. He looks at the golden sovereigns, and he says, "What is the use of these to me?" Tell him that a rich man has left him heir to a wide estate. "Yes," says he, "but how can I enjoy it? I am condemned to die." He is always in his dreams hearing his death-knell, and picturing to himself the dreary scene when he is to be launched into eternity. If you could only whisper in his ear, "Her Majesty has granted you a free pardon," he would say, "You may take away the feast; I feel too happy to eat. All the gold in the world could not make me more delighted than I am now, as a pardoned man." When men have come out of prison, after they have been shut up for years, everything has been a joy to them. Though they went home, perhaps, and found everybody dead that they once knew, and saw their own hair turned grey through having lain so long in a moldy den, yet the sweets of liberty made the stones of the streets shine as if they were made of gold, and the fields seemed like fairy-land to them. Such is the joy of pardon when it comes from our God. A man must have forgiveness, or else everything will be emptiness to him; but when he is absolved he goes forth with joy, and is led forth with peace.

Pardon of sin makes all our sorrows light. If a condemned man is permitted to live, he will not ask whether he is to live like a gentleman or like a peasant. When some kind-hearted men struggle to get the life of a condemned criminal spared, the man's friends think of nothing but his life. When a judge sentences a man to penal servitude for life, it may be thought a hard sentence; but you never hear of complaints, when a condemned criminal has his life spared, if we find that he is to be kept a prisoner as long as he lives. The heaviest punishment seems nothing if life be spared. You heave a sigh of relief to think that the gallows will bear one sad fruit the less, and you forget all about the servitude or the imprisonment which the convict will have to endure. So, depend upon it, if you get sin pardoned, and so are saved from the eternal wrath of God, you will make no bargain with God whether you have meat to eat and raiment to put on, or are left hungry and naked. No, Lord, I will shiver in a beggar's rags with full content, if I be but pardoned. I will dwell in prison with a dry crust for my food if I be but delivered from thy wrath. Thus it is clear that the blotting out of sin takes the sting from every other sorrow.

Let me add, *it makes death itself light.* I remember the story of a felon in those days when they used to hang people for very little indeed. A poor man who had committed some offence was condemned to die: while he lay waiting for the sentence, the Lord sent a choice minister of the gospel to him, and his heart was enlightened so that he found Christ. As he was on the way to the gallows tree, what, think you, was this man's cry? He was overwhelmed with joy, and lifting up his hands he said many times, "Oh, he is a great forgiver! He is a great forgiver!" Death was no terror now that he had found forgiveness through Jesus Christ. Poverty repines not when sin is removed. Sickness frets no longer when conscience is at ease. It may cost you many a pang to feel yourself melting away in consumption; but what matters it now that transgression is forgiven? Every breath may be a labor, every pulse may be a pang; but, when sin is forgiven, the Lord has created such a spring of joy within the heart that the soul can never faint.

Yet again, dear friend, remember that *he pardon of sin is the guarantee of every other blessing.* When Christ said, "Thy sins be forgiven thee," was there any question at all as to whether that paralytic man would be healed? Certainly not; for the love which had forgiven the sufferer's sin was there to prompt the Savior to say afterwards, "Take up thy bed and walk." Reader, if your sin be pardoned, it is written concerning you, "No good thing will I withhold from them that walk uprightly," and again, "All things work together for good to them that love God." Everything between here and heaven is secured by the covenant of grace for your best benefit.

> If sin be pardoned, I'm secure:
> Death has no sting beside.

You shall never have a need but God will assuredly supply it, since he has already bestowed on you the major blessing, the all-comprehending blessing of forgiveness. Covenant mercies follow each other like links of a chain. "Who forgiveth all thine iniquities; who healeth all thy diseases; who redeemeth thy life from destruction; who crowneth thee with loving-kindness and tender mercies; who satisfieth thy mouth with good things, so that thy youth is renewed like the eagle's." Do you think that God forgives men their sins and then leaves them to perish? Such cruel mercy would be more worthy of a demon than of the Deity. Pardon is the pledge of everlasting love, and the pledge will never be forfeited.

"Alas," cries one, "perhaps after the Lord has forgiven me he may yet turn again and punish me." Listen. "The gifts and calling of God are without repentance." That is, God never repents of what he does in the way of grace. If he forgives, he forgives once for all and forever. It would be blasphemy to represent God as making a transient truce with men instead of an eternal peace. The Lord casts the iniquities of his people into the depths of the sea, and their transgressions he remembers against them no more forever. Is not this a blessed act of grace? It secures the removal of all the evil results of sin, and the guarantee of all that will be needed this side of heaven, yea, and of glory forever. Oh, dear reader, if you do but hear Jesus say, "Thy sins be forgiven thee," you may also hear him say, "Be of good cheer," for there is everything in the fact of pardon to make your heart dance for joy.

We will not linger longer upon the doctrine, but make our meditation personally practical by pressing home the work of self-examination.

II. Let us consider THE QUESTION: *Are you forgiven?* Reader, has God, for Christ's sake, forgiven you? "Ah," cries one, "do not judge us." I shall not attempt to do so, but I would beg you to judge yourselves. "We cannot be sure of our salvation," answers another. Can you not? Then you ought never to be happy; for a man who is in doubt about a matter so vital as this, which involves his all, ought never to enjoy a moment's peace. How can we rest in fear of hell? In danger of eternal wrath?

Do you not long for certainties? A great novelist began a favorite story with the sentence, "What I want is facts." In that he expressed the longing of many a thoughtful soul; many of us feel that we want indisputable facts. Our proverb hath it, "Fast bind, fast find!" Prudent men will take double care about this weightiest of all concerns and will not be content till they are infallibly assured. I will help you to answer this question by remarking that there is a way by which we may know if we are *not* forgiven.

We may know that we are not forgiven if we have never felt that we need forgiveness. Where guilt has never been perceived it has never been removed. "If we say that we have no sin, we deceive ourselves, and the truth is not in us." If I feel that I am as good as most people, and perhaps a little better, if I justify myself and think of gaining heaven by my own endeavors, then I am under condemnation. God has never healed the man who was never wounded, nor has he made the man alive who was never dead. If you have never been humbled before God so as to acknowledge your sinnership, then you abide under his wrath. Think of that, I pray you, you who are at ease, wrapping yourself about in the garments of your own deservings. "Because thou sayest, I am rich, and increased with goods, and have need of nothing," thou mayest be sure that in God's sight "thou art wretched, and miserable, and poor, and blind, and naked." Dear reader, I hope it is not so with you.

Again, he has never been forgiven who does not at this moment hate sin. Jesus never came to save us *in* our sins, but *from* our sins, and wherever he takes away the guilt of sin he also kills the love of it. Sin never seems so black as when we see it put away by Jesus' blood. At the sight of the cross we grow angry with ourselves for having slain our Lord by our transgressions. Never dream that you can be pardoned and then be allowed to live as you did before: the very wish to do so would show that you are under condemnation still.

Again, you are not forgiven if you have never sought Christ and his atoning blood. If you have labored by other means to procure mercy, you have not found it; for no one else can give it but the one appointed Mediator. Can your priest grant pardon? Did you offend the priest? Then the priest can forgive you for offending him; but he cannot forgive you for offending God. None but God in Christ Jesus can blot out sin, and you must go to him; and, if you do not, you are not forgiven, whatever you may dream.

Once more, have you forgiven everybody else? This is a home question to some minds; but remember how needful it is to answer it. If ye do not forgive everyone his brother his trespasses, neither will your heavenly Father forgive you. There it stands, "Forgive us our debts as we forgive our debtors." If you cannot pardon everyone, no matter how grievous the offence, neither has God pardoned you. A malicious heart is an unrenewed heart A revengeful spirit is clean contrary to the Spirit of God who passeth by transgression, iniquity, and sin. This truth may be little preached, but Holy Scripture makes it very prominent, and the reader will be unwise if in any measure he ignores it. You are not forgiven if you cannot forgive.

Let me now help the reader to see whether he is forgiven by some positive test. Only one is needed: *you are pardoned if you are a true believer in Jesus Christ.* It is written, "Jesus seeing their faith"—that is, the faith of the four bearers and the faith of the man that lay upon the bed—said, "Thy sins be forgiven thee." The poor palsied man so believed in Jesus that his very face beamed with confidence when he came into Jesus's presence; and so Jesus, seeing his faith, said to him, "Thy sins are forgiven thee." Do you believe in Jesus?

Reader, I know that thou believest that Jesus Christ is God and a great Savior; but is this a mere matter of doctrine to thee? Do you believe *in* him? You know what it is to believe in a man so that you can trust him, and leave your affairs in his hand: do you in this way believe in Jesus? That is the faith which saves. When a man believes in Christ so as to commit himself to Christ for salvation he believes aright; for believing is but another word for trusting, relying, depending upon.

Do not trifle with this question. It is my hope that you can answer, "Yes, unless I am awfully deceived, I am trusting the blood and merits of the Lord Jesus Christ, and I am so trusting him that I endeavor to follow in his footsteps, and copy his example." Then you are saved for "there is therefore now no condemnation to them which are in Christ Jesus." Dwell on that word, "Therefore being justified by faith, we have peace with God." If you really trust Christ, though you have only done so during the last hour, your transgressions are put away, and your iniquity is covered, for he immediately pardons those who come to him. "If we confess our sins, he is faithful and just to forgive us our sins, and to cleanse us from all unrighteousness." If you have confessed your sin to him and trusted him, you are most assuredly cleansed by his blood.

Now for the last word. It is this. Jesus said, "Be of good cheer; thy sins are forgiven thee." Come, then, let us be of good cheer. Let us be happy. Let us be merry in the Lord. Let us begin to sing for very joy of heart, because our sins are forgiven us. We are very poor, but our sin is forgiven us. We are very weak, but our sin is forgiven us. We are perhaps getting very old and near to our end, but our sin is forgiven us! We are full of infirmity and vexed with temptations, but our sin is forgiven us for his name's sake! "Son, be of good cheer," said the Savior, and shall we be otherwise? What if our room is a very small one, what matters, if our sin is forgiven? "Ah, but there is a sick one at home." "Son, be of good cheer; thy sins are forgiven thee." You know how the Master, when the disciples found another joy, turned them back to this—"Nevertheless, rejoice not in this, but rather rejoice that your names are written in heaven;" and so when you find a multitude of troubles, follow the like good advice, and return to this old-fashioned joy—"Son, be of good cheer; thy sins are forgiven thee." Does the reader say, "I am over head and ears in trouble, for I am in great straits"? Let me lay my hand upon your shoulder, and say, "Brother, be of good cheer; thy sins are forgiven thee." "Oh, but I have very little to live upon." True, but you have this—"Thy sins be forgiven thee." Be of good cheer. The Lord make thee to be so. Thy sins are forgiven thee.

If you are not happy, it will be disobedience to Christ, for he commands you to "be of good cheer." It will look as if you did not value the blessing that cost him his blood. "Thy sins be forgiven thee." It cost him his life to buy you this redemption; and are you going to groan when you get it? No doubt you are pleased to give good things to poor persons, and, if so, you like to see their gratitude. I gave something, not many days ago, to a man, and he just put it in his pocket, and walked off without a word, as if he would say, "I thought you would have given me at least ten times as much." I thought, "If I had seen the way you would take it, my man, I should not have been in such a hurry with my gift." When you give your children a little treat, you like to see them pleased and thankful; but if they sit down and fret over your kindness you are disappointed, and are in no great haste to indulge them again. Our heavenly Father's gifts must be valued and delighted in: if he has forgiven us our sins, let us be happy.

"Son, be of good cheer." Have some regard to the outside world, for if they see pardoned men and women with gruesome countenances they will infer that there is not much comfort in God after all. "My wife," says one, "declares that her sins are forgiven her, and I am sure when there is a little trouble in the house she is more downhearted than I am." "There," cries a woman, "my husband tells me that his sins are washed away, but he grumbles and murmurs till we are all made miserable by him." Do not let it be so. If we have a cross to

carry, let us bear it joyfully for Jesus' sake. If we have work to do for Christ, let us do it with delight. Let us live to music. Let us march to heaven to a gladsome tune, rejoicing in the Lord because our sins are forgiven, and he hath said—
BE OF GOOD CHEER.

3

Good Cheer from Grace Received

"And, behold, a woman, which was diseased with an issue of Mood twelve years, came behind him, and touched the hem of his garment: for she said within herself, If I may but touch his garment, I shall be whole. But Jesus turned him about, and when he saw her, he said, Daughter, be of good comfort; thy faith hath made thee whole. And the woman was made whole from that hour" (Matt. 9:20–22).

"But as he went the people thronged him. And a woman having an issue of blood twelve years, which had spent all her living upon physicians, neither could be healed of any, came behind him, and touched the border of his garment: and immediately her issue of blood stanched. And Jesus said, Who touched me? When all denied, Peter and they that were with him said, Master, the multitude throng thee and press thee, and sayest thou, Who touched me? And Jesus said, Somebody hath touched me: for I perceive that virtue hath gone out of me. And when the woman saw that she was not hid, she came trembling, and falling down before him, she declared unto him before all the people for what cause she had touched him, and how she was healed immediately. And he said unto her. Daughter, be of good comfort: thy faith hath made thee whole; go in peace" (Luke 8:42–48).

The words of good cheer which our Savior spoke to this woman were not given to her while she was coming to him, for it would have been premature. She had not avowed her desire to be healed, she had uttered no prayer, she had actually as yet sought nothing at the Savior's hands, and hence she had not reached the stage at which comfort is fitting. She does not appear to have required comfort in taking her first step; she was resolved upon that, and she took it without fail. It is one of the unwisest things under heaven to comfort people who do not require it. When we are dealing with enquirers, our love may bring them loss if we offer them words of cheer when they need admonition or rebuke. I tried to show in a previous chapter that any comfort which keeps a soul short of Christ is dangerous, and I would now repeat the caution. Our business is to get to Jesus himself, to exercise personal faith in the personal Savior, and we have no right to a gleam of comfort until we have heartily and honestly trusted in Christ. If encouragements to believe are used as a sort of halfway house to rest in before actually believing, they are mischievously used, and may ruin our souls.

This afflicted woman did not require to be cheered so soon, for she had such confidence in Christ, and such a resolve to put her confidence to the test, that difficulties could not hinder her, nor crowds keep her back; the Savior was in the press, she joined the throng, and with a holy boldness mixed with a sacred modesty she came behind him, only wishing to touch his garment, or even the fringe of it, feeling persuaded that if she did but come into contact with the Lord, no matter how, she would be healed. According to her faith so was it to her, and *it was after she had been healed that our Lord spoke comfortingly to her.* He brought not forth the cup of cordial till the need for it had fully come. After she had touched him and her faith had made her whole a trial awaited her, and her spirit was ready to faint, and then the tender One cheered her by saying, "Thy faith hath made thee whole; go in peace."

It happens to many and many a heart that after it has obtained the blessing of salvation, and has been healed of the disease of sin, a time of fear occurs. After it has made its confession of faith a season of trembling follows, occurring perhaps as a reaction from the joy of salvation, a rebound of the spirit from excessive delight. We eat the heavenly provision eagerly, and it is sweet to our taste, and yet afterwards, our long hunger having weakened us, we do not digest the food with ease, and pains ensue for which medicine is required. We fear and tremble because of the greatness of the mercy received, and then this word is wanted: "Be of good comfort: thy faith hath made thee whole."

We will meditate, first, upon *this woman's need of comfort*; secondly, upon *the comfort which Jesus gave her*; and then, in the third place, we will enter a little further into that comfort, and think of *the faith which Jesus Christ declared had made her whole*—the faith to which he pointed her for comfort.

I. Come, then, dear reader, and attentively consider THIS WOMAN'S NEED OF GOOD CHEER. She felt in her body that she was made whole, and yet she stood in urgent need of comfort. This necessity arose from several causes.

First, *she had hoped to obtain the blessing secretly, and she was found out.* She thought that by coming behind the Lord Jesus in the press she should not be observed; and secrecy she anxiously desired because the peculiarity of her bodily disorder caused her to dread publicity. She aimed at gaining her end and retreating unnoticed into the multitude. Truth to say, she stole the cure. Her touch was given in stealth, no eye resting upon her. No disciple seems to have spied her out, nor had any one in the throng perceived the deed, or else, when the Master said, "Who touched me?" one or other of them would have pointed her out. So far she had shunned observation, and even the Savior himself had not seen her with his bodily eyes; but faith such as hers could not be hid. It was not meet that such a flower should bloom unseen. She is called for and she stands discovered, the center of all eyes.

You, perhaps, dear friend, have hoped to find salvation and to keep it a secret. You entered the house of prayer a stranger to the things of God, but very anxious; there you sat and wept; but you tried to conceal your feelings from those who sat near you. You have gone in and out of the place of worship, seeking the Savior, but fearing to be suspected of it. Nobody spoke to you, or, if they did, you evaded their questions, for you were as jealous of your secret as if you carried diamonds and were afraid of thieves. Now you have believed in the Savior, or at least you hope so, but you court secrecy just as much. You have found honey, and you have tried to eat it all alone, not because you grudge others, but because you are afraid of them. You did not wish mother or father, kinsfolk or acquaintance to suspect you of religion; you shrank from the blessed charge, and desired to be a secret friend of Jesus, a Nicodemus, or a Joseph of Arimathea. To your great amazement you have been found out. Like Saul, you hid among the stuff, but the people have called you forth. Your love to Jesus has oozed out, and is spoken of by many. Do you wonder? How can fire be hidden? Your speech has betrayed you. Your manner and spirit have discovered you, as odors betray sweet flowers. And now that it is out, you feel a sinking of spirit at the notice you have attracted. Your modesty cries, "They take me for a Christian. Can I live like a Christian? Shall I be able to adorn my profession? They have discovered me in the family: my brothers and sisters see that there is a change in me: is it a real change? or shall I turn out to be one of those deceivers who have a name to live and are dead?" Your heart fails you for fear of future backsliding and apostasy, and well it may, for flesh is weak, and the world is bewitching, and Satan is subtle, and sin is deceitful. Whatever comfort there is in the present meditation will be meant for you, since it is intended for persons embarrassed by being forced out of the shade of solitude into the glare of observation, troubled because they fear that they shall not honor the holy name which is named upon them. To you who are in that condition Jesus says at this moment, "Be of good comfort: thy faith hath made thee whole."

This poor woman, in addition to being found out, *had been constrained to make a public personal testimony.* As we have already noticed, her case was a very special one, in which privacy would naturally be courted; but that secrecy had been invaded, the Savior had looked for her, and had demanded—"Who touched me?" and she, all trembling and afraid, had been constrained to fall down before him and to tell him all the truth: do you wonder that the excitement was too much for her? The people had been astonished as they heard of the wondrous power which had emanated from the person of Christ, even through the fringe of his garment, and that astonishment in a great measure referred to her. She was the observed of all observers. Of her cure she had to make a public acknowledgment. She was equal to the task. Being brought to bay she did her work bravely, and bore full and telling testimony. Take careful note that our Lord did not bid her be of good cheer till she had so done. She trembled before she confessed the Lord's deed of grace which had been wrought upon her; but as soon as she had made a public avowal her Lord said, "Daughter, be of good comfort."

I have known certain timid ones who have wished to unite with the church on the sly, and to make no open confession either by word of mouth or by baptism: I have refused to be a party to the breeding of cowards, and they have lived to thank me for what seeemed a harsh demand. Yet when the confession has been made once for all, many brave hearts have been full of anxiety and downcastings. They have confessed Christ before men, they have told out what the Lord has done for their souls; and after it has been all over, they have been overwhelmed with a sense of responsibility, and have said within themselves, "What great things will be expected of me! What have I had the courage to say? Shall I be able to live up to it all?" After the bold, open confession comes the inward shrinking: though they are not sorry that they made the avowal, for, on the contrary, they would make it a thousand times over if they could glorify Christ thereby—yet they see their weakness, and tremble lest they should ever behave themselves so as to prove unworthy of the cause of their beloved Redeemer. If you, dear friend, have just come out from the world and have newly said, "I am for the Lord," do not feel surprise if what you have just done should, upon calm consideration, look almost like presumption. A sense of fear is natural when you see to what a service your dedication vows have bound you. At such a time Jesus will give you the comfort of the text, "Be of good cheer; thy faith hath made thee whole." May you have grace to receive it by faith and to drink in all its consolation.

This, however, is not quite all the reason for the woman's needing encouragement at the moment the Lord bestowed it. This woman, no doubt, *had a very deep reverence for the Lord Jesus Christ.* She had such an esteem for him that even his garments were thought by her to be saturated with healing energy; and now, when she found herself immediately in his presence, she trembled and was afraid. She had come behind him, no doubt, to a great extent out of modesty and humility as well as out of timidity; and now she finds herself face to face with the glorious Lord, and he is asking her questions, and in full view of all the people she has to avow her faith in him. I hardly think that she was afraid of the people, but I do think that her faith was so reverential that she felt an awe at being found immediately in the presence of the Lord. Beloved friend, you have been singing lately, "Happy day, when Jesus washed my sins away"; and you have joined in meetings where all have been filled with a sacred delight because they have met with Jesus; and I should not wonder if, when you have been at home afterwards alone, and you have thought the matter over, it has seemed too gracious a thing to be really true that the Lord of glory had lovingly communed with you. As your thoughts of him have risen in reverential love, you have said, "Is it possible? Is it possible? Am I not dreaming? Has the Son of God looked on me with love? Can it be true that he who wears the majesty of heaven has set his heart upon me and has come to tabernacle in my breast? This is a miracle of miracles! Is it indeed a fact?" You have felt pressed down by the weight of the divine goodness. I remember well not only the joy I had when I found the Savior, but the horror of great darkness which fell upon me within a very short time after I had rejoiced with joy unspeakable. It was on this account: I knew that I had found the Lord; I was fully assured of my salvation and full of joy as to my possession of his love; but then I asked, "Is it not too good to be true? Is salvation altogether of free grace? Is there an everlasting love of God, and is it fixed on me? Am I indeed an heir of God, joint-heir with Jesus Christ?" The brightness of the glory blinded my weak eyes: by floods of amazing love I was carried off my feet. Are you in such a condition? Then it is time for the Savior's gentle words to sound in your heart—"Be of good comfort: thy faith hath made thee whole." When a reverent sense of the Lord's amazing condescension causes us to swoon at heart he will stay us with apples and comfort us with flagons. This is a sweet melancholy which infinite love can soon relieve.

Perhaps the greatest reason for the trembling of the woman in the narrative, lay in *a sense of her faulty coming*. When she looked back at the way in which she had approached the Lord, she saw a mass of faults in it, as we may well do in ours. When she had been made whole her faith would say to her, "The blessed Lord did not deserve that you should come behind him and touch his garment in that *unbelieving* fashion. See what a Savior he is! What love, what tenderness shines in his face! Why did not you come to him openly? You crouched in the rear, why did you not look him full in the face and crave his mercy? He would have received you freely, why did you suspect his grace? You may have wounded him by doubting his willingness to bless you. You should not have indulged such unbelief." After a seeker has found the Lord and has experienced salvation, he is sometimes tempted to question whether he is really a believer in Jesus. He reasons within himself thus: "My faith is so mixed with unbelief that I am ashamed of it. Why did I come to Jesus in such a way as I did come? It was well to come, but oh that I had come to Jesus before! O that I had come in a more childlike spirit, and that I had done him the justice to have a greater confidence in him!" Does my reader know this experience? If so, to him and to all others who are thus exercised, the comfort of our text is addressed.

Very likely conscience would charge the trembling woman with a dishonest *stealth* in her way of getting her cure. "You felt at the time that you had no right to the blessing, but you snatched at it, and did not ask leave. You thought that you would be healed and then run away, and none would be any the wiser;

thus you robbed the Lord of his glory. Can a blessing rest on such a way of acting?" Conscience made her tremble, and therefore the Savior as good as said, Daughter, do not suspect your faith, for it has made you whole, and therefore it is good faith. However it acted, it has brought you healing, therefore do not distress yourself about its imperfections, but go in peace. He pointed her for comfort to the fact that, however faulty might be the way of her coming, it had healed her, and therefore she might well be content. Is there not a word of cheer in this for us also? If we have been renewed in heart and life the faith by which this change was wrought cannot but be good.

Perhaps, too, she might have felt that it was sadly *too bold* of her, a woman unclean according to the law, to push among the throng, and dare to touch the Lord himself. Many and many a time my heart has whispered to itself, "How could you be so bold as to trust Christ?" The devil has called it presumption, and my trembling heart has feared it might be so. One thing I know, I am certain that I am healed, even as the woman knew that the cure was wrought in her. This I do know, that I am not what I once was, but I am made a new creature through faith in Christ Jesus: yet the question will propose itself, "How can it be that you dared to dash in and seize on mercy, being such a sinner, and so utterly unworthy?" For my own part, I confess that I acted toward the Lord Jesus somewhat like a poor starving dog who saw meat in the butcher's shop and could not restrain himself from laying hold thereon, and running away with it.

Many a butcher would chase the wretched creature and take the meat from him, but our Savior is of a nobler temper. If our Lord Jesus sees us grasp his mercy he will never take it away from us. He says, "Him that cometh to me I will in no wise cast out." Oh, you who are quite unfit to come to Christ, and altogether unworthy of his favor, you are the very people who may come and welcome. Oh, you who say that you have no warrant to come to Jesus, he would have you come without warrant but his word, which saith, "Whosoever will let him come." Let your want of inward warrant be your warrant: you are needy and sinful; be this your passport. Come along with you! Make bold to grasp the covenanted mercy. It will not be theft, for Jesus has already given over himself and all that he has to all who are willing to have him. Have courage to take freely what the Lord freely gives.

Yet it may be that after you have done so, and after you have felt the blessing, you will fall into a fainting fit and swoon with fear because you question your own right. Hearken to a word of comfort. Possession is nine points of the law, and it is all the points of the gospel. So long as you have Christ there is no need to ask how you got him. Yet the trembling conscience whispers, "You had no right to believe. You are not the man who should have ventured to rest in Jesus." Then you will need a cheering word, and then will you have it, even as our dear Master said, "Daughter, be of good comfort; thy faith hath made thee whole." Let what grace has done for you plead your justification for having believed in Jesus. If you are indeed changed and renewed, question not your faith, but believe yet more, and you shall see greater things than these.

Thus, then, I set forth the woman's need of comfort, and if he who reads these lines is in like case, let him look up, and be of good cheer, for other feet have trodden the way of fear before him.

II. May the Holy Spirit rest upon us while we next notice THE COMFORT WHICH JESUS GAVE HER. He said, "Be of good comfort, daughter; thy faith hath made thee whole." *There was comfort in the loving title.* To call her "daughter" was most kind and tender. I suppose that she must have been of much the same age as our Lord himself, and therefore he did not call her "daughter" because of her youth. When our Lord said "daughter," he expressed his tender consideration for her, which made him feel towards her as tenderly as a father to a child. "Sister" would have been the word, if he had only meant human relationship, but "daughter" meant careful affection. While Jesus is our brother, there is a sense in which he is our father also, and he exercises towards his poor, downcast children a father's pity and care. Such a title must have dispelled her fears. To be so near of kin to him who had wrought a matchless cure upon her was consolation enough.

Let our tried and cast-down friends rest with us concerning this matter: you have believed in Jesus and you have confessed his name, and you are made whole; go your way in peace. Henceforth you belong to Christ, and you are related to Christ as his daughter or son; do not, therefore, question your right, since the grace of adoption has confirmed it. If the Lord calls you his daughter, you did no wrong when you touched your father's garment. If he avows you as his child, be not so unwise as to question the divine declaration. Your rights and privileges henceforth are almost boundless. You may do much more than touch his garment's hem, you may lean on his breast. He gives you greater privileges than those which you have yet enjoyed, yea, favors beyond what you ask or even think. To those who believe on him he gives the privilege to become the sons of God, even to as many as believe on his name, so that all question about your right to do this or that may be ended, for he calls you his own beloved and says, "Be of good comfort."

The main point of consolation was that she was cured: Jesus said, "Thy faith hath made thee whole," which would bring her comfort in several ways; for, first, *it was a great consolation that her impurity was gone.* So, my brother, if you have believed in Jesus you are no longer regarded as unclean before the Lord. The blood of the Lord Jesus has removed your defilement. You are accepted in the Beloved: your faith, like the hyssop which David sang of, has purged you, and you are clean. Do not look upon yourself as being what you are not: but know yourself to be whiter than snow in Christ Jesus. In the removal of your guilt and the renewal of your nature, the source of your defilement is destroyed. Do not, therefore, hide your face and stand afar off from God, but come boldly to the throne of grace, since grace has made you meet to come. When, my anxious brother, you come before the Lord with the recollection of all your past transgressions, you may well be ashamed and confounded, and feel as if you could never open your mouth anymore; but know of a surety that your sins have ceased to be, they shall not be mentioned against you any more for ever: God, even the God of judgment, has blotted out the record.

Humble yourself for having been a transgressor, but let a sense of perfect forgiveness embolden you in coming to your Savior. Whatever you were, God views you not as you were in yourself, but as what you are in Christ Jesus. When you come to his table, and feast among his family, do not hesitate to feel at home, although it cannot be denied that you once stood at the swine-trough, and hungered after husks. Say within your believing heart, "Whatever I was, my Father has kissed me, and put a ring on my hand, and shoes on my feet, therefore I will eat and drink as he bids me, and I will not mar the music and the merriment by unbelieving lamentations. My Father rejoiced over me because he had received me safe and sound, and shall I not be glad at being thus received?" God be thanked that, though ye were the servants of sin, ye have obeyed from the heart that form of doctrine which was delivered unto you, and you are brought into glorious liberty. Though you were once unclean, polluted and polluting, it may be said of you, "But ye are washed, but ye are sanctified." Perhaps your old name will stick to you as it did to Rahab the harlot, and to Simon the leper; but do not feel degraded, since the Lord has turned away your reproach. Hear Jesus Christ say to you, "Daughter, thy faith hath made thee whole."

Remember that, and rejoice in his presence. You have a right to be among his people, for "your faith has made you whole," and this is the mark which all his people wear. You are a sinner, it is true; but you are a sinner saved from wrath through infinite love. You are no longer a miserable sinner, and why should you call yourself so? You are a happy, blessed, forgiven child, whom the Lord has taken from the dunghill, to set among his princely children. Rejoice, therefore, because your faith has made you whole. Is not this a theme for boundless gratitude? Come boldly into the church; come boldly to the throne of grace; for you are so cleansed by the blood of atonement that you may come unquestioned into the holy of holies. Has not Jesus said, "He that is washed is clean every whit"?

The woman was comforted by being made to see in her cure that Jesus was not angry with her. Our Lord in effect said to the saved woman, "Have you been afraid that you did wrong in touching me? Are you fearful lest I should be grieved because you did not believe enough in me to come and face me, but must needs steal behind me? Do you suspect that I shall blame you because of the littleness of your faith? Now"—he puts it so sweetly—"do not think so, but be of good comfort, for thy faith hath made thee whole." Though her faith dared only to touch his garment, it was evidently acceptable faith, for because of it the Lord had made her whole. It is clear that the Lord has not rejected our faith when he owns and honors it. He cannot be vexed at a confidence which he has evidently rewarded.

Beloved reader, has your faith been such that it has made you abhor sin? Has it been such that the things you once loved you now hate, and the things you once hated you now love? Has your faith made a change in you? Are you a new man in Christ Jesus? Have you been made whole, morally and spiritually? Then, be sure that no wrong faith could have wrought this good work in you: a faith that produces wholeness or holiness of life cannot have been a mistake. Whether in your coming to Jesus you came behind him or before him, whether you touched his hand or touched his hem, whether you did it secretly or did it publicly, all these enquiries are interesting, but not essential; for if a change of heart has been wrought in you and you are saved, then the Lord Jesus must be pleased with you. He could not have wrought a great work in you and yet be angry with you; and therefore you need not be troubled as to the way in which you came to him. "Be of good comfort; thy faith hath made thee whole," is a most sweet and effectual way of lulling fears to rest! Possibly the poor woman may have been haunted by the fear that she would suffer a relapse; but our Lord consoles her by *the assurance that her faith had effectually made her whole*. She had not obtained a little time of deliverance from the evil, so that it would recur again, but she was made *whole*. The Lord gives her a medical certificate; he sends her forth with a clean bill of health.

Oh, how sweet it is when Jesus Christ gives a full assurance to any one of us of complete salvation, so that we are delivered from all fear of the malady's return, and can walk abroad free from fear. I know that some Christians think that, after Christ has saved us and given us new hearts, the old hearts may come back, and though his grace is in us a well of water which he promises shall spring up to everlasting life, yet they think that it may dry up to the last drop. Beloved, I do not thus read the word, but the very opposite is clear to me in sacred writ. The work of God in the soul is a lasting and an everlasting work; and if you are once healed by Christ, he has wrought in you an effectual cure, which will hold good throughout time and eternity. I know that whatsoever God doeth it shall be forever. He who has made you whole will keep you whole, for his gifts and calling are without repentance.

The comfort to the woman in the narrative was meant, as we have seen, to meet the trial occasioned by her open confession. She had been driven to reveal her secret, and this to a large extent caused her trembling. She would rather have hidden in the press, but she was called to the front and made to confess Jesus before all. The Savior, in effect, says, "You need not be ashamed to tell your story, for *it ends well*, since you are made whole; you need not be ashamed to let everybody know that your faith has healed you; what does it matter what your sickness was, if you are now recovered from it?" It will be no disgrace to us to confess our guilt if at the same moment we are assured of full forgiveness. It is annoying to hear persons talk flippantly of their sins before conversion as though they were proud of them; they seem to glory in them as a Greenwich pensioner might boast of his battles and his broken bones: such things are to be mentioned with blushes and tears. Say as little as you can about those things whereof you are now ashamed, and let what you do say be spoken in lowliest penitence.

Still, there are times when you are bound to tell out your case to the praise of the glory of the grace which so abounded when your sin abounded, and then you need not be afraid to tell your story, for grace has made it end so well. Let the world know that though foully defiled, you came into contact with the Savior by simply, humbly believing in him, and that by this simple means you are saved. Once more, if any reader is conscious that faith has saved him, he may take to himself the good cheer of the text and use it wherever he goes, *for nothing can happen to him so bad as that which has been removed.* "Thy faith has saved thee" is an antidote for many ills. "I am very poor," says one; so was this woman, for she had spent all that she had upon physicians: but Jesus said, "Thy faith hath saved thee." "I am very sick," cries a friend, "I feel low and ill:" but "thy faith hath *saved* thee." Is not this joy enough? Oh, what a blessing it is to be saved! That you are saved is enough to set all your nature on a blaze with joy. I am sure that the healed woman felt rich, though she had not two pence to chink together in her pocket; she was made whole by faith, and that was wealth enough for her. To be one of the Lord's saved ones is joy enough to upbear the heart under every affliction.

Do you not see that if your faith has changed your character and delivered you from the desperate plague of sin, there remains no longer any impossibility or even difficulty in the way of duty? You have been half afraid to try to teach the children in the Sunday school, but surely since your faith has made you whole you can teach a few little children! You have been afraid to address a score of people in a village chapel, but you need not be afraid to try if God has called you, for the faith which has made you whole can give you a word in season. What is there that faith cannot do? Why, if my faith has had the power to drop the burden of my sin into the sepulcher of my Lord, what is there that it cannot accomplish? If by that faith my soul has risen from among the dead, and taken her seat at the right hand of the Father in the heavenly places, what shall stand in its way? If we have to force a passage through a throng of devils we need not hesitate; and though all the world combined and stood against us, we need not fear. Our faith has made us whole: who can undo the miracle?

A faith which by divine grace brings us out of hell, and secures us for heaven, what is there that it cannot accomplish? It laughs at impossibilities, and marches from strength to strength in majestic serenity. Holy confidence shall win victory upon victory, till at last it shall cry, "I have finished my course; I have kept the faith; henceforth there is laid up me for a crown of life, that fadeth not away." Beloved reader, I cannot imagine a sweeter consolation than this: "Thy faith hath saved thee: go in peace:" endeavor to suck the honey out of it.

III. We will close this meditation by considering THE FAITH WHICH OUR LORD COMMENDED. It made her whole: that is its best certificate of excellence. There is much to note in reference to that faith, but a few brief hints may suffice. Her faith is to be commended because *it outlived a long season of discouragement.* She had been twelve years afflicted—think of that! Patience had had its perfect work in her. But she believed in Christ for a cure, and the cure came. So will it be with everyone who will believe in Jesus. If there could be a soul found which had been living in sin twelve hundred years, if it had faith in Jesus, he would make it whole. After half a century of impenitence he that believeth in Christ Jesus is saved at once. Eighty years of sin vanish in a moment when a man trusts in the great atonement. Come, dear unconverted reader, and cast yourself at Christ's feet at this quiet hour, for Jesus will not cast you out.

The faith which healed this poor woman had *survived many failures;* she had been deceived by all sorts of quacks and medicine-men, and yet she had not lost the capacity for faith. It is said that she had "suffered many things of many physicians," and I can well believe it, for if you read the prescriptions of the old doctors you will quite agree that poor humanity has suffered many things from the faculty. The way in which the ancient doctors went to work to cure their patients much resembled that which a man would follow who was eager to kill them. Dr. Sangrado by his bleeding and drenching has sent many into a premature grave; and, in Christ's time, if you wanted to be well, the first rule was to avoid all physicians. I will tell you the names of a few spiritual doctors to whom I beseech you not to go; for if you do, you will suffer a great deal from them, but get no good. There is one whose name is Dr. Self-Confidence, who is in partnership with a relative called Dr. Self-Righteousness. Dr. Legality, and his son Mr. Civility, are another popular pair of cheats. You will find them at home, whenever you call, and they will give you bitter doses or silver-coated pills as they see fit, but never a whit the better will you be. There is a doctor about just now, who was educated by the Jesuits, and practices the Romeopathic system—wafers and wine-and-water are his specific; to this school belong Mr. Surgeon Ceremonies, and Doctor Sacraments. None of these can heal a sick soul: have done with them, and apply to the beloved Physician, even the Lord Jesus. Some of us went round to most of these pretenders and gave them a long trial; and though we were disappointed in them all, yet we still were enabled to believe in Jesus Christ.

Dear friend, do the same. Though you have been disappointed everywhere else, yet go and knock at Jesus' door; and that faith of yours, which leaps over discouragement, will make you whole. Her faith *believed in simple touching:* she used no ceremonies, she only believed. It was a faith which believed that she would be healed *without payment.* She took the cure gratis; she offered no fee. That is gospel faith which takes Christ's forgiveness without money and without price, just as he presents it in the gospel. Hers was a great faith, for she believed that Christ could heal her *when he was occupied with healing another.* He was hastening to the house of Jairus to work a miracle there, and yet she believed that he could heal her on the way. Can you, dear reader, believe in this fashion? Do you know of a surety that however Jesus may be now occupied, he can without difficulty at this moment pardon and save you? If you have reached so great a confidence, then give the saving touch and trust him once for all.

The poor sick soul had a faith which assured her that *Christ could bless her when his back was turned.* Can my reader reach this point? Some of God's own children can hardly trust him when they see the light of his countenance, but this woman could trust him when his back was turned towards her. I would to God that we had each such confidence in Jesus that we would not doubt, under any circumstances, his power and willingness to save all who trust him. He must save those who rely upon him. It is a necessity of his nature that those who touch him should receive healing from him.

Trusting in Jesus is a man's best evidence that he is saved, for it is written, "He that believeth in him is not condemned." Faith has made its possessor whole, whoever he may be, and if the reader is resting alone in Jesus and his finished work the life of the holy has begun in him, and he may therefore: BE OF GOOD CHEER.

4

Good Cheer From Christ's Real Presence

"And straightway he constrained his disciples to get into the ship, and to go to the other side before unto Bethsaida, while he sent away the people. And when he had sent them away, he departed into a mountain to pray. And when even was come, the ship was in the midst of the sea, and he alone on the land. And he saw them toiling in rowing; for the wind was contrary unto them: and about the fourth watch of the night he cometh unto them, walking upon the sea, and would have passed by them. But when they saw him walking upon the sea, they supposed it had been a spirit, and cried out: For they all saw him, and were troubled. And immediately he talked with them, and saith unto them, Be of good cheer: it is I; be not afraid. And he went up unto them into the ship; and the wind ceased: and they were sore amazed in themselves beyond measure, and wondered. For they considered not the miracle of the loaves: for their heart was hardened" (Mark 6:45–52).

We have here a word of comfort given to a ship-load of believers *who were where their Lord had sent them.* They had been unwilling to put out to sea, though it was probably calm enough at the time, but they did not wish to leave the Lord Jesus. He constrained them to go, and thus their sailing was not merely under his sanction, but by his express command. They were in their right place, and yet they met with a terrible storm. The little inland sea upon which they sailed lies in a deep hollow, and from the shore there pours a sudden downdraft of tremendous wind for which it is not possible to be prepared. By one of these whirlwinds the whole sea was stirred up to boiling, as only those little lakes can be. So, though they were where Jesus bade them go, they were in desperate peril. Reader, you must not think that you are in a wrong position because you are in trouble. Do not consider that adverse circumstances are a proof that you have missed your road; for they may even be an evidence that you are in the good old way, since the path of believers is seldom without trial. You did well to embark and to leave the shore; but remember, though your Lord has insured the vessel, and guaranteed that you shall reach your haven, he has not promised that you shall sail over a sea of glass; on the contrary, he has told you that "in the world you shall have tribulation," and you may all the more confidently believe in him because you find his warning to be true.

Their Lord had bidden his disciples make for the other side, and therefore they did their best, and continued rowing all night, but making no progress whatever because the wind was dead against them. It was with difficulty that they could keep what little way they had made, and not be blown back again to the starting place. Probably you have heard it said that, if a Christian man does not go forward, he goes backward: that is not altogether true, for there are times of spiritual trial, when, if a man does not go backward, he is really going forward. "Stand fast" is a precept which, when well kept, may involve as much virtue as "press forward." A master of a steam-vessel will put on all steam, and drive right into the teeth of a hurricane, and remain perfectly satisfied if the good ship can only keep from being driven on shore. The apostolic crew rowed, and rowed, and rowed, and it was no fault of theirs that they made no progress, "for the wind was contrary." The Christian man may make little or no headway, and yet it may be no fault of his, for the wind is contrary. Our good Lord will take the will for the deed, and reckon our progress, not by our apparent advance, but by the hearty intent with which we tug the oars.

Often when a believer groans in prayer, and cannot pray, he has offered the best prayer; and when he tries to win men's hearts and does not win them, his zeal is as acceptable as if it convinced a nation: and when he would do good and finds evil present with him, there is good in the desire. If he threw up the oars and drifted with the wind, that would be another thing; but if our Lord sees him toiling and rowing, albeit no progress is made, he has never a word to say against his servant, but he will bid him "be of good cheer."

It does not appear from the narrative that the disciples had any fear about the storm, except such as might naturally arise even in the minds of fishermen when they were dreadfully tossed upon the sea. They probably said to one another: "Did not our Master constrain us to put forth? Though we meet with this storm, we are not to be blamed." Certain believers who have lately known the Lord have been great losers in temporal things by becoming Christians. What then? Let them not be terrified by this fact; even Christ's ship is tossed with tempest. Let them row on against the wind, and if the storm increases in fury let them not lose heart. One who knew the seas right well exclaimed, "Though he slay me, yet will I trust in him"; and in so doing he glorified God, and ere long found himself in a great calm. Does Jesus bid us make for the shore? Then let us row on, even if we cannot make headway, for Jesus knows all about it, and orders all things well.

Why, then, did our Savior, when he came to this ship-load of Apostles who had been toiling and rowing, say to them, "Be of good cheer"? They were bold, brave men, and were not at all afraid of the sea. What, then, did they fear? He would not have so spoken unless they had been afraid of something, and on looking at the text we see to our astonishment that they were *afraid of Jesus Himself*. They were not afraid of winds and storms and waves and tempests, but they were afraid of their best friend. That is the point which he aimed at by saying, "Be of good cheer: *it is I*; be not afraid."

We will first think over *the cause of their fear*; then, secondly, we will meditate upon *the method by which Jesus cheered them*; and thirdly, we will reflect upon *the times when we shall need just such a good word as this*.

I. First, then, dear reader, consider with me THE CAUSE OF THEIR FEAR. If we had not sailed over the same lake—I mean, if we had not suffered the same experience—it might surprise us that they were afraid of their Lord. He was appearing for them, and coming to their rescue. He was about to still the tempest for them, but they were afraid *of him*—of him whom they loved and trusted. So holden were their eyes, so hardened were their hearts, that they were afraid of their Lord—afraid of him when he was giving them the best reasons for trusting him. Before their eyes he was displaying himself as Lord over all, Master of wind and wave, and yet they were afraid of him. The greatness of his power would have comforted them had they understood the truth, but they did not consider the miracle of the loaves, and therefore they were in a state of perplexity, and were sore afraid.

Jesus was acting meanwhile in great gentleness to them: he was displaying his power, but it was not in a dazzling and overwhelming manner. Admire the sacred gentleness which made him move as though he would have passed by them. If he had suddenly appeared in brilliant light in the middle of the ship he might well have astounded them and driven them to fright. If in a moment he had shone forth just at the stern, or alighted from the heavens upon the deck they would have been petrified with alarm, but he began by showing himself away there on the crest of the billow, and one cried to his fellow, "See you that strange light yonder?" They watch, and Jesus comes nearer! They can discern a figure; they can see a man step from wave to wave with majestic tread. In tenderness he will not flash upon them all at once. As when the morning breaketh by slow increase of light, so Jesus came to his timid followers. Even then he moved as though he would pass by, that they might not be alarmed by his appearing to bear down upon them as an adversary. Even thus he manifests himself to us in the riches of his grace in all wisdom and prudence. The fears of the trembling crew were sufficiently aroused by even seeing him at a distance; they were so afraid that they cried out thinking that they saw a ghost. What would they have done had he not, in gentleness to their weakness, manifested himself gradually to them, and set himself in a side light?

Take what way the Master might, his disciples were still afraid, and we are not much wiser nor much more courageous than they. The manifestation of the Christ of God in all his glory to us will have to be by degrees as long as we are in this body, and, mayhap, even in heaven it may not be at the very first that we shall be able to endure the fullness of its joy: even there he may have to lead us to fountains of water which at the first we did not discover, and guide us into more and more of that superlative knowledge which will utterly eclipse all acquaintance that we have of him now, as the sunlight puts out the stars.

To return to our subject. The disciples were afraid of Jesus when he was revealing his power to help them; afraid of him when he was acting in the gentlest possible manner, and treating them as a nurse doth her child. Ah me, that we should be afraid of Jesus!

The Lord, after all, was doing nothing more than they knew he could do. Twenty-four hours had not passed since they had seen him perform a work of creation; for he had taken bread and fish and multiplied them so as to make a festival for five thousand, and leave far more when all had eaten, than had been in store when first the loaves and fish had been counted. After this they ought not to have been surprised that he should traverse the sea. To walk the waters is to suspend a law, but to make loaves and fishes is to exercise the supreme power of creation, which must forever remain with God himself: knowing this, they ought not to have been astonished—not so soon, at any rate. The memory of that festival ought not to have vanished quite so quickly from the most forgetful minds. Yet when they saw him only doing what they knew he could do, only doing something not a jot more difficult than he was accustomed to do, they cried out for fear. Was it not because *they dreaded contact with the spiritual, the mysterious, and the supernatural*? Although we are talking now about them, and perhaps half saying in our minds, "If we had been there we should not have been afraid of Jesus, and have cried out"; we do not know what we say; it takes very little of the supernatural to make one's flesh creep, let the man be who he may.

When Belshazzar saw the handwriting upon the wall he trembled most because of the mystery involved in a moving hand with which no visible body was connected. The unseen is the birthplace of fear. Imagination exaggerates, and conscience whispers that some great ill will befall us. We are nearing the confines of the mysterious world where God and spirits dwell, and hence we tremble. Yet, beloved, the spirit-world is the last thing which Christians should tremble at, for there can be nothing in the supernatural world which we have cause to dread. If there be such a thing as a ghost walking the earth, I, for one, should like to meet it, either at dead of night or noon of day.

I have not the least particle of faith in rambling spirits. Those who are in heaven will not care to be wandering in these foggy regions; and those in hell cannot leave their dread abode. Whence, then, shall they come? Are they devils? Even so, and what then? A devil is no new personage; we have fought with devils full often, and are prepared to resist them again and make them fly. The Lord will tread Satan, who is the master of evil spirits, under our feet shortly; why, then, should we be afraid of his underlings? Nothing supernatural should cause any Christian man the slightest alarm. We are expressly forbidden to fear the fear of the heathen, and that is one of their greatest horrors—their dread of witchcraft and necromancy, and other supposed manifestations of evil spirits. We who believe in Jesus are to be ashamed of such superstitions, lest a lie should have dominion over us.

If saintly spirits and holy angels can appear among men, what then? It would be a joy and a privilege to meet them. We are come to an innumerable company of angels; they bear us up in their hands lest we dash our feet against a stone.

Brethren, I am more afraid of the natural than of the supernatural, and far more fearful of the carnal than of the spiritual. Yet the disciples were afraid of Jesus because they were fearful of the supernatural, and when a person falls under that dread he will be afraid of anything. We have known such persons to be frightened by cattle, alarmed by a cat, and distressed at the croak of a raven. Some foolish ones have even died with fear at the click of an insect in an old post, for they call it a "death watch." Let us shake off all such childish folly, for if we once fall into it we may even go the length of these Apostles and be afraid of our Master himself.

II. Let us consider, secondly, THE METHOD BY WHICH OUR MASTER CHEERED HIS FOLLOWERS WHEN THEY WERE AFRAID OF THE SUPERNATURAL.

First of all he assured them that he was not a disembodied spirit. He said, "It is I," and that "I" was a man who did eat and drink with them, a man of flesh and blood, whom they had seen and heard and touched. They were comforted when they knew that it was really no disembodied spirit, but a man in flesh and blood.

I beg the reader always to remember concerning our Lord Jesus Christ, that he is not to be regarded as an unclothed spirit, for he wears a body like our own. It would greatly detract from our comfort if we doubted the real personality of Christ, and the truth of his resurrection. Our Lord has taken into heaven our human nature in its entirety, body as well as soul, and he ever liveth, not as a spirit, but as a man like ourselves, all sin excepted, and he lives there as the pledge that we shall be there too in the completeness of our manhood, when the trumpet of the resurrection sounds. As a real man Jesus reigns above; he is no phantom, no ghost, no spirit, but a risen man, touched with the feeling of our infirmities, who pities us and loves us, and feels for us; and in that capacity he speaks to us out of the glory of heaven, and he saith, "It is I; be not afraid."

Another thought lies on the surface of the passage: *He comforted them by the assurance that it was really himself.* They were not looking upon a fiction, they were looking upon Christ himself.

Friend, be sure of the reality of the Christ you trust in. It is very easy to use the name of Jesus, but not quite so easy to know his person; it is common to talk about what he did, and not to feel that he lives just as truly as we do, and that he is a person to be loved and to be trusted in just as much as our own brother, or father, or friend. We want a real, living, personal Christ! A phantom Christ will not cheer us in a storm; it is rather the cause of fright than hope: but a real Christ is a real consolation in a real tempest. May every one of my readers truly know a personal Savior to whom they can speak with as much certainty as if they could touch his hand.

The Christ of two millennia ago wrought out our salvation, but the Christ of today must apply it, or we are lost. Seeing he ever liveth, he is able to save to the uttermost them that come unto God by him. Believe in his true manhood, and never allow your idea of him to become thin and unsubstantial. Those are substantial Christians to whom Christ is substantial.

But the pith of the comfort lay in this, he said "It is I; be not afraid," which being interpreted means, *it is Jesus*, be not afraid. When our Lord met Paul on the road to Damascus, he said to him, "I am Jesus." But when he spoke to those who knew his voice and were familiar with him he did not quote his name, but said, "It is I." They were sheep that had been long enough with the shepherd to know his voice, and they had only to hear him speak, and without a name being mentioned they perceived that it was the Lord. To this conclusion they should have come at first. But as they blundered and said, "It is a spirit," the loving Master corrected them by saying, "It is I,—it is Jesus." It is not possible for any to convey to you what richness of consolation lies in the thought that Jesus is Jesus, which is, being interpreted, a Savior. That one character and office is cheering, but the same is true of all the names he wears. All the glorious titles and the blessed emblems under which he is set forth are rich in good cheer.

It is Jesus who walks the water of your trouble and comes to you—Jesus the Son of God. The Alpha and Omega, the Head over all things to his church, the All in All of all his people.

When Jesus wished to encourage John in the first chapter of Revelations, the comfort he gave to him was, "I am the first and the last." The comfort of the Lord's people lies in the person and character of Jesus. Here is their solace—"*IT IS I*." But what a big "I" it is. Compound in one all that is conceivable of goodness, and mercy, and grace, and faithfulness, and love; add perfect humanity, and infinite Godhead, and all the sovereign rights, powers, and possessions of the Highest, and these are all contained in the one little letter "I," when Jesus says, "It is I, be not afraid."

You have not reached the bottom of it yet. The Greek is ἐγώ εἰμί, "I am." Literally rendered, the word which Jesus said was not "It is I," but "I am." When he would cheer his people the Lord bade Moses comfort Israel by saying, "I AM hath sent me unto you." The self-existence of their God was to be the joy of the tribes. When Jesus said to those who came to take him in the garden, " I am," they fell backward, such was the power of that word; but when he said to these his cowering disciples, "I am," they were drawn towards him, and yet they lost not the awe which must ever go with that incommunicable name "I AM." Believing reader, Jesus saith to you "I am." Is your wife dead? Is the child to be buried? Have possessions failed? Is health departing? Are joys declining? Alas, it is a dying, fleeting world, but there is One who is always the same, for Jesus says to you, "I am, and because I live you shall live also." Be comforted; whatever else is gone, wherever else the arrows of death may fly, your Jesus still lives. "I am": blessed word of rich comfort to be heard amid the darkness of the night by weary mariners whose spirits had been sinking within them.

The glory of it all was brought out by the fact that he came up into the ship, and as he stood amid them the stillness all around proved that the "I am" was there. Had he not moved upon the face of the deep, as once the Spirit moved there, and did there not come order out of the tempest's chaos even as at the beginning? Where the great "I AM" is present the winds and the seas perceive their ruler and obey.

Then the men knew that Jesus was not only "I AM," but "Immanuel," God with us. "I AM" had come to the rescue, and was in the ship with them. Here, dear reader, is *your* comfort and mine. We will not fear the supernatural, or the unseen, for we see Jesus, and in him we see the Father, and are of good cheer.

III. Our third point for consideration is this: THERE ARE TIMES WHEN WE SHALL BE LIKELY TO NEED SUCH COMFORT. Jesus spoke it to believers, tossed with tempest, and we need it *when we are depressed by the surroundings of these evil times.* In seasons of depressed trade, great sickness, terrible wars, and public disasters, it is balm to the spirit to know that Jesus is still the same. Sin may abound yet more, the light of the gospel may burn low, and the prince of darkness may widely sway his destroying scepter; but, nevertheless, this standeth sure, that Jesus is the "I AM." At certain periods diabolical influence seems paramount; the reins of nations appear to be taken out of the hand of the great

Governor: and yet it is not so. Look through the darkness, and you shall see your Lord amid the hurricane, walking the waters of politics, ruling national convulsions, governing, over-ruling, arranging all, making even the wrath of man to praise him, and restraining it according to his wisdom. Above the howling of the blast I hear his voice announcing, "It is I." When men's hearts sink for fear, and the rowers feel their oars ready to snap by the strain of useless toil, I hear that word which is the soul of music, "It is I; be not afraid—I am ruling all things. I am coming to the rescue of the barque, my church: she shall yet float on smooth waters and reach her desired haven."

Another time of need will surely be *when we reach the swellings of Jordan*. We shall near the spirit world, the soul will begin to strip off her material garment to enter on a new form of life. How shall we feel as we enter the unknown world? Shall we cry out as we salute the first who meets us, "It is a spirit!" It may be so—but then a sweet voice will destroy death's terror, and end all our alarms, and this shall be its utterance—"It is I; be not afraid." This new world is not new to Jesus; our pains and dying throes are not unknown to him! The disembodied state, wherein the spirit sojourns for a while unclothed, he knows it all, for he died and entered into the spirit land, and can sympathize with us in every step of the way. In what sweet company shall we pass through the valley of death shade! Surely its gloom will turn to brightness, as when a cavern wrapped in blackness is lit up with a hundred torches, and myriads of gems sparkle from roof and walls. Passing through the sepulcher, its damp darkness shall flash and glow with unexpected joys and marvelous revelations of the Ever-Blessed, because Jesus will be with us, and "the Lamb is the light." If in that dread hour we shall feel the least trembling at our Lord as the Judge of all the earth, that dread shall vanish as he cries, "It is I."

This comfort may serve us *when we suffer great tribulation*. May my friend, the reader, be spared this trial; but should it come he will all the better understand me. They that "do business on great waters" know that our troubles are at times so pressing that we lose our heads, and are not able to cope with our trials. Forebodings fill the air, and our sinking spirits chill the very marrow of our life. We become like men distraught; or as David put it, we reel to and fro and stagger like a drunken man, and are at our wits' end. Then, ah then, the voices of our comrades in the ship are of little value, and even the echoes of former words from the Lord are of small account; nothing will serve but the present and sure consolations of the Lord Jesus. We must hear him say, "It is I," or we shall faint outright. Then is the soul braced to breast the next billow, and while she cries, "All thy waves and thy billows have gone over me," she is still able to add, "Yet the Lord will command his loving-kindness in the daytime, and in the night his song shall be with me." When Jesus is with a man troubles have lost their power to trouble him.

We shall need this same word of comfort *whenever the Lord graciously reveals himself to us*. His glory is such that we are not able to bear much of it. Its very sweetness overpowers the heart. Saints have had to ask for a staying of the intense delight which seemed to overbear their natural faculties. Those who have enjoyed those transporting manifestations can quite understand why John has written, "When I saw him I fell at his feet as dead." An awful delight—or shall I say a delightful awe?—throws the man upon his face. John had lain in Jesus' bosom, and yet when he had a clear manifestation of his glorified Savior he could not bear it till his tender Friend laid his hand upon him and said, "Fear not." So will it be with each of us when we are favored with the visits of the Well-beloved, we shall greatly need that he should say to us, "It is I, your brother, your friend, your Savior, your husband; be not afraid. Great as I am, tremble not in my presence, for I am Jesus the Lover of your soul."

Once more, there is a day coming *when the Son of man will be revealed in the clouds of heaven*. We know not when it will be, but we are solemnly warned that when men look not for him he will suddenly appear. He will come as a thief in the night to the mass of men; but as for believers, they are not in darkness that that day should come upon them as a thief: to them he comes as a long expected friend. When he cometh there will be seen tokens, signs in the heavens above and in the earth beneath, which we shall recognize. We may then, perhaps, be distressed by these supernatural portents, and begin to tremble. What, then, will be our delight when we hear him say, "It is I; be not afraid"? Lift up your heads, ye saints, for the coming of the Lord draweth nigh, and to you it is not darkness, but day: to you it is not judgment and condemnation, but honor and reward. What bliss it will be to catch the first glimpse of our Lord on the throne! Men will wring their hands, and weep and wail because of him; but we shall know his voice and welcome his appearing. When the last trumpet rings out clear and loud, happy shall we be to hear that gladsome sound, "It is I; be not afraid." Rolling earth and crumbling mountains, darkened sun and blackened moon, flames of fire, and shocks of earthquake, gathering angels and chariots of God, none of these things shall amaze us while Jesus whispers to our soul, "I am," and yet again, "It is I; be not afraid."

5

Good Cheer from Christ's Victory Over the World

"These things have I spoken unto you, that in me ye might have peace. In the world ye shall have tribulation; but be of good cheer; I have overcome the world" (John 16:33).

The believer is in two places, and he lives two lives. In the text there are two places spoken of: "in me," and, "in the world."

The saint's noblest life is hid "with Christ in God": this is his new life, his spiritual life, his incorruptible life, his everlasting life. Rejoice, beloved reader, if you are in Christ, and enjoy the privilege which belongs to that condition: Jesus says, "In me ye shall have peace." Do not be satisfied without it; it is your right through your relationship to the Prince of Peace. Because you are in Christ your life of lives is always safe, and should be always restful. Your greatest interests are all secure, for they are guaranteed by the covenant of which Jesus is the surety. Your treasure, your eternal portion is laid up with him in heaven where neither rust nor robber can enter. Therefore be of good cheer. Be restful and happy, for you are in Christ, and he has said, "In me ye shall have peace."

You are sorrowfully conscious that you also live another life, for you dwell in the midst of evil men, or, as the text puts it, you are "in the world." I need not enlarge upon that fact; for probably, dear friend, every time you go out to business or to daily labor you find by the ungodly speeches of graceless men that you are in the world which lieth in the wicked one. Even while you dwell in the sweet seclusion of domestic life, though your family has been graciously visited, and your dear ones are all believers, yet even there matters occur which make you feel that you are "in the world,"—a world of sin and sorrow. You are not in heaven yet; do not dream that you are. It would be a pity for a sailor to expect the sea to be as stable as the land, for the sea will be the sea to the end; and the world will be the world to you as long as you are in it.

The Savior warns his people, "In the world ye shall have tribulation": that is to say, your condition will at times be as unpleasant as that of wheat under the flail; for the Latin word "tribulation" signifies threshing. Many blows of the flail are needed to separate your chaff from your wheat, and therefore while you are in this world you are on the threshing floor. The *Greek* word which Jesus used is not quite of the same import as our English-Latin word, but it means pressing grief and searching trial. You must at times experience trial while you are in the world, though not always to the same degree; for God gives some of his people much rest even while here below; but this does not arise out of the world, it is his own special gift. "In the world ye shall have tribulation" is as sure a fact as that in Christ you shall have peace.

Now, because of this tribulation and the sorrow which is likely to come of it, our Savior gives us the words of good cheer to which the reader is now directed. We have already four times considered the words, "Be of good cheer," and we shall continue the same method: first, showing *what sorrow the comfort is aimed at*; and, secondly, *what is the actual comfort here bestowed*.

WHAT IS THIS TRIBULATION IN THE WORLD AT WHICH THE SAVIOR'S WORDS OF COMFORT ARE AIMED? It includes *the afflictions which come upon us because we are men living among men*, and not yet at home among angels and glorified saints. We dwell among beings who are born to trouble as the sparks fly upward. Between us and other men there are many points of difference; but we share with them in the common infirmities, labors, sicknesses, bereavements, and necessities of our fallen race. We are outside of Eden's gate with the rest of Adam's family. We may be greatly beloved of God and yet be poor. God's love to Lazarus did not prevent his lying at the rich man's gate, nor hinder the dogs from licking his sores. Saints may be sick as well as other men: Job and David and Hezekiah felt sore diseases. Saints go into the hospital as well as sinners, for their bodies are liable to the same accidents and ailments. Such diseases as men bring upon themselves by vice the godly escape, and therefore as a rule God's people have a great advantage over the reckless and reprobate in point of health; but still in this respect the best of men are only men, and it will often be said, "Lord, he whom thou lovest is sick." Upon the bodies of the godly the elements have the same power as upon others; upon them the hot sirocco blows, or through their garments the cold penetrates; the sun scorches them in the fierceness of his summer heat, or chilling damps threaten the flame of life: in this respect one event happeneth unto all, though not without mysterious and blessed differences. No screen is set around the godly to protect them from physical suffering; they are not living in the land of Goshen so that light cheers their dwellings while the dense fog hangs over the rest of the land. Scant is the need to dwell upon this theme, for it is well known that many are the afflictions of the righteous, because they are in a world which for a while is made subject to vanity.

Nor may we forget that we endure a second set of tribulations *because we are Christian men*. Ishmael was not mocked, but Isaac was, for he was born after the promise. Esau's posterity never suffered bondage in Egypt, but Israel must be trained by hard service. Persecution is for the righteous, wicked men are in honor among their ungodly associates. Slander shoots her poisoned arrows, not at the vicious, but at the virtuous. Birds do not peck at sour fruit, but they wage war upon the sweet and ripe. Holy men must expect to be misrepresented, misinterpreted, and often wilfully maligned, while hypocrites have their reward in undeserved homage. Carry what load you choose upon your shoulders and no one will notice it, unless indeed they obey the good old rule and "respect the burden;" but if you take up Christ's cross and bravely bear it, few will respect the burden or praise the bearer. Graceless men will add weight to your load, for the offence of the cross has not ceased. The seed of the serpent has still enmity against the seed of the woman, and one and another will commence biting at the heel which treads the sacred way of Christ.

It is the nature of the wicked to hate the righteous, even as the wolf rages against the sheep. This world cannot be the friend of the friend of God, unless, indeed, Belial can have concord with Christ, and this we know is impossible. In one form or another, the Egyptian will oppress the Israelite till the day of the bringing out with a high hand and an outstretched arm. If today the enmity is restrained in its manifestation it is because the law of the land, by the good providence of God, does not now allow the rack, the stake, or the dungeon. Our Lord said to his first disciples, "In the world ye shall have tribulation," and he explained it to mean that men would put them out of the synagogues; yea, that the time would come when those that killed them would think that they did God service. Tribulation of that sort remains up to the measure in which it is not hindered by divine power; the spirit out of which it sprang cannot die till men are renewed. A man's foes are still they of his own household. "All that will live godly in Christ Jesus shall suffer persecution."

Nor is the opposition of the world confined to persecution, but it sometimes takes the far more dangerous form of flattery—pleasing baits are held out, and allurements are used to decoy the believer from his Lord. Let not my reader be unaware of this. Many have been grievously wounded by the world when it has met them with the kiss of Judas on its lip and a dagger in its right hand wherewith to slay the soul. Woe unto those who are ignorant of its devices. This is a sore trouble under the sun, that men are false: their words are softer than butter, but inwardly they are drawn swords. This has often surprised young Christians. They imagined that, since the godly were charmed at the sight of their early graces, all others would be equally pleased; they are stumbled when they find that their good is evil spoken of. Is my reader one of these raw recruits? Let him learn that to be a soldier of the cross means real war, and not a sham fight. He is in an enemy's country, and the time will yet come when as a veteran warrior he will be surprised if he lives a day without a conflict, or is able for an hour to sheathe his sword.

Certain tender hearts are not only surprised, but they are daunted and grieved, by the world's opposition. Gentle, loving spirits, who would not oppose anybody if they could help it, keenly feel the wanton assaults of those whom they would rather please than provoke. The sensitiveness of love renders the choicest characters the most susceptible of pain under cruel opposition, especially when it comes from beloved kinsfolk. To those who love God and man it is at times an agony to be compelled to appear as the cause of strife, even for Christ's sake. We would fain follow peace with all men, yet are we often forced to cry:

> My soul with him that hateth peace
>   Hath long a dweller been;
> I am for peace; but when I speak,
>   For battle they are keen.

> My soul distracted mourns and pines
>   To reach that peaceful shore,
> Where all the weary are at rest,
>   And troublers vex no more.

We are sent forth as sheep among wolves, and this jars upon our gentleness, which loves far better to lie down in the green pastures near the shepherd and in the midst of his flock.

We are most of all grieved to think that men should not love Christ. It makes us deeply sorrowful that they should not see the beauties of the Man of Sorrows. In our inmost hearts we are wounded when they wound our Wellbeloved. That they oppose *us* is little; but that they stumble at the great foundation stone, upon which they will surely be broken, is terrible to perceive. They sin against light and love; they sin against their own souls, and this is a tribulation which bruises every holy heart, and causes every loving spirit to bleed.

This calls for constant watchfulness, since our very love to men might become, unless salted by the grace of God, a cause of decay to our purity. Some spirits love fighting, and are never more happy than when they can denounce, resist, secede, and contend. These are members of the church militant in another than the best sense. When the grace of God enters their hearts, and consecrates their obstinacy into firmness, they make fine men in a way; but if we measure them by the scale of love, and that, I take it, is the standard of the sanctuary—for he is most like God who loves most, and he has come nearest to the image of Christ whose heart is fullest of tenderness—these rougher spirits turn out to be rather dwarfs than giants in the kingdom of God. We must have backbone, and must be prepared to contend earnestly for the faith; but yet, the more love we exhibit the better, and hence the more pain it will cost us to be continually at war with unloving spirits. This is a part of the tribulation which we must endure, and the more bravely we face it the more thoroughly shall we win the battles of peace and purity.

Is not this enough upon the darker side of the picture?

Dear friend, let us now consider WHAT THE COMFORT IS WHICH JESUS GRACIOUSLY OFFERS US. "Be of good cheer," he says, "I have overcome the world."

This is a glorious sentence, spoken by the greatest conqueror that ever lived, in whom all his people shall yet be "more than conquerors."

Here let us view our Lord in his blessed person, for there is much of good cheer in the contemplation. Remember, first, that *our blessed Lord was a man.* Believe all that this means, for many are apt to think that, because he was God as well as man, therefore he was not so fully a man. The tendency is to separate him from the race, and so from ourselves; but I pray the reader to reflect that Jesus was in some respects more a man than any one of us.

There are some points in which no one man is all that manhood is; but Jesus was the summary of all manhood. I might almost venture to say that he had about him the whole nature of mankind, as it respects the mental conformation of both man and woman, for he was as tender as woman, though as strong as man. Holy women, as much as godly men, find in Jesus all that is in their own souls. There is nothing effeminate in him, and yet all the loveliness which is feminine: read his life story and see. He was man in the broadest sense of the term, taking up into one the whole genus. Men are of certain ranks and grades, but Christ is without limit, save only that in him was no sin. Though a Jew, he bore no special national peculiarity, for Gentiles find in him their next of kin. You apply no descriptive word to the Son of man, except it be that you call him "the man of sorrows." He was a man who greatly suffered in body and in mind, and displayed his manhood by the bravery of his endurance: a man joying in man's joy, depressed in man's grief; a man who ran up the entire scale of humanity, from its deepest to its highest tone. Now, if a typical man has overcome the world, then man has done it, and man can be enabled to do it again. This inspires courage and banishes despair. It was the mighty power of the Holy Ghost dwelling in him by which Jesus overcame the world, and that same quiet power, if it dwell in us, will make us win the like victory by faith. The arch enemy has been conquered by man, and our hearts may be comforted by the conviction that, by God working in us, we, too, shall bruise Satan under our feet shortly.

It is cheering to remember, that wherein our Lord's was a special case, it is to our comfort; for he, as man, entered into the conflict under serious disadvantages, which we cannot labor under. He was weighted with a care unique and unexampled. Be our charge what it may, it cannot be comparable to his heavy burden as the Shepherd of souls. We think ourselves over weighted, and speak of life as though it were rendered too stern a conflict by the load of our cares and responsibilities; but what comparison is there between our load and that of Jesus? A pastor with a great flock is not without his hourly anxieties; but what are those to the cares of the Chief Shepherd? He watched over the great multitude which no man can number, who were committed to him of the Father, and for these he carried all their griefs: here was a burden such as you, dear reader, and your friend, the writer, cannot even imagine; and yet, without laying aside the weight, he fought the world and overcame it. Let his name be praised and let his victory be the comfort of all that labor and are heavy laden.

Recollect, next, that he was loaded with substitutionary sorrows which he bore for us. These are not ours. He came into the world to suffer griefs that were not his own. He had human guilt laid upon him to bear, and, because of that, he was bowed down till he was exceeding sorrowful even unto death. Some seem to think we are to imitate Christ in being men of sorrows as he was. No, no, the argument is the other way. Because Jesus took our sorrows, we may leave them all with him, rolling our burden upon the Lord. Because he was grieved for me and in my stead, it is mine to rejoice with joy unspeakable in full redemption. No weight of sin remains to press us to the dust. Christ has carried it all away, and in his sepulcher he has buried it forever. Yet never let us forget what an inconceivable pressure our sin put upon him; for, remembering this, it becomes the more a comfort to us that, notwithstanding all, he could say, "I have overcome the world."

Recollect, again, that our Lord in the battle with the world was the center of the attack. When the whole host marches to the fight, we each one take our place in the ranks, and the war goes on against us all; but where, think you, did the arrows fly most thickly? Where were the javelins hurled one after the other, thick as hail? "The standard bearer among ten thousand" was the chief target. It seems to me as if the prince of darkness had said to his armies, "Fight neither with small nor great, save only with the King of Israel;" for he was tempted in all points like as we are. You and I encounter some temptations, but he endured them all. I have mine and you have yours, but he had mine and yours, and such as are common to all his saints; and yet, standing in the thick of the fray, he remained unwounded, and cried aloud, "I have overcome the world." Grace, then, can clothe us also with triumph, for against us no such supreme charges of hosts upon hosts will ever be led. The whole band was gathered together against him, but never against any one of his feeble followers.

Remember also, again, that the Redeemer was, in many respects, a lonely man. If we want spiritual succor we know someone to whom we can go. If we need converse with a superior mind, we can find such a one among our brethren; but our blessed Master could scarcely find a kindred spirit, and never an adviser. Like some lone mountain top which towers above all surrounding heights, he stood alone where winter's snowstorms beat full upon him, spending all their fury on his unshielded height. We are but valley dwellers, and rise not to his loftiness. To whom could he tell his secret griefs? To Peter, James, John? As well might a mother whisper to her babe the throes that rend her heart. He did once in deep distress resort to the three noblest spirits among the twelve apostles; but they slept for sorrow, and could not watch with him one hour. O lonely Christ, if thou didst overcome the world alone, how surely shall thy warrior brethren overcome it, when they stand shoulder to shoulder, cheering each man his fellow, and, above all, when thou thyself art in the field communicating thy victorious valor to the whole host.

I have not finished this setting forth of the disadvantage under which the Savior lay; for I beg my friend to notice that there were possibilities about our Lord that were never ours. A man who does not know his letters is little tempted to be proud of his learning, and the man who lives from hand to mouth and never has a penny to lay by can hardly be tempted to be purse-proud. We poor creatures could not be tempted to the same degree as our great Lord. The multitude would have taken him by force and made him a king; nay, more, all the kingdoms of the earth were proffered him, and instead of suffering poverty and yielding himself up to death he might have pushed Caesar from his throne. The world with all its honors, the cattle on a thousand hills, and secret mines, and rocks of gold and silver were all his, and he might have left his life-work to be the greatest, richest, mightiest monarch that ever reigned,—had he not been Jesus, to whom such things were as the dirt beneath his feet. But none of us have such great offers and brilliant opportunities, and therefore we have not such a battle to fight as he had. Shall we not by his help overcome the lesser temptations since he went on to victory over the greatest that can be imagined?

Recollect, too, that the intense zeal that burned in his spirit, had he been capable of ever yielding to a temptation, might have suggested to him, in a hundred ways, a turning aside from his own chosen line of action by which he had resolved to conquer the world. He came to vanquish evil by the force of love and truth, through his Spirit. If some of his followers had been girt with his power, they would not have kept to his order of battle. I stood in Rome one day at the bottom of the Scala Sancta and watched the poor votaries of superstition creeping up those so-called sacred steps upon their knees, imagining them to be the very stairs which our Lord descended, when Pilate said, "Behold the man." As I saw certain priests watching their dupes, I longed for a thunderbolt or two with which to make a clearance of Pope, cardinals, and priests. But the spirit of our Lord Jesus was not so hot; for when John asked, "Lord, wilt thou that we command fire to come down from heaven and consume them?" his Lord replied, "Ye know not what manner of spirit ye are of."

We may never have been tempted to ask fire from heaven, because we knew that we could not get it; but our Lord had only to ask his Father and he would presently have sent him legions of angels. See with grief what a part of the church has done: certain professors easily fell into the snare which their Lord avoided. Suppose the Lord Jesus had been made a king and had marshalled an army, he might have set up an established church, and have maintained it by the power and wealth of the State. A temple might have been built in every parish in the Roman Empire, and the heathen might have been compelled to pay tithes for the support of the ministry and the apostleship. By the help of imperial prestige and patronage, nominal professors of the faith would have been multiplied by millions, and, outwardly, religion would have prevailed.

Would it not have been as great a blessing as our established church is to us? But the Lord Jesus Christ did not choose this method, for his kingdom is not to be set up by other force than by that of truth and love. It was his to die for men, but not to lift the mailed hand of power, or even the jeweled finger of rank to bring them into subjection. Jesus *loves* men to himself: love and truth are his battle-axe and weapons of war. Thus he overcame the world in that most insidious form of worldliness—the suggestion to make alliance with it and set up a mongrel society, a kingdom at once earthly and heavenly, a state church, a society loyal both to God and Mammon, fearing the Lord, and serving the High Court of Parliament. It might have appeared to us to be the readiest means to bless the world; but it was not his Father's way, nor the way of holiness, and therefore he would not follow it, but overcame the world. No force may be put on conscience; the altar of God must not be polluted by forced offerings; Caesar must not step beyond his province. However great the proffered benefit, the Lord never did evil that good might come.

Let us now observe that the main point of the comfort lies in the fact that not only did our Lord overcome the world as an individual, but *he vanquished it as the representative man*. Clear a space! Clear a space! A deadly fight is to be fought. Here comes into the lists, stalking along, a monster man, towering high above his fellows. He is for Philistia! Here comes the champion of Israel, a youth and ruddy. These two are to decide the day. Anxious eyes are turned towards the field of duel. Philistia, look to thy champion! Israel, watch thy stripling with beating heart! O, maids of Judah, lift up your prayers for the son of Jesse that he play the man this day. As we watch that fight and see the stone sink into the champion's brow, and behold the youth taking off the giant's head, and bringing it to the camp, we are ready to join in the dances of the jubilant women, for David has won the victory. See the result of his deed—the victory of David is the triumph of every man in Israel's land. It was a representative conflict—Israel against Philistia, and when Philistia's hero fell, Israel was the conqueror. Up to the spoil, O sons of Jacob! They fly! The uncircumcised are utterly routed! Pursue them and scatter them as dust before the whirlwind! Even so, when Christ overcame the world, the victory was won on the behalf of all his people, and to-day we face a vanquished foe. Up, and spoil the enemy! Let your infirmities become the subject of your glorying. Let your tribulations become the themes of your thanksgivings; and if you are persecuted for righteousness' sake, do not whine and whimper as though some dread calamity had come upon you; but rejoice that ye are made participators of the honors of prophets and saints, and of your great Leader who won the battle as your champion.

In closing, let us remember that here we have not merely representation, but *union*. "I have overcome the world," means more than, "I overcame in your name." All believers have virtually overcome the world, for they are one with Christ. Did my hand win the victory? Then my foot triumphs. Did my head achieve the conquest? Then my heart shares the honor. The sole of my foot is victorious when my head is crowned. When Jesus Christ, the Head of the Church, was victorious over the foe, every member of his mystical body, even the most uncomely, was, virtually, a conqueror in the conquering Head. So let us shout the victory and wave the palm branch, for we are more than conquerors through him that hath loved us. Said he not well when he bade us be of good cheer, for he had overcome the world? Wherefore, struggling brother, obey his word, and *BE OF GOOD CHEER*.

6

Good Cheer from Past and Future Service

"And when there arose a great dissension, the chief captain, fearing lest Paul should have been pulled in pieces of them, commanded the soldiers to go down, and to take him by force from among them, and to bring him into the castle. And the night following the Lord stood by him, and said, Be of good cheer, Paul: for as thou hast testified of me in Jerusalem, so must thou bear witness also at Rome. And when it was day, certain of the Jews banded together, and bound themselves under a curse, saying that they would neither eat nor drink till they had killed Paul. And they were more than forty which had made this conspiracy" (Acts 23:10–13).

From the midnight whisper of the Lord to Paul we may draw forth sweet encouragement. Those of the Lord's children who have been engaged in his work and are called to suffer in it have here a special word of consolation.

Paul had been in a great tumult, and had been roughly rescued from the wrath of the people by the chief captain, who saw that otherwise he would be pulled in pieces. Paul was like the rest of us, made of flesh and blood, and therefore liable to be cast down: he had kept himself calm at first, but, still, the strong excitement of the day had no doubt operated upon his mind, and when he was lying in prison all alone, thinking upon the perils which surrounded him, he needed *good cheer*, and he received it. The bravest man may find his spirit sinking after the battle, and so perhaps it was with the apostle.

In these words let the reader note the Good Cheer that came to Paul in the dungeon. This consisted, first, in *his Master's presence*: "The Lord stood by him." If all else forsook him, Jesus was company enough; if all despised him, Jesus' smile was patronage enough; if the good cause seemed in danger, in the presence of his Master victory was sure. The Lord who had stood *for* him at the cross, now stood *by* him in prison: the Lord, who had called to him out of heaven, who had washed him in his blood, who had commissioned him to be his servant, who had sustained him in labors and trials oft, now visited him in his solitary cell. It was a dungeon, but the Lord was there; it was dark, but the glory of the Lord lit it up with heaven's own splendor. Better to be in a dungeon with the Lord than to be in heaven without him. The harps above could make no heavenly place without Jesus; and Jesus being there, the clanking fetters and the cold pavement of the stony cell could not suggest a sorrow.

"The Lord stood by him." This shall be said of all who diligently serve God. Dear friend, if you are a worker for the Lord Jesus, depend upon it he will not desert you. If in the course of your endeavors you are brought into sadness and depression, you shall then find it sweetly true that the Lord stands by you. Did *you* ever forsake a friend who was spending his strength for you? If you have done so, you ought to be ashamed of yourself; but I think I hear you say, indignantly, "No, I have always been faithful to my faithful friend." Do not, therefore, suspect your Lord of treating you ungenerously, for he is faithful and true. All your former helpers may desert you; Sadducees, Pharisees, and scribes may all set themselves to oppose you; but with the Lord at your right hand you shall not be moved. Cheer up, desponding brother,

> God is near thee, therefore cheer thee,
>   Sad soul!
> He'll defend thee when around thee,
>   Billows roll.

The next comfort for Paul was the reflection that *the Lord's standing by him proved that he knew where he was, and was aware of his condition.* The Lord had not lost sight of Paul because he was shut up in the common jail. One is reminded of the Quaker who came to see John Bunyan in prison, and said to him, "Friend, the Lord sent me to thee, and I have been seeking thee in half the prisons in England." "Nay, verily," said John, "that cannot be; for if the Lord had sent thee to me, thou wouldst have come here at once, for he knows I have been here for years." God has not a single jewel laid by and forgotten "Thou God seest me" is a great consolation to one who delights himself in the Lord. Many and diverse are the prisons of affliction in which the Lord's servants are shut up: it may be that the reader is lying in the prison of pain, chained by the leg or by the hand, through accident or disease; or perhaps he is shut up in the narrow cell of poverty, or in the dark room of bereavement, or in the dungeon of mental depression; but the Lord knows in what ward his servant is shut up, and he will not leave him to pine away forgotten, "as a dead man out of mind."

The Lord stood by Paul despite doors and locks; he asked no warder's leave to enter, nor did he stir bolt or bar; but there he was, the companion of his humble servant. The Lord can visit his chosen when nobody else could be allowed to do so, because of contagion, or from fear of exciting the fevered brain. If we come into such a peculiar position that no friend knows our experience, none having been tempted as we are, yet the Lord Jesus can enter into our special trial and sympathize in our peculiar grief. Jesus can stand side by side with us, for he has been afflicted in all our afflictions.

What is more, that part of our circumstances which we do not know ourselves, Jesus knows, and in these he stands by us; for Paul was not aware of the danger to which he was exposed, he did not know that certain Jews, to the number of forty, had banded together to kill him; but he who was his shield and his exceeding great reward had heard the cruel oath, and arranged to disappoint the bloodthirsty ones. Reader, the Lord knows your troubles before they come to you; he anticipates them by his tender foresight. Before Satan can draw the bow the Preserver of men will put his beloved beyond the reach of the arrow. Before the weapon is forged in the furnace, and fashioned on the anvil, he knows how to provide us with armor of proof which shall turn the edge of the sword and break the point of the spear. Let us therefore sing with holy boldness, "In the time of trouble he shall hide me in his pavilion: in the secret of his tabernacle shall he hide me; he shall set me up upon a rock." How safe we are, for Jehovah hath said, "No weapon that is formed against thee shall prosper; and every tongue that shall rise against thee in judgment thou shalt condemn." With joy let us draw water out of these two wells of salvation: the Lord is present with us, and he knows us altogether. Putting the two thoughts together, we may hear him say to our inmost souls—

> I, the Lord, am with thee,
> Be thou not afraid!

> I will help and strengthen,
>   Be thou not dismayed!
>
> Yea, I will uphold thee
>   With my own right hand;
> Thou art called and chosen
>   In my sight to stand.
>
> Onward then, and fear not,
>   Children of the day!
> For His word shall never,
>   Never pass away.

When the Lord Jesus came to Paul he gave him a third reason for courage. He said, "Be of good cheer, Paul: for thou hast testified of me in Jerusalem." *There was much comfort in this assurance that his work was accepted of his Master.* We dare not look for much joy in anything that we have done, for our poor works are all imperfect; and yet the Lord sometimes gives his servants honey in the carcasses of lions which they have themselves slain, by pouring into their souls a sweet sense of having walked in integrity before him. Before the great day of reward the Lord whispers into the ear, "Well done, good and faithful servant;" or he says openly before all men, "She hath done what she could."

Herein is good cheer, for if the Lord accepts, it is a small matter if men condemn. The Lord says to Paul, "Thou hast testified of me in Jerusalem." The apostle had done so, but he was too humble to console himself with that fact till his Lord gave him leave to do so by acknowledging the brave deed. Perhaps, dear friend, by this little book you shall be made to remember that you have borne witness for Jesus, and that your life has not been altogether in vain. It may be that your conscience makes you more familiar with your faults than with your services, and you rather sigh than sing as you look back upon your Christian career; yet your loving Lord covers all your failures, and commends you for what his grace has enabled you to do in the way of witness-bearing. It must be sweet to you to hear him say, "I know thy works; for thou hast a little strength, and hast kept my word, and hast not denied my name."

Be faithful to your Lord, dear reader, if you are now in prosperity; for thus you will be laying up a store of cheering memories for years to come. To look back upon a well-spent life will not cause an atom of legal boasting to an experienced believer; but it will justly create much holy rejoicing. Paul was able to rejoice that he had not run in vain—neither labored in vain—and happy are we if we can do the same. If it be right for us to chasten our conscience on account of omissions, it must be lawful ground for thankful joy that our heart condemns us not, for then have we confidence towards God. If we fall into straitened circumstances it will be a comfort to be able to say, "When I was rich I freely used my wealth for my Lord." If we are ill it will be a satisfaction to remember that when we were in health we used our strength for Jesus. These are reflections which give light in the shade, and make music at midnight. It is not out of our own reflections that the joy arises, but out of the witness of the Holy Spirit that the Lord is not unrighteous to forget our work of faith and labor of love.

A fourth comfort remained for Paul in the words, "As thou hast testified of me in Jerusalem, so must thou bear witness also at Rome." The Lord would have us take comfort from *the prospect of future service and usefulness*. We are not done with yet, and thrown aside as vessels in which the Lord hath no more pleasure. This is the chief point of comfort in our Lord's word to the apostle. Be of good courage, *there is more for you to do*, Paul; they cannot kill you at Jerusalem, for you must bear witness also at Rome.

Brace yourself up, O weary, working brother, for your day's work is not over yet, and your sun cannot go down till, like Joshua, you have finished your conflict with Amalek. The old saying is true, "You are immortal till your work is done." Possibly not one half of your work is even begun, and therefore you will rise again from sickness, you will soar above depression, and you will do more for the Lord than ever. It will yet be said of you as of the church in Thyatira, "I know thy works, and the last to be more than the first." Wycliffe could not die though the malicious monks favored him with their best wishes in that direction. "Nay," said the reformer, "I shall not die, but live, and declare all the evil deeds of the friars." The sight of rogues to be exposed roused his flickering life, and revived its flame. Disease could not carry off Melanchthon because he had eminent service yet to do, side by side with Luther. I have admired the way in which the great Reformer dragged his coadjutor back to life by assuring him that the great work needed him, and he must recover. "He devoutly prayed, 'We implore thee, O Lord our God, we cast all our burdens on thee;

and will cry till thou hearest us, pleading all the promises which can be found in the Holy Scriptures respecting thy hearing prayer, so that *thou must indeed hear us* to preserve at all future periods our entire confidence in thine own promises.' After this, he seized hold of Melanchthon's hand, and said, 'Be of good courage, Philip, YOU SHALL NOT DIE.'" He prayed his friend back from the mouth of the grave, and sent him on his way comforted with the truthful prediction that he had yet to bear more testimony for the truth. Surely there is no restorative from sickness, and no insurance for continued life, like the confidence that our task is not done, and our race is not ended.

Godly George Whitefield, when smitten with a dangerous illness, rose again to renew his seraphic activities after his death had become matter of daily expectation. It is said, in connection with this event that shortly after his recovery a poor colored woman insisted on having an interview with him. On being admitted, she sat down upon the ground, and, looking earnestly into his face, said to him in broken language, "Massa, you just go to heaven's gate, but Jesus Christ said, Get you down; you must not come here yet, but go first and call some more poor negroes." And who would not be willing to tarry here to win more poor negroes for Jesus? Even heaven may be cheerfully postponed for such a gain.

Come, then, ailing and desponding one, there is no use in lying down in despair; for a life of usefulness is still in reserve for you. Up, Elijah, and no more ask to die; for God has further errands for his servant. Neither the lion nor the bear can kill thee, O David, for thou hast yet to fight a giant and cut off his head! Be not fearful, O Daniel, of the rage of Babylon's drunken king, for thou art yet to outlive the rage of hungry lions. Courage, O thou mistrustful spirit; thou hast only run with the footmen as yet, thou shalt yet contend with horses and prove more than a match for them, wherefore lift up the hands that hang down. "Thou *must* stand before Caesar"; a divine decree ordains for thee greater and more trying service than as yet thou hast seen. A future awaits thee, and no power on the earth or under the earth can rob thee of it; therefore BE OF GOOD CHEER.

7

Good Cheer from Faith in the Divine Truthfulness

"And we being exceedingly tossed with a tempest, the next day they lightened the ship; and the third day we cast out with our own hands the tackling of the ship. And when neither sun nor stars in many days appeared, and no small tempest lay on us, all hope that we should be saved was then taken away. But after long abstinence Paul stood forth in the midst of them, and said, Sirs, ye should have hearkened unto me, and not have loosed from Crete, and to have gained this harm and loss. And now I exhort you to be of good cheer: for there shall be no loss of any man's life among you, but of the ship. For there stood by me this night the angel of God, whose I am, and whom I serve, saying, Fear not, Paul; thou must be brought before Caesar: and, lo, God hath given thee all them that sail with thee. Wherefore, sirs, be of good cheer: for I believe God, that it shall be even as it was told me" (Acts 27:18–25).

Here we see a believer full of comfort cheering others: it is time that our reader should endeavor to rise to a like position. The words of good cheer now before us are from a man; but inasmuch as he does but repeat what the Lord had spoken to him, they are none the less precious, and they may be all the more profitable if they move us by their example to speak words of cheer to others.

The believer is sure to come to the front. He may be hidden away in the crowd, and his condition and circumstances may put him in the rear rank for a time; but his light will by some means rise out of obscurity. Paul is nothing but a prisoner all the time the ship sails safely: he is courteously entreated, yet he holds rank among others who are being carried to Rome for trial; but the storm comes on and the ship is driven before the tempest, and he who was only a prisoner becomes practically the chief man in the ship. The owner, the captain, the centurion—these are very small figures in the picture; you scarcely notice them in the group huddled together in the laboring barque. Paul is the center of the whole company, the observed of all. He is as much the master of the ship as Caesar was when in the tempest he encouraged the mariners with the words, "Fear not, you carry Caesar and all his fortunes." Paul is greater than Caesar, for he says less of himself, and more of the Eternal God. He is evidently reverenced and esteemed even by those who hold him in charge.

Paul on board that vessel was strikingly like the Lord Jesus when he came into the ship upon the Galilean lake. There are many parallels between every true believer and his Lord. Albeit that he is great, and everything about him is colossal, we, if we follow Jesus, are like him, and in this world we are as he was, we are miniatures of his life-size portrait, shadows of his glorious substance. When Paul on board the ship sees the fears of those about him, and lovingly cries, "Be of good cheer," his voice has a consoling ring borrowed from his Master's. If you, dear friend, are thoroughly and strongly a believer, you will find a place in which you shall illustrate to others the character of your Lord. If I might so speak, on board that ship Paul was prophet, priest, and king. In our text he spoke prophetically; for he declared to them their perfect safety.

He acted like a priest in his prayers for them all; and I had almost added that in his breaking of bread he was dimly like Melchizedek, blessing men, and refreshing them with bread and wine. As for the kingly office, was not Paul truly royal? No mortal brow was ever more worthy of a crown. Amid that crowded ship he was more imperial than Caesar, and all on board acknowledged it. They felt constrained to obey him, for he stood superlatively above them all—unassuming, modest, gentle, self-denying, sympathetic, yet evidently a superior being. If we had more faith we should sink in our own esteem, but we should greatly rise in our influence upon others, for we, too, should dwell among men as prophets, priests, and kings. Are not the saints the twice-born, of a higher lineage and a nobler race, the excellent of the earth in whom is the delight of holy men?

Dear reader, let us think of the apostle's character as set forth in his cheery speech, and view him under three aspects. First, let us see in him *the avowed believer*, secondly, let us consider him as *the bold prophet*; thirdly, as *the sympathetic comforter*. May we, by God's good Spirit, be made to bear each of these characters.

I. First, the apostle will be seen, if we read our text, as THE AVOWED BELIEVER. Hear him as he says, "*I believe God, that it shall be even as it was told me.*"

He commences his statement of his faith by saying that *he believed God*. We cannot have a better basis of faith than that. We must settle in our minds that there is a God, that the word of God must certainly be true, absolutely infallible, and beyond all question. "I believe God"—if a man can say no more than this means in the very mildest sense of it, he is on the way towards faith; but he that can say, "I believe God," in such a sense as the apostle intended, has reached to an eminent height of faith, and has obtained the elements of spiritual strength.

"I believe God." Sometimes it quite staggers me that it should be difficult for us to believe God. Dear friend, do you not sympathize with me in my wonder? If our hearts and minds were as they should be, faith in God would be a matter of course, and even now, imperfect as we are, it ought to need a crushing argument to persuade us to entertain the slightest doubt of God. It is most of all surprising that God's children should ever doubt him; especially those who have been so highly favored as some of us- have been. Let writer and reader be amazed that we should ever dare to say that we find faith in God to be difficult. It is a grievous imputation upon God when we talk about faith as hard.

If we were to say of a neighbor, "I find it hard to believe him," I do not know what worse we could say. If a child were to say of his father, "You know my father: he is in high repute, but I find it quite a struggle to believe him." What rumors would get abroad! What whisperings! "That man's own child confesses that he finds it hard to believe him!" Will not this bring forth from us the blush of shame and the tear of repentance, to think that we should ever have spoken thus of our Father God? Is there any proof of our fall more conclusive? Is there any token of the natural depravity of our heart more glaring than that we should be so out of order as to doubt the living God? Why do we not trust him altogether and implicitly? How is it that when we get a great promise we begin to say, "And is this true"? When we come into deep trouble, how is it that we mistrust his goodness? How is it that we do not rest in God in all things great or small? He that is true to his covenant and to his oath will be true in the very jots and tittles of his promises. He that is true to Christ will be true to every member of Christ's body. He cannot lie. It is impossible that he should deny himself; ought it not to be impossible for us to suspect him? The apostle is worthy to be called "the master of the sentences" in this brave utterance, "I believe God." Take this one line to heart, beloved reader, and repeat it for yourself full many a time: "I believe God." Whatever else you question, always believe God.

Paul's firm faith was grounded upon revelation; for he says, "I believe God *that it shall be even as it was told me.*" He believed, then, that God had told him something. He says of a certain "it" that it was told him. An angel had told it him, but we need not envy him the channel of communication, since the written word of God is a more sure word of testimony than anything else can be. Even the word which came on the holy mount in the transfiguration, when Peter and James and John saw Christ in his glory, though it was a true and pure and bright word, yet is it spoken of by Peter as second to the Scriptures: he says, "We have a more sure word of testimony,"—more sure even than speech heard by the ear.

Nothing is so sure as the inspired Book: the man who cavils at the inspiration of the word of God has given up the foundation of faith. You and I, kind friend, at any rate are able to say that we believe that God has told *us* something, for we accept the Bible as his word to us—even to us. We are not of those who say of a certain chapter, "That is for the Jews;" for in Christ Jesus there is neither Jew nor Gentile, but all the promises are yea and amen in Christ Jesus, to the glory of God *by us*. We are the true Israel which worship God in the spirit, and have no confidence in the flesh, and the promises are sure to all the seed. We believe in inspiration and revelation, and we ground our faith thereon, even as Paul did. "I believe that it was told me," is our unmistakable avowal.

Observe carefully that Paul's faith, grounded upon God and the fact of a revelation, went on to a conviction of the absolute certainty of that revelation. "*It shall be even as it was told me.*" "*It* shall be." You can apply this to everything that God has told you. Whatever promise he has made, whatever declaration he has set forth in his Holy Word, *it* shall be even as *it* was told you. Just as when the press comes down upon the paper the type leaves its own impress in each line and letter, so shall the eternal purpose and promise of God leave its impress in your life and mine, fulfilling in actual fact all that the Lord God has promised. We shall try the word and we shall prove it true. We shall expect the promise to be faithful, and we shall find it so. "It shall be *as it was told me:*" there shall be no errata at the end of the chapter, no emendations and obliterations. What God has written he has written, and it must be even so. Augustine wrote confessions and retractions at the close of his life; but not so Augustine's God. At the last day, when the roll of history shall be complete, and *"finis"* shall be put to it, it will tally with the forecasts of God's word in every respect. Has he said, and shall he not do it? Has he spoken, and shall it not come to pass? Heaven and earth shall pass away, but God's word shall never pass away. Here is the joy of the believer; he can say, "I believe God, that it shall be even as it was told me."

The faith of Paul was most blessedly comprehensive. I want the reader to note the fact; for God had told him that he had given him all them that sailed with him, and he believes it for their comfort. It is a great thing for faith to make a sweep as wide as God's word. I have known some to whom God has said, "Believe in the Lord Jesus Christ, and thou shalt be saved *and thy house;*" and they have only gone as far as, "Thou shalt be saved," and according to their faith it has been to them. As yet they have not believed the other three words, "and thy house;" and when their children grow up and grieve their hearts by their ill manners, what is the cause of it but the parents' unbelief? If we have not prayed believingly for our children, is it any marvel that they are not saved? It often comes to pass that by clipping a promise we shear off a blessing which we might have had if our faith had accepted the sacred word in its entirety.

Oh, for a comprehensive faith as to all that is in the gracious covenant. Have you looked long enough at the promise to see all that is in it? What sheaves of blessing are tied up in a single promise, though it may only consist of a dozen words. I like to make up my troubles into bundles. Do you ever do that? If a man has nine, ten, twelve, fourteen parcels to carry, they may be all little ones, but what a worry they are. Here are some in this pocket and some in that, and they are more than he can manage, for they drop about everywhere. If he is a wise man he finds a bag and puts the separate items together. True, they are no lighter, but they are much easier to carry. Bind your troubles into one burden, and then roll it upon the Lord. With your mercies do just the opposite; cut the string and open the package: they will be no more, but they will give you more joy as you count them and examine them one by one. Take care that your faith grasps the whole mass of blessing stored away in the promise, and mind you believe that it shall be even as God has told you.

Further, note that Paul believed this when to outward appearance "all hope that they should be saved was taken away." *Paul's faith hoped against hope.* When Hope mourns, "I cannot find rest for the sole of my foot," Faith cries, "Use your wings." When there seems nothing for faith to rest on but the bare word, then faith is glad, for now she can commune with her Creator without being entangled by outward means and instrumentalities. Did not the Lord hang the world upon nothing but his word? And cannot we hang our souls there too? It is grand to stand like the arch of heaven, unpillared and yet unmoved, resting only upon the invisible God. Only, did I say? Is not that resting upon everything that is worth trusting since God is all in all?

Before we leave this point we ought to notice that while Paul thus believed God, that it should be as it was told him, *he very plainly and boldly expressed this faith.* He did not conceal his confidence, but he proclaimed it even before those who did not share his belief. No matter whether they could sympathize with him or not, he spoke out boldly. He did not cast pearls before swine by needlessly parading his faith; but as it was necessary to speak of it for the comfort of others he did not hesitate for a single moment, but confessed, in the hearing of soldiers and sailors, "I believe God." Nowadays people are so dreadfully modest that they are afraid to glorify God. God save us from such cowardice. Infidelity brawls in every street: shall faith be dumb?

If you believe, there is at this time grave necessity that you should declare your faith, for unbelief is rampant. Look at the high-class reviews, look at popular literature: these things reek with unbelief of the worst kind. Alas that ever it should come to this—that men who call themselves Christians should lend their pens to suggest and spread infidel principles, and even enter into pulpits to insinuate mistrust of the verities which they were ordained to preach! Honesty seems to have fled the earth, and men have lost all conscience. Let believers then speak out at once, though men will call us narrow-minded, destitute of culture, incapable of enlarged views, and other pretty things. What does it matter what they say? All that they say or insinuate should only make us the more vehemently declare, "I believe God." Why, it has become a rare thing to meet a man who believes anything now, for the reputed wise man of the period is he who says, "I do not believe in anything in particular. I hold certain views, but I am quite prepared to change them, for there is a great deal to be said on the other side." This is not after the manner of Christ, nor according to the ways of the faithful in the olden time, who held fast the form of sound words, and were ready to die for the truths which had taken possession of their souls. It is time now, if ever in the world's history, for those who are believers to speak with all confidence. Fear nothing. Can there be anything to fear in believing God? Can there be any shame in avowing an implicit faith in the God of truth? For my own part, I had rather be ridiculed for bigotry than be applauded for "advanced and liberal views." I would sooner be despised with the orthodox than reign with "the intellectual."

We have thus gone over Paul's words as an avowed believer, and now we may turn to look at him as *A BOLD PROPHET*.

Far be it from any one of us to set ourselves up as prophets, for thereunto we are not called. Yet every truly instructed Christian is in some sense a prophet, and may prophesy according to the proportion of faith, if he will follow the true method. Paul was not rash in his prophecies; he confined himself to revelation. He said, "It shall be." But what shall be? "It shall be as it was told me." You may always go that length; and you will be to many men a wonderful personage. If you go only as far as that, they will marvel that you dare say, "It shall be even as it was told me." We speak positively where they can only guess and dream. We cannot see behind that veil which hides the future; but we know what is to come as to some matters, for God has told us, and we can therefore prophesy that it shall be according to his declaration. Learn from Paul not to be a presumptuous dreamer, but a prudent speaker.

On what he foretold he staked the honor of God, for he said, "It shall be as it was told me." But why? Because "I believe God." If God be not worthy of belief, then it may not be as it was told me: but his word must be fulfilled, and his promise kept, since he is a faithful God. Never recklessly compromise the honor of God by any rash assertion of your own; but you may always challenge the veracity of God as to his own promises or threatenings, and be quite sure that he will vindicate both himself and his servant, by making it to be as he told you.

The apostle uttered this prophecy of his before all that were in the ship. Most of them were unbelievers, but he boldly said to them, "It shall be even as God has told me." Some of them were his superiors in station—officers of the Roman army; but he told them, "It shall be even as it was told me." It is sometimes hard to confess Christ in polite society, in the presence of those who are considered to be superior persons; but let not my reader yield to fear. Say with David,

> I'll speak thy word, though kings should hear,
>   Nor yield to sinful shame.

Paul made his avowal of faith in the presence of very rough men—selfish sailors, cruel soldiers, and criminal prisoners; but what of that? An avowal of faith in God might be made before all the fiends of hell; and you could not say a better thing before the angels of heaven. In no place and in no company can the testimony of faith in the living God, and his Son Jesus Christ, be out of place; therefore fear not to make it. My friend, make the world conscious of your solemn conviction that God is to be believed. Protest, and so act as a true Protestant; confess Christ, and so be his disciple indeed. Speak like a prophet in the name of the Lord that which he has told you in his word, and fear no man. Let the fear of God forbid all other fear.

Paul so truly, so practically believed God that the power of his faith told on all that were around him. If they did not themselves believe, yet that calm face amid the storm, that practical action in bidding them take bread and eat, that common-sense proceeding in cutting away the boat that the sailors might remain to manage the ship—all this made them see that he was not a man who merely talked of faith, but one to whom believing was part and parcel of his life, the fountain of the common-sense which fitted him to be a leader. He acted like a man who believed in God in a business-like way: faith was real in him, and therefore practical. Many Christians appear to hold their religion as a pious fiction, regarding the promises of God as pretty things for sentimentalism to play with, and his providence as a poetical idea. We must get out of that, and make God to be the greatest factor in our daily calculations—the chief force and fact of our lives. We must each one boldly act on the conviction that "It shall be even as he has told us."

Paul was all this while himself in trouble, for he was in the ship with those whom he comforted, suffering the same discomforts, and yet he said, "I believe God." It is very fine for those who have a good income, and enjoy good health, and are in excellent spirits, to sit down by the side of some poor half-starved woman, who is full of disease, and near to die, and say, "My good woman, you should have faith in God." Do you hear that landsman teaching sailors how to go to sea? That is true faith which believes God when it is *in* the sinking ship; in the same peril and trouble with others, and yet unmoved where they are filled with alarm. How I wish that my friend the reader may be able to do this.

May God make you to be so far a prophet that you may be prophetic on several points: in the first place, always declaring that God will hear believing prayer; and, next, that a wrong thing cannot have the divine blessing resting upon it. Be prophet enough to say these two things, and act upon them as downright matters of fact. You can also foretell that if the gospel be faithfully and simply preached, with the Holy Ghost sent down from heaven, it must win souls. You may prophesy that, and never fail; and you may prophesy also, that if the biggest sinner in the world will come to Christ he shall be forgiven; that if the vilest heart will yield itself to the Savior it shall be renewed; that if the most rebellious and obstinate man that ever lived is touched by the finger of God, and is led to repentance and faith, he is capable of becoming one of the brightest of the sons of God. No one shall ever shame you by proving that you spoke falsely if you speak for God in this fashion. Speak out, then, and banish guilty silence.

The apostle may be viewed in a third character—as *A SYMPATHETIC COMFORTER*.

They were all in trouble, for they were all in danger of drowning. The ship was going to pieces, death stared them in the face, dismay was written on every countenance; but Paul says to them, "Sirs, be of good cheer." Doubtless, his cheerful tones and manly voice helped to banish their fears, and to prevent a panic. Beloved Christian friend, should it not be our effort, wherever we are, to make troubled ones happy? Next to loving God, the first duty of a Christian is to spread peace on earth, and goodwill to men. Whenever we meet with a person in trouble—I do not mean spiritual trouble only—we should administer relief. Even when we meet with a child that has lost a penny, or has broken a jug, we should take pleasure in soothing its grief. His mother will scold him. Buy him another jug if you can, and try and cheer his little heart. What a mass of happiness you can buy for a few pence, if you will spend them on poor children. Where money is not needed, you may give sympathy and consolation, and these will be much valued. Do not reply that you are unable to act as a comforter. Learn the art. If you cannot *speak* well, there is a better way than speech. A little child once said to her mother, "Mother, I stopped with Widow Brown, for she said that I comforted her so." "Well, I dare say you did, my dear," the mother replied. "But, mother, I do not see that I am of any use, for I cannot tell her anything, but I put my cheek against hers, and when she cries I cry too, and she says that it comforts her." Exactly so. This little child shall lead us. Herein is wisdom. "Weep with them that weep:" you cannot more effectually console them. Comfort others with the comfort wherewith you yourself are comforted of God; for Paul said, "Be of good cheer. I believe God that it shall be even as it was told *me*." He had been comforted of the Lord, and with this consolation he could cheer others.

The Lord grant us grace to be looking out for those who are in any sort of affliction, that we may cheer their hearts; but let us be doubly watchful over those in spiritual distress. Let no one in our neighborhood ever complain, "No man careth for my soul." Comfort God's people, and labor at the same time to win sinners to Jesus, and the love of your heart shall bring untold blessings into your own bosom. Happiness is contagious, and the cheerfulness of your piety will be so attractive that the careless and indifferent will be allured to the ways of piety. Do not run about with ill news, but make your communications joyous by mixing up the glad tidings of salvation with your cheerful daily talk; so shall you imitate your Lord by saying, BE OF GOOD CHEER.

www.ingramcontent.com/pod-product-compliance
Lightning Source LLC
Chambersburg PA
CBHW070721240426
43673CB00003B/101